Film and Literature

The Routledge new edition of this classic book functions as an accessible introduction to the historical and theoretical exchanges between film and literature and also includes the key critical readings necessary for an understanding of this increasingly vibrant and popular field of adaptation studies.

This new edition has been fully updated and is usefully separated into three sections: in the first section Timothy Corrigan guides readers through the history of film and literature to the present; the second section has expanded to reprint 28 key essays by leading theorists in the field including André Bazin, Linda Hutcheon, and Robert Stam, as well as new essays by Timothy Corrigan and William Galperin; and the third section offers hands-on strategies and advice for students writing about film and literature.

Film and Literature will fill a gap on many film and literature courses and courses concentrating on the interplay between the two.

Timothy Corrigan is Professor of English and Cinema Studies at the University of Pennsylvania, USA. His work in Cinema Studies has focused on modern American and contemporary international cinema. His books include *New German Film: The Displaced Image*, *The Films of Werner Herzog: Between Mirage and History*, *Writing about Film*, *A Cinema without Walls: Movies and Culture after Vietnam* and *The Essay Film: From Montaigne, After Marker*. He is an editor of the journal *Adaptation*.

Film and Literature

An Introduction and Reader

Second Edition

Edited by

Timothy Corrigan

Routledge
Taylor & Francis Group

LONDON AND NEW YORK

This edition published 2012
by Routledge
2 Park Square, Milton Park, Abingdon, Oxon OX14 4RN

Simultaneously published in the USA and Canada
by Routledge
711 Third Avenue, New York, NY 10017

Routledge is an imprint of the Taylor & Francis Group, an informa business

First edition published by Prentice-Hall 1999

British Library Cataloguing in Publication Data
A catalogue record for this book is available from the British Library

Library of Congress Cataloging in Publication Data
Corrigan, Timothy.
    Film and literature : an introduction and reader / Timothy Corrigan. – 2nd ed.
        p. cm.
    Includes bibliographical references and index.
    1. Motion pictures and literature. I. Title.
    PN1995.3.C68 2012
    791.43'6--dc23   2011019007

ISBN 13: 978-0-415-56009-2 (hbk)
ISBN 13: 978-0-415-56010-8 (pbk)

Typeset in Perpetua and Bell Gothic
by HWA Text and Data Management, London

Printed and bound in Great Britain by the MPG Books Group

For Cecilia, Graham, and Anna,
my wonderful companions
through so many books and movies

Contents

PART 2
Major documents and debates

This textbook is supported by a companion website at www.routledge.com/cw/corrigan

Acknowledgments

I WISH TO THANK Marcia Ferguson, who read this manuscript at various stages with both encouragement and criticism. Rick Prouty, Annalisa Castaldo, Sara Brenes-Akerman, and Cecilia Corrigan helped with the research, and Dana Polan gave me excellent advice early on, the wisdom of which sank in only later. Three of the most important scholars of contemporary adaptation studies have provided much direct and indirect support for this second edition: Deborah Cartmell, Thomas Leitch, and Imelda Whelehan. A study leave from the University of Pennsylvania allowed me to complete the second edition, and James Fiumara provided crucial assistance for this edition. I also wish to thank the following reviewers for their suggestions: Susan Scrivner, Bemidji State University; Anthony J. Mazzella, William Paterson University; Jere Real, Lynchburg College; Melissa Croteau, California Baptist University; Geoffrey A. Wright, Samford University; Rebecca L. Bell-Metereau, Texas State University; Pamela Demory, UC Davis; Helen Hanson, University of Exeter; Kamilla Elliott, Lancaster University; William J. Christmas, San Francisco State University; Jack Boozer, Georgia State University; Shelley Cobb, University of Southampton; Judith Buchanan, University of York; Laura Knight, Mercer County Community College; and Nancy West, University of Missouri. Finally, my undergraduate and graduate students have demonstrated through their patience and enthusiasm that scholarship and research can be an exciting and integral part of teaching and learning on every level.

Preface to the second edition

I WROTE AND ASSEMBLED THIS BOOK because I teach film and literature and know the challenges and rewards in dealing with this combination of subjects. The heart of most courses on film and literature is usually specific movies and different works of literature, and any one course will follow its own focus in selecting individual novels, poems, plays, and movies. Studying and discussing film and literature also involves, however, other crucial materials that enrich any particular work of film or literature and how we understand it. These include materials about film history as part of a larger cultural history, about film forms that clarify and differentiate the connections between film and literature, and about the different approaches used to analyze film and literature throughout the twentieth century. These important materials are what this book aims to provide.

Given the enormous scope of the topic, an introductory text such as this must be fairly modest and very flexible. With those guidelines, I aim here, first, to suggest a range of issues and approaches and, second, to provide tools and signposts that will allow readers to follow their own interests in further exploring certain topics. An introduction can, of course, only go so far, and one of its chief functions is, I believe, to emphasize where introductory discussion ends and where more advanced work begins, to highlight places in the readings that are in fact openings for more thinking and debate. Through the various inserts and questions that punctuate the book, I hope I've accomplished that.

In this new edition, many of the original features of the book have been improved and expanded. The historical survey of Part 1 now accounts for the last ten years in the changing rapport between film and literature, and the pedagogical material (now in Part 3) includes an added guide to writing essays about film and literature. Part 3 also features short discussions of and introductions to "Major Topics in Adaptation Studies." The most significant change in this edition, however, is the increase in the number of theoretical and analytical essays about film and literature. While retaining most of the essays from the first edition, I have nearly doubled the number in this edition, adding more recent work by Linda Hutcheon, Henry Jenkins, and others, and reorganized them according to six categories. This expansion is a measure of the broad and continuing vibrancy of the topic, while the reorganization aims to reflect current critical thinking about "adaptation studies" as theoretical, historical, and generic approaches. This central section also includes new essays that serve as focused cases studies of adaptations of William Shakespeare's *Macbeth* and Jane Austen's *Emma,* and a final section introduces some of the most significant new directions in the relation of film and literature.

Timothy Corrigan
March 2011

Permissions

THE AUTHOR AND PUBLISHER would like to thank the following copyright holders for permission to reprint material:

André Bazin, "Adaptation, or the Cinema as Digest" from André Bazin, *Bazin at Work: major essays and reviews from the forties and fifties* (NY: Routledge, 1997). Taylor & Francis Ltd, http://www.informaworld.com, reprinted by permission of the publisher.

Dudley Andrew, "Adaptation" from *Concepts in Film Theory* (1985) 4761w from pp.96-106 © 1984 by Oxford University Press, Inc. By permission of Oxford University Press, Inc.

Robert Stam, "Beyond Fidelity: The Dialogics of Adaptation" in James Naremore, ed., *Film Adaptation*. New Brunswick: Rutgers UP, 2000. pp. 54-76. Copyright © 2000 by Rutgers, the State University. Reprinted by permission of Rutgers University Press.

Lawrence Venuti, "Adaptation, Translation, Critique" in *Journal of Visual Culture* (6.1) pp. 25-43, copyright © 2007 by Sage Publications. Reprinted by Permission of SAGE.

Thomas Leitch "Twelve Fallacies in Contemporary Adaptation Theory" in *Criticism: A Quarterly for Literature and the Arts*, Vol. 45, No. 2. Copyright © 2003 Wayne State University Press, with the permission of Wayne State University Press.

Kristin Thompson, "Novel, Short Story, Drama: The Conditions for Influence" in *The Classical Hollywood Cinema: Film Style and Mode of Production to 1960*, David Bordwell, Janet Staiger and Kristin Thompson, Copyright 1988 Routledge. Reproduced by permission of Taylor & Francis Books UK.

Walter Benjamin, excerpts from "The Work of Art in the Age of Mechanical Reproduction" from *Illuminations*, copyright © 1955 by Suhrkamp Verlag, Frankfurt a.M., English translation by Harry Zohn copyright © 1968 and renewed 1996 by Houghton Mifflin Harcourt Publishing Company, reprinted by permission of Houghton Mifflin Harcourt Publishing Company.

INTRODUCTION

THE HISTORY of the relationship between film and literature is a history of ambivalence, confrontation, and mutual dependence. From the late nineteenth century to the present, these two ways of seeing and describing the world have at different times despised each other, redeemed each other, learned from each other, and distorted each other's self-proclaimed integrity. In 1859 the French poet Charles Baudelaire had already expressed fear and anger about how photographic images would "corrupt" traditional arts. By 1915 literary spectacles would increasingly become the material for the movies in attempts to distinguish the cinema from its vaudevillian heritage and to offer a new social respectability to a mechanical art (most notably with the 1913 Italian filmed version of the Polish novel *Quo vadis?* and D. W. Griffith's 1916 epic *Intolerance,* which used a visual refrain from the poet Walt Whitman to link the New Testament, two historical tales, and a modern melodrama). With a mixture of regret and pride about the failure to have his novel *The Magic Mountain* adapted for the cinema, Thomas Mann would characterize the position of many respected modern writers in 1932 when he wrote about the film industry, "I despise it myself—but I love it too" (Geduld 1972: 131). By 1996, Emma Thompson's mostly faithful *Sense and Sensibility* (1995), a tongue-in-cheek version of *Emma* called *Clueless* (1995), and several other recent adaptations of Jane Austen novels would start a whole new generation reading that nineteenth-century writer, while the blockbuster *Harry Potter* films (2001–2011) would concomitantly draw masses of young readers to movie theaters and lines of moviegoers into bookstores.

Today the topic of film and literature and the extended field of adaptation studies are more lively than ever before, both inside and outside the classroom. The reasons are many: From the cultural questioning of artistic hierarchies and canons to the increased mixing of different media in both literary and film practices, film and literature clash against and invigorate each other in more and more complicated fashions. Once isolated media and literature departments now share materials, students, and methods. Students recognize the intricacies of poetry in the rhetoric of experimental films. Elia Kazan's 1951 film version of Tennessee Williams's *A Streetcar Named Desire* becomes what Maurice Yacowar has called "an invaluable record of a legendary production ... which introduced Method acting to the mass audience" (1977: 24). More today than ever before, adaptations proliferate, novelizations follow rapidly on a movie's success, and debates continue about film as literature and film versus literature. One estimate claims that at least 30 percent of the movies today derive from novels and that 80 percent of the books classified as best sellers have been adapted to the cinema (Holt 1979). If the connection between the two practices has persisted so adamantly through the years, it seems especially pressing now, at the beginning of the twentieth-first century, as an index of why the movies are important, why literature still matters, and what both have to offer a cultural period in which boundaries are continually being redrawn.

One of the consequences of this renewed interest, as well as a consequence of the historical development of film studies over the past 40 years, is that the intersections of film and literature need to be viewed from an unprecedented variety of angles, as we admit and take seriously many different exchanges between literary works and films. Novels, dramatic literature, short stories, poetry, and even the essay have particular counterparts in film form; films influence literary imagery in a myriad of ways; and each of these paths lead to other issues: about the production and reception of movies and literature, about writing and scriptwriting, about reading and viewing. Encompassing this proliferation of practices and directions, four critical frameworks are important to this book.

First, the exchange between film and literature demands, especially now, rigorous historical and cultural distinctions. The connection between French surrealist poetry and experimental silent film of the late 1920s, for instance, evokes different terms and issues than those used to discuss the Broadway adaptations by Hollywood in the next decade. The more carefully these terms and issues can be situated in terms of their specific historical, national, and cultural contexts, the more accurate a discussion of this literature and these films will be.

Second, the usual cultural hierarchy that places serious literature above supposedly less serious film has been brought usefully into question in recent decades. This is not to say that the movies have as long and as complex a history as literature does but rather to recognize the limited value of assuming commonplaces like "the book is better than the movie." Once there may have been little debate about the fact that a theatrical performance of Shakespeare was far superior to a filmic reproduction. By 1948, Laurence Olivier's *Hamlet* could, however, provoke enormous interest and debate about his controversial filmic interpretation of Shakespeare, and nine years later Akira Kurosawa's *Throne of Blood* had cinema communities lavishing praise on that film as an exceptional recreation and translation of Shakespeare's *Macbeth*. Whether because of its massive social impact, because of the aesthetic development of film art, or because of shifts in cultural literacy, the cinema now demands equal time and attention when we argue the relative value and meaning of movies and literature.

Third, critical and theoretical perspectives that align and distinguish film and literature are no longer confined to how film is or is not like a language or how expressive film may be of an author or how representative of a reality. When the relationship of literature to the cinema began to expand as a critical topic in the 1930s through the 1950s, much energy was devoted to how fully or how accurately one or the other mirrored the human experience. In the 1960s and 1970s, the topic shifted its ground to how both were (or were not) like a language that allowed similar formal strategies. Today there are many other issues that complement these. The literary art of scriptwriting versus story writing, acting technique as it differs in the theater and on the screen, the ideological underpinnings that inform an adaptation of a particular work, the different ways readers and spectators make sense of their experience before a page or screen, and the impact of new media and the Internet on adaptation studies are just some of the rich and resonant perspectives that are reopening film and literary history in this century.

As a fourth framework for this book, film and literature can now be discussed on the common grounds provided by interdisciplinary and cultural studies. Both film and literature, for instance, can be seen as businesses and industries that participate in technological constraints and advantages. Both enlist or engage dominant figures of gender, race, and class. These and other expanded cultural perspectives then reverberate back through film and literary history. To what extent, for example, is the demand for "quality films" adapted from older and well-known classic literature a response, at certain times in history, to social and political turbulence? How did Bertolt Brecht's legal battles over the screen adaptation of *The Threepenny Opera* focus acute economic and legal distinctions between film and literature in the early 1930s? Within a larger cultural panorama of cultural studies, apparently unrelated films and texts—such as the gendered territory of American slasher films and Harlequin novels—may have more to say to each other than previously considered.

There are numerous academic agendas that should fit this book, but the primary aim is to serve students and scholars, new and old, who wish to begin or to continue reading about and thinking about the relationship between literature and the movies. This subject could be concentrated on any one particular genre or author—say, the novel and film or Shakespeare and film. My aim, however, has been to provide a broad-based foundation for the issues and histories that pervade this topic, and to allow instructors and readers to supplement or refocus their concerns according to their own needs and their particular choices of literary works and films. The specific readings provide, above all else, historical and theoretical perspectives that, at the same time, address different genres and offer different approaches to the question of how the movies and literature interact. While one of my first priorities has been to choose materials that would be accessible to students, there are also essays here that are challenging and demanding. I did this not only because this mix reflects a range of methods and views but because the book hopes to promote a reader's advancing sense of the subject. Vachel Lindsay's writings on film and literature are rich but not overly complex; Rober Stam's essay assumes readers will have more experience or more guidance with the questions he raises.

The organization of this book aims, in short, to be at once historical, methodological, and pedagogical, representing a variety of historical periods, cultural practices, and critical methods. Part 1 attempts to delineate the historical differences and dynamics that have shaped the topic, emphasizing distinctions and heritages that follow the debate into 2011. Here I wish to contextualize and highlight those economic, technological, and social issues that add depth and complexity to the specific aesthetic arguments. A reader interested in Cocteau on film or the "angry young" dramatists and filmmakers of England, for instance, will thus have a historical background against which to place their thinking.

Part 2 is the pedagogical centerpiece of the book, featuring the major statements on the relationship of film and literature that have appeared in the twentieth century and into the twenty-first. Such an immensely popular topic has produced, of course, numerous other essays, and many readers will know other essays that might have been included. My goal here, however, is to represent the path of the debates as it has sprung from different cultures, addressed different genres, and taken sometimes very different stances. In this I have also tried to choose texts that might have the most use and flexibility in different classrooms. Instructors and students and general readers should be able to formulate from this selection an arrangement and direction that responds to more particular concerns.

In my experience teaching film and literature, individuals frequently need a basic vocabulary to allow them to discuss and compare cinematic and literary techniques and form. Many of the debates about film and literature can become rather lofty, and it is obviously important that a reader have some basic sense of, for instance, how narrative point of view has been traditionally defined in the two practices, or what *mise-en-scène* means in the cinema, before (or while) they work through the more complex issues binding film and literature. In Part 3 there is, therefore, a brief presentation of key critical concepts that film and literature share and that often distinguish their particular practices, including narrative structure, genres, and formal devices such as camera techniques and figurative languages. In addition, this section of the book includes short discussions of more specific research topics, such as novels as films, copyright, authors and auteurism, novelizations, and so forth. The final section provides succinct guidelines for writing about film and literature, as well as an example of a student essay on this topic. Finally, the book includes a list of pertinent journals and websites and a bibliography.

What makes the discussions and debates about the connections between film and literature more compelling and topical today than the many other discussions and debates about film or about literature? Why do these issues across film and literature continue to claim our attention? One of the presumptions informing many of these debates is that the interaction of film and literature has special relevance to our culture and times, and the basis for this assumption needs to be examined. One preliminary answer to the question is that film has historically depended on literature for so much of its material. Put simply, movies very often base their scripts on literary texts and traditions. Yet, the complexity, logic, and centrality of the topic goes well beyond this industrial or artistic reliance, I believe, and much of that complexity is what this book intends to open up. Since the end of the nineteenth century, the tension between visuality and literacy has dominated much of Western culture. It has served as a barometer for questions about class, human intelligence, political action, the different statuses of races and genders, and the use and abuse of leisure time. We continue to ask how movies, television, and the Internet affect reading habits of children; we continue to fear or to embrace the power of the image to transcend different languages and speech itself. Twentieth-century and twenty-first-century history, perhaps more than any other epoch in history, has positioned itself between the "traditional word" and the "technological image," and tracing the directions of this debate through this century as it works through movies, books, and culture dramatizes one of the most pressing motifs of these times.

PART 1

Film and literature in the crosscurrents of history

THE HISTORY OF FILM ADAPTATIONS involves over a century of cultural, industrial, and textual complexities. Paralleling and entwined with the separate histories of literature and film, this history would be impossible to survey fully as part of a short introduction. Since historical and cultural differences have always provided the critical base for different adaptation practices and theories, history must be a starting point and, ideally, an opening toward the many other historical debates and issues that surround adaptation studies.

This opening section thus aims to provide historical contexts and cultural overviews for approaching the dynamics which have linked film and literature since the nineteenth century and into the twenty-first century. Some moments and events stand out, and, those key turns in the history of adaptation have been emphasized as a way to frame different critical perspectives (such as those in Part 2) and as a way to evaluate specific adaptations from different periods of history.

Chapter 1

THE PREHISTORY OF FILM AND LITERATURE

I T WOULD BE IMPOSSIBLE to mark and describe here all the different sources, forms, and arguments that anticipate the twentieth- and twenty-first-century encounters between film and literature, since the relationship between the word and the image can be traced back to the beginnings of various civilizations. Indeed, many students and scholars of film locate the first connections between film and literature in prehistoric cave drawings, Egyptian hieroglyphics, or the various picture writings of early civilizations, such as Chinese ideograms. In these practices that combine verbal signs and visual images, critics and historians recognize early attempts to record events, tell stories, or evoke spiritual power in a manner that anticipates the combinations of literary forms and technological images used in movies centuries later to present their histories, recount their tales, and generate their own magical charms. From the times of those more ancient civilizations, developments in most Western and non-Western cultures would continue to feature a rich source of materials and debates about the relationship between verbal and visual signs. From illuminated manuscripts and religious iconography to sixteenth-century verbal and visual exercises for memory, from the construction of Renaissance theaters as the visual forum for elaborate dialogue to the storytelling amusements of camera obscuras and other precursors to the camera, the pre-cinematic relationships between seeing and saying would be debated and practiced as central arguments about knowledge, identity, spiritual truth, pleasure, politics, and the meaning of culture.

Publics and cultures

The historical tale of the relationship between film and literature gains considerable momentum in the late eighteenth and early nineteenth centuries when the recognizable precedents in the debate began to appear. One of these precedents is a social and cultural anxiety about the proliferation of writings, spectacles, and entertainments attracting lower- and middle-class

Three fascinating
and well illustrated
accounts of the cultural
interactions between
literature and different
forerunners of the
movies are C. W.
Ceram's *Archeology of the
Cinema*, Richard Altick's
The Shows of London,
and Martin Meisel's
Realizations.

The first photograph
was made in 1826
by Joseph Nicéphore
Niépce and the process
later refined by Louis
Daguerre in 1839 with
his "daguerreotype."

audiences. By the late eighteenth century, the industrial revolution is underway, and the technological implications of this revolution appear throughout the visual and literary arts. Developments in the printing industry and its mechanics revolutionize many societies, for instance, through the introduction of the iron press in 1798 and later of the steam press. With these inventions, both books and prints proliferate through mass production, and these new technological powers to produce and disseminate words and images parallel, and in some ways helped to prepare, corresponding social revolutions that were ushering in an expanding middle class of readers, spectators, and cultural consumers.

Throughout this period, from roughly 1750–1830, Western cultures grow increasingly fascinated by visual images and spectacles that drew on but transformed the traditional pictorial arts, as well as by the similarities and differences in images and words as separate means of communication. On the one hand, this fascination with the visual promotes immense scientific and cultural development of new mechanisms for reproducing images, theatrical spectacles, and optical toys. These include new methods for mass production of prints in books (welcomed by artists such as William Hogarth, who develops methods for telling satirical tales through a series of engravings), popular illusory dioramas and panoramas that appear somewhere between legitimate dramatic theater and carnivalesque sideshow (in the 1790s Étienne Gaspard Robertson's Phantasmagoria attracted crowds with fantastic specters of Rousseau, Marat, and other celebrities of revolutionary France), and innumerable scientific oddities (such as the kaleidoscope invented by Sir David Brewster in 1814) that anticipate the discovery of photographic methods and instruments between 1826 and 1839.

On the other hand, these various cultural and scientific inventions and amusements, not surprisingly, stir continual debates among literary men and women about the two media and the place of literature in a culture that, even in the early nineteenth century, seem to be coming more and more under the spell of fascinating images rather than the discriminating power of crafted words.

Although he does not single out the showdown between literature and the technologies of the image, Raymond Williams rightly suggests that what is at stake in these debates in the early nineteenth century (and beyond) is the formation and defense of some notion of "culture," a term that, since then, has figured in many arguments about film and literature. The poet William Wordsworth, defender of the literary tradition in the early nineteenth century, rails against what he sees as the blunt lack of discrimination in this growing image culture (Wordsworth calling on a literary "people" to distinguish itself from the easily amused and less cultured "public"). His contemporary William Blake, however, envisions a new public and takes advantage of experimental methods for reproducing printed images, setting them as a complex counterpoint to the poetry that faced those images (in his celebrated lyrics such as *Songs of Innocence and Experience* or his epic *Jerusalem*). This particular period in Western history is an especially rich prelude to the cultural, aesthetic, and political issues that would appear full-blown by the end of the nineteenth century. Writers, artists, scientists, philosophers, and entrepreneurs raise questions early that remain unresolved, often in the context of the relationship of literary culture and a new culture of images, about high culture versus popular culture, active reading versus passive fascination, individual sense versus mass sensibility, creative expression versus mechanical reproduction, words versus images as pedagogical tools, and realistic pictures of history versus literary descriptions.

Nineteenth-century realism and melodrama

By the second quarter of the nineteenth century, the encounter between literature and this new image culture would become as much about realism as about the cultural terrain mapped by these two ways of presenting the world. Although foreshadowed by earlier movements toward more realism (in the characters, settings, and events of literature from Shakespeare through the eighteenth century), the scientific developments in photography in the 1830s mark a major shift in the discussions of painting, literature, theater, and other arts. From then till now, questions about the amount and accuracy of realistic fact and figure dominate much of the debate about connections and differences between new technological modes of representation and the more traditional forms of art and literature. From the novels of Sir Walter Scott at the beginning of this century through the naturalistic narratives of Émile Zola at the other end, an aesthetic of historical realism parallels and competes with the evolution of photography and early experiments with moving images such as Eadweard Muybridge's famous studies of animal motion in the 1870s.

See The Compleat Eadweard Muybridge for an abundance of materials and images tracing Muybridge's work and continuing influence today: http://www. stephenherbert.co.uk/ muybCOMPLEAT.htm

Indeed, much of the literature of the period seems to aim specifically at integrating the detailed objectivity of the photograph into the movement of narrative. In the novels of Gustave Flaubert and George Eliot, readers find shocking close-ups or precise panoramas of local scenes; in Nathaniel Hawthorne's *The House of Seven Gables* (1850), the work of a central character, Holgrave, as a daguerrotypist (or early photographer) turns the plot climactically. Even the historical snapshots of Renaissance artists and aristocrats found in Robert Browning's poetry might be seen developing their perspectives through the minute historical, geographical, and physical details associated with the new realism of photography.

At the center of the separate practices of film and literature, new blends and composite works appear: magic lanterns project scenes of Walter Scott novels and other literary narratives, and, as J. Hillis Miller has noted, serial novels become a compelling blend of the drawn or photographic illustrations and narrative storytelling supported by lithographic images or, after 1880, even halftone photo-engravings. Often these stories would first appear in the commercial format of newspapers, magazines, and other periodicals that functioned as the commercial forebears of the mass media that would later describe the movie business. One of the most innovative literatures that appears during the second half of this century is appropriately a similar hybrid: The photo essay that arrives late in this century (Jacob Riis's *How the Other Half Lives*, for example) combines news, personal reflection, and social commentary with the power of illustrative photographs. Its creative blend of the photographic and the literary would continue to evolve through the twentieth century in various kinds of photo essays (from W. Eugene Smith to Cindy Sherman) and documentary novels (from John Dos Passos to the New Journalism of Norman Mailer in the 1960s). As A. Nicholas Vardac has pointed out in his book *Stage to Screen*, however, the theater is clearly the center stage for these cross currents between an established literary tradition and the beginnings of cinematic realism:

> The times rather than the men controlled the ultimate arrival of the motion picture, for at just the point beyond which stage realism would have broken down and in many instances did, the cinema came to meet the need for a greater pictorial realism. By coming at the very peak of the nineteenth century cycle of realism, it upset normal expectations in theatre itself ... Naturally, in these early years, the film and the stage were hardly differentiated from one another; the cinema frequently borrowed from the theatre, while the theatre, in an attempt to counter the new attraction, in its turn borrowed from the film ... The result was that the two styles which defined the nineteenth-century theatre, realism and romanticism, and which most probably would have seen alteration in the early years of the twentieth century, were given a new lease on life. (1949: xxvi)

Especially as the nineteenth century proceeds, the divisions between the established traditions of literature and the technological precursors to the film are never neatly and clearly marked off, and it is more accurate to see both the practices and arguments as moving back and forth in a series of responses and assertions, most prominently about realism. Certainly, some positions are highly oppositional. In 1859, the French poet Charles Baudelaire's disdain is typical of the suspicion of many in the literary and artistic community of the "unworthy tricks" of photography: "If photography is allowed to supplement art in some of its functions, it will soon have supplanted or corrupted it altogether" (1983: 19, 20). Versions of this position underlie much of the poetic practice in the second half of this century, where the sometimes extreme emphasis placed on private experience or dreamlike, imaginative states—in poetic movements such as those of the Pre-Raphaelites (the poetry of D. G. and Christina Rossetti, for instance) or the Symbolists (the French poetry of Stéphane Mallarmé and Arthur Rimbaud)—become clear moves away from the powerful realism of photography. Similarly, while the revolutionary realist theater of Henrik Ibsen and other nineteenth-century dramatists can usefully be discussed in the context of the incisive and realistic eye of the camera, many of the most notable theatrical achievements of this time are either a reaction to the onslaught of a technological realism or a reinvention of drama in the light of this new realism. Beginning with the so-called "closet drama" of romantic theater and continuing through highly symbolic versions of this practice in the theater of August Strindberg, Maurice Maeterlinck, and William Butler Yeats, this other kind of drama works primarily in the invisible regions of the mind and the emotions rather than in the visible centers of society and nature.

In many cases, this tension between the realism of public life and art and the emotional escapisms of private life and art describes less separate spheres dividing individual practices than contested fields within many single works. From one direction there are the forces of society, historical determinism, and realism; from the other, the forces of individualism, personal desire, and imagination. One of the most significant productions of the collision is melodrama, that nineteenth-century form of emotional need and suspense that pits personal desire and dreams against the restrictions of social realism.

Melodramatic plots and situations become a dominant chord in much of the respected literatures of the age (from the poetry of Lord Byron and Goethe to the novels of Charlotte Brontë and Thomas Hardy), but they appear in their most transparent forms in the popular entertainments that were outlining the beginnings of a cultural place for cinema. Following the trends of the first part of the century, lower-and middle-class cultures develop popular institutions and forms, such as music halls, pantomime fantasies, and lavish dramatic spectacles built around special effects. In these institutions and entertainments, melodramatic feelings and desires are often played out against massive backgrounds and tableaux of history and nature. These kinds of melodramatic entertainments would, according to Peter Brooks, transform classical theater into a "mute text," "a visual summary of the emotional situation" (1976: 47); as it engages that other dominant literary concern, realism, melodrama would become one of the prominent linchpins uniting nineteenth-century literature and the forms, audiences, and institutions of the cinema.

Chapter 2

FILMING LITERATURE
From early film and literature to classical form, 1895–1925

1895 is considered the start of film history with the first projection of movies by the Lumière brothers on March 22 to a small group of friends and then on December 28 to a more public gathering. On December 8 of the same year, Emil and Max Skladanowsky also projected movies publicly in Berlin.

Watch these two early films at http://www.youtube.com/watch?v= 1dgLEDdFddk and http://www.youtube.com/watch?v= 7JDaOOw0MEE

A COMMON SCHEME for distinguishing the two major trends at the origins of film history (from 1895 to 1913) is to oppose the films of the Lumière brothers to those of Georges Méliès, the first associated with documentary realism and the second with fantasy. While this is no doubt too simplistic a summary of the many different strategies taking part in the birth of the cinema, it does highlight two of the main tendencies that early film practice inherits from the confluence of literature and the image cultures of the nineteenth century. The Lumières made short films intended to document various activities and realities in a way that emphasizes the scientific powers of film to investigate the actuality of events as historical realities. Méliès exploits the theatrical magic of the movies in developing film as an entertainment and imaginative play. The early Lumière shorts (like *Arrival of a Train at a Station* [1895]) usually last about a minute and work as moving snapshots of the world, while Georges Méliès's dramas (like *A Trip to the Moon* [1902]) create illusions staged theatrically before a stationary camera. Both kinds of early cinema participate in what Tom Gunning has dubbed "a cinema of attraction," a cinema that, like the mass entertainments that precede them, relies less on the form or matter of the image than on its sheer novelty and excitement—in this case on the pleasure of seeing a moving spectacle and, possibly, a literary text come to life.

The attraction of the literary

For students of film and literature, there are three important dimensions to film practice in these early years: (1) film practice and its connection with literature follow the social and aesthetic directions and developments established in the nineteenth century, especially the demands for realism and a class-oriented fascination with spectacle; (2) early cinema tends to find its formal literary precedents in the staged perspectives of the theater and less in narrative traditions; and (3) even at this early stage, film turns to literary materials of all kinds for subject matter. The first of these has already been signaled in our discussion of the cultural tensions evolving through the nineteenth century, and it acquires even more weight in the United States at the turn of the century when large immigrant audiences discover in their neighborhood nickelodeons (storefront movie theaters) fascinating images and entertainments that seemed to transcend all their linguistic differences, promising, for some proponents of the early cinema, to fulfill the dream of a universal language or "esperanto" in the immediately comprehensible realism of the movies. The second point, the theatricality of early films, derives from many influences, including the combination of realism and melodrama found on nineteenth-century stages, the historical dominance of popular theater traditions such as music halls and vaudeville performances, and, perhaps most important, the necessarily stationary position of the camera that could most easily recreate the perspective of a spectator in a center seat before the stage. The third point calls attention to the immediate appearance of literary subjects in film history, since documentary events could entertain audiences only to a limited degree. Along with topical historical and sporting events, literary figures and topics are a natural choice for early cinema. These literary films are sometimes as much about the performance of a famous player as about the story itself (as with the 1896 film of the actor Joseph Jefferson performing *Rip Van Winkle*), but filmmakers are also quick to use the cultural and popular currency of well-known literary tales, such as the filming of staged versions of *Cinderella* (1900), *Robinson Crusoe* (1902), *Gulliver's Travels* (1902), *Uncle Tom's Cabin* (1903), and *The Damnation of Faust* (1904). Besides the condensation of these literary classics as costume spectacles, early movies also turn to less canonized literary sources: bourgeois melodramas or so-called middle-class fiction, dramas and tales from folklore, and many different kinds of vaudevillian traditions.

The literary attraction in these early adaptations, staged often as "action-tableau" but eventually as narratives, is in many ways pragmatic. As the demand for movies increases exponentially and audiences grow more demanding and sophisticated about what they wanted to see on film, literature provides an abundance of ready-made materials that could be transposed to film. Looking for an image, a scene, a concept, or a story, a filmmaker could turn to a literary work to represent on film. That the audiences might sometimes be familiar with the literary precedent could also work to the filmmaker's advantage since part of the interest in the film would be seeing words brought to life, and this piqued interest would dovetail, of course, with the expanding financial possibilities the cinema contained as a growing form of mass entertainment.

Condensed versions of Shakespeare's plays are especially popular adaptations during this period. See Judith Buchanan's *Shakespeare on Silent Film: An Excellent Dumb Discourse*

Watch selections of the 1902 *Gulliver's Travels* and Edison's 1903 *Uncle Tom's Cabin*: http:// www.youtube.com/ watch?v=dGg9j0BdyEM and http://www. youtube.com/ watch?v=408ms-P2nVk

At the same time, this tendency to use literature for early movies is more than just a pragmatic way to find new subject matter. As Roberta Pearson and William Uricchio's *Reframing Culture* demonstrates in its discussion of the Vitagraph Company between 1907 and 1910, adapting literature also became a way of negotiating a new, respectable cultural position for movies and their audiences. Perceived in these first years of development as a curiosity and amusement geared toward lower-class audiences, film could, by adapting classics and popular literary figures and types, position itself closer and closer to traditional art and respectable cultural practices and thus add other classes of audiences as patrons. One of the most significant examples of this move toward respectability on the coattails of theater is the film d'art movement. Started by the French Société Film d'Art in 1908, this project makes films featuring celebrated performances and performers from the Comédie Française, such as Sarah Bernhardt in *La Dame aux Camélias* (1912). The success of these productions inspire a spate of imitations using theatrical actors and sets, most notably in the United States by Adolph Zukor and his Famous Players Film Corporation. One of the important side effects of the widespread success of these movies and their famous players is the birth of a star system that dictated higher prices for the movies and stories centered on a highly visible and recognizable character.

Especially pertinent to this period in film history is Vachel Lindsay's "Progress and Endowment" (p. 125).

D. W. Griffith and the birth of classical cinema from literature

For most historians of cinema, classical film develops its main shape and elements in the first quarter of the twentieth century, predominantly through the work of D. W. Griffith after 1913. There are certainly other influential moviemakers who worked alongside Griffith in these efforts, and one of the most important is Giovanni Pastrone, whose grand epic *Cabiria* (1913–1914) features intertitles written by Gabriele D'Annunzio, one of the most celebrated Italian writers of the late nineteenth and early twentieth centuries. Yet most historians credit Griffith with implementing and popularizing the aesthetic and technological changes that move the cinema from its early cinematic to classical stage, in an effort, as Griffith put it, "to place pictures on par with the spoken word as a medium of expression appealing to thinking people" (Schickel 275–276). The chief formal features of this shift from early cinema to classical cinema center on narrative elements inherited from the nineteenth-century novel: a narrative linearity that progresses according to a cause-and-effect logic, propelled by the demands and desires of primary characters, represented through an objective point of view and editing continuity.

For most historians, the transition from early short "scenic" or "topical" films to clearly formulated narrative cinema takes place between 1904 and 1917. For further reading, see Thomas Elsaesser and Adam Barker's collection of essays in *Early Cinema: Space, Frame, Narrative.*

While Griffith directly or indirectly adapts the formal figures, character types, or references from the nineteenth-century novels, other literary forms are equally influential in the transition to classical film form. Often overlooked in this context, for instance, are Griffith's use of serial novels (such as the Perils of Pauline) that supply the short episodic tales that fit the one-reel screenings of early cinema and that, through the course of several screenings, could develop a longer tale. As with other filmmakers, melodramatic theater is another source for Griffith's films, but equally important is poetry, as evidenced in the refrain from Walt Whitman's *Leaves of Grass* that punctuates *Intolerance* in 1916, or in his adaptation of Alfred Lord Tennyson's Victorian poem "Enoch Arden" in 1911. *Enoch Arden*, in fact, figures as a marker of the crucial transition from the early cinema of short one-reel movies (approximately ten to twenty minutes long) to the longer narratives of classical cinema. After making a one-reel version of the poem "After Many Years" (1908), Griffith made a more faithful, longer adaptation as the two-reeler *Enoch Arden*. Although Biograph, the producer, tried to distribute the film as two distinct parts (believing audiences would not sit still for the long version), the full version proved a success that would alter the direction of the cinema and its relationship with literature.

See *Enoch Arden* at http://www.youtube.com/watch?v=vhs-ez0JVdg

More than just an idiosyncratic episode in Griffith's career, this incident, marking the evolution of the cinema from one-reel shorts that ran for ten or twenty minutes to longer narratives of ninety to one hundred minutes, comes from the desire to tell stories. This desire, in turn, would draw filmmakers to different sorts of literary models and practices. During the first fifteen years of the twentieth century, a program of short films would stress their variety and their spectacular images, and both the length and the need to differentiate one film from another suggests a specific literary model for the movies: the short stories found in magazines like *The Saturday Evening Post* (with whom they also competed for those stories and their audiences). When movie cultures move to larger theatrical venues and begin to expand the kind and size of its audiences, the longer, feature length of the movies begins to accommodate the more substantial size of novels and dramatic literature, thus allowing movies to compete or align with these putatively more respected forms of cultural entertainment. This literary tradition of longer narrative fiction, specifically the novels of Charles Dickens, is what the Russian filmmaker Sergei Eisenstein, in "Dickens, Griffith, and the Film Today" (p. 144), describes as the source of Griffith's landmark experiments with classical narrative form and editing techniques such as cross-cutting.

Kristin Thompson's "Novel, Short Story, Drama: The Conditions for Influence" (p. 130) details these important literary influences and industries impacting films at this time.

Although always in touch with his theatrical background (he was a stage actor before becoming a filmmaker), Griffith is one of the first filmmakers to recognize, through his explorations of longer narrative literature, the power of freeing the image from its theatrical position as a stationary point of view, watching action as if it took place on a stage. Through the use of different camera angles and distances from the action, as well as editing techniques such as irises and fades, Griffith introduces into movies a version of the unconstrained visual and temporal movement and rhetoric found in and derived from the novel and other forms of narrative fiction. Like the novels and short stories on which so many of these films were based, this allows for a spatial opening up of movies (moving the action quickly from one locale to a different one) and the coexistence of several temporal registers (whereby actions could take place simultaneously or flashback suddenly to another moment), all within a linear chronology associated with the nineteenth-century novel and now classical film form.

No wonder then that so many of Griffith's films and those of other early directors turn increasingly to narrative fiction for materials that would respond to film's developing technical prowess: Griffith's own inflammatory *Birth of a Nation* (1915) is adapted from Thomas E. Dixon's *The Clansman*, and the silent movies throughout the period from 1915–1925, such as Maurice Tourneur and Clarence Brown's 1920 *The Last of the Mohicans*, consistently used popular and classical fiction for their storylines. Along with the narrative and technical mobility to imitate the spatial and temporal activity found in novels, the movies also become the ideal place to recreate that narrative objectivity that had become the crucial foundation for the nineteenth-century novel. As an interesting parallel, the emphasis at this point in film history on a realistic point of view contrasts sharply with the narrative experiments found in many modernist novels written about this time. While filmmakers like Griffith are perfecting a classical style associated with the historical objectivity of the nineteenth-century novel, writers like James Joyce, Virginia Woolf, and other novelists are experimenting with perspectives aimed to subvert notions of narrative objectivity. Indeed, in some cases, these literary experiments may be seen as conscious reactions to film's popular realism.

Along with these narrative developments that linked the early cinema to nineteenth-century literature, models for movie characters naturally follow the models of novelistic characters. Unlike stock characters found in melodramatic and comic plays and unlike epic characters defined by physical actions, film characters like the characters of nineteenth-century novels gradually develop a psychological depth of fears and longings that serve to motivate the action of a film. The star system that begins to appear around 1910 was indeed partially related to this evolution, for when the individuality that focused and drove nineteenth-century narratives moves to the center of a film narrative, the actors who inhabited those characters soon become the most prominent attraction at the movies. Readers learn to empathize and sympathize with literary characters like Dickens's Little Nell, and because real people and personalities perform movie characters, one consequence is perhaps a more potent form of empathy and identification with faces and personalities, an empathetic attraction on which a star system is built. Here, at this juncture at the beginnings of classical cinema, the forces of literary narrative and its psychology of character meet the materials of the theater; here famous actors could (or could not) choose to be converted into the famous movie stars who propel film narratives.

Watch a clip of *Birth of a Nation* at http://www.youtube.com/watch?v=vPxRIF1c2fI

Chapter 3

TESTING AND EXPANDING THE VALUE OF FILM AND LITERATURE, 1915–1940

I T IS APPROPRIATE THAT, just as classical cinema develops culturally and formally to a state that remains its foundation today, the formulas of classical cinema are tested by one of the most controversial and daring adaptations of all time: Erich von Stroheim's adaptation of Frank Norris's *McTeague,* retitled as *Greed* (1924). Originally completed as a ten-and-one-half-hour silent film, *Greed* attempts to retain all the pessimistic complexity of the novel through elaborate and incisive use of filmic techniques and visual detail: editing techniques that suggest the nuanced themes of greed and determinism; a camera focus that makes ironic connections between characters and their inevitable fates; and almost obsessive framing of narrative details all work to create filmic equivalents for the linguistics of the novel. The film culminates in a stunningly long sequence in Death Valley, giving the film's relentless temporal motifs physical contours that may even surpass the novel. In these attempts to push film's literary and artistic powers to new extremes, however, *Greed* becomes one of the first of many cases in which the commercial necessities of the film industry stepped in to restrain the literary and artistic visions of the filmmaker. When the studio, Metro-Goldwyn-Mayer, became justifiably concerned about marketing a movie of such an exorbitant length, the film was taken from von Stroheim and cut to two-and-one-half hours. Throughout this period of film history, the growing literary aspirations of many other movie adaptations would be tested by the commercial and formal differences of the cinema.

For the most part, literary men and women in the first two decades of the twentieth century avoid and often attack the movie business. By the 1920s, however, notable shifts of sentiment and practice begin to appear as the literary world starts to recognize (1) the claims of film as

Watch a clip of the final sequence *of Greed* at http:// www. youtube.com/ watch?v–0ECZW9R16EY, and read more about the film at http:// en.wikipedia.org/ wiki/ Greed_%28film%29 a poetic and narrative art with aesthetic and social powers particularly attuned to modern life, and (2) the possibility of using the themes and forms of the movies as part of their literary work. In line with these observations and intimations, the 1920s and 1930s represent one of the most active periods of creative exchange, rather than dependence, between film and literature, one in which film begins to assert its aesthetic claims for creative powers equal to literature. Two kinds of historical activities connecting film and literature during the 1920s and 1930s need to be signaled here: The first relates to the various imagistic movements of modernism and the avant-garde and their indirect relation to a new realism of social reform; the second outlines the massive impact of the coming of sound on literary adaptations. Through these and other trends, film and literature interact to test and develop their value to society: Film begins to assume new cultural and artistic value, while literature must reevaluate its own abilities to reflect and engage social change.

Modern Images and social imperatives

Before and after *Greed,* there is a great deal of successful and unsuccessful experimentation with the relationship between film and literature, most notably with how film could assimilate or potentially surpass traditional literature in its efforts to create new perspectives and ideas. This is, in part, an aesthetic project that overlaps with various avant-garde practices; frequently the movies borrow from literature to demonstrate how film could not only accommodate poems, novels, and theater but could transform those literary materials into truly modernist works of art. Following some developing precepts of modernism, the technological art of film seems especially able to organize fragmentary images (as edited "shots") even more

Figure 3.1 Like a modernist poem, Jean Cocteau's *The Blood of a Poet* (1930) creates a dreamscape of images that resist easy explanation. Statues come to life and rooms lose their gravity in a shared space of avant-garde literature and film.

graphically and dynamically than the linear and nonlinear patterns explored by the "less modern" modernisms of traditional literature and art.

This modernist interface between film and literature produces movies from a variety of countries and in numerous aesthetic shapes, commercial and noncommercial, narrative and non-narrative, poetic and theatrical. German Expressionist cinema and its most famous product *The Cabinet of Dr. Caligari* (1919)—a film scripted by the artist Carl Mayer and the Czech poet Hans Janowitz—are perhaps the best known and anticipatory examples of this movement toward art and poetry in the cinema: like some of the most inventive literature and paintings of this period, Caligari specifically questions realist notions of time and place before the power of dreams and desires. As part of the same movement but with roots in the earlier *film d'art* movement, director Max Reinhardt translates theater into film through remarkably inventive *mise-en-scènes* orchestrating lighting, crowds, and set designs (still recognizable in his American-made *A Midsummer Night's Dream* of 1935). Similarly, F. W. Murnau's filmed versions of *Tartuffe* (1925) and his 1922 *Nosferatu* (loosely adapted from Bram Stoker's 1897 *Dracula*) would use film idioms and techniques to retell those stories with an imagistic force that visually actualized shifts in human identity that the literature may only be able to describe; in *Nosferatu* he employs the special effects of the film image to present the horrifying figure of a body there but not there, alive but dead.

With many of these efforts, aesthetic experiments with film and literature are also political and social reevaluations of the relationship

Especially important in this context is Hugo Münsterberg's "The Means of Photoplay" (p. 137) which examines the new visual potentials in film representation.

Figure 3.2 Adapted from Bram Stoker's 1897 novel *Dracula*, the 1922 *Nosferatu* would use film idioms and techniques to retell those stories with an imagistic force that the literature may only be able to describe.

between art and culture. In Italy, the Futurist movement of Tommaso Marinetti and others would influence both the avant-garde cinema and the experimental theater movements of the 1920s and early 1930s by freely trading on the supposed revolutionary powers of technology and technological perspectives to suggest the new velocities and energies of modern society. In Russia, Vsevolod Meyerhold experiments throughout the 1920s with radical theatrical techniques transposed from the cinema, much of this interdisciplinary energy being passed onto filmmaker Sergei Eisenstein, who would envision a renovated social order brought to life by the new theatrics of the cinema. In France, the surrealist overlappings of drama, poetry, and film found in the work of Antoine Artaud and Jean Cocteau reappear in their films and in the more narrative films of Abel Gance, *J'accuse* (1919), *La Roue* (1922–1923), and his tryptiched-screen epic *Napoléon* (1927), the latter demonstrating how modern history could only be apprehended through multiple viewpoints. For all the distinctions and differences in these projects, their creative crossings between various artistic and literary fields demonstrate a deep belief in the way film, at the cultural intersection of art, literature, and technology, might best present the twentieth century that was taking shape. In many cases, these writers, artists, and filmmakers believe that the older forms of literature and the traditional arts could not adequately represent modern society. As a technological art with new ways of imagining people and events, film would thus move to the forefront of culture where it could absorb literary traditions and transform them. The result would be images and literatures demonstrating the new movements, speeds, industrial powers, unconscious minds, and the expanding social masses of a brave new world.

Note this passage in Crane's 1930 modernist epic "The New Technological Wonder of the Brooklyn Bridge":
"I think of cinemas,
  panoramic sleights
With multitudes bent
  toward some flashing
  scene
Never disclosed, but
  hastened to again,
Foretold to other eyes
  on the same screen"

Not surprisingly then, the direction of the exchange between film and literature often shifts during this period from the adaptation of literature by the movies to the adaptation of film and its techniques by literature. Certain writers, such as Hart Crane (*The Bridge*), Gertrude Stein (*Tender Buttons*), and John Dos Passos (*U.S.A.*), experiment with the metaphors and rhetoric of the cinema to challenge the limitations of literary language, recasting in language, for instance, film's panoramic visual movements, its fragmentary montages of images, or its documentary clarity. If film assimilates literature for both its aesthetic and social value, the literature of this period would often attempt to take advantage of the imagistic energy of film to make the literary more responsive to the visual patterns of the twentieth century.

By the early 1930s those poetic and avant-garde directions meet a second powerful direction in film history, that of the social documentary. These two general directions should not be viewed as opposites but as complementary counterpoints, since both sought to challenge cultural assumptions and formulas deemed inadequate to the social and experiential realities of contemporary life. For both the aesthetic experimenters and the social realists the film medium becomes a tool for redefining the peoples and problems that, from one point of view, conventional literature and other traditional forms of representation excluded. In this sense, the power of modern technology and industry, as manifested in film practice, might supplement or replace those literary forms, and so expand or alter the older social values associated with literature. From some quarters— the defenders of the cultural sanctuaries of literature, for instance—those traditional values are defended vigorously against the new energies and liberalities of the movies, as many critics during this period condemn what they considered the distorted views disseminated by the movies. For others, however, the values of traditional art and literature remade through the language of film could reveal the possibilities of changing the world for the better. As part of a lively cross-cultural debate about cinematic realism and its ability to engage its audiences, Walter Benjamin's celebrated essay on "The Work of Art in the Age of its Technological Reproducibility" (p. 147) represents, in this historical context, one of the most important and dramatic statements about the radical social value of film in the changing history of art and literature.

The work of many movements and filmmakers should be seen in this context of changing relationship between film and literature. In Germany there is, besides the aesthetics of expressionism, the "street realism" of Murnau, G. W. Pabst, and others, in which—as in Pabst's *The Love of Jeanne Ney* (1927) or Phil Jutzi's 1931 version of Alfred Döblin's *Berlin Alexanderplatz*—the complex plots of literary narratives would be reduced and intensified through darkly realistic images. In France, one of the most important periods in cinema history, from 1934–1940, has been dubbed "poetic realism," a combination of two of the period's central literary and filmic terms. Film historian George Sadoul defines the poetic realism of French cinema as a combination of poetry and realism developing out of novelist Émile Zola's literary naturalism and the work of several poet/ filmmakers, including the avant-garde films of Louis Delluc (*The Woman from Nowhere* [1921]) and the lyrical films of Jean Vigo (*À propos de Nice* [1929] and *Zero for Conduct* [1933]). Two of the most important filmmakers associated with poetic realism are Jean Renoir and Marcel Carné whose films—such as Renoir's 1934 adaptation of Flaubert's *Madame Bovary*, his 1937 *Grand Illusion*, and Carné's 1938 collaboration with poet-screenwriter Jacques Prévert on *Port of Shadows*—brilliantly develop careful and sometimes elaborate cinematic styles to portray social and historical flashpoints in human and class relations.

Watch a selection of *À propos de Nice*: http://www.youtube. com/watch?v= mAY5KNSoS2o

Although the worldwide Depression years that defined much of the 1930s promote escapist fare of nostalgic and sentimental adaptations, Hollywood is not immune to these demands to produce socially conscious films as part of a new aesthetic. In the United States, the combination of documentary realism and stylistic innovation inspire one of the decade's finest movies and finest literary adaptations of all times: Lewis Milestone's 1930 *All Quiet on the Western Front* (based on Erich Maria Remarque's novel about World War I) begins a Hollywood decade that would conclude most famously with the socially stark and disgruntled *The Grapes of Wrath* (1940).

Yet, in the United States commercial and political pressures intended to assure certain middle-class values at the movies would largely temper the movement toward formal experimentation and social realism. This is illustrated most concretely in the 1930–1931 battle over Theodore Dreiser's *An American Tragedy*, a melodramatic but searing critique of modern American society. At the center of this adaptation by Paramount Studios were, besides one of America's greatest novelists, two European directors who embodied the best of the political and artistic potential in film, Sergei Eisenstein and Josef von Sternberg. When Eisenstein submitted a script that Dreiser favored, studio executives rejected the treatment because it was too political (since Eisenstein carefully followed Dreiser in complicating the hero's guilt and assigning some of it to his dire social predicament). Over Dreiser's protest, von Sternberg took over the adaptation and made it into a more politically palatable tale of an individual's erotic obsession. Writing for the avant-garde film review *Close Up* (which featured some of the most important literary figures of the time), Harry Potamkin would defend Dreiser's novel and Eisenstein's script by returning to one of the central themes binding film and literature during the period: "The fight for the integrity of this experience [depicted in the novel] is not a personal one, nor even for the rights of authorship. It is a struggle against the debasing of the intellectual and social level of an experience" (1977: 186).

Read more about this important event in adaptation history at http://www.britannica.com/bps/additionalcontent/18/6593698/AN-AMERICAN-TRAGEDY

Hollywood, the Code, sound, and literature

As the case of *An American Tragedy* indicates, a very significant, if indirect, force in the increased development of literary adaptations is the Production Code or, as it is commonly known, the Hays Code. Established in 1922, the Motion Picture Producers and Distributors Association (MPPDA) aimed to correct the growing image of Hollywood as a den of iniquity, scandal, and social subversion, and by the early 1930s the Hays Code had established clear guidelines for the censorship of sexual language and behavior, graphic violence, and other actions that might be deemed immoral or reprehensible. In the 1930s, other positions and groups, such as the 1932–1933 studies by the Payne Fund and the Catholic League of Decency, also attempt to argue guidelines that would prevent movies from becoming too offensive or too far outside the moral mainstream. Of the many effects of these rules and guidelines, one is the growing attraction of literary classics, since literature, even when the subject matter was morally suspect, could often carry a cultural weight sufficient to deflect the censors. In that sense, the Hays Code's encouragement of and the fashion for the cinematic adaptation of literary classics works as a visible variation on the motif of the 1930s culture attempting to measure and ensure certain social values.

Perhaps even more important to the dialogue between literature and the movies, however, is the coming of sound to the cinema in the late 1920s (usually marked by the phenomenal success of the 1927 *The Jazz Singer*). In her wide-ranging discussion of the theoretical and historical links between film and literature, Marie-Claire Ropars-Wuilleumier has highlighted the critical impact of the introduction of recorded sound on the cinema in the late 1920s. The coming of sound alters and revolutionizes many dimensions of film form and film history, but new sound technologies are especially significant in the relationship between film and literature in four far-reaching ways, ways that extend and complicate tendencies already dominating classical cinema: (1) Sound reinforces and expands the possibilities for realism in the cinema; (2) sound allows the rapid development of theatrical dialogue within the cinema; (3) the introduction of sound provokes fierce reactions against commercial sound movies since some felt it subverted film's unique artistic potential (and so, ironically watered down its ability to compete aesthetically with literature and other arts) by making the spoken word a major component of film form; and (4) as spoken language enlarged the development of character and character motivation, it expands narrative or novelistic form as the main structural principle for the movies. In the transition from silent to sound films, from the late 1920s through the early 1930s, these directions for the cinema both confirm the power of realistic narrative and initiated a reaction against it.

Indeed, the spate of adaptations that appear in the 1930s is one indication of the importance of sound in drawing film and literature closer together. In many ways, the decade of the 1930s (and into the 1940s) represents the golden era of traditional literary adaptations in Hollywood, producing many of the finest examples of literature adapted to classical film form: James Whale's *Frankenstein* (1931); Josef von Sternberg's *Crime and Punishment* (1935); George Cukor's *Dr. Jekyll and Mr. Hyde* (1932) and *Camille* (1936); Rouben Mamoulian's *Becky Sharp* (1935); William Wyler's *Wuthering Heights* (1939); Robert Leonard's *Pride and Prejudice* (1940); and Alfred Hitchcock's *Rebecca* (1940). All of these bear the marks of the technological and stylistic struggles and innovations of the period, upon which literary sources become rich foundations for experimentation and development.

Throughout this period the relationship between the theater world and the film world is especially lively, as elements of the theater once again emerge to counterpoint the forces of narrative realism in the cinema. During this period, theater and film develop particularly strong financial ties as they compete for and exchange literary materials, as well as personnel, such as director George Cukor, actress Katharine Hepburn, and writer Clifford Odets. The exchange also produces a genre of movies called "backstage musicals" that has continued to the present. Including *On with the Show*

The official arrival of sound in 1927, the same year of the first transatlantic flight by Charles Lindbergh, makes this date one of the landmark years in film history. For wide-ranging discussion of film sound, see Rick Altman's collection *Sound Theory, Sound Practice.*

(1929), *The Gold Diggers of Broadway* (1929), and *Swingtime* (1936), and later *Singin' in the Rain* (1952), these are movies whose subject matter is the theatrical life behind and in front of the curtain, and they occasionally turn those stories into a commentary on the differences in the two media. In Europe and America, the interplay between theater and film also moves into less commercial ventures, bringing more artistically demanding works from the stage to the screen, such as the 1930 British adaptation of Sean O'Casey's *Juno and the Paycock* and Paul Robeson's 1933 screen incarnation of Eugene O'Neill's drama *The Emperor Jones.*

Following the swift developments in sound cinema, the surge of dramatic adaptations and novelistic adaptations draw together in a highly creative blend of two regularly contending forces in film history—one emphasizing the external conflictual forces associated with traditional drama and the other exploring character psychology in which internal forces drive a narrative forward. From this creative merger of contending literary forces would appear some of the most accomplished, polished, and successful films in and outside Hollywood, assimilating not only the developing technologies of sound but also, in some cases, the new Technicolor processes of the 1930s. In 1939–1940 Hollywood produces three of the grandest adaptations in the history of cinema, each in its different way fashioning stunning spectacles of human desire overcoming numerous social and personal obstacles along its narrative path: *The Wizard of Oz* (1939), from L. Frank Baum's 1900 tale; *Gone with the Wind* (1939), based on Margaret Mitchell's 1936 bestseller; and *The Grapes of Wrath* (1940), adapted from John Steinbeck's 1939 novel. With all their differences, these films mark, for many, the culmination of the classical film as the most modern of classical literatures.

Despite the remarkable number and quality of film adaptations of literature in the 1930s, at the end of the decade there are signs of strain and unease. Appearing in 1939 alongside that remarkable collection of movies (which also included John Ford's *Stagecoach*, Frank Capra's *Mr. Smith Goes to Washington*, and, in France, Jean Renoir's *Rules of the Game*), Nathaniel West's 1939 novel *The Day of the Locust*, for instance, is one of the most justly celebrated intersections of literature and the movies. Employing a pictorial style that describes life as if lived through different movie shots and scenes, the novel sets the desperation of an alienated artist against the numbing frustrations and hysterias produced by the mass media and popular culture of Hollywood. West's novel paints an extremely bleak picture of what movie culture—or at least Hollywood—has to offer individuals struggling to retain their individuality and meaningful social relations. At a moment when narrative and dramatic histories are growing and spreading rapidly as the myths of the movie screen, West's novel sounds a note of suspicion and warning about the nature and truth of that cinematic literature, a warning that clearly anticipates the next decade.

Especially pertinent here is Judith Mayne's "Readership and Spectatorship" (p. 252).

Chapter 4

PENS, PULP, AND THE CRISIS OF THE WORD, 1940–1960

THAT THE EVENTS OF WORLD WAR II altered the perspectives of literature, the cinema, and the relationship between the two is a fundamental fact of this period. For many, the events preceding and informing World War II (as it grew out of the 1914–1918 World War I) represent the violent twists and disruptions of an Enlightenment vision that sees human civilization always progressing through intellectual, technological, and cultural advancements. In a sense, all sides in that global conflict participate, through their increasing technological and industrial resources, in superhuman aspirations: to conquer nature and space, to know more than ever before, to create ideal societies, to make imaginative myths real. The ghastly results of that vision, however, rapidly reveal themselves in the unthinkably inhuman products of those visions: Auschwitz and other Nazi concentration camps and the nuclear victims of Hiroshima and Nagasaki are only the most infamous testimonies to the reversal of a progressive direction in cultural and human history.

Precisely because both had been the vehicles for cultural identities and their myths throughout the twentieth century, film and literature could not help but be affected by this global trauma, a trauma that visibly rattled their confidence in the humanizing truth each claimed to purvey. If during the 1920s and 1930s literature assimilated film as the new vehicle for social change and modern visions, during the 1940s and into the 1950s the failures and inadequacies of that redemption became abundantly clear. Out of these concerns there are two dominant trends that surfaced through the next two decades: (1) the cinema explored and in some cases "deauthorized" the monumental powers of the cultural myths and histories, found often in literary classics and embodied in the figure of the writer and his or her authority; (2) in the cultural rubble left over by the war, claims for personal expression in film, modeled after the individual creativity of writing, attempted to reclaim or to "reauthorize" film as a more personal and human instrument.

Film exploring literature

The years of World War II in Europe (1939–1945) continue to produce some of the most accomplished, often literary, epics in film history, featuring such classic movies as *Stagecoach* and *Gone with the Wind* in 1939, *Citizen Kane* in 1941, David Lean's *Brief Encounter* in 1945, and Marcel Carné's *Children of Paradise* in 1945. Like many films of this era, these examples sometimes have less a direct relation with a literary source than with the larger cultural place of literary visions. Thus, even though Ford's *Stagecoach* derives directly from an Ernest Haycox story and less directly from Guy de Maupassant's "Boule de suif," it appears an almost archetypal homage to the literary western as an American cultural myth. Cinematic paeans like this are, moreover, only one of many possible ways to represent these stories and myths, which might also be retrieved by the movies as a kind of nostalgia or as an object of criticism. Following these and other strategies, movies throughout this period tend to retrieve a literary or cultural past to measure, sharply or vaguely, the distance between those past cultures and the troubled world of the 1940s. One thematic thread that runs through much of this work is appropriately the struggle to define and understand the history of individuals and nations and the intersection of film and literature during this period often replays this issue of cultural history and its relation to personal and public memory.

From this angle, Orson Welles's *Citizen Kane* functions as almost an allegory for the relationship between film and literature during this period. Leaving his rocketing stage and radio career to come to Hollywood to make an adaptation of Joseph Conrad's *Heart of Darkness*, Welles instead made *Citizen Kane*, a film that still bears the oblique marks of that original idea in its story of an obsessive individual whose greed and ideals ultimately alienate him from the world he hoped to remake in his image. The narrative complexities of Conrad's novel also leave their traces on Welles's movie as both construct convoluted narratives in which the search through words and images never finally reveals the truth. Indeed, that Conrad's novel suggests that its demonic hero, Kurtz, is the product of the history of European culture provides a charged link with Welles's cultural icon Kane, who hobnobs proudly with Hitler and other political forces on the brink of World War II and who proudly identifies himself as first and foremost an American.

Two other important films that adapt cultural masterpieces and memories to address the trauma of history are Carné's *Children of Paradise* and Laurence Olivier's *Henry V* (1944). The first tells the story of the theatrical world of nineteenth-century Paris when the culture of classical theater and the popular boulevard entertainments of mimes and other street performers interact. Its elaborate narrative and complex theatrical *mise-en-scènes* move in two directions: Most prominently, the film creates

Read more about this connection between the famous novel and film in Robert Carringer's *The Making of* Citizen Kane.

Figure 4.1 One of the most celebrated adaptations of a Shakespearean play, Laurence Olivier's *Henry V* (1944) faithfully recreates the stage of Shakespeare's Globe Theatre, only to shift its perspective to the Technicolor realism of the movies. In this way the movie both acknowledges its past and draws attention to the historical distance between the sixteenth and twentieth centuries.

a homage to the artistic brilliance of an older period of cultural and social change, yet, concomitantly, its shadowy and wistful perspective on those former times serves to ironize that lost world, making the human vivacity of that former historical moment seem, from the perspective of the 1940s, an illusory dream. With Olivier's film, too, much of the appreciative analysis that has surrounded it seems fully justified, not simply for its inventive stylistic and structural engagements with Shakespeare's play, but also in how those formal features index critical historical shifts in the relationship between film and literature. As the film moves between the staged world of Shakespeare's Elizabethan theater and the cinematic open spaces of Henry's Technicolored forces leaving for France, the film becomes as much about historical distance as about continuities. Although the patriotic fever of the original play pervades this remake completely, the Technicolor orchestrations of its ancient war makes its classic vision an inspiring memory of tropes and gestures, whose distance from the horrors of modern times means that they can only be *performed* in a highly self-conscious way.

In the United States, notable contributors to these reflections on classical forms, literatures, and their value during these times are the immigrant filmmakers, technicians, and actors. Spurred on by the Parufamet agreement of 1926 (a three-way agreement between the American studios,

One of the earliest and most important arguments about Olivier's adaptation appears in André Bazin's "Theater and Cinema" (p. 223).

Paramount and MGM, and the German studio UFA), the movement of immigrant artists and movie craftsmen continues through the 1930s and begins to impact Hollywood throughout the 1930s and 1940s. Influx of Europeans such as von Stroheim, Fritz Lang, Max Ophuls, Billy Wilder, Douglas Sirk, and others brings with it a deep commitment to art and poetic cinema; when movies begin to question the forms and assumptions of their cultural heritage in the 1940s, these directors and their films often contribute significantly to the shift toward other relationships for film and literature. Those relationships extend the questioning of history and its instabilities beyond the classical paradigms that thrived on adaptations of literary classics.

Some of the most important films following these alternative literary perspectives in the movies are the detective films and other dark and violent movies associated with the *film noir* movement. In part a product of the style imported from German Expressionism, these movies—from *The Maltese Falcon* (1941) to *Double Indemnity* (1944), *The Big Sleep* (1946), and *Touch of Evil* (1958)—are characterized by plots of dark passions and crime in which the law can no longer be trusted and a visual style that emphasizes shadows and spatial confusion. More important in the relationship of film and literature, these films of the 1940s and early 1950s turn toward popular (usually detective) fiction and often swerve from the clear linearity and chronologies of classical literature and cinema to foreground multiple plot lines and narrative gaps in the action. Often constructed around a first-person literary narrative recreated through a voice-over film narration, this popular fiction, sometimes dubbed "hard-boiled fiction" or "pulp fiction," concentrates on socially isolated and morally marginal characters in a threatening and shifting world.

There can be little doubt that these new literary inspirations indirectly mirror the larger historical and social disturbances beginning in the 1930s and climaxing in World War II. They likewise reconfirm, first, a move away from classical literature and its association with certain cultural traditions and hierarchies, and, second, a willingness to explore, in search of new realisms, more experimental narrative patterns and characters outside the literary mainstream, specifically through the work of the detective fiction of writers such as Dashiell Hammett, James Cain, and Raymond Chandler. Indeed, one suggestive moment in this shift between critically canonized literatures and minor literatures is the tale of adaptation of *To Have and Have Not* (1944), produced when director Howard Hawks dared Ernest Hemingway to let him have what Hawks considered the writer's worst novel to transform into a successful film. With the screenwriting help of another celebrated American novelist, William Faulkner, this "bad" work of literature became one of the finest examples of a cinema inspired by the rough edges of troubled fiction. Throughout the United States, minor literature and unpolished stories increasingly became the source for some of the most trenchant films of the next decade, including numerous Hitchcock movies of the 1950s and the 1955 films *Night of the Hunter*, produced from a minor Davis Grubb novel, and *Rebel without a Cause*, from the short story "The Blind Run."

That *film noir* and other innovative kinds of movies throughout this period attracted some of the most important writers of twentieth-century fiction—Faulkner, Bertolt Brecht, Graham Greene (whose novels were often adapted for the screen, such as the 1944 Fritz Lang film *Ministry of Fear*), and many others—adds to the paradoxes and contradictions that describe the rapport between the two arts during the 1940s and 1950s. Serious theatrical and literary writers (including journalists) from the 1930s through the 1940s began to gravitate to a film industry that was formerly viewed with deep suspicion; at the same time films and screenplays begin to break away from the dominance of literary culture and to innovate by creatively adapting the much less intimidating forms of popular literature. It is no wonder that scriptwriting during this period drew so many celebrated writers to experiment in a new idiom.

Finally, two cataclysmic industrial and political events add to the turbulence surrounding writers, literature, and movies as the 1940s turned into the 1950s. The first is the 1948 Paramount Decision in which the courts ruled that the main studios (Paramount, Warner Brothers, Loew's [MGM], Twentieth Century-Fox, RKO, Universal, Columbia, and United Artists) violated antitrust laws by monopolizing the film business (through control of theater chains, block-booking, and other means of keeping out independent production and distribution practices). This decision in effect initiates the dispersal of the studio system through which classical Hollywood movies had flourished. As a consequence, independent filmmaking begins its expansion (between 1946 and 1956 the number of independent films doubled to 150), and this growth of independence in turn encourages the more active kind of relationship between writers, books, and movies that *film noir* and similar films were encouraging in other ways.

The second event strikes directly at writers in Hollywood—the investigations of the House Un-American Activities Committee (HUAC) hearings. Adding to the tensions in the relationship between writing and

See Peter Lurie's *Vision's Immanence: Faulkner, Film, and the Popular Imagination* for a discussion of how the work of theAmerican novelist Faulkner interacts with film aesthetics.

Figure 4.2 Sunset Blvd. (1950) is a movie about a delusory movie queen and a dead screenwriter who paradoxically acts as the voice-over narrator of the story of his own death. Beyond the drama of the murder mystery, the film suggests a wry perspective on the turbulent role of the writer in a changing Hollywood.

film of this period, political conservatives, led by Senator Joseph McCarthy, seek out members of the Hollywood movie community—most notably the screenwriters—whom they suspected of being communists. Dalton Trumbo and Bertolt Brecht are just two of the writers called before the committee that condemned some to serve jail time for refusing to cooperate with the hearings. Others, who were, or were not necessarily, part of the famous "Hollywood Ten" called before the committee, are blacklisted from working in Hollywood. Jules Dassin and Joseph Losey, two of the most creative writers to cross between theater and film, are casualties of this process and end up doing most of their later work outside Hollywood (Losey in Europe as a renowned interpreter of Harold Pinter's plays). In 1949, Robert Rossen adapts Robert Penn Warren's *All the King's Men* as a bitter tale of political machinery and demagoguery, and, ironically or predictably, HUAC subpoenas him as a member of the "Hollywood Nineteen."

If the Hollywood studios were being forced to make way for more independent relations between writers and filmmaking, the HUAC hearings make clear the massive challenges facing independent and creative writing in Hollywood then. Two useful examples of this paradox and problem are *Sunset Blvd.* (1950) and *Native Son* (1951). With some irony, the winner of three Oscars in 1950 (including best screenplay), *Sunset Blvd.,* tells the gloomy and disturbing tale of a murdered screen writer from the voice-over perspective of that same writer, present but dead. In it the writer-protagonist cynically remarks that "audiences don't know [that] anyone writes a picture. They think the actors make it up as they go along."

This contradictory position in which the writer is both acknowledged and denied (fictionally, politically, or industrially) becomes nearly an allegory of the "deauthorizing" of the writer that characterizes the relationship of film and literature during these years. A second illustration of this deauthorization of the writer of a literary tradition, as a twisted engagement with literary authority and tradition, is the saga of the adaptation of Richard Wright's 1940 novel *Native Son.* Given the novel's blistering attack on racism in the United States, Wright felt that it could be adequately adapted only outside Hollywood—specifically in Argentina, in 1951. The result, however, is a desperately lame film that even in its muted form, was banned and repressed when it first appeared in the United States, marginalizing outside the movie mainstream one of the central voices in African-American writing. Here, and in many other cases of new writing and the movies, a central irony appears: so many dramas of deauthorization occur, throughout the 1950s, just as the writer as an independent literary force becomes the model for a new creativity in a film industry undergoing major changes and looking for new directions.

A similar deauthorizing and suspicion of the traditions of high culture informs the major changes that were occurring in film cultures around the world. In Europe, we see somewhat different versions of these dramas about film, literature, writing, and language. After World War II, many

See the trailer and opening of the problematic adaptation of *Native Son:* http://www.youtube.com/watch?v= ckBvNE0qc9Y salient parts of European film culture seem to turn sharply from the literary traditions that had supported the cinema since the beginning, but which now become suspect when viewed across the horrific products of Western culture. Most famously, Italian neorealism initiates a call for a depiction of the social realities left out of the grand fictions and theatrical displays of Hollywood films, and this movement would produce numerous decidedly unliterary and flatly realistic dramas of postwar life in Italy, such as Roberto Rossellini's *Rome, Open City* (1945) and Vittorio De Sica's *The Bicycle Thieves* (1948). While film and literature are exploring their relationship most fruitfully and creatively in some corners of Europe and Hollywood, one of the celebrated spokespersons for Italian neorealism, Cesare Zavattini, calls for the removal of the story from the screenplay. Even off the Italian screens, the postwar concern with the social realism of shattered lives produces stark literary landscapes in the writings of Elio Vittorini, Vasco Pratolini, Cesare Pavese, and later the fiction of Pasolini.

Besides the Italians, other European film cultures and literary movements participate in this call for a new realism sprung from the devastations and insecurities unleashed and recorded by World War II. By the mid-1950s, for example, the British Free Cinema provides its own form of this realism in short documentary films. Later it would join the parallel work being done by the "angry young men" of the British theater and literary world, and produce filmmaker Tony Richardson's adaptation of John Osborne's play *Look Back in Anger* (1959) and Karel Reisz's version of Alan Sillitoe's novel *Saturday Night and Sunday Morning* (1960), both hugely successful literary accommodations of the tough realism that punctuated the 1950s. These and other films of the British New Cinema of the 1960s would foster film/literary collaborations between Joseph Losey and Harold Pinter (*The Servant* [1963] and *The Accident* [1967]) and William Golding and Peter Brook (*Lord of the Flies* [1963]), among others.

One final and tangentially related instance of this renegotiation of authors, authority, and realism in the 1950s is the spread of method acting in drama and film. Usually identified with the Actor's Studio of Elia Kazan and Lee Strasberg and derived to a large extent from Stanislavsky's work in the Moscow Art Theater, method acting alters acting on the stage and screen for the next several decades, as a tactic in which actors would intensely "inhabit" the role being played in order to forsake the authority of the actor's own personality and to recreate the full reality of the character. This encounter between a literary character and the filmic or dramatic performance of that character's reality quickly becomes the heart of much modern film or theater. One of the most powerful examples of it is Marlon Brando's performance in Kazan's screen version of Tennessee Williams's *A Streetcar Named Desire* (1951). In this particular example, not only does Williams's play become a literature confronting an illusory past to unveil the sordid realism of the present, but Brando's and Kazan's performances of that play (as a character and a film) permanently instantiate

See Leo Braudy's "Acting: Stage vs. Screen" (p. 232).

that work as a literature with particularly real bodies, actual movements, and historically determined spaces.

In an important sense, the film *A Streetcar Named Desire* deauthorizes and reauthorizes a literary character and work in terms of a more visceral and more historical realism. In this context, it shares a common ground with film performances from Orson Welles's remakings of Shakespeare's *Macbeth* (1948) and *Othello* (1952) to Akira Kurosawa's astonishingly original recreation of Shakespeare's *Macbeth* as *Throne of Blood* (1957). Whereas realism since the nineteenth century functions as a way of measuring the distance between film and literature, realism of the 1950s now appears — in the United States and other societies around the world — as a way of binding new filmmakers and new writers in a common effort to rethink and recreate, in terms of the *present historical reality,* the authorities and authors of both the literary and the cinematic past. Masters of literature now provide very malleable material for the new authors of cinema.

See Evelyn Tribble's "'When Every Noise Appalls Me': Sound and Fear in *Macbeth* and Akira Kurosawa's *Throne of Blood*" (p. 297).

Reauthoring film

As a continuation of the unease that closed the 1940s, films in the 1950s mark a major shift in the rapport between film and literature. Literature begins, decisively I believe, to lose its hierarchical control over film, and films begin to claim their own rights and powers as an independent way of examining and employing the literary paradigms of the past and the harsh realities of a postwar world. Whether intentionally or not, the movies seem no longer to need the authority of a sanctioned literary work, and can now promote their own rebellious independence by choosing works of popular literary culture outside the respected literary mainstream, works that often provide enough intellectual space for the filmmaker to do what he or she wishes to do in filmic form. Despite being described as a filmmaker with "such a great reliance on literature, with such a pronounced affinity with his country's literary culture," the Swedish director Ingmar Bergman — one of the most singularly influential filmmakers to emerge from the 1950s — would claim "Film has nothing to do with literature; the character and substance of the two art forms are usually in conflict" (quoted in Winston 1973: 96). Dismissing the authority of literature, other filmmakers, as well, would position themselves as the creative authors of the new cinema.

Like Bergman, many individuals behind the French New Wave (Jean-Luc Godard, François Truffaut, Alain Resnais, Agnès Varda, and others) often argued that a dependence on literary sources was an uncreative and retrograde way to make films. This attitude becomes distilled in François Truffaut's famous attack on a "cinema of quality" and its dependence on the literal adaptation of well-known classics (in his essay "A Certain Tendency of the French Cinema"). In 1948, however, André Bazin, with

Figure 4.2 In Truffaut's *400 Blows* (1959) the struggles of the young Antoine Doinel to find a way to express himself marks a landmark moment in the French New Wave and the possibility of writing with a camera.

typical prescience for the new directions of film history, notes the contradictions and paradoxes in this claim suggesting that even Italian neorealists, with their public criticism of literary films, remained indebted to literature. Like several other postwar cinemas, Bazin argued Italian neorealism sprang from a close rapport with the American novel as it developed decades earlier. Citing the novels of William Faulkner, John Dos Passos, and Ernest Hemingway specifically, he stresses a more creative notion of adaptation. For Bazin, these instances of adaptation worked across historical and cultural differences, allowing film to seek past literature that would accord with present times:

One of Bazin's most innovative and suggestive discussions is his "Adaptation, or the Cinema as Digest" (p. 57).

> So then, while Hollywood adapts bestseller after bestseller at the same time moving further away from the spirit of this literature, it is in Italy, naturally with an ease that excludes any notion of willful and deliberate imitation, that the cinema of American literature has become a reality. ... It is a long while since the modern novel created its realist revolution, since it combined behaviorism, a reporter's technique, and the ethic of violence. Far from the cinema having the slightest effect on this revolution, as is commonly held today, a film like *Paisa* [*Paisan*] proves that the cinema was twenty years behind the contemporary novel. It is not the least of the merits of the Italian cinema that it has been able to find the truly cinematic equivalent for the most important literary revolution of our time. (1971: II, 39–40)

In France as well, despite different filmmakers' denunciation of one literary tradition, the movies begin to reinvent themselves out of other literary paradigms and institutions. Poet, dramatist, and filmmaker Jean Cocteau is a well-known transitional figure in the appearance of the French

New Wave. He had insisted, since his 1930 film *The Blood of the Poet* and through his 1946 *Beauty and the Beast,* that "poetry" encompassed many practices, including filmmaking. Historically related to popular ciné-clubs (where important, as well as obscure, films would be screened and discussed), Henri Langlois's Cinémathèque Française defines the 1950s in France (after going underground during World War II) by becoming a library of modern film culture, replacing books with the texts of films from different nations and historical eras. The cinémathèque and those other ciné-clubs become institutional classrooms for a growing number of journals, including *La Revue du cinéma* (started in 1946), *Positif* (1952), and the *Cahiers du cinéma* (1951). These journals, mirroring the literary journals and reviews that had been arbitraters and promoters of literary culture since 1800, argue for and educate a developing cinema culture that would see and discriminate about films as readers and critics do about literature.

Appropriately, the critical writer who promotes and privileges creative films in these journals becomes the cinematic auteur aspiring to use the camera like a pen. In 1959–1960, the landmark years for the French new cinema, three of these writer/critics would show the world what the revitalized authors of the film image could bring forth: Truffaut's *400 Blows*, an intensely personal story of a delinquent boy rebelling against encrusted traditions and a failed family; Resnais and Duras's *Hiroshima mon amour*, the struggle of two illicit lovers to find a language for their wartime memories in France and Japan; and Jean-Luc Godard's *Breathless*, a wry portrait of outlaw behavior in an equally wry and ironic play with the powers of cinematic idioms.

The idea that the movie camera can be used like a writer's pen becomes one of the most suggestive and inspiring metaphors for alternative film practices in this decade, both as a vehicle for a more "personal" cinema and as a pathway to more and more complex arguments for a language of the cinema comparable to a literary language. That film technology makes available a new lightweight Arriflex camera (and later other models) during this period dovetails with those other social shifts toward independent cinema and aesthetic claims for a more critical and creative cinema. With this more mobile equipment filmmakers could work more quickly and individually, as one might express oneself through words on a page.

Well removed from Hollywood, then, the attention to the language and writing of cinema received a more intellectual and less overtly social twist in the 1950s and 1960s. Whereas the first quarter-century saw movie culture working to absorb and accommodate literary traditions as a way of solidifying a respectable position in that culture, in the 1950s and later, film cultures begin to stress the distinctions of film and literature, or the more creative possibilities in that relationship, by emphasizing its unique artistic practices—modeled, somewhat paradoxically, after literary figures and paradigms. This argument about a distinctive cinematic language has

Watch the remarkable concluding sequence of *400 Blows*: http://www.youtube.com/watch?v=5TTUJQdzSvA

appeared before—from claims about film's hieroglyphic heritage and form that many saw in early cinema to the defenders of the pure language of silent cinema. But now, that language of cinema is endowed with the power of personal expression. Alexandre Astruc's famous essay "The Birth of a New Avant-Garde: La Caméra-Stylo" (p. 181) articulates this position most definitively in 1948: "The cinema is quite simply becoming a means of expression, just as all the other arts have been before it, and in particular painting and the novel ... cinema, like literature, is not so much a particular art as a language which can express any sphere of thought" (p. 182). In 1960, filmmaker Maya Deren goes even farther than Astruc's equation of literary language and a filmic language in asking film to break entirely with its literary heritages and to choose subjects and forms suited to its own unique language:

> If cinema is to take its place beside the others as a full-fledged art form, it must cease merely to record realities that owe nothing of their actual existence to the film instrument. Instead, it must create a total experience so much out of the very nature of the instrument as to be inseparable from its means. It must relinquish the narrative disciplines it has borrowed from literature and its timid imitation of the causal logic of narrative plots, a form which flowered as a celebration of the earthbound, step-by-step concept of time, space and relationship which was part of the primitive materialism of the nineteenth century. Instead, it must develop the vocabulary of filmic images and evolve the syntax of filmic techniques which relate those. It must determine the disciplines inherent in the medium, discover its own structural modes, explore the new realms and dimensions accessible to it and so enrich our culture artistically as science has done in its own province. (Deren 1992: 70)

Situated between the deauthorization of literature and the reauthorization of themselves as authors, many other emerging and independent cinemas use language as a model for film, not, however, simply to underline the expressive possibilities of film but to expand its connections with the other "languages" of society, especially popular culture. In this way, the French New Wave articulates the paradox of film as and beyond literature. As T. Jefferson Kline remarks about this most influential of the new waves: "In usurping the place of the writer, these filmmakers simply recast the meta-literary concerns of the 1950s into meta-cinematic ones" (1992: 3–4). Using film as a language, but a more mobile and critical language than literary words, these filmmakers aim to call into question the classical claims of literature to transparently reveal reality and to replace that tradition and authority with a filmic language that, often through its association with popular culture, could create critical arguments about the dominant forms and languages of culture. The new writers of film, in short, would, like the Beat poets and other alternative literary movements of this time, work to create a language of cinema fully aware of its limitations and relativity, willfully enlisted with cultural fields and personal voices that avoid literary hierarchies and centers.

Chapter 5

ACADEMIC CINEMA AND INTERNATIONAL SPECTACLES, 1960–1980

WHAT CHARACTERIZES THE 1960S in most world cultures is a pervasive rattling of social cages: the Vietnam War, the Paris student riots, the Soviet invasion of Czechoslovakia in 1968, both the black and women's liberation movements, and youth cultures promoting the freedom of sexuality and drugs, all contribute to societies around the world questioning and reacting to rapid cultural and historical changes. As an extension of the anxieties, suspicions, and restlessness of the 1950s, traditional views about family and gender, race and religion, and education and entertainment are sometimes radically confronted during these times. In this context, one trend that figures most prominently in the relationship of film and literature is the continued internationalization of film as perspectives and languages to be examined on both personal and ideological grounds. From this, however, three more specific directions appear: (1) literatures of the 1950s and the 1960s provide film with stories and other materials to challenge the status quo positions that, in the first half of the century, movies helped to establish; (2) as literature turns to film for structures and forms more in touch with modern experience, film declares not only its independence but to a certain extent its privileged status, allowing it to recuperate and remake classic and contemporary literature as "intertextual arguments" or collaborations; and (3) Hollywood films particularly continue the imperative to transform big literature into big spectacles.

Fueling these changes in the relationship between film and literature are three demographic changes in the movie business, all of which start in the 1950s and all of which relate to those three aesthetic patterns. First, the primary audience for the movies grows younger and younger, and this "teenaging" of the moviegoer leads to more youthful, energetic, restless, and often discontented films. Second, as an extension of the ciné-club tradition in France, film culture becomes a central part of colleges and universities, from unofficial film societies to regular film courses in the classrooms, and this academization of movie culture shapes, sometimes directly and sometimes indirectly, the self-conscious and reflective audiences and practices at the movies. Third, the social and geographic movement of urban populations to the suburbs encourages different types of moviegoing habits and different types of movies that must compete with television and draw audiences out of the isolation of their homes by casting movies as major, if not spectacular, events that often turn to controversial or best selling literary sources.

The subversive power of literature as film

Although movies in the 1960s describe other directions and activities, one prominent rapport between film and literature suggests a more pronounced stage of the historical reversals begun in the 1950s. Unlike the relationship in the first three decades of the twentieth century, literature during the 1960s does not become a traditional source for textual and cultural respectability but rather the source for social and aesthetic challenges. Following larger social trends, American movies during the 1950s and 1960s risk more confrontational and daring subject matter, which results in a particularly rich relationship with works of literature outside the mainstream and outside the classical traditions. In the expanding literature of the 1950s and 1960s, sexuality becomes a more explicit subject to be examined and celebrated; the sanctities of the family come into question; and political and historical flashpoints, scandals, and nightmares are exposed and derided.

Contemporary literature becomes, then, an invigorating source for a film culture dissatisfied with the status quo and mainstream. Movies like Joseph Strick's 1963 film of Jean Genet's play *The Balcony* and his daring attempt in 1967 to adapt James Joyce's monumental *Ulysses* were two of several provocative literary adaptations by Strick that struck an appropriately confrontational chord. *The Pawnbroker* (1965) and *Who's Afraid of Virginia Woolf?* (1966)—the first derived from Edward Lewis Wallant and the second from Edward Albee's play—are two notable examples of movies whose grating depictions of society failed to pass the censors and were released without an MPAA certificate. Even the 1963 *Tom Jones* turns the eighteenth-century novel into a gleefully scandalous celebration of sensual pleasures. Indeed, a contributing factor and an inevitable result of this outbreak of a new and subversive breed of literary adaptations is the revision of the MPAA rating system to allow more flexibility and experimentation with the matter and manner of movies. Faced with the image of unsettling but acclaimed literary works, even the censors seem to acknowledge that literature should be allowed to provide film with ways to challenge middle-class perspectives rather than to comfort and secure that group the way classical literary adaptations once did.

Read more about the MPAA rating system and its relation to the earlier Hays Code at http://en.wikipedia. org/wiki/Motion_ Picture_Association_of_ America_film_rating_ system

Collaborative enterprises

One striking tendency in the late fifties that continues through the 1960s was an increasing number of literary and film collaborations not only on

Of the many studies of postmodern film and literature, a usefully wide-ranging collection is Thomas Docherty's *Postmodernism: A Reader* Of the many definitions and commentaries on postmodernism and postmodernity, several shared features stand out: an emphasis on imagistic simulation rather than mimesis, a subversion of traditional narrative cohesion, and a formal aesthetic of pastiche or collage.

the subject matter of the movies but also with a foregrounding of the metaphors, tropes, perspectives, and structural organizations of the film. In those literature/film exchanges in the immediate postwar period, we identified a process of deauthorization and reauthorization, whereby filmmakers critically examined or rejected one literary tradition and rediscovered another in their films. Gradually, however, that pattern of exchange becomes more and more an equitable sharing in which each sees the other as participating in common theoretical and aesthetic concerns. Similar to but distinctive from the modernity that film brought to literature in the 1920s and 1930s, the imagistic structures of film in the 1960s interacted with the verbal play of contemporary literature to create a shared project often called postmodernity, a vision of life and culture as a place of decentered, surface images.

During this period, film offers literature another way of perceiving the world, a visual rhetoric that captures the crisis and desires of a new "society of spectacle." One of the advocates of the so-called new novel, Alain Robbe-Grillet accepts this offer — in novels like *The Voyeur* (1955) and *Snapshots* (1962), in a theoretical study *For a New Novel* (1963), and a landmark film *Last Year in Marienbad* (1961), and makes both his films and novels exercises in external visual form and the imagistic constructions of presence without meaning. "Man looks at the world" he writes, "and the world does not look back at him" (1965: 58). Profoundly influenced by the new cinema of the 1950s and 1960s, poet Adrienne Rich writes poems that internalize the collage structures of alternative movies, explaining in her "Images for Godard" (1975: 53):

> the mind of the poet is the only poem
> the poet is at the movies
> dreaming the film-maker's dream but differently
> free in the dark as if asleep

Indicative of the fragmented, dislocated, and imagistic sensibility shared by writers and filmmakers during this time is this observation by the alienated protagonist of Walker Percy's 1961 *The Moviegoer*: "Other people treasure memorable moments in their lives. ... What I remember is the time John Wayne killed three men with a carbine as he was falling to the dusty street in *Stagecoach,* and the time the kitten found Orson Welles in the doorway of *The Third Man*." About his 1960 novel *Laughter in the Dark*, Vladimir Nabokov says he tried to write "the entire book as if it were a film" (Appel 1974: 258).

More than the exchanges of themes, characters, and stories, and more than a logic according to which film would simply transfer the structures of literature to the screen (such as narrative forms), now film and literature offer each other textual and formal systems whose languages were compatible enough to create an "intertextual" dialogue on problems of representation and interpretation. Godard's 1962 *My Life to Live* transforms Émile Zola's novelistic *Nana* into a thoroughly modern techno-industrial image of the life of a prostitute in Paris. In Italy, Pasolini releases both the novel and the film *Teorema* (1968) the same year, with the assumption that they represent the same argument but with somewhat different textual idioms. As much as Michelangelo Antonioni alters and expands the plot and characters of Julio Cortazar's short story for his 1967 film *Blow Up*, he maintains its obsession with its dynamics of visuality and indeterminancy. Stanley Kubrick's film adaptations of contemporary literature are, from the beginning of the decade with his *Lolita* (1962), creative dialogues with the novelists, but by the time of his 1971 version of Anthony Burgess's *A Clockwork Orange*, the filmmaker seems to work with novels whose imagistic textuality already approaches cinematic forms. In the same spirit, Austrian writer Peter Handke and German director Wim Wenders collaborate from 1969 through the 1970s on films such as an adaptation of Handke's novel *The Goalie's Anxiety at the Penalty Kick* (1972); the full textual parity of this collaboration crystallizes in Handke's virtually simultaneous production and publication of a film and a novel titled *The Left-Handed Woman*, the story of a woman/translator isolated in the images around her.

The role of the universities and other educational institutions in this period of cinema history cannot be overestimated, especially since these institutions begin to defend more vigorously than ever before the place of cinema as the cultural equal of literature, painting, and other traditional arts. While European (and particularly French) universities had occasionally introduced film studies into academia in the 1950s, the 1960s are the period when film studies begin to proliferate in many Western countries, including the United States. That new film courses are claimed more often by English and comparative literature professors is not a trivial point. Film would no longer be presented simply as a question of industrial craft and production nor as an entertainment that students could learn to appreciate. Rather it grew rapidly as an aesthetic discipline whose histories and screenplays more often than not shared an office shelf with Shakespeare, George Eliot, Flaubert, and W. H. Auden. As part of this academic status in the 1960s and 1970s, film becomes a subject for theoretical studies that developed complex arguments for film as an imagistic sign system that parallels the linguistic systems of literature. Rooted in the structuralism of Lévi-Strauss and the early semiotics of Umberto Eco, Roland Barthes, and others, these new theoretical models are instant allies of film (1) because they turn serious intellectual attention to culture at large, including popular cultural forms like the movies, and (2) because they offer rigorous models for discussing how shared "sign systems" (such as film and literature) could both differ and productively interact.

See especially Robert Stam's "Beyond Fidelity: The Dialogics of Adaptation" (p. 74) for a theoretical argument that reflects these historical shifts.

Figure. 5.1   For many, Franco Zeffirelli's 1968 *Romeo and Juliet* epitomizes both the directions and the larger goals of modern literary spectacles with lavish sets and youthful stars.

Figure 5.2 Nearly thirty years later, Baz Luhrmann's *William Shakespeare's Romeo + Juliet* (1996) continues this tradition, featuring stars Claire Danes and Leonardo DiCaprio, an urban setting and a pop-music soundtrack.

Movie spectaculars and cinematic theatricality

Meanwhile, a very different relationship between film and literature develops as one of the dominant tendencies of modern movie culture, mainly through mainstream commercial centers such as Hollywood. Here, literature maintains a more recognizable and traditional connection with the cinema; aiming to attract audiences (drifting into the suburbs or television), it provides materials to be transformed into movie spectacles in which images of literature are made even grander through the power of the cinema. This literature as movie spectacle describes a traditional merger of the literary and the cinematic as commercial theatrics. Alongside and counterpointing these commercial theatrics, however, is a very different sort of theatrical film during this same stretch of years: These are the variety of mostly noncommercial theatrical adaptations that foreground their theatricality in order to align themselves with the art film traditions that grew out of the 1950s.

Revived in the late 1950s and evolving into the contemporary blockbusters that continue into the twenty-first century, movie spectaculars have existed since the silent films and have always had a close relationship with literary works. King Vidor made one of the most expensive films ever seen when he adapted *War and Peace* in 1956; Cecil B. DeMille returned his earlier biblical epic, *The Ten Commandments,* to an even bigger screen in the same year, now with Oscar-winning special effects; and in 1959 the new three-and-a-half hour Cinemascope production of *Ben-Hur* adds more momentum to a literary trend that would continue through the 1960s in huge box-office successes such as *Lawrence of Arabia* (1962) and *Doctor Zhivago* (1965). For many, Franco Zeffirelli's 1968 *Romeo and Juliet* epitomizes both the directions and the larger goals of these modern literary spectacles: An international production (British and Italian), it successfully targets the restless discontent of a large youth audience, while still managing a wonderfully operatic interpretation of the play, purporting to return Shakespeare to popular culture with artistic integrity.

With the dissolution of the old studio system and the subsequent rising cost of making movies, blockbusters like these could draw audiences away from their television sets through the scale of the movie production values (widescreens, Technicolor processes, and stars) and, just as important, the aura of their established literary values.

Paralleling these commercial theatrics, however, another, more alternative, kind of cinema turns to theater and its theatrics to create complex dialogues between film and theatrical drama, often with self-conscious political or aesthetic aims. After a number of extraordinary adaptations in the 1950s, Orson Welles continues his work with theater and film in his 1966 version of Shakespeare's *Henry IV*, Part I and II, *Chimes at Midnight,* a curiously personal film in which Welles casts himself as Falstaffian collaborator and victim. Peter Brook's adaptation of Peter Weiss's *Marat/Sade: The Persecution and Assassination of Jean Paul Marat as Performed by the Inmates at the Asylum of Charenton* (1966) uses film to critique the political theatrics of modern life in his excessively theatricalized staging of Marquis de Sade's asylum revolutionaries; and Eric Rohmer's later adaptations— *The Marquise of O* (1976), based on Heinrich von Kleist's novella, and *Perceval* (1978), based on an unfinished twelfth-century poem, Chrétien de Troyes—abandon all vestiges of historical realism to create stunningly artificial sets, costumes, and acting styles as contemporary updatings of a theater of the mind. In Germany, R. W. Fassbinder's 1972 *The Bitter Tears of Petra Von Kant*, based on his own

Watch the opening of Weiss's *Marat/Sade* at http://www.youtube.com/watch?v=a ur-t-RtOJM.

play, exhausts a single theatrical space as an exploration of the theatrics of gender and power; and his 1979 *Despair*, an English language collaboration with Vladimir Nabokov's novel, playwright Tom Stoppard's screenplay, and global star Dirk Bogarde, ironically deconstructs the very logic of films as commercial spectacles whose pleasures and entertainments, for Fassbinder, often disguise a brutal politics.

After the heydays of their relationship in the thirties, theater and drama return, in short, full force to film practice in the 1960s, 1970s, and 1980s, but the situation is, of course, quite different from that in the 1960s. For many of these alternative films (including Robert Altman's *Come Back to the 5 & Dime Jimmy Dean, Jimmy Dean* [1982] and *Fool for Love* [1985]), theatricality now represents not a similar set of mechanisms with which to capture images of the world, but mechanisms and styles whose artificiality and spatial limitations could expose or critique the false realism of traditional social identities, as well as the commodified realism of traditional movies.

Much of this energy and creative movement between film and literature during these decades is a consequence of an evolving audience for the cinema. By the early 1970s, American, European, and many Asian film cultures could assume an audience saturated from childhood through college with television and movies, and this audience is both more casually and more seriously familiar with media culture than ever before. Moviegoers are now able, if not always willing, to watch and follow films with remarkably sophisticated competencies, and in that sense the old tensions and showdowns over the cultural authority of literature or the movies have already dissipated significantly. One of the consequences of this maturing film audience is an exceptionally dynamic and creative period in film's use of literature through the 1970s.

Indeed, this implicit presumption of an audience with a cinematic literacy perhaps comparable to high points of verbal literacy, an audience able to appreciate the complexities of film and its many relationships with literature, is a crucial backdrop for Francis Coppola's 1972 transformation of the popular novel *The Godfather*, a best seller with quite unremarkable literary value, into a blockbuster art film. Mario Puzo's novel offers Coppola a confrontational subject that sometimes violently questions the sacred cows of the American family and political system, but Coppola transforms that material into *The Godfather I* and *The Godfather II* (1974), with intricate cinematic texts and theatrical spectacles that fully overshadow the book. The *Godfather* films become one of the most celebrated achievements of modern cinema, involving all three of those salient motifs characterizing film and literature from the sixties through the 1970s: subversive material, collaborative cinematics, and commercial theatrics. Following *The Godfather* and its new audiences, other movies from *The Exorcist* (1973) through *Jurassic Park* (1993), would take books and plays where they have never gone before—sometimes as finer artistic achievements and often with much larger economic success. Once highlighted as a textual issue, collaborations between film and literature are now becoming much more transparently financial matters, which an ingenious director could sometimes work to an artistic advantage.

Chapter 6

BOOKS AND MOVIES AS MULTIMEDIA
Into the new millennium

THE FILMS OF STANLEY KUBRICK stand out as intricate and fascinating examples of the trends and changes that occur during the last decades of the twentieth century. From *Lolita* to A *Clockwork Orange*, Kubrick's adaptations through the 1960s and early 1970s align best with the auteurist experiments to collaborate with and creatively remake the literary as the filmic. In each of these movies, the literature provides a respected creative perspective that the filmmaker, often with the assistance of the novelist, transforms into a film. With his 1980 *The Shining*, based on the bestseller by writer Stephen King, however, the relationship becomes a more antagonistic whirlpool of art and commerce. Whereas Nabokov revised *Lolita* as a screenplay for Kubrick and ultimately accepted the director's many changes as a "first-rate film with magnificent actors" (Phillips 1977: 105), King's relationship with Kubrick is more territorial and hostile from the outset. With scriptwriter Diane Johnson, Kubrick strips down King's horror novel and largely reinvents it. Although initially flattered that Kubrick would adapt his novel, King quickly turned on Kubrick and his film; he was most horrified at Kubrick's intention to change the ending (in which Hallorann would be shockingly killed) and by the choice of Jack Nicholson to play Jack Torrance. The choice of Nicholson, according to Kubrick, was economics (since Nicholson is always "bankable") but for King the film became a beautiful image emptied of its inner meaning. This seems, however, hardly a question of literature versus film since King's novels are always films in the making, and in 1997 King would reclaim his novel with the ABC mini-series version of *The Shining*, an adaptation he produced, acted in, and even partly rewrote. As this case suggests, from the 1980s through 2010, film and literature battle mostly for the media image of a work, not for some untranslatable quality in the literature but as part of an open financial and technological circulation in which the proliferation of images of and from literature demonstrates increasingly less concern about authenticity or authority.

Through these recent decades, within and outside Hollywood, film and literature arguably attend especially to their commercial and industrial terms. Whereas the decades immediately preceding this period can be said to have promoted expressive powers, linguistic and textual structures, and a re-imagining of the politics associated with the relationship between film and literature, by the mid-1970s both film and literature are more transparently enmeshed in the commercial shapes that determined their artistic possibilities. In this context, the values and meanings of both film and literature become increasingly determined by their status as saleable commodities, and what they share as entertainment products begins to overshadow their past differences. From this perspective, (1) the value and meaning of both forms are fundamentally determined by a marketplace economics rather than by aesthetic or social discourses, and (2) within this commodification of form and meaning, writers and filmmakers, necessarily or by choice, learn to use the other's commodified textuality as the focus for a self-promotion, a critique, or a play for consumer choice.

Multimedia conglomerates, blockbusters, and home viewing

Recent decades in film history have been most significantly defined by two forces: the reorganization of the movie industry in the hands of multimedia conglomerates and the technological expansion of the ways movies are exhibited, most obviously through home video technologies. The first change begins in the 1960s and early 1970s when industrial giants such as Gulf & Western and Transamerica Corporation take over studio production units like Paramount and United Artists in pursuit of the large profits promised by blockbuster films like *The Godfather* or *Jaws* (1975). The logic here is not complicated: By investing more and more capital into fewer movies (including the investment of paying more money for a blockbuster novel or play), these conglomerates could generate from the movies the kinds of revenues they found in oil, hotels, and other holdings. By the late 1980s, however, another industrial change is afoot: The conglomerate powers behind the movies refocus and downsize as exclusively media empires. Directing their energies more exclusively toward television, movies, records, or book and magazine publication, Gulf & Western became Paramount Communications; in 1989 Kinney became the multimedia mogul Time Warner; Fox joined Rupert Murdoch's News Corporation in 1985; and Sony extended its media powers by buying Columbia in 1989.

Movies have been a commercial, industrial enterprise practically since their inception at the end of the nineteenth century; literature too, since at least the eighteenth century, has been inescapably connected to the economics and industry of publishing or theatrical production. But the restructuring of the film industry through conglomerate and media giants has major consequences for film and literature: (1) conglomerates encourage a continued transformation of literature into commodified spectacles that typically tends to reduce the importance of narrative and character; and

A detailed background for this interaction of adaptations within the changing economics of "high concept" is Justin Wyatt's *High Concept: Movies and Marketing in Hollywood.*

(2) sharing the same spreadsheets, books now must compete commercially within the corporate marketplace, meaning that fewer and fewer risky or experimental works of literature find their way through publishing houses. "High concept" became a buzzword for condensing the marketability of movie projects, and one of the most effective high concepts is to simply match a bestseller or classic novel with a well-known star or director. Conversely, literary publishers and Broadway producers begin to view manuscripts and plays for their potential as blockbusters—the now common media measure for stage, literary, and film work—and, as the 1997 Broadway production of the movie *The Lion King* reminds us, the traditional cultural and aesthetic values that have informed the exchanges between film and literature become overshadowed by financial value.

Even film cultures outside of Hollywood learn to use literature as part of high concept competition: From Volker Schlöndorff's *The Tin Drum* (1979) through Jean Paul Rappeneau's *Cyrano de Bergerac* (1990) and *The Lord of the Rings* trilogy (2001–2003), literature sells films and films sell literature. Most telling perhaps, the two most commercially successful adaptations of literature in the 2000s, the eight *Harry Potter* films (2001–2011) and the three *Lord of the Rings* films, represent the blockbuster return of one of the earliest and most persistent relationships between film and literature (including the 1912–1913 French adaptations of the *Fantomas* stories), the adaptation of books and stories as serialized movies aimed to maintain a continual recycling of audiences eager to see the evolving plot and characters visualized and actualized on screens. The extraordinary success of these films, however, suggests how that older pattern has been refashioned as shrewd promotional and commercial strategies by massive media industries with a common financial interest in the interaction of books and films they produce.

The rapid advance of home video technology has been the second important change from the mid-1970s to the present, creating a situation in which the majority of movies are now seen through home video players, cable networks, and computers. Watching movies on television is, of course, not an entirely new phenomenon, and literature on television is a kind of adaptation that has been prevalent since the 1950s. The recent explosion of DVD technologies and the recent expansion of ways to watch movies with computer technologies influence, however, the ways individuals and audiences watch films and bear significantly on the intersection of film and literature. Most obviously, watching movies is now more often a domestic or private experience that comes, in some ways, closer to the conditions of reading a work of literature. Unlike the experience of seeing a movie blockbuster in theater, the private control that a home viewer has over a film approaches that of reading at a certain pace or rereading certain lines or passages, and many original films and many recent adaptations seem geared toward this more readerly relationship between the film and the viewer, a relationship in which the spectator becomes a

Simone Murray's "Materializing Adaptation Theory: The Adaptation Industry" (p. 365) is an astute and detailed discussion of these issues.

LIBRARY, UNIVERSITY OF CHESTER

Watch a selection from the "Book of Mythologies" in *Prospero's Books:* http://www.youtube.com/watch?v=zA_ofR8MFak

View a clip from the Bollywood *Bride and Prejudice:* http://www.youtube.com/ watch?v=ocNFQioWM5c

For a study of how DVD technology has shifted movie viewing towards the literary dynamics of reading a book, see Deborah Parker and Mark Parker's *The DVD and the Study of Film: The Attainable Text.*

more active participant in the address and style of the movie. Peter Greenaway's 1991 *Prospero's Books,* David Cronenberg's 1991 version of William Burrough's novel *Naked Lunch,* and Gurinder Chadha's 2004 *Bride and Prejudice* may map a new field for the relationship between film and literature, where movies do not assimilate literature to their own visual theatrics but develop a unique relationship with their film audiences analogous to the more concentrated activity of private readings.

The return of the classics: choosing a version

In recent decades, even a casual viewer would note the unusual proliferation of adaptations of classic novels and other classic literature, a tendency used to characterize especially British films as part of a "heritage cinema" that aims to recreate past historical people and places (originally appearing in the 1980s as, in part, a commercial strategy to market British films in the U.S. and also as a way to reframe controversial contemporary issues by relocating those issues in images of the past). From the spate of Jane Austen and Henry James novels and Shakespeare plays to the less commonly adapted works of Thomas Hardy, Edith Wharton, and Virginia Woolf, reputable literature and canonized names compete vigorously today with blockbusters and action films for contemporary movie audiences around the world. From James Ivory's adaptation of Henry James's *The Europeans* (1979) through his version of E. M. Forster's *Howard's End* (1992) and, more recently, the 2006 adaptation of *Twelfth Night* as *She's the Man,* some of this fashion may be attributable to the usual industry problem of finding basic material to make into films or of finding sufficiently recognizable works of classic literature to make into a literary spectacle. There are, however, four other ways to view this widespread return of literary classics in the 1980s and 1990s: (1) as a reaction against contemporary filmmaking trends to diminish traditional plot and character; (2) as a conservative or at least therapeutic turn from the cultural complexity of the present; (3) as a reflection of contemporary film audiences and their increasing concern with manner over matter; and (4) as the vehicle to reexamine and reinvent new political or cultural perspectives within traditional narratives.

The exceptional prevalence of nineteenth-century adaptations in the last two decades might, first, be seen as a reaction to certain tendencies in filmmaking today, a period when the force and reliability of narrative (as a way of knowing the world) has been devalued or marginalized. Since the 1980s, even mainstream movies have tended to abandon or undermine complex or coherent characters, tight plot lines, and causal logics. In a range of movies from Oliver Stone's *Natural Born Killers* (1994) through *Hellboy* (2004) and *Avatar* (2009), characters are, by choice or default, constructed more and more as surface images lacking much psychological depth; their frequently unmotivated actions create dynamic performances but are often based only on the slightest of plot lines as intentionally fragmented stories. In this context, literary masterpieces present the fresh, and ironically alternative, possibility of both full characters and classical narrative logics. Much of the fascination with nineteenth-century novels or Shakespearean drama may be, in short, what some have identified as a post-postmodern yearning for good plots and characters with depth.

There is, at the same time, more than a trace of a cultural conservatism in these literary reactions to the unmooring of plot and character in contemporary society. Choosing the stories and settings of past cultures alone might indicate nostalgia for long-ago worlds of coherency, romance, adventure, and some degree of psychological and social order. This should not be interpreted, however, to mean that a Jane Austen heroine or a Shakespearean society does not struggle with choices and balances. Nor is it to suggest that contemporary life is truly or factually more complex or violent than life in the eighteenth or nineteenth centuries. What does seem true is that media cultures of contemporary societies have inundated individuals with more information and more images than ever before and, as today's global perspective grows larger and more rapid, individual and social identities find themselves shaped by those fast and disorienting images. In contrast, movie adaptations of classic literature combine images of other times and places (with at least more civilized violence and articulate fears of race and gender) and the conceptual and imagistic reductions needed to make and market literary films today (as the "high concept" images of "great literature"). The result is a literary image that acts as a packageable and comprehensible alternative to the other, much less comprehensible, images audiences live through today.

There is a third attraction and activity embedded in the numerous classics offered up on the contemporary screens and monitors and in the numerous versions of the same work of literature that audiences can now watch. Today, literary classics on film are multiple and redundant in two ways. Not only are different versions of a novel or film sometimes produced by different filmmakers within a few years of each other (including several *Emmas* in the 1990s or almost simultaneous versions of Laclos's *Dangerous Liaisons* by Stephen Frears [1988] and Milos Forman [the 1989 *Valmont*]) but home video and computer technologies have made it possible for viewers to watch and compare even more versions of an adaptation from other periods of film history. After seeing those different contemporary versions of Austen's and Laclos's novels, audiences today might have the option of watching on video Clarence Brown's 1932 *Emma* or Roger Vadim's 1960 *Dangerous Liaisons*, and these, of course, could be sampled next to the original novels and, in the case of *Dangerous Liaisons*, next to Christopher Hampton's play. Contemporary film culture offers more versions and more opportunities to see and compare the relationships between film and literature as historical practices and textual performances, and one consequence of this redistribution of literature through the media may be that questions of fidelity or authenticity may be less and less a concern for both filmmakers and their audiences. As Scorsese's *Age Of Innocence* (1993) seems to suggest in its almost fetishistic obsession with the surface of gowns, wall coverings, and dinner table settings, audiences today may be more interested in the different textures of adaptation than in the textual accuracy of any one adaptation.

Finally, the return to classic literatures as source material for film adaptations can often represent progressive engagements as these films rework and reinvent classic plots and characters as reflections of new gender, cultural, and political positions. In these cases, the fundamentals of the original novels or plays may remain intact—the plots, the characters, and even the settings—but these are inflected and transformed in ways that often recreate the meanings of those characters and their worlds to reflect more contemporary points of view. Beyond questions of fidelity to the Henry James novel *The Portrait of a Lady*, for instance, Jane Campion's Isabel Archer is a 1996 portrait of a lady who, like many women today, moves through a cross-fire of social perspectives and desires but successfully assumes an agency that resists its nineteenth-century heritage. Similarly, the title of Campion's 2009 *Bright Star* refers to a poem written by the celebrated nineteenth-century poet John Keats, yet this adaptation of Keats's world and poem becomes mainly the background against which the creativity and imagination of Fanny Brawne, Keats's lover, stand out as feminist future. While these types of cinematic transformations of classical literature can sometimes appear as mainly accommodations of one historical period and cultural place by another, as when *The Taming of the Shrew* becomes renewed as the contemporary *10 Things I Hate about You* (1999), at other times these accommodations are better seen as ideological transformations: thus, *Bride and Prejudice* (2004) recreates Jane Austen's plot as also a subtle critique of the colonialism implicit in the original novel, and Julia Taymour's *The Tempest* (2010) unmistakably rethinks the sexual politics of Shakespeare's play by remaking Shakespeare's powerful male Prospero as the female Prospera.

See Hilary Schor's "Emma, Interrupted: Speaking Jane Austen in Fiction and Film" (p. 329) and William Galperin's "Adapting Jane Austen: The Surprising Fidelity of *Clueless*" (p. 351).

Literature, film, and digital convergence

New directions in filmmaking already point to new and alternative relationships between film and literature in the 2000s. Thanks in part to expanding possibilities of DVD and digital distribution venues, a growing number of examples of the exchanges between oral and folk literatures and film from Asian, African, and Arab cultures have begun to revise the global landscape of how literatures reconfigure film (and vice versa). Television and cable programming now attract and offer more opportunities for writers in ways different from those historically provided by the cinema since the 1950s. Finally, if home video already demands a rethinking of how audiences watch film or read literature in both different and similar ways, these issues have only become more exciting and complicated as various computer technologies—part of the broad "digital turn" in contemporary representation—redefine future ways of seeing and reading. Two trends in particular stand out as the new millennium starts to take shape: 1) the widespread and popular adaptation of fantasy literatures such as graphic novels, comic book narratives, and children's literature, and 2) the circulation of literature through video games, computer sites, and other interactive forums that create more open systems that encourage viewers and readers to more freely interact with literature as part of a screen culture.

Figure 6.1 The 2007 *Persepolis* (2007) is one of the most successful adaptations of a graphic novel in which the animated visuals of the cinema creatively bring to life the images of the novel.

Figure 6.2 Tim Burton's *Alice in Wonderland* (2010) is part of a contemporary trend to explore the bond between film and literature within the realm of fantasy.

Since the 1990s especially, movies have commercially expanded the cinematic potentials of comic book literatures, anime, and graphic novels and other unconventional literary forms. Along with the stream of various *Batman* films (1989–2008), comic books and graphic novels have been the source of *The X-Men* series (2000–2011), two *The Spider-Man* films (2002, 2004), *Hellboy* and *Hellboy II* (2004, 2008), *Sin City* (2005), *Persepolis* (2007), *Iron Man* and *Iron Man 2* (2008, 2010), and *Watchmen* (2009), to name just a well-known handful. Although this kind of material has many historical precedents, its popular proliferation today suggests a visibly significant move towards the combination of fantasy literature and films, a hybrid of graphic literature and film in which creative potential of graphic animation provides a common ground more important perhaps than narrative or character.

This move towards fantasy graphics can also be associated with the equally prominent and popular adaptation of children's literature during the last decade, such as Tim Burton's *Charlie and the Chocolate Factory* (2005), *The Chronicles of Narnia* series (2005–2010), Burton's *Alice in Wonderland* (2010), and *Shrek Forever After* (2010). Certainly there are major differences across these many films, but, as a salient tendency, it suggests that, rather than film providing literature with realistic incarnations (as so traditionally common in the relationship between film and literature), literature today provides film with powerful imaginative visions that encourage the technological transformations of cinematic realism.

A movie about an underground comic book artist, *American Splendor* (2003) is an unusual variation on this cinematic turn towards graphic literature fantasies, and overlaps with another literary direction of the last decade, namely, biopics about real writers, artists, intellectuals, and other powerful personalities representing the creativity of individual minds and personal desires. In the last ten years, these films include *Quills* (2000), adapted from the life of the eighteenth-century writer Marquis de Sade, *The Diving Bell and the Butterfly* (2007), recreated from a memoir by the paralyzed magazine editor Jean-Dominique Bauby, *Into the Wild* (2007), based on the non-fiction autobiography about the wilderness adventures of Christopher McCandless, and *Julie & Julia* (2009), adapted from Julia Child's *My Life in France* and Julie Powell's memoir *Julie & Julia: 365 Days, 524 Recipes, 1 Tiny Apartment*. In their own way, each of these films recreates a literature in which individuals seek to control or conquer a world of real obstacles and limitations, not, strictly speaking, as forms of fantasy but as powerful personal imaginations and determinations that, in very different ways, fantastically remake the world.

In film's recent pursuit of fantasy literatures and literatures of personal fantasy, there are without doubt, economic and commercial motives related to the digital revolution that has propelled the film and media industries since the 1990s. Digital technologies not only allows for the visual freedoms and representational inventions that support and urge creative and

Watch the trailer for *American Splendor*: http://www.youtube.com/watch?v=APpxQm7sH5k

imaginative ideas and subjects, but the rapid move into digital media also makes film production and distribution considerably less expensive.

A third and widespread effect of this digital revolution, specifically as it impacts the exchanges between literature and film, is the potential transformation of age-old hierarchies about authorship and textual authority. Writing about these transformations, Henry Jenkins has identified a "convergence culture" of the last two decades in which multiple sites of interactivity have made readers and viewers mobile participants within each of those fields and the exchanges between them (p. 403). Legally and illegally, readers of popular novels and films commonly rewrite and remake original books, films, and television programs into new texts, new YouTube videos, and interactive internet sites. In the contemporary world of digital convergences, literature, film, and the many screens and traditions that surround and bind them are constantly expanding as new activities and interactivities. In this context, it may now be more appropriate to think of the relations between film and literature as less about texts and screens or about readers and viewers than about creative and interactive players. No wonder that video and computer games, like *Lara Croft: Tomb Raider* (2001) and the *Pokemon* movies (1998–2008), have in recent years become a primary material and different type of literature that films eagerly adapt. No wonder that classic works of literature are now adapted not only as films but as video programs like the 2010 computer games of *Dante's Inferno*, *Hamlet*, and *Treasure Island*.

As in the past, the present and future intersections of film and literature are thus about more than just movies and books. The evolving relationship tells us not only about individual works of film and literature but also about how each, as part of changing cultural, economic, and technological environments, works to change the other's meaning and value as part of complex historical ratios. To read a book, to attend a play, to hear a poem, to view a film, to watch a television broadcast, to play a computer game, or to interact with an Internet site today are experiences that frequently offer discrete and particular meanings. Like all discrete experiences, however, they open up larger debates and questions—about history, about aesthetics, and about human value. When those experiences are visibly multiplied as dual or triple engagements in which film and literature regard and react to each other on different experiential planes, those debates and questions become, I think, more specific and more pressing—about cultural literacy, about the psychologies of different arts, about the social politics of entertainment, and about the varieties of human and technological expression. This is why the questions provoked by the dialogues between film and literature have been and will continue to be so central in their relentless particularity.

See Nicholas Rombes's *Cinema in the Digital Age* for more on the digital revolution in cinema

For an expansive model of how texts and films interact with each other and how audiences engage those interactions, see Linda Hutcheon's "How? (Audiences)" (p. 385).

PART 2

Major documents and debates

THIS SECTION OF THE BOOK features a wide selection of critical writings on film and literature. They represent various approaches to both specific and general questions about the relationships of film and literature. Some may be concerned with cultural issues and survey a large number of examples; others may use models derived from psychology, semiotics, or political science and may concentrate on a single film or filmmaker; still others direct their analysis at specific cinematic adaptations. The following essays also represent various historical periods and cultures, and their arguments may implicitly or explicitly be responding to how the movies and literature interact in a particular period or particular culture—such as the silent film era in Europe or the field of contemporary popular culture in Hollywood.

As a general rule through this section of the book, I recommend three guidelines. First, consider each essay as a product of a particular social and historical environment that generates specific issues about the relationship between film and literature. Second, see each argument as addressing and responding to certain films or kinds of films that determine the range of questions and answers available in writing about film and literature. Third, approach the argument of each essay as an open debate—as a point of departure for other questions and discussions about film and literature.

2.1 ADAPTATION STUDIES

Chapter 7

André Bazin

ADAPTATION, OR THE CINEMA AS DIGEST

CO-FOUNDER OF *CAHIERS DU CINÉMA* IN 1951, French film critic André Bazin has inspired generations of filmmakers and film critics. Bazin frequently argued for the productive relationship between cinema and other art forms such as theater, literature, and painting rather than considering any one form as inferior to another. In this study Bazin presents a theory of adaptation which argues against "faithfulness to form" as the predominant criterion for film adaptation. Instead, Bazin calls for a process of adaptation that seeks cinematic "equivalences in meaning." He ultimately argues that the underlying characters, stories, and meanings of a novel (like myths) exist beyond the confines of surface "style" and can therefore be represented equally—albeit with different formal equivalences— in different media.

■ ■ ■

ADAPTATION, OR THE CINEMA AS DIGEST
ANDRÉ BAZIN

From Bert Cardullo, *Bazin at Work*. New York: Routledge, 1997, first published in French in *Esprit*, 16, no. 146 (July 1948), pp. 32–40.

The problem of digests and adaptations is usually posed within the framework of literature. Yet literature only partakes of a phenomenon whose amplitude is much larger. Take painting, for instance: one might even consider an art museum as a digest, for we find *collected* there a *selection* of paintings that were intended to exist in a completely different architectural and decorative context. Nonetheless, these works of art are still original. But now take the imaginary museum proposed by Malraux: it refracts the original painting into millions of facets thanks to photographic reproduction, and it substitutes for that original images of different dimensions and colors that are readily accessible to all. And by the way, photography for its part is only a modern substitute for engraving, which previously had been the only approximate "adaptation" available to connoisseurs.[1] One must not forget that the "adaptation" and "summary" of original works of art have become so customary and so frequent that it would be next to impossible to question their existence today. For the sake of argument, I'll take my examples from cinema.

More than one writer, more than one critic, more than one film-maker even, has challenged the aesthetic justification for the adaptation of novels to the screen; however, there are few examples of those who take actual exception to this practice, of artists who refuse to sell their books, to adapt other people's books, or to direct them when a producer comes along with the right blandishments. So their theoretical argument doesn't seem altogether justified. In general, they make claims about the specificity or distinctness of every authentic literary work. A novel is a unique synthesis whose molecular equilibrium is automatically affected when you tamper with its form. Essentially, no detail in the narrative can be considered as secondary; all syntactic characteristics, then, are in fact expressions of the psychological, moral, or metaphysical content of the work. André Gide's simple pasts[2] are in a way inseparable from the events of *The Pastoral Symphony* (1919), just as Camus's present perfects are inherent in the metaphysical drama of *The Stranger* (1942).

Even when it is posed in such complex terms, however, the problem of cinematic adaptation is not absolutely insolvable, and the history of the cinema already proves that this problem has often been solved in various ways. I'll take only incontestable examples here: Malraux's *Man's Hope* (*Espoir*, a.k.a. *Sierra de Teruel*; 1939), Jean Renoir's *A Day in the Country* (1936), after Maupassant, and the recent *Grapes of Wrath* (1940; dir. John Ford) from Steinbeck. I find it easy to defend even a qualified success such as *The Pastoral Symphony* (1949; dir. Jean Delannoy). It's true that everything in the film isn't a success, but this is certainly not due to what some consider to be the ineffable aspect of the original. I don't care much for Pierre Blanchar's acting, but I do think that Michèle Morgan's beautiful eyes—which are able to communicate the blind Gertrude's innermost thoughts—and the omnipresent motif of the ironically serene snow are acceptable substitutes for Gide's simple pasts.[3] All it takes is for the filmmakers to have enough visual imagination to create the cinematic equivalent of the style of the original, and for the critic to have the eyes to see it.

To be sure, this theory of adaptation comes with the following warning: that one not confuse prose style with grammatical idiosyncrasies or, more generally still, with formal constants. Such confusion is widespread—and unfortunately, not merely among French teachers. "Form" is at most a sign, a visible manifestation, of style, which is absolutely inseparable from the narrative content, of which it is, in a manner of speaking and according to Sartre's use of the word, the metaphysics. Under these circumstances, faithfulness to a form, literary or otherwise, is illusory: what matters is the *equivalence in meaning of the forms*. The *style* of Malraux's film is completely identical to that of his book, even though we are dealing here with two different artistic forms, cinema on the one hand and literature on the other. The case *of A Day in the Country* is subtler: it is faithful to the spirit of Maupassant's short story at the same time that it benefits from the full extent of Renoir's genius. This is the refraction of one work in another creator's consciousness. And there isn't a person who will deny the beauty of the result. It took somebody like Maupassant, but also someone like Renoir (both of them, Jean and Auguste), to achieve it.

The hard-liners will respond that the above-mentioned examples prove only that it is perhaps not metaphysically impossible to make a cinematic work inspired by a literary one, with sufficient faithfulness to the spirit of the original and with an aesthetic intelligence that permits us to consider the film the equal of the book; but they will also say that this is no longer the kind of "adaptation" I was talking about at the beginning of this piece. They'll say that *A Day in the Country* on screen is a different work, that's all, equal or superior to its model because Jean Renoir is, in his own right, an artist of the same rank as Maupassant, and because he has of course benefitted from the work of the writer, which is anterior to his own. They'll claim that, if we examine the countless American and European novels that are adapted to the screen every month, we will see that they are something completely different, that they are the condensed versions, summaries, film "digests" of which I spoke earlier. For instance, take aesthetically indefensible films such as *The Idiot* (1946; dir. Georges Lampin) and *For Whom the Bell Tolls* (1943; dir. Sam Wood), or those never-ending "adaptations" of Balzac, which seem to have more than amply demonstrated that the author of *The Human Comedy*[4] is the least "cinematic" of all novelists. To be sure, one must first know to what end the adaptation is designed: for the cinema or for its audience. One must also realize that most adaptors care far more about the latter than about the former.

The problem of adaptation for the audience is much more evident in the case of radio. Indeed, radio is not quite an art like the cinema: it is first and foremost a means of reproduction and transmission. The digest phenomenon resides not so much in the actual condensing or simplification of works as in the way they are consumed by the listening public. The cultural interest of radio— precisely the aspect of it that scares Georges Duhamel[5]—is that is allows modern man to live in an environment of sound comparable to the warm atmosphere created by central heating. As for me, although I've had a radio set for barely a year now, I feel the need to turn it on as soon as I get home; often I even write and work with the radio on as my companion. Right now, as I write this article, I'm listening to Jean Vittold's[6] excellent, daily morning broadcast on the great musicians. Earlier today, while I was shaving, Jean Rostand,[7] juggling with chromosomes, told me why only female cats (or was it male cats?) can be of three colors simultaneously, and I don't remember who explained to me while I was having breakfast how, through simple scraping with sand, the Aztecs carved extraordinary masks of polished quartz that one can see at the Musée de l'Homme.[8] Jules Romains's[9] appalling hoax on extraocular vision was itself seriously adapted for radio.

Radio has created an atmospheric culture that is as omnipresent as humidity in the air. For those who think that culture can only be achieved through hard work, the ease of physical access that radio allows to works of art is at least as antagonistic to the nature of these works as any tampering with their form. Even if it is well rendered or integrally performed on radio, the *Fifth Symphony* is no longer Beethoven's work when you listen to it while in your bathtub; music must be accompanied by the ritual of attending a concert, by the sacrament of contemplation. However, one can also see in radio the spreading of culture to everyone—the physical spread of culture, which is the first step toward its spiritual ascendance. Radio comfortably provides, like one more modern convenience, "culture for everyone." It represents a gain of time and a reduction of effort, which is the very mark of our era. After all, even M. Duhamel will take a cab or the metro to get to the concert hall.

The clichéd bias according to which culture is inseparable from intellectual effort springs from a bourgeois, intellectualist reflex. It is the equivalent in a rationalistic society of the initiatory rites in primitive civilizations. Esoterism is obviously one of the grand cultural traditions, and I'm not pretending that we should completely banish it from ours. But we could simply put it back in its place, which should in no way be absolute. There is a definite pleasure in cracking or conquering the hermeticism of a work of art, which then refines our relationship to that work of art. So much the better. But mountain climbing has not yet replaced walking on level ground. In place of the classical modes of cultural communication, which are at once a defense of culture and a secreting of it behind high walls, modern technology and modern life now more and more offer up an extended culture reduced to the lowest common denominator of the masses. To the defensive, intellectual motto of "No culture without mental effort," which is in fact unconsciously elitist, the up-and-coming civilization now responds with, "Let's grab whatever we can." This is progress—that is, if there really is such a thing as progress.

As far as the cinema is concerned, my intention is not to defend the indefensible. Indeed, most of the films that are based on novels merely usurp their titles, even though a good lawyer could probably prove that these movies have an indirect value, since it has been shown that sales of a book always increases after it has been adapted to the screen. And the original work can only profit from such an exposure. Although *The Idiot*, for example, is very frustrating on the screen, it is undeniable that many potential readers of Dostoyevsky have found in the film's oversimplified psychology and action a kind of preliminary trimming that has given them easier access to an otherwise difficult novel. The process is somewhat similar to that of M. de Vogüe, the author of "abridged" classics for schools in the nineteenth century. These are despicable in the eyes of devotees of the Russian novel (but they have hardly anything to lose by this process, and neither does Dostoyevsky), yet extremely useful to those who are not yet familiar with the Russian novel and who thus can benefit from an introduction to it. In any event, I won't comment further on this, for it has more to do with pedagogy than with art. I'd much prefer to deal with a rather *modern* notion for which the critics are in large part responsible: that of the untouchability of the work of art.

The nineteenth century, more than any other, firmly established an idolatry of form, mainly literary, that is still with us and that has made us relegate what has in fact always been essential for narrative composition to the back of our critical consciousness: the invention of character and situation. I grant that the protagonists and events of a novel achieve their aesthetic existence only through the form that expresses them and that somehow brings them to life in our mind. But this precedence is as vain as that which is regularly conveyed to college students when they are asked to write an essay on the precedence of language over thought. It is interesting to note that the novelists who defend so fiercely the stylistic or formal integrity of their texts are also the ones who sooner or later overwhelm us with confessions about the tyrannical demands of their characters. According to these writers, their protagonists are *enfants terribles* who completely escape from their control once they have been conceived. The novelist is totally subjected to their whims, he is the instrument of their wills. I'm not doubting this for a minute, but then writers must recognize that the true aesthetic reality of a psychological or social novel lies in the characters or their environment rather than in what they call the "style." The style is in the service of the narrative: it is a reflection of it, so to speak, the body but not the soul. And it is not impossible for the artistic soul to manifest itself through another incarnation. This assumption, that the style is in the service of the narrative, appears vain and sacrilegious only if one refuses to see the many examples of it that the history of the arts gives to us, and if one therefore indulges in the biased condemnation of cinematic adaptation. With time, we do see the ghosts of famous characters rise far above the great novels from which they emanate. Don Quixote and Gargantua dwell in the consciousness of millions of people who have never had any direct or complete contact with the works of Cervantès and Rabelais. I would like to be sure that all those who conjure up the spirit of Fabrice and Madame Bovary have read (or reread, for good measure) Stendhal and Flaubert, but I'm not so sure. Insofar as the style of the original has managed to create a character and impose him on the public consciousness, that character acquires a greater autonomy, which might in certain cases lead as far as quasi-transcendence of the work. Novels, as we all know, are mythmakers.

The ferocious defense of literary works is, to a certain extent, aesthetically justified; but we must also be aware that it rests on a rather recent, individualistic conception of the "author" and of the "work," a conception that was far from being ethically rigorous in the seventeenth century and that started to become legally defined only at the end of the eighteenth. In the Middle Ages, there were only a few themes, and they were common to all the arts. That of Adam and Eve, for instance, is to be found in the mystery plays, painting, sculpture, and stained-glass windows, none of which were ever challenged for transferring this theme from one art form to another. And when the subject of the Rome Prize for Painting is "the love of Daphnis and Chloë,"[10] what else is it but an adaptation? Yet nobody is claiming that copyright has been violated. In justification of the artistic multiplication of Biblical and Christian themes during the Middle Ages, it would be wrong to say that they were part of a common fund, a land of public domain of Christian civilization: the copiers or imitators had no more respect for the *chansons de gestes*, the Old French epic poems, than they did for religious literature. The reason is that the work of art was not an end in itself; the only important criteria were its content and the effectiveness of its message. But the balance between the public's needs and the requirements for creation was such in those days that all the conditions existed to guarantee the excellence of the arts. You may perhaps observe that those days are over and that it would be aesthetic nonsense to want to anachronistically reverse the evolution of the relationship among the creator, the public, and the work of art. To this I would respond that, on the contrary, it is possible that artists and critics remain blind to the birth of the new, aesthetic Middle Ages, whose origin is to be found in the accession of the masses to power (or at least their participation in it) and in the emergence of an artistic form to complement that accession: the cinema.

But even if this thesis is a rather risky one that would require additional arguments in its support, it remains true that the relatively new art of cinema is obliged to retrace the entire evolution of art on its own, at an extraordinarily quickened pace, just as a fetus somehow retraces the evolution of mankind in a few months. The only difference is that the paradoxical evolution of cinema is contemporaneous with the deep-seated decadence of literature, which today seems designed for an audience of individualist elites. The aesthetic Middle Ages of the cinema finds its fictions wherever it can: close at hand, in the literatures of the nineteenth and twentieth centuries. It can also create its own fictions, and has not failed to do so, particularly in comic films, from the first French ones to the American comedies of, say, Mack Sennett and above all Charlie Chaplin. The defenders of seriousness in the cinema will name instead examples like the Western epics and those of the Russian revolution, or such unforgettable pictures as *Broken Blossoms* (1919; dir. D. W. Griffith) and *Scarface* (1932; dir. Howard Hawks). But there's nothing that can be done to bring back the halcyon past. Youth is transient, and grandeur with it; another grandeur will take its place, if perhaps a bit more slowly. In the meantime, the cinema borrows from fiction a certain number of well-wrought, well-rounded, or well-developed characters, all of whom have been polished by twenty centuries of literary culture. It adopts them and brings them into play; according to the talents of the screenwriter and the director, the characters are integrated as much as possible into their new aesthetic context. If they are not so integrated, we naturally get these mediocre films that one is right to condemn, provided one doesn't confuse this mediocrity with the very principle of cinematic adaptation, whose aim is to simplify and condense a work from which it basically wishes to retain only the main characters and situations. If the novelist is not happy with the adaptation of his work, I, of course, grant him the right to defend the original (although he sold it, and thus is guilty of an act of prostitution that deprives him of many of his privileges as the creator of the work). I grant him this right only because no one has yet found anyone better than parents to defend the rights of children until they come of age. One should not identify this natural right with an a priori infallibility, however.

Instead of Kafka's *Trial*, which was adapted to the stage by André Gide (1947) from a translation by André Vialatte, I'll take the more appropriate example of *The Brothers Karamazov*, adapted by Jacques Copeau *(Les Frères Karamazov*, 1911), in my defense of the condensed adaptation. The only thing Copeau has done—but he did it more skillfully than M. Spaak[11] in *The Idiot*—is to extract the characters from Dostoyevsky's novel and condense the main events of their story into a few dramatic scenes. There's something slightly different about these theatrical examples, however: the fact that today's theater-going public is educated enough to have read the novel. But Copeau's work would remain artistically viable even if this were not the case.

To take another example, I suffered when I saw *Devil in the Flesh* (1947; dir. Claude Autant-Lara), because I know Raymond Radiguet's book; the spirit and "style" of that book had somehow been betrayed. But it remains true that this adaptation is the best one that could be made from the novel and that, artistically, it is absolutely justified. Jean Vigo would probably have been more faithful to the original, but it's reasonable to conclude that the resulting film would have been impossible to show to the public because the reality of the book would have ignited the screen. The work of the screenwriters Aurenche and Bost consisted, so to speak, in "transforming" (in the sense that an electric transformer does) the voltage of the novel. The aesthetic energy is almost all there, but it is distributed—or perhaps better, dissipated—differently according to the demands of the camera lens. And yet, although Aurenche and Bost have succeeded in transforming the absolute amoralism of the original into an almost too decipherable moral code, the public has been reluctant to accept the film.

In summary, adaptation is aesthetically justified, independent of its pedagogical and social value, because the adapted work to a certain extent exists apart from what is wrongly called its "style," in a confusion of this term with the word "form." Furthermore, the standard differentiation among the arts in the nineteenth century and the relatively recent, subjectivist notion of the author as identified with the work no longer fit in with an aesthetic sociology of the masses, in which the cinema runs a relay race with drama and the novel and doesn't eliminate them, but rather reinforces them. The true aesthetic differentiations, in fact, are not to be made among the arts but within genres themselves: between the psychological novel and the novel of manners, for example, rather than between the psychological novel and the film that one would have made from it. Of course, adaptation for the public is inseparable from adaptation for the cinema, insofar as the cinema is more "public" than the novel.

The very word "digest," which sounds at first contemptible, can have a positive meaning. "As the word indicates," Jean-Paul Sartre writes, "it is a literature that has been previously digested, a literary chyle."But one could also understand it as a literature that has been made more accessible through cinematic adaptation, not so much because of the oversimplification that such adaptation entails (in *The Pastoral Symphony*, the narrative on screen is even more complex than the one in the novel), but rather because of the mode of expression itself, as if the aesthetic fat, differently emulsified, were better tolerated by the consumer's mind. As far as I'm concerned, the difficulty of audience assimilation is not an a priori criterion for cultural value.

All things considered, it's possible to imagine that we are moving toward a reign of the adaptation in which the notion of the unity of the work of art, if not the very notion of the author himself, will be destroyed. If the film that was made of Steinbeck's *Of Mice and Men* (1940; dir. Lewis Milestone) had been successful (it could have been so, and far more easily than the adaptation of the same author's *Grapes of Wrath)*, the (literary?) critic of the year 2050 would find not a novel out of which a play and a film had been "made," but rather a single work reflected through three art forms, an artistic pyramid with three sides, all equal in the eyes of the critic. The "work" would then be only an ideal point at the top of this figure, which itself is an ideal construct. The chronological precedence of one part over another would not be an aesthetic criterion any more than the chronological precedence of one twin over the other is a genealogical one. Malraux made his film of *Man's Hope* before he wrote the novel of the same title, but he was carrying the work inside himself all along.

■ ■ ■

Questions and projects

1. What exactly does Bazin mean by "digest"? Describe two different films that could be part of the same core digest but that find different ways to create "equivalences of meaning."
2. Identify a text or story that functions as a central "myth" in contemporary culture. What is the primary literary source for that myth and which are the prominent adaptations that circulate that myth as films?

Notes

1   Bazin's note: In a recent radio broadcast of *French Cancan*, during which Messieurs Pierre Benoit [1886–1962; French novelist, member of the Académie Française, author of *Königsmark* and *L'Atlantide*], Labarthe [obscure French literary figure of Bazin's time, co-author, with Marcel Brion, Jean Cocteau, Fred Bérence, Emmanuel Berl, Danielle Hunebelle, Robert Lehel, Jean-Lucas Dubreton, and Jean-Jaques Salomon, of a volume entitled *Léonard de Vinci* (1959)], and several others exchanged a great number of utter platitudes, we heard Curzio Malaparte [1898–1957; Italian novelist, the celebrated author of *Kaputt* and many other works, who contributed one film to Italian cinema, *Il Cristo Proibita* (*Forbidden Christ*, 1950), which he wrote, directed, and scored. The film was released in the United States in 1953] ask the speaker what he would think of a "condensed version" of the Parthenon, for example. In his mind, this was supposed to be the ultimate argument against the "digest." Nobody was there to respond that such a condensed version had been realized a long time ago in the casts that were made of the Parthenon's friezes, and above all in the photo albums of the Acropolis that anybody can buy at a reasonable price in a gift shop.

2   Editor's note: Bazin is here using the term "passé simple" in French. This tense does not exist in English. It is a form of the simple past, which itself is called "imparfait" in French. "Imparfait" tends to be used more often in everyday language, whereas "passé simple" is a more literary form of the same tense.

3   Bazin's note: There are types of stylistic transfer that are indeed reliable, however, such as those "simple pasts" of André Gide that unfortunately were not built into the actual cutting of *The Pastoral Symphony*, i.e., its filmic syntax, but did show up in the eyes of an actress and in the symbolism of the snow.

4   Editor's note: This was the title given by Honoré de Balzac to his collected stories and novels, thus casting his copious fictions as a single, secular reply to Dante's *Divine Comedy*. *La Comédie Humaine* was published in 16 volumes by Furne, Paulin, Dubochet, and Hetzel between 1842 and 1846; a seventeenth supplementary volume appeared in 1847.

5   Editor's note: Georges Duhamel (1884–1966), now a largely forgotten figure, achieved fame before World War II, being elected to the Académie Française in 1935. He is remembered for two cycles of novels: *Vie et Aventures de Salavin* (1920–32) and the popular *Chronique des Pasquier* (1933–5). Writing with warmth and humor, Duhamel used the saga of the Pasquier family to attack materialism and defend the rights of the individual against the collective forces of society.

6   Editor's note: Vittold was a famous French musicologist.

7   Editor's note: Rostand was a well-known French biologist who did much to popularize the study of science.

8   Editor's note: Famous anthropological museum in Paris.

9   Editor's note: Jules Romains (pseudonym of Louis Farigoule, 1885–1972) was a French novelist, dramatist, poet, and essayist, elected to the Académie Française in 1946. *La Vie Unanime*, a collection

of poems published in 1908, and much of his later verse and prose, were influenced by Unanimist theories of social groups and collective psychology. Before the outbreak of war in 1914 he published more collections of poetry, a verse play, *L'Armée dans la Ville* (1911), and two novels, *Mort de Quelqu'un* (1911) and the farcical *La Copains* (1913).

The farcical comedies *Knock, ou le Triomphe de la Médecine* (1923), *M. Le Trouhadec Saisi par la Débauche* (1923), and *Le Mariage de M. Le Trouhadec* (1925) earned him much popularity after the war. Interesting collections of essays include *Hommes, médecins, machines* (1959) and *Lettre Ouverte contre une Vaste Conspiration* (1966) with its strictures on modern cultural attitudes and standards.

10   Editor's note: Daphnis and Chloë were two lovers in an old Greek pastoral romance of the same name, attributed to Longus (of the third century A.D. [?]). Daphnis himself is a Sicilian shepherd renowned in Greek myth as the inventor of pastoral poetry.

11   Charles Spaak was a Belgian screenwriter whose credits include *Carnival in Flanders* (1935) and *La Grande Illusion* (1937).

Chapter 8

Dudley Andrew

ADAPTATION

CONCENTRATING ON THE SINGLE ISSUE OF ADAPTATION, Dudley Andrew's 1981 study uses contemporary semiotics, theories of representation and interpretation, and finally sociological and historical determinants to situate the exchanges between film and literature. Within these frameworks, Andrew provides two directions in thinking about adaptation. First, adaptation becomes part of larger philosophical and epistemological projects in interpretation and thus connects adaptation with other questions linking the human and social sciences today. Second, unlike past tendencies to generalize about fundamental theoretical relations between film and literature, this framework allows a person to discriminate and distinguish between different tactics in individual acts of adaptation, placing each interpretive strategy in a specific social context. In that sense, this essay has a clear pragmatic direction, as Andrew's three modes of adaptation provide a starting point for differentiating individual acts of adaptation and for examining how a single film may attempt to convert a literary work.

■ ■ ■

ADAPTATION
DUDLEY ANDREW

From *Concepts in Film Theory*, New York: Oxford University Press, 1985, pp. 96–106.

The sources of films

Frequently the most narrow and provincial area of film theory, discourse about adaptation is potentially as far-reaching as you like. Its distinctive feature, the matching of the cinematic sign system to prior achievement in some other system, can be shown to be distinctive of all representational cinema.

Let us begin with an example, *A Day in the Country*. Jean Renoir set himself the task of putting his knowledge, his troupe, and his artistry at the service of a tale by Guy de Maupassant. No matter how we judge the process or success of the film, its "being" owes something to the tale that was its inspiration and potentially its measure. That tale, "A Country Excursion," bears a transcendent relation to any and all films that adapt it, for it is itself an artistic sign with a given shape and value, if not a finished meaning. A new artistic sign will then feature this original sign as either its signified or its referent. Adaptations claiming fidelity bear the original as a signified, whereas those inspired by or derived from an earlier text stand in a relation of referring to the original.

The notion of a transcendent order to which the system of the cinema is beholden in its practice goes well beyond this limited case of adaptation.[1] What is a city symphony,[2] for example, if not an adaptation of a concept by the cinema? A definite notion of Berlin pre-existed Walter Ruttman's 1927 treatment of that city. What is any documentary for that matter except the signification by the cinema of some prior whole, some concept of person, place, event, or situation. If we take seriously the arguments of Marxist and other social theorists that our consciousness is not open to the world but filters the world according to the shape of its ideology, then every cinematic rendering will exist in relation to some prior whole lodged unquestioned in the personal or public system of experience. In other words, no filmmaker and no film (at least in the representational mode) responds immediately to reality itself, or to its own inner vision. Every representational film *adapts* a prior conception. Indeed the very term "representation" suggests the existence of a model. Adaptation delimits representation by insisting on the cultural status of the model, on its existence in the mode of the text or the already textualized. In the case of those texts explicitly termed "adaptations," the cultural model which the cinema represents is already treasured as a representation in another sign system.

The broader notion of the process of adaptation has much in common with interpretation theory, for in a strong sense adaptation is the appropriation of a meaning from a prior text. The hermeneutic circle, central to interpretation theory, preaches that an explication of a text occurs only after a prior understanding of it, yet that prior understanding is justified by the careful explication it allows.[3] In other words, before we can go about discussing and analyzing a text we must have a global conception of its meaning. Adaptation is similarly both a leap and a process. It can put into play the intricate mechanism of its signifiers only in response to a general understanding of the signified it aspires to have constructed at the end of its process. While all representational films function this way (as interpretations of a person, place, situation, event, and so forth), we reserve a special place for those films which foreground this relation by announcing themselves as versions of some standard whole. A standard whole can only be a text. A version of it is an adaptation in the narrow sense.

Although these speculations may encourage a hopelessly broad view of adaptation, there is no question that the restricted view of adaptation from known texts in other art forms offers a privileged locus for analysis. I do not say that such texts are themselves privileged. Indeed, the thrust of my earlier remarks suggests quite the opposite. Nevertheless, the explicit, foregrounded relation of a cinematic text to a well-constructed original text from which it derives and in some sense strives to reconstruct provides the analyst with a clear and useful "laboratory" condition which should not be neglected.

The making of film out of an earlier text is virtually as old as the machinery of cinema itself. Well over half of all commercial films have come from literary originals—though by no means all of these originals are revered or respected. If we confine ourselves to those cases where the adaptation process is foregrounded, that is, where the original is held up as a worthy source or goal, there are still several possible modes of relation between the film and the text. These modes can, for convenience, be reduced to three: borrowing, intersection, and fidelity of transformation.

Borrowing, intersecting, and transforming sources

In the history of the arts, surely "borrowing" is the most frequent mode of adaptation. Here the artist employs, more or less extensively, the material, idea, or form of an earlier, generally successful text. Medieval paintings featuring biblical iconography and miracle plays based on Bible stories drew on an exceptional text whose power they borrowed. In a later, secular age the artworks of an earlier generation might be used as sacred in their own right. The many types of adaptations from Shakespeare come readily to mind. Doubtless in these cases, the adaptation hopes to win an audience by the prestige of its borrowed title or subject. But at the same time it seeks to gain a certain respectability, if not aesthetic value, as a dividend in the transaction. Adaptations from literature to music, opera, or paintings are of this nature. There is no question of the replication of the original in Strauss's *Don Quixote*. Instead the audience is expected to enjoy basking in a certain pre-established presence and to call up new or especially powerful aspects of a cherished work.

To study this mode of adaptation, the analyst needs to probe the source of power in the original by examining the use made of it in adaptation. Here the main concern is the generality of the original, its potential for wide and varied appeal; in short, its existence as a continuing form or archetype in culture. This is especially true of that adapted material which, because of its frequent reappearance, claims the status of myth: *Tristan and Isolde* for certain, and *A Midsummer Night's Dream* possibly. The success of adaptations of this sort rests on the issue of their fertility not their fidelity. Frank McConnell's ingenious *Storytelling and Mythmaking* catalogues the garden of culture by examining borrowing as the history of grafting and transplantation in the fashion of Northrop Frye or even Carl Jung.[4] This direction of study will always elevate film by demonstrating its participation in a cultural enterprise whose value is outside film and, for Jung and others, outside texts altogether. Adaptation is the name of this cultural venture at its most explicit, though McConnell, Frye, and Jung would all immediately want to extend their theories of artistic fertility to "original" texts which upon inspection show their dependence on the great fructifying symbols and mythic patterns of civilization.

This vast and airy mode of borrowing finds its opposite in that attitude toward adaptation I choose to call "intersecting." Here the uniqueness of the original text is preserved to such an extent that it is intentionally left unassimilated in adaptation. The cinema, as a separate mechanism, records its confrontation with an ultimately intransigent text. Undoubtedly the key film exhibiting this relation is Robert Bresson's *Diary of a Country Priest*. André Bazin, championing this film and this mode,[5] claimed that in this instance we are presented not with an adaptation so much as a refraction of the original. Because Bresson featured the writing of the diary and because he went out of his way to avoid "opening up" or in any other way cinematizing the original, Bazin claims that the film *is* the novel as seen by cinema. To extend one of his most elaborate metaphors,[6] the original artwork can be likened to a crystal chandelier whose formal beauty is a product of its intricate but fully artificial arrangement of parts while the cinema would be a crude flashlight interesting not for its own shape or the quality of its light but for what it makes appear in this or that dark corner. The intersection of Bresson's flashlight and the chandelier of Bernanos's novel produces an experience of the original modulated by the peculiar beam of the cinema. Naturally a great deal of Bernanos fails to be lit up, but what is lit up is only Bernanos, Bernanos, however, as seen by the cinema.

The modern cinema is increasingly interested in just this sort of intersecting. Bresson, naturally, has given us his *Joan of Arc* from court records and his *Mouchette* once again from Bernanos. Straub has filmed Corneille's *Othon* and *The Chronicle of Anna Magdalena Bach*. Pasolini audaciously confronted Matthew's gospel with many later texts (musical, pictorial, and cinematic) which it inspired. His later *Medea, Canterbury Tales*, and *Decameron* are also adaptational events in the intersecting mode. All such works fear or refuse to adapt. Instead they present the otherness and distinctiveness of the original text, initiating a dialectical interplay between the aesthetic forms of one period with the cinematic forms of our own period. In direct contrast to the manner scholars have treated the mode of "borrowing," such intersecting insists that the analyst attend to the *specificity* of the original within the *specificity* of the cinema. An original is allowed its life, its own life, in the cinema. The consequences of this method, despite its apparent forthrightness, are neither innocent nor simple. The disjunct experience such intersecting promotes is consonant with the aesthetics of modernism in all the arts. This mode refutes the commonplace that adaptations support only a conservative film aesthetics.

Unquestionably the most frequent and most tiresome discussion of adaptation (and of film and literature relations as well) concerns fidelity and transformation. Here it is assumed that the task of adaptation is the reproduction in cinema of something essential about an original text. Here we have a clear-cut case of film trying to measure up to a literary work, or of an audience expecting to make such a comparison. Fidelity of adaptation is conventionally treated in relation to the "letter" and to the "spirit" of the text, as though adaptation were the rendering of an interpretation of a legal precedent. The letter would appear to be within the reach of cinema for it can be emulated in mechanical fashion. It includes aspects of fiction generally elaborated in any film script: the characters and their inter-relation, the geographical, sociological, and cultural information providing the fiction's context, and the basic narrational aspects that determine the point of view of the narrator (tense, degree of participation and knowledge of the storyteller, and so on). Ultimately, and this was Bazin's complaint about faithful transformations, the literary work can readily become a scenario written in typical scenario form. The skeleton of the original can, more or less thoroughly, become the skeleton of a film.

More difficult is fidelity to the spirit, to the original's tone, values, imagery, and rhythm, since finding stylistic equivalents in film for these intangible aspects is the opposite of a mechanical process. The cinéaste presumably must intuit and reproduce the feeling of the original. It has been argued variously that this is frankly impossible, or that it involves the systematic replacement of verbal signifiers by cinematic signifiers, or that it is the product of artistic intuition, as when Bazin found the pervasive snowy decor in *Symphonie Pastorale* (1946) to reproduce adequately the simple past tense which Gide's verbs all bear in that tale.[7]

It is at this point that the specificity of these two signifying systems is at stake. Generally film is found to work from perception toward signification, from external facts to interior motivations and consequences, from the givenness of a world to the meaning of a story cut out of that world. Literary fiction works oppositely. It begins with signs (graphemes and words) building to propositions which attempt to develop perception. As a product of human language it naturally treats human motivation and values, seeking to throw them out onto the external world, elaborating a world out of a story.

George Bluestone, Jean Mitry, and a host of others find this opposition to be most graphic in adaptations.[8] Therefore they take pleasure in scrutinizing this practice even while ultimately condemning it to the realm of the impossible. Since signs name the inviolate relation of signifier to signified, how is translation of poetic texts conceivable from one language to another (where signifiers belong to different systems); much less how is it possible to transform the signifiers of one material (verbal) to signifiers of another material (images and sounds)? It would appear that one must presume the global signified of the original to be separable from its text if one believes it can be approximated by other sign clusters. Can we attempt to reproduce the meaning of the *Mona Lisa* in a poem, or of a poem in a musical phrase, or even of a musical phrase in an aroma? If one accepts this possibility, at the very least one is forced to discount the primary articulations of the relevant language systems. One would have to hold that while the material of literature (graphemes, words, and sentences) may be of a different nature from the materials of cinema (projected light and shadows, identifiable sounds and forms, and represented actions), both systems may construct in their own way, and at higher levels, scenes and narratives that are indeed commensurable.

The strident and often futile arguments over these issues can be made sharper and more consequential in the language of E. H. Gombrich or the even more systematic language of semiotics. Gombrich finds that all discussion of adaptation introduces the category of "matching."[9] First of all, like Bazin he feels one cannot dismiss adaptation since it is a fact of human practice. We can and do correctly match items from different systems all the time: a tuba sound is more like a rock than like a piece of string; it is more like a bear than like a bird; more like a romanesque church than a baroque one. We are able to make these distinctions and insist on their public character because we are matching equivalents. In the system of musical instruments the tuba occupies an equivalent position to that enjoyed by the romanesque in its system of architectural styles. Nelson Goodman has treated this issue at length in *The Language of Art* pointing to the equivalence not of elements but of the position elements occupy vis-à-vis their different domains.[10] Names of properties of colors may thus metaphorically, but correctly, describe aspects of the world of sound (a blue note, a somber or bright tone). Adaptation would then become a matter of searching two systems of communication for elements of equivalent position in the systems capable of eliciting a signified at a given level of pertinence, for example, the description of a narrative action. For Gombrich adaptation is possible, though never perfect, because every artwork is a construct of elements built out of a traditional use of a system. Since humans have the general capacity to adapt to new systems with different traditions in achieving a like goal or construct, artistic adaptation poses no insurmountable obstacles. Nevertheless attention to such "proportional consistencies" demands that the study of adaptation include the study of both art forms in their proper *historic* context.

Gombrich and Goodman anticipated the more fashionable vocabulary of semiotics in their clarification of these issues. In *Film and Fiction, The Dynamics of Exchange*, Keith Cohen tries to justify this new, nearly scientific approach to questions of relations between these arts; he writes, citing Metz:

> A basic assumption I make is that both words and images are sets of signs that belong to systems and that, at a certain level of abstraction, these systems bear resemblances to one another. More specifically, within each such system there are many different codes (perceptual, referential, symbolic). What makes possible, then, a study of the relation between two separate sign systems, like novel and film, is the fact that the same codes may reappear in more than one system. ... The very mechanisms of language systems can thus be seen to carry on diverse and complex interrelations: "one function, among others, of language is to name the units segmented by vision (but also to help segment them), and ... one function, among others, of vision is to inspire semantic configurations (but also to be inspired by them)."[11]

Cohen, like Metz before him, suggests that despite their very different material character, despite even the different ways we process them at the primary level, verbal and cinematic signs share a common fate: that of being condemned to connotation. This is especially true in their fictional use where every signifier identifies a signified but also elicits a chain reaction of other relations which permits the elaboration of the fictional world. Thus, for example, imagery functions equivalently in films and novels. This mechanism of implication among signs leads Cohen to conclude that "narrativity is the most solid median link between novel and cinema, the most pervasive tendency of both verbal and visual languages. In both novel and cinema, groups of signs, be they literary or visual signs, are apprehended consecutively through time; and this consecutiveness gives rise to an unfolding structure, the diegetic whole that is never fully *present* in any one group yet always *implied* in each such group."[12]

Narrative codes, then, always function at the level of implication or connotation. Hence they are potentially comparable in a novel and a film. The story can be the same if the narrative units (characters, events, motivations, consequences, context, viewpoint, imagery, and so on) are produced equally in two works. Now this production is, by definition, a process of connotation and implication. The analysis of adaptation then must point to the achievement of equivalent narrative units in the absolutely different semiotic systems of film and language. Narrative itself is a semiotic system available to both and derivable from both. If a novel's story is judged in some way comparable to its filmic adaptation, then the strictly separate but equivalent processes of implication which produced the narrative units of that story through words and audio-visual signs, respectively, must be studied. Here semiotics coincides with Gombrich's intuition: such a study is not comparative between the arts but is instead intensive within each art. And since the implicative power of literary language and of cinematic signs is a function of its use as well as of its system, adaptation analysis ultimately leads to an investigation of film styles and periods in relation to literary styles of different periods.

We have come round the other side of the argument now to find once more that the study of adaptation is logically tantamount to the study of the cinema as a whole. The system by which film involves us in fictions and the history of that system are ultimately the questions we face even when starting with the simple observation of an equivalent tale told by novel and film. This is not to my mind a discouraging arrival for it drops adaptation and all studies of film and literation out of the realm of eternal principle and airy generalization, and onto the uneven but solid ground of artistic history, practice, and discourse.

The sociology and aesthetics of adaptation

It is time for adaptation studies to take a sociological turn. How does adaptation serve the cinema? What conditions exist in film style and film culture to warrant or demand the use of literary prototypes? Although adaptation may be calculated as a relatively constant volume in the history of cinema, its particular function in any moment is far from constant. The choices of the mode of adaptation and of prototypes suggest a great deal about the cinema's sense of its role and aspirations from decade to decade. Moreover, the stylistic strategies developed to achieve the proportional equivalences necessary to construct matching stories not only are symptomatic of a period's style but may crucially alter that style.

Bazin pointed to an important instance of this in the immediate postwar era when adaptations from the stage by Cocteau, Welles, Olivier, Wyler, and others not only developed new ways for the cinema to be adequate to serious theater, but also developed a kind of discipline in *mise-en-scène* whose consequences go far beyond the production of *Macbeth, Les Parents terribles, The Little Foxes*, and *Henry V*.[13] Cocteau's film, to take one example, derives its style from Welles's use of interior shooting in *Kane* and *Ambersons,* thus responding to a new conception of dramatic space, but at the same time his film helped solidify a shooting style that would leave its mark on Alexandre Astruc and André Michel among others. Furthermore his particular cinematic *ecriture* would allow

Truffaut to set him against the cinema of quality in the famous 1954 diatribe.[14] It is instructive to note that while Truffaut railed against the status quo for its literariness and especially for its method of adaptation, the directors he praised were also working with literary originals: Bresson adapting Bernanos, Ophuls adapting Maupassant and Schnitzler, and Cocteau adapting his own theater pieces. Like Bazin, Truffaut looked upon adaptation not as a monolithic practice to be avoided but as an instructive barometer for the age. The *cinéma d'auteur* which he advocated was not to be pitted against a cinema of adaptation; rather one method of adaptation would be pitted against another. In this instance adaptation was the battleground even while it prepared the way for a stylistic revolution, the New Wave, which would for the most part avoid famous literary sources.

To take another sort of example, particular literary fashions have at times exercised enormous power over the cinema and, consequently, over the general direction of its stylistic evolution. The Romantic fiction of Hugo, Dickens, Dumas, and countless lesser figures originally set the stylistic requirements of American and mainstream French cinema at the end of the silent era. Similarly Zola and Maupassant, always of interest to French cinéastes, helped Jean Renoir muscularly reorient the style of world cinema in the 1930s. Not only that, through Luchino Visconti this naturalist impulse directly developed one strain of neorealism in his adaptations of Giovanni Verga (*La Terra Trema*) and James M. Cain (*Ossessione*).

This latter case forces us to recall that the "dynamics of exchange," as Cohen calls it, go both ways between film and fiction. Naturalist fiction helped cinema develop its interest in squalid subjects and a hard-hitting style. This in turn affected American hard-boiled novelists like Cain and Hammett, eventually returning to Europe in the film style of Visconti, Carné, Clouzot, and others. This general trading between film and literature in the currency of naturalism had some remarkable individual incidents associated with it. Renoir's adaptation of *The Lower Depths* can serve as an example. In 1881 Zola had cried out for a naturalist theater[15] and had described twenty years before the time precisely the sort of drama Gorki would write in *The Lower Depths*: a collection of real types thrown together without a domineering plot, the drama driven by the natural rhythms of little incidents and facts exposing the general quality of life in an era. Naturalism here coincided with a political need, with Gorki's play preceding the great uprisings in Russia by only a few years.

In another era and in response to a different political need, Renoir leapt at the chance to adapt the Gorki work. This was 1935, the year of the ascendancy of the Popular Front, and Renoir's treatment of the original is clearly marked by the pressures and aspirations of that moment. The film negotiates the mixture of classes which the play only hints at. Louis Jouvet as the Baron dominates the film, descending into the social depths and helping organize a collective undoing of Kastylylov, the capitalist landlord. Despite the gloomy theme, the murder, jailing, deaths by sickness and suicide, Renoir's version overflows with a general warmth evident in the airy setting by the Marne and the relaxed direction of actors who breathe languidly between their lines.

Did Gorki mind such an interpretation? We can never know, since he died a few months before its premier. But he did give Renoir his imprimatur and looked forward to seeing the completed version, this despite the fact that in 1932 he declared that the play was useless, out of date, and unperformable in socialist Russia. Perhaps these statements were the insincere self-criticism which that important year elicited from many Russian artists. I prefer, however, to take Gorki at his word. More far-sighted than most theorists, let alone most authors, he realized that *The Lower Depths* in 1932 Russia was by no means the same artwork as *The Lower Depths* in the France of the Popular Front. This is why he put no strictures on Renoir assuming that the cinéaste would deal with his play as he felt necessary. Necessity is, among other things, a product of the specific place and epoch of the adaptation, both historically and stylistically. The naturalist attitude of 1902, fleshing out the original plans of Zola, gave way to a new historic and stylistic moment, and fed that style that Renoir had begun elaborating ever since *La Chienne* in 1931, and that despite its alleged looseness and airiness in comparison to the Gorki, would help lead European cinema onto the naturalist path.

This sketch of a few examples from the sociology of adaptation has rapidly taken us into the complex interchange between eras, styles, nations, and subjects. This is as it should be, for adaptation, while a tantalizing keyhole for theorists, nevertheless partakes of the universal situation of film practice, dependent as it is on the aesthetic system of the cinema in a particular era and on that era's cultural needs and pressures. Filmmaking, in other words, is always an event in which a system is used and altered in discourse. Adaptation is a peculiar form of discourse but not an unthinkable one. Let us use it not to fight battles over the essence of the media or the inviolability of individual art works. Let us use it as we use all cultural practices, to understand the world from which it comes and the one toward which it points. The elaboration of these worlds will demand, therefore, historical labor and critical acumen. The job of theory in all this is to keep the questions clear and in order. It will no longer do to let theorists settle things with a priori arguments. We need to study the films themselves as acts of discourse. We need to be sensitive to that discourse and to the forces that motivate it.

■ ■ ■

Questions and projects

1. Must a single film operate in only one of Andrew's three modes of adaptation or might a film move between all three? Select either a single film (such as the provided example of Jean Renoir's *A Day in the Country* [1946] and Guy de Maupassant's "A Country Excursion") or a different filmed version of the same literary source (such as the Oz story in Victor Fleming's *Wizard of Oz*, David Lynch's version of *Wild at Heart* [1990], and perhaps Martin Scorsese's *After Hours* [1985]) to illustrate or test, concretely and precisely, one or more of Andrew's three adaptation strategies.
2. Using these or other films, argue how a particular style and tactic of adaptation is "symptomatic" of the movie styles and forms of the period in which it was made. Do, for instance, silent adaptations use tactics specific to the period to interpret literature? Is there a postmodern style of interpretation that influences how literature is adapted for the movies?

Notes

1   For this idea I am indebted to a paper written by Dana Benelli in a class at the University of Iowa, autumn term 1979.
2   The "city symphony" is a genre of the 1920s which includes up to fifteen films all built on formal or abstract principles, yet dedicated to the presentation of a single city, be it Berlin, Paris, Nice, Moscow, or the like.
3   In the theory of interpretation this is generally attributed to Wilhelm Dilthey, although Martin Heidegger has made much of it in our century.
4   Frank McConnell, *Storytelling and Mythmaking* (New York: Oxford University Press, 1979).
5   André Bazin, *What Is Cinema?* (Berkeley, CA: University of California Press, 1968), p. 142.
6   Ibid., p. 107.

7   Ibid., p. 67.

8   George Bluestone, *Novels into Film* (Berkeley, CA: University of California Press, 1957), and Jean Mitry, "Remarks on the Problem of Cinematic Adaptation," *Bulletin of the Midwest Modern Language Association* 4, no. 1 (Spring 1971): 1–9.

9   E.H. Gombrich, *Art and Illusion* (Princeton, NJ: Princeton University Press, 1961), p. 370.

10   Nelson Goodman, *Languages of Art* (Indianapolis, IN: Hackett, 1976), esp. pp. 143–148.

11   Keith Cohen, *Film and Literature: The Dynamics of Exchange* (New Haven, CT: Yale University Press, 1979), p. 4. Cohen's citation from Metz comes from Christian Metz, *Langage et cinéma* (Paris: Albatros, 1977), pp. 20–21.

12   Ibid., p. 92.

13   Bazin, *What Is Cinema?* p. 76.

14   François Truffaut, "A Certain Tendency in French Cinema," in Bill Nichols, *Movies and Methods* (Berkeley, CA: University of California Press, 1976), pp. 224–36.

15   Émile Zola, "Naturalism and the Theater," in *The Experimental Novel and Other Essays*, tr. by Belle Sherman (New York: Haskell House, 1964).

Chapter 9

Robert Stam

BEYOND FIDELITY
The dialogics of adaptation

ROBERT STAM HAS WRITTEN WIDELY on the topics of film theory, multicultural media, and the relationship between film and literature. Here Stam draws on structural and post-structural theories of literature and cinema in order to move beyond the restrictive notion of "fidelity" in adaptation studies. Stam argues against the notion that literary works contain a single extractable "essence" hidden within. Rather every text exists within a matrix of intertextual reference, transformation, recycling, and transmutation. While this process does not preclude one from making judgments about the value of a cinematic adaptation, Stam suggests that we avoid "moralistic" notions of fidelity and instead pay more attention to "dialogic responses" activated as different kinds of viewings, critiques, and interpretations.

■ ■ ■

BEYOND FIDELITY: THE DIALOGICS OF ADAPTATION
ROBERT STAM

From James Naremore (ed.), *Film Adaptation,* New Brunswick: Rutgers University Press, 2000, pp. 54–76

The language of criticism dealing with the film adaptation of novels has often been profoundly moralistic, awash in terms such as *infidelity, betrayal, deformation, violation, vulgarization*, and *desecration*, each accusation carrying its specific charge of outraged negativity. *Infidelity* resonates with overtones of Victorian prudishness; *betrayal* evokes ethical perfidy; *deformation* implies aesthetic disgust; *violation* calls to mind sexual violence; *vulgarization* conjures up class degradation; and *desecration* intimates a kind of religious sacrilege toward the "sacred word." In this chapter I would like to move beyond a moralistic approach to propose specific strategies for the analysis of adaptations. Rather than develop a full-blown narratological theory of novel and film, my agenda is modest and practical. But first I need to deal with the issue of "fidelity."

The chimera of fidelity

Let me begin by acknowledging that the notion of the fidelity of an adaptation to its source novel does contain its grain of truth. When we say an adaptation has been "unfaithful" to the original, the term gives expression to the disappointment we feel when a film adaptation fails to capture what we see as the fundamental narrative, thematic, and aesthetic features of its literary source. The notion of fidelity gains its persuasive force from our sense that some adaptations are indeed better than others and that some adaptations fail to "realize" or substantiate that which we most appreciated in the source novels. Words such as *infidelity* and *betrayal* in this sense translate our feeling, when we have loved a book, that an adaptation has not been worthy of that love. We read a novel through our introjected desires, hopes, and utopias, and as we read we fashion our own imaginary *mise-en-scène* of the novel on the private stages of our minds. When we are confronted with someone else's phantasy, as Christian Metz pointed out long ago, we feel the loss of our own phantasmatic relation to the novel, with the result that the adaptation itself becomes a kind of "bad object."[1] To paraphrase the Georges Perec lines borrowed by Godard in *Masculin Féminin*, "We left the theatre sad. It was not the adaptation of which we had dreamed. ... It wasn't the film we would have liked to make. Or, more secretly, that we would have liked to live."[2]

But the partial persuasiveness of "fidelity" should not lead us to endorse it as an exclusive methodological principle. The notion of fidelity is highly problematic for a number of reasons. First, it is questionable whether strict fidelity is even possible. A counter-view would insist that an adaptation is automatically different and original due to the change of medium. Here we can take as our own Fritz Lang's response (in *Contempt*) to the producer Prokosch's accusation of infidelity to the script: "Yes, Jerry, in the script it's written, in a film it's images and sounds ... a motion picture it's called." The words of a novel, as countless commentators have pointed out, have a virtual, symbolic meaning; we as readers, or as directors, have to fill in their paradigmatic indeterminances. A novelist's portrayal of a character as "beautiful" induces us to imagine the person's features in our minds. Flaubert never even tells us the exact color of Emma Bovary's eyes, but we color them nonetheless. A film, by contrast, must choose a specific performer. Instead of a virtual, verbally constructed Madame Bovary open to our imaginative reconstruction, we are faced with a specific actress, encumbered with nationality and accent, a Jennifer Jones or an Isabelle Huppert.

This "automatic difference" between film and novel becomes evident even in fairly straightforward adaptations of specific novelistic passages. Take, for example, the passage from Steinbeck's *The Grapes of Wrath* in which Ma Joad contemplates her memorabilia just before leaving her Oklahoma home for California:

> She sat down and opened the box. Inside were letters, clippings, photographs, a pair of earrings, a little gold signet ring, and a watch chain braided of hair and tipped with gold swivels. She touched the letters with her fingers, touched them lightly, and she smoothed a newspaper clipping on which there was an account of Tom's trial.
>
> (*The Grapes of Wrath*, London: Penguin, 1976, p. 118)

In this case a realist director (John Ford) adapted a realist novel just a few months after the novel's publication, attempting a "faithful" rendition of the specific passage. In the film we see Ma Joad sit down, open the box, and look at letters, clippings, photographs, and so forth. But even here the "cinematization" generates an inevitable supplement. Where Steinbeck wrote "photographs," Ford had to choose specific photographs. The mention of "earrings" in the novel does not dictate

Ford's choice of having Ma Joad try them on. The newspaper account of Tom's trial requires the choice of a specific newspaper, specific headlines, specific illustrations, and specific fonts, none of which is spelled out in the original. But beyond such details of *mise-en-scène*, the very processes of filming—the fact that the shots have to be composed, lit, and edited in a certain way—generates an automatic difference. Nothing in the novel prepares us for the idea that Ma Joad will look at the memorabilia by the light of a fire or that the fire's reflection will flicker over her face. Nothing dictates the point-of-view cutting that alternates close shots of Ma Joad's face with what she is looking at, the contemplative rhythm of shot and reverse shot, or the interplay of on-screen and off-screen space, all of which is arguably in the spirit of the novel but not literally in the written text. Nor does the Steinbeck passage mention music, yet the Ford version features a melancholy accordion version of a song ("Red River Valley"). And even if the text had mentioned "Red River Valley," that would still be quite different from our actually hearing it performed. And even if the passage had mentioned both the music and the firelight and the light's flickering over Ma Joad's face, that would still not be anything like our seeing her face (or Jane Darwell's) and hearing the music at the same time.

The shift from a single-track, uniquely verbal medium such as the novel, which "has only words to play with," to a multitrack medium such as film, which can play not only with words (written and spoken), but also with theatrical performance, music, sound effects, and moving photographic images, explains the unlikelihood—and I would suggest even the undesirability—of literal fidelity. Because novels do not usually feature soundtracks, for example, should the filmmaker deprive him or herself of music as an expressive resource?[3] But quite apart from this change in signifying materials, other contingencies also render fidelity in adaptation virtually impossible. The demand for fidelity ignores the actual processes of making films—for example, the differences in cost and in modes of production. A novel is usually produced by a single individual; the film is almost always a collaborative project, mobilizing at minimum a crew of four or five people and at maximum a cast and crew and support staff of hundreds. Although novels are relatively unaffected by questions of budget, films are deeply immersed in material and financial contingencies. Therefore, grand panoramic novels such as *War and Peace* might be difficult to film on a low budget, whereas interiorized novellas such as *Notes from Underground* seem more manageable. With a novel, questions of material infrastructure enter only at the point of distribution, whereas in the cinema they enter at the phase of production of the text itself. Although a novel can be written on napkins in prison, a film assumes a complex material infrastructure—camera, film stock, laboratories—simply in order to exist. Although it costs almost nothing for a novelist to write "The Marquis left Versailles palace at 5:00 p.m. on a cold and wintry day in January 1763," the filmmaker requires substantial funding in order to stage a simulacral Paris (or to shoot on location), to dress the actors in period costume, and so forth.

The notion of "fidelity" is essentialist in relation to both media involved. First, it assumes that a novel "contains" an extractable "essence," a kind of "heart of the artichoke" hidden "underneath" the surface details of style. Hidden within *War and Peace*, it is assumed, there is an originary core, a kernel of meaning or nucleus of events that can be "delivered" by an adaptation. But in fact there is no such transferable core: a single novelistic text comprises a series of verbal signals that can generate a plethora of possible readings, including even readings of the narrative itself. The literary text is not a closed, but an open structure (or, better, structuration, as the later Barthes would have it) to be reworked by a boundless context. The text feeds on and is fed an infinitely permutating intertext, which is seen through ever-shifting grids of interpretation.

This process is further complicated by the passage of time and by change of place. The verbal signals are not always communicated in the same way in a changed context. References obvious to eighteenth-century readers of *Robinson Crusoe* are not necessarily obvious to twentieth-century readers. References clear to English readers of the novel are not necessarily clear to French readers. At the same time, certain features of Defoe's hero, such as his misogyny and latent homo-eroticism, might be *more* visible to present-day than to eighteenth-century readers precisely because contemporary critical discourses have made feminist and homosexual readings available. The greater the lapse in time, the less reverence toward the source text and the more likely the reinterpretation through the values of the present. Thus Jack Gold's adaptation of *Robinson Crusoe, Man Friday*, "sees" the Defoe novel through the contemporary values of the counter-culture— spontaneity, sexual freedom, antiracism.

The question of fidelity ignores the wider question: Fidelity to what? Is the filmmaker to be faithful to the plot in its every detail? That might mean a thirty-hour version of *War and Peace*. Virtually all filmmakers condense the events of the novels being adapted, if only to conform to the norms of conventional theatrical release. Should one be faithful to the physical descriptions of characters? Perhaps so, but what if the actor who happens to fit the description of Nabokov's Humbert also happens to be a mediocre actor? Or is one to be faithful to the author's intentions? But what might they be, and how are they to be inferred? Authors often mask their intentions for personal or psychoanalytic reasons or for external or censorious ones. An author's expressed intentions are not necessarily relevant, since literary critics warn us away from the "intentional fallacy," urging us to "trust the tale not the teller." The author, Proust taught us, is not necessarily a purposeful, self-present individual, but rather "un autre moi." Authors are sometimes not even aware of their own deepest intentions. How, then, can filmmakers be faithful to them? And to what authorial instance is one to be faithful? To the biographical author? To the textual implied author? To the narrator? Or is the adapter-filmmaker to be true to the style of a work? To its narrative point of view? Or to its artistic devices?[4]

Much of the discussion of film adaptation quietly reinscribes the axiomatic superiority of literary art to film, an assumption derived from a number of superimposed prejudices: *seniority*, the assumption that older arts are necessarily better arts; *iconophobia*, the culturally rooted prejudice (traceable to the Judaic-Muslim-Protestant prohibitions on "graven images" and to the Platonic and Neoplatonic depreciation of the world of phenomenal appearance) that visual arts are necessarily inferior to the verbal arts; and *logophilia*, the converse valorization, characteristic of the "religions of the book," of the "sacred word" of holy texts.

Structuralist and poststructuralist theoretical developments, meanwhile, indirectly undermine some of these prejudices in ways that have implications for our discussion of adaptation. The structuralist semiotics of the 1960s and 1970s treated all signifying practices as productive of "texts" worthy of the same close attention as literary texts. The Bakhtinian "translinguistic" conception of the author as the orchestrator of pre-existing discourses, meanwhile, along with Foucault's downgrading of the author in favor of a pervasive anonymity of discourse, opened the way to a "discursive" and nonoriginary approach to all arts. With poststructuralism the figure of the author, rather like the Robin Williams character in *Deconstructing Harry*, loses focus and firmness. Derridean deconstruction, meanwhile, by dismantling the hierarchy of "original" and "copy," suggests that both are caught up in the infinite play of dissemination. A film adaptation seen as a "copy," by analogy, would not necessarily be inferior to the novel as the "original." And if authors are fissured, fragmented, multidiscursive, hardly "present" even to themselves, how can an adaptation communicate the "self-presence" of authorial intention? In the same vein, Roland Barthes's provocative leveling of the hierarchy between literary criticism and literature tends, by analogy, to rescue the film adaptation as a form of criticism or "reading" of the novel, one not necessarily subordinate to the source novel.

From essence to specificity

A variation on the theme of fidelity suggests that an adaptation should be faithful not so much to the source text, but rather to the essence of the medium of expression. This "medium-specificity" approach assumes that every medium is inherently "good at" certain things and "bad at" others.[5] A cinematic essence is posited as favoring certain aesthetic possibilities and foreclosing others, as if a specific aesthetic were inscribed on the celluloid itself. Here is film critic Pauline Kael (in *Deeper into Movies*) on the subject of the "natural" propensities of the film medium:

> Movies are good at action; they're not good at reflective thought or conceptual thinking. They're good at immediate stimulus, but they're not a good means of involving people in the other arts or in learning about a subject. The film techniques themselves seem to stand in the way of the development of curiosity.

Kael seems to be saying that films cannot be intelligent or reflective—and this is from someone who claims to be a "fan" of the movies. Despite her self-proclaimed populism, Kael shares with certain literary elitists the assumption that the cinema inevitably lacks the depth and dignity of literature. But apart from her factitious hierarchizing of the arts, Kael makes suspect generalizations about the cinema. Are films good at portraying only action and not subjective states? What about surrealism and expressionism, not to mention music and video or the work of Alfred Hitchcock? Should film not be "theatrical"? Should all the films inspired by Brecht in their dramaturgy or by Stanislavsky in their acting be dismissed as "uncinematic"? Notions of filmic and literary essence, in this sense, impose an oppressive straitjacket on an open-ended and "non-finalized" set of practices.

A more satisfying formulation would emphasize not ontological essence, but rather diacritical specificity. Each medium has its own specificity deriving from its respective materials of expression. The novel has a single material of expression, the written word, whereas the film has at least five tracks: moving photographic image, phonetic sound, music, noises, and written materials. In this sense, the cinema has not lesser, but rather greater resources for expression than the novel, and this is independent of what actual filmmakers have done with these resources. (I am arguing not superiority of talent, but only complexity of resources. Indeed, one could credit literary fictioners with doing a lot with little, whereas filmmakers could be censured for doing so little with so much.) In a suggestive passage, Nabokov's Humbert Humbert laments the prodding deliberateness of prose fiction, with its subordination to linear consecution, its congenital incapacity to seize the moment in its multifaceted simultaneity. Gleefully reporting his wife Charlotte's providential death by car crash, he deplores having to put "the impact of an instantaneous vision into a sequence of words." The "physical accumulation on the page," he complains, "impairs the actual flash, the sharp unity of impression" (*Lolita* [New York: Berkley Medallion, 1977], p. 91). By contrast, the same crash as staged by Kubrick's *Lolita* offers precisely this simultaneity of impression: we see the crash as we hear it, along with the commentative music that conveys a specific attitude toward the events presented. Yet I am in no way arguing the superiority of the Kubrick rendition. Nabokov, paradoxically, conveys more sense of discontinuity (for example, between the tragic theme of untimely death on the one hand and Humbert's flip, cynical, self-regarding style of presentation on the other) than does Kubrick, despite the discontinuous multiplicity of the film tracks.

Although Humbert Humbert lusts after the cinema's "fantastic simultaneousness," he might also envy its potential for nonsimultaneity, its capacity for mingling apparently contradictory times and temporalities. Each of the filmic tracks can potentially develop an autonomous temporality entering into complex relations with the other tracks. Film's multitrack nature makes it possible to stage contradiction between music and image—for example, Kubrick's underscoring of the opening shot of nuclear bombers, in *Dr. Strangelove,* with the instrumental version of "Try a Little Tenderness." A quoted piece of music, with its own rhythm and continuity, can "accompany" an image track characterized by a different rhythm and continuity. Thus the cinema offers possibilities of disunity and disjunction not immediately available to the novel. The possible contradictions between tracks become an aesthetic resource, opening the way to a multitemporal, polyrhythmic cinema.

The novelistic character also potentially undergoes a kind of fissure or fragmentation within the film adaptation. Although the novelistic character is a verbal-artifact, constructed quite literally out of words, the cinematic character is an uncanny amalgam of photogenie, body movement, acting style, and grain of voice, all amplifed and molded by lighting, *mise-en-scène*, and music. And although novels have only character, film adaptations have both character (actantial function) and performer, allowing for possibilities of interplay and contradiction denied a purely verbal medium. In the cinema a single actor can play many roles: Peter Sellers played three roles in *Dr. Strangelove,* Eddie Murphy five roles in *The Nutty Professor.* Conversely, multiple performers can play a single role: different actors portrayed the four incarnations of Christ in Rocha's *Age of the Earth,* and two actresses (Angela Molina and Carole Bouquet) played Conchita in Buñuel's adaptation of *The Woman and the Puppet* (*That Obscure Object of Desire*).

In the cinema the performer also brings along a kind of baggage, a thespian intertext formed by the totality of antecedent roles. Thus Lawrence Olivier brings with him the intertextual memory of his Shakespeare performances, just as Madonna brings the memory of the various personae of her music videos. By casting Jack Palance as the hated film producer Prokosch in *Contempt,* the auteurist Godard brilliantly exploited the sinister memory of Palance's previous roles as a barbarian (in *The Barbarians,* 1959), and as Atilla the Hun (in *Sign of the Pagans,* 1959). This producer, the casting seems to be telling us, is both a gangster and a barbarian, a suggestion confirmed by the brutish behavior of the character. The director can also have the performer play against the intertext, thus exploiting a realm of tension not available to the novel. To appreciate the force of this difference, we need only contemplate the consequences of other casting choices. What would have happened if Fritz Lang had played the Prokosch role in *Contempt* or if Marlon Brando—or Pee Wee Herman—had played Humbert Humbert in *Lolita?*

Along with character and performer, the cinema offers still another entity denied the novel: the dubber (postsynchroniser), allowing for further permutations of character and voice. In India playback singers, who dub the moving lips of the stars on the image track, become famous in their own right. This third instance enables filmmakers to make thematic points about characters. Thus Glauber Rocha, in his *Deus e Diabo na Terra do Sol* (*Black God, White Devil,* 1964), has actor Othos Bastos dub the voices of both the "black God" and the "white devil," thus insinuating a deeper subterranean unity linking these apparently antagonistic characters.

Both novel and film have consistently cannibalized other genres and media. The novel began by orchestrating a polyphonic diversity of materials—courtly fictions, travel literature, allegory, and jestbooks—into a new narrative form, repeatedly plundering or annexing neighboring arts, creating novel hybrids such as poetic novels, dramatic novels, cinematic novels, and journalistic novels. But the cinema carries this cannibalization to its paroxysm. As a rich, sensorially composite language characterized by what Metz calls "codic heterogeneity," the cinema becomes a receptacle open to all kinds of literary and pictorial symbolism, to all types of collective representation, to all ideologies, to all aesthetics, and to the infinite play of influences within cinema, within the other arts, and within culture generally.

The cinema is both a synesthetic and a synthetic art, synesthetic in its capacity to engage various senses (sight and hearing) and synthetic in its anthropophagic capacity to absorb and synthesize antecedent arts. A composite language by virtue of its diverse matters of expression— sequential photography, music, phonetic sound, and noise—the cinema "inherits" all the art forms associated with these matters of expression. Cinema has available to it the visuals of photography and painting, the movement of dance, the decor of architecture, and the performance of theater. Both the novel and the fiction film are summas by their very nature. Their essence is to have no essence, to be open to all cultural forms. Cinema can literally include painting, poetry, and music, or it can metaphorically evoke them by imitating their procedures; it can show a Picasso painting or emulate cubist techniques or visual dislocation, cite a Bach cantata, or create montage equivalents of fugue and counterpoint. Godard's *Passion* not only includes music (Ravel, Mozart, Ferre, Beethoven, and Fauré), but is conceived musically, and not only includes animated tableaux based on celebrated paintings (Rembrandt's *Night Watch,* Goya's *The Third of May,* and Delacroix's *Turkish Bathers*), but also expresses a painterly concern with light and color. The famous definitions of cinema in terms of other arts—"painting in motion" (Canudo), "sculpture in motion" (Vachel Lindsay), "music of light" (Abel Gance), and "architecture in movement" (Elie Faure)—merely call attention to the synthetic multiplicity of signifiers available to the cinema.

Translations and transformations

If "fidelity" is an inadequate trope, we must then ask, What tropes might be more appropriate? One trope, I would suggest, is "translation." The trope of adaptation as translation suggests a principled effort of intersemiotic transposition, with the inevitable losses and gains typical of any translation.[6] The trope of translation undergirds the textual mechanisms of Godard's *Le Mépris* (*Contempt,* 1963), itself an adaptation of the Moravia novel *Il Disprezzo,* a novel whose partial subject is the issue of the adaptation of Homer's *The Odyssey* for film. The film deals with various kinds of translations, literal and figurative. The translation is literal both in its implicit reference to the translation of *The Odyssey* from classical Greek into contemporary European vernaculars and in its literal inclusion of a translator (not present in the novel)—the interpreter Francesca (Georgia Moll)— who mediates linguistically between the monolingual American producer Prokosch and his more polyglot European interlocutors. (When Italian laws concerning obligatory postsynchronization led Italian dubbers to eliminate the role of Francesca, Godard disassociated himself from the Italian version of the film.) Francesca's hurried translations of Fritz Lang's poetic quotations prove that, in art as in language, "traduire, c'est trahir." [to translate is to betray] Her translations invariably miss a nuance, smooth over an aggression, or exclude an ambiguity. But the film also concerns less literal translations: the generic "translation" of Homer's epic poetry into contemporary novelistic prose and the intersemiotic "translation" of Moravia's novel into Godard's photographic images and sounds. In this sense, *Contempt* can be seen as a meditation on the richly ambiguous nature of all translation and adaptation. At the same time, the film suggests, art renews itself through creative mistranslation.

In fact, adaptation theory has available a whole constellation of tropes—translation, reading, dialogization, cannibalization, transmutation, transfiguration, and signifying—each of which sheds light on a different dimension of adaptation. For example, the trope of adaptation as a "reading" of the source novel—a reading that is inevitably partial, personal, and conjectural—suggests that just as any text can generate an infinity of readings, so any novel can generate any number of adaptations. Why should we assume that one director—for example, John Huston—has said everything that needs to be said about *Moby-Dick*? (If one has nothing new to say about a novel, Orson Welles once suggested, why adapt it at all?) A single novel can thus generate any number of critical readings and creative misreadings. Indeed, many novels have been adapted repeatedly. *Madame Bovary* has been adapted at least nine times, in countries as diverse as France, Portugal, the United States, India, and Argentina. Each adaptation sheds a new cultural light on the novel; the Hindi version, entitled *Maya* (*Illusion*) not only envisions Bovary through the grid of Hindu philosophy ("the veil of illusion"), but also links Emma's romanticism, quite logically, to the conventions of the Bombay musical. ...

Adaptation as intertextual dialogism

Adaptations, then, can take an activist stance toward their source novels, inserting them into a much broader intertextual dialogism. An adaptation, in this sense, is less an attempted resuscitation of an originary word than a turn in an ongoing dialogical process. The concept of intertextual dialogism suggests that every text forms an intersection of textual surfaces. All texts are tissues of anonymous formulae, variations on those formulae, conscious and unconscious quotations, and conflations and inversions of other texts. In the broadest sense, intertextual dialogism refers to the infinite and open-ended possibilities generated by all the discursive practices of a culture, the entire matrix of communicative utterances within which the artistic text is situated, which reach the text not only through recognizable influences, but also through a subtle process of dissemination.

Intertextuality, then, helps us transcend the aporias of "fidelity." But intertextuality can be conceived in a shallow or in a deep manner. Bakhtin spoke of the "deep generating series" of literature—that is, the complex and multidimensional dialogism, rooted in social life and history, comprising both primary (oral) and secondary (literary) genres—which engendered literature as a cultural phenomenon. Bakhtin attacked the limitation of the literary scholar-critic's interest exclusively to the "literary series," arguing for a more diffuse dissemination of ideas as interanimating all the "series," literary and nonliterary, as they are generated by what he called the "powerful deep currents of culture." Literature and by extension the cinema, must be understood within what Bakhtin called the "differentiated unity of the epoch's entire culture" (Bakhtin, "Response to a Question from *Novy Mir*," in *Speech Genres and Other Late Essays* [ed. Carl Emerson and Michael Holquist, Austin: University of Texas Press, 1986], p.3).

Building on Bakhtin and Julia Kristeva, in *Palimpsestes* (1982) Gérard Genette offers other analytic concepts useful for our discussion, of adaptation. Genette proposed a more inclusive term, *transtextuality*, to refer to "all that which puts one text in relation, whether manifest or secret, with other texts." Genette posited five types of transtextual relations, some of which bear relevance to adaptation. He defined the first type, "intertextuality" as the "effective co-presence of two texts" in the form of quotation, plagiarism, and allusion. Adaptation, in this sense, participates in a double intertextuality, one literary and the other cinematic.

"Paratextuality," Genette's second type of transtextuality, refers to the relation within the totality of a literary work, between the text proper and its "paratext"—titles, prefaces, postfaces, epigraphs, dedications, illustrations, and even book jackets and signed autographs—in short, all the accessory messages and commentaries that come to surround the text and at times become virtually indistinguishable from it. In the case of film, the paratext might include widely quoted prefatory remarks by a director at a film's first screening, reported remarks by a director about a film, or widely reported information about the budget of a film.

"Metatextuality," Genette's third type of transtextuality, consists of the critical relation between one text and another, whether the commented text is explicitly cited or only silently evoked. In this sense, *The Other Francisco* can be seen as a metatextual critique of the Suárez y Romero novel. "Architextuality," Genette's fourth category, refers to the generic taxonomies suggested or refused by the titles or infratitles of a text. Architextuality has to do with an artist's willingness or reluctance to characterize a text generically in its title. Because most adaptations of novels simply carry over the title of the original, if only to take advantage of a preexisting market, this term would seem irrelevant to our discussion. Yet in some cases a changed title signals the transformations operative in the adaptation. Giral's title *The Other Francisco* alerts us to Giral's radical transfiguration of the politics and aesthetics of the source novel. The title *Clueless*, disguises the Jane Austen source (*Emma*) while signaling the film's milieu: rich, upper-middle-class adolescents. As we shall see, the title of *Man Friday,* an adaptation of *The Adventures of Robinson Crusoe,* signals a change in voice and perspective from those of the colonizer Crusoe to those of the colonized Friday, now no longer the "boy" of colonialist discourse, but a "man."

"Hypertextuality," Genette's fifth type of transtextuality, is perhaps the most suggestive of Genette's categories. It refers to the relation between one text, which Genette calls "hypertext," to an anterior text, or "hypotext," which the former transforms, modifies, elaborates or extends. In literature the hypotexts of *The Aeneid* include *The Odyssey* and *The Iliad*, whereas the hypotexts of Joyce's *Ulysses* include *The Odyssey* and *Hamlet*. Both *The Aeneid* and *Ulysses* are hypertextual elaborations of a single hypotext, *The Odyssey*. Filmic adaptations, in this sense, are hypertexts derived from preexisting hypotexts that have been transformed by operations of selection, amplification, concretization, and actualization. The diverse filmic adaptations of *Madame Bovary* (by Renoir and Minnelli) or of *La Femme et le Pantin* (by Duvivier, von Sternberg, and Buñuel) can be seen as variant hypertextual "readings" triggered by the same hypotext. Indeed, the diverse prior adaptations can form a larger, cumulative hypotext that is available to the filmmaker who comes relatively "late" in the series.

Film adaptations, then, are caught up in the ongoing whirl of intertextual reference and transformation, of texts generating other texts in an endless process of recycling, transformation, and transmutation, with no clear point of origin. Let us take as an example *The Adventures of Robinson Crusoe*, one of the seminal source novels of a specific European tradition, the realistic mimetic novel supposedly based on "real life" and written in such a way as to generate a strong impression of factual reality. Yet this "realistic" novel is itself rooted in various intertexts: the Bible, the literature of religious meditation, the journalistic texts about Crusoe's prototype, Alexander Selkirk, and sensationalist travel literature, to mention just a few. Defoe's 1719 novel, rooted in this complex and variegated intertext, also generated its own textual "afterlife" or "post-text." In France the exemplars of this post-text were called Robinsonades. Already in 1805, less than a century after the publication of the Defoe novel, a German encyclopedia (*Bibliothek der Robinsone*) offered a comprehensive guide to all the works inspired by *Robinson Crusoe*. Nor did this novelistic post-text end in the nineteenth century, as both Michel Tournier's *Vendredi, ou l'Île de la Pacifique* and Derek Walcott's *Pantomime*, in both of which *Crusoe* is reread through an anticolonialist grid, clearly attest.

The *Crusoe* post-text also has ramifications in the world of film, where a long pageant of adaptations has rung in changes on the themes of the original. *Miss Crusoe* (1919) performs a variation in gender, which is interesting because the novel, against the grain of the "desert island" genre, scarcely mentions women at all. *Little Robinson Crusoe* (1924), carrying out the logic of *Crusoe*-as-children's-book, changes the age of the protagonist, with Jackie Coogan coming to the island on wings to be worshiped by the naive natives. *Mr. Robinson Crusoe* (1932) keeps Crusoe but supplies him with a feminine companion, perhaps inevitably called not Friday; but Saturday. *Swiss Family Robinson* (1940) permutates the number and social status of the characters, changing the solitary Crusoe to an entire family. The Laurel and Hardy film *Robinson Crusoeland* (1950) performs a shift in genre, from colonial adventure story to slapstick comedy. Similarly, *Robinson Crusoe on Mars* (1964) turns the novel into science fiction: the "pioneer" on earth becomes a pioneer in space. In *Lieutenant Robinson Crusoe* (1965) there are transformations both professional and zoological, as Defoe's protagonist becomes the sailor played by Dick van Dyke, and Crusoe's parrot is replaced by a chimpanzee. ...

The grammar of transformation

To sum up what has been argued thus far, one way to look at adaptation is to see it as a matter of a source novel hypotext's being transformed by a complex series of operations: selection, amplification, concretization, actualization, critique, extrapolation, analogization, popularization, and reculturalization. The source novel, in this sense, can be seen as a situated utterance produced in one medium and in one historical context, then transformed into another equally situated utterance that is produced in a different context and in a different medium. The source text forms a dense informational network, a series of verbal cues that the adapting film text can then take up, amplify, ignore, subvert, or transform. The film adaptation of a novel performs these transformations according to the protocols of a distinct medium, absorbing and altering the genres and intertexts available through the grids of ambient discourses and ideologies, and as mediated by a series of filters: studio style, ideological fashion, political constraints, auteurist predilections, charismatic stars, economic advantage or disadvantage, and evolving technology. The film hypertext, in this sense, is transformational almost in the Chomskian sense of a "generative grammar" of adaptation, with the difference that these cross-media operations are infinitely more unpredictable and multifarious than they would be were it a matter of "natural language."

Central to the transformational grammar of adaptation are permutations in locale, time, and language. The Renoir and the Chabrol adaptations of *Madame Bovary* feature continuity between the language and locale of the source novel and the language and locale of the film adaptations. The Minnelli adaptation, by contrast, features discontinuity; studio lots "stand in" for France, and the actors speak English, with occasional use of French words and intermittent use of French accents. The filmmaker adapting a novel written in another country and in another language is confronted with a series of options: Should the director find performers from the country in question? Should he have actors from the "home" country speak with an accent? Or should the adapter "Americanize" the source novel? The bored provincial protagonist of Woody Allen's *Purple Rose of Cairo* (played by Mia Farrow), deluded by artistic fictions, can on some levels be seen as an American Bovary. The director must also confront questions of temporality and epoch. Is the film adaptation a costume drama that respects the historical time frame of the original, or does it "update" the novel? The history of the theater features innumerable updatings of Shakespeare, for example, yet the practice is less common in film. Of the recent spate of Jane Austen films, only *Clueless* updated the original, but without referencing the novel explicitly. ...

The question of intertext also brings up the question of parody. Although some adaptations, such as the Richardson and Osborne *Tom Jones,* pick up on the parodic cues of their source novels, others ignore them. Both the Chabrol and the Renoir adaptations of *Madame Bovary,* for example, do surprisingly little with a recurrent feature of the source novel, its rendering of Emma's interior consciousness, in *le style indirect libre,* through parodic exaggerations of the stylistic vices of such writers as Chateaubriand and Sir Walter Scott. Minnelli emphasizes Emma's early reading of romantic novels, but has James Mason's voice-over condemn her "illusions" and "dreams" in a univocal fashion that has little to do with Gustave ("Madame-Bovary-c'est-moi") Flaubert's "complicitous critique" of his heroine. Kubrick's version of *Lolita,* similarly, does almost nothing with the densely parodic prose of the Nabokov source novel or, for that matter, with all the self-flauntingly cinematic and self-referential ideas proposed in Nabokov's screenplay, partly as a function of Kubrick's instrumental view (at the time) of prose style as what the artist uses to fascinate the beholder and thus to convey feelings and thoughts.[7]

Transmutations of plot and character

Much of the literature on adaptation has concentrated on specifically textual operations having to do with plot events and characters. Often we find a kind of condensation of characters. The many Okie families of *The Grapes of Wrath* are foreshortened into the Joads of the John Ford version. The bevy of female lovers of Jules and Jim in the Henri Pierre Roché novel are condensed into Catherine (Jeanne Moreau) in the Truffaut adaptation. Film adaptations have a kind of "Sophie's choice" about which characters in the novel will live or die. But although adaptations tend to sacrifice "extra" characters from novels, occasionally the opposite process takes place, as we saw in the case of *El Otro Francisco.* The Minnelli version of *Madame Bovary* adds the character of Flaubert himself, who is being tried for obscenity in the courts of France. Godard adds the character of the translator Francesca in *Contempt,* precisely in order to highlight the polyglot ambiance of international coproductions in the 1960s, as well as to make a more metaphorical point about adaptation as a process of translation.

Characters can also be subtly changed. The white judge in Thomas Wolfe's *Bonfire of the Vanities* became the black judge played by Morgan Freeman in the Brian de Palma adaptation, presumably as a way of sidestepping and warding off the accusations of racism leveled against the novel. Film adaptations often ignore key passages in the source books. None of the *Madame Bovary* adapters, to my knowledge, chose to stage the opening passage in which a group of pupils "nous étions a l'étude, quand le Proviseur entra, suivi d'un nouveau. ..." And most of the adaptations downplay Charles's first wife in order to concentrate on the relationship between Emma and Charles.

Film adaptations usually make temporal changes as well. Therefore, two months in the Alberto Moravia source novel become just two days in the Godard adaptation (*Contempt*), part of a Brechtian "theatricalization" of the source novel. On the other hand, events in the source novel can be amplified, as when, in the case of *Tom Jones,* a few sentences regarding Squire Western's love of hunting became in the film the pretext for a spectacular fox hunt staged in an attempt to make the film more "cinematic" but also in order to strengthen the satire of the landed gentry. Film adaptations can also add events—for example, in the form of Peter Sellers's inspired improvisations in the Kubrick *Lolita.* These additions can have any number of motivations: to take advantage of a brilliant actor, to suggest contemporary relevance, or to "correct" the novel for aesthetic reasons. In the case of Godard's *Masculine Feminine,* supposedly an adaptation of a Guy de Maupassant story, very little was retained from the source novel. Godard kept only a few of the characters' names and almost nothing else, to the point that those who sold the rights concluded that those rights had not even been used.

There is also the complex question of point of view. Does the film adaptation maintain the point of view and the focalization (Genette) of the novel? Who tells the story in the novel vis-à-vis the film? Who focalizes the story—that is, who sees within the story? Genette distinguishes between the instance that tells (the narrator), the instance that sees and experiences (the character), and the instance that knows (the filter). In Godard's *Contempt* there is a clear shift in point of view or, to change the metaphor, to a change in voice, a "transvocalization." Although the novel is narrated as a reminiscence in the first person by screenwriter Ricardo Molteni (Paul in the film), the film is neither narrated in the first person, nor is it a reminiscence, nor is it told from any particular point of view except that, perhaps, of the cinema itself. What was therapeutic first-person rumination in the novel—"I decided to write these memoirs in hopes of finding [Camille] again"—becomes a kind of no-person point of view in the film. The unreliable narrator of the novel—we slowly realize that he is highly disturbed, paranoid, almost hallucinatory—gives way to the impersonal narration of the film, all as part of a drift toward a Brechtian depersonalization and depsychologizing. The emphasis shifts from one character's mind to the relations between five characters belonging to the same film milieu.

This is not the place to attempt to perform an ambitious extrapolation of Genette's categories concerning novelistic discourse to filmic discourse. Suffice it to say that such categories as "variable focalization" and "multiple focalization" are very suggestive for film analysis. The former evokes the tag-team approach to point of view that characterizes Hitchcock's films, moving between major characters such as Mitch and Melanie in *The Birds* but also moving to minor characters such as the boy who whistles at Melanie in the opening shots, the man who observes her from the dock at Bodega Bay, or even the birds who oversee her departure in the shot/reverse shot structure of the final sequence. "Multiple focalization" evokes not only the multiple perspectives of a film such as *Rashomon* or *Citizen Kane,* but also the multiple focalizations of a dispersed narrative such as that of Altman's *Nashville.*

Film adaptations of novels often change novelistic events for (perhaps unconscious) ideological reasons. In the case of the Minnelli *Madame Bovary,* Charles Bovary is made to refuse to operate on Hippolyte (whereas in the novel he bungles the operation), presumably out of respect for Hollywood pieties concerning the *pater familias* figure. Film adaptations of novels thus become entangled in questions of ideology. Does the film "push" the novel to the left or the right in terms of sexual, racial, and class politics? Spielberg's *The Color Purple* plays down the lesbianism of the Alice Walker novel. And by having Shug reconcile with her censorious preacher father, the adaptation "repatriarchalizes" a feminist novel. The John Ford version of *The Grapes of Wrath* shies away from the socialist drift of the Steinbeck novel. But the drift is not always rightward. *Man Friday,* as we have seen, pushes *Robinson Crusoe* to the antiracist, anticolonialist, antireligious left. The narrative sequencing can also be rearranged, with clear ideological overtones. The circular structure of the Kubrick *Lolita* clearly draws attention away from Humbert Humbert's nympholepsy and toward the murderous rivalry between Humbert and Quilty in ways that lead one to suspect that this was a sop to the censors. In the John Ford *Grapes of Wrath,* as has often been pointed out, the sequencing of the three camps—the Hooverville, the New Deal "Wheatpatch," and the Keane Ranch—is altered so as to transform what was a spiraling descent into oppression into an ascent into New Deal benevolence and good order.[8]

Just as interesting as what in the source novel is eliminated or bypassed is why certain materials are ignored. The intercalary, essayistic chapters of *The Grapes of Wrath* were largely eliminated from the John Ford adaptation, presumably because they were seen as "uncinematic" but also because those chapters happen to be the places in which John Steinbeck's (then) socialist opinions were most in evidence. The philosophical meditations that dot Melville's *Moby-Dick* were largely ignored in the John Huston adaptation, again because of their "uncinematic" nature but also perhaps because film producers assumed that the mass audience would not be "up to" such lofty and allusive materials. The adaptations of reflexive novels such as *Tom Jones* or *Lolita,* in the same vein, tend to downplay the literary-critical excursuses that mark the source novels. Although reflexive in certain respects, the Osborne and Richardson *Tom Jones* does not try to recreate the film equivalents of Fielding's essays in literary criticism—for example, by proffering film criticism—presumably because tampering too much with the filmic illusion would spoil the "sport" of the fiction.

Here we enter the fraught area of comparative stylistics. To what extent are the source novel and the film adaptation innovative in aesthetic terms, and if they are innovative, are they innovative in the same way? *Madame Bovary* was extremely innovative at its time for its decentered approach to narrative, its subversion of norms of character, its mobile approach to point of view, and its systemic frustration of the reader's expectations. To what extent do the various film versions provide an equivalent sense of such innovations? To what extent do they go beyond the novel to innovate in cinematic terms? The answers to these questions become crucial when we realize that *Madame Bovary,* although written prior to the advent of the cinema, can reasonably be called protocinematic. Eisenstein famously cited the "agricultural fair" chapter in the Flaubert novel as a brilliant precinematic example of montage. The concept of the "cinematic novel" has, admittedly, often been abused, bandied about so imprecisely as to mean anything from a book that has sharply imagined physical action to a book that uses certain techniques reminiscent of film. Despite this danger, it is nonetheless fruitful, I think to see a novel such as *Madame Bovary* as protocinematic. Flaubert was an author at a crucial transitional moment within the history of the novel, one distinct from both the sober documentary realism of Defoe and the playful reflexivity of a Cervantes or a Fielding. I am referring to the moment when a kind of mobilized regard crystallized the altered perceptions associated with modernity—an altered gaze associated both with impressionism in painting, where the artist is attentive to what intervenes between the object and the eye, and with modernism in the novel, where point of view and filters of consciousness become paramount organizing principles—instantiating a subjectification and a relativization of the stabilities of the classical realist model.

Flaubert's *Madame Bovary* might be called both proleptically modernist and protocinematic in a number of senses: in its film script—like notation of precise gestures (see, for example, the account of Charles Bovary's first arrival at Emma's family farm); in its artful modulation, à la Hitchcock, of point of view, whereby we experience flickering moments of identification not only with major characters such as Emma and Charles, but also with minor characters and even with unnamed characters who never again appear in the text; in its precise articulation, reminiscent of camera "setups," of character vantage points within voyeuristic structures (for example, the two gossips who observe Emma from their attic post or the "curieux" of the final pages who peeks at Charles from behind a bush); in its kinetic, destabilized portraiture of characters as a kind of flowing composition in time; in its verbal recreation of the "feel" of seeing, especially encumbered seeing (Emma's squinting, her intermittent loss of focus, her attempts to discern objects in the distance); in its "impressionist" attention to the vapors and gases jostling one another in the atmosphere, as well as to the dynamic agency of light in modifying appearances, as seen in the use of such light-active words as *blanchissaient, vernissait,* and *veloutant*; in the corporeal empathy with which it identifies the reader with the very body of the heroine (for example, the account of Emma's milky orgasm with Rodolphe); in the kinesthetic quality of Flaubert's prose, its manner of mobilizing the reader's gaze (for example, the accounts of the passing world as seen from the moving *hirondelle*); and in the ironic manipulation of "focal length"—for instance, in the abrupt move from the long view of the cab containing the fornicating Leon and Emma to the close view of "the torn-up note," followed by the extremely long view that turns Emma into a generic "femme" descending from a vehicle.

Compared with the novel, the film adaptations of *Madame Bovary* are much less innovative, and much more concerned with adapting the text to a mainstream audience. In other words, the phenomenon of "mainstreaming" is not limited to ideological issues; there also exists the phenomenon of aesthetic mainstreaming. Despite its surface modernity and its technological razzle-dazzle, dominant cinema has maintained, on the whole, a premodernist aesthetic corresponding to that of the nineteenth-century mimetic novel. In its dominant mode it became a receptacle for the mimetic aspirations abandoned by the most advanced practitioners of the other arts. Film inherited the illusionistic ideals that impressionism had relinquished in painting, that Jarry had attacked in the theater, and that Proust, Joyce, and Woolf had undermined in the novel. Aesthetic censorship, in this sense, might be in some ways more severe and deeply rooted than political self-censorship. Adaptation, in this sense, seems to encounter the most difficulty with modernist novels such as Joyce's *Ulysses*, Nabokov's *Lolita*, or Duras's *L'Amant*. When Jean-Jacques Annaud turns Marguerite Duras's modernist, feminist novel *L'Amant* into a linear, masculinist, mainstream film, we are not entirely wrong to regret that the director has misrecognized the most salient traits of Durasian *écriture*. When a modernist, discontinuous novel is made relatively continuous through the dumb inertia of convention; when a filmic adaptation is thought to need a sympathetic male protagonist in order, to be palatable for a mass audience (whence Minnelli's idealized Charles Bovary); when the hero cannot die or the villain must be punished; when a digressive, disruptive style must be linearized into a classical three-act structure with exposition, conflict, and climax; when morality must be reconfigured to suit preestablished Manichean schemas; when a difficult, reflexive novel must be made transparent and redundant; when the spectator must be led by the hand—in such cases, I would suggest, we find a kind of ideologically driven failure of nerve to deal with the aesthetic implications of novelistic modernism.

By adopting the approach to adaptation I have been suggesting, we in no way abandon our rights or responsibilities to make judgments about the value of specific film adaptations. We can—and, in my view, we should—continue to function as critics; but our statements about films based on novels or other sources need to be less moralistic, less panicked, less implicated in unacknowledged hierarchies, more rooted in contextual and intertexual history. Above all, we need too to be less concerned with inchoate notions of "fidelity" and to give more attention to dialogical responses—to readings, critiques, interpretations, and rewritings of prior material. If we can do all these things, we will produce a criticism that not only takes into account, but also welcomes, the differences among the media.

■   ■   ■

Questions and projects

1. Explain what Stam means by "intertextuality" and choose a contemporary adaptation of a work of literature that demonstrates how that intertextuality appears visibly in a single film.
2. Part of Stam's argument about "intertextual dialogism" develops from Gérard Genette's five types of transtextuality. Briefly identify each type and provide an example of each from a film adaptation.

Notes

1   See Christian Metz, *The Imaginary Signifier* (Bloomington: Indiana University Press, 1977), p. 12.
2   Georges Perec, *Les Choses* (Paris: L. N. Julliard, 1965), p. 80 (translation mine).
3   One of the side effects of reading a novel after having seen its cinematic adaptation, for me at least, is

that I tend to "hear" the music track as I read.

4   Julio Bressane, in his film adaptation of the Machado de Assis novel *Memorias Postunas de Bras Cubas*, professed a lack of interest in the novel's plot while rigorously attempting to find film equivalents of its devices. The literary device of the posthumous narrator, for example, is "translated" by a filmmaker's sound boom's banging up against a skeleton.

5   For a critique of medium-specificity arguments, see Noel Carroll, *Theorizing the Moving Image* (Cambridge: Cambridge University Press, 1996).

6   For a systematic, even technical, exploration of adaptation as translation, see Patrick Cattrysse, *Pour une Théorie de l'Adaptation Filmique: Le Film Noir Américain* (Paris: Peter Lang, 1995).

7   One regrets that the later, more reflexive, Kubrick of *Clockwork Orange* and *Dr. Strangelove* did not return to the Nabokov text and process it through a more stylistically self-conscious grid.

8   See Warren French, *Filmguide to The Grapes of Wrath* (Bloomington: Indiana University Press, 1973).

Chapter 10

Lawrence Venuti

ADAPTATION, TRANSLATION, CRITIQUE

L AWRENCE VENUTI is an internationally renowned expert in translation studies. In this essay, Venuti applies concepts from recent advances in translation studies as a means of rethinking cinematic adaptation. Similar to other contemporary models, Venuti seeks to move adaptation studies beyond the restrictive criterion of "fidelity," yet unlike most, Venuti encourages a more self-conscious critical methodology that recognizes the critic's own act of interpretation in the process of evaluating an adaptation in relation to the source work, arguing for a third term existing between the poles of "fidelity" and "intertextuality"—what Venuti calls an "interpretant."

■ ■ ■

ADAPTATION, TRANSLATION, CRITIQUE
LAWRENCE VENUTI

Journal of Visual Culture, vol 6, no. 1 (2007), pp. 25–43.

Translation theory advances thinking about film adaptation by enabling a more rigorous critical methodology. The relation between such second-order creations and their source materials is not communicative but hermeneutic, depending on the translator's or filmmaker's application of an interpretant. The hermeneutic relation can be seen not only as interpretive, fixing the form and meaning of the source materials, but as interrogative, exposing the cultural and social conditions of those materials and of the translation or adaptation that has processed them. The critic in turn applies an interpretant, whether a critical methodology or specific interpretation, to formulate the hermeneutic relation and its interrogative effects.

Communicative vs hermeneutic models

The study of film adaptation has long been impeded by the lack of a rigorous methodology that enables the examination of adaptations as cultural objects in their own right, distinct both from the materials they adapt and from films that do not make the adaptation of prior materials central to their signifying process. This methodological lack has been due to a variety of factors, but two in particular seem to be decisive, one conceptual, the other institutional (for a survey that aims to be exhaustive, see Stam, 2005a: 3–8). The literary texts that are usually considered in studies of film adaptations are assigned a greater value that reflects not only the assumption of a romantic concept of original, self-expressive authorship and hence the marginalization of second-order creations like adaptations, but also the disciplinary sites to which film studies was most often affiliated in its emergence, particularly academic departments and programs of literature, where romantic assumptions about authorship continue to hold sway. As a result, the film adaptation has generally been described and evaluated on the basis of its adequacy to the literary text, whereby it tends to be judged as an unfaithful or distorted communication of the author's expressive intention. Such a judgement, however, routinely involves the unwitting application of a third term, a dominant or authoritative interpretation of the text, which the critic applies as a standard on the assumption that the film should somehow inscribe that and only that interpretation (for examples, see Orr, 1984). In adaptation studies informed by the discourse of fidelity, the film is not compared directly to the literary text, but rather to a version of it mediated by an interpretation.

This critical practice is perhaps most evident with adaptations of canonical literary texts around which a substantial body of commentary has accumulated and a limited range of interpretations has achieved authority. Yet the communicative model on which the practice depends can also be detected in studies that pay closer and more sophisticated attention to aspects of film form. Brian McFarlane (1996) construes the film version of a novel as effectively a complicated act of communication, an interplay between the 'transfer' of 'narrative' (story, setting, character) and the 'adaptation' of 'enunciation' (plot, tone, point of view). He argues that narrative is 'transferable because [it is] not tied to one or other semiotic system', whereas the 'effects' of enunciation 'are closely tied to the semiotic system in which they are manifested' and therefore 'involve intricate processes of adaptation' (pp. 19–20). Although McFarlane acknowledges that a film can put the novel it adapts to diverse uses (following such previous theorists as Andrew, 1984: 98–104), he ignores the fact that even a seemingly invariant narrative element like setting is transformed when it moves from a novelistic description to a filmic representation (McFarlane, 1996: 14). Given the multiple dimensions of film, at once verbal, visual and aural, filmmakers must make numerous choices that are never entirely specified in or capable of being inferred from a text. Robert Stam (2005a) neatly makes this point by analyzing a scene from a 'fairly straightforward adaptation' of a 'realist novel', John Ford's 1940 version of John Steinbeck's *The Grapes of Wrath*, where 'the very processes of filming – the fact that the shots have to be composed, lit, and edited in a certain way – generates an "automatic difference"' (p. 18).

Subsequent developments in film studies have abandoned the communicative model by considering adaptation as essentially a form of intertextuality. Here the film is viewed as necessarily transformative of prior materials and therefore demands analytical tools designed specifically to describe and assess the significance of the transformations. Stam argues that a film version of a novel should be seen as performing various operations on both the formal and thematic features of the literary text so as to recast it in characteristically filmic terms. These operations may include 'selection, amplification, concretization, actualization, critique, extrapolation, popularization, reaccentuation, transculturization' (p. 45; see also Stam, 2000: 68). The film adaptation is thus treated as relatively autonomous from the materials it adapts because its relationship to those materials consists of a simultaneous resemblance and difference, mimetic but never an identity. For Stam, an adaptation is most productively seen not as communicative, but as hermeneutic, as an interpretation of prior materials that is inscribed by the transformative operations in accordance with various factors peculiar to the medium of film (the screenplay, elements of film form, intertextual or intersemiotic relations to film and other cultural traditions and practices, and the institutional and social conditions of film production). The interpretation, furthermore, is overdetermined by the cultural situation and historical moment in which the adaptation is produced, so that in interpreting prior materials the adaptation intervenes in a specific conjuncture of social relations and developments, regardless of whether the filmmaker intends to intervene in political struggles or to take sides in social divisions.

Still, in examining the recent work in which Stam and his collaborators have deployed this hermeneutic model – a monograph (Stam, 2005b) and two edited volumes (Stam and Raengo, 2004, 2005) – it becomes clear that another set of methodological blinders has appeared. Despite the enormous theoretical sophistication of this research, the studies show a strong tendency to privilege the film adaptation over the literary text it adapts, thereby reversing the implicit evaluation found in the critics who assume the communicative model. 'A filmic adaptation is *automatically* different and original due to the change of medium', Stam (2005a) asserts, and 'by revealing the prisms and grids and discourses through which the novel has been reimagined, adaptations grant a kind of objective materiality to the discourses themselves, giving them visible, audible, and perceptible form' (pp. 17, 45, original emphasis). Yet if an adaptation is by definition a second-order creation, if it consists of numerous intertextual and intersemiotic relations to prior materials, not just the literary text it adapts, in what sense can it be called 'original'? And how can the 'discourses' that the critic articulates in the adaptation ever assume 'a kind of objective materiality' when those discourses are seen as ideological and the critic's interpretation of them more often than not consists of an ideological critique, mounted from a specific political position that may not be shared by the film?

'Many of the changes between novelistic source and film adaptation', states Stam (2005a), have to do with ideology and social discourses. The question becomes whether an adaptation pushes the novel to the 'right,' by naturalizing and justifying social hierarchies based on class, race, sexuality, gender, region, and national belonging, or to the 'left' by interrogating or leveling hierarchies in an egalitarian manner. There are also 'uneven developments' in this respect; for example, in adaptations which push the novel to the left on some issues (e.g. class) but to the right on others (e.g. gender or race) (pp. 42–3).

With few exceptions, Stam and his collaborators treat the 'ideology and social discourses' in film adaptations as if they were readily available, 'perceptible' in an unmediated form, as if the critics themselves had not selected which 'changes' between novel and film enable them to describe the ideological standpoint of the film and to evaluate it as a progressive or reactionary interpretation of the novel (or other prior material). In their hands, the hermeneutic model involves the deliberate but usually unremarked application of a third term, if not always a dominant or authoritative interpretation of a novel or film, then at the very least a dominant critical methodology based on a political position (broadly democratic, although capable of further specification according to various social categories), which the critic applies as a standard on the assumption that the film should somehow inscribe that and only that ideology. In adaptation studies informed by the discourse of intertextuality, the film is not compared directly to the literary text, but rather to a version of it mediated by an ideological critique.

Stam's approach to film adaptation, admittedly 'something less than a grandly ambitious theory yet more substantive than a methodology' (pp. 31–2), remains the most advanced in the field, and his trilogy of books demonstrates how productive it can be. Yet even though I share his politics, I find the lacunae in his methodological exposition not only limiting to the study of film, but potentially damaging to the political position he wishes to bring to it. And I want to suggest that translation theory can be useful in addressing the problems. In fact, if my discussion so far has at all clarified the differences between the two theoretical discourses that prevail in adaptation studies, fidelity and intertextuality, this must be attributed to my reliance on translation research, on a basic distinction between different concepts of language and the translation theories to which they give rise: an instrumental concept of language as expressive of thought and representing reality leads to a theory of translation (and adaptation) as the communication of a univocal meaning inherent in the source text, whereas a hermeneutic concept of language as constitutive of thought and determining reality leads to a theory of translation (and adaptation) as an interpretation that fixes a form and meaning in the source text in accordance with values, beliefs and representations in the translating language and culture (Venuti, 2004: 6; Kelly, 1979: Ch. 1).

Adaptation as translation

The choice of translation theory as a source of concepts for adaptation studies is far from arbitrary. The analogy between adaptation and translation frequently recurs in the literature, but it is usually applied without comment, rarely examined in any detail (see, for instance, Stam, 2000: 62). When the analogy is explored, the understanding of translation turns out to be hampered by the very communicative model that the critic aims to banish from adaptation studies. 'As a trope', states R. Barton Palmer (2004), 'translation is useful because it emphasizes the (at least normally) shared identity of source and adaptation. But translation is also distorting, for it postulates a "carrying over" of some irreducible set of features or qualities from one text to another', so that 'translation makes it difficult to theorize any adaptation as a separate entity' (pp. 262, 263). For Palmer, a translation, unlike a film adaptation, is an untroubled communication of an invariant in the source text. Yet this view betrays an ignorance of developments in translation studies over the past three decades (see Venuti, 2004).

Today, to be sure, translation and adaptation are carefully distinguished by publishers and translators, filmmakers and screenwriters, even if copyright law classifies both cultural practices as 'derivative works'. Contemporary translators are required by their publishers, often explicitly in contracts, to render the source text without any deletions and with only such additions as might be necessary to make that text intelligible in the translating language and culture. An adaptation, in contrast, might depart widely from its prior materials, submitting them to various kinds of manipulation and revision. Nonetheless, a translation can never simply communicate in whole or in part the text that it translates; it can only inscribe an interpretation that inevitably varies the form and meaning of that text. Translation can be regarded as intercultural communication only if we recognize that it communicates one interpretation among other possibilities. This is not to suggest that no formal or semantic correspondences can exist between the source and translated texts, but rather that any such correspondences are subject to the exigencies of an interpretive labor that is decisively determined by the translating language and culture.

Translation enacts an interpretation, first of all, because it is radically decontextualizing. The structural differences between languages, even between languages that bear significant lexical and syntactical resemblances stemming from shared etymologies or a history of mutual borrowing, require the translator variously to dismantle, rearrange, and finally displace the chain of signifiers that make up the source text. Three source-language contexts are lost. The first is intratextual and therefore constitutive of the source text, of its linguistic patterns and discursive structures, its verbal texture. The second is intertextual yet equally constitutive since it comprises the network of linguistic relations that endows the source text with significance for readers who have read widely in the source language. The third, which is also constitutive but both intertextual and intersemiotic, is the context of reception, the various intermedia through which the source text continues to accrue significance when it begins to circulate in its originary culture, ranging from book jackets and advertisements to periodical reviews and academic criticism to editions and adaptations, depending on the genre or text type. By 'constitutive', I mean that this triple context is necessary for the signifying process of the source text, for its capacity to support meanings, values and functions which therefore never survive intact the transition to a different language and culture.

A film adaptation similarly initiates its inscription of an interpretation by detaching its prior materials from their contexts. These contexts are also multiple, both originary and subsequent, and they determine the meanings, values and functions of the materials, whether the latter consist of literary, dramatic or musical texts such as novels, plays, operas and songs, nonfiction texts, such as memoirs, biographies, histories and archival documents, or visual forms, such as other films, television programs, paintings and comic strips – even the screenplay that a director might take as a point of departure. In contrast to contemporary translation practices, however, an adaptation is likely to decontextualize these materials in a much more extensive and complex way, not only because of the change in medium, but because of the license routinely taken by filmmakers. Portions of the prior materials might be eliminated or altered because a filmmaker has chosen not to incorporate them in the film at all or in the same form, including subplots and plot twists, scenes and dialogue, characters and descriptions of settings, images from visual art, and historical figures and events.

The interpretive force of a translation also issues from the fact that the source text is not only decontextualized, but *re*contextualized. These two processes occur simultaneously, as soon as a text is chosen and the translator begins to render it. Translating rewrites a source text in terms that are intelligible and interesting to receptors, situating it in different patterns of language use, in different literary traditions, in different cultural values, in different social institutions, and often in a different historical moment. The recontextualizing process entails the creation of another network of intertextual relations established by and within the translation, a receiving intertext, and the process continues in the emergence of another context of reception, whereby the translation is mediated by promotion and marketing strategies, various kinds of commentaries, and the uses to which diverse readers put it. When translated, then, the source text undergoes not only various degrees of formal and semantic loss, but also an exorbitant gain: in attempting to fix the form and meaning of that text, the translator develops an interpretation in the translating language that ultimately proliferates cultural differences so that the translation can signify in the receiving situation. Although these differences undoubtedly relate to features of the source text, they work only in the translating language and culture and therefore release different effects.

A film adaptation likewise recontextualizes its prior materials, but once again the process is much more extensive and complex because of the shift to a different, multidimensional medium with different traditions, practices and conditions of production. Not only do aspects of film form (*mise-en-scène*, montage, soundtrack, genre) contribute to the construction of a different context that creates a substantially different signifying process, but they are further inflected by distinct styles of acting, directing and studio production, by the trajectory of a particular actor's, director's or screenwriter's career, by economic and political factors, and by the hierarchy of values, beliefs and representations in the cultural situation where the adaptation is produced. Working within these parameters, filmmakers might add to or alter the prior materials, creating or substituting different plots and characters, settings and scenes, and establishing different intertextual and intersemiotic relations. Because of the multidimensionality of the filmic medium, the interpretation inscribed by an adaptation can be so powerful as to compete against and forever complicate the viewer's experiences of the adapted materials.

The interpretant

Yet what exactly is the mechanism of interpretation at work in translating? What principles guide the choice of a source text and the verbal choices made by the translator and editors of the translated text, principles of selection that always constitute interpretive moves? An interpretation is inscribed through the application of a category that mediates between the source language and culture, on the one hand, and the translating language and culture, on the other, a method of choosing the source text and transforming it into the translation. This category consists of *interpretants,* which can be either formal or thematic. Formal interpretants may include a relation of equivalence, such as a semantic correspondence based on dictionary definitions or philological research, or a particular style, such as a lexicon and syntax characteristic of a genre. Thematic interpretants are codes: an interpretation of the source text that has been articulated independently in commentary; a discourse in the sense of a relatively coherent body of concepts, problems, and arguments linked to a genre and housed in a social institution; or values, beliefs and representations affiliated with specific social groups. Interpretants are rooted primarily in the receiving situation even if in some cases they may incorporate materials specific to the source culture. It is the translator's application of interpretants that guides the process of decontextualizing and recontextualizing the source text, replacing intertextual relations in the source language and culture with a receiving intertext, with relations to the translating language and culture which are built into the translation.

The interpretant is a category that has yet to receive sufficient attention in adaptation studies, although it has led an active but clandestine life there. It is what I called earlier the implicit 'third term' in the competing discourses of fidelity and intertextuality, a dominant interpretation or critical methodology applied without reflection by many critics in their analyses and critiques. But it is absent from most efforts to theorize the hermeneutic relation between an adaptation and its prior materials. Two exceptions repay closer examination by helping to develop further the analogy between adaptation and translation.

Mikhail Iampolski (1998) uses the term 'interpretant' in his suggestive treatment of intertextuality in film. For him, the interpretant is a 'third text' that the viewer introduces in order to understand the relation between a film and its 'intertext', which in Iampolski's terminology is defined as a text that exists prior to the film but is explicitly present in it, such as the references to Samuel Taylor Coleridge's poem 'Kubla Khan' in Orson Welles's 1941 film *Citizen Kane* (pp. 42–4). This notion of the interpretant, however, does not clarify or explain the interpretation that the film inscribes in the intertext. On the contrary, it opens up a potentially interminable range of other intertexts, bound only by the viewer's memory of cultural forms. In fact, Iampolski describes the interpretant as 'a term to be understood very broadly to mean a whole field of artistic creation, a kind of "superarchitext"' (p. 57). This open-ended quality effectively limits the explanatory power of the term in Iampolski's critical discourse, although he does make clear that his interest lies elsewhere. In taking up Welles's film, Iampolski wants to show 'how structural isomorphism between intertextually connected texts can create meaning as an enigma or mystery, and how the interpretant is involved in the creation of this enigma', and so his analysis simply multiplies 'parallels' to the basic plot details by citing other, similar literary texts (pp. 43, 45). The methodological lack in his discourse is caused by his privileging of non-narrative elements in film: 'The enigmatic literary subtexts', he states, 'destroy the clarity of the narrative *mode* and create a structure that allows for a slippage from the diegetic level (the level of narrative) to the discursive level (the level of the formal organization of the story)' (p. 47, original emphasis). The interpretant that enables Iampolski's own critical acts is a poststructuralist concept of indeterminacy, an endless proliferation of interpretive possibilities that produce the sublime effect of escaping the viewer's cognitive mastery. 'In this struggle for meaning', he concludes, 'the real victory belongs to the characters in the film, since they are the ones who know that there is in fact no real solution' (p. 47).

The open-ended quality of Iampolski's terms highlights the restrictedness of Patrick Cattrysse's unique application of translation theory to the study of film adaptation. Central to Cattrysse's synthesis is Gideon Toury's concept of norms, the values that govern cultural practices like translation. 'Whereas adherence to source norms determines a translation's *adequacy* as compared to the source text', Toury (1995) states, 'subscription to norms originating in the target culture determines its *acceptability*' (pp. 56–7, original emphasis; see also Toury, 1980). As a result, equivalence is reconceptualized as a dynamic category that functions solely in the translating culture: criteria of acceptability may be either source-oriented or target-oriented, and standards of equivalence can vary according to different cultural constituencies and different historical moments. Cattrysse (1990) develops these concepts for adaptation studies by distinguishing between norms that are 'semiotic', specific to the signifying processes of literature or film, and norms that are 'pragmatic', defined as 'socio-communicative determinations' that are exemplified by style or genre or by economic and political factors, among other possibilities (pp. 40–1, my translation here and later). To formulate the norms in a 'corpus' of film adaptations, according to Cattrysse, the films must be compared to their prior materials (his corpus is American film noir between 1940 and 1960) so as 'to locate divergences and resemblances, shifts and non-shifts'; the comparison ultimately reveals 'the equivalence [that] is realized through the compromise between the norms of adequacy and the norms of acceptability' (pp. 38–9).

The concept of norms would seem to do the work of the interpretant for Cattrysse. Yet in setting equivalence as the goal of the analysis, his application of translation theory devolves into a more flexible and sophisticated but nonetheless recognizable version of the discourse of fidelity. Not only are norms too narrowly defined and too simply applied to encompass the multiple factors that enable and constrain film production, but the emphasis on equivalence stops short of describing the hermeneutic relation between an adaptation and its prior materials. Cattrysse (1992) later realized some of these limitations when he observed that shifts are complex in their effects and cannot be reduced to a specific norm (pp. 56–7). Nonetheless, his work has the virtue of reinstalling the concept of equivalence in adaptation studies since it has been treated too dismissively in the discourse of intertextuality. Equivalence is definitely one relationship into which a film can enter with its prior materials, however that concept may be defined.

I want to suggest that the interpretant is an essential category for studying adaptation. Interpretants enable the film to inscribe an interpretation by mediating between its prior materials, on the one hand, and the medium and its conditions of production, on the other – by providing, in other words, a method of selecting those materials and transforming them into the adaptation through the multimedial choices made by the filmmakers. As in the case of translation, the interpretants in adaptation can be either formal or thematic. Formal interpretants may include a relation of equivalence, such as a structural correspondence maintained between the adapted materials and the film (cf. Iampolski's 'structural isomorphism' between plot details), a particular style, such as a distinctive set of formal features that characterize the work of a director or studio, or a concept of genre that necessitates a manipulation or revision of the adapted materials (cf. Cattrysse, 1992: 57, where a 'norm of suspense' typical of noir is cited to account for narrative divergences between novels and films). Thematic interpretants are codes, values, ideologies. They may include an interpretation of the adapted materials that has been formulated elsewhere, a morality or cultural taste shared by the filmmakers and used to appeal to a particular audience, or a political position that reflects the interests of a specific social group.

Given the complexity of the medium, a number of interpretants will be applied in any adaptation, even if in the long run they might be grouped into more general categories as the analysis proceeds and the field is articulated in an overall interpretation. To analyze the interpretants, as Cattrysse's work has hinted, the critic would need to focus on shifts, on the additions, deletions and substitutions that come to light in the adaptation when it is compared to its prior materials. This procedure can avoid the unwitting or automatic introduction of an interpretation of the materials themselves: the aim is to elucidate the interpretive operation performed by the film, allowing it to expose significant formal and thematic features of the materials, both those features that the filmmakers have chosen to adapt in some way and those that they have omitted or replaced. The shifts can therefore be useful in indicating a concept of equivalence, among other kinds of interpretants. Yet it must not be thought that a shift is somehow neutral, immediately perceptible without any critical processing. Locating a shift between an adaptation and its prior materials assumes some effort to fix the form and meaning of those materials in order to establish that a resemblance or divergence exists in the adaptation and reflects a specific interpretant applied by the filmmakers. Locating a shift, then, reveals the critic's own application of an interpretant, which may be thematic (an interpretation of the prior materials) or formal (a critical methodology). The critic's interpretants enable the inference of interpretants in the adaptation by singling out specific features and operations for analysis and by processing them according to the critic's own methodology.

Consider an example from a close adaptation of a novel, Paul Schrader's 1991 version of Ian McEwan's *The Comfort of Strangers*. The very beginning of the film presents a rapid sequence of images, all of Venice. The first image, coinciding with the last credit, is a blazing sunset on the Grand Canal which evokes J.M.W. Turner's luminous, atmospheric paintings of comparable Venetian scenes; the next images show the skyline and smaller canals, evoking conventional Italian postcards. This montage has no direct counterpart in McEwan's novel, which plunges immediately into a description of a British couple on a summer holiday at an unnamed seaside resort. The peculiar absence of any explicit reference to Venice throughout the novel would be noticed by an attentive reader, but it becomes even more conspicuous when the film is juxtaposed to the text because the visual images cannot but show the Italian city. In the first chapter, the setting is no more than implied through a succession of markers that gradually become identifiable: 'the iron barges', 'the hotel café pontoon', 'the clouded, late afternoon heat', 'the fine old churches, the altar pieces, the stone bridges over canals', 'the crowds who swarmed over the canal bridges and down every narrow street' (McEwan, 1981: 9, 10, 12). The absence of the word 'Venice' in the text triggers the reader's identification of the setting, foregrounding its sheer recognizability. A similar effect, I would argue, is produced by the intersemiotic relations I have cited in the opening montage of the film, its evocation of paintings and postcards that exceed a mere indication of the setting and convey a sense of familiarity, even conventionality. Although the film actually deviates from the novel here by inserting images that do not conform to any extended descriptions in the text, a formal interpretant can still be inferred, a relation of equivalence – but only if the critic interprets the lack of any mention of Venice in the novel as well as the visual allusions in the montage that opens the film.

As a rule, shifts show the film altering its prior materials so as to signify a particularly strong interpretation of them. This can be seen in two controversial film biographies of seventeenth-century Italian painters which adapt the historical record by revising it: Derek Jarman's *Caravaggio* (1986) and Agnès Merlet's *Artemisia* (1998). Jarman takes a figure whom in contemporary accounts Caravaggio is reported to have fought and killed, Ranuccio Tomassoni, and turns him into a violent motor mechanic for whom the painter develops a homoerotic attraction (for the biographical details, see Hibbard, 1983). The shift reveals a thematic interpretant, an ideology that is at once aesthetic and sexual: Jarman characterizes a canonical figure in art history as bisexual in order to enlist him in a queer cultural politics that associates the avant-garde with sexual transgression. Merlet departs from the transcript of Artemisia Gentileschi's rape trial by representing her relationship with the painter Agostino Tassi as consensual rather than coerced (the transcript is presented in the appendix to Garrard, 1989). This shift likewise reveals a thematic interpretant that can be read as political, a gender ideology: although feminist art historians have seen the rape as a brutal form of male oppression, Merlet's own feminist agenda connects Artemisia's sexual awakening to her artistic coming-of-age, so that her affair with Tassi becomes a bid to wrest her sexuality as well as her art from her father Orazio's control. 'You want everything for yourself', Merlet's Artemisia tells Orazio after the trial, 'me and the frescoes'. In Merlet's adaptation, the rape is a trumped-up charge that conceals the commercial rivalry between two male painters vying for commissions.

Complaints that Jarman and Merlet have wrongly introduced historical inaccuracies apply a rather rigid critical interpretant, an empiricist concept of history that effectively preempts any understanding of the revisionary moves made by the filmmakers. Such complaints are also likely to rest on sexual and gender ideologies that are inimical to the cultural political agendas of the films. In treating adaptations as interpretations of their prior materials, it is important that, at least initially, the critic apply an interpretant that does not disallow the interpretants applied by the filmmakers. Just as no translation can be judged through a simple comparison to the source text it translates because of the manifold losses and gains that necessarily result from the translation process, so no film adaptation can be judged merely through a comparison to its prior materials because of the extensive and complicated ways it processes them. The contexts in which the translation or adaptation was produced and received, the traditions and practices of translating and filmmaking as well as the social conditions of reading and viewing, must be taken into account to avoid rendering essentialist judgements that ignore historical contingencies (for a historical survey of adaptation, see Corrigan, 1998).

Aesthetics of production and reception

The interpretants deployed in a film adaptation may be complementary, mutually reinforcing an overall interpretation inscribed in the prior materials, or disjunctive, resulting in opposing and even contradictory interpretations that may in turn be perceived differently by different audiences. The viewer's interpretant thus becomes a central factor in assessing the significance of an adaptation, raising the question of whether an academic critical discourse can or should take precedence over other, more popular forms of reception. A particularly illuminating example is offered by Franco Zeffirelli's 1968 adaptation of Shakespeare's *Romeo and Juliet*, where two thematic interpretants seem to figure in the filmmakers' choices: on the one hand, a dominant idealization of the heterosexual love between the two leads; on the other hand, a recurrent homoeroticism in the treatment of the male characters.

The screenplay initiates the idealization by making two revealing deletions from the beginning of the play. The first is the opening dialogue between Capulet's servants, which is filled with double entendres that link sexual aggression to violence. The second is the extended dialogue between Benvolio and Romeo, in which the latter shows himself to be not just enamored of a woman who will not requite his affection, but frustrated that she will not have sex with him — even if he pays her for it. In Romeo's words, she will not 'ope her lap to saint-seducing gold' (I.i.206). In the film, the first deletion is supplied to some extent by costumes and camera movements that emphasize the servants' genitals. They wear brightly colored tights and codpieces, and when they are introduced, the camera pans from toe to head so that the viewer is forced to look at their bulging crotches before they pick a quarrel with the Montagues. Here the filmmakers' choices are guided, at least partly, by a formal interpretant of equivalence, although the critic needs to interpose a gender-oriented reading of the play to draw this conclusion. As Peter Donaldson (1990) observes, admittedly influenced by a 'generation of feminist Shakespeareans' in the academy, 'a central feature of the sex-gender system in place in Shakespeare's text is the obsessive verbal equation of erect penis and sword', and the camera works to 'replicate the verbal texture of anxious phallic wordplay' (pp. 153, 154). Yet the deletion of both the servants' coarse language and Romeo's questionable desire for another woman points to a thematic interpretant that is more significant in its impact: the film romanticizes the representation of love and sexuality in the text, removing it from any language that would taint its ideal purity, and this romanticization coincides with a rehabilitation of Romeo, a suppression of any questions about his integrity as a lover. The film carries out the rehabilitation most strikingly in its first depiction of Romeo. In Donaldson's careful description,

> [Romeo's] entrance, in a long shot accompanied by a lyrical musical cue followed by a lingering close-up, shows him carrying a mint blossom plucked on his morning walk, a delicate spike of tiny white florets [which] connotes nonaggressive, pacific masculinity. (p. 156)

Whereas in the play Romeo uses the elevated language of Petrarchan love poetry to mystify his lustful designs, in the film he enters as the sincere, sensitive lover.

Juxtaposed with this idealization of heterosexual love, however, is a strain of homoeroticism. This second interpretation, in Donaldson's metaphor, 'hovers at the edges of the film' (pp. 145–6), although we can better understand how the filmmakers' choices support opposing interpretations of Shakespeare's text if we employ Roland Barthes' (1978) concept of the 'third meaning'. Take the provocative codpieces. This costume detail contains what Barthes calls an informational level of meaning, communicating a sense of historicity, even historical authenticity, that indicates the sixteenth century as the period in which the action is set. As Donaldson's gender-oriented reading makes clear, the codpieces also contain a symbolic level, signifying a theme of masculinity as phallic aggression which finds its counterpart in the text. Yet they release still another meaning that Barthes would describe as 'obtuse' or 'discontinuous', resisting easy assimilation to the other levels of signification, possibly unintentional because clearly subversive, 'indifferent to the story', in fact 'the epitome of a counternarrative' (pp. 61, 63). With the panning that focuses on the codpieces, the film can also be seen as transforming the male actors into objects of homoerotic desire, especially insofar as that particular camera movement has been often used to signify a male heterosexual gaze directed towards female characters. In *The Postman Always Rings Twice* (dir. Tay Garnett, 1946), for example, when the drifter Frank Chambers first encounters his employer's wife, the seductive Cora, the camera represents his eye movements by panning across the floor from the lipstick holder that rolls towards him to a shot of her legs cropped at the knees. No such point-of-view shots are used in Zeffirelli's film when the viewer is presented with homoerotic images. They appear repeatedly and take various forms: the dramatic panning at Tybalt's appearance in the opening scene, the effeminate handsomeness of the youthful male actors, the physical affection that Romeo shows for Mercutio during his increasingly distraught delivery of the Queen Mab speech, and the long shots of Romeo's buttocks, clad in tights when he weeps hopelessly in Friar Laurence's cell and naked in the love scene with Juliet. Donaldson's (1990) typically careful description indicates the peculiarity of this scene: 'Romeo is on screen naked for more than seventeen seconds in three shots, during which he is the sole object of attention; Juliet's nude "scene" lasts less than a second' (p. 169).

The opposing interpretations that Zeffirelli's film inscribes in Shakespeare's text can be viewed as different aesthetics of production that appeal to different aesthetics of reception or different audiences. Here Pierre Bourdieu's (1984) distinction between elite and popular taste can prove helpful. For Bourdieu, elite taste rests on the application of specialized knowledge in the detached formal appreciation of a cultural object, drawing the boundary between art and life, whereas popular taste aims to erase that boundary through a vicarious participation in the object, a sympathetic identification with characters as real people which often leads to the inference of moralistic lessons for conduct. Hence some adaptations cater to elite taste by building an intertextual and intersemiotic network and thereby assuming a broad familiarity with cultural traditions and practices as well as a willingness to pay critical attention to forms and themes that may be discontinuous or unconventional. Other adaptations cater to popular taste by deploying formal and thematic features that solicit identification, such as editing for narrative continuity, modelling scenes on popular film genres, and treating familiar themes in conventional ways. These distinctions are certainly not hard-and-fast: both elite and popular elements can function in the production and reception of the same film, just as elite filmmaking might appeal to popular taste and vice versa. The aesthetic categories 'elite' and 'popular' are heuristic devices that need to be specified according to various factors – formal and thematic, cultural and social – when applied in the analysis of a film.

For the most part, Zeffirelli's film presents a popular interpretation of the text through its idealization of heterosexual love. The romanticizing screenplay, the casting of two leads who were unknown as actors and relatively close in age to Shakespeare's characters, a scene suggestive of Hollywood musicals with dances and a theme song (which became a hit according to *Billboard*'s charts) all invite the audience to identify with the images, to take the actors as the real incarnations of Romeo and Juliet, and to participate in the representation of their emotional lives. Other popular elements include the jerky, hand-held camera movements in the fight scenes, which generate suspense by immersing the viewer in the violence, and the deletion of Paris's death in the tomb scene, a detail that could limit the tragic impact of the lovers' deaths. The effectiveness of the filmmakers' popularizing choices was proved at the box office: the film earned over $50 million on an investment of $1.5 million (Zeffirelli, 1986: 229). Yet reviewers also attested to its popular appeal: *Newsweek* remarked that 'while it takes the Ph.D.-ism out of Shakespeare, [the film] jams back in as much idealism, sex, love, hate, desire, recklessness, passion as the human mind, body, heart and soul can contain' (Plate, 1968: 102).

Nevertheless, the homoeroticism signifies a more elite interpretation that in effect opposes the popular aesthetic governing much of the film. This aspect should be considered elite not only because it reflects the interests of a sexual minority, but because it requires the viewer to pay attention to film form, to be distanced from the narrative and open to discontinuities that may actually subvert it. Donaldson's reading demonstrates that an academic critical discourse, informed by developments in feminist and gay/lesbian studies may also be necessary to perceive the homoeroticism, although viewers familiar with gay visual culture might see it immediately. The importance of these kinds of knowledge to an elite appreciation of Zeffirelli's film was also made evident in its popular reception. In a rare comment on camera movement, the *Newsweek* reviewer confessed a telling ignorance: 'it is hard to know what to make of the camera's occasional introduction of a character by panning from toe to head' (Plate, 1968: 102). Yet not only were the homoerotic images generally invisible when the film was released, but some of them could also function as supports for the heterosexual desire of popular viewers. Leonard Whiting, the actor who played Romeo, became a heart-throb among teenage girls.

Adaptation as critique

In recontextualizing prior materials, a second-order creation like a translation or adaptation submits them to a transformation that changes their significance – even as an effort is made to maintain a resemblance. As a result, the application of an interpretant in establishing the new context is never simply interpretive, but potentially interrogative: the formal and thematic differences introduced by the translation or adaptation, the move to a different language and culture or to a different cultural medium with different conditions of production, can invite a critical understanding of the prior materials as well as their originary or subsequent contexts, the linguistic patterns, cultural traditions and social institutions in which they were positioned. Yet once an interrogation is set going, it need not stop at the prior materials; they may in turn be used to probe the translation or adaptation, along with the cultural forms and practices that constitute it as well as the traditions and institutions to which it is affiliated. It is essential to recognize, however, that any interrogation is no more than potential: not only does it assume the translator's or filmmaker's application of interpretants that allow the second-order creation to be construed as a critique, but it once again requires the critic's own application of interpretants that specifically emphasize interrogative effects.

These points can be developed by turning again to translation theory, particularly Philip Lewis's (1985) concept of 'abusive fidelity'. Lewis challenges the communicative model of translation that tends 'to privilege the capture of signifieds, to give primacy to message, content or concept over language texture', and he instead articulates a new formal interpretant, a concept of equivalence 'that requires attention to the chain of signifiers, to syntactic processes, to discursive structures, to the incidence of language mechanisms on thought and reality formation' (p. 42). The application of this interpretant in a translation zeroes in on whatever in the source text 'abuses' or deviates from normal patterns of linguistic usage, 'points or passages that are in some sense forced, that stand out as clusters of textual energy – whether they constituted by words, turns of phrase, or more elaborate formulations' (p. 43). Thus a stylistic feature or node of intertextuality is abusive in Lewis's sense insofar as it resists the direct communication of a signified and demands a fairly aggressive interpretation of the signifier. For Lewis, a translation should seek to recreate source-text abuses analogically by deviating from linguistic norms in the translating culture. In so doing, however, the translation will also abuse or deviate from the source text, exposing linguistic and cultural conditions that remain implicit or unstated in it. The abusively faithful translation possesses a double interrogative function – on the one hand, that of forcing the linguistic and conceptual system of which it is a dependent, and on the other hand, of directing a critical thrust back toward the text that it translates and in relation to which it becomes a kind of unsettling aftermath (p. 43).

Yet a third interrogative function might be located here: the source text can be seen as equally abusive of the translation. A comparison between them will always uncover shifts or deviations that indicate the limitations of the translation, not merely of its mimetic aim, but of the interpretation that it inscribes during the recontextualizing process. Only the most skeptical critic will stage this sort of dialectic, in which source text and translation submit each other to a mutual interrogation. And the precise nature of the interrogative effects will be determined by the very choice of forms and themes on which to focus the analysis.

Stam (2005a) glances at a filmic analogue to this critical dialectic when he observes that in an adaptation 'a source work is reinterpreted through new grids and discourses', and 'each grid, in revealing aspects of the source text in question, also reveals something about the ambient discourses in the moment of reaccentuation' (p. 45). Yet his emphasis on ideological critique displaces attention from the adaptation itself to the 'ambient discourses' in its historical 'moment'. This move limits not only the analysis of the adaptation as a critique, but also the critique of the adaptation that can be drawn from its prior materials. Moreover, the critic's application of interpretants is elided, removing the possibility that they too might be submitted to a searching critique. A more productive starting point, as Lewis's work suggests, would be to consider what formal and thematic features of the prior materials stand out as 'clusters of textual energy' vis-à-vis the film and can therefore be useful in bringing to light the interpretants that guided the filmmakers' recontextualization of those materials through various multimedial choices.

Zeffirelli's adaptation of *Romeo and Juliet* shows a keen interest in the gender relations depicted in Shakespeare's play. Yet the recurrent homoeroticism runs counter not only to the romanticizing treatment of heterosexual love in the film, but to the homosocial relations that prevail in the text, underpinning the violent feud as well as the male domination of women. These disjunctions between film and text constitute the bases of a critique: the homoeroticism in Zeffirelli's adaptation can be viewed as a demystification of the male rivalry in the text, an implicit indication that homosociality may in fact mask homoerotic desire. Yet the text also comes back to worry Zeffirelli's film by revealing that the homoeroticism is linked both to violence, as in the phallic aggressiveness symbolized by the codpieces, and to the exclusion of women, perhaps most obvious in the love scene where Juliet's body is visually marginalized. The discourse of fidelity that informs Donaldson's (1990) analysis, resting on feminist and queer interpretations, leads him to praise the film for 'extend[ing] Shakespeare's critique' of 'patriarchal values' and for 'bringing to the surface homoerotic aspects of Shakespeare's art' (pp. 153, 145). Yet this optimism effaces the many differences between film and text, particularly Zeffirelli's idealization of heterosexuality against Shakespeare's ambivalent treatment, as well as the gender hierarchy that is reinstalled through the homoeroticism. Donaldson has not allowed these differences to probe the limitations of his own ideological critique.

The double interrogation that adaptation makes possible is perhaps more readily seen in films that push their manipulation of prior materials to a revisionary extreme. Jarman's *Caravaggio* and Merlet's *Artemisia* fasten on key figures and events to facilitate their own political agendas in representing the painters' lives and thereby question the very reliability of the historical record, implicitly treating it as incomplete or prejudiced, as official accounts that do not make clear the degree of falsification they contain. Yet the record of course remains to throw into high relief the filmmakers' ideologically loaded interpretations, demonstrating that their presentations of the past answer to present contigencies, current political struggles. The critic or viewer who possesses the pertinent historical data is thus compelled to take sides with these films, to decide whether to accept the historical record at face value or to doubt it and join the queer or feminist struggles in which the filmmakers aim to intervene. Once this question is posed, however, a critical self-awareness has been forced upon the analysis, and the contradictions in such political filmmaking have been made explicit.

The intertextual or intersemiotic relations that a film establishes in adapting prior materials must also be figured into its interrogative potential, since the cultural forms introduced through those relations are altered as well. The visual allusions at the start of Schrader's *The Comfort of Strangers* (1991) not only construct an equivalence to the unnamed setting in McEwan's novel through their shared familarity or conventionality; they also point to the heterogeneous cultural conditions of the text. On the one hand, McEwan's descriptions stress the popular attractions of Venice, referring repeatedly to the crowds of camera-toting tourists, lingering on the most frequented sites that would be covered in tour guides, and even mentioning kiosks 'with tiers of postcards showing famous views', while on the other hand passages incorporate largely verbatim quotations of what has become a most elite literary work, John Ruskin's *The Stones of Venice* (McEwan, 1981: 19; d'Elia and Williams, 1986: 233–6). Schrader's opening montage, the decision to follow a Turneresque sunset with postcard shots of domes and canals, evokes a similar combination of elite and popular cultural forms (knowledgeable viewers may also recall that Ruskin was one of Turner's strongest champions). Yet because the filmic images are so different in composition and color, their juxtaposition intensifies their heterogeneity, allowing the postcards to defamiliarize Turner and vice versa, producing an unsettling strangeness even with such 'famous views'. Nonetheless, the subtlety of McEwan's intertext, his uncredited use of a canonical author, can work as a reminder that Schrader's visual effects will not be perceptible to every audience: they require both a specialized knowledge of art (and possibly literary) history and a sophisticated analytical technique. The formal interpretant I located in Schrader's adaptation, the equivalence between the filmic images and the novelistic descriptions, enables the articulation of a critical dialectic between film and novel on the basis of a thematic interpretant, cultural taste, ultimately calling attention to the social or institutional limits of my own analysis – which is obviously an academic reading.

I have argued that translation theory can advance thinking about film adaptations by contributing to the formulation of a more rigorous methodology for studying them. If we abandon the communicative model of translation and instead consider its relation to a source text as hermeneutic, the interpretant can assume crucial importance in analyzing both translations and adaptations as well as the critical act that performs the analysis. The hermeneutic relation can be seen not only as interpretive, fixing the form and meaning of the prior materials, but as interrogative, exposing the cultural and social conditions of those materials and of the translation or adaptation that has processed them. The critic's application of an interpretant, whether a particular interpretation or critical methodology, finally determines the formulation of the hermeneutic relation and its interrogative effects. But the critical dialectic that might be located in these effects can also help to avoid privileging either the prior materials or the second-order creation and to turn the critic's work into an act of self-criticism. At a moment when ideological critique remains the most prevalent move in literary and cultural studies, all too ready to foreclose interpretive possibilities by reducing them to political positions, it seems urgent that the critic's position not be put beyond interrogation. A critical methodology that presents itself as democratic or emancipatory cannot afford to let its own hierarchies and exclusions go unexamined.

■ ■ ■

Questions and Projects

1. Consider an adaptation in which translation (between different languages or between different cultures, for instance) becomes an explicit or implicit theme in a film (for instance, the 1963 *Contempt* or the 2004 *Bride and Prejudice*). How does that thematic issue shed light on the process of adaptation that the film puts into practice?

2. Explain what Venuti means by the role of an "interpretant" in an audience's engagement with an adaptation. How do these kinds of viewers impact an adaptation in a specific manner? Provide an example.

References

Andrew, Dudley (1984) *Concepts in Film Theory*. New York: Oxford University Press.
Barthes, Roland (1978) 'The Third Meaning: Research Notes on Some Eisenstein Stills', in *Image/Music/Text*, trans. Stephen Heath, pp. 44–68. New York: Hill and Wang.
Bourdieu, P. (1984) *Distinction: A Social Critique of the Judgment of Taste*, trans. Richard Nice. Cambridge, MA:

Harvard University Press.

Cattrysse, Patrick (1990) *Pour une théorie de l'adaptation filmique: Le film noir américain*. Frankfurt: Peter Lang.

Cattrysse, Patrick (1992) 'Film (Adaptation) as Translation: Some Methodological Proposals', *Target* 4(1): 53–70.

Corrigan, Timothy (ed.) (1998) *Film and Literature: An Introduction and Reader*. Upper Saddle River, NJ: Prentice Hall.

D'Elia, Gaetano and Williams, Chrisopher (1986) *La nuova letteratura inglese: Ian McEwan*. Fasano: Schena.

Donaldson, Peter S. (1990) *Shakespearean Films / Shakespearean Directors*. Boston, MA: Unwin Hyman.

Garrard, Mary D. (1989) *Artemisia Gentileschi: The Image of the Female Hero in Italian Baroque Art*. Princeton, NJ: Princeton University Press.

Hibbard, Howard (1983) *Caravaggio*. New York: Harper & Row.

Iampolski, Mikhail (1998) *The Memory of Tiresias: Intertextuality and Film*, trans. Harsha Ram. Berkeley: University of California Press.

Kelly, Louis G. (1979) *The True Interpreter: A History of Translation Theory and Practice in the West*. Oxford: Blackwell.

Lewis, Philip E. (1985) 'The Measure of Translation Effects', in Joseph Graham (ed.) *Difference in Translation*, pp. 31–62. Ithaca, NY: Cornell University Press.

McEwan, Ian (1981) *The Comfort of Strangers*. London: Jonathan Cape.

McFarlane, Brian (1996) *Novel into Film: An Introduction to the Theory of Adaptation*. Oxford: Oxford University Press.

Naremore, James (ed.) (2000) *Film Adaptation*. New Brunswick, NJ: Rutgers University Press.

Orr, Christopher (1984) 'The Discourse on Adaptation', *Wide Angle* 6(2): 72–6.

Palmer, R. Barton (2004) 'The Sociological Turn of Adaptation Studies: The Example of *Film Noir*', in Robert Stam and Alessandra Raengo (eds) *A Companion to Literature and Film*, pp. 258–77. Oxford: Blackwell.

Plate, Thomas Gordon (1968) 'The Teen-agers of Verona', *Newsweek*, 14 October: 102.

Stam, Robert (2000) 'Beyond Fidelity: The Dialogics of Adaptation', in James Naremore (ed.) *Film Adaptation*, pp. 54–76. New Brunswick, NJ: Rutgers University Press.

Stam, Robert (2005a) 'Introduction: The Theory and Practice of Adaptation', in Robert Stam and Alessandra Raengo (eds) *A Companion to Literature and Film*, pp. 1–52. Oxford: Blackwell.

Stam, Robert (2005b) *Literature Through Film: Realism, Magic, and the Art of Adaptation*. Oxford: Blackwell.

Stam, Robert, and Raengo, Alessandra (eds) (2004) *A Companion to Literature and Film*. Oxford: Blackwell.

Stam, Robert and Raengo, Alessandra (eds) (2005) *Literature and Film: A Guide to the Theory and Practice of Film Adaptation*. Oxford: Blackwell.

Toury, Gideon (1980) *In Search of a Theory of Translation*. Tel Aviv: Porter Institute for Poetics and Semiotics.

Toury, Gideon (1995) *Descriptive Translation Studies and Beyond*. Amsterdam: Benjamins.

Venuti, Lawrence (ed.) (2004) *The Translation Studies Reader*, 2nd edn. London: Routledge.

Zeffirelli, Franco (1986) *Zeffirelli: The Autobiography of Franco Zeffirelli*. New York: Weidenfeld & Nicolson.

Chapter 11

Thomas Leitch

TWELVE FALLACIES IN CONTEMPORARY ADAPTATION THEORY

W HILE LEITCH'S ESSAY advocates moving beyond restrictive criteria such as fidelity, he takes this position further than some by arguing against a number of received notions (his "twelve fallacies") that continue to hold sway and marginalize adaptation studies within the larger field of cinema studies. Leitch's primary complaint is that adaptation studies lack a sufficient underlying theoretical structure and instead often rely on individual case studies. Arguing that the marginal status of adaptation studies often derives from institutional reasons more so than aesthetic or theoretical reasons, Leitch calls for the establishment of a synthetic field of "textual studies" incorporating adaptation studies, cinema studies, and literary studies.

■ ■ ■

TWELVE FALLACIES IN CONTEMPORARY ADAPTATION THEORY
THOMAS LEITCH

Criticism, vol. 45, no. 2, (2003), pp. 149–171

What could be more audacious than to argue that the study of moving images as adaptations of literary works, one of the very first shelters under which cinema studies originally entered the academy, has been neglected? Yet that is exactly what this essay will argue: that despite its venerable history, widespread practice, and apparent influence, adaptation theory has remained tangential to the thrust of film study because it has never been undertaken with conviction and theoretical rigor. By examining a dozen interlinked fallacies that have kept adaptation theory from fulfilling its analytical promise, I hope to claim for adaptation theory more of the power it deserves.

1. There is such a thing as contemporary adaptation theory

This is the founding fallacy of adaptation studies, and the most important reason they have been so largely ineffectual—because they have been practiced in a theoretical vacuum, without the benefit of what Robert B. Ray has called "a presiding poetics."[1] There is, as the preceding sentence acknowledges, such a thing as adaptation studies. It is pursued in dozens of books and hundreds of articles in *Literature/Film Quarterly* and in classrooms across the country, from high school to graduate school, in courses with names like "Dickens and Film" and "From Page to Screen." But this flood of study of individual adaptations proceeds on the whole without the support of any more general theoretical account of what actually happens, or what ought to happen, when a group of filmmakers set out to adapt a literary text. As Brian McFarlane has recently observed: "In view of the nearly sixty years of writing about the adaptation of novels into film ... it is depressing to find at what a limited, tentative stage the discourse has remained."[2] Despite the appearance of more recent methodologies from the empiricism of Morris Beja to the neo-Aristotelianism of James Griffith, the most influential general account of cinema's relation to literature continues to be George Bluestone's tendentious *Novels into Film*, now nearly half a century old. Bluestone's categorical and essentialist treatment of the relations between movies and the books they are based on neglects or begs many crucial questions, and more recent commentators, even when they are as sharp as McFarlane (who will therefore claim particularly close attention in this essay) in taking exception to Bluestone, have largely allowed him to frame the terms of the debate.

Hence several fundamental questions in adaptation theory remain unasked, let alone unanswered. Everyone knows, for example, that movies are a collaborative medium, but is adaptation similarly collaborative, or is it the work of a single agent—the screenwriter or director—with the cast and crew behaving the same way as if their film were based on an original screenplay? Since virtually all feature films work from a pre-existing written text, the screenplay, how is a film's relation to its literary source different from its relation to its screenplay? Why has the novel, rather than the stage play or the short story, come to serve as the paradigm for cinematic adaptations of every kind? Given the myriad differences, not only between literary and cinematic texts, but between successive cinematic adaptations of a given literary text, or for that matter between different versions of a given story in the same medium, what exactly is it that film adaptations adapt, or are supposed to adapt? Finally, how does the relation between an adaptation and the text it is explicitly adapting compare to its intertextual relationships with scores of other precursor texts?

The institutional matrix of adaptation study—the fact that movies are so often used in courses like "Shakespeare and Film" as heuristic intertexts, the spoonful of sugar that helps the Bard's own text go down; the fact that studies of particular literary texts and their cinematic adaptations greatly out-number more general considerations of what is at stake in adapting a text from one medium to another; the fact that even most general studies of adaptation are shaped by the case studies they seem designed mainly to illuminate—guarantees the operation of adaptation studies on a severe economy of theoretical principles which have ossified into a series of unvoiced and fallacious bromides most often taking the form of "binary oppositions that poststructuralist theory has taught us to deconstruct: literature versus cinema, high culture versus mass culture, original versus copy."[3] Precisely because these bromides are rarely articulated, they have retained the insidious power of Ibsen's ghosts: the power to direct discussion even among analysts who ought to know better.

2. Differences between literary and cinematic texts are rooted in essential properties of their respective media

This fallacy was first promulgated by Bluestone and by Siegfried Kracauer's roughly contemporaneous *Theory of Film*, which opens with the sweeping statement, "This study rests upon the assumption that each medium has a specific nature which invites certain kinds of communications while obstructing others."[4] More recently, it has been one of the rare articles of faith that has actually come under such general debate that few theorists would probably admit to subscribing to it these days. Nonetheless, it has been given new impetus in the past ten years by the reprinting in the last two editions of the Oxford anthology *Film Theory and Criticism* of Seymour Chatman's accurately but fallaciously entitled essay, "What Novels Can Do That Films Can't (and Vice Versa)."[5] The most influential attacks on the essentialist view that novels and films are suited to fundamentally different tasks—in Chatman's view, assertion and depiction respectively—because of the features specific to their media have taken two forms. One is the empirical argument advanced by F. E. Sparshott and V. F. Perkins[6] that many films and not a few novels break the rules the essential qualities of their media apparently prescribe. The other is the more general attack Noël Carroll has mounted against what he calls Rudolf Arnheim's "specificity thesis" on the grounds of its philosophical gratuitousness: "There is no rationale for the system [of arts], for in truth it is only a collection. Thus, we have no need for the specificity thesis, for the question it answers—'Why is there a system of different arts?'—is not really an admissible question at all."[7] But these attacks can be usefully supplemented by a closer consideration of the alleged specifics of film and fiction.

Chatman, for instance, dismisses explicitly descriptive voiceover commentary in movies as uncinematic on the grounds that "it is not cinematic description but merely description by literary assertion transferred to film."[8] Would anybody writing today argue that the highly assertive and descriptive voiceover commentary by the murdered Joe Gillis in *Sunset Boulevard*, a film not adapted from a literary source, was inessential to the film's effect because, as McFarlane notes, voiceover narration by its nature "cannot be more than intermittent as distinct from the continuing nature of the novelistic first-person narration"—or, in Chatman's terms, that it was uncinematic *because* it was literary?[9] Chatman argues that such "arguably descriptive" closeups as Professor Jordan's amputated finger in *The 39 Steps*, the poisoned coffee cup in *Notorious*, and Marion Crane's staring dead eye in *Psycho* are actually hermeneutic rather than descriptive because "for all their capacity to arrest our attention, these close-ups in no way invite aesthetic contemplation."[10] But a generation of Hitchcock commentary has disagreed. These shots *do* invite aesthetic contemplation because they *are* descriptive and assertive.

In arguing from the other side that the camera's essential function of depicting without describing is confirmed by the use of terms like "the *camera eye* style"[11] to characterize passages of neutral, Hemingwayesque detail in novels that approach the condition of cinema, Chatman is again beguiled by his essentialism into mistaking how both novels and films work.

Consider one the most famous "camera eye" passages in fiction, this description of Sam Spade awakened in *The Maltese Falcon* by the news that Miles Archer, his partner, has been shot to death:

> Spade's thick fingers made a cigarette with deliberate care, sifting a measured quantity of tan flakes down into curved paper, spreading the flakes so that they lay equal at the ends with a slight depression in the middle, thumbs rolling the paper's inner edge down and up under the outer edge as forefingers pressed it over, thumbs and fingers sliding to the paper cylinder's ends to hold it even while tongue licked the flap, left forefinger and

thumb pinching their end while right forefinger and thumb smoothed the damp seam, right forefinger and thumb twisting their end and lifting the other to Spade's mouth.[12]

According to Chatman, this depiction of Spade rolling a cigarette should be utterly neutral rather than assertive. But it is not only not neutral; it is much less neutral, much more assertive, than it would be if it had been included, for instance, in John Huston's 1941 film version of *The Maltese Falcon*, which substitutes a brief but highly revealing telephone call Spade makes to his secretary Effie Perrine ("You'll have to break the news to Iva. I'd fry first") before dissolving to Spade's arrival at Bush and Stockton Streets. The perspective of aesthetic history has offered several ways to read this passage. It is first of all a stylistic tour de force, an imitation of the dogged routines Nick Adams follows in pitching camp and making pancakes in Hemingway's "Big Two-Hearted River." In addition, its apparent neutrality can be read as a commentary on Spade's mechanical coldness, the emotional detachment from his partner's murder that will make him Archer's ironically perfect avenger. What it figures most powerfully, however, is Spade's remoteness, not from Archer, but from us. Like Nick Adams, Spade is presumably in the grip of powerful emotions during this scene. Not only are the emotions not described; the resolute eschewing of psychological description makes the suppression of these emotions, whether it is Spade's or Dashiell Hammett's, the scene's leading issue. Pauline Kael once remarked that "Huston was a good enough screenwriter to see that Hammett had already written the scenario."[13] But Hammett's novel, though it suppresses any explicit indication of Spade's thoughts or feelings as completely as Huston's film, is much more disturbing, and most disturbing in its most apparently 'cinematic' passages, because readers of novels, unlike viewers of movies, *expect* a certain amount of psychological description and are troubled, even if they do not know why, if it is suppressed.

This line of reasoning might seem to substitute one essentialist argument for another. Novels are not assertive and descriptive, as Chatman claims, in contradistinction to films; instead novels are the medium that gravitates toward psychological analysis, so that the absence of such analysis becomes a highly marked, non-novelistic or cinematic device. It would be more accurate, however, to consider all Chatman's arguments together and conclude that they apply not to essential properties of novels and films, but to specific reading habits that are grounded in the history of fashion, taste, and analysis rather than in any specific technical properties of novels and films.

Hence voiceover commentary has come to seem less uncinematic because of the perceptive analysis of its salient effects by J. P. Telotte and Sarah Kozloff. Hitchcock's closeups seem more worthy of aesthetic contemplation because commentators have refashioned Hitchcock the storyteller into Hitchcock the artist. Hammett's silence about Sam Spade's thought seems more disturbing at least in part because Huston's film has shown by contrast how such silence can be naturalized instead of emphasized. Contemporary film scholars are much more likely to mine movies for assertions, from economic subtexts to gender politics, as if they were novels, but that only means that film analysis, not films themselves, has become, as Chatman might say, more novelistic—or, to be fair, more effective. Though novels and films may seem at any given moment in the history of narrative theory to have essentially distinctive properties, those properties are functions of their historical moments and not of the media themselves.

3. Literary texts are verbal, films visual

Of all the explicitly stated fallacies that have substituted for theoretical principles in adaptation study, this is the most enduring and pernicious. Although the more general principle that literature and film are distinguished by essential properties of their presentational media has at least come in for lively debate by theorists ever since Sparshott and Perkins, film scholars have been much less inclined to reconsider the implications of this more specific bromide. Yet it is obviously untrue, not because literary texts are not verbal, but because films are not strictly speaking visual. At least they have not been purely visual for at least seventy-five years—most of film history. Films since the coming of synchronized sound, and perhaps even before, have been audio-visual, not visual, depending as they do on soundtracks as well as image tracks for their effects. Commentators who continue to brush aside synchronized sound as a mere appendage to the visual essence of cinema are overlooking several powerful developments in film history. Movies like *Citizen Kane* have introduced sound-driven radio aesthetics into cinema; even stripped of its spectacular visuals, Orson Welles's landmark film makes perfect sense because of the radio-shaped continuity of its soundtrack. More recent filmmaking has overlapped increasingly with television, a medium whose narratives are so largely driven by their soundtracks rather than their image tracks that Welles called television "illustrated radio." [14] In an even more recent move toward greater synergy, movies have been marketed through their musical soundtracks as well as vice-versa.

Cinema since the silent era has been an audio-visual medium that depends on engaging exactly two of its audience's five senses as if they were sufficient to constitute the sensory envelope of an entire world. It would make more sense to define cinema as a non-olfactory medium—that is, a medium that has the technological capacity to incorporate smells but chooses not to do so—than to define it as a visual medium. Anyone who doubts the dependence of contemporary cinema on the complex interrelations of visual and auditory stimulation should teach a course on silent melodrama, whose visual track requires viewing habits quite as foreign as those of Sanskrit interpreters from modern audiences' acculturated dependence on a finely-calculated series of combinations of sounds and images. But movies as we know them are not simply an audio-visual medium, since, as McFarlane observes, "the novel draws on a wholly *verbal* sign system, the film variously, and sometimes simultaneously, on *visual, aural,* and *verbal* signifiers." [15] Fifty years ago, Laurence Olivier recognized that in bringing *Henry V* and *Hamlet* to the screen, he was not merely responsible for translating Shakespeare's poetry into cinematic images; he was equally responsible for staging poetic set-pieces his audience would have come to the movies specifically to hear, speeches like "To be or not to be" and "Once more into the breach, my friends." Movies cannot therefore legitimately be contrasted with literary texts on the grounds of their visual signifying system, because their actual signifying system, combining images and sounds and excluding information that might be processed by the other three senses, is a great deal more subtle and complex than visual iconicity.

Instead of saying that literary texts are verbal and movies aren't, it would be more accurate to say that movies depend on prescribed, unalterable visual and verbal *performances* in a way literary texts don't. [16] Cary Grant, James Stewart, John Wayne, even Marilyn Monroe are as well-remembered for their distinctive voices as for their distinctive looks. This is not necessarily a good thing. An audience watching a film version of *The Importance of Being Earnest* is constrained to hear Oscar Wilde's epigrams in exactly the way the performers are delivering them, whereas the audience reading Wilde's play can imagine them paced and inflected any way they like. One of the often-remarked differences between movies and plays, in fact, is that the iterative, interactive nature of dramatic performance allows performers to adjust their performances from night to night so that there will never be a single definitive performance of *Everybody Comes to Rick's* in the way there is a definitive performance of *Casablanca,* at least in the absence of a film remake that might threaten the original's primacy.

Because films depend on screenplays which in turn often depend on literary source material, in fact, they are doubly performative. Actors and actresses are translating into performance a written script which is itself an adaptation of a prior literary source, with the important difference that the script is a performance text—a text that requires interpretation first by its performers and then by its audience for completion—whereas a literary text requires only interpretation by its readers.

4. Novels are better than films

I have specified novels rather than literary texts here for two reasons. Using the term "literary texts" instead would already beg the question because "literature" carries an honorific charge "cinema" does not. Since even the term "classic cinema" is a long way from having the same implication as "literary classic," written texts themselves, unlike films, would seem to fall into two distinct orders, and any film that sought to adapt a work of literature could only hope to fall into a category of films that does not yet have a name. Although theater critics have always condescended to the canned nature of cinema, which freezes a single performance text forever instead of allowing retakes every night, the more general assumption that literary texts are richer, subtler, or more sophisticated than cinematic texts is confined largely to the novel. No critic to my knowledge has claimed that short stories are better than movies.

The tenacity of the prejudice in favor of novels and against films is due no doubt in part to the impossibility of refuting it. Though it takes less time for most audiences to sit through most feature films than it does for them to read most novels, films, as many commentators realized long ago, can contain quite as many telling details as novels. If their stories are unlikely to be as intricate, they can register behavioral traits and background details more fully, and during their more limited running time they are capable of commanding closer attention from a mass audience, even though they will still be comprehensible to less attentive viewers. The old saw that movies can be read in fewer different ways than novels because their critical history is shorter becomes for better or worse less relevant every year, as the flood of Internet commentary on *Pulp Fiction* and *Memento* does its best to make up for the hundred years' head start that has made "The Turn of the Screw" a classic of interpretive debate.

Since there is no prima facie reason why novels should be assumed to be better than movies, the question to ask is not why this assumption is wrong but why it is so stoutly, albeit tacitly, maintained. Entrenched representational forms have always greeted new rivals with a suspicion amounting to hostility, especially if economic power is at stake, as it was in the rise of the novel as the predominant mode of entertainment for the rising middle class two centuries ago. So the snobbery opera lovers feel for devotees of Broadway musicals is echoed by the snobbery with which fans of Rodgers and Hammerstein dismiss their cinematic incarnations. It is possible, in addition, that the reason that "once there may have been little debate about the fact that a theatrical performance of Shakespeare was far superior to a filmic reproduction" was simply that in the bad old days before Olivier and Welles, movies were worse than plays. In these more enlightened times, however, "the cinema now demands equal time and attention when we argue the relative value and meaning of movies and literature"[17] because the arguments against cinema concern "film-as-it-was" under the Hollywood moguls, the star system, and the undifferentiated target audience rather than "film-as-it-is"[18] in the age of quasi-independent production and niche marketing. Even now, of course, movies remain notoriously a mass medium that seeks as broad an audience as possible. A film like *Titanic* is disdained because it tries to provide something for everyone—historical re-creation, epic sweep, class warfare, adolescent romance, hissable villains, state-of-the-art visual effects, broken china—even though Shakespeare is praised for the corresponding reason. And of course cinema is a capital-intensive, publicity-intensive medium whose overhyped failures, unlike the failed novels that sink in merciful silence, become negative media events in their own right. How could a medium that produced *Heaven's Gate, Ishtar,* and *Mom and Dad Save the World* ever compete with the great tradition of the novel, the vast majority of whose exemplars have long faded from memory? Beyond all these prejudices, however, there is one final fallacious assumption that must be examined in closer detail.

5. Novels deal in concepts, films in percepts

These terms are derived from Bluestone's observation that "where the moving image comes to us directly through perception, language must be filtered through the screen of conceptual apprehension. And the conceptual process, though allied to and often taking its point of departure from the precept, represents a different mode of experience, a different way of apprehending the universe."[19] On its own terms this observation seems unexceptionable. The visual markers films use for dogs, for instance, including such different markers as Rin Tin Tin, Lassie, and Huckleberry Hound, are all iconic rather than indexical, like the words *dog, hound,* and *pooch*. The auditory markers films use for dogs—barking, whining, growling—are so much more obviously iconic that most audiences cannot distinguish these recorded sounds from their sources. Fallacies enter only when the conceptual is defined in contradistinction to the perceptual, as an exclusive property of verbal texts, and the pleasures movies offer their audiences are defined in terms that privilege the perceptual.

Such steps have often been taken both by ontologists and apologists for movies. In reserving the notion of "conceptual process"[20] for readers of prose fiction, for example, Gerald Mast evidently assumes that the kind of competence required to make sense of a fictional film is non-conceptual and that moviegoers watch films only for their kinesthetic images, not for their conceptual implications. But this argument overlooks the fact that virtually all films screened for the purpose of entertainment are fictional narratives which invoke not only visual codes but auditory codes, narrative codes, fictional codes, and a rhetoric of figuration. Interpreting and integrating these codes into the single signifying system of a given film surely requires as much conceptual initiative and agility as interpreting the verbal (and narrative and fictional and figural) signifying system of a given novel. Images may be percepts, but the fictional narratives that overwhelmingly draw audiences into movie theaters are not.

Nor are cinematic images as neutral and innocent as Bluestone and Mast assume. In "A Future for the Novel" (1956), Alain Robbe-Grillet contrasted novels and their film adaptations by arguing that in the initial novel, the objects and gestures forming the very fabric of the plot disappeared completely, leaving behind only their significations:

> the empty chair became only absence or expectation, the hand placed on a shoulder became a sign of friendliness, the bars on the window became only the impossibility of leaving. ... But in the cinema, one sees the chair, the movement of the hand, the shape of the bars. What they signify remains obvious, but instead of monopolizing our attention, it becomes something added, even something in excess ... because what affects us ... are the gestures themselves ... to which the cinema has suddenly (and unintentionally) restored their reality.[21]

But it would be impossible to maintain such a distinction today in view not only of novels like Robbe-Grillet's own, which seeks to restore the "reality" to objects and gestures by frustrating any definitive account of their significations, but of the digitized dinosaurs of *Jurassic Park* and the impossible acrobatics of *Spider-Man* and *Minority Report,* which depend not on their intimacy with the pre-existing physical reality they misleadingly imply but on producing a reality effect quite as loaded as Robbe-Grillet's empty chair.

Even though "concept" versus "percept," as James Griffith has pointed out, "offers critical certainty and shuts off discussion,"[22] the dichotomy has proved lamentably tenacious. Brian McFarlane, in the most acute recent general study of adaptation, follows Bluestone in arguing that

> the verbal sign, with its low iconicity and high symbolic function, works conceptually, whereas the cinematic sign, with its high iconicity and uncertain symbolic function, works directly, sensuously, perceptually.[23]

The implication McFarlane draws from this contrast is that adaptation study should not rest content with "impressionistic" comparisons that emphasize films' alleged "fail[ure] to find satisfactory visual representations of key verbal signs," but should "consider to what extent the film-maker has picked up visual suggestions from the novel in his representations of key verbal signs—and how the visual representation affects one's 'reading' of the film text."[24] McFarlane goes on to argue that at several crucial points in the 1946 *Great Expectations,* David Lean succeeds not only in capturing a sense of Pip's first-person narrative voice but in grounding symbolic functions in a realistic *mise-en-scène* rather than imposing them by fiat. The result is that "the realistic meaning of the action seems to me to melt into the symbolic. ... The symbolic is a function of the *mise-en-scène,* inextricably interwoven into the realist texture."[25] McFarlane acknowledges, however, that "as one very familiar with the film, I find it hard to be sure how far on a single or first viewing a spectator might be aware of the symbolic functions I now discern"[26] in Magwitch's floundering in the mud, Jaggers' towering over Pip and Estella, and the stormy night sky that heralds Magwitch's return. The difference between percept and concept may well be more properly a function of rereading, and of a specifically analytical kind of rereading, than of a difference between movies, which are commonly assumed against mounting evidence to be watched only once, and novels, which are assumed to be endlessly rereadable, with each rereading converting more percepts to concepts.

6. Novels create more complex characters than movies because they offer more immediate and complete access to characters' psychological states

The ability to enter the minds of fictional characters directly is of course one of the glories, as it is one of the constitutive distinctions, of prose fiction—the only medium whose conventions allow third-person sentences beginning "she thought"—and it is indeed hard for movies to compete with novels in this regard. But it is just as hard for other media whose representation of complex characters has long been accepted. Since most novels take longer to read than two hours, it stands to reason that they have more leisure to develop characters who change over time. But I have never read an argument that long novels create more compelling characters than shorter novels, or even than short stories. The stricture against brevity seems to condemn movies alone.

Nor will the argument that cinema's characters are limited by its inability to present thought directly stand up to analysis. When Bluestone notes that "the film, having only arrangements of space to work with, cannot render thought, for the moment thought is externalized it is no longer thought,"[27] his observation is equally apt to drama as to film. Yet no one questions the ability of playwrights from Euripides to Chekhov to create complex characters. It is true, of course, that

Shakespeare's dramaturgy allows him soliloquies and asides that make it easier to dramatize thought, but Hamlet's thoughts are still necessarily externalized. The conclusion that follows is not that externalized thought is no longer thought, but that the pleasures of many non-novelistic media are based to a large extent in the invitation they extend to audiences to infer what characters are thinking on the basis of their speech and behavior, and that thoughts that are inferred can be just as subtle and profound as thoughts that are presented directly.

This last point deserves closer consideration. Novels, plays, and movies can each hardly help leaving out many details from their discourse. Wolfgang Iser, calling these omissions "gaps" or "blanks," has analyzed at length the processes by which readers are encouraged to fill them in, the freedom they have in choosing from among alternative possibilities, and the limitations on that freedom that define "failure" as "filling the blank exclusively with one's own projections."[28] What Iser does not consider is the necessity of gaps, not as an inevitable corollary of a given story's incompleteness, but as the very basis of its appeal. For it is precisely the business of fictional narratives to create a field in which audiences are invited to make inferences about what the characters are feeling or planning, where the story is going, what particular details will mean, and how everything will turn out. Such inferences are the product of the same increasingly educated guesswork that derives concepts from percepts. These inferences confer both the sense of intimacy with fictional characters that makes them more memorable than most real people and the assurance that the fictional field at hand comprises a world more satisfyingly coherent than the world outside. Novels and plays and movies might be said paradoxically to display their gaps in the sense that they depend for the pleasures they provide on audiences noticing and choosing to fill some of them but not others.[29]

The importance of this invitation to the audience is confirmed by the fact that few moviegoers read screenplays for pleasure—not because screenplays have no gaps (they specify many fewer details than either the literary texts they are based on or the movies that are based on them), but because their gaps are designed to be filled once and for all by the cast and crew, not displayed as an invitation to nonprofessional audiences' active participation. It is one of Shakespeare's most underappreciated gifts that the plays generations of readers have revered are nothing more than performance texts whose verbal texture happens to support an incomparably richer sense of reality than that of any screenplay to date.

Novels and movies, to stick with the two media most often contrasted in this regard, typically depend for their effects on different kinds of gaps. Because Jane Austen's novels, for example, though exceptionally precise in revealing the thoughts of each of their fictional heroines, limit themselves to exactly one such heroine per novel, cinematic adaptations of her work typically narrow the gap between the intimacy viewers feel with her heroines and the corresponding lack of intimacy they feel with other characters. Leo Braudy has contended that:

> the basic nature of character in film is omission. ... Film character achieves complexity by its emphasis on incomplete knowledge, by its conscious play with the limits a physical, external medium imposes upon it.[30]

But Sam Spade's disturbingly unreadable rolling of a cigarette in Hammett's novel raises the possibility that the basis of *all* character may well be incompleteness and omission—that characters are by definition figures whose gaps allow readers or viewers to project for them a life that seems more vivid, realistic, and complex than their explicitly specified thoughts and actions. At the very least, it does not follow either that novels and movies are condemned to certain kinds of gaps that are specific to their media, or that one sort of gap is better than another. What determines the success of a given work is neither the decision to withhold nor the decision to specify a character's thoughts, but the subtlety, maturity, and fullness of the pattern that emerges from thoughts and actions specified or inferred. These are not criteria on which any particular medium has a monopoly.

7. Cinema's visual specification usurps its audience's imagination

Perhaps dismayed that television has killed the novel-reading tastes of a generation of students who lack the patience to appreciate psychological fiction or to wait for a slow payoff, commentators like McFarlane have often concluded more generally that "because of its high iconicity, the cinema has left no scope for the imaginative activity necessary to the reader's visualization of what he reads."[31] This assumption amusingly manages to invert the assumption that novels' ability to present thought directly makes their characters potentially deeper and richer than movie characters while still condemning movies as inferior. In fact, the argument often urged against cinema's overspecification would make more sense if it were directed against novelists like Henry James, since the details movies are compelled to specify—the shape of the settee on which two lovers are sitting, the distance between them, the color of the wallpaper behind them—are often inconsequential, whereas the thoughts going through their minds, which novels are much more likely than films to specify with great precision, are crucial.

Despite this logical contradiction, the argument against cinema's overspecification is in important ways consistent with the argument against its lack of direct access to characters' minds. The basis of the charge in both cases is that films are incapable of translating the unique properties of verbal texts without transforming, diminishing, or otherwise betraying them. Hence McFarlane notes the impossibility of translating Dickens's descriptions to the screen despite their apparent wealth of visual detail, as in Pip's first description of Wemmick as:

> a dry man, rather short in stature, with a square wooden face whose expression seemed to have been imperfectly chipped out with a dull-edged chisel. There were some marks in it that might have been dimples, if the material had been softer and the instrument finer, but which, as it was, were only dints. The chisel had made three or four of these attempts at embellishment over his nose, but had given them up without any effort to smooth them off.[32]

McFarlane aptly notes that such a passage, which "may seem like a rich visual invitation to a film-maker," in truth "offer[s] little in the way of actual physical detail and a good deal of purely verbal energy working toward a sense of the grotesque."[33] The fallacy lies in two assumptions about the nature of imagery in prose fiction, the first of which McFarlane partly identifies himself. When Dickens describes Wemmick's face as carved out of wood, or when he describes Scrooge's home in *A Christmas Carol* as:

> a gloomy suite of rooms, in a lowering pile of building up a yard, where it had so little business to be, that one could scarcely help fancying it must have run there when it was a young house, playing at hide-and-seek with other houses, and have forgotten the way out again,[34]

his imagery depends more on fanciful ideas and rhythmically stylized rhetoric than on any set of images. It is not the reader's job to translate such passages into visually realized or narrativized images of Wemmick's face under the chisel (how broad a chisel, and how long did the operation take?) or Scrooge's house playing hide-and-seek with other houses (how many other houses? was Scrooge's house the smallest? how long did the other houses look for it before they gave up?) but to enjoy them as concepts whose sensory appeal is at least as much to the ear as to the eye. The dauntingly rich visual field of films does not inhibit viewers' imagination, because imagining, as Chatman has pointed out, cannot legitimately be reduced to "picturing."[35]

The deeper fallacy, which McFarlane does not identify, is the assumption that it would be an advantage to a film adaptation if Dickens were to specify Wemmick's visual reality more closely because the fewer gaps the novelist leaves, the easier it is to fill them without transgressing.[36] On this analysis, it would be a hopeless endeavor to adapt Austen's novels to film because their visual texture is so remarkably thin that adapters are compelled to draw on ancillary historical accounts to dress all the characters and furnish their rooms. Austen's novels would be much better suited to radio, which would emphasize her subtlety in distinguishing her characters' voices without the necessity of supplying extraneous visual details. But even the most deferential film adapters commonly approach such gaps not with trepidation but with a sense of opportunity to supply their own details because they assume that films will differ from their sources in myriad ways and are eager to invent details whenever the novel's discourse gives them leave to do so. Just as gaps are the engine of narrative engagement for the audience, they are the license for the kinds of filmmaking inventions that elevate adaptations above servile transcriptions. Even to talk of the inventiveness of deferential adapters, however, anticipates the next fallacy.

8. Fidelity is the most appropriate criterion to use in analyzing adaptations

McFarlane's restive description of "the near-fixation with the issue of fidelity" that has "inhibited and blurred" adaptation study since its inception is all too accurate.[37] Fidelity to its source text—whether it is conceived as success in re-creating specific textual details or the effect of the whole—is a hopelessly fallacious measure of a given adaptation's value because it is unattainable, undesirable, and theoretically possible only in a trivial sense. Like translations to a new language, adaptations will always reveal their sources' superiority because whatever their faults, the source texts will always be better at being themselves. Even if the adaptations are remakes in the same medium, their most conscientious attempts to replicate the original will betray their differences, and thus their inferiority, all the more plainly—a point made particularly clear in the critical discourse on Gus Van Sant's instructive 1998 remake of Alfred Hitchcock's *Psycho*. Van Sant's film prompted critics across the country to complain not only that Vince Vaughn and Anne Heche were inadequate substitutes for Anthony Perkins and Janet Leigh but that it didn't matter that Julianne Moore was a better actress than Vera Miles because her performance was *different*, and every departure from Hitchcock's text, which Van Sant had promised to follow line by line and shot by shot, was by definition a betrayal. The only remake that would have maintained perfect fidelity to the original text would have been a re-release of that text. But as McFarlane broadly implies in his discussion of Martin Scorses's *Cape Fear* (1991) as a remake and commentary on J. Lee-Thompson's 1961 version, even a re-release of the original film might well have a profoundly different effect on audiences influenced by thirty years of changes in social mores, generic prestige, family values, and industry self-censorship.[38]

Given the indefensibility of fidelity as a criterion for the analysis of adaptations, why has it maintained such a stifling grip on adaptation study? The likely reasons seem less theoretical than institutional. The assumption of fidelity is really an appeal to anteriority, the primacy of classic over modern texts which are likely to come under suspicion by exactly the teachers trained in literary studies—for example, the Shakespeareans giving courses in "Shakespeare on Film" or using the Kenneth Branagh and Mel Gibson *Hamlets* as classroom anodynes—who are most likely to be interested in adaptations.[39] At least until the infant study of novelizations adapted from cinematic originals becomes a full-fledged discipline, the valorization of fidelity amounts to a valorization of literature as such in the face of the insurgent challenge of cinema studies. And the theoretical poverty of fidelity as a touchstone of value, which begs analytical questions that might bedevil other approaches, is no stumbling block to commentators who are suspicious of theory in the first place.

These explanations, however, still leave unquestioned the more general assumption that the main business of commentators who are considering film adaptations is evaluating them, whether vis-à-vis their source texts or on their own merits. The peculiarity of this assumption can hardly be overstated. Evaluation may well be "one of the most venerable, central, theoretically significant, and pragmatically inescapable set of problems" in criticism.[40] Yet the whole tendency of cinema studies since universities first took it up thirty years ago has been away from evaluation as a critical project—except in the area of adaptation study. The Top Ten lists that so roiled readers of *Sight and Sound* in the years before cinema studies made it into the academy have now lost the headlines to newspaper reviewers' annual roundups and the American Film Institute, freeing film scholars to focus on analytical and theoretical problems. Only adaptation study, whether or not it uses the source text as a touchstone, remains obsessed with asking whether a given film is any good as a preliminary, a precondition, or a substitute for asking how it works.

9. Source texts are more original than adaptations

A primary reason that adaptation study remains obsessed with fidelity as a criterion for evaluation is that adaptations raise questions about the nature of authorship that would be difficult to answer without the bulwark of fidelity. It is much easier to dismiss adaptations as inevitably blurred mechanical reproductions of original works of art than to grapple with the thorny questions of just what constitutes originality and in what sense Robert James Waller's phenomenally popular novels are themselves less mechanically reproduced than Clint Eastwood's film version of *The Bridges of Madison County*.

The basis for the assumption that literary texts are to be valued for an originality that adaptations lack is clarified by considering the apparently exceptional case of William Shakespeare, nearly all of whose plays are adaptations, often to a new medium, of earlier material from sources as diverse as Holinshed's *Chronicles* and Greene's *Pandosto*. The originality of Shakespeare, his defenders asseverate, depends precisely on his seeing the artistic potential of inert source materials; he is an alchemist, not an adapter, as one can see by comparing any of his plays with its base original. But this defense demonstrates only that some adaptations are better than others, not that the best adaptations aren't really adaptations at all. Nor does it demonstrate that only writers can escape the label of adapter, since there are several noted film adapters sanctified by the name of auteur. Orson Welles wrote most of his own screenplays, typically based on earlier source material. Stanley Kubrick's films, all of them similarly adaptations of literary source texts, are universally recognized as distinctively his. Perhaps most startling of all are Walt Disney's animated versions of children's classics (*Alice in Wonderland*), folk classics (*Snow White and the Seven Dwarfs*), demi-classics (*Bambi*), and non-classics (*101 Dalmations*), in which the producer continues his successful career as auteur some forty years after his death.

Perhaps the best illustration of the slippery nature of originality in adaptation is the critical reception of Hitchcock, who emerged as an auteur in France in the 1950s and in America ten years later precisely to the extent that his champions were able to make a case for thematic affinities among his many films that ran deeper than recycled genre formulas. The further Hitchcock's star rose as the only begetter of his films, the less "a film criticism centred on directors" was "concerned to follow up Hitchcock's statements … of indebtedness to English literary figures,"[41] even though only a handful of Hitchcock films—*The Ring, Champagne, Saboteur, North by Northwest, Torn Curtain*—are based on original screenplays.[42] Only with the decline of auteurism as a critical framework did critics like Charles Barr turn to a closer examination of Hitchcock's sources.

The moral implicit in the shifting fortunes of writers and directors as creative artists seems to be the enduring appeal of *someone's* originality as an artistic value and the need commentators continually feel to identify a single shaping intelligence as a given work's creator. The reason that originality maintains a central position in adaptation study but not cinema studies generally is that cinema studies has long rejected aesthetics as its leading methodology in favor of analytical and theoretical critique. The antipathetic tendencies of cinema studies and adaptation study have so exacerbated each other that adaptation study is now the safest refuge for film scholars unsympathetic to the prevailing currents in cinema studies today, whose discourse, if it took any notice of adaptation at all, would no doubt dismiss it with the observation that all texts are intertexts. That is, all texts quote or embed fragments of earlier texts, in Mikhail Bakhtin's terms, typically without explicit acknowledgment, often without conscious intention, and never with any attempt at straightforward replication of the original's force. Indeed, the novel, which Bakhtin hailed as the dialogic mode par excellence because in "the rich soil of novelistic prose," the "internally dialogized discourse" Bakhtin describes as double-voiced or heteroglot "sinks its roots deep into a fundamental, socio-linguistic speech diversity and multi-languaged-ness,"[43] has long been eclipsed by the junkyard aesthetics of the cinema. Movies are a mode whose elastic form, by turns comic, ironic, and parodic, can tolerate heteroglossia that would wreck more narrowly defined forms. Indeed, movies themselves may already in turn have been eclipsed by television series like *The Simpsons*, surely the most carnivalistic work of fiction enjoyed by a large contemporary audience— except of course for the World Wide Web in its entirety.

10. Adaptations are adapting exactly one text apiece

It might seem commonsensical to assume a one-to-one correspondence between film adaptations and their literary sources. But just as a novel like *Frankenstein* may serve as the vehicle for over a hundred adaptations, each individual adaptation invokes many precursor texts besides the one whose title it usually borrows. When McFarlane begins his disapproving discussion of the criterion of fidelity by asking satirically, "Is it really 'Jamesian'? Is it 'true to Lawrence'? Does it 'capture the spirit of Dickens'?",[44] he is invoking authorial intention as a possible regulatory function. But the phrases he chooses, especially "Jamesian" and "capture the spirit of Dickens," are reminders that adaptations of the works of famous and prolific novelists are customarily measured not only against the novels they explicitly adapt but against the distinctive world or style or tone associated with the author in general. Adaptations of *Great Expectations* invoke not only textual particulars of Dickens's novel but more general conventions of the Dickens world: genial satire, sentimental benevolence, comically grotesque minor characters, happy endings. Hence the "more buoyant ending" tacked onto David Lean's *Great Expectations*, an ending McFarlane finds so charmingly redolent of British aspirations at the end of World War II that "one is led to have more in mind than the famous novel whose title Lean's film bears,"[45] is arguably more Dickensian than the uncharacteristically downbeat ending Dickens himself supplied.

Nor is the world or style or career of the author the only precursor text that competes with the particular novel or play or story for attention. Hollywood adaptations of foreign novels invariably foreground their particular nationalities and historical moments in ways their source novels rarely do. American adaptations make much more of the Surrey of *Emma* and the London of *The Picture of Dorian Gray*, and the innumerable adaptations of Agatha Christie beginning with *Murder on the Orient Express* mark their historical period more emphatically than their forerunners do. Dozens of adaptations that open with screens showing copies of the books on which they are based, from *A Christmas Carol* to *The Postman Always Rings Twice*, invoke not only their specific precursor texts but the aura of literature as such to confer a sense of authority. And as McFarlane himself points out, films as different as *Great Expectations* and *Cape Fear* inevitably comment on their own cultural and historical contexts. Nor will it do to argue that the author, a collection of national characteristics or historical periods, or the institutions of literature and cultural history themselves are not textualized in the same way novels and plays are, since even if they were not textualized before their adaptation, the adaptations confer a specifically textual status on them by the mode of their reference, which can borrow only the authority it grants its subjects. Hence Imelda Whelehan has observed that:

> when … we study a text such as *Hamlet* which has been subjected to countless adaptations … [we] recognize that in untangling one adaptation from another, we have recourse to many sources outside both the play and subsequent films.[46]

Commentators on adaptations like McFarlane often recognize the richness of their heteroglossia but rarely pursue its leading implication: that no intertextual model, however careful, can be adequate to the study of adaptation if it limits each intertext to a single precursor. As Bakhtin argues of the novel:

> The real task of stylistic analysis consists in uncovering all the available orchestrating languages in the composition of the novel, grasping the precise degree of distancing that separates each language from its most immediate semantic instantiation in the work as a whole, and the varying angles of refraction of intentions within it, understanding their dialogic interrelationship and—finally—if there is direct authorial discourse, determining the heteroglot background outside the work that dialogizes it.[47]

Adaptation study requires as sensitive and rigorous attention to the widest possible array of a film's precursor texts as McFarlane devotes to the novels the films he considers adapt.

11. Adaptations are intertexts, their precursor texts simply texts

This is the assumption that underlies the last two assumptions about originality and the one-to-one congruence adaptations are widely held to betray. An adaptation is assumed to be a window into a text on which it depends for its authority, and the business of viewers and analysts is to look through the window for signs of the original text. But texts themselves are assumed to be not windows but paintings that invite readers to look at or into them than through them. This assumption vitiates even so perceptive an analysis as Seymour Chatman's discussion of Harold

Pinter's adaptation of John Fowles's novel *The French Lieutenant's Woman* for Karel Reisz's 1981 film, which focuses on a single question: "How do intelligent film adaptations grapple with the overtly prominent narrator, the expositor, describer, investigator of characters' states of mind, commentator, philosophizer?"[48] His answer is that despite the film's much more narrow and limited focus—its "only real theme is love" compared to the novel's broadly discursive treatment of its exotic Victorian "panorama"—and its "simpler and less determinate" treatment of its characters' psychology, it doubles the novel's Victorian narrative with a highly original modern frame tale of the relationship between a pair of contemporary actors who are filming the story that "attempts to dramatize the novel's *commentary*.[49]

Chatman's analysis is so sensitive and acute that it is easy to overlook the reductive terms that frame it. Since he is considering Reisz's film strictly as a case study in the successful adaptation of a highly resistant text, he naturally measures its success against the success of the novel, which plays the text to the film's intertext. This parasitism does not require the film to stick to the novel's thematic material any more than it requires the film to stick to the actions the novel represents. Indeed Chatman, who is warmly appreciative of the film's presentation of "the impossible search for a fictional woman out of a bygone era ... not a subject proposed by the novel, which handles the modern repercussions of Victorian thought only in the expository-argumentative mode," notes approvingly that "the film is less sanguine than the novel about the progress of evolution in the emotional sphere."[50] But his project requires him to accept the novel as establishing a criterion of value for the film. Hence he dismisses Joy Gould Boyum's attack on the "coyness" of Fowles's often tiresomely "chatty" narrator as "a narrow Lubbockian view"[51] because if the narrator's ruminative commentary were in any way flawed, there would be no toilsome need to find a cinematic equivalent for it. When adapters approach source texts, he seems to suggest, they should assume that whatever is, is right.

More generally, Chatman contends that "film cannot reproduce many of the pleasures of reading novels, but it can produce other experiences of parallel value."[52] The key word here is "parallel," which absolves the adaptation from the responsibility of slavish imitation to its source even as it invokes the source's regulatory function in setting the standard for those parallel experiences. My point is not to ask whether a film labeled *The French Lieutenant's Woman* has an intertextual responsibility to its source novel, but to ask why the novel itself should be treated so uncritically as a criterion of value that adaptations seek to create non-parallel experiences at their peril. Although it is certainly true that adaptations are intertexts, it is equally true that their precursors are intertexts, because every text is an intertext that depends for its interpretation on shared assumptions about language, culture, narrative, and other presentational conventions.

Chatman might well object here that the constitutive difference between adaptations and their originals is that adaptations invite the consideration of a single precursor text as primary whereas their originals combine many influences into a new synthesis that does not privilege any one of them. Adaptations imitate novels, novels imitate life, or at least Victorian life, itself. But this distinction cannot be seriously maintained in an age that abounds in such ironic, parodic, or heteroglot adaptations as *The Birds, The Three Musketeers* (and *The Four Musketeers*), *Batman, Clueless*, and *Everything You Always Wanted to Know about Sex (But Were Afraid to Ask)*. The most capacious novels, to the extent that they choose subjects more specific than life—the First Reform Bill, the intrigue Cardinal Richelieu provoked at the court of Louis XIII, the effects of Napoleon's campaign against Russia—take on the responsibility of illuminating those particular subjects. Even the *Aeneid*, whose avowed subject is arms and the man, and *Tom Jones*, whose subject Fielding grandly announces as "HUMAN NATURE,"[53] approach their forbiddingly general subjects in terms of far more specific historical narratives and behavioral types. As Deborah Cartmell points out, "instead of worrying about whether a film is 'faithful' to the original literary text (founded in the logocentric belief that there is a single meaning), we read adaptations for their generation of a plurality of meanings. Thus the intertextuality of the adaptation is our primary concern."[54]

12. Adaptation study is a marginal enterprise

This is the only one of my twelve fallacies that is actually true. Adaptation study has indeed for many years been marginal to the study of moving images in general. But does it need to be marginal? Dudley Andrew, describing adaptation study as "frequently the most narrow and provincial area of film theory," called for the integration of adaptation study into cinema studies by noting that "its distinctive feature, the matching of the cinematic sign system to prior achievement in some other system, can be shown to be distinctive of all representational cinema."[55] Andrew called for a generalizing of adaptation study to cover all the varieties of signification, quotation, and reference that make cinema possible and an analysis of connotation and a sociology of adaptation to complement its aesthetic assumptions about fidelity. Nothing like this has happened in the twenty years since Andrew wrote. Even acute contemporary analysts like McFarlane and Chatman who have deplored the crippling dependence of adaptation study on concepts like fidelity and monistic claims of literature's superiority to film (or vice versa) have retained an unhelpful emphasis on notions of essentialism, originality, and cinematic equivalents to literary techniques.

The broad implication of this essay is that adaptation study has sought a separate place less for aesthetic or theoretical than for institutional reasons: to defend literary works and literature against the mass popularity of cinema, to valorize authorial agency and originality in a critical climate increasingly opposed to either, and to escape from the current orientation of film theory and from theoretical problems in general. In other words, adaptation study has been marginalized because it wishes to be. Just as the apparently essential properties of novels and films stipulated by Chatman turn out on closer analysis to be functions of specific historical contexts, however, institutional battles can be resolved in the same ways they arose, by changing the way the institution does business. Adaptation study will emerge from its ghetto not when cinema studies accepts the institutional claims that would make cinema a poor relation of literature or succeeds in refashioning analysts of adaptation into loyal citizens of cinema studies, but in some larger synthesis that might well be called Textual Studies—a discipline incorporating adaptation study, cinema studies in general, and literary studies, now housed in departments of English, and much of cultural studies as well.

This is not to suggest that this omnivorous new field would take its marching orders from adaptation study. The question adaptation study has most persistently asked—in what ways does and should an intertext resemble its precursor text in another medium?—could more usefully be configured in dialogic terms: How and why does any one particular precursor text or set of texts come to be privileged above all others in the analysis of a given intertext? What gives some intertexts but not others the aura of texts? More generally, in what ways are precursor texts rewritten, as they always are whenever they are read? Such questions, though not subsuming dialogism to adaptation, would extend both dialogism and adaptation study in vitally important ways. If they don't watch out, analysts of adaptation who are willing to trade their historical valorization of literature for broader theoretical range and greater theoretical rigor are apt to find themselves in a most unlikely place: at the very center of intertextual—that is, of textual—studies.

■　■　■

Questions and projects

1. Identify three of Leitch's "fallacies" that seem most prevalent in critical reactions to adaptations today, and provide examples that one might use to support the claims of those positions.
2. Add two or three fallacies not addressed in the essay that you believe impede adaptation studies today. To what extent are these a product of "institutional" pressures?

Notes

1   Robert B. Ray, "The Field of 'Literature and Films,'" in James Naremore, ed., *Film Adaptation* (New Brunswick, NJ: Rutgers University Press, 2000), 44.
2   Brian McFarlane, *Novel to Film: An Introduction to the Theory of Adaptation* (Oxford: Clarendon, 1996), 194.
3   James Naremore, Introduction to *Film Adaptation*, 2.
4   Siegfried Kracauer, *Theory of Film: The Redemption of Physical Reality* (London: Oxford University Press, 1960), 1. For a later version of the essentialist argument, see Geoffrey Wager, *The Novel and the Cinema* (Rutherford, NJ: Fairleigh Dickinson University Press, 1975): "Language is a completion, an entelechy, and film is not. By its nature it cannot be. Film is a diffusion" (12).
5   See Seymour Chatman, "What Novels Can Do That Films Can't (and Vice Versa)," *Critical Inquiry* 7 (1980–81): 121–40. Chatman's view of adaptation is better represented by his more recent and subtle discussion of the topic in *Coming to Terms: The Rhetoric of Narrative in Fiction and Film* (Ithaca, NY: Cornell University Press, 1990), about which I will have more to say later on.
6   See F. E. Sparshott, "Basic Film Aesthetics," in Gerald Mast and Marshall Cohen, eds., *Film Theory and Criticism: Introductory Readings,* 3rd edition (New York: Oxford University Press, 1985), 286–87, and V. F. Perkins, *Film as Film: Understanding and Judging Movies* (1972; rpt. Harmondsworth: Penguin, 1986), 59. For more recent empirically based attacks on the essentialist argument, see Morris Beja, *Film and Literature: An Introduction* (New York: Longman, 1979), 54–59, and James Griffith, *Adaptations as Imitations* (Newark, DE: University of Delaware Press, 1997), 30–35.
7   Noël Carroll, *Philosophical Problems of Classical Film Theory* (Princeton, NJ: Princeton University Press, 1988), 88.
8   Chatman, "What Novels Can Do," 128.
9   McFarlane, 16. In "Jane Campion and the Limits of Literary Cinema," Ken Gelder has attacked this essentialist argument by noting that commentators on Jane Campion and Kate Pullinger's novelization of Campion's film *The Piano* have consistently identified it "as somehow *less* literary than the film: as if the film was more of a novel than the novel itself" (Deborah Cartmell and Imelda Whelehan, eds., *Adaptations: From Text to Screen, Screen to Text* [London: Routledge, 1999], 157).
10   Chatman, "What Novels Can Do," 128–29.
11   Ibid., 128.
12   Dashiell Hammett, *Complete Novels* (New York: Library of America, 1999), 398.
13   Pauline Kael, *5001 Nights at the Movies* (New York: Holt, Rinehart and Winston, 1982), 355.
14   André Bazin, *Orson Welles: A Critical View,* trans. Jonathan Rosenbaum (New York: Harper & Row, 1978), 133.
15   McFarlane, 26.
16   In *Made into Movies: From Literature to Film* (New York: Holt, Rinehart and Winston, 1985), James Y. McDougal, who is practically alone among analysts of adaptation in noting that "casting ... considerably shapes the process of adaptation," avers that casting is "extrinsic to the medium of film" (6).
17   Timothy Corrigan, *Film and Literature: An Introduction and Reader* (Upper Saddle River, NJ: Prentice

Hall, 1999), 3.

18 Joy Gould Boyum, *Double Exposure: Fiction into Film* (New York: New American Library, 1985), 21.

19 George Bluestone, *Novels into Film* (1957; rpt. Berkeley and Los Angeles: University of California Press, 1971), 20.

20 Gerald Mast, *Film/Cinema/Movie: A Theory of Experience* (New York: Harper & Row, 1977), 64.

21 Alain Robbe-Grillet, *For a New Novel: Essays on Fiction,* trans. Richard Howard (New York: Grove, 1965), 20.

22 Griffith, 229, 230.

23 McFarlane, 26–27.

24 Ibid., 27.

25 Ibid., 132.

26 Idem.

27 Bluestone, 47–48.

28 Wolfgang Iser, *The Act of Reading: A Theory of Aesthetic Response* (Baltimore, MD: Johns Hopkins University Press, 1978), 167.

29 Boyum goes so far as to argue that since readers cannot read novels without visualizing them as films, they "inevitably expect … the movie projected on the screen to be a shadow reflection of the movie … [they] have imagined" (60).

30 Leo Braudy, *The World in a Frame: What We See in Films* (Garden City, NY: Anchor/ Doubleday, 1976), 184.

31 McFarlane, 27.

32 Charles Dickens, *Great Expectations* (Oxford: Oxford University Press, 1953), 161.

33 McFarlane, 133.

34 Dickens, *Christmas Novels* (Oxford: Oxford University Press, 1954), 14.

35 Chatman, *Coming to Terms,* 162.

36 Compare Chatman: "The central problem for film adapters is to transform narrative features that come easily to language but hard to a medium that operates in 'real time' and whose natural focus is the surface appearance of things" (*Coming to Terms,* 162). The fallacy is not only in the explicitly stated essentialist assumption that film has "a natural focus" but also in the implied assumption that exemplary narratives in any medium concentrate on exploiting the features that "come easily" to that medium, marginalizing departures from those features as a "problem." Hence Chatman, in continuing his general rejection of voiceover commentary, observes that "historically, the best filmmakers have preferred purely visual solutions" to the problems of narratorial commentary (163).

37 McFarlane, 194.

38 See McFarlane, 187–93.

39 Imelda Whelehan has suggested that "it is possibly the 'literariness' of the fictional text which itself appears to give credence to the study of adaptations at all" (Cartmell and Whelehan, 17).

40 Barbara Herrnstein Smith, *Contingencies of Value: Alternative Perspectives for Critical Theory* (Cambridge, MA: Harvard University Press, 1988), 17. For a contrasting view, see for example Northrop Frye, who asserts in *Anatomy of Criticism: Four Essays* (Princeton, NJ: Princeton University Press, 1957) that "the demonstrable value-judgment is the donkey's carrot of literary criticism" (20).

41 Charles Barr, *English Hitchcock* (Moffat: Cameron & Hollis, 1999), 8.

42 To be sure, *Shadow of a Doubt* and *Lifeboat* are based on unpublished stories, and many other Hitchcock films, from *The Man Who Knew Too Much* to *Foreign Correspondent, Spellbound,* and *The Birds,* have only a nominal connection to the sources they credit.

43 M. M. Bakhtin, *The Dialogic Imagination: Four Essays,* trans. Caryl Emerson and Michael Holquist (Austin, TX: University of Texas Press, 1981), 324, 325–36.

44 McFarlane, 8.

45 McFarlane, 111.

46 Cartmell and Whelehan, 16.

47 Bakhtin, 416.

48 Chatman, *Coming to Terms,* 163–64.
49 Ibid., 169, 168, 173, 174.
50 Ibid., 180.
51 Ibid., 172. See Boyum, 107.
52 Ibid., 163.
53 Henry Fielding, *The History of Tom Jones, a Foundling,* ed. Fredson Bowers (Middle-town, CN: Wesleyan University Press, 1975), 32.
54 Cartmell and Whelehan, 28.
55 Dudley Andrew, *Concepts in Film Theory* (Oxford: Oxford University Press, 1984), 96.

2.2 ADAPTATION IN HISTORY

Chapter 12

Vachel Lindsay

PROGRESS AND ENDOWMENT

ONE OF THE EARLY PIONEERS in serious discussions of the movies as an art, Vachel Lindsay was also a determined poet who saw film as a revolutionary vehicle for bringing the spirit of poetry to masses of individuals. *The Art of the Moving Picture* was written in 1915 and revised in 1922, and many of its assumptions and arguments are a product of the silent films (especially the work of D. W. Griffith) that defined film culture at the time. Along with a number of sharp insights into a new way of telling stories, Lindsay's work represents a still resonant argument about the real and potential place of movies within society and, more specifically, their place on book shelves in universities and within other institutions of knowledge and culture. Here and at other points in his book, Lindsay demonstrates a sense of the universal potential of film language as it translates social ideas and poetic visions into pictorial terms that all audiences understand. Both this utopian faith in the new language of the cinema and its revolutionary power to claim a place in culture next to literature were shared by Griffith and other early filmmakers.

■ ■ ■

PROGRESS AND ENDOWMENT
VACHEL LINDSAY

From *The Art of the Moving Picture*, New York: Liveright Publishing Corporation, 1970, pp 253–271

The moving picture goes almost as far as journalism into the social fabric in some ways, further in others. Soon, no doubt, many a little town will have its photographic news-press. We have already the weekly world-news films from the big centres.

With local journalism will come devices for advertising home enterprises. Some staple products will be made attractive by having film-actors show their uses. The motion pictures will be in the public schools to stay. Text-books in geography, history, zoölogy, botany, physiology, and other sciences will be illustrated by standardized films. Along with these changes, there will be available at certain centres collections of films equivalent to the *Standard Dictionary* and the *Encyclopaedia Britannica*.

And sooner or later we will have a straight-out capture of a complete film expression by the serious forces of civilization. The merely impudent motion picture will be relegated to the leisure hours with yellow journalism. Photoplay libraries are inevitable, as active if not as multitudinous as the book-circulating libraries. The oncoming machinery and expense of the motion picture is immense. Where will the money come from? No one knows. What the people want they will get. The race of man cannot afford automobiles, but has them nevertheless. We cannot run away into non-automobile existence or non-steam-engine or non-movie life long at a time. We must conquer this thing. While the more stately scientific and educational aspects just enumerated are slowly on their way, the artists must be up and about their ameliorative work.

Every considerable effort to develop a noble idiom will count in the final result, as the writers of early English made possible the language of the Bible, Shakespeare, and Milton. We are perfecting a medium to be used as long as Chinese ideographs have been. It will no doubt, like the Chinese language, record in the end massive and classical treatises, imperial chronicles, law-codes, traditions, and religious admonitions. All this by the *motion picture* as a recording instrument, not necessarily the *photoplay* [short film], a much more limited thing, a form of art.

...

High-minded graduates of university courses in sociology and schools of philanthropy, devout readers of *The Survey*, *The Chicago Public*, *The Masses*, *The New Republic*, *La Follette's*, are going to advocate increasingly, their varied and sometimes contradictory causes, in films. These will generally be produced by heroic exertions in the studio, and much passing of the subscription paper outside.

Then there are endowments already in existence that will no doubt be diverted to the photoplay channel. In every state house, and in Washington, DC, increasing quantities of dead printed matter have been turned out year after year. They have served to kindle various furnaces and feed the paper-mills a second time. Many of these routine reports will remain in innocuous desuetude. But one-fourth of them, perhaps, are capable of being embodied in films. If they are scientific demonstrations, they can be made into realistic motion picture records. If they are exhortations, they can be transformed into plays with a moral, brothers of the film *Your Girl and Mine*. The appropriations for public printing should include such work hereafter.

The scientific museums distribute routine pamphlets that would set the whole world right on certain points if they were but read by said world. Let them be filmed and started. Whatever the congressman is permitted to [be] frank to his constituency, let him send in the motion picture form when it is the expedient and expressive way.

When men work for the high degrees in the universities, they labor on a piece of literary conspiracy called a thesis which no one outside the university hears of again. The gist of this research work that is dead to the democracy, through the university merits of thoroughness, moderation of statement, and final touch of discovery, would have a chance to live and grip the people in a motion picture transcript, if not a photoplay. It would be University Extension. The relentless fire of criticism which the heads of the departments would pour on the production before they allowed it to pass would result in a standardization of the sense of scientific fact over the land. Suppose the film has the coat of arms of the University of Chicago along with the name of the young graduate whose thesis it is. He would have a chance to reflect credit on the university even as much as a football player.

Large undertakings might be under way, like those described in the chapter on Architecture-in-Motion. But these would require much more than the ordinary outlay for thesis work, less, perhaps, than is taken for Athletics. Lyman Howe and several other world-explorers have already set the pace in the more human side of the educative film. The list of Mr. Howe's offerings from the first would reveal many a one that would have run the gantlet of a university department. He points out a new direction for old energies, whereby professors may become citizens.

Let the cave-man, reader of picture-writing, be allowed to ponder over scientific truth. He is at present the victim of the alleged truth of the specious and sentimental variety of photograph. It gives the precise edges of the coat or collar of the smirking masher and the exact fibre in the dress of the jumping-jack. The eye grows weary of sharp points and hard edges that mean nothing. All this idiotic precision is going to waste. It should be enlisted in the cause of science and abated everywhere else. The edges in art are as mysterious as in science they are exact.

Some of the higher forms of the Intimate Moving Picture play should be endowed by local coteries representing their particular region. Every community of fifty thousand has its group of the cultured who have heretofore studied and imitated things done in the big cities. Some of these coteries will in exceptional cases become creative and begin to express their habitation and name. The Intimate Photoplay is capable of that delicacy and that informality which should characterize neighborhood enterprises.

The plays could be acted by the group who, season after season, have secured the opera house for the annual amateur show. Other dramatic ability could be found in the high-schools. There is enough talent in any place to make an artistic revolution, if once that region is aflame with a common vision. The spirit that made the Irish Players, all so racy of the soil, can also move the company of local photoplayers in Topeka, or Indianapolis, or Denver. Then let them speak for their town, not only in great occasional enterprises, but steadily, in little fancies, genre pictures, developing a technique that will finally make magnificence possible.

There was given not long ago, at the Illinois Country Club here, a performance of *The Yellow Jacket* by the Coburn Players. It at once seemed an integral part of this chapter.

The two flags used for a chariot, the bamboo poles for oars, the red sack for a decapitated head, etc., were all convincing, through a direct resemblance as well as the passionate acting. They suggest a possible type of hieroglyphics to be developed by the leader of the local group.

Let the enthusiast study this westernized Chinese play for primitive representative methods. It can be found in book form, a most readable work. It is by G. C. Hazelton, Jr., and J. H. Benrimo. The resemblance between the stage property and the thing represented is fairly close. The moving flags on each side of the actor suggest the actual color and progress of the chariot, and abstractly suggest its magnificence. The red sack used for a bloody head has at least the color and size of one. The dressed-up block of wood used for a child is the length of an infant of the age described and wears the general costume thereof. The farmer's hoe, though exaggerated, is still an agricultural implement.

The evening's list of properties is economical, filling one wagon, rather than three. Photographic realism is splendidly put to rout by powerful representation. When the villager desires to embody some episode that if realistically given would require a setting beyond the means of the available endowment, and does not like the near-Egyptian method, let him evolve his near-Chinese set of symbols.

The Yellow Jacket was written after long familiarity with the Chinese Theatre in San Francisco. The play is a glory to that city as well as to Hazelton and Benrimo. But every town in the United States has something as striking as the Chinese Theatre, to the man who keeps the eye of his soul open. It has its Ministerial Association, its boys' secret society, its red-eyed political gang, its grubby Justice of the Peace court, its free school for the teaching of Hebrew, its snobbish chapel, its fire-engine house, its milliner's shop. All these could be made visible in photoplays as flies are preserved in amber.

Edgar Lee Masters looked about him and discovered the village graveyard, and made it as wonderful as Noah's Ark, or Adam naming the animals, by supplying honest inscriptions to the headstones. Such stories can be told by the Chinese theatrical system as well. As many different films could be included under the general title: "Seven Old Families, and Why they Went to Smash." Or a less ominous series would be "Seven Victorious Souls." For there are triumphs every day under the drab monotony of an apparently defeated town: conquests worthy of the waving of sun-banners.

Above all, *The Yellow Jacket* points a moral for this chapter because there was conscience behind it. First: the rectitude of the Chinese actors of San Francisco who kept the dramatic tradition alive, a tradition that was bequeathed from the ancient generations. Then the artistic integrity of the men who readapted the tradition for western consumption, and their religious attitude that kept the high teaching and devout feeling for human life intact in the play. Then the zeal of the Drama League that indorsed it for the country. Then the earnest work of the Coburn Players who embodied it devoutly, so that the whole company became dear friends forever.

By some such ladder of conscience as this can the local scenario be endowed, written, acted, filmed, and made a real part of the community life. *The Yellow Jacket* was a drama, not a photoplay. This chapter does not urge that it be readapted for a photoplay in San Francisco or anywhere else. But a kindred painting-in-motion, something as beautiful and worthy and intimate, in strictly photoplay terms, might well be the flower of the work of the local groups of film actors.

Harriet Monroe's magazine, "Poetry" (Chicago), has given us a new sect, the Imagists:—Ezra Pound, Richard Aldington, John Gould Fletcher, Amy Lowell, F. S. Flint, D. H. Lawrence, and others. They are gathering followers and imitators. To these followers I would say: the Imagist impulse need not be confined to verse. Why would you be imitators of these leaders when you might be creators in a new medium? There is a clear parallelism between their point of view in verse and the Intimate-and-friendly Photoplay, especially when it is developed from the standpoint of the last part of chapter nine, *space measured without sound plus time measured without sound.*

There is no clan to-day more purely devoted to art for art's sake than the Imagist clan. An Imagist film would offer a noble challenge to the overstrained emotion, the overloaded splendor, the mere repetition of what are at present the finest photoplays. Now even the masterpieces are incontinent. Except for some of the old one-reel Biographs of Griffith's beginning, there is nothing of Doric restraint from the best to the worst. Read some of the poems of the people listed above, then imagine the same moods in the films. Imagist photoplays would be Japanese prints taking on life, animated Japanese paintings, Pompeian mosaics in kaleidoscopic but logical succession, Beardsley drawings made into actors and scenery, Greek vase-paintings in motion.

Scarcely a photoplay but hints at the Imagists in one scene. Then the illusion is lost in the next turn of the reel. Perhaps it would be a sound observance to confine this form of motion picture to a half reel or quarter reel, just as the Imagist poem is generally a half or quarter page. A series of them could fill a special evening.

The Imagists are colorists. Some people do not consider that photographic black, white, and gray are color. But here for instance are seven colors which the Imagists might use: (1) The whiteness of swans in the light. (2) The whiteness of swans in a gentle shadow. (3) The color of a sunburned man in the light. (4) His color in a gentle shadow. (5) His color in a deeper shadow. (6) The blackness of black velvet in the light. (7) The blackness of black velvet in a deep shadow. And to use these colors with definite steps from one to the other does not militate against an artistic mystery of edge and softness in the flow of line. There is a list of possible Imagist textures which is only limited by the number of things to be seen in the world. Probably only seven or ten would be used in one scheme and the same list kept through one production.

The Imagist photoplay will put discipline into the inner ranks of the enlightened and remind the sculptors, painters, and architects of the movies that there is a continence even beyond sculpture and that seas of realism may not have the power of a little well-considered elimination.

The use of the scientific film by established institutions like schools and state governments has been discussed. Let the Church also, in her own way, avail herself of the motion picture, wholeheartedly, as in mediaeval time she took over the marvel of Italian painting. There was a stage in her history when religious representation was by Byzantine mosaics, noble in color, having an architectural use, but curious indeed to behold from the standpoint of those who crave a sensitive emotional record. The first paintings of Cimabue and Giotto, giving these formulas a touch of life, were hailed with joy by all Italy. Now the Church Universal has an opportunity to establish her new painters if she will. She has taken over in the course of history, for her glory, miracle plays, Romanesque and Gothic architecture, stained glass windows, and the music of St. Cecilia's organ. Why not this new splendor? The Cathedral of St. John the Divine, on Morningside Heights, should establish in its crypt motion pictures as thoroughly considered as the lines of that building, if possible designed by the architects thereof, with the same sense of permanency.

This chapter does not advocate that the Church lay hold of the photoplays as one more medium for reillustrating the stories of the Bible as they are given in the Sunday-school papers. It is not pietistic simpering that will feed the spirit of Christendom, but a steady church-patronage of the most skilful and original motion picture artists. Let the Church follow the precedent which finally gave us Fra Angelico, Botticelli, Andrea del Sarto, Leonardo da Vinci, Raphael, Michelangelo, Correggio, Titian, Paul Veronese, Tintoretto, and the rest.

Who will endow the successors of the present woman's suffrage film, and other great crusading films? Who will see that the public documents and university researches take on the form of motion pictures? Who will endow the local photoplay and the Imagist photoplay? Who will take the first great measures to insure motion picture splendors in the church?

Things such as these come on the winds of to-morrow. But let the crusader look about him, and where it is possible, put in the diplomatic word, and coöperate with the Gray Norns.

■   ■   ■

Questions and projects

1. Compare a film to a work of late nineteenth-century theater or fiction on which it is based. How does the film fail to communicate all that the work of literature does? Are there ways, as Lindsay would claim, that the film expands or surpasses the literary work in communicating certain ideas or emotions?

2. Examine a current issue or question regarding film and its relation to education, such as the use of film in science, literature, or history classrooms or the arguments about how movies affect the reading habits of children. How should Lindsay's great claims for the movies as education be tempered or challenged in these instances? Or, can one show, with some detailed analysis, how film does educate in its own manner?

Chapter 13

Kristin Thompson

NOVEL, SHORT STORY, DRAMA
The conditions for influence

O NE OF THE MORE PRODUCTIVE DIRECTIONS in recent film criticism has attended to the precise historical details that shape films and film culture. This perspective holds that careful historical and cultural discriminations need to be made when investigating film forms—where they originate, and how they change. In this excerpt from *The Classical Hollywood Cinema* (1985), Kristin Thompson examines the social and industrial pressures that promoted the development of movies not only from drama and novels but also from short stories and magazine culture. Detailed historical groundings such as this lead to more precise evaluations of how certain forms and patterns in the movies (like those derived from literary subjects and structures) were employed and understood at the time and how they should be understood now by the viewer attuned to history.

■ ■ ■

NOVEL, SHORT STORY, DRAMA: THE CONDITIONS FOR INFLUENCE
KRISTIN THOMPSON

From *The Classical Hollywood Cinema*, New York: Columbia University Press, 1985, pp. 163–167.

As films grew longer, the status of the individual film on a program changed. Initially, eight or so short films might fill a twenty-minute slot in a vaudeville program of several hours. The overall emphasis was on variety, and the disparate films formed an act. As a consequence, no individual film was expected to stand by itself. But with the advent of the nickelodeon and the standardized 1,000-foot reel, a program would typically consist of only three or four films; each occupied a distinct place within the complete show, separated by song-slide presentations and possibly other live acts. Internal coherence became a more central issue. And when the feature film came to occupy virtually an entire evening's program (with overture and other entertainment often tailored to the film), it had to carry the burden of sustaining audience interest. Expanded length and the change in viewing circumstances undoubtedly played a large part in turning filmmakers away from a vaudeville model of narrative toward fiction and the drama.

In the early years, films had competed only with other vaudeville acts for a place on a program in an art form that had an established audience. But with the phenomenal growth of the film industry, its product began to vie with other entertainment commodities for customers. By the first half of the teens, films were competing with inexpensive popular fiction—short-story magazines and novels, *The Saturday Evening Post* and *Collier's*, for instance, offered 'one or two nights enjoyment of the best serials and short stories for five cents.'[18] To lure those readers in at a similar price for a shorter period, film producers felt they had to raise the quality of their offerings. Thus, for the short film at least, the popular short story offered an existing model to be emulated.

The feature film, on the other hand, offered a more expensive, often lengthier evening's entertainment, one directly comparable to that offered by a play, and entrepreneurs showed early features in legitimate theaters with prices based upon live-drama admissions. The situation in the theater industry of the early teens gave film a competitive advantage and probably fostered the industry's move into features during that period. That advantage derived from the organization of the theatrical business around the turn of the century.

The legitimate theater in the early years of this century operated as a cluster of touring troupes, controlled by a small number of entrepreneurs centralized in New York. This centralized touring system had replaced the country's earlier theatrical organization, the individual local professional repertory company, around 1870. Theater historian Jack Poggi sums up the changes in the theater industry:[19]

> What to the American theater after 1870 was not very different from what happened to many other industries. First, a centralized production system replaced many local, isolated units. Second, there was a division of labor, as theater managing became separate from play producing. Third, there was a standardization of product, as each play was represented by only one company or by a number of duplicate companies. Fourth, there was a growth of control by big business.

The characteristics which Poggi lists have obvious parallels to the development of the film industry as described in Part Two. Film was able to compete successfully with legitimate drama because it provided a more efficient, more centralized system for staging a performance only once, recording it, and reproducing it for the mass audience with minimal transportation costs.[20] Because of its success in competing with the drama, the film industry was able to standardize the multiple-reel feature, which in turn encouraged the move to a classical continuity system. But again, in order to compete with the drama for its audience, filmmakers realized the necessity of raising the quality of their offerings.

To a considerable extent, raising the quality of films to attract consumers of short fiction, novels, and plays required drawing directly or indirectly upon these other arts. Chapter 12 has shown that the film companies did this by adapting plays, stories, and novels. So for sources of subject matter, films turned definitively away from vaudeville skits. Producers also wanted to lure personnel, particularly established stars, away from the theater; adaptations of drama and literature, plus a general elevation of film's status among the arts, helped accomplish this.

But film drew upon these other arts in ways other than the direct appropriation of stories and personnel. The original scenarios used by the companies, whether done by their own staff writers or by freelancers, already felt the indirect impact of existing literary models. The film industry was fortunate in being able to tap a huge marketplace for popular fiction and drama. The writers working in this marketplace were often trained in popularized versions of traditional rules, and they could apply these rules to film scenarios as well.

The large freelance market for novels and short fiction had arisen only a few years before the invention of film. The development of a wide-spread native fiction had been discouraged by the lack of an international copyright law. Publishers tended to bring out editions of European novels and stories, which they could obtain without payment, rather than to pay American authors to write for them. Before 1891, when an international copyright law took effect, there had been only a very limited output of American short stories.[21] From about 1824 into the 1840s, literary annuals, ladies' magazines, and later gentlemen's magazines, fostered a brief flowering of the tale or sketch; these were generally considered hack work, although at their best such periodicals brought out the works of Hawthorne, Irving, and Poe. The 1850s were a fallow period for short fiction, but the tremendous commercial successes in America of Dickens's novels and of Stowe's *Uncle Tom's Cabin* (1852) marked the rise of the popular novel in America. With the founding during the 1860s of *The Atlantic Monthly* and *The Nation*, short fiction became increasingly respectable, and by the mid-1880s, the writing of short stories was becoming lucrative. The number of writers increased steadily.[22]

After the new international copyright law of 1891, popular fiction underwent a huge growth. Brander Matthews, a leading critic of the period, commented in 1898:

> This is perhaps the most striking fact in the history of the literature of the nineteenth century—this immense vogue of the novel and of the short story. Fiction fills our monthly magazines, and it is piled high on the counters of our bookstores.[23]

Novels were relatively easy to sell but took more time to write. Also, short stories were so popular at the time that a payment for a single story often was as great as the total royalties on a novel. For the vast number of part-time or casual writers, the short story proved attractive. By the late 1890s, there were so many weekly magazines and newspaper supplements that the writing of short stories could be considered an industry. And by 1900, syndicates existed to write, buy, and sell stories.[24]

There were also freelance playwrights, although this market was much smaller. A writer could not sell a play nearly so easily as a piece of fiction; the financial rewards, however, were potentially greater.[25]

Although there is far more pecuniary profit to the author from a successful play than from the average successful novel, and although in some countries, notably in France, the authorship of a play brings more instant personal recognition, playwriting demands a long and arduous period of apprenticeship. Even after years of familiarity with technical stagecraft, it is far more difficult to get a manuscript play accepted than it is to secure publication for a manuscript novel. Most authors choose, or are forced to follow, the easier path.

Authors could mail plays directly to managers or to stars, but many worked through agents. Chances of a sale were relatively slim. One 1915 playwriting manual described how an author could expect to wait while his or her manuscript languished for months on a manager's shelf.[26] Once a playwright succeeded in getting one play produced, however, she or he usually would be considered a professional, receiving reasonably high, regular royalties. There was also a small market for freelance writers of vaudeville playlets.[27] Again, the procedure involved royalties rather than outright sales.

The film industry entered the literary market in part by hiring established writers and in part by inviting submissions of synopses and scenarios. Staff writers and scenario editors came to the studios from a variety of backgrounds, but the most common previous occupations were journalism and popular-fiction writing. Journalists were presumably well-suited to the task because they had professional experience in writing and editing synoptic narratives. A trade journal noted in 1916:

> The best school for the would-be photoplay writer is the newspaper office. Many who were formerly newspaper men are now successful as writers for the silent drama. They know life, a good story, and the value of a gripping situation.[28]

Edward Azlant's examination of screenwriting before 1920 discusses several dozen prominent scenarists at the studios.[29] The largest number of this group came from journalism, followed by magazine-fiction writing, novel writing, and playwriting. These divisions are not hard and fast, however. Many writers worked in several or all of these fields. Given the huge, lucrative freelance story market, few writers of any type failed to submit something to the magazines. Reporters, copy readers and editors working for magazines and newspapers wrote short stories. (Stephen Crane, Edna Ferber, Willa Cather, James Cabell, Irwin Cobb, and Sinclair Lewis were among those who got their starts this way.)[30] Writers who worked at the studios or sent in their freelance efforts would usually have some experience with the popular fiction forms of the period.

Historians have dealt extensively with the impact of the drama and the novel on film form and style.[31] The concomitant influence of the short story, however, has been largely overlooked. An examination of the close relations between the freelance short story and scenario markets will demonstrate some of the conditions which encouraged narrative principles from all of these arts to enter the cinema.

In order to make narrative films on a regular, efficient basis, producers began to use the detailed division of labor described in Part Two. Narrative filmmaking necessitated a steady source of stories, a need which eventually resulted in the scenario staff. These workers performed specialized tasks: among other things, they wrote many of the original stories used and read the freelance synopses or scenario-scripts submitted to the studio. Chapter 12 has suggested that the heyday of the amateur scenarist was actually brief (from about 1907 to 1914), but these were important years in the transition from primitive to classical filmmaking. Vast changes took place in ideas about how a narrative film should be constructed. The backgrounds of both studio and freelance writers, as well as the normative advice they received, helped shape those ideas.

By 1910, the methods of obtaining stories for purposes resembled those of the popular fiction magazines, which, as we have seen, had become popular in the 1890s. The prominent *Black Cat* magazine, for instance, started a trend toward using contests to encourage submissions of short stories. Motion-picture companies followed this strategy, and there were scenario contests conducted through the trade journals in the early teens.

Whether encouraged by prizes or by flat-fee purchases, amateur and professional freelance writers flooded the studios with scenarios. Usual estimates in the trade journals and scenario guides suggest that only about one in a hundred scripts was actually accepted, and scenario editors frequently complained about the poor quality of the material they had to plow through. Very quickly, the studios' dependence on such submissions declined. By 1912, copyright problems and the expanding production of multiple-reel films made unsolicited stories less attractive; contract writers in scenario departments proved a more reliable, efficient source, and the most promising freelancers could be hired. Amateur scenarios were used almost exclusively for one- or two-reel films, the production of which declined as the feature became the standard basis for production in the mid-teens.

Little direct evidence indicates what proportion of the freelance material came from writers who had also tried their hand at short stories. Few films of this period credited their scenarists. But some indirect evidence suggests the importance of popular short fiction as a model for film narrative. For one thing, some of the books on how to write scenarios of the period came from authors who also provided advice on short-story writing.[32] In addition, a few major scenarists of the time have recalled their beginnings as short-story freelancers. Frances Marion wrote fiction until requests for the screen rights to her stories led her to try doing scenarios; she eventually became a staff writer for several West Coast companies. Clifford Howard, who later became scenario editor for the Balboa and the American companies, wrote of having turned his outlines for short-story plots into scenarios when he heard how easy they were to sell. Others who had written short stories (usually in addition to work in other prose or dramatic forms) include: Roy L. McCardell, Lloyd Lonergan, Emmett Campbell Hall, Epes Winthrop Sargent, James Oliver Curwood, Eustace Hale Ball, Mary H. O'Connor, Beulah Marie Dix, and Clare Beranger.[33] There were undoubtedly others, but most freelancers remained anonymous, and their backgrounds are now untraceable. At least some, however, had learned their craft from magazine freelancing, rather than from the stage.

Most explicitly, trade journals recognized a parallel between the scenario and popular short-story markets. These comparisons tend to come a little later in the period, during the middle and late teens, but they indicate an awareness that writers were often working for both markets. By about 1915 the industry began to realize that it was competing with the popular fiction magazines for good stories. *Motography* noted in early 1915:

> An able and recognized short story writer can command from five to ten cents a word for his manuscript. To such a writer an average short story of three thousand words brings a check for one hundred to three hundred dollars.

The article contrasted this with the average payment for a scenario, which ranged well below $100, and pointed out that 'at present the short story writer is only tempted to submit something made over from an oft-rejected story manuscript.' The author concluded:

> The film producers can afford to pay better prices than the magazines. Encourage the writer to try his ideas in scenario form first; he can make over his rejected scenarios into magazine articles as easily as he can do the opposite.[34]

A *Motion Picture News* editorial pointed out that fiction magazines attracted a large middle-class audience and educated it to appreciate good stories:[35]

> They are sharp critics, these readers. They want pictures up to their established fiction standards.
>
>   It is regrettable, but it is a fact, that up to a few years ago, the large percentage of pictures released were of the same ordinary adventurous or sentimental or funny character of the fiction in our popular publications of *thirty years* ago.
>
>   What is to be done then to get good stories?
>
>   Simply this: Pay the price. ...
>
>   Go directly to the best magazine writers and get their work by *paying at least what the magazine will pay.*

Throughout 1915 and into 1916, similar articles in the trade press called for the producers to raise their fee for scenarios, to attract something beyond the leavings of the fiction magazines.[36]

The possibility for influence from the short story, then, came in part from the contact with writers who sold stories in both the magazine and film markets. In addition, many of the writers who were employed as permanent staff members came from a similar background. Along with the novel and the drama, the short story provided classical models upon which the early film could draw.

■ ■ ■

Questions and projects

1. Investigate the social or economic "conditions of influence" at a specific point in history between the film industry and the world of literary publications or theatrical productions.
2. Compare a work of literature from one period to its adaptation in another period to show how different historical conditions for the production and reception of those works can alter or determine their meanings.

Notes

18 'The Weakness of the strong,' *MPN*, 11, no. 1 (9 January 1915): 29.

19 Jack Poggi, *Theater in America: The Impact of Economic Forces 1870–1967* (New York: Cornell University Press, 1968), p. 26.

20 The touring theater company, the touring vaudeville act, and the film can all be seen as ways of distributing a theatrical entertainment to a farflung mass audience. ... See *ibid.*, pp. 6, 78, 36.

21 C. Alphonso Smith, *The American Short Story* (Boston, MA: Ginn & Co., 1912), p. 39; Fred Lewis Pattee, *The Development of the American Short Story* (New York: Harper & Bros, 1923), pp. 81, 130.

22 Pattee, *The Development of the American Short Story*, pp. 31, 70–5, 145, 150, 167, 191, 310.

23 Brander Matthews, 'The study of fiction,' [1898], in his *The Historical Novel and Other Essays* (New York: Charles Scribner's Sons, 1901), p. 81.

24 Bliss Perry, *A Study of Prose Fiction* (Boston/New York: Houghton, Mifflin & Co., 1902), p. 330; Pattee, *The Development of the American Short Story*, p. 337.

25 Perry, *A Study of Prose Fiction*, p. 65.

26 Charlton Andrews, *The Technique of Play Writing* (Springfield, MA: Home Correspondence School, 1915), p. 230.

27 At least one book-length guide appeared to dispense advice on writing playlets and other vaudeville forms: Page's *Writing for Vaudeville.*

28 Gilson Willets [Selig staff writer], 'Photoplay writing not an easy art,' *Motography*, 16, no. 14 (30 September 1916): 763.

29 Edward Azlant, 'The theory, history, and practice of screenwriting, 1897–1920' (PhD dissertation, University of Wisconsin, 1980).

30 Pattee, *The Development of the American Short Story*, p. 337.

31 Concentration on film and the nineteenth-century novel ... stemm[ed] primarily from Colin MacCabe's 'Realism and the cinema: notes on some Brechtian theses,' *Screen*, 15, no. 2 (Summer 1974): 7–27. In *Film and the Narrative Tradition* (Norman, OK: University of Oklahoma Press, 1974), John L. Fell relates early film to a variety of nineteenth-century narrative arts.

32 Besides his manuals on *The Photodrama* ... and *The Feature Photoplay,* ... Henry Albert Phillips also authored *The Plot of the Short Story* and *Art in Short Story Narration.* ... J. Berg Esenwein was editor of the Home Correspondence School's 'Writer's Library.' In addition to coauthoring *Writing the Photo-*

play, … he contributed many works on short fiction to the series.

33   'Film stories change rapidly,' *Motography*, 18, no. 16 (20 December 1917): 813; Clifford Howard, 'The cinema in retrospect,' *Close Up*, 3, no. 5 (November 1928): 18; Azlant, *The Theory, History, and Practice of Screenwriting.*

34   'The need for more originality,' *Motography*, 13, no. 5 (30 January 1915): 167.

35   William A. Johnston, 'About stories,' *MPN*, 11, no. 21 (29 May 1915): 35. Emphases in original.

36   See also, 'The story writers' opportunity,' *Motography*, 14, no. 20 (13 November 1915): 1025; 'The weakness of the strong,' *MPN*, 11, no. 1 (9 January, 1915): 29, 48.

Chapter 14

Hugo Münsterberg

THE MEANS OF PHOTOPLAY

I F LINDSAY WAS PRIMARILY INTERESTED in the social force of movies as it advanced the spirit of traditional literature, Münsterberg, writing at about the same time (1916), approached the film/literature debate from a very different point of view: using a psychology and aesthetics of perception, he investigates how film organizes human experience in a way that distinguishes it from other artistic and literary forms. For him, that unique organization is a function of film's intimate access to an internal movement and a psychological space that other literatures can only approach or describe. With these more abstract matters addressed in the first part of his book, he turns in the second part to a discussion of film as an art form distinguished from traditional literature and art. One of the significant historical points about the following excerpt from *The Film: A Psychological Study* is that it practices film criticism and theory as rigorously as academic philosophy and social sciences, employing an interdisciplinary approach that assumes from the start that film is as complex as literature and theater. If Lindsay draws the debate about film and literature into a social arena, Münsterberg delineates a psychological aesthetic that would become, despite his archaic description of film as a "photoplay," a rich framework for discussion of the illusory forms of the art cinema—of German Expressionism, French Surrealism, and others—that flourished from 1917 to 1930.

■ ■ ■

THE MEANS OF PHOTOPLAY
HUGO MÜNSTERBERG

From *The Film: A Psychological Study*, New York: Dover Publications, 1970, pp 253–271.

We have now reached the point at which we can knot together all our threads, the psychological and the esthetic ones. If we do so, we come to the true thesis of this whole book. Our esthetic discussion showed us that it is the aim of art to isolate a significant part of our experience in such a way that it is separate from our practical life and is in complete agreement within itself. Our esthetic satisfaction results from this inner agreement and harmony, but in order that we may feel such agreement of the parts we must enter with our own impulses into the will of every element, into the meaning of every line and color and form, every word and tone and note. Only if everything is full of such inner movement can we really enjoy the harmonious coöperation of the parts. The means of the various arts, we saw, are the forms and methods by which this aim is fulfilled. They must be different for every material. Moreover the same material may allow very different methods of isolation and elimination of the insignificant and reënforcement of that which contributes to the harmony. If we ask now what are the characteristic means by which the photoplay succeeds in overcoming reality, in isolating a significant dramatic story and in presenting it so that we enter into it and yet keep it away from our practical life and enjoy the harmony of the parts, we must remember all the results to which our psychological discussion in the first part of the book has led us.

We recognized there that the photoplay, incomparable in this respect with the drama, gave us a view of dramatic events which was completely shaped by the inner movements of the mind. To be sure, the events in the photoplay happen in the real space with its depth. But the spectator feels that they are not presented in the three dimensions of the outer world, that they are flat pictures which only the mind molds into plastic things. Again the events are seen in continuous movement; and yet the pictures break up the movement into a rapid succession of instantaneous impressions. We do not see the objective reality, but a product of our own mind which binds the pictures together. But much stronger differences came to light when we turned to the processes of attention, of memory, of imagination, of suggestion, of division of interest and of emotion. The attention turns to detailed points in the outer world and ignores everything else: the photoplay is doing exactly this when in the close-up a detail is enlarged and everything else disappears. Memory breaks into present events by bringing up pictures of the past: the photoplay is doing this by its frequent cut-backs, when pictures of events long past flit between those of the present. The imagination anticipates the future or overcomes reality by fancies and dreams; the photoplay is doing all this more richly than any chance imagination would succeed in doing. But chiefly, through our division of interest our mind is drawn hither and thither. We think of events which run parallel in different places. The photoplay can show in intertwined scenes everything which our mind embraces. Events in three or four or five regions of the world can be woven together into one complex action. Finally, we saw that every shade of feeling and emotion which fills the spectator's mind can mold the scenes in the photoplay until they appear the embodiment of our feelings. In every one of these aspects the photoplay succeeds in doing what the drama of the theater does not attempt.

If this is the outcome of esthetic analysis on the one side, of psychological research on the other, we need only combine the results of both into a unified principle: *the photoplay tells us the human story by overcoming the forms of the outer world, namely, space, time, and causality, and by adjusting the events to the forms of the inner world, namely, attention, memory, imagination, and emotion.*

We shall gain our orientation most directly if once more, under this point of view, we compare the photoplay with the performance on the theater stage. We shall not enter into a discussion of the character of the regular theater and its drama. We take this for granted. Everybody knows that highest art form which the Greeks created and which from Greece has spread over Asia, Europe, and America. In tragedy and in comedy from ancient times to Ibsen, Rostand, Hauptmann, and Shaw we recognize one common purpose and one common form for which no further commentary is needed. How does the photoplay differ from a theater performance? We insisted that every work of art must be somehow separated from our sphere of practical interests. The theater is no exception. The structure of the theater itself, the framelike form of the stage, the difference of light between stage and house, the stage setting and costuming, all inhibit in the audience the possibility of taking the action on the stage to be real life. Stage managers have sometimes tried the experiment of reducing those differences, for instance, keeping the audience also in a fully lighted hall, and they always had to discover how much the dramatic effect was reduced because the feeling of distance from reality was weakened. The photoplay and the theater in this respect are evidently alike. The screen too suggests from the very start the complete unreality of the events.

But each further step leads us to remarkable differences between the stage play and the film play. In every respect the film play is further away from the physical reality than the drama and in every respect this greater distance from the physical world brings it nearer to the mental world. The stage shows us living men. It is not the real Romeo and not the real Juliet; and yet the actor and the actress have the ringing voices of true people, breathe like them, have living colors like them, and fill physical space like them. What is left in the photoplay? The voice has been stilled: the photoplay is a dumb show. Yet we must not forget that this alone is a step away from reality which has often been taken in the midst of the dramatic world. Whoever knows the history of the theater is aware of the tremendous rôle which the pantomime has played in the development of mankind. From the old half-religious pantomimic and suggestive dances out of which the beginnings of the real drama grew to the fully religious pantomimes of medieval ages and, further on, to many silent mimic elements in modern performances, we find a continuity of conventions which make the pantomime almost the real background of all dramatic development. We know how popular the pantomimes were among the Greeks, and how they stood in the foreground in the imperial period of Rome. Old Rome cherished the mimic clowns, but still more the tragic pantomimics. "Their very nod speaks, their hands talk and their fingers have a voice." After the fall of the Roman empire the church used the pantomime for the portrayal of sacred history, and later centuries enjoyed very unsacred histories in the pantomimes of their ballets. Even complex artistic tragedies without words have triumphed on our present-day stage. *L'Enfant Prodigue* which came from Paris, *Sumurun* which came from Berlin, *Petroushka* which came from Petrograd, conquered the American stage; and surely the loss of speech, while it increased the remoteness from reality, by no means destroyed the continuous consciousness of the bodily existence of the actors.

Moreover the student of a modern pantomime cannot overlook a characteristic difference between the speechless performance on the stage and that of the actors of a photoplay. The expression of the inner states, the whole system of gestures, is decidedly different: and here we might say that the photoplay stands nearer to life than the pantomime. Of course, the photoplayer must somewhat exaggerate the natural expression. The whole rhythm and intensity of his gestures must be more marked than it would be with actors who accompany their movements by spoken words and who express the meaning of their thoughts and feelings by the content of what they say. Nevertheless the photoplayer uses the regular channels of mental discharge. He acts simply as a very emotional person might act. But the actor who plays in a pantomime cannot be satisfied with that. He is expected to add something which is entirely unnatural, namely a kind of artificial demonstration of his emotions. He must not only behave like an angry man, but he must behave like a man who is consciously interested in his anger and wants to demonstrate it to others. He exhibits his emotions for the spectators. He really acts theatrically for the benefit of the bystanders. If he did not try to do so, his means of conveying a rich story and a real conflict of human passions would be too meager. The photoplayer, with the rapid changes of scenes, has other possibilities of conveying his intentions. He must not yield to the temptation to play a pantomime on the screen, or he will seriously injure the artistic quality of the reel.

The really decisive distance from bodily reality, however, is created by the substitution of the actor's picture for the actor himself. Lights and shades replace the manifoldness of color effects and mere perspective must furnish the suggestion of depth. We traced it when we discussed the psychology of kinematoscopic perception. But we must not put the emphasis on the wrong point. The natural tendency might be to lay the chief stress on the fact that those people in the photoplay do not stand before us in flesh and blood. The essential point is rather that we are conscious of the flatness of the picture. If we were to see the actors of the stage in a mirror, it would also be a reflected image which we perceive. We should not really have the actors themselves in our straight line of vision; and yet this image would appear to us equivalent to the actors themselves, because it would contain all the depth of the real stage. The film picture is such a reflected rendering of the actors. The process which leads from the living men to the screen is more complex than a mere reflection in a mirror, but in spite of the complexity in the transmission we do, after all, see the real actor in the picture. The photograph is absolutely different from those pictures which a clever draughtsman has sketched. In the photoplay we see the actors themselves and the decisive factor which makes the impression different from seeing real men is not that we see the living persons through the medium of photographic reproduction but that this reproduction shows them in a flat form. The bodily space has been eliminated. We said once before that stereoscopic arrangements could reproduce somewhat this plastic form also. Yet this would seriously interfere with the character of the photoplay. We need there this overcoming of the depth, we want to have it as a picture only and yet as a picture which strongly suggests to us the actual depth of the real world. We want to keep the interest in the plastic world and want to be aware of the depth in which the persons move, but our direct object of perception must be without the depth. That idea of space which forces on us most strongly the idea of heaviness, solidity and substantiality must be replaced by the light flitting immateriality.

But the photoplay sacrifices not only the space values of the real theater; it disregards no less its order of time. The theater presents its plot in the time order of reality. It may interrupt the continuous flow of time without neglecting the conditions of the dramatic art. There may be twenty years between the third and the fourth act, inasmuch as the dramatic writer must select those elements spread over space and time which are significant for the development of his story. But he is bound by the fundamental principle of real time, that it can move only forward and not backward. Whatever the theater shows us now must come later in the story than that which it showed us in any previous moment. The strict classical demand for complete unity of time does not fit every drama, but a drama would give up its mission if it told us in the third act something which happened before the second act. Of course, there may be a play within a play, and the players on the stage which is set on the stage may play events of old Roman history before the king of France. But this is an enclosure of the past in the present, which corresponds exactly to the actual order of events. The photoplay, on the other hand, does not and must not respect this temporal structure of the physical universe. At any point the photoplay interrupts the series and brings us back to the past. We studied this unique feature of the film art when we spoke of the psychology of memory and imagination. With the full freedom of our fancy, with the whole mobility of our association of ideas, pictures of the past flit through the scenes of the present. Time is left behind. Man becomes boy; today is interwoven with the day before yesterday. The freedom of the mind has triumphed over the unalterable law of the outer world.

It is interesting to watch how playwrights nowadays try to steal the thunder of the photoplay and experiment with time reversals on the legitimate stage. We are esthetically on the borderland when a grandfather tells his grandchild the story of his own youth as a warning, and instead of the spoken words the events of his early years come before our eyes. This is, after all, quite similar to a play within a play. A very different experiment is tried in *Under Cover*. The third act, which plays on the second floor of the house, ends with an explosion. The fourth act, which plays downstairs, begins a quarter of an hour before the explosion. Here we have a real denial of a fundamental condition of the theater. Or if we stick to recent products of the American stage, we may think of *On Trial*, a play which perhaps comes nearest to a dramatic usurpation of the rights of the photoplay. We see the court scene and as one witness after another begins to give his testimony the courtroom is replaced by the scenes of the actions about which the witness is to report. Another clever play, *Between the Lines*, ends the first act with a postman bringing three letters from the three children of the house. The second, third, and fourth acts lead us to the three different homes from which the letters came and the action in the three places not only precedes the writing of the letters, but goes on at the same time. The last act, finally, begins with the arrival of the letters which tell the ending of those events in the three homes. Such experiments are very suggestive but they are not any longer pure dramatic art. It is always possible to mix arts. An Italian painter produces very striking effects by putting pieces of glass and stone and rope into his paintings, but they are no longer pure paintings. The drama in which the later event comes before the earlier is an esthetic barbarism which is entertaining as a clever trick in a graceful superficial play, but intolerable in ambitious dramatic art. It is not only tolerable but perfectly natural in any photoplay. The pictorial reflection of the world is not bound by the rigid mechanism of time. Our mind is here and there, our mind turns to the present and then to the past: the photoplay can equal it in its freedom from the bondage of the material world.

But the theater is bound not only by space and time. Whatever it shows is controlled by the same laws of causality which govern nature. This involves a complete continuity of the physical events: no cause without following effect, no effect without preceding cause. This whole natural course is left behind in the play on the screen. The deviation from reality begins with that resolution of the continuous movement which we studied in our psychological discussions. We saw that the impression of movement results from an activity of the mind which binds the separate pictures together. What we actually see is a composite; it is like the movement of a fountain in which every jet is resolved into numberless drops. We feel the play of those drops in their sparkling haste as one continuous stream of water, and yet are conscious of the myriads of drops, each one separate from the others. This fountainlike spray of pictures has completely overcome the causal world.

In an entirely different form this triumph over causality appears in the interruption of the events by pictures which belong to another series. We find this whenever the scene suddenly changes. The processes are not carried to their natural consequences. A movement is started, but before the cause brings its results another scene has taken its place. What this new scene brings may be an effect for which we saw no causes. But not only the processes are interrupted. The intertwining of the scenes which we have traced in detail is itself such a contrast to causality. It is as if different objects could fill the same space at the same time. It is as if the resistance of the material world had disappeared and the substances could penetrate one another. In the interlacing of our ideas we experience this superiority to all physical laws. The theater would not have even the technical means to give us such impressions, but if it had, it would have no right to make use of them, as it would destroy the basis on which the drama is built. We have only another case of the same type in those series of pictures which aim to force a suggestion on our mind. We have spoken of them. A certain effect is prepared by a chain of causes and yet when the causal result is to appear the film is cut off. We have the causes without the effect. The villain thrusts with his dagger—but a miracle has snatched away his victim.

While the moving pictures are lifted above the world of space and time and causality and are freed from its bounds, they are certainly not without law. We said before that the freedom with which the pictures replace one another is to a large degree comparable to the sparkling and streaming of the musical tones. The yielding to the play of the mental energies, to the attention and emotion, which is felt in the film pictures, is still more complete in the musical melodies and harmonies in which the tones themselves are merely the expressions of the ideas and feelings and will impulses of the mind. Their harmonies and disharmonies, their fusing and blending, is not controlled by any outer necessity, but by the inner agreement and disagreement of our free impulses. And yet in this world of musical freedom, everything is completely controlled by esthetic necessities. No sphere of practical life stands under such rigid rules as the realm of the composer. However bold the musical genius may be he cannot emancipate himself from the iron rule that his work must show complete unity in itself. All the separate prescriptions which the musical student has to learn are ultimately only the consequences of this central demand which music, the freest of the arts, shares with all the others. In the case of the film, too, the freedom from the physical forms of space, time, and causality does not mean any liberation from this esthetic bondage either. On the contrary, just as music is surrounded by more technical rules than literature, the photoplay must be held together by the esthetic demands still more firmly than is the drama. The arts which are subordinated to the conditions of space, time, and causality find a certain firmness of structure in these material forms which contain an element of outer connectedness. But where these forms are given up and where the freedom of mental play replaces their outer necessity, everything would fall asunder if the esthetic unity were disregarded.

This unity is, first of all, the unity of action. The demand for it is the same which we know from the drama. The temptation to neglect it is nowhere greater than in the photoplay where outside matter can so easily be introduced or independent interests developed. It is certainly true for the photoplay, as for every work of art, that nothing has the right to existence in its midst which is not internally needed for the unfolding of the unified action. Wherever two plots are given to us, we receive less by far than if we had only one plot. We leave the sphere of valuable art entirely when a unified action is ruined by mixing it with declamation, and propaganda which is not organically interwoven with the action itself. It may be still fresh in memory what an esthetically intolerable helter-skelter performance was offered to the public in *The Battlecry of Peace.* Nothing can be more injurious to the esthetic cultivation of the people than such performances which hold the attention of the spectators by ambitious detail and yet destroy their esthetic sensibility by a complete disregard of the fundamental principle of art, the demand for unity. But we recognized also that this unity involves complete isolation. We annihilate beauty when we link the artistic creation with practical interests and transform the spectator into a selfishly interested bystander. The scenic background of the play is not presented in order that we decide whether we want to spend our next vacation there. The interior decoration of the rooms is not exhibited as a display for a department store. The men and women who carry out the action of the plot must not be people whom we may meet tomorrow on the street. All the threads of the play must be knotted together in the play itself and none should be connected with our outside interests. A good photoplay must be isolated and complete in itself like a beautiful melody. It is not an advertisement for the newest fashions.

This unity of action involves unity of characters. It has too often been maintained by those who theorize on the photoplay that the development of character is the special task of the drama, while the photoplay, which lacks words, must be satisfied with types. Probably this is only a reflection of the crude state which most photoplays of today have not outgrown. Internally, there is no reason why the means of the photoplay should not allow a rather subtle depicting of complex character. But the chief demand is that the characters remain consistent, that the action be developed according to inner necessity and that the characters themselves be in harmony with the central idea of the plot. However, as soon as we insist on unity we have no right to think only of the action which gives the content of the play. We cannot make light of the form. As in music the melody and rhythms belong together, as in painting not every color combination suits every subject, and as in poetry not every stanza would agree with every idea, so the photoplay must bring action and pictorial expression into perfect harmony. But this demand repeats itself in every single picture. We take it for granted that the painter balances perfectly the forms in his painting, groups them so that an internal symmetry can be felt and that the lines and curves and colors blend into a unity. Every single picture of the sixteen thousand which are shown to us in one reel ought to be treated with this respect of the pictorial artist for the unity of the forms.

The photoplay shows us a significant conflict of human actions in moving pictures which, freed from the physical forms of space, time, and causality, are adjusted to the free play of our mental experiences and which reach complete isolation from the practical world through the perfect unity of plot and pictorial appearance.

■ ■ ■

Questions and projects

1. Choose a film made between 1900 and 1925 (perhaps F. W Murnau's *Nosferatu* [1922] or *The Last Laugh* [1924] or an early Fritz Lang movie) and a work of literature written about the same time (August Strindberg's play *The Ghost Sonata*, the prose fiction of James Joyce, or a poem by T. S. Eliot, for example) that best demonstrates or that best refutes Münsterberg's position about the different capacities of film and literature to represent psychological experiences.

2. Select a novel or other work of literature and demonstrate how it attempts to approximate psychological experiences as they are shown on film. To what extent do literary techniques such as "stream of consciousness" validate Münsterberg's argument about the psychological limitations of literature and advantages of film? Are there psychological experiences that literature can represent that the movies cannot?

Chapter 15

Sergei Eisenstein

DICKENS, GRIFFITH, AND THE FILM TODAY

AFTER DECADES OF ARGUMENTS about what distinguishes film as an art form, this 1944 essay by Russian filmmaker Eisenstein (director of *The Battleship Potemkin* [1925], *Alexander Nevsky* [1938], and other films) reclaims the crucial connections between literature and film but only as films create an historical and critical engagement with their literary forerunners. He specifically credits the novels of Charles Dickens as anticipating the editing methods that Griffith transposed to film—which he calls montage. Yet, keeping with the general trends of the 1940s, Eisenstein's historical perspective on the connections is more complex than arguments about what film shares with literature or how it differs from literature. He is quick to argue that film evolves from the social and industrial traditions that redefined space and time for the individual in the nineteenth century, but for him—as he argues in other sections of this essay—film offers possibilities of moving beyond the heritage of Western individualism shared by Dickens and Griffith and, through montage, of creating the new, more liberating visions of the individual in society.

■ ■ ■

DICKENS, GRIFFITH, AND THE FILM TODAY
SERGEI EISENSTEIN

From *Film Form*, trans. Jay Leyda, New York: Harcourt Brace, 1947, pp. 195, 198–201, 204–213, and 232–233

What were the novels of Dickens for his contemporaries, for his readers? There is one answer: they bore the same relation to them that the film bears to the same strata in our time. They compelled the reader to live with the same passions. They appealed to the same good and sentimental elements as does the film (at least on the surface); they alike shudder before vice, they alike mill the extraordinary, the unusual, the fantastic, from boring, prosaic and everyday existence. And they clothe this common and prosaic existence in their special vision.

Illumined by this light, refracted from the land of fiction back to life, this commonness took on a romantic air, and bored people were grateful to the author for giving them the countenances of potentially romantic figures.

...

Perhaps the secret lies in Dickens's (as well as cinema's) creation of an extraordinary plasticity. The observation in the novels is extraordinary—as is their optical quality. The characters of Dickens are rounded with means as plastic and slightly exaggerated as are the screen heroes of today. The screen's heroes are engraved on the senses of the spectator with clearly visible traits, its villains are remembered by certain facial expressions, and all are saturated in the peculiar, slightly unnatural radiant gleam thrown over them by the screen.

It is absolutely thus that Dickens draws his characters—this is the faultlessly plastically grasped and pitilessly sharply sketched gallery of immortal Pickwicks, Dombeys, Fagins, Tackletons, and others.

...

We can see for ourselves that his descriptions offer not only absolute accuracy *of detail*, but also an absolutely *accurate drawing of the behavior* and actions of his characters. And this is just as true for the most trifling details of behavior—even gesture, as it is for the basic generalized characteristics of the image. Isn't this piece of description of Mr. Dombey's behavior actually an exhaustive regisseur-actor directive?

> He had already laid his hand upon the bell-rope to convey his usual summons to Richards, when his eye fell upon a writing-desk, belonging to his deceased wife, which had been taken, among other things, from a cabinet in her chamber. It was not the first time that his eye had lighted on it. He carried the key in his pocket; and he brought it to his table and opened it now—having previously locked the room door—with a well-accustomed hand.

Here the last phrase arrests one's attention: there is a certain awkwardness in its description. However, this "inserted" phrase: *having previously locked the room door*, "fitted in" as if recollected by the author in the middle of a later phrase, instead of being placed where it apparently should have been, in the consecutive order of the description, that is, before the words, *and he brought it to his table*, is found exactly at this spot for quite *un*fortuitous reasons.

In this deliberate "montage" displacement of the time-continuity of the description there is a brilliantly caught rendering of the *transient thievery* of the action, slipped between the preliminary action and the act of reading another's letter, carried out with that absolute "correctness" of gentlemanly dignity which Mr. Dombey knows how to give to any behavior or action of his.

...

I don't know how my readers feel about this, but for me personally it is always pleasing to recognize again and again the fact that our cinema is not altogether without parents and without pedigree, without a past, without the traditions and rich cultural heritage of the past epochs. It is only very thoughtless and presumptuous people who can erect laws and an esthetic for cinema, proceeding from premises of some incredible virgin-birth of this art!

Let Dickens and the whole ancestral array, going back as far as the Greeks and Shakespeare, be superfluous reminders that both Griffith and our cinema prove our origins to be not solely as of Edison and his fellow inventors, but as based on an enormous cultured past; each part of this past in its own moment of world history has moved forward the great art of cinematography. Let this past be a reproach to those thoughtless people who have displayed arrogance in reference to literature, which has contributed so much to this apparently unprecedented art and is, in the first and most important place: the art of viewing—not only the *eye*, but *viewing*—both meanings being embraced in this term.

This esthetic growth from the *cinematographic eye* to the *image of an embodied viewpoint on phenomena* was one of the most serious processes of development of our Soviet cinema in particular; our cinema also played a tremendous rôle in the history of the development of world cinema as a whole, and it was no small rôle that was played by a basic understanding of the principles of film-montage, which became so characteristic for the Soviet school of film-making.

None the less enormous was the rôle of Griffith also in the evolution of the system of Soviet montage: a rôle as enormous as the rôle of Dickens in forming the methods of Griffith. Dickens in this respect played an enormous rôle in heightening the tradition and cultural heritage of preceding epochs; just as on an even higher level we can see the enormous rôle of those social premises, which inevitably in those pivotal moments of history ever anew push elements of the montage method into the center of attention for creative work.

■ ■ ■

Questions and projects

1. Analyze in detail how a specific literary work (say, from another Victorian novel like Thackeray's *Vanity Fair*) and a specific film (say, Rouben Mamoulian's 1935 version of the novel retitled as *Becky Sharp*) juxtapose and contrast images or scenes. Do these juxtapositions correspond to Eisenstein's model of montage? Or is there some other, more appropriate way to describe the logic and ideas behind how these works construct and edit actions, images, and scenes?

2. Besides montage and editing techniques, which other film forms have their sources in literature (or vice versa)? Voice-over narration? Chapter breaks? Narrative frames? Examine a film that may self-consciously use one of these literary techniques (such as Kenneth Branagh's use of a narrative frame in his 1994 *Mary Shelley's Frankenstein*). What is gained and what is lost?

Chapter 16

Walter Benjamin

THE WORK OF ART IN THE AGE OF ITS TECHNOLOGICAL REPRODUCIBILITY

WRITTEN IN 1935, BENJAMIN'S "The Work of Art in the Age of its Technological Reproducibility" is one of the most widely cited and quoted essays in studies of film and studies of twentieth-century aesthetics. The reasons are many, but for students of the relationship between film and literature, this essay is especially central as it combines and extends some of the ideas introduced by Lindsay and Münsterberg: namely, that film offers a radical social relationship with modern audiences and this new relationship—supported by the technological differences of the cinema—is decidedly different from the one implied in classical art and literature. Literature itself is not discussed in much detail in this excerpt; Benjamin provides only suggestive remarks about the French poet Stéphane Mallarmé, Italian playwright Luigi Pirandello, Max Reinhardt's adaptation of *A Midsummer Night's Dream,* and the literature of Dadaism. Yet his concern with how audiences relate to and comprehend film, in what he considered a new age, opens enormously important questions about film culture versus literary culture. These questions not only reflect the changes in the 1930s in how the two arts looked at each other, but they have continued to influence debates about language, literacy, and literature/film discussions since then. Indeed, his comments on the vexed issue of "authenticity" provide a powerful starting point for arguments about adaptation.

■ ■ ■

THE WORK OF ART IN THE AGE OF ITS TECHNOLOGICAL REPRODUCIBILITY
WALTER BENJAMIN

from "The Work of Art in the Age of its Technological Reproducibility: Second Version," in *Selected Writings, vol. 3, 1935–1938,* Cambridge, MA: Belknap Press, 2008, pp. 21–34.

III

In even the most perfect reproduction, *one* thing is lacking: the here and now of the work of art—its unique existence in a particular place. It is this unique existence—and nothing else—that bears the mark of the history to which the work has been subject. This history includes changes to the physical structure of the work over time, together with any changes in ownership. Traces of the former can be detected only by chemical or physical analyses (which cannot be performed on a reproduction), while changes of ownership are part of a tradition which can be traced only from the standpoint of the original in its present location.

The here and now of the original underlies the concept of its authenticity and on the latter in turn is founded the idea of a tradition which has passed the object down as the same, identical thing to the present day. *The whole sphere of authenticity eludes technological—and of course not only technological—reproduction.* But whereas the authentic work retains its full authority in the face of a reproduction made by hand, which it generally brands a forgery, this is not the case with technological reproduction. The reason is twofold. First, technological reproduction is more independent of the original than is manual reproduction. For example, in photography it can bring out aspects of the original that are accessible only to the lens (which is adjustable and can easily change viewpoint) but not to the human eye; or it can use certain processes, such as enlargement or slow motion, to record images which escape natural optics altogether. This is the first reason. Second, technological reproduction can place the copy of the original in situations which the original itself cannot attain. Above all, it enables the original to meet the recipient halfway, whether in the form of a photograph or in that of a gramophone record. The cathedral leaves its site to be received in the studio of an art lover; the choral work performed in an auditorium or in the open air is enjoyed in a private room.

These changed circumstances may leave the artwork's other properties untouched, but they certainly devalue the here and now of the artwork. And although this can apply not only to art but (say) to a landscape moving past the spectator in a film, in the work of art this process touches on a highly sensitive core, more vulnerable than that of any natural object. That core is its authenticity. The authenticity of a thing is the quintessence of all that is transmissible in it from its origin on, ranging from its physical duration to the historical testimony relating to it. Since the historical testimony is founded on the physical duration, the former too, is jeopardized by reproduction, in which the physical duration plays no part. And what is really jeopardized when the historical testimony is affected is the authority of the object, the weight it derives from tradition. One might focus these aspects of the artwork in the concept of the aura, and go on to say: what withers in the age of the technological reproducibility of the work of art is the latter's aura. This process is symptomatic; its significance extends far beyond the realm of art. *It might be stated as a general formula, that the technology of reproduction detaches the reproduced object from the sphere of tradition. By replicating the work many times over, it substitutes a mass existence for a unique existence. And in permitting the reproduction to reach the recipient in his or her own situation, it actualizes that which is reproduced.* These two processes lead to a massive upheaval in the domain of objects handed down from the past—a shattering of tradition which is the reverse side of the present crisis and renewal of humanity. Both processes are intimately related to the mass movements of our day. Their most powerful agent is film. The social significance of film, even—and especially—in its most positive form, is inconceivable without its destructive, cathartic side: the liquidation of the value of tradition in the cultural heritage. This phenomenon is most apparent in the great historical films. It is assimilating ever more advanced positions in its spread. "When Abel Gance fervently proclaimed in 1927, "Shakespeare, Rembrandt, Beethoven will make films.... All legends, all mythologies, and all myths, all the founders of religions, indeed, all religion ... await their celluloid resurrection, and the heroes are pressing at the gates," he was inviting the reader, no doubt unawares, to witness a comprehensive liquidation.

IV

Just as the entire mode of existence of human collectives changes over long historical periods, so too does their mode of perception. The way in which human perception is organized—the medium in which it occurs—is conditioned not only by nature but by history. The era of the migration of peoples, an era which saw the rise of the late-Roman art industry and the Vienna Genesis, developed not only an art different from that of antiquity but also a different perception. The scholars of the Viennese school Riegl and Wickhoff, resisting the weight of the classical tradition beneath which this art had been buried, were the first to think of using such art to draw conclusions about the organization of perception at the time the art was produced. However far-reaching their insight, it was limited by the fact that these scholars were content to highlight the formal signature which characterized perception in late-Roman times. They did not attempt to show the social upheavals manifested in these changes in perception—and perhaps could not have hoped to do so at that time. Today, the conditions for an analogous insight are more favorable. And if changes in the medium of present-day perception can be understood as a decay of the aura, it is possible to demonstrate the social determinants of that decay.

What, then, is the aura? A strange tissue of space and time: the unique apparition of a distance, however near it may be. To follow with the eye—while resting on a summer afternoon—a mountain range on the horizon or a branch that casts its shadow on the beholder is to breathe the aura of those mountains, of that branch. In the light of this description, we can readily grasp the social basis of the aura's present decay. It rests on two circumstances, both linked to the increasing emergence of the masses and the growing intensity of their movements. Namely: *"the desire of the present-day masses to 'get closer' to things, and their equally passionate concern for overcoming each thing's uniqueness [Überwindung des Einmaligen jeder Gegebenheit] by assimilating it as a reproduction."* Every day the urge grows stronger to get hold of an object at close range in an image *[Bild]* or, better, in a facsimile *[Abbild],* a reproduction. And the reproduction *[Reproduktion],* as offered by illustrated magazines and newsreels, differs unmistakably from the image. Uniqueness and permanence are as closely entwined in the latter as are transitoriness and repeatability in the former. The stripping of the veil from the object, the destruction of the aura, is the signature of a perception whose "sense for all that is the same in the world" has so increased that, by means of reproduction, it extracts sameness even from what is unique. Thus is manifested in the field of perception what in the theoretical sphere is noticeable in the increasing significance of statistics. The alignment of reality with the masses and of the masses with reality is a process of immeasurable importance for both thinking and perception.

V

The uniqueness of the work of art is identical to its embeddedness in the context of tradition. Of course, this tradition itself is thoroughly alive and extremely changeable. An ancient statue of Venus, for instance, existed in a traditional context for the Greeks (who made it an object of worship) that was different from the context in which it existed for medieval clerics (who viewed it as a sinister idol). But what was equally evident to both was its uniqueness—that is, its aura. Originally, the embeddedness of an artwork in the context of tradition found expression in a cult. As we know, the earliest artworks originated in the service of rituals—first magical, then religious. And it is highly significant that the artwork's auratic mode of existence is never entirely severed from its ritual function. In other words: *the unique value of the "authentic" work of art always has its basis in ritual*. This ritualistic basis, however mediated it may be, is still recognizable as secularized ritual in even the most profane forms of the cult of beauty. The secular worship of beauty, which developed during the Renaissance and prevailed for three centuries, clearly displayed that ritualistic basis in its subsequent decline and in the first severe crisis which befell it. For when, with the advent of the first truly revolutionary means of reproduction (namely photography, which emerged at the same time as socialism), art felt the approach of that crisis which a century later has become unmistakable, it reacted with the doctrine of *l'art pour l'art*—that is, with a theology of art. This in turn gave rise to a negative theology, in the form of an idea of "pure" art, which rejects not only any social function but any definition in terms of a representational content. (In poetry, Mallarmé was the first to adopt this standpoint.)

No investigation of the work of art in the age of its technological reproducibility can overlook these connections. They lead to a crucial insight: for the first time in world history, technological reproducibility emancipates the work of art from its parasitic subservience to ritual. To an ever-increasing degree, the work reproduced becomes the reproduction of a work designed for reproducibility. From a photographic plate, for example, one can make any number of prints; to ask for the "authentic" print makes no sense. *But as soon as the criterion of authenticity ceases to be applied to artistic production, the whole social function of art is revolutionized. Instead of being founded on ritual it is based on a different practice: politics.*

VI

Art history might be seen as the working out of a tension between two polarities within the artwork itself, its course being determined by shifts in the balance between the two. These two poles are the artwork's cult value and its exhibition value. Artistic production begins with figures in the service of magic. What is important for these figures is that they are present, not that they are seen. The elk depicted by Stone Age man on the walls of his cave is an instrument of magic, and is exhibited to others only coincidentally; what matters is that the spirits see it. Cult value as such even tends to keep the artwork out of sight: certain statues of gods are accessible only to the priest in the cella; certain images of the Madonna remain covered nearly all year round; certain sculptures on medieval cathedrals are not visible to the viewer at ground level. *With the emancipation of specific artistic practices from the service of ritual, the opportunities for exhibiting their products increase.* It is easier to exhibit a portrait bust that can be sent here and there than to exhibit the statue of a divinity that has a fixed place in the interior of a temple. A panel painting can be exhibited more easily than the mosaic or fresco which preceded it. And although a mass may have been no less suited to public presentation than a symphony, the symphony came into being at a time when the possibility of such presentation promised to be greater.

The scope for exhibiting the work of art has increased so enormously with, the various methods of technologically reproducing it that, as happened in prehistoric times, a quantitative shift between the two poles of the artwork has led to a qualitative transformation in its nature. Just as the work of art in prehistoric times, through the exclusive emphasis placed on its cult value, became first and foremost an instrument of magic which only later came to be recognized as a work of art, so today, through the exclusive emphasis placed on its exhibition value, the work of art becomes a construct *[Gebilde]* with quite new functions. Among these, the one we are conscious of—the artistic function—may subsequently be seen as incidental. This much is certain: today, film is the most serviceable vehicle of this new understanding. Certain, as well, is the fact that the historical moment of this change in the function of art—a change which is most fully evident in the case of film—allows a direct comparison with the primeval era of art not only from a methodological but also from a material point of view.

Prehistoric art made use of certain fixed notations in the service of magical practice. In some cases, these notations probably comprised the actual performing of magical acts (the carving of an ancestral figure is itself such an act); in others, they gave instructions for such procedures (the ancestral figure demonstrates a ritual posture); and in still others, they provided objects for magical contemplation (contemplation of an ancestral figure strengthens the occult powers of the beholder). The subjects for these notations were humans and their environment, which were depicted according to the requirements of a society whose technology existed only in fusion with ritual. Compared to that of the machine age, of course, this technology was undeveloped. But from a dialectical standpoint, the disparity is unimportant. What matters is the way the orientation and aims of that technology differ from those of ours. Whereas the former made the maximum possible use of human beings, the latter reduces their use to the minimum. The achievements of the first technology might be said to culminate in human sacrifice; those of the second, in the remote-controlled aircraft which needs no human crew. The results of the first technology are valid once and for all (it deals with irreparable lapse or sacrificial death, which holds good for eternity). The results of the second are wholly provisional (it operates by means of experiments and endlessly varied test procedures). The origin of the second technology lies at the point where, by an unconscious ruse, human beings first began to distance themselves from nature. It lies, in other words, in play.

Seriousness and play, rigor and license, are mingled in every work of art, though in very different proportions. This implies that art is linked to both the second and the first technologies. It should be noted, however, that to describe the goal of the second technology as "mastery over nature" is highly questionable, since this implies viewing the second technology from the standpoint of the first. The first technology really sought to master nature, whereas the second aims rather at an interplay between nature and humanity. The primary social function of art today is to rehearse that interplay. This applies especially to film. *The function of film is to train human beings in the apperceptions and reactions needed to deal with a vast apparatus whose role in their lives is expanding almost daily.* Dealing with this apparatus also teaches them that technology will release them from their enslavement to the powers of the apparatus only when humanity's whole constitution has adapted itself to the new productive forces which the second technology has set free.

VII

In photography, exhibition value begins to drive back cult value on all fronts. But cult value does not give way without resistance. It falls back to a last entrenchment: the human countenance. It is no accident that the portrait is central to early photography. In the cult of remembrance of dead or absent loved ones, the cult value of the image finds its last refuge. In the fleeting expression of a human face, the aura beckons from early photographs for the last time. This is what gives them their melancholy and incomparable beauty. But as the human being withdraws from the photographic image, exhibition value for the first time shows its superiority to cult value. To have given this development its local habitation constitutes the unique significance of Atget, who, around 1900, took photographs of deserted Paris streets. It has justly been said that he photographed them like scenes of crimes. A crime scene, too, is deserted; it is photographed for the purpose of establishing evidence. With Atget, photographic records begin to be evidence in the historical trial [Prozess]. This constitutes their hidden political significance. They demand a specific kind of reception. Free-floating contemplation is no longer appropriate to them. They unsettle the viewer; he feels challenged to find a particular way to approach them. At the same time, illustrated magazines begin to put up signposts for him—whether these are right or wrong is irrelevant. For the first time, captions become obligatory. And it is clear that they have a character altogether different from the titles of paintings. The directives given by captions to those looking at images in illustrated magazines soon become even more precise and commanding in films, where the way each single image is understood seems prescribed by the sequence of all the preceding images.

VIII

The Greeks had only two ways of technologically reproducing works of art: casting and stamping. Bronzes, terra cottas, and coins were the only artworks they could produce in large numbers. All others were unique and could not be technologically reproduced. That is why they had to be made for all eternity. *The state of their technology compelled the Greeks to produce eternal values in their art.* To this they owe their preeminent position in art history—the standard for subsequent generations. Undoubtedly, our position lies at the opposite pole from that of the Greeks. Never before have artworks been technologically reproducible to such a degree and in such quantities as today. Film is the first art form whose artistic character is entirely determined by its reproducibility. It would be idle to compare this form in detail with Greek art. But on one precise point such a comparison would be revealing. For film has given crucial importance to a quality of the artwork which would have been the last to find approval among the Greeks, or which they would have dismissed as marginal. This quality is its capacity for improvement. The finished film is the exact antithesis of a work created at a single stroke. It is assembled from a very large number of images and image sequences that offer an array of choices to the editor; these images, moreover, can be improved in any desired way in the process leading from the initial take to the final cut. To produce *A Woman of Paris,* which is 3,000 meters long, Chaplin shot 125,000 meters of film. *The film is therefore the artwork most capable of improvement. And this capability is linked to its radical renunciation of eternal value.* This is corroborated by the fact that for the Greeks, whose art depended on the production of eternal values, the pinnacle of all the arts was the form least capable of improvement—namely sculpture, whose products are literally all of a piece. In the age of the assembled [montierbar] artwork, the decline of sculpture is inevitable.

IX

The nineteenth-century dispute over the relative artistic merits of painting and photography seems misguided and confused today. But this does not diminish its importance, and may even underscore it. The dispute was in fact an expression of a world-historical upheaval whose true nature was concealed from both parties. Insofar as the age of technological reproducibility separated art from its basis in cult, all semblance of art's autonomy disappeared forever. But the resulting change in the function of art lay beyond the horizon of the nineteenth century. And even the twentieth, which saw the development of film, was slow to perceive it.

Though commentators had earlier expended much fruitless ingenuity on the question of whether photography was an art—without asking the more fundamental question of whether the invention of photography had not transformed the entire character of art—film theorists quickly adopted the same ill-considered standpoint. But the difficulties which photography caused for traditional aesthetics were child's play compared to those presented by film. Hence the obtuse and hyperbolic character of early film theory. Abel Gance, for instance, compares film to hieroglyphs: "By a remarkable regression, we are transported back to the expressive level of the Egyptians. . . . Pictorial language has not matured, because our eyes are not yet adapted to it. There is not yet enough respect, not enough *cult* for what it expresses." Or; in the words of Séverin-Mars: "What other art has been granted a dream ... at once more poetic and more real? Seen in this light; film might represent an incomparable means of expression, and only the noblest minds should move within its atmosphere, in the most perfect and mysterious moments of their lives." It is instructive to see how the desire to annex film to "art" impels these theoreticians to attribute elements of cult to film—with a striking lack of discretion. Yet when these speculations were published, works like *A Woman of Paris* and *The Gold Rush* had already appeared. This did not deter Abel Gance from making the comparison with hieroglyphs, while Séverin-Mars speaks of film as one might speak of paintings by Fra Angelico. It is revealing that even today especially reactionary authors look in the same direction for the significance of film—finding, if not actually a sacred significance, then at least a supernatural one. In connection with Max Reinhardt's film version of *A Midsummer Night's Dream,* Werfel comments that it was undoubtedly the sterile copying of the external world—with its streets, interiors, railway stations, restaurants, automobiles, and beaches—that had prevented film up to now from ascending to the realm of art. "Film has not yet realized its true purpose, its real possibilities... These consist in its unique ability to use natural means to give incomparably convincing expression to the fairylike, the marvelous, the supernatural."

X

To photograph a painting is one kind of reproduction, but to photograph an action performed in a film studio is another. In the first case, what is reproduced is a work of art, while the act of producing it is not. The cameraman's performance with the lens no more creates an artwork than a conductor's with the baton; at most, it creates an artistic performance. This is unlike the process in a film studio. Here, what is reproduced is not an artwork, and the act of reproducing it is no more such a work than in the first case. The work of art is produced only by means of montage. And each individual component of this montage is a reproduction of a process which neither is an artwork in itself nor gives rise to one through photography. What, then, are these processes reproduced in film, since they are certainly not works of art?

To answer this, we must start from the peculiar nature of the artistic performance of the film actor. He is distinguished from the stage actor in that his performance in its original form, from which the reproduction is made, is not carried out in front of a randomly composed audience but before a group of specialists—executive producer, director, cinematographer, sound recordist, lighting designer, and so on—who are in a position to intervene in his performance at any time. This aspect of filmmaking is highly significant in social terms. For the intervention in a performance by a body of experts is also characteristic of sporting performances and, in a wider sense, of all test performances. The entire process of film production is determined, in fact, by such intervention. As we know, many shots are filmed in a number of takes. A single cry for help, for example, can be recorded in several different versions. The editor then makes a selection from these; in a sense, he establishes one of them as the record. An action performed in the film studio therefore differs from the corresponding real action the way the competitive throwing of a discus in a sports arena would differ from the throwing of the same discus from the same spot in the same direction in order to kill someone. The first is a test performance, while the second is not.

The test performance of the film actor is, however, entirely unique in kind. In what does this performance consist? It consists in crossing a certain barrier which confines the social value of test performances within narrow limits. I am referring now not to a performance in the world of sports, but to a performance produced in a mechanized test. In a sense, the athlete is confronted only by natural tests. He measures himself against tasks set by nature, not by equipment—apart from exceptional cases like Nurmi, who was said to run against the clock. Meanwhile the work process, especially since it has been standardized by the assembly line, daily generates countless mechanized tests. These tests are performed unawares, and those who fail are excluded from the work process. But they are also conducted openly, in agencies for testing professional aptitude. In both cases, the test subject faces the barrier mentioned above.

These tests, unlike those in the world of sports, are incapable of being publicly exhibited to the degree one would desire. And this is precisely where film comes into play. *Film makes test performances capable of being exhibited, by turning that ability itself into a test.* The film actor performs not in front of an audience but in front of an apparatus. The film director occupies exactly the same position as the examiner in an aptitude test. To perform in the glare of arc lamps while simultaneously meeting the demands of the microphone is a test performance of the highest order. To accomplish it is to preserve one's humanity in the face of the apparatus. Interest in this performance is widespread. For the majority of city dwellers, throughout the workday in offices and factories, have to relinquish their humanity in the face of an apparatus. In the evening these same masses fill the cinemas, to witness the film actor taking revenge on their behalf not only by asserting *his* humanity (or what appears to them as such) against the apparatus, but by placing that apparatus in the service of his triumph.

XI

In the case of film, the fact that the actor represents someone else before the audience matters much less than the fact that he represents himself before the apparatus. One of the first to sense this transformation of the actor by the test performance was Pirandello. That his remarks on the subject in his novel *Si gira* [Shoot!] are confined to the negative aspects of this change, and to silent film only, does little to diminish their relevance. For in this respect, the sound film changed nothing essential. What matters is that the actor is performing for a piece of equipment—or, in the case of sound film, for two pieces of equipment. "The film actor," Pirandello writes, "feels as if exiled. Exiled not only from the stage but from his own person. With a vague unease, he senses an inexplicable void, stemming from the fact that his body has lost its substance, that he has been volatilized, stripped of his reality, his life, his voice, the noises he makes when moving about, and has been turned into a mute image that flickers for a moment on the screen, then vanishes into silence. ... The little apparatus will play with his shadow before the audience, and he himself must be content to play before the apparatus." The situation can also be characterized as follows: for the first time—and this is the effect of film—the human being is placed in a position where he must operate with his whole living person, while forgoing its aura. For the aura is bound to his presence in the here and now. There is no facsimile of the aura. The aura surrounding Macbeth on the stage cannot be divorced from the aura which, for the living spectators, surrounds the actor who plays him. What distinguishes the shot in the film studio, however, is that the camera is substituted for the audience. As a result, the aura surrounding the actor is dispelled—and, with it, the aura of the figure he portrays.

It is not surprising that it should be a dramatist such as Pirandello who, in reflecting on the special character of film acting, inadvertently touches on the crisis now affecting the theater. Indeed, nothing contrasts more starkly with a work of art completely subject to (or, like film, founded in) technological reproduction than a stage play. Any thorough consideration will confirm this. Expert observers have long recognized that, in film, "the best effects are almost always achieved by 'acting' as little as possible. ... The development," according to Rudolf Arnheim, writing in 1932, has been toward "using the actor as one of the 'props,' chosen for his typicalness and ... introduced in the proper context." Closely bound up with this development is something else. *The stage actor identifies himself with a role. The film actor very often is denied this opportunity.* His performance is by no means a unified whole, but is assembled from many individual performances. Apart from incidental concerns about studio rental, availability of other actors, scenery, and so on, there are elementary necessities of the machinery that split the actor's performance into a series of episodes capable of being assembled. In particular, lighting and its installation require the representation of an action—which on the screen appears as a swift, unified sequence—to be filmed in a series of separate takes, which may be spread over hours in the studio. Not to mention the more obvious effects of montage. A leap from a window, for example, can be shot in the studio as a leap from a scaffold, while the ensuing fall may be filmed weeks later at an outdoor location. And far more paradoxical cases can easily be imagined. Let us assume that an actor is supposed to be startled by a knock at the door. If his reaction is not satisfactory, the director can resort to an expedient: he could have a shot fired without warning behind the actor's back on some other occasion when he happens to be in the studio. The actor's frightened reaction at that moment could be recorded and then edited into the film. Nothing shows more graphically that art has escaped the realm of "beautiful semblance," which for so long was regarded as the only sphere in which it could thrive.

XII

The representation of human beings by means of an apparatus has made possible a highly productive use of the human being's self-alienation. The nature of this use can be grasped through the fact that the film actor's estrangement in the face of the apparatus, as Pirandello describes this experience, is basically of the same kind as the estrangement felt before one's appearance *[Erscheinung]* in a mirror—a favorite theme of the Romantics. But now the mirror image *[Bild]* has become detachable from the person mirrored, and is transportable. And where is it transported? To a site in front of the masses. Naturally, the screen actor never for a moment ceases to be aware of this. While he stands before the apparatus, he knows that in the end he is confronting the masses. It is they who will control him. Those who are not visible, not present while he executes his performance, are precisely the ones who will control it. This invisibility heightens the authority of their control. It should not be forgotten, of course, that there can be no political advantage derived from this control until film has liberated itself from the fetters of capitalist exploitation. Film capital uses the revolutionary opportunities implied by this control for counterrevolutionary purposes. Not only does the cult of the movie star which it fosters preserve that magic of the personality which has long been no more than the putrid magic of its own commodity character, but its counterpart, the cult of the audience, reinforces the corruption by which fascism is seeking to supplant the class consciousness of the masses.

XIII

It is inherent in the technology of film, as of sports, that everyone who witnesses these performances does so as a quasi-expert. Anyone who has listened to a group of newspaper boys leaning on their bicycles and discussing the outcome of a bicycle race will have an inkling of this. In the case of film, the newsreel demonstrates unequivocally that any individual can be in a position to be filmed. But that possibility is not enough. *Any person today can lay claim to being filmed.* This claim can best be clarified by considering the historical situation of literature today.

For centuries it was in the nature of literature that a small number of writers confronted many thousands of readers. This began to change toward the end of the past century. With the growth and extension of the press, which constantly made new political, religious, scientific, professional, and local journals available to readers, an increasing number of readers—in isolated cases, at first—turned into writers. It began with the space set aside for "letters to the editor" in the daily press, and has now reached a point where there is hardly a European engaged in the work process who could not, in principle, find an opportunity to publish somewhere or other an account of a work experience, a complaint, a report, or something of the kind. Thus, the distinction between author and public is about to lose its axiomatic character. The difference becomes functional; it may vary from case to case. At any moment, the reader is ready to become a writer. As an expert—which he has had to become in any case in a highly specialized work process, even if only in some minor capacity—the reader gains access to authorship. Work itself is given a voice. And the ability to describe a job in words now forms part of the expertise needed to carry it out. Literary competence is no longer founded on specialized higher education but on polytechnic training, and thus is common property.

All this can readily be applied to film, where shifts that in literature took place over centuries have occurred in a decade. In cinematic practice—above all, in Russia—this shift has already been partly realized. Some of the actors taking part in Russian films are not actors in our sense but people who portray *themselves*—and primarily in their own work process. In western Europe today, the capitalist exploitation of film obstructs the human being's legitimate claim to being reproduced. The claim is also obstructed, incidentally, by unemployment, which excludes large masses from production—the process in which their primary entitlement to be reproduced would lie. Under these circumstances, the film industry has an overriding interest in stimulating the involvement of the masses through illusionary displays and ambiguous speculations. To this end it has set in motion an immense publicity machine, in the service of which it has placed the careers and love lives of the stars; it has organized polls; it has held beauty contests. All this in order to distort and corrupt the original and justified interest of the masses in film—an interest in understanding themselves and therefore their class. Thus, the same is true of film capital in particular as of fascism in general: a compelling urge toward new social opportunities is being clandestinely exploited in the interests of a property-owning minority. For this reason alone, the expropriation of film capital is an urgent demand for the proletariat.

■ ■ ■

Questions and projects

1. From the late 1920s through the 1930s there were many superior film adaptations of liter-
    ary works: from Marcel L'Herbier's updating of an Émile Zola novel as *L'Argent* (1929)
    to George Cukor's (1937) *Camille*. Do these provoke the new ways of 'reading' and under-
    standing that Benjamin hopes for? How or how not? Are there better examples of films that
    achieve Benjamin's aims, such as Russian director Alexander Dovzhenko's *Earth* (1930)
    or Eisenstein's aborted project with American novelist Upton Sinclair, *Qué viva Mexico!*
    (1933)?
2. Are Benjamin's arguments still valid today? Does literature, in short, participate in a cultur-
    al "aura" that the movies are free of? Choose a particularly good contemporary example of
    a film that transforms a literary work into an experience that is more politically accessible
    or socially relevant. Analyze how this is accomplished in terms of the style of the film and
    the audience's relation to it.

Chapter 17

Mark A. Reid

LITERARY FORCES ENCOURAGING THE USE OF BLACK WRITERS

Q UESTIONS OF RACE and related ideological concerns can often figure in adaptations or other movements between film and literature. While the 1950s were a turbulent and creative period for many writers connected to the movies, Mark A. Reid's examination of the predicament of African-American writers opens a rich dimension within it. He makes clear that writing itself, and especially writing for the movies, is fraught with politics and other visible or hidden concerns. For black writers and other groups marginalized by the film industry (then and now) such social and professional politics can create thorny and frustrating contexts in which opportunities are the product of many historical forces, such as the growing box-office power of those groups. For Reid, strong writers and filmmakers find a way to challenge the dominant forces on their own terms and produce a "textual dialogue" within the finished work that reveals a vision that, in the best cases, still retains its racial origin.

■ ■ ■

LITERARY FORCES ENCOURAGING THE USE OF BLACK WRITERS
MARK A. REID

From *Redefining Black Film*, Berkeley, CA: University of California Press, 1993, pp. 47–49 and 57–68

Hollywood did not produce black family films written by African-American writers until the late 1950s. The new opportunities for black film writers in Hollywood resulted in part from studio interest in film adaptations and partly from Hollywood's recognition of the popularity of African-American literature. The industry's preference for screen adaptations of popular works is evidenced by the Academy of Motion Picture Arts and Sciences 1956 creation of the Best Writing Award for the Best Adapted Screenplay. This move affected the subject matter and themes that studio films would choose to dramatize.[2]

Between 1940 and 1960 one short story and a few novels by African-Americans had received such acclaim that film studios decided to adapt them for the screen. Frank Yerby's best seller, *The Foxes of Harrow* (1946), was produced by Twentieth Century-Fox in 1947. Willard Motley's two novels *Knock on Any Door* (1947) and *Let No Man Write My Epitaph* (1958) were produced by Columbia in 1949 and 1960, respectively. MGM produced *Bright Road* (1953), a screen adaptation of Mary E. Vroman's short story "See How They Run" (1951).

Moreover, black-oriented dramas written by African-Americans were increasingly accepted by mainstream American theaters and professional critics during the 1950s. In 1953, Louis Peterson's *Take a Giant Step* appeared on Broadway. *Take a Giant Step* was revived off-Broadway in 1956 and received critical acclaim. The off-Broadway Greenwich Mews Theatre produced William Branch's historical dramatization of John Brown and Frederick Douglass, *In Splendid Error* (1954). Alice Childress's satire on black stereotypes, *Trouble in Mind* (1957), and Loften Mitchell's dramatic treatment of school desegregation in *A Land Beyond the River* (1957) were also produced for the stage. In 1959, the most significant event of the decade for black theater occurred when Hansberry received the Critics Circle Award for *A Raisin in the Sun*.[3]

By the end of the fifties, major studios were hiring African-Americans to write scenarios for studio-produced black-oriented films. With the integration of black writers came more pressure for studios to broaden their depiction of African-American life and experiences. The development of a third subtype of African-American family film is the result of the hiring of black scenarists, the increasing popularity of black-oriented film fare, and the impact of the civil rights movement.

The literary exchange between studio executives and black writers during this period resembles the relationship that newly independent African nations enjoyed with their former colonial administrators. The black writer, like the newly independent African nation, was still beholden to the system of production, distribution, and consumption. Individual writers or nations could not disrupt the flow and if they tried, other blacks would eagerly replace them. In fact, the film industry now engaged in a sort of neocolonial relationship between black artists, their audience, and mass-produced black art. Only through the processes of negotiation and resistance could African-American writers and white studio executives generate a filmic portrait of the African-American family. On the one hand, this neocolonial relationship usually ensured that formal conventions were respected. On the other hand, black scenarists used subversive rhetorical strategies that obscured the over-determined nature of the American film industry, which demanded adherence to the generic form. For example, in accordance with the requirements of the film industry, most early black-authored family films, such as *Take a Giant Step, The Learning Tree*, and *Black Girl* (1972), focus on the qualities of one family member.

During this period, there were a few short-lived rebels who penned scenarios that broke with the genre's insistent focus on one member of the family. *A Raisin in the Sun* and *The River Niger* brought attention to the dreams of individual family members and thereby revealed the genre's ability to speak to a multitude of black others whose voices were not confined to one black hero(ine). The neocolonial partnership between studio and black writer requires one to study how the industry packages a black-authored film for consumption by an audience. This requirement is as important as a close reading of the film text. Film analysis must include descriptions of the industry, the product, and consumer-related issues as well as aesthetic concerns that involve the relationship between film and spectator.

Regardless of the film industry's assumption of an "average" African-American moviegoer and attempts to market films to such, black audiences employ different reading strategies based on their class, ethnicity, gender, and sexual orientation. Even within the limited confines of neocolonial black film production, the reactions of black *or* white audiences are far from predetermined. Finally, the reception of this subtype is equally indeterminate if one views these films as examples of the disjointed nature of products issued from a relationship between the colonizer (the master or patriarchal discourse) and the colonized (those bound to masters or confined within a patriarchal system).

...

A Raisin in the Sun

One of the earliest major examples of a black family film that was written by a black scenarist and independently produced for a major studio is the David Susskind and Philip Rose Production of *A Raisin in the Sun*. The film was directed by Daniel Petrie, and Hansberry adapted her original play for the screen.

Susskind was interested in producing *Raisin* because he recognized that it would be a financially and critically successful Broadway play. *Variety*'s coverage of the play's pre-Broadway tryouts was one way in which Susskind may have developed an interest in *Raisin*. On 28 January 1959, *Variety* reported,

> Whatever the theatre shortage in Gotham may be, there must be room for "A Raisin in the Sun." Already of solid substance in tryout form, the Lorraine Hansberry drama is loaded with smash potentials that should ripen into substantial Broadway tenancy.

Variety also heralded the fact that the play was "written, directed and acted by Negroes, (with only one white role in the cast)." This mode of production, which entailed black control over three major aspects of dramatic art, was adopted by a mainstream American entertainment institution— Broadway. Later, Hollywood would institute a similar mode of production and thereby rejuvenate the black commercial film movement within the dominant structure of Hollywood studios.

The content of *Raisin* seemed to be far different from the content of plays made by whites about blacks, and *Variety* hinted at this:

> Raisin stands out as a shining example of talent potential if given the opportunity. The play should draw comment not only for the quality of its presentation but also for the depth of its message.

On March 11, 1959, *Raisin* opened on Broadway and received rave reviews. Two days later, Susskind wrote to Sam Briskin, Columbia Pictures vice-president in charge of production, and expressed his interest in a screen adaptation of *Raisin*. Susskind wrote:

> I have an inside track on this property as a consequence of my relationship with the author and her attorney. I think if you were to manifest real interest I could be granted a pre-empt right on the play for motion pictures at the best price offered by any competitor. At this writing, United Artists, Harry Belafonte, Metro-Goldwyn-Mayer, Paramount, Fox, Hall-Bartlett and the Mirisch Brothers have expressed strong interest in purchasing the play.[14]

At this early date, at least six major film producers were interested in a screen adaptation of the play. Susskind, writing in the same letter, recognized that the play presented "a warm, frequently amusing and profoundly moving story of [N]egro life in which *for once*, the race issue is not paramount." He reassured Briskin that a film version featuring Poitier would attract an audience: "after *The Defiant Ones* and the upcoming *Porgy and Bess*, Sidney Poitier would be an important box office element."

By the 16th of March, Briskin wrote "we [Columbia] have had this interest ... since we first learned of the play and its pre-New York openings ... we have been approached by others both in and out of the studio."[15] Before a month had passed, *Variety* reported on 1 April 1959 that Columbia Pictures in association with Susskind and Rose had acquired the film rights to *Raisin* for $300,000. Susskind formulated the preproduction package that had been accepted by the studio. The package included himself and Rose as co-producers, Hansberry as scenarist, Poitier as featured star, and costars Claudia McNeil, Ruby Dee, and Diana Sands.

Martin Baum, the agent for Poitier and *Raisin*'s black stage-director Lloyd Richards, initially suggested that Richards direct the film version. Columbia's vice-president of publicity and advertising Paul Lazarus discussed this possibility with Briskin, who inquired about Richards's CBS-TV videotape production of *Raisin*. In a letter to Lazarus, Briskin reported that "when it got down to the last couple of days of rehearsal and the cameras were placed on the act he [Richards] seemed lost and CBS had to throw in a TV director to help him."[16]

Thus, Columbia refused to give Richards an opportunity to direct the film adaptation of the Broadway play that he directed. Columbia studio executives were both cautious and backward. They wanted to produce *Raisin* because of its financial and critical success, yet they did not want to make the same gamble that Broadway had made with Richards, one of the first blacks to direct a Broadway play. When Columbia executives approved Susskind's three-picture contract with director Daniel Petrie, *Raisin* had its director.[17] Petrie had made one film, *The Bramble Bush* (Warner, 1960), and was safe according to Columbia's standards.

Even though Columbia executives rejected Richards as the director, they accepted Hansberry as the scenarist. The primary reason that Columbia accepted Hansberry was *Raisin*'s status as a very hot property which gave its writer some leverage in deals with the studio. However, Briskin would not allow Hansberry any changes or additions to the screenplay which might threaten a mass audience. For example, Hansberry's first draft of the screenplay included Travis Younger having to bring fifty cents to school for special books about African-Americans. Columbia production executives Briskin and Arthur Kramer and the story editors William Fadiman and James Crow "agreed that this should be deleted from the screenplay," because it was not in the play. In addition, the Columbia production team "agreed that the addition of race issue material ... should be avoided." because "the introduction of further race issues may lessen the sympathy of the audience, give the effect of propagandistic writing, and so weaken the story, not only as dramatic entertainment, but as propaganda too."[18]

The production team also sought to eliminate Beneatha's comment that "all Africans are revolutionaries today," calling it an example of "surplus in the race issue category and potentially troublesome to no purpose." In addition, executives argued that "Beneatha's dialogue about Africans needing salvation 'from the British and French' could give the picture needless trouble abroad."[19]

These suggested deletions are examples of the sort of censorship that occurs in Hollywood-produced and -distributed black commercial films. Since Hollywood films are produced for international markets and most black commercial films include social criticisms, studios usually tone down criticism of their potential audiences.

In *Raisin*'s case, Columbia story editors and executives were quick to reject Beneatha Younger's pan-African consciousness because their audience was not going to be limited to black pan-Africanists and white liberals like Susskind and Rose. Columbia's intended audience for *Raisin* included British and French colonialist sympathizers, and Columbia's recommended deletions acknowledged their presence. The audience for whom a black-oriented film is made determines film content and form and thus affects the filmic representation of black culture. Critics must identify the studio's estimation of an "intended audience" and describe and interpret the underlying ideology.

In the above instance, Columbia's executives suggested three deletions in *Raisin*'s sociopolitical and cultural elements. The power to delete certain ideological expressions of black culture highlights the limitations that Hollywood places on black scenarists and black directors involved in black commercial cinema. Film theoretician Gladstone Yearwood writes, "if the practice of black cinema is derived from that of Hollywood, then it will serve to reproduce the unequal relations characteristic of blacks in society."[20]

When black artists are involved in the mode of production as writers and directors, however, then these films become something other than mere Hollywood films. The presence of blacks in positions of power forces the critic to reformulate terms and elaborate new definitions. This critical process involves defining variables of image control (as in Beneatha's pan-African remarks, which were not cut) and determining the studio's actual exercised power. I use the term "colonized" to describe major studio productions, such as King Vidor's *Hallelujah* (MGM, 1929), which are written or solely directed by whites. In addition, I use the term "neocolonized" to refer to major studio productions, such as *Raisin*, which are written or directed by black people. These two categories distinguish the two forms of black-oriented major studio productions.

The critical success of the film adaptation of *Raisin* is demonstrated by the letters that Susskind received from people in the film and television industries. NBC special projects producer-director Robert K. Sharpe wrote,

> Perhaps more in this industry than any other we are judged by what we do when we have the opportunity to do it. In "Raisin in the Sun" I feel not only have you been loyal to a property which could have been changed in so many ways for expediency, but you and your associates have produced an even more immediate and compelling piece than the play itself. It is indeed a credit to the movie industry and certainly will be to this country overseas.[21]

This congratulatory letter conveys the prestige value *Raisin* had for its studio and the United States. However, the owner of William Goldman Theatres expressed an important reservation when he thanked Susskind:

> We are presently in consultation with Columbia as to the best approach ad-wise in order to garner the greatest possible return at the box office. I am sure you realize that the picture does present a problem from a selling standpoint due to its subject matter. It is imperative that we reach a mass rather than just a class audience.[22]

One way in which Columbia attempted to solve this problem, as well as exploit what Sharpe had discerned as "a credit to the movie industry," involved promoting *Raisin* as a prestige picture. Columbia made *Raisin* a United States entry in the 1961 Cannes Film Festival. The film thereby acquired an international prestige that grew when the festival gave *Raisin* a special award. The Screenwriters Guild also nominated it for the Best Screenplay of the Year award that same year. This award and nomination helped increase Hollywood's acceptance of black writers and the black family film genre.

On 10 January 1962, *Variety* reported that *Raisin*'s domestic rentals amounted to $1,100,000.[23] *Variety*'s estimated domestic rentals for *Raisin* nearly equaled Columbia Picture's $1,500,000 production costs reported in *Ebony* magazine.[24] Thus, *Raisin* was neither a financial disaster nor a box-office success. *Raisin* offered the studios proof that a low-budget, skillfully written black scenario about a black family which features well-known black performers can accrue prestige as well as return a moderate amount of money to its distributor. The film's effect on audiences and film critics, however, did not equal the play's critical acclaim and popularity among both black and white theater audiences. This imbalance may have resulted from the different expectations of theater and film audiences. Major film productions like *Raisin* require mainstream audience approval, but theater productions like *Raisin* can attract an interracial audience and still focus on topics that would offend a mainstream film audience. It is understandable that the film had little effect on mainstream film audiences, and that most film critics ignored the importance of this film.

It is an unquestionable fact that the first priority of the film industry is to avoid products that threaten its major markets. Nonetheless, if one performs a close reading of the black family films adapted from African-American literary sources, one discovers the resiliency of the ongoing struggle that black writers have waged against dehumanized images of black family life.

Textual dialogue in *A Raisin in the Sun*

Like most committed black artists, Hansberry developed the story of the Younger family by experiencing its sociological equivalent. Hansberry attended Englewood High School on Chicago's southside, where she made friends with the black working-class youth who attended her school. James Baldwin wrote that "much of the strain under which Lorraine worked was produced by her knowledge of this reality, and her determined refusal not to be destroyed by it." Baldwin observed that he "had never in (his) life seen so many black people in the theatre. And the reason was that never before, in the entire history of the American theater, had so much of the truth of black people's lives been seen on [the Broadway] stage. Black people had ignored the theater because the theater had always ignored them."[25]

Granted, it is problematic to assert that an imaginative work like *Raisin* reflects the collective voices of working-class black America. But Hansberry's working film script generates a dialogic language that empowers a black working-class family in a particular region and at a particular time   post-World War II Chicago. The following discussion of the Youngers will serve as a case study of the filmic dramatization of political diversity within a black working-class family.

In *Raisin*, textual dialogism results from the family members who express different aspirations and political and religious beliefs. Lena's religious beliefs are an area of conflict between herself and her children. Walter Lee, her thirty-five-year-old son, wants to purchase a liquor store while Ruth, the wife of Walter Lee, considers abortion. Beneatha, Lena's daughter at college, freely questions the existence of God and the value of marriage.

Raisin attempts verbally and visually to affirm Afro-American working-class interests, especially through the two white male characters who interact with Walter Lee and the Younger family. Mr. Arnold is the representative *sign* of white corporate America. His relationship to Walter is determined by the socioeconomic relationship between unskilled, black America and a postindustrialized America. Walter represents black men who live in northern, industrialized cities. Karl Lindner portrays the intra-class racial hostility of working-class American ethnics. Lindner's relationship to the Younger family signifies the white working-class that practices racially restrictive housing covenants that forbid blacks from purchasing homes in white neighborhoods. Thus, Lindner is the representative *sign* of this white collectivity. The interaction between Lindner and the Youngers occasions a dialogic discourse that wealthy Mr. Arnold and corporate America resist. *Raisin* explores linear mobility along class lines *the integration of predominantly white working-class neighborhoods* but neglects or is unable to suggest an integration of the unskilled black into white corporate America.

The Younger family articulates desirous dream discourses that generate an inter-familial dialogue. Lena's dreams encompass three different actions: placing $3000 in a savings account for her daughter's (Beneatha) medical school education, placing a $3500 down payment on a home for the Younger family, and giving her son $3500 to open a checking account. It is Lena Younger's three-fold dream that includes the dreams of Beneatha, Ruth, and her deceased husband Big Walter. The promise of a medical school education for her college-trained daughter represents the advancement of black women. The purchase of a home for the Younger family shows a desire for better housing and permits the family melodrama to critically discuss the issue of racially segregated housing.

Raisin begins with Ruth Younger leaving the bedroom and entering the living room where her son, Travis, is asleep on the couch. Travis must sleep in the living room because there is not enough room in the two-bedroom apartment in which five family members live. Ruth awakens Travis and rushes him into the hallway bathroom that the Youngers share with their neighbors. Returning to the bedroom, she proceeds to do the same to her husband. He responds with two questions that reveal their marriage is "festering like a sore." Walter's first response questions the logic behind waking him up to go to a bathroom already occupied by his son. His second response illustrates his growing obsession with the $10,000 insurance money. He asks Ruth about the money and then asks her to persuade Lena to give him the insurance money so he can purchase a liquor store with his two friends Willie and Bobo. Ruth rejects Walter's request because she believes that the money belongs to Lena.

The opening dialogue and action establish that Walter Lee has displaced the collective Younger voice for that of an individual desire. Walter has assimilated the rhetoric of small business without its necessary requirement—experience and training. When Ruth rejects Walter's request, he counters with "I'm trying to talk to you about me!" Here, the reference "me" does not include the promise of a medical education for his sister Beneatha, nor does it include placing a down payment on a new home for the Younger family. Walter's desire does not encompass a group consciousness, and his entrepreneurial desire ignores the collective dreams that sustain the Younger family.

It is a bit obtuse to characterize Lena as a matriarch who dominates the members of her household. Throughout the play, Lena refers to her deceased husband Big Walter as an agent of her actions. Her son Walter Lee, on the other hand, repudiates Lena's dreams and the mythic qualities of Big Walter. In the assimilative mode, he constantly compares himself to wealthy Mr. Arnold and similar white men. Walter develops an entrepreneurial interest in a liquor store as a means to escape poverty and says that he must have the $10,000 insurance money that Lena will receive for the death of her husband.

The scene that presents Big Walter as the imaginary significer of the black working-class and Lena as its poet takes place when Walter has left the apartment. Lena is "paying witness" to the memory of her deceased husband. She says, "You know Big Walter always hated the idea of being a servant. Always says man's hands wasn't meant to carry nobody's slop jars and make their beds. Always used to say they was meant to turn the earth with, make things. That husband of yours, Walter Lee, he's just like him." Lena's statement precedes a scene that presents Walter in his chauffeur uniform busily polishing Mr. Arnold's black limousine. The off-camera voice of Mr. Arnold is heard over a loud speaker: "Walter, bring the car around. Please." The camera follows Walter as he drives the car around the expanse of Mr. Arnold's mansion. Then the camera fades in on Walter rushing to open Mr. Arnold's car door. Arnold exits from the car, hands Walter a newspaper, leaves the camera frame, and enters a downtown office building. Walter, like many who aspire to enter corporate America through unskilled beginnings, is exposed to the world of Mr. Arnold and wants to be like him. But Mr. Arnold only offers Walter a newspaper. Walter lacks the education and the opportunities that would admit him into the office building that towers over him. Walter stands outside the building. He does not participate in corporate deals, he observes them with a sense of frustration.

Walter's position as a passive onlooker with frustrated dreams results in an oppositional language that explores the dynamics of the frustrated, black, male ego. His ego, having disregarded the myth of Big Walter, tells us about Mr. Arnold's myth. In Walter's attempt to measure up to Arnold, he totally neglects the survival strategies of Big Walter and the memories of Lena his mother.

Lena encourages aspiration through education and racio-familial memory; these are elements that transcend the individualistic aspirations of Walter. Unlike her son, Lena wants to devote the $10,000 insurance payment to three different purposes: education, housing, and savings. The purchase of a two-flat house represents the failed dream of Big Walter and Lena. The dream is secured but it remains the responsibility of the family to pay the mortgage. Lena says that she will use "part of the insurance money for a down payment and everybody kind of pitch in." The house is a collective sign that signifies the possibility of achieving a group aspiration. The two-flat is no mere signifier of middle-class desires for home ownership nor does it represent a desire to live in an integrated neighborhood. The new home carries forth Big Walter's dream since it connects his past struggle with the present state of the family's crowded living quarters. The house also becomes the collective sign of the Youngers' ability to resist the white Clybourne Park Improvement Association's bribe to forego their civil rights.

When Walter is entrusted with the responsibility to open the savings account for Beneatha and the checking account for himself, he gives the $6500 to Willie Harris, who absconds with the money. Walter's entrepreneurial dreams are crushed but they resurface when Mr. Lindner appears. Lindner is the representative of the Clybourne Park Improvement Association, a group of white homeowners who want to buy the two-flat from the Youngers at an inflated price. Earlier in the story, Walter had refused Lindner's offer but he now reconsiders it. After being swindled by Willie Harris, Walter asks Lindner to return to the Younger apartment because he now will accept the bribe. Lindner returns and Ruth tries to send Travis downstairs to prevent him from witnessing Walter accept the bribe. But Lena insists that Travis witness his father's actions. Lena says, "No. Travis, you stay right here. And you [Walter] make him [Travis] understand what you're doing. … You teach him good. Like Willie Harris taught you. You show where our five generations done come to. Go ahead son." Walter takes on the mantle of his deceased father and the five generations of Youngers. He affirms the collective memory and thereby educates the sixth generation in the resistance struggle. Walter says,

> I have worked as a chauffeur most of my life—and my wife she does domestic work in people's kitchens. So does my mother. My father … was a laborer most of his life. And that's my sister over there, and she's going to be a doctor. This is my son, who makes the sixth generation of our family in this country. We have thought of your offer and have decided to move into our home because my father … my father, he earned it.

Walter Lee's monologue articulates a collective working-class voice, a racial consciousness, and a vision of black womanhood as mothers, laborers, and soon-to-be professionals.

Raisin explores, then, three major issues: race, class, and gender. The film shows the constant friction between the laboring class of white Mr. Lindners and the equally laboring class of black Youngers. It portrays the racial and class differences between the wealthy, white Mr. Arnold, and the dreams and vision of an unskilled, black Walter Lee. It mirrors the black woman's growing awareness of her right to reject motherhood and plan parenthood around her professional career. The film celebrates the African-American vision of a collective consciousness in which polyphony reigns.

Raisin simultaneously portrays a black matriarchal family structure that is rooted in several value systems—capitalism, black feminism, religious fundamentalism, and pan-Africanism. In *Raisin,* family members discuss residential segregation, abortion, atheism, and the liberation of African nations. The presence of conflicting desires between family members and those outside the family circle permits interfamilial and extrafamilial dialogue and, simultaneously, avoids the erasure of black generative discourses.

The film industry's increasing need to attract African-American audiences requires it to create black-oriented products. But to understand this industrial necessity, one must also discern the ways in which blacks participated in the artistic construction of black-oriented films. Film industry executives, even during the period of independently-produced, studio-distributed films, such as *Take a Giant Step* and *A Raisin in the Sun,* reaffirmed the dominant visual representation of the black family. However, black screenwriters such as Peterson and Hansberry used dialogue to undermine a film's apparent middle-class values. This indeterminacy of meaning is only one of the levels at which tension occurs. Similarly, certain forms of reception can assimilate, appropriate, and resist any visual representation of black family life.

The illusory nature of dominant racial-gender discourses generated by most films helps to circumvent the threatening nature of a popularized "black" form and its reception. Consequently a subversive black character, such as Beneatha in *A Raisin in the Sun*, is unthreatening in her affirmation of black socialism. Beneatha's indeterminate reception permits the production of subversive works. Her pan-African and black feminist subjectivity refuses assimilation by a mass audience. Her dialogue on Africa, planned parenthood, and feminism invites a resistant spectatorial positioning. The indeterminate receptive quality of black family films, then, permits dominant and subversive readings.

By the seventies, the independently-produced, studio-distributed African-American family film permitted a broader vision of black American life. Black middle-class family melodramas, such as *Take a Giant Step* and *A Raisin in the Sun*, spoke to the era of integration and polite militancy.

During this period the black film market required films that spoke to despairing urban youths, rather than to parents who remained hopeful that social programs would return. Black and white youths demanded and regularly paid the price of admission. Urban black youths frequented inner city movie theaters while white youths went to those in the suburbs. Many inner city theaters showed films that attracted a black youth audience. Consequently, black family films no longer hid the single-parent welfare family behind smiles of hope. They revealed the grim reality of urban uprisings, abandoned buildings, gang violence, and a new generation locked into economic dependency and psychological poverty. Some of the films that document this period are J. E. Franklin's screen adaptation *Black Girl*, Eric Monte's screenplay *Cooley High* (AIP, 1975), and Joseph A. Walker's screen adaptation *The River Niger.*

The hybrid black family narrative, like the hybrid minstrelsy humor of Eddie Murphy, can conceal its racist, sexist, and homophobic elements. Such an ability to conceal becomes equal to the hybrid's ability to reveal itself as one with the majority of its *imagined* audience at a particular time in history.

■ ■ ■

Questions and projects

1. Look closely at the 1961 *A Raisin in the Sun* and analyze in as much detail as possible the elements in it that reveal both the presence of mainstream cinema and the counter-forces of an African-American literary voice.

2. The exchanges between literature and film can dramatize a politics of race in many ways. Select another racially charged work—such as Spike Lee's *Malcolm X,* David Lean's 1984 *A Passage to India,* or the 1998 big-budget adaptation of Tony Morrison's *Beloved*—and discuss how race informs many of the questions or problems that surround these scripts and movies.

Notes

...

2   Andrew Dowdy, *The Films of the Fifties* (New York: William Morrow and Company, 1973), 90. Dowdy writes, "The decline of original scripts in favor of films based on popular novels [and plays] inextricably tied the larger studios to the increasing permissiveness of American fiction."

3   Genevieve Fabre, *Drumbeats, Masks, and Metaphor: Contemporary Afro-American Theatre* (Cambridge, MA: Harvard University Press, 1983), 13.

...

14   David Susskind to Sam Briskin, 13 March 1959. This and all other Susskind letters cited are in the David Susskind Papers, Wisconsin State Historical Society, Madison, Wisconsin.

15   Sam Briskin to David Susskind, 16 March 1959.

16   Sam Briskin to Paul Lazarus, 5 November 1959.

17   Harold Stern to Bernard Birnbaum, 1 June 1960. This letter is from Petrie's attorney to Columbia Pictures assistant treasurer-secretary Birnbaum. Also see Jack Pittman, "Real Things vs. Studio Mockups," *Variety*, 20 July 1960, 23.

18   Arthur Kramer to David Susskind, 30 December 1959.

19   It should be noted that, during the late 1950s and well into 1960, Africa was witnessing the Mau Mau liberation movement against British colonialists in Kenya, the Algerian liberation movement against its French colonialist government, and civil unrest in the Belgium Congo.

20   Gladstone L. Yearwood, "Toward a Theory of a Black Cinema Aesthetic," in *Black Cinema Aesthetics*, ed. Gladstone L. Yearwood (Athens, OH: Ohio University Center for Afro-American Studies, 1982), 71.

21   Robert K. Sharpe to David Susskind, 21 March 1961.

22   William Goldman to David Susskind, 3 April 1961.

23   "1961: Rentals and Potentials," *Variety*, 10 Jan. 1962, 58.

24   In "A Raisin in the Sun," *Ebony* (April 1961): 53, the author states: "with all obstacles overcome and the movie an accomplished fact, Columbia is eagerly awaiting the day when it can recoup its $1½ million investment."

25   James Baldwin, introduction to *To Be Young, Gifted and Black*, by Lorraine Hansberry (New York: New American Library, 1970), xii.

Chapter 18

Sarah Cardwell

LITERATURE ON THE SMALL SCREEN
Television adaptations

S ARAH CARDWELL'S INSIGHTFUL AND ACCESSIBLE PIECE successfully brings
together the fields of adaptation and television studies. Cardwell argues against
long-standing critical contentions that adaptations of classic novels made specifically for
television are often conservative, unimaginative, and formulaic in comparison with cinematic
adaptations of classic literature which are often positioned as more aesthetically sophisticated
and challenging. Despite certain important connections between cinematic and television
literary adaptations, Cardwell makes the case that the aesthetic choices made in television
adaptation are best explained by the medium-specific origins of television and its institutional,
technological, cultural, and formal features.

■ ■ ■

LITERATURE ON THE SMALL SCREEN: TELEVISION ADAPTATIONS
SARAH CARDWELL

From Deborah Cartmell and Imelda Whelehan (eds), *The Cambridge Companion to Literature on Screen*. Cambridge: Cambridge University Press, 2007, pp. 181–196

Practices, perceptions, and prejudices: film versus television adaptations

Since the birth of cinema, filmmakers have adapted an eclectic range of sources, including many and
varied sub-genres of literature – from classic eighteenth- and nineteenth-century novels to 'pulp'
fiction, from thrillers to romances, from melodramas to ghost stories. The breadth and variety of
film adaptations is clearly visible to most cinema-goers. When one speaks of television adaptations,
in comparison, one tends to refer more particularly to prolific 'classic serials': relatively faithful

adaptations of classic, mostly nineteenth-century, works of literature. So-called classic serials have formed a flourishing and prominent genre on television since the earliest days of broadcasting, and have constituted a significant portion of television's dramatic output.

Television adaptations of classic novels are comparatively more prominent than adaptations of other kinds of sources, not necessarily because they outnumber them, but for two powerful reasons. First, they are more frequently advertised *as adaptations*, rather than being subsumed into other generic categories – compare *The Mayor of Casterbridge* (1978), *Middlemarch* (1994), and *Pride and Prejudice* (1995) which are clearly marked as classic-novel adaptations, with series such as *Miss Marple* (1985–1992), *Inspector Morse* (1987–2000), and *The Ruth Rendell Mysteries* (1987–2000), which are regarded primarily as detective serials, and only secondarily (if at all) as adaptations. Second, classic-novel adaptations share a generic identity: they 'look' similar to one another (or so it is claimed), so that their visibility is heightened, along with their tendency to be categorized straightforwardly as adaptations.

The strong generic or group identity of television classic-novel adaptations has led, somewhat inevitably, to pejorative judgments from scholars and critics; as John Caughie notes, 'academic television criticism … has treated the classic serial with a certain disdain.'[1] One of the most commonly held prejudices against these television adaptations is that they reflect television's tendency towards conservative, staid, and unimaginative programming in contrast with cinema's more vibrant, eclectic, and innovative offerings. It is argued that television returns again and again to the same core canon of texts, by Austen, Dickens, Eliot and the like and, moreover, adapts their works in familiar ways, employing generic norms that inhibit originality, imagination and individuality; and substituting recycled conventions and simplistic 'translations' from novel to screen for truly innovative (re)interpretations of the sources. While film adaptations exhibit variety in their choice of sources, and directorial individuality and flair in their particular reinterpretations, television adaptations are often regarded as dull, formulaic products, further subsumed into categories with vaguely derogatory labels (heritage television, or costume drama, for example), rather than being regarded as potentially good, 'serious' drama.

However, television's predilection for generically consistent classic-novel adaptations is not, on its own, sufficient evidence to uphold an accusation of a lack of imagination or enterprise. Rather, such artistic choices are better explained with reference to the medium-specific origins of television, and its arising technological, institutional, cultural, and formal features. One consequence of these distinctive features is that adaptation is particularly well suited to the medium; television's serial form, for example, is often better suited to adapting expansive classic novels than is cinema. It is this close 'fit' between television and adaptation that partly explains the comparatively high rate of production of such programmes, and thus the establishment of a more clearly defined and longstanding genre of classic-novel adaptations than one encounters in the cinema.

This is not to underplay the creative and commercial connections and correlations that can be found between television and film adaptations, as selected historical instances reveal. In the 1980s and early 1990s, for example, at the height of the 'heritage film', film adaptations such as *A Room with a View* (1985), *Maurice* (1987), and *Howards End* (1992) bore striking resemblances to their renowned televisual counterparts *Brideshead Revisited* (1981) and *The Jewel in the Crown* (1984). Similarly, the popularity of Raj epics such as *Jewel* and *Staying On* (1980) was echoed in the production of cinema-release films, *Heat and Dust* (1983) and *A Passage to India* (1984). Noticeably, in these cases of correspondence between cinema and television, it is not the case (as is sometimes assumed) that television 'jumped on the bandwagon' and followed in the footsteps of pioneering filmmakers. *Brideshead* was the forerunner of Merchant Ivory's famous run of successful heritage films, and *Jewel* was contemporaneous with Lean's

Passage to India. What is clear is that one can observe creative influences amongst and between filmmakers and television makers, especially once television technology had advanced beyond studio-based techniques.

That said, it is crucial that television adaptations are considered independently of film adaptations, and that the powerful influences of medium-specific technologies, institutions, and ideals are recognized as determinants of aesthetic practices. These medium-specific roots created the differences between film and television adaptations that may be perceived even today. Furthermore, the long-standing tradition of classic-novel adaptation within television underlines the value of considering this particular group of television adaptations as a genre or sub-genre that exhibits its own norms and conventions, which do not always correspond with those found in cinematic adaptations.

Classic-novel adaptations

Classic-novel adaptations are often termed classic serials, though this is a less accurate name, as there are some programmes that fit within this 'genre' which are not serials, and it is not the serials themselves that are necessarily regarded as classic, but their sources. It is more accurate, therefore, to use the term classic-novel adaptations. These programmes form a striking and coherent generic group, and their collective identity has been recognized in a concentrated range of academic writing that tends to highlight continuities and similarities across the texts.

The programmes mostly tend to draw upon well-known literature of the nineteenth century, and sometimes of the eighteenth and early twentieth centuries. Until the mid 1990s, there was also a strong proclivity for *British* classic novels, reflecting the prevailing notion of 'educating and informing' the public about British cultural heritage. Thus adaptations of Austen, Dickens, and the Brontës have proved particularly popular on British television: *Pride and Prejudice*, *Great Expectations*, and *Jane Eyre* have each been adapted five times, and *Wuthering Heights* six times. Interestingly, although British cinema has often spurned Hardy as a source, television has retained an interest in him: since 1950, there have been only three British cinematic Hardy adaptations (and two co-productions with other countries), but eleven television versions. This proclivity for broadcasters to favour nationally specific sources is mirrored across the Atlantic: Henry James is far more frequently adapted for American television than for television in other countries.

Some critics have alleged that all classic-novel adaptations look broadly the same, and that they iron out the significant differences between the source novels. This is an exaggeration. Instead, popular perceptions of the source novels' authors have had a great influence on the style and mood of the arising adaptations: while Austen's novels are mostly adapted into whimsical, lighthearted, gently ironic romances, Dickens adaptations have generally exhibited a darker tone and have rejected straightforward naturalism, bringing out the expressionistic qualities of the sources. But it is true, nevertheless, that adaptations of Dickens (and the Brontës) to some extent mark their differences from the conventions or norms of the group; Austen and, perhaps surprisingly, Hardy adaptations are more representative of television classic-novel adaptations, with their emphasis on high production values, their 'heritage aesthetic', and their apparent nostalgia for a simpler rural past.

Compared with film adaptations, then, television adaptations have exhibited a greater interest in British classics. They have also placed a proportionately greater emphasis on dialogue, and on the slow development of characters and their interrelations. In order to make sense of this difference in approach, one must consider the early days of television.

The roots of television adaptation: early television to the 1970s

The technologies, institutions, and ideals of early television shaped classic-novel adaptations, and the impact of these factors lingers today within the genre.

The impact of medium-specific technologies on aesthetic practices

The technologies of television have always affected the stylistic choices that could be made by practitioners. At the most fundamental level, there are powerful historical reasons for the prominence of classic-novel adaptations within television. It is sometimes observed that television as a medium originated from a fascination with transmitting live moving images from one place to another, and that this fascination preceded considerations about what the technology might be used *for*. That is, at the point at which the technology to achieve this relay of moving images was invented, there had been little discussion about what precisely those images might be. Thus at first television was regarded as a valuable means of broadcasting live, 'real' events, and although its dramatic potential was soon realized, there was a need to seek out ideas for dramatic content. Understandably, broadcasters turned to existing dramatic sources for inspiration: first, theatrical sources (play texts and theatrical performances) and then literary ones (novels and short stories). These provided broadcasters with ready-made material: good stories and credible characters. In 1930, before the BBC had established regular broadcasts, they screened Pirandello's play *The Man With a Flower in His Mouth*. In 1937, when national broadcasting had only just begun, the first live television drama to be broadcast was a literary adaptation: *Journey's End*, adapted from R. C. Sherriff's play. The first drama serial was also an adaptation: *Little Women*, which ran from December 1950 to January 1951. Adaptations from plays and from literary sources dominated television's schedules.

Early television had to contend with several technological limitations in comparison with contemporary film. First, it was almost entirely studio based, and the cameras were cumbersome, heavy, and difficult to move. This meant that changes of perspective and pace had to be created through vision mixing (cutting from one camera to another, in a three or four camera set-up), rather than through moving the cameras themselves, as in film. Moreover, the ability to record the material was not developed until 1947 (and very few of those recordings were kept, until the mid 1950s). A 'repeat' was not a re-broadcasting of a previous recording, as it is today, but was an actual re-performance, as of a stage play, in which the actors reprised their roles. These conditions bore significant consequences for the aesthetics of programmes: with no post-production editing, for example, it was difficult to gain the fine, subtle control over pace and movement that was within reach for a film editor. The combination of relatively still cameras, infrequent changes of *mise-en-scène* and lack of post-production editing led to an aesthetic that we would today consider staid and rigid, especially in contrast with contemporary cinema. Finally, the quality of sound and image were comparatively poor, undermining the potential for atmospheric demarcations on the soundtrack or intricate delineations of detail within the images.

Modes of performance were also influenced by these medium-specific conditions, leading to distinctively different methods of portraying characters from those found in film. The limited movement of characters meant that the actors were restricted to moving within a demarcated area, contributing to a 'stagy' feel. Given the relative lack of physical and spatial movement available to the actors, and the limitations of the television camera in terms of cutting rapidly from one person to another in order to pick up tiny details of performance, verbal aspects of performance were of crucial importance. The screenwriter was regarded as the originator of the drama (in contrast with the director in cinema), and television established a tradition of valuing writing, and words, above other aesthetic aspects. (In this it also reflected its predecessor: radio.)

Interestingly, while some television programmes fruitfully exploited later advances in technology that provided the opportunity for innovation, classic-novel adaptations conventionalized many of these early aesthetic traits and one can find them in adaptations up to and into the 1970s. The 1971 adaptation of *Persuasion*, for example, is noticeably still and subdued in terms of camerawork, and lacking in stylistic flair. It is also conventionally 'wordy', relying upon verbal communication to convey not just story but also theme, mood, and pace. In this, adaptations consciously echoed their sources (play texts and literature), which were literally 'wordy'. Despite the possibility for alternative modes of adaptation, many adaptors chose to persist with well-established televisual practices, retaining as many as possible of the words of the source text, reproducing dialogue and translating some descriptive passages into spoken words. Thus the desire for 'fidelity' that is apparent in the aesthetic choices made in these classic-novel adaptations arose not just from an abiding sense of attachment to and respect for the original source, but also from the historical necessities and conventions of television production. This contrasts with film's early silent adaptations, which set aside words altogether and attempted to retell the stories in images. Television classic-novel adaptations have retained to this day a commitment to the careful and expressive use of verbal language, albeit alongside an expansion of the medium's audio-visual repertoire.

Given that a single set might form the location for an entire play or episode, early adaptations exhibited increased attention to details of setting and decor, compensating to some degree for a lack of shot variation and movement. One of the motivations behind such attention was an attempt to attain textual fidelity to the source, in the sense of accurately reproducing its historical and cultural moment, although unsurprisingly the programmes inevitably reflect their contemporary contexts rather more than their sources' contexts. (Compare for example the aforementioned *Persuasion* of 1971 with the 1995 version, or the 1980 *Pride and Prejudice* with its 1995 counterpart.)

A strong emphasis on the importance of the spoken word and on detailed *mise-en-scène* compensated to some extent for the considerable limitations of early television. Moreover, such limitations must be offset against the medium's particular possibilities. First, the medium has a potential for intimacy that arises from its domestic setting and its consequent role within our everyday lives. Secondly, in terms of adaptations in particular, it has one significant advantage: the serial form. Caughie argues that

> If there is a classical form of television narrative, it may be the dramatic serial. While the television film emulates, to a greater or lesser extent, the form of the cinema feature film, and the single play derives its form from the theatre play, the drama serial, having failed to establish itself as a continuing tradition in cinema, now seems specific to television and radio.[2]

Cinematic films are ordinarily limited to around two hours; television serials can be much longer, enabling fuller, more slowly and complexly developed adaptations – especially of expansive books such as those classed as 'great' literature. In this, television exhibits a closer relationship with nineteenth-century literature than does film, for much of the literature of that period was written and published in instalments. When audiences gathered to hear Dickens read the latest instalment of one of his tales aloud, they took part in a form of ongoing, communal engagement with the work that is most clearly approximated today by the audience of a television serial.

BBC Radio broadcast a regular Sunday evening serial, and this tradition was picked up by BBC Television. As mentioned previously, the first televised drama serial was an adaptation (*Little*

Women, 1950–1), which was followed by another adaptation: *The Warden*, adapted from Trollope, in 1951. That enduring favourite with adaptors, *Pride and Prejudice*, was first adapted for television in 1952. The potential for gradual, extended development across the duration of a serial can be seen in such long-running serials as *The Pallisers* (January to November 1974), adapted from six novels by Trollope, and *Clayhanger* (January to June 1976), from Arnold Bennett's novel; both serials ran for over twenty-six episodes. This is a form with which commercial cinema cannot compete. In this way, television adaptations are able not only to retain more of the source's narrative, but also to open out the details of the novel – its intricacies of plot, mood, and atmosphere – to build characters and our relationships with them more incrementally and carefully, and to sustain a sense of contemplation.

The impact of institutions and ideals on aesthetic practices

Many of the stylistic conventions of classic-novel adaptations have their roots in television's early history and technology: sedate camerawork; an emphasis on words and on detailed *mise-en-scène*, as a means for attaining fidelity; and careful exploitation of the possibilities of seriality. But adaptations on television have also been influenced by prevailing ideas about television's (social) purpose. A Reithian notion of public service broadcasting (PSB) has been crucial in shaping adaptations. Lord John Reith was the first Director General of the British Broadcasting Corporation and is associated with its public service ideals: to inform, educate, and entertain; 'Reithian' has become a shorthand for those ideals. PSB is a useful shorthand for those television channels which are state-funded, or funded by a license fee, and whose remit is to some degree determined by the state, rather than the market. They are usually required to devote a percentage of their broadcasting to programmes that further the public good, such as those that proffer education or information about important aspects of national and international culture. The remit of the BBC, which was the sole broadcaster until 1955, was to 'educate, inform, and entertain'. Adaptations were seen as a perfect way to achieve all these aims, bringing great literature (whether classic or contemporary, but especially the former) to the public. The sources most often chosen for adaptation support this analysis: acclaimed writers such as Austen, Hardy, Dickens, Eliot, and Tolstoy tend to be favoured over those outside the canon. Moreover, despite massive changes in the landscape of television, the Reithian ideal still has currency today with broadcasters, critics, and audiences, especially when discussion turns to the role of the BBC (even if challenges to the license fee pose a threat to such values).

Such PSB ideals should not be dismissed, especially if one is interested in exploring the specific aesthetic practices of television adaptation. The impact of broader ideals and purposes is too often overlooked when simplistic comparisons are made between cinema and television, and when television adaptations are accused of being more obsessed with fidelity and with a narrow range of British literature. Historically speaking, a television adaptation, unlike a film, cannot be regarded as mere entertainment. Its aim is not limited to being financially viable or even artistically successful; its accomplishments are also measured with reference to these broader conceptions of television's public role. This in part explains television adaptations' preoccupation with fidelity. If the public is to depend upon these representations of great literature for their educative and informative value, then the adaptations must provide a fair representation of the source novels. Thus the fidelity that has been encouraged by medium-specific features is endorsed by the ideals and institutions of the specifically televisual context.

Furthermore, given this emphasis on conveying accurate 'content', the medium was required to remain just that: a means by which something, some pre-televisual event, could be accessed, just as it was when broadcasting original live events. Up to the 1970s, it was preferred that the medium itself remain invisible, or at least transparent, when adapting classic literature, and the relative stillness of the camera and corresponding lack of emphasis on 'directorial style' such as that found in cinema enhanced this. In this way, adaptations developed as stylistically distinct from other television drama, where the form/content balance was struck differently, and where transparency was more often rejected in favour of formal experimentation, innovation, or reflexivity.

Consolidating and expanding the genre: classic-novel adaptations from the 1980s to the 2000s

By the 1980s, television had grown into what may be regarded as a multi-channel environment (ITV had begun broadcasting in 1955, and Channel Four followed in 1982). Improvements in television technology, and the rise of videotapes and then DVDs, broadened television's aesthetic potential and meant that programme makers could foresee endurance, even longevity, for their work. In addition, the opening up of the television market had a positive impact upon the development of television adaptations. Whilst the BBC had already established its reputation for reliable, well-produced adaptations of the classics, the commercial channel ITV made its mark with several innovative and successful adaptations, and indeed it was independent company Granada who was responsible for both *Jewel in the Crown* and the ground-breaking serial *Brideshead Revisited*.

Brideshead was shot on 16 mm, which enabled a greater variety of shots and camera movements, and allowed these 'filmic' aspects to play as vital a role as the dialogue. Indeed, the serial's most significant achievement – the reproduction of the source novel's distinctively nostalgic tone – was attained through the careful integration of music, camerawork, dialogue, and performance, which in turn developed subtleties of pace, momentum, colour, and tone. Again, the advantages of televisual serial form were fully exploited here, as the story was slowly and carefully unravelled, creating possibilities for reflection and contemplation on the part of the characters and the viewers.

The popularity and success of *Brideshead* revitalized the genre of classic-novel adaptations, and the 1980s saw a consolidation of the conventions that are now so familiar, and which include: high production values; 'authentic', detailed costumes and sets; 'great British actors'; light classical music; slow pace; steady, often symmetrical framing; an interest in landscapes, buildings, and interiors as well as characters; strong, gradually developed protagonists accompanied by entertaining cameo roles; and intelligent, 'faithful' dialogue. These characteristics were not just repeated, but also deepened during the 1980s, as the genre became more familiar and programme makers thus endeavoured to distinguish their work from others', through ever-increasing attention to the integration of stylistic details.

At the start of the 1990s, the genre was at risk of becoming stale. It seemed that the classic-novel adaptation might founder, as it appeared resolved to repeating the same fundamental conventions, like a stuck record. Another glut of Austen adaptations did little to alter this, although *Persuasion* (1992) stood out, combining fidelity to the dialogue and spirit of the source text whilst breaking away from norms of the genre and employing multi-strand narrative and even some hand-held camerawork. Andrew Davies's phenomenally successful *Pride and Prejudice*, in 1995, was saturated with the norms of the genre. Impressive and successful in its own right, this adaptation had an impact upon the viewing public that rivalled that of *Brideshead*, and revealed that the 'multi-channel environment' did not disallow the kinds of mass television events that were possible in earlier eras. At the same time, though, the programme marked a turning point. Having intensified every convention and exaggerated every code, it seemed that ensuing adaptations had nowhere to go. Interestingly, Davies himself was one of the first to recognize this, and true to his history of innovation and reinvention, he reshaped the genre yet again with his notable adaptations of *Moll Flanders* (1996) and *Vanity Fair* (1998), among others.

The efforts of programme makers to revitalize classic-novel adaptations around the turn of the century can be seen in two areas in particular. First, there was a marked broadening in the range of source novels chosen for adaptation, in particular incorporating novels from outside Britain, such as *Madame Bovary* (2000), *Anna Karenina* (2000), *Doctor Zhivago* (2002,) and *Crime and Punishment* (2002). Second, adaptations became stylistically more innovative, varied and reflexive. Thus we find the Brechtian deployment of direct address in *Moll Flanders*; the humorous undermining of generic norms in order to draw out buffoonish and satirical elements in *Vanity Fair*; the subtle yet sharp puncturing of generic expectations, especially nostalgic tone, in *The Tenant of Wildfell Hall* (1996); and the overturning of generic conventions in the experimental *Crime and Punishment*. Accompanying these changes are shifts in performance style, with acting becoming more varied across different adaptations. The reflexive styles of performance in much of Davies's work (such as *Moll Flanders* and *Vanity Fair*) are palpably distinct from the more naturalistic performances found in *The Tenant of Wildfell Hall*, for example.

Scholarship

Given the sheer range within the genre today, it is somewhat surprising that many critics and theorists continue to paint a very narrow picture of it. Adaptation theorists frequently overlook television altogether, and focus only on literature/film adaptations.[3] Current television scholarship tends to subsume adaptations into other categories, often regarding them simply as 'costume dramas'. Lez Cooke, for example, lumps together costume drama and classic-novel adaptations from the mid 1990s – at exactly the point at which the genre becomes more varied – with the justification that these programmes are all a part of the 'heritage export' which makes British programmes like these so popular in other countries;[4] Robin Nelson also conflates the two.[5] Yet if there is a group of programmes called 'costume dramas', these include, alongside classic-novel adaptations, adaptations from popular novels, and original programmes, and any seasoned viewer is able to recognize that these programmes are distinct from one another. Costume dramas based on popular novels, such as Catherine Cookson adaptations (of which there was a glut in the 1990s), or original screenplays, such as *Upstairs Downstairs* (1971–5) and *House of Elliot* (1991–4) exhibit different emphases, scope, and values. Compared with their classic-novel counterparts, these programmes place less emphasis on dialogue and rarely contend with issues of fidelity, and they intensify their use of melodramatic conventions, raising the emotional temperature through melodramatic music and performance styles. To subsume classic-novel adaptations into costume dramas is to over-simplify these televisual forms and underplay their differences.

Frequent and persistent recourse to notions of 'heritage' also limits understanding of classic-novel adaptations. The heritage debate has long appealed to critics and theorists (myself included): Cooke writes about heritage television,[6] and Nelson argues that adaptations are concerned no longer with fidelity but with the nostalgic presentation of heritage.[7] But taken alone, this is too simplistic a view of the genre. It is true that the television classic-novel adaptation is closely related to the heritage film, but since the late 1990s in particular, it is simply not the case that the genre can be defined by its obsession with heritage – nor by a 'nostalgic' tone – as is demonstrated by the exceptions named above.

Adaptations of contemporary and popular literature

While television classic-novel adaptations have historically had a high profile, this is not true of adaptations of contemporary and/or popular novels. These adaptations are relatively fewer, and they are much less visible, especially because many of them correspond quite easily to existing television genres and they thus find their place within pre-established forms, alongside non-adapted sources. In a sense, these are the 'hidden' adaptations, which make little noise about their adapted status. For example, *Inspector Morse*, *The Ruth Rendell Mysteries*, and Catherine Cookson adaptations are commonly regarded not as adaptations but primarily as detective series, murder-mystery series, and romance, respectively. A similar logic applies with many science fiction adaptations: *The Time Machine* (adapted in 1949) is well known as a novel by H. G. Wells, but has been readapted so many times that it also forms part of a sub-genre of 'time-travel' films and programmes. The 1954 television version of *Nineteen Eighty-Four*, despite the fame of its source, is usually explored as part of the history of science fiction television, rather than as an adaptation; even Jason Jacobs, in his excellent and detailed discussion of the programme, limits his acknowledgment of its adapted status to a discussion of the comparative reception of the novel and the programme.[8]

Adaptations of popular novels that are non-generic are rarer, but include adaptations as varied as those of R. F. Delderfield's *To Serve Them All My Days* (1980), Kingsley Amis's *The Old Devils* (1992), Hanif Kureishi's *The Buddha of Suburbia* (1993), Angela Lambert's *A Rather English Marriage* (1998), Mervyn Peake's *Gormenghast* (2000), Anthony Trollope's *The Way We Live Now* (2001), and Zadie Smith's *White Teeth* (2002). Of course these adaptations differ in terms of their success, but in opening up a range of genres, sources, perspectives, and voices, adaptations of contemporary and popular literature contribute to the breadth of television drama today.

Television and film adaptations today

Television adaptations have seen immense changes in their technological, institutional and creative contexts. Yet some fundamental features of early adaptations linger. Despite the broadening of the classic-novel adaptation canon, British television retains a penchant – and a reputation – for adapting great British classics and for working within some kind of public service remit; cinema, after the height of the heritage film, remains less clearly nationally specific. The issue of fidelity persists in the case of classic-novel adaptations, primarily because of the special status of these highly regarded and much-loved sources. Yet while this is as true for film classic-novel adaptations as it is for television ones, still the latter exhibit a more overt historical commitment to fidelity, perhaps because of television's enduring PSB role. The consequences of this are that television produces some of the strongest, most sensitive adaptations of lengthy and/or complex novels, such as *Far From the Madding Crowd* (1998) and *Daniel Deronda* (2002). These two examples reveal that the modern competitive marketplace within television sometimes results in successful collaborations – the former is one in a long line of acclaimed BBC co-productions with the American PSB company WGBH Boston, and the latter was made by the producers of *Brideshead*: Granada, in collaboration with WGBH Boston and Mobil Masterpiece Theatre.

The historical legacy of television's establishment, consolidation, and development of the classic-novel adaptation should not be regarded as a hindrance, or as something which today's adaptors need to move on from, or away from. Of course, there will always be weak, formulaic and dull 'generic products', but the presence of historically established traditions and structures also open up immense possibilities. Programme makers are able to take a certain generic literacy for granted, and therefore have greater freedom to use generic shorthand, to play with and subvert formal conventions, and open up greater reflexivity within programmes. These possibilities have been most clearly taken up in the adaptations of the late 1990s, especially in those scripted by Andrew Davies, who has made the genre his specialism, and is the closest it has to an auteur.

Davies's high profile draws attention to the fact that television still places a much stronger emphasis on writing than that found in the cinema, and despite technological and creative developments, and the notable increase in directorial flair within the medium, the screenwriter retains his status, and is comparable with the director in cinema. Not only does this allow an individual like Davies to build a career within television, it also means that he can endow this television genre with an artistic personality. Moreover, his work is the ultimate case-study for those interested in the progression of television adaptation: he has adapted popular and classic texts; he was a major contributor to the establishment of the genre of classic-novel adaptations; and he has always been eclectic in his choice of sources, but has become more interested in international sources in the late 1990s.[9]

Fidelity remains important – but it is also the case that notions of fidelity have altered. While in early adaptations it implied faithfulness to the words of the novel, in later adaptations, as television has developed stylistically, and greater expressive opportunities have opened up, fidelity has been reconfigured and adaptors have become more concerned with conveying the 'spirit' of the source text. Adaptations have become more courageous and imaginative, and viewers seem more willing to accept changes to plot and dialogue if they perceive some underlying attempt to achieve fidelity to the style, tone, or spirit of the original. Perhaps this can be regarded as a shift in understanding: the affiliation to the source text remains, but it is possibly better conceptualized as a desire to show *respect* to that text, rather than to be *faithful* to it. In the early days of television, fidelity to the 'content' – specifically the plot and the words – of the source was the dominant method through which an adaptor could express his or her respect for that former text; now with technological, cultural, and creative advances, there are many alternative ways. It also appears that adaptors have broadened their artistic impulses and updated the Reithian aim of educating and informing the audience to one of inspiring enthusiasm in the viewers for the source text and for the adaptation itself. This would explain why television adaptations today now rival the levels of variety and innovation that can be seen in cinematic versions.

While the small screen can suffer in contrast with the large screen (such as in the reception of the recent television version of *Doctor Zhivago*, in contrast with Lean's classic cinematic version), it can also fare well in comparison. The best television adaptations continue to use one of television's major strengths – its serial form   and exploit this in combination with a strong emphasis on writing high-quality dialogue, and the medium's greater capacity for intimate equality with the viewer. Thus lengthy, episodic, or picaresque novels often adapt more successfully to television: consider the feisty and fascinating television serial *Moll Flanders*, or the witty and reflexive television version of *Vanity Fair*, both of which overshadow the most recent cinematic versions (1996 and 2004).

This chapter opened with some of the more negative ways in which television adaptations have been characterized and dismissed. When examining television adaptation, one has the usual problem of a lack of archive material from before the 1950s, but this is less frustrating a barrier than having to counter common perceptions of the genre. Television scholars are able to get away with gross generalizations, most often derisive, which would not be tolerated in film studies. Characterizations of classic-novel adaptations, in particular, are frustratingly slow to change, and do not reflect the genre as it currently stands. Those of us who outlined the 'genre' of classic-novel adaptations, drawing upon work on the heritage film, perhaps did not expect that these necessarily broad and tentative sketches would be perpetuated without further reflection, challenge, and refinement.[10] The 'generic' approach has been extremely valuable in distinguishing television from film adaptations, and future studies may use it to delineate classic-novel adaptations from, for example, costume dramas. It has also steered television scholars away from simplistic comparative evaluations of adaptations with their source texts. But the generic approach should not replace a close attention to the distinctive qualities of individual texts, most of which do not fit straightforwardly within generic norms and boundaries. The generic context is only one of the contexts that have influenced television adaptations. It would be fruitful to move towards a greater understanding of and responsiveness to the particularities of the television medium, accepting its limitations and recognizing its special capacities, and to evaluate adaptations from within such a comprehension. It is also vital to recognize television's different historical purposes and principles. Television adaptations are not a branch of film adaptations but are a distinct medium-specific form.

■ ■ ■

Questions and projects

1. Succinctly summarize what distinguishes television adaptations of literature from cinematic adaptations. The technology of the image? Sound? Viewing conditions? Are certain works of literature, such as Evelyn Waugh's *Brideshead Revisited* or any Dickens novel, more suited to these conditions than others?
2. Compare successful film and television adaptations by a single author or of a single work of literature (for instance, the 1945 film *Mildred Pierce* with Todd Haynes's 2011 television adaptation of the novel). How do they use their respective media to draw out different themes and ideas?

Notes

1   John Caughie, *Television Drama: Realism, Modernism, and British Culture* (Oxford Television Studies: Oxford University Press, 2000), p. 207.
2   Caughie, *Television Drama*, p. 205.
3   Three important recent publications in the field exemplify this tradition of excluding consideration of television adaptations, as their titles imply: Robert Stam and Alessandra Raengo's *Literature and Film: A Guide to the Theory and Practice of Film Adaptation* (Malden, MA and Oxford: Blackwell, 2005); its companion volume, also edited by Stam and Raengo and published simultaneously by Blackwell, *A Companion to Literature and Film*; and Kamilla Elliott's *Rethinking the Novel/Film Debate* (Cambridge: Cambridge University Press, 2003). All three books extend their scope beyond adaptation studies, yet ignore television adaptations.
4   Lez Cooke, *British Television Drama: A History* (London: BFI Publishing, 2003), pp. 166–9.
5   Robin Nelson, 'Costume Drama (Jane Austen adaptations)', in Glen Creeber (ed.), *The Television Genre Book* (London: BFI Publishing, 2001), pp. 38–41.
6   Cooke, *British Television Drama*, p. 83.
7   Nelson, 'Costume Drama', p. 39.
8   Jason Jacobs, *The Intimate Screen: Early British Television Drama* (Oxford Television Studies: Clarendon Press, 2000), pp. 139–55.
9   Sarah Cardwell, *Andrew Davies: The Television Series* (Manchester: Manchester University Press), 2005.
10   Sarah Cardwell, *Adaptation Revisited: Television and the Classic Novel* (Manchester: Manchester University Press), 2002.

2.3   AUTHORS AND AUTEURS

Chapter 19

Alexandre Astruc

THE BIRTH OF A NEW AVANT-GARDE
La caméra-stylo

T HIS 1948 ESSAY BY ALEXANDRE ASTRUC is considered by many to be a seminal
statement in the appearance of New Wave directors in France, other European countries,
and eventually the United States. It is a dramatic and compelling assertion that filmmakers
could use the camera as a writer uses a pen or as an essayist expresses thoughts. The analogy
is a fragile one, given the collaborative teamwork necessary to make a film and the economic
and technological obstacles that stand between an individual's idea and its filmic expression.
Yet, the timing of the statement is historically precise: film and filmmakers were positioning
themselves on separate but equal terms with literature; the industrial monolith of Hollywood
cinema was beginning to give way to alternative practices; and camera technology would
soon introduce more mobile, lightweight equipment that could be used by individuals rather
than teams. Following Astruc, the debates about film and literature would include notions of
film as personal expression, the filmmakers as author or auteur, and an increasingly complex
sense of what the "language" of film is or is not.

■ ■ ■

THE BIRTH OF A NEW AVANT-GARDE: LA CAMÉRA-STYLO
ALEXANDRE ASTRUC

From Peter Graham (ed.), *The New Wave*, New York: Doubleday, 1968, pp 17–23

What interests me in the cinema is abstraction.
—Orson Welles

One cannot help noticing that something is happening in the cinema at the moment. Our sensibilities
have been in danger of getting blunted by those everyday films which, year in year out, show their
tired and conventional faces to the world.

The cinema of today is getting a new face. How can one tell? Simply by using one's eyes. Only a film critic could fail to notice the striking facial transformation which is taking place before our very eyes. In which films can this new beauty be found? Precisely those which have been ignored by the critics. It is not just a coincidence that Renoir's *La Règle du Jeu*, Welles's films, and Bresson's *Les Dames du Bois de Boulogne*, all films which establish the foundations of a new future for the cinema, have escaped the attention of critics, who in any case were not capable of spotting them.

But it is significant that the films which fail to obtain the blessing of the critics are precisely those which myself and several of my friends all agree about. We see in them, if you like, something of the prophetic. That's why I am talking about *avant-garde*. There is always an *avant-garde* when something new takes place. ...

To come to the point: the cinema is quite simply becoming a means of expression, just as all the other arts have been before it, and in particular painting and the novel. After having been successively a fairground attraction, an amusement analogous to boulevard theatre, or a means of preserving the images of an era, it is gradually becoming a language. By language I mean a form in which and by which an artist can express his thoughts, however abstract they may be, or translate his obsessions exactly as he does in the contemporary essay or novel. That is why I would like to call this new age of cinema the age of *caméra-stylo* (camera-pen). This metaphor has a very precise sense. By it I mean that the cinema will gradually break free from the tyranny of what is visual, from the image for its own sake, from the immediate and concrete demands of the narrative, to become a means of writing just as flexible and subtle as written language. This art, although blessed with an enormous potential, is an easy prey to prejudice; it cannot go on for ever ploughing the same field of realism and social fantasy which has been bequeathed to it by the popular novel. It can tackle any subject, any genre. The most philosophical meditations on human production, psychology, ideas, and passions lie well within its province. I will even go so far as to say that contemporary ideas and philosophies of life are such that only the cinema can do justice to them. Maurice Nadeau wrote in an article in the newspaper *Combat*: 'If Descartes lived today, he would write novels.' With all due respect to Nadeau, a Descartes of today would already have shut himself up in his bedroom with a 16mm camera and some film, and would be writing his philosophy on film: for his *Discours de la Méthode* would today be of such a kind that only the cinema could express it satisfactorily.

It must be understood that up to now the cinema has been nothing more than a show. This is due to the basic fact that all films are projected in an auditorium. But with the development of 16mm and television, the day is not far off when everyone will possess a projector, will go to the local bookstore and hire films written on any subject, of any form, from literary criticism and novels to mathematics, history, and general science. From that moment on, it will no longer be possible to speak of *the* cinema. There will be *several* cinemas just as today there are several literatures, for the cinema, like literature, is not so much a particular art as a language which can express any sphere of thought.

This idea of the cinema expressing ideas is not perhaps a new one. Feyder has said: 'I could make a film with Montesquieu's *L'Esprit des Lois*.' But Feyder was thinking of illustrating it 'with pictures' just as Eisenstein had thought of illustrating Marx's *Capital* in book fashion.

What I am trying to say is that cinema is now moving towards a form which is making it such a precise language that it will soon be possible to write ideas directly on film without even having to resort to those heavy associations of images that were the delight of the silent cinema. In other words, in order to suggest the passing of time, there is no need to show falling leaves and then apple trees in blossom; and in order to suggest that a hero wants to make love there are surely other ways of going about it than showing a saucepan of milk boiling over on the stove, as Clouzot does in *Quai des Orfèvres.*

The fundamental problem of the cinema is how to express thought. The creation of this language has preoccupied all the theoreticians and writers in the history of the cinema, from Eisenstein down to the scriptwriters and adaptors of the sound cinema. But neither the silent cinema, because it was the slave of a static conception of the image, nor the classical sound cinema, as it has existed right up to now, has been able to solve this problem satisfactorily. The silent cinema thought it could get out of it through editing and the juxtaposition of images. Remember Eisenstein's famous statement: 'Editing is for me the means of giving movement (i.e., an idea) to two static images.' And when sound came, he was content to adapt theatrical devices.

One of the fundamental phenomena of the last few years has been the growing realization of the dynamic, i.e., significant, character of the cinematic image. Every film, because its primary function is to move, i.e., to take place in time, is a theorem. It is a series of images which, from one end to the other, have an inexorable logic (or better even, a dialectic) of their own. We have come to realize that the meaning which the silent cinema tried to give birth to through symbolic association exists within the image itself, in the development of the narrative, in every gesture of the characters, in every line of dialogue, in those camera movements which relate objects to characters and characters to objects. All thought, like all feeling, is a relationship between one human being and another human being or certain objects which form part of his universe. It is by clarifying these relationships, by making a tangible allusion, that the cinema can really make itself the vehicle of thought. From today onwards, it will be possible for the cinema to produce works which are equivalent, in their profundity and meaning, to the novels of Faulkner and Malraux, to the essays of Sartre and Camus. Moreover we already have a significant example: Malraux's *L'Espoir,* the film which he directed from his own novel, in which, perhaps for the first time ever, film language is the exact equivalent of literary language.

Let us now have a look at the way people make concessions to the supposed (but fallacious) requirements of the cinema. Script writers who adapt Balzac or Dostoievsky excuse the idiotic transformations they impose on the works from which they construct their scenarios by pleading that the cinema is incapable of rendering every psychological or metaphysical overtone. In their hands, Balzac becomes a collection of engravings in which fashion has the most important place, and Dostoievsky suddenly begins to resemble the novels of Joseph Kessel, with Russian-style drinking-bouts in night-clubs and troika races in the snow. Well, the only cause of these compressions is laziness and lack of imagination. The cinema of today is capable of expressing any kind of reality. What interests us is the creation of this new language. We have no desire to rehash those poetic documentaries and surrealist films of twenty-five years ago every time we manage to escape the demands of a commercial industry. Let's face it: between the pure cinema of the 1920s and filmed theatre, there is plenty of room for a different and individual kind of film-making.

This of course implies that the scriptwriter directs his own scripts; or rather that the scriptwriter ceases to exist, for in this kind of film-making the distinction between author and director loses all meaning. Direction is no longer a means of illustrating or presenting a scene, but a true act of writing. The film-maker/author writes with his camera as a writer writes with his pen. In an art in which a length of film and sound-track is put in motion and proceeds, by means of a certain form and a certain story (there can even be no story at all—it matters little), to evolve a philosophy of life, how can one possibly distinguish between the man who conceives the work and the man who writes it? Could one imagine a Faulkner novel written by someone other than Faulkner? And would *Citizen Kane* be satisfactory in any other form than that given to it by Orson Welles?

Let me say once again that I realize the term *avant-garde* savors of the surrealist and so-called abstract films of the 1920s. But that *avant-garde* is already old hat. It was trying to create a specific domain for the cinema; we on the contrary are seeking to broaden it and make it the most extensive and clearest language there is. Problems such as the translation into cinematic terms of verbal tenses and logical relationships interest us much more than the creation of the exclusively visual and static art dreamt of by the surrealists. In any case, they were doing no more than make cinematic adaptations of their experiments in painting and poetry.

So there we are. This has nothing to do with a school, or even a movement. Perhaps it could simply be called a tendency: a new awareness, a desire to transform the cinema and hasten the advent of an exciting future. Of course, no tendency can be so called unless it has something concrete to show for itself. The films will come, they will see the light of day—make no mistake about it. The economic and material difficulties of the cinema create the strange paradox whereby one can talk about something which does not yet exist; for although we know what we want, we do not know whether, when, and how we will be able to do it. But the cinema cannot but develop. It is an art that cannot live by looking back over the past and chewing over the nostalgic memories of an age gone by. Already it is looking to the future; for the future, in the cinema as elsewhere, is the only thing that matters.

■　■　■

Questions and projects

1. Choose a specific filmmaker (say, Marguerite Duras, Rainer Werner Fassbinder, or David Lynch) whose films seem to be about personal expression. What are the most important textual or thematic signs of this personal expression? Does that work also suggest differences between literary writing and filmmaking?
2. How has the idea and image of a film director as a literary writer or auteur changed over the last four decades? Contrast the films of two or three filmmakers from different periods or places, and compare the different ways they use the cinema to position themselves as versions of the writer expressing his or her thoughts or perspectives.

Chapter 20

Peter Wollen

THE AUTEUR THEORY

THEORIST, WRITER, AND FILMMAKER, PETER WOLLEN has had an immense impact on the field of contemporary film studies. In this piece, drawn from his seminal 1969 work *Signs and Meaning in the Cinema,* Wollen deftly brings together the individual artistry of auteurism or film authorship with an account of textual meaning informed by structuralism and semiotics. Ultimately, Wollen argues that the auteur theory does not imply a transparent transfer of meaning from auteur to audience, but rather requires active interpretation to trace core themes and motifs across a body of work.

■ ■ ■

THE AUTEUR THEORY
PETER WOLLEN

From *Signs and Meaning in the Cinema*, Bloomington, IN: Indiana University Press, 1972, pp. 74–105

The *politique des auteurs* – the *auteur* theory, as Andrew Sarris calls it – was developed by the loosely knit group of critics who wrote for *Cahiers du Cinéma* and made it the leading film magazine in the world. It sprang from the conviction that the American cinema was worth studying in depth, that masterpieces were made not only by a small upper crust of directors, the cultured gilt on the commercial gingerbread, but by a whole range of authors, whose work had previously been dismissed and consigned to oblivion. There were special conditions in Paris which made this conviction possible. Firstly, there was the fact that American films were banned from France under the Vichy government and the German Occupation. Consequently, when they reappeared after the Liberation they came with a force – and an emotional impact – which was necessarily missing in the Anglo-Saxon countries themselves. And, secondly, there was a thriving ciné-club movement, due in part to the close connections there had always been in France between the cinema and the intelligentsia: witness the example of Jean Cocteau or André Malraux. Connected with this ciné-club movement was the magnificent Paris *Cinémathèque*, the work of Henri Langlois, a great *auteur*, as Jean-Luc Godard described him. The policy of the *Cinémathèque* was to show the maximum number of films, to plough back the production of the past in order to produce the culture in which the cinema of the future could thrive. It gave French *cinéphiles* an unmatched perception of the historical dimensions of Hollywood and the careers of individual directors.

The *auteur* theory grew up rather haphazardly; it was never elaborated in programmatic terms, in a manifesto or collective statement. As a result, it could be interpreted and applied on rather broad lines; different critics developed somewhat different methods within a loose framework of common attitudes. This looseness and diffuseness of the theory has allowed flagrant misunderstandings to take root, particularly among critics in Britain and the United States. Ignorance has been compounded by a vein of hostility to foreign ideas and a taste for travesty and caricature. However, the fruitfulness of the *auteur* approach has been such that it has made headway even on the most unfavourable terrain. For instance, a recent straw poll of British critics, conducted in conjunction with a Don Siegel Retrospective at the National Film Theatre, revealed that, among American directors most admired, a group consisting of Budd Boetticher, Samuel Fuller and Howard Hawks ran immediately behind Ford, Hitchcock and Welles, who topped the poll, but ahead of Billy Wilder, Josef Von Sternberg and Preston Sturges.

Of course, some individual directors have always been recognised as outstanding: Charles Chaplin, John Ford, Orson Welles. The *auteur* theory does not limit itself to acclaiming the director as the main author of a film. It implies an operation of decipherment; it reveals authors where none had been seen before. For years, the model of an author in the cinema was that of the European director, with open artistic aspirations and full control over his films. This model still lingers on; it lies behind the existential distinction between art films and popular films. Directors who built their reputations in Europe were dismissed after they crossed the Atlantic, reduced to anonymity. American Hitchcock was contrasted unfavourably with English Hitchcock, American Renoir with French Renoir, American Fritz Lang with German Fritz Lang. The *auteur* theory has led to the revaluation of the second, Hollywood careers of these and other European directors; without it, masterpieces such as *Scarlet Street* or *Vertigo* would never have been perceived. Conversely, the *auteur* theory has been sceptical when offered an American director whose salvation has been exile to Europe. It is difficult now to argue that *Brute Force* has ever been excelled by Jules Dassin or that Joseph Losey's recent work is markedly superior to, say, *The Prowler*.

In time, owing to the diffuseness of the original theory, two main schools of *auteur* critics grew up: those who insisted on revealing a core of meanings, of thematic motifs, and those who stressed style and *mise en scène*. There is an important distinction here, which I shall return to later. The work of the *auteur* has a semantic dimension, it is not purely formal; the work of the *metteur en scène*, on the other hand, does not go beyond the realm of performance, of transposing into the special complex of cinematic codes and channels a pre-existing text: a scenario, a book or a play. As we shall see, the meaning of the films of an *auteur* is constructed *a posteriori*; the meaning – semantic, rather than stylistic or expressive – of the films of a *metteur en scène* exists *a priori*. In concrete cases, of course, this distinction is not always clear-cut. There is controversy over whether some directors should be seen as *auteurs* or *metteurs en scène*. For example, though it is possible to make intuitive ascriptions, there have been no really persuasive accounts as yet of Raoul Walsh or William Wyler as *auteurs*, to take two very different directors. Opinions might differ about Don Siegel or George Cukor. Because of the difficulty of fixing the distinction in these concrete cases, it has often become blurred; indeed, some French critics have tended to value the *metteur en scène* above the *auteur*. MacMahonism sprang up, with its cult of Walsh, Lang,

Losey and Preminger, its fascination with violence and its notorious text: 'Charlton Heston is an axiom of the cinema'. What André Bazin called 'aesthetic cults of personality' began to be formed. Minor directors were acclaimed before they had, in any real sense, been identified and defined.

Yet the *auteur* theory has survived despite all the hallucinating critical extravaganzas which it has fathered. It has survived because it is indispensable. Geoffrey Nowell-Smith has summed up the *auteur* theory as it is normally presented today:

> One essential corollary of the theory as it has been developed is the discovery that the defining characteristics of an author's work are not necessarily those which are most readily apparent. The purpose of criticism thus becomes to uncover behind the superficial contrasts of subject and treatment a hard core of basic and often recondite motifs. The pattern formed by these motifs ... is what gives an author's work its particular structure, both defining it internally and distinguishing one body of work from another.

It is this 'structural approach', as Nowell-Smith calls it, which is indispensable for the critic.

The test case for the *auteur* theory is provided by the work of Howard Hawks. Why Hawks, rather than, say, Frank Borzage or King Vidor? Firstly, Hawks is a director who has worked for years within the Hollywood system. His first film, *Road to Glory*, was made in 1926. Yet throughout his long career he has only once received general critical acclaim, for his wartime film, *Sergeant York*, which closer inspections reveals to be eccentric and atypical of the main *corpus* of Hawks's films. Secondly, Hawks has worked in almost every genre. He has made westerns, (*Rio Bravo*), gangsters (*Scarface*), war films (*Air Force*), thrillers (*The Big Sleep*), science fiction (*The Thing from Another World*), musicals (*Gentlemen Prefer Blondes*), comedies (*Bringing up Baby*), even a Biblical epic (*Land of the Pharaohs*). Yet all of these films (except perhaps *Land of the Pharaohs*, which he himself was not happy about) exhibit the same thematic preoccupations, the same recurring motifs and incidents, the same visual style and tempo. In the same way that Roland Barthes constructed a species of *homo racinianus*, the critic can construct a *homo hawksianus*, the protagonist of Hawksian values in the problematic Hawksian world.

Hawks achieved this by reducing the genres to two basic types: the adventure drama and the crazy comedy. These two types express inverse views of the world, the positive and negative poles of the Hawksian vision. Hawks stands opposed, on the one hand, to John Ford and, on the other hand, to Budd Boetticher. All these directors are concerned with the problem of heroism. For the hero, as an individual, death is an absolute limit which cannot be transcended: it renders the life which preceded it meaningless, absurd. How then can there be any meaningful individual action during life? How can individual action have any value – be heroic – if it cannot have transcendent value, because of the absolutely devaluing limit of death? John Ford finds the answer to this question by placing and situating the individual within society and within history, specifically within American history. Ford finds transcendent values in the historic vocation of America as a nation, to bring civilisation to a savage land, the garden to the wilderness. At the same time, Ford also sees these values themselves as problematic; he begins to question the movement of American history itself. Boetticher, on the contrary, insists on a radical individualism. 'I am not interested in making films about mass feelings. I am for the individual.' He looks for values in the encounter with death itself: the underlying metaphor is always that of the bull-fighter in the arena. The hero enters a group of companions, but there is no possibility of group solidarity. Boetticher's hero acts by dissolving groups and collectives of any kind into their constituent individuals, so that he confronts each person face-to-face; the films develop, in Andrew Sarris's words, into 'floating poker games, where every character takes turns at bluffing about his hand until the final showdown'. Hawks, unlike

Boetticher, seeks transcendent values beyond the individual, in solidarity with others. But, unlike Ford, he does not give his heroes any historical dimension, any destiny in time.

For Hawks the highest human emotion is the camaraderie of the exclusive, self-sufficient, all-male group. Hawks's heroes are cattlemen, marlin-fishermen, racing-drivers, pilots, big-game hunters, habituated to danger and living apart from society, actually cut off from it physically by dense forest, sea, snow or desert. Their aerodromes are fog-bound; the radio has cracked up; the next mail-coach or packet-boat does not leave for a week. The *élite* group strictly preserves its exclusivity. It is necessary to pass a test of ability and courage to win admittance. The group's only internal tensions come when one member lets the other down (the drunk deputy in *Rio Bravo*, the panicky pilot in *Only Angels Have Wings*) and must redeem himself by some act of exceptional bravery, or occasionally when too much 'individualism' threatens to disrupt the close-knit circle (the rivalry between drivers in *Red Line 7000*, the fighter pilot among the bomber crew in *Air Force*). The group's security is the first commandment: 'You get a stunt team in acrobatics in the air – if one of them is no good, then they're all in trouble. If someone loses his nerve catching animals, then the whole bunch can be in trouble.' The group members are bound together by rituals (in *Hatari!* blood is exchanged by transfusion) and express themselves univocally in communal sing-songs. There is a famous example of this in *Rio Bravo*. In *Dawn Patrol* the camaraderie of the pilots stretches even across the enemy lines: a captured German ace is immediately drafted into the group and joins in the sing-song; in *Hatari!* hunters of different nationality and in different places join together in a song over an intercom radio system.

Hawks's heroes pride themselves on their professionalism. They ask: 'How good is he? He'd better be good.' They expect no praise for doing their job well. Indeed, none is given except: 'The boys did all right.' When they die, they leave behind them only the most meagre personal belongings, perhaps a handful of medals. Hawks himself has summed up this desolate and barren view of life:

> It's just a calm acceptance of a fact. In *Only Angels Have Wings*, after Joe dies, Cary Grant says: 'He just wasn't good enough.' Well, that's the only thing that keeps people going. They just have to say: 'Joe wasn't good enough, and I'm better than Joe, so I go ahead and do it.' And they find out they're not any better than Joe, but then it's too late, you see.

In Ford films, death is celebrated by funeral services, an impromptu prayer, a few staves of 'Shall we gather at the river?' – it is inserted into an ongoing system of ritual institutions, along with the wedding, the dance, the parade. But for Hawks it is enough that the routine of the group's life goes on, a routine whose only relieving features are 'danger' (*Hatari!*) and 'fun'. Danger gives existence pungency: 'Every time you get real action, then you have danger. And the question, "Are you living or not living?" is probably the biggest drama we have.' This nihilism, in which 'living' means no more than being in danger of losing your life – a danger entered into quite gratuitously – is augmented by the Hawksian concept of having 'fun'. The word 'fun' crops up constantly in Hawks's interviews and scripts. It masks his despair.

When one of Hawks's *élite* is asked, usually by a woman, why he risks his life, he replies: 'No reason I can think of makes any sense. I guess we're just crazy.' Or Feathers, sardonically, to Colorado in *Rio Bravo*: 'You haven't even the excuse I have. We're all fools.' By 'crazy' Hawks does not mean psychopathic: none of his characters are like Turkey in Peckinpah's *The Deadly Companions* or Billy the Kid in Penn's *The Left-Handed Gun*. Nor is there the sense of the absurdity of life which we sometimes find in Boetticher's films: death, as we have seen, is for Hawks simply a routine occurrence, not a *grotesquerie*, as in *The Tall T* ('Pretty soon that well's going to be chock-a-block') or *The Rise and Fall of Legs Diamond*. For Hawks 'craziness' implies difference, a sense of apartness from the ordinary, everyday, social world. At the same time, Hawks sees the ordinary world as being 'crazy' in a much more fundamental sense, because devoid of any meaning or values. 'I mean crazy reactions – I don't think they're crazy, I think they're normal – but according to bad habits we've fallen into they seemed crazy.' Which is the normal, which the abnormal? Hawks recognises, inchoately, that to most people his heroes, far from embodying rational values, are only a dwindling band of eccentrics. Hawks's 'kind of men' have no place in the world.

The Hawksian heroes, who exclude others from their own *élite* group, are themselves excluded from society, exiled to the African bush or to the Arctic. Outsiders, other people in general, are perceived by the group as an undifferentiated crowd. Their role is to gape at the deeds of the heroes whom, at the same time, they hate. The crowd assembles to watch the showdown in *Rio Bravo*, to see the cars spin off the track in *The Crowd Roars*. The gulf between the outsider and the heroes transcends enmities among the *élite*: witness *Dawn Patrol* or Nelse in *El Dorado*. Most dehumanised of all is the crowd in *Land of the Pharaohs*, employed in building the Pyramids. Originally the film was to have been about Chinese labourers building a 'magnificent airfield' for the American army, but the victory of the Chinese Revolution forced Hawks to change his plans. ('Then I thought of the building of the Pyramids; I thought it was the same kind of story.') But the presence of the crowd, of external society, is a constant covert threat to the Hawksian *élite*, who retaliate by having 'fun'. In the crazy comedies ordinary citizens are turned into comic butts, lampooned and tormented: the most obvious target is the insurance salesman in *His Girl Friday*. Often Hawks's revenge becomes grim and macabre. In *Sergeant York* it is 'fun' to shoot Germans 'like turkeys'; in *Air Force* it is 'fun' to blow up the Japanese fleet. In *Rio Bravo* the geligniting of the badmen 'was very funny'. It is at these moments that the *élite* turns against the world outside and takes the opportunity to be brutal and destructive.

Besides the covert pressure of the crowd outside, there is also an overt force which threatens: woman. Man is woman's 'prey'. Women are admitted to the male group only after much disquiet and a long ritual courtship, phased round the offering, lighting and exchange of cigarettes, during which they prove themselves worthy of entry. Often they perform minor feats of valour. Even then though they are never really full members. A typical dialogue sums up their position:

WOMAN: You love him, don't you?
MAN   (embarrassed):Yes … I guess so. …
WOMAN: How can I love him like you?
MAN: Just stick around.

The undercurrent of homosexuality in Hawks's films is never crystallised, though in *The Big Sky*, for example, it runs very close to the surface. And he himself described *A Girl in Every Port* as 'really a love story between two men'. For Hawks men are equals, within the group at least, whereas there is a clear identification between women and the animal world, most explicit in *Bringing Up Baby*, *Gentlemen Prefer Blondes* and *Hatari!* Man must strive to maintain his mastery. It is also worth noting that, in Hawks's adventure dramas and even in many of his comedies, there is no married life. Often the heroes were married or at least intimately committed, to a woman at some time in the distant past but have suffered an unspecified trauma, with the result that they have been suspicious of women ever since. Their attitude is 'Once bitten, twice shy.' This is in contrast to the films of Ford, which almost always include domestic scenes. Woman is not a threat to Ford's heroes; she falls into her allotted social place as wife and mother, bringing up the children, cooking, sewing, a life of service, drudgery and subordination. She is repaid for this by being sentimentalised. Boetticher, on the other hand, has no obvious place for women at all; they are phantoms, who provoke action, are pretexts for male modes of conduct, but have no authentic significance in themselves. 'In herself, the woman has not the slightest importance.'

Hawks sees the all-male community as an ultimate; obviously it is very retrograde. His Spartan heroes are, in fact, cruelly stunted. Hawks would be a lesser director if he was unaffected by this, if his adventure dramas were the sum total of his work. His real claim as an author lies in the presence, together with the dramas, of their inverse, the crazy comedies. They are the agonised exposure of the underlying tensions of the heroic dramas. There are two principal themes, zones of tension. The first is the theme of regression: of regression to childhood, infantilism, as in *Monkey Business*, or regression to savagery: witness the repeated scene of the adult about to be scalped by painted children, in *Monkey Business* and in *The Ransom of Red Chief*. With brilliant insight, Robin Wood has shown how *Scarface* should be categorised among the comedies rather than the dramas: Camonte is perceived as savage, child-like, subhuman. The second principal comedy theme is that of sex-reversal and role-reversal. *I Was A Male War Bride* is the most extreme example. Many of Hawks's comedies are centred round domineering women and timid, pliable men: *Bringing Up Baby* and *Man's Favourite Sport*, for example. There are often scenes of male sexual humiliation, such as the trousers being pulled off the hapless private eye in *Gentlemen Prefer Blondes*. In the same film, the Olympic Team of athletes are reduced to passive objects in an extraordinary Jane Russell song number; big-game hunting is lampooned, like fishing in *Man's Favourite Sport*; the theme of infantilism crops up again: 'The child was the most mature one on board the ship, and I think he was a lot of fun.'

Whereas the dramas show the mastery of man over nature, over woman, over the animal and childish; the comedies show his humiliation, his regression. The heroes become victims; society, instead of being excluded and despised, breaks in with irruptions of monstrous farce. It could well be argued that Hawks's outlook, the alternative world which he constructs in the cinema, the Hawksian heterocosm, is not one imbued with particular intellectual subtlety or sophistication. This does not detract from its force. Hawks first attracted attention because he was regarded naïvely as an action director. Later, the thematic content which I have outlined was detected and revealed. Beyond the stylemes, semantemes were found to exist; the films were anchored in an objective stratum of meaning, a plerematic stratum, as the Danish linguist Hjelmslev would put it. Thus the stylistic expressiveness of Hawks's films was shown to be not purely contingent, but grounded in significance.

Something further needs to be said about the theoretical basis of the kind of schematic exposition of Hawks's work which I have outlined. The 'structural approach' which underlies it, the definition of a core of repeated motifs, has evident affinities with methods which have been developed for the study of folklore and mythology. In the work of Olrik and others, it was noted that in different folk-tales the same motifs reappeared time and time again. It became possible to build up a lexicon of these motifs. Eventually Propp showed how a whole cycle of Russian fairy-tales could be analysed into variations of a very limited set of basic motifs (or moves, as he called them). Underlying the different, individual tales was an archi-tale, of which they were all variants. One important point needs to be made about this type of structural analysis. There is a danger, as Lévi-Strauss has pointed out, that by simply noting and mapping resemblances, all the texts which are studied (whether Russian fairy-tales or American movies) will be reduced to one, abstract and impoverished. There must be a moment of synthesis as well as a moment of analysis; otherwise, the method is formalist, rather than truly structuralist. Structuralist criticism cannot rest at the perception of resemblances or repetitions (redundancies, in fact), but must also comprehend a system of differences and oppositions. In this way, texts can be studied not only in their universality (what they all have in common) but also in their singularity (what differentiates them from each other). This means of course that the test of a structural analysis lies not in the orthodox canon of a director's work, where resemblances are clustered, but in films which at first sight may seem eccentricities.

In the films of Howard Hawks a systematic series of oppositions can be seen very near the surface, in the contrast between the adventure dramas and the crazy comedies. If we take the adventure dramas alone it would seem that Hawks's work is flaccid, lacking in dynamism; it is only when we consider the crazy comedies that it becomes rich, begins to ferment: alongside every dramatic hero we are aware of a phantom, stripped of mastery, humiliated, inverted. With other directors, the system of oppositions is much more complex: instead of there being two broad strata of films there are a whole series of shifting variations. In these cases, we need to analyse the roles of the protagonists themselves, rather than simply the worlds in which they operate. The protagonists of fairy-tales or myths, as Lévi-Strauss has pointed out, can be dissolved into bundles of differential elements, pairs of opposites. Thus the difference between the prince and the goose-girl can be reduced to two antinomic pairs: one natural, male versus female, and the other cultural, high versus low. We can proceed with the same kind of operation in the study of films, though, as we shall see, we shall find them more complex than fairy-tales. ...

It is instructive, for example, to consider three films of John Ford and compare their heroes: Wyatt Earp in *My Darling Clementine*, Ethan Edwards in *The Searchers* and Tom Doniphon in *The Man Who Shot Liberty Valance*. They all act within the recognisable Ford world, governed by a set of oppositions, but their *loci* within that world are very different. The relevant pairs of opposites overlap; different pairs are foregrounded in different movies. The most relevant are garden versus wilderness, plough-share versus sabre, settler versus nomad, European versus Indian, civilised versus savage, book versus gun, married versus unmarried, East versus West. These antimonies can often be broken down further. The East, for instance, can be defined either as Boston or Washington and, in *The Last Hurrah*, Boston itself is broken down into the antipodes of Irish immigrants versus Plymouth Club, themselves bundles of such differential elements as Celtic versus Anglo-Saxon, poor versus rich, Catholic versus Protestant, Democrat versus Republican, and so on. At first sight, it might seem that the oppositions listed above overlap to the extent that they become practically synonymous, but this is by no means the case. As we shall see, part of the development of Ford's career has been the shift from an identity between civilised versus savage and European versus Indian to their separation and final reversal, so that in *Cheyenne Autumn* it is the Europeans who are savage, the victims who are heroes.

The master antinomy in Ford's films is that between the wilderness and the garden. As Henry Nash Smith has demonstrated, in his magisterial book *Virgin Land*, the contrast between the image of America as a desert and as a garden is one which has dominated American thought and literature, recurring in countless novels, tracts, political speeches, and magazine stories. In Ford's films it is crystallised in a number of striking images. *The Man Who Shot Liberty Valance*, for instance, contains the image of the cactus rose, which encapsulates the antinomy between desert and garden which pervades the whole film. Compare with this the famous scene in *My Darling Clementine*, after Wyatt Earp has gone to the barber (who civilises the unkempt), where the scent of honeysuckle is twice remarked upon: an artificial perfume, cultural rather than natural. This moment marks the turning-point in Wyatt Earp's transition from wandering cowboy, nomadic, savage, bent on personal revenge, unmarried, to married man, settled, civilised, the sheriff who administers the law.

Earp, in *My Darling Clementine*, is structurally the most simple of the three protagonists I have mentioned: his progress is an uncomplicated passage from nature to culture, from the wilderness left in the past to the garden anticipated in the future. Ethan Edwards, in *The Searchers*, is more complex. He must be defined not in terms of past versus future or wilderness versus garden compounded in himself, but in relation to two other protagonists: Scar, the Indian chief, and the family of homesteaders. Ethan Edwards, unlike Earp, remains a nomad throughout the film. At the start, he rides in from the desert to enter the log-house; at the end, with perfect symmetry, he leaves the house again to return to the desert, to vagrancy. In many respects, he is similar to Scar; he is a wanderer, a savage, outside the law: he scalps his enemy. But, like the homesteaders, of course, he is a European, the mortal foe of the Indian. Thus Edwards is ambiguous; the antinomies invade the personality of the protagonist himself. The oppositions tear Edwards in two; he is a tragic hero. His companion, Martin Pawley, however, is able to resolve the duality; for him, the period of nomadism is only an episode, which has meaning as the restitution of the family, a necessary link between his old home and his new home.

Ethan Edwards's wandering is, like that of many other Ford protagonists, a quest, a search. A number of Ford films are built round the theme of the quest for the Promised Land, an American re-enactment of the biblical exodus, the journey through the desert to the land of milk and honey, the New Jerusalem. This theme is built on the combination of the two pairs: wilderness versus garden and nomad versus settler; the first pair precedes the second in time. Thus, in *Wagonmaster*, the Mormons cross the desert in search of their future home; in *How Green Was My Valley* and *The Informer*, the protagonists want to cross the Atlantic to a future home in the United States. But, during Ford's career, the situation of home is reversed in time. In *Cheyenne Autumn* the Indians journey in search of the home they once had in the past; in *The Quiet Man*, the American Sean Thornton returns to his ancestral home in Ireland. Ethan Edwards's journey is a kind of parody of this theme: his object is not constructive, to found a home, but destructive, to find and scalp Scar. Nevertheless, the weight of the film remains orientated to the future: Scar has burned down the home of the settlers, but it is replaced and we are confident that the homesteader's wife, Mrs Jorgensen, is right when she says: 'Some day this country's going to be a fine place to live.' The wilderness will, in the end, be turned into a garden.

The Man Who Shot Liberty Valance has many similarities with *The Searchers*. We may note three: the wilderness becomes a garden – this is made quite explicit, for Senator Stoddart has wrung from Washington the funds necessary to build a dam which will irrigate the desert and bring real roses, not cactus roses; Tom Doniphon shoots Liberty Valance as Ethan Edwards scalped Scar; a log-home is burned to the ground. But the differences are equally clear: the log-home is burned after the death of Liberty Valance; it is destroyed by Doniphon himself; it is his own home. The burning marks the realisation that he will never enter the Promised Land, that to him it means nothing; that he has doomed himself to be a creature of the past, insignificant in the world of the future. By shooting Liberty Valance he has destroyed the only world in which he himself can exist, the world of the gun rather than the book; it is as though Ethan Edwards has perceived that by scalping Scar, he was in reality committing suicide. It might be mentioned too that, in *The Man Who Shot Liberty Valance*, the woman who loves Doniphon marries Senator Stoddart. Doniphon when he destroys his log-house (his last words before doing so are 'Home, sweet home!') also destroys the possibility of marriage.

The themes of *The Man Who Shot Liberty Valance* can be expressed in another way. Ransom Stoddart represents rational-legal authority, Tom Doniphon represents charismatic authority. Doniphon abandons his charisma and cedes it, under what amounts to false pretences, to Stoddart. In this way charismatic and rational-legal authority are combined in the person of Stoddart and stability thus assured. In *The Searchers* this transfer does not take place; the two kinds of authority remain separated. In *My Darling Clementine* they are combined naturally in Wyatt Earp, without any transfer being necessary. In many of Ford's late films – *The Quiet Man, Cheyenne Autumn, Donovan's Reef* – the accent is placed on traditional authority. The island of Ailakaowa, in *Donovan's Reef*, a kind of Valhalla for the homeless heroes of *The Man Who Shot Liberty Valance*, is actually a monarchy, though complete with the Boston girl, wooden church, and saloon made familiar by *My Darling*

Clementine. In fact, the character of Chihuahua, Doc Holliday's girl in *My Darling Clementine*, is split into two: Miss Lafleur and Lelani, the native princess. One represents the saloon entertainer, the other the non-American in opposition to the respectable Bostonians, Amelia Sarah Dedham and Clementine Carter. In a broad sense, this is a part of a general movement which can be detected in Ford's work to equate the Irish, Indians, and Polynesians as traditional communities, set in the past, counterposed to the march forward to the American future, as it has turned out in reality, but assimilating the values of the American future as it was once dreamed.

It would be possible, I have no doubt, to elaborate on Ford's career, as defined by pairs of contrasts and similarities, in very great detail, though – as always with film criticism – the impossibility of quotation is a severe handicap. My own view is that Ford's work is much richer than that of Hawks and that this is revealed by a structural analysis; it is the richness of the shifting relations between antinomies in Ford's work that makes him a great artist, beyond being simply an undoubted *auteur*. Moreover, the *auteur* theory enables us to reveal a whole complex of meaning in films such as *Donovan's Reef*, which a recent filmography sums up as just 'a couple of Navy men who have retired to a South Sea island now spend most of their time raising hell'. Similarly, it throws a completely new light on a film like *Wings of Eagles*, which revolves, like *The Searchers*, round the vagrancy versus home antinomy, with the difference that when the hero does come home, after flying round the world, he trips over a child's toy, falls down the stairs and is completely paralysed so that he cannot move at all, not even his toes. This is the macabre *reductio ad absurdum* of the settled.

Perhaps it would be true to say that it is the lesser *auteurs* who can be defined, as Nowell-Smith put it, by a core of basic motifs which remain constant, without variation. The great directors must be defined in terms of shifting relations, in their singularity as well as their uniformity. Renoir once remarked that a director spends his whole life making one film; this film, which it is the task of the critic to construct, consists not only of the typical features of its variants, which are merely its redundancies, but of the principle of variation which governs it, that is its esoteric structure, which can only manifest itself or 'seep to the surface', in Lévi-Strauss's phrase, 'through the repetition process'. Thus Renoir's 'film' is in reality a 'kind of permutation group, the two variants placed at the far ends being in a symmetrical, though inverted, relationship to each other'. In practice, we will not find perfect symmetry, though as we have seen, in the case of Ford, some antinomies are completely reversed. Instead, there will be a kind of torsion within the permutation group, within the matrix, a land of exploration of certain possibilities, in which some antinomies are foregrounded, discarded, or even inverted, whereas others remain stable and constant. The important thing to stress, however, is that it is only the analysis of the whole *corpus* which permits the moment of synthesis when the critic returns to the individual film.

Of course, the director does not have full control over his work; this explains why the *auteur* theory involves a kind of decipherment, decryptment. A great many features of films analysed have to be dismissed as indecipherable because of 'noise' from the producer, the cameraman, or even the actors. This concept of 'noise' needs further elaboration. It is often said that a film is the result of a multiplicity of factors, the sum total of a number of different contributions. The contribution of the director – the 'directorial factor', as it were – is only one of these, though perhaps the one which carries the most weight. I do not need to emphasize that this view is quite the contrary of the *auteur* theory and has nothing in common with it at all. What the *auteur* theory does is to take a group of films – the work of one director – and analyse their structure. Everything irrelevant to this, everything non-pertinent, is considered logically secondary, contingent, to be discarded. Of course, it is possible to approach films by studying some other feature; by an effort of critical ascesis we could see films, as Von Sternberg sometimes urged, as abstract light-show or as histrionic feasts. Sometimes these separate texts – those of the cameraman or the actors – may force themselves into prominence so that the film becomes an indecipherable palimpsest. This does not mean, of course, that it ceases to exist or to sway us or please us or intrigue us; it simply means that it is inaccessible to criticism. We can merely record our momentary and subjective impressions.

Myths, as Lévi-Strauss has pointed out, exist independently of style, the syntax of the sentence, or musical sound, euphony or cacophony. The myth functions 'on an especially high level where meaning succeeds practically in "*taking off*" from the linguistic ground on which it keeps rolling'. *Mutatis mutandis,* the same is true of the *auteur* film. 'When a mythical schema is transmitted from one population to another, and there exist differences of language, social organization, or way of life which make the myth difficult to communicate, it begins to become impoverished and confused.' The same kind of impoverishment and confusion takes place in the film studio, where difficulties of communication abound. But none the less the film can usually be discerned, even if it was a quickie made in a fortnight without the actors or the crews that the director might have liked, with an intrusive producer and even, perhaps, a censor's scissors cutting away vital sequences. It is as though a film is a musical composition rather than a musical performance, although, whereas a musical composition exists *a priori* (like a scenario), an *auteur* film is constructed *a posteriori*. Imagine the situation if the critic had to construct a musical composition from a number of fragmentary, distorted versions of it, all with improvised passages or passages missing. ...

What the *auteur* theory demonstrates is that the director is not simply in command of a performance of a pre-existing text; he is not, or need not be, only a *metteur en scène*. Don Siegel was asked on television what he took from Hemingway's short story for his film, *The Killers*; Siegel replied that 'the only thing taken from it was the catalyst that a man has been killed by somebody and he did not try to run away'. The word Siegel chose – 'catalyst' – could not be bettered. Incidents and episodes in the original screenplay or novel can act as catalysts; they are the agents which are introduced into the mind (conscious or unconscious) of the *auteur* and react there with the motifs and themes characteristic of his work. The director does not subordinate himself to another author; his source is only a pretext, which provides catalysts, scenes which fuse with his own preoccupations to produce a radically new work. Thus the manifest process of performance, the treatment of a subject, conceals the latent production of a quite new text, the production of the director as an *auteur*.

Of course, it is possible to value performances as such, to agree with André Bazin that Olivier's *Henry V* was a great film, a great rendering, transposition into the cinema, of Shakespeare's original play. The great *metteurs en scène* should not be discounted simply because they are not *auteurs*: Vincente Minnelli, perhaps, or Stanley Donen. And, further than that, the same kind of process can take place that occurred in painting: the director can deliberately concentrate entirely on the stylistic and expressive dimensions of the cinema. He can say, as Josef Von Sternberg did about *Morocco*, that he purposely chose a fatuous story so that people would not be distracted from the play of light and shade in the photography. Some of Busby Berkeley's extraordinary sequences are equally detached from any kind of dependence on the screenplay: indeed, more often than not, some other director was entrusted with the job of putting the actors through the plot and dialogue. Moreover, there is no doubt that the greatest films will be not simply *auteur* films but marvellous expressively and stylistically as well: *Lola Montès, Shinheike Monogatari, La Règle du Jeu, La Signora di Tutti, Sansho Dayu, Le Carrosse d'Or.*

The *auteur* theory leaves us, as every theory does, with possibilities and questions. We need to develop much further a theory of performance, of the stylistic, of graded rather than coded modes of communication. We need to investigate and define, to construct critically the work of enormous numbers of directors who up to now have only been incompletely comprehended. We need to begin the task of comparing author with author. There are any number of specific problems which stand out: Donen's relationship to Kelly and Arthur Freed, Boetticher's films outside the Ranown cycle. Welles's relationship to Toland (and − perhaps more important − Wyler's), Sirk's films outside the Ross Hunter cycle, the exact identity of Walsh or Wellman, the decipherment of Anthony Mann. Moreover there is no reason why the *auteur* theory should not be applied to the English cinema, which is still utterly amorphous, unclassified, unperceived. We need not two or three books on Hitchcock and Ford, but many, many more. We need comparisons with authors in the other arts: Ford with Fenimore Cooper, for example, or Hawks with Faulkner. The task which the critics of *Cahiers du Cinéma* embarked on is still far from completed.

1969

At this point, it is necessary to say something about the *auteur* theory since this has often been seen as a way of introducing the idea of the creative personality into the Hollywood cinema. Indeed, it is true that many protagonists of the *auteur* theory do argue in this way. However, I do not hold this view and I think it is important to detach the *auteur* theory from any suspicion that it simply represents a 'cult of personality' or apotheosis of the director. To my mind, the *auteur* theory actually represents a radical break with the idea of an 'art' cinema, not the transplant of traditional ideas about 'art' into Hollywood. The 'art' cinema is rooted in the idea of creativity and the film as the expression of an individual vision. What the *auteur* theory argues is that any film, certainly a Hollywood film, is a network of different statements, crossing and contradicting each other, elaborated into a final 'coherent' version. Like a dream, the film the spectator sees is, so to speak, the 'film façade', the end-product of 'secondary revision', which hides and masks the process which remains latent in the film 'unconscious'. Sometimes this 'façade' is so worked over, so smoothed out, or else so clotted with disparate elements, that it is impossible to see beyond it, or rather to see anything in it except the characters, the dialogue, the plot, and so on. But in other cases, by a process of comparison with other films, it is possible to decipher, not a coherent message or world-view, but a structure which underlies the film and shapes it, gives it a certain pattern of energy cathexis. It is this structure which *auteur* analysis disengages from the film.

The structure is associated with a single director, an individual, not because he has played the role of artist, expressing himself or his own vision in the film, but because it is through the force of his preoccupations that an unconscious, unintended meaning can be decoded in the film, usually to the surprise of the individual involved. The film is not a communication, but an artefact which is unconsciously structured in a certain way. *Auteur* analysis does not consist of retracing a film to its origins, to its creative source. It consists of tracing a structure (not a message) within the work, which can then *post factum* be assigned to an individual, the director, on empirical grounds. It is wrong, in the name of a denial of the traditional idea of creative subjectivity, to deny any status to individuals at all. But Fuller or Hawks or Hitchcock, the directors, are quite separate from 'Fuller' or 'Hawk' or 'Hitchcock', the structures named after them, and should not be methodologically confused. There can be no doubt that the presence of a structure in the text can often be connected with the presence of a director on the set, but the situation in the cinema, where the director's primary task is often one of coordination and rationalisation, is very different from that in the other arts, where there is a much more direct relationship between artist and work. It is in this sense that it is possible to speak of a film *auteur* as an unconscious catalyst.

However, the structures discerned in the text are often attacked in another way. Robin Wood, for example, has argued that the '*auteur*' film is something like a Platonic Idea. It posits a 'real' film, of which the actual film is only a flawed transcript, while the archi-film itself exists only in the mind of the critic. This attack rests on a misunderstanding. The main point about the Platonic Idea is that it predates the empirical reality, as an archetype. But the '*auteur*' film (or structure) is not an archi-film at all in this sense. It is an explanatory device which specifies partially how any individual film works. Some films it can say nothing or next-to-nothing about at all. *Auteur* theory cannot simply be applied indiscriminately. Nor does an *auteur* analysis exhaust what can be said about any single film. It does no more than provide one way of decoding a film, by specifying what its mechanics are at one level. There are other kinds of code which could be proposed, and whether they are of any value or not will have to be settled by reference to the text, to the films in question.

Underlying the anti-Platonic argument, however, there is often a hostility towards any kind of explanation which involves a degree of distancing from the 'lived experience' of watching the film itself. Yet clearly any kind of serious critical work – I would say scientific, though I know this drives some people into transports of rage – must involve a distance, a gap between the film and the criticism, the text and the meta-text. It is as though meteorologists were reproached for getting away from the 'lived experience' of walking in the rain or sunbathing. Once again, we are back with the myth of transparency, the idea that the mark of a good film is that it conveys a rich meaning, an important truth, in a way which can be grasped immediately. If this is the case, then clearly all the critic has to do is to describe the experience of watching the film, reception of a signal, in such a way as to clear up any little confusions or enigmas which still remain. The most that the critic can do is to put the spectator on the right wavelength so that he can see for himself as clearly as the critic, who is already tuned in.

The *auteur* theory, as I conceive it, insists that the spectator has to work at reading the text. With some films this work is wasted, unproductive. But with others it is not. In these cases, in a certain sense, the film changes, it becomes another film – as far as experience of it is concerned. It is no longer possible to look at it 'with the same eyes'. There is no integral, genuine experience which the critic enjoys and which he tries to guide others towards. Above all, the critic's experience is not essentially grounded in or guaranteed by the essence of the film itself. The critic is not at the heart of the matter. The critic is someone who persists in learning to see the film differently and is able to specify the mechanisms which make this possible. This is not a question of 'reading in' or projecting the critic's own concerns in to the film; any reading of a film has to be justified by an explanation of how the film itself works to make this reading possible. Nor is it the single reading, the one which gives us the true meaning of the film; it is simply a reading which produces more meaning.

Again, it is necessary to insist that since there is no true, essential meaning there can therefore be no exhaustive criticism, which settles the interpretation of a film once and for all. Moreover, since the meaning is not contained integrally in any film, any decoding may not apply over the whole area of it. Traditional criticism is always seeking for the comprehensive code which will give the complete interpretation, covering every detail. This is a wild goose chase, in the cinema, above all, which is a collective form. Both Classical and Romantic aesthetics hold to the belief that every detail should have a meaning – Classical aesthetics because of its belief in a common, universal code; Romantic aesthetics because of its belief in an organic unity in which every detail reflects the essence of the whole. The *auteur* theory argues that any single decoding has to compete, certainly in the cinema, with noise from signals coded differently. Beyond that, it is an illusion to think of any work as complete in itself, an isolated unity whose intercourse with other films, other texts, is carefully controlled to avoid contamination. Different codes may run across the frontiers of texts at liberty, meet and conflict within them. This is how language itself is structured, and the failure of linguistics, for instance, to deal with the problem of semantics, is exemplified in the idea that to the unitary code of grammar (the syntactic component of language) there must correspond a unitary semantic code, which would give a correct semantic interpretation of any sentence. Thus the idea of 'grammaticality' is wrongly extended to include a quite false notion of 'semanticity'. In fact, no headway can be made in semantics until this myth is dispelled.

The *auteur* theory has important implications for the problem of evaluation. Orthodox aesthetics sees the problem in predictable terms. The 'good' work is one which has both a rich meaning and a correspondingly complex form, wedded together in a unity (Romantic) or isomorphic with each other (Classical). Thus the critic, to demonstrate the value of a work, must be able to identify the 'content', establish its truth, profundity, and so forth, and then demonstrate how it is expressed with minimum loss or leakage in the signals of the text itself, which are patterned in a way which gives coherence to the work as a whole. 'Truth' of content is not envisaged as being like scientific truth, but more like 'human' truth, a distillation of the world of human experience, particularly interpersonal experience. The world itself is an untidy place, full of loose ends, but the artefact can tie all these loose ends together and thus convey to us a meaningful truth, an insight, which enables us to go back to the real world with a reordered and recycled experience which will enable us to cope better, live more fully, and so on. In this way art is given a humanistic function, which guarantees its value.

All this is overthrown when we begin to see loose ends in works of art, to refuse to acknowledge organic unity or integral content. Moreover, we have to revise our whole idea of criteria, of judgement. The notion behind criteria is that they are timeless and universal. They are then applied to a particular work and it is judged accordingly. This rigid view is varied to the extent that different criteria may apply to different kinds of works or that slightly different criteria may reflect different points of view or kinds of experience, though all are rooted in a common humanity. But almost all current theories of evaluation depend on identifying the work first and then confronting it with criteria. The work is then criticised for falling short on one score or another. It is blemished in some way. Evidently, if we reject the idea of an exhaustive interpretation, we have to reject this kind of evaluation. Instead, we should concentrate on the *productivity* of the work. This is what the 'modern movement' is about. The text, in Octavio Paz's words, is something like a machine for producing meaning. Moreover, its meaning is not neutral, something to be simply absorbed by the consumer.

The meaning of texts can be destructive – of the codes used in other texts, which may be the codes used by the spectator or the reader, who thus finds his own habitual codes threatened, the battle opening up in his own reading. In one sense, everybody knows this. We know that *Ulysses* or *Finnegans Wake* are destructive of the nineteenth-century novel. But it seems difficult to admit this destructiveness into court when judgements are to be made. We have to. To go to the cinema, to read books, or to listen to music is to be a partisan. Evaluation cannot be impartial. We cannot divorce the problem of codes from the problem of criteria. We cannot be passive consumers of films who then stand back to make judgements from above the fray. Judgements are made in the process of looking or reading. There is a sense in which to reject something as unintelligible is to make a judgement. It is to refuse to use a code. This may be right or wrong, but it is not the same thing as decoding a work before applying criteria. A valuable work, a powerful work at least, is one which challenges codes, overthrows established ways of reading or looking, not simply to establish new ones, but to compel an unending dialogue, not at random but productively.

■ ■ ■

Questions and projects

1. Attempt to offer an auteurist analysis of two or three films by a filmmaker (other than Ford or Hawks). Are there certain structural formations, thematic clusters, or oppositional motifs that identify the filmmaker as an auteur? Can a similar analysis illuminate most literary authors? Provide an example.
2. Wollen suggests that an auteur uses a literary text as 'catalyst' for his or her own cinematic vision. What does he mean by that? Examine an adaptation to show this kind of exchange can work.

Chapter 21

Jack Boozer

THE SCREENPLAY AND AUTHORSHIP IN ADAPTATION

JACK BOOZER'S PIECE BEGINS with the observation that adaptation studies frequently overlook a central process through which a source text is transformed into a film; namely, the screenplay. For Boozer, the screenplay serves as a textual mediating point between the "single-track medium of published writing" and the "multi-track medium of film." Boozer argues that it is the screenplay, not the source text, which serves as the foundation for the eventual film indicating such crucial features as story structure and themes, but just as importantly what will be excluded or altered from the source text. Ultimately, Boozer reminds us of the important intertextual and industrial mediations across source text, screenplay, and film that any critical engagement with studying adaptation must be attentive to.

■ ■ ■

THE SCREENPLAY AND AUTHORSHIP IN ADAPTATION
JACK BOOZER

From *Authorship in Film Adaptation*, Austin, TX: University of Texas Press, 2008, pp. 1–30

Historically, the adapted screenplay has been viewed only as an interim step in the binary focus on the source literature (usually the novel) and on the film. The script has been deemed merely a skeletal blueprint for the adapted film and thus unworthy of serious consideration in its own right. There are several reasons for this binary critical emphasis, beginning with the essential point that a work of fiction or drama typically has a single author and a readily consumable existence in published form, just as an adapted film can be recognized as a finished entity on screen. The adapted screenplay, however, has had no comparable existence as a finished artifact for public consumption (with the exception of published transcripts). Interest in the adapted screenplay mainly follows from an initial critical or public interest in the adapted film. But whereas the audience of an adapted film might rush to purchase copies of the source text (underscoring an adapted film's direct value to publishers), a much smaller readership will seek the film transcript, and only a tiny group will seek a late screenplay draft or shooting script, assuming such is even available. Other reasons for disregarding the screenplay in adaptation study include the multiple revisions a script undergoes during development (at times by different hands), Hollywood's traditional low regard for the screenwriter generally, and a resistance to any sort of transposition of esteemed canonic literature (the "hallowed word") to another medium, especially one that has been associated with mass entertainment.

In respect to this last issue, the adaptation of high-profile best-sellers to the screen can prove as controversial as the adaptation of literary classics. In the recent adaptation of Dan Brown's best-selling mystery thriller, *The Da Vinci Code*, the film version was criticized for softening the book's main thematic thrust, namely, that since antiquity, conservatives within the Catholic Church have suppressed the role of women, including the role of Mary Magdalene, with whom Jesus may have sired children to produce a still extant lineage. Did film director Ron Howard (who at an early point worked with other producers and the screenwriter) already commit to deemphasizing that theme to stem possible boycotts and thus increase ticket sales? Often overlooked but also notable in this regard is that modern writers and directors tied to studio support are frequently asked to work with studio promotional departments to consider a film's marketing in relation to its final story construction.[1] The who and why surrounding the process of adaptation at the screenwriting stage, then, can begin to answer these kinds of preproduction questions and issues. Meanwhile, the closed fixation only on literary source and finished film both in journalistic reviews and scholarly study has often shown an indifference to the evolving intentions of producers, writers, and directors and their shifting levels of input and authority.

In scholarly and trade publications, several articles and a few chapters in collections over the years have given some attention to specific cases of adapted screenplays (see especially *Literature/ Film Quarterly*, in publication since 1973), although the script per se has received little extended treatment as the key step in the process of adaptation. Excluding the numerous how-to texts on screenwriting and marketing and at least two recent manuals on writing adaptations, only a handful of publications on the subject of screenwriting and screenwriters have mentioned adaptation even casually.[2] Adaptation study as a whole has, however, received considerable academic focus, with no fewer than eleven books on the subject appearing since 1996,[3] and three more from Robert Stam in 2005 alone.[4] Kamilla Elliott, in her introduction to the collection *Rethinking the Novel/ Film Debate* (2003), notes that "recent critics rightly protest novel and film studies' neglect of … screenplays" (p. 6). Overall, then, the growing interest in the theory and critical assessment of adaptation supports the need for a closer look at the screenplay/screenwriter and writer-director collaboration in the genesis of adaptation.

For the movie-going public in general, the screenplay has largely remained no more visible than a category on film credits or on film awards lists. In awards ceremonies that include recognition of the screenplay, the scriptwriter stands in for a document that few ever see or read. Those who have tracked down the screenplay have usually had to locate specialty libraries, vendors, or Internet sources, only then to have to rely either on an uncertain script draft dating or on a film's verbatim transcript, which is the version typically published when a feature screenplay is offered as a book. Such transcripts imitate the finished film in standard or nonstandard script form on the page and hence reveal little of the process of adaptation. To uncover that process requires comparing the completed film with the last script draft prior to shooting. Also helpful in understanding the process of adaptation are interviews with or commentaries from the principal figures responsible for a film—producers, writers, directors, and actors. Although such commentaries are often largely anecdotal, their increasing availability through publications, the Internet, DVD supplementary material, and television commentary has made investigating the adaptation process and the centerpiece screenplay more than ever viable.

It is the screenplay, not the source text, that is the most direct foundation and fulcrum for any adapted film. As the film's narrative springboard, it guides the screen choices for story structure, characterization, motifs, themes, and genre. It indicates what will or will not be used from the source, including what is to be altered or invented, and in what settings and tonal register. Because the modern adapted screenplay at the point of input from the director includes so many key decisions relative to the source, it remains the essential conceptual and creative bible for the film's construction. The writing births the overriding narrative that all the filmmaking participants serve during production. Unlike the original source text, which can be read at the reader's pace, the screenplay is the directive for the film performance in a designated time frame. Whatever alterations are made during shooting and editing, the adapted screenplay as it exists just before production starts is the most prescriptive guide to the film in the mind's eye of writer and director.

An adapted screenplay that is recognizable for its quality increases the likelihood that a successful film might be made. This belief is associated with the Hollywood truism that you can make a bad film from a good script but you can't make a good film from a bad script. A director may have the benefit of the screenplay *and* the source text for consideration in production, but script quality, irrespective of the quality of the source text, remains essential for production. In adaptive film projects, the lack of a relatively complete screenplay when production begins can cause great anxiety on the set and hurt the quality of the finished product.[5] Since modern directors work out the transmediation of their source text in the screenplay (usually in conjunction with the adaptive scriptwriter), their interpretation of the literary property and its presentation is already largely decided on. Virtually all of Alfred Hitchcock's films were rather loose adaptations, but he was known for adhering closely during shooting to his finished scripts. Other auteur directors, such as John Ford and Robert Altman, have a reputation for improvising even adapted scripts on the set, although the script remains the jumping-off point for innovation, thus necessitating script rewrites after the fact to accommodate changes made along the way.[6]

The basic format of narrative film scripts conveys their practical specificity. Their goal is to portray drama through concrete descriptive passages and character dialogue within individual scenes, which are designated as either interior or exterior locations. Scenes form the building blocks of sequences and story or character arcs that make up the larger sections or "acts" of the narrative. Because Hollywood scripts are usually written to fit within exhibitors' preferred two-hour maximum running time (120 script pages), as well as to appeal to mass audiences, efficiency and clarity in story and characterization have been standard practice. The adapted screenplay usually pares down dialogue and avoids metaphorical style in description. All of this is intended to set a mood and tone, as well as tell a story in the eventual service of an audiovisual design. The expressive language of fiction in paragraph and chapter form describes circumstances, attitudes, and feelings that readers are left to invoke ("imagine") directly for themselves, while the screenplay is structured to work in the service of a narrative that is read in the moving scenic terms of imaging for the camera. The screenplay must organize and telegraph audiovisual codes to directors, actors, and technicians for the sake of production. The script format thus appears intrusive to a reader, and its written style is less intimate and rich than fiction. It points to the potential specificity and power of fully realized, framed, and mobile iconic imagery ready for editing. The page layout and story elements of the adapted script demonstrate its media-transformational function for the performance of film narrative.

Unlike the solitary, imaginative origin of most fiction (however informed by a cultural milieu), the composition of an adapted screenplay takes place not only under the shadow of myriad narrative expectations but in a complex environment of business, industrial, and artistic considerations. Some version of a screenplay must answer in preproduction to a producer and director. It is usually required by a producer not only to generate specific project funding but also to initiate the attachment to the production of other above-the-line personnel, including the director, director of photography, and stars. Screenplays determine specific production budgets and can also leverage immediate capital from speculative investors, from upfront theatrical distribution deals, and from potential DVD sales for a film, including possible ancillary product contracts. The director, meanwhile, mandates the script required for performance and editing needs. This script presumes its eventual technical and aesthetic performance in an audiovisual space of specific time, pacing, and place. As the central narrative cog in all three stages of film production, the screenplay determines the contributions of the hundreds of individuals who typically work on any given project.[7]

Given its many functions, then, there tend to be at least two main versions of a script. In the preproduction stage, there is first the one that helps bring together budget resources and key personnel, and then the one that is coordinated by the director for production. In modern film development; William Goldman observes,

> There are two entirely different versions of any screenplay. There is stuff that is written before the film is a go project, and there is what's written once the movie is actually going to be shot. And sometimes they have very little to do with each other. The purpose of the earlier version is to make it happen. The purpose of the latter version or versions is to be as supportive to your director as you can.[8]

Goldman's last sentence also points up the service role that the Hollywood screenwriter plays in relation to the producer and director. Once the director approves the final draft, that screenplay is arranged into a shooting script for production, and notations on this script during shooting become the continuity script.[9]

In one case, Stanley Kubrick, who wanted to work through his own extended visual conception for the adaptation of Arthur Clarke's *The Sentinel*, first composed a 40,000-word descriptive prose piece with Clarke in preparation for their writing the initial screenplay for what became 2001.[10] Kubrick sought to fully develop the visual details that would be indicative of an atmosphere and mood for his largely style-driven narrative. This circumstance also highlights how some later auteurs, who often locate and purchase their own source material, already have some connection to the source material and some intention in relation to it, which they continue to develop throughout the scriptwriting stage. Directors use the screenwriting stage of development in collaboration with the writer to invent and refine their story and image conceptions.[11] The scripting process may even suggest a whole new unity of narrative emphasis and meaning, or at least may encourage a director to see further possibilities for cinematic forms of storytelling. How a critical analyst interprets the information provided by a late script draft can therefore make all the difference not only in assigning specific authorship to the quantity and degree of intended source alterations but also to recognizing how the initial screenplay conception may have been altered by performative and technical factors in the production and postproduction stages. A critic's familiarity with a late script can enhance awareness of where the subsequent production soared beyond its original scripted intent, became waylaid, or simply changed direction.

The scholarly study of the screenplay in Hollywood studio cinema has already helped shed light on some well-known examples of scriptwriting confusion. For instance, a famous controversy has surrounded what transpired in the writing of the original script for *Citizen Kane*. Although not technically an adaptation, since the life of William Randolph Hearst had not been published in a biography used directly in the writing of the screenplay, the film nevertheless played fast and loose with the life story of a living person (and the producers had to negotiate screenplay changes because of it, owing to the threat of a lawsuit). Long a matter of contention among film critics over screenplay authorship between Herman Mankiewicz and Orson Welles, the puzzle seems largely now to be laid to rest. As Tom Stempel writes in *Framework*:

> While Mankiewicz had the energy and the early enthusiasm to whip out a lengthy first draft (the two written on his own at 250 and then at 325 pages that provide the basic structure for the eventual film), he did not necessarily have the dedication to do the fine-tuning any script required. Welles, on the other hand, did not necessarily have the patience to do all the creative work required on a first draft, but was brilliant as an editor/rewrite man. As a screenwriting collaboration, they were well matched.[12]

Another factor that is obvious in this historic if nonsimultaneous "collaboration" is the assumption during the writing by both Mankiewicz and Welles that Orson would play the main role. It may be assumed that Welles's script editing in particular was oriented not only to story conflation but to the fine-tuning of the dialogue that he and his colleagues among the Mercury Theatre cast would deliver.

Specific challenges for adaptive writers and filmmakers usually include ways to visualize the fiction narrator's exposition, metaphors, and interior character observations and their thought processes, all of which help to convey story tone as well as character psychology. The determination of filmic equivalents for some or all of these fictional devices is part of the craft and art of the adaptation process. Ruth Prawer Jhabvala, the constant screenwriter on the Ishmael Merchant and James Ivory producer-director team, wrote several publicly successful and close adaptations of heritage literature (particularly by Henry James and E. M. Forster). She has observed that she sometimes changes and also typically cuts even the dialogue in novels down to about one-fourth, noting that "dialogue in a novel is always full of artifice" and is therefore often unwieldy in the mouths of actors on the screen.[13] The exchange or alteration of certain literary for filmic devices in adaptation is thus a given, and the screenwriter and director must make choices in this regard either to enhance cinematic drama or to address unforeseen production issues.

These issues frequently involve casting and performance, which can change a screenplay in all three stages of production. Casting actors, of course, is not determined by the screenwriter unless the writer also happens to have a producer or director role in the film.[14] American cinema offers numerous examples of adapted scripts that have been written and produced with certain performers in mind. It is also true that best-sellers have been written with a movie version and a film star in mind, as in the case of John Grisham's novel *The Pelican Brief*. The author projected Julia Roberts for the lead role in the inevitable film adaptation, and the screen rights were also purchased before the novel was actually written. Furthermore, of course, the attachment of "bankable" stars to a production after the adapted script is completed can push certain roles in certain directions on the set to the point that character and story directions are significantly changed.

Adaptations also typically have more limited options in the casting of lead characters because of the expectations of audiences relative to the given character profiles in the source text. Close matching can bring success, as attested to by the definitive performances of leads Anthony Hopkins and Jodie Foster in *The Silence of the Lambs* (1991, Jonathan Demme), who mirror the physiognomy of their characters and convincingly project their traits just as described in the novel. Certain actors may have the look of a fictional character but lack the affect, while others may not look the part detailed in the source but may nevertheless succeed in capturing the inner life of the character in the film role. An example of the latter is the full-figured version of Renée Zellweger as Ruby in *Cold Mountain* (2003, Anthony Minghella), who was critically praised for her energetic portrayal in this supporting role. The character Ruby, however, is described in Charles Frazier's novel as "broad-nosed," "frail chested," and "corded through the neck and arms." Another example is that of Denzel Washington, whom writer-director Carl Franklin brought in for the role of detective Easy Rawlins in his adaptation of *Devil in a Blue Dress* (1995). The lead actor felt that his characterization of Rawlins should be more active and skilled than in the novel or in Franklin's initial screenplay, and the director agreed and made adjustments to script and film.[15] Whether an actor's performance is attuned to the adapted script or the script is adjusted to the actor depends finally on the director's intent in relation to the source text.

Adaptive screenplays and films face the inevitable question of their specific orientation to their source, and there is no simple answer about what is appropriate that could possibly satisfy all readers and audiences. In critical approaches, the direct matching of the content of a literary source with its film version may serve useful descriptive goals concerning transmediation, but it has also long encouraged an evaluative form of "fidelity criticism" that has necessarily privileged the original literary work, particularly literary classics, to the detriment of the cinematic "derivation." The versatility of the visual and sound palette available to screenwriters and filmmakers, however, can provide a wealth of alternative ways to convey the intricacies of the source text, and therefore disobliges a simplistic comparative cataloging across the two media. In this line of thought, critical writing on film adaptation has frequently suggested that the screenplay and film should mainly seek to capture "the essence" of the source text through audiovisual "equivalents." Because exact iconic images of fiction in film are impossible (owing to the variations of each fiction reader's particular imagination) and in any case are likely to fail dramatically (owing to film's need to establish its own "live" scenic rhythms as opposed to literary ones), it is essential to locate the goal that any particular adaptation sets for itself. To this end, the screenplay can reveal the transformational decisions that account for a change in medium, as well as the initial story and dialogue alterations that point to the conceptual goal of the film adaptation.

The issue of authorial intent, therefore, must be a part of any discussion of fidelity in adaptation. One way that critics and theorists of adaptation have repeatedly addressed this issue of allegiance has been to assign labels to what is usually presented as three levels of a film's distance from its source. Most of these labels, which have been used over the years,[16] offer some variation on the following terminology:

1. a literal or close reading (such as the Ishmael Merchant-James Ivory adaptation of *Howards End*, with Ruth Prawer Jhabvala as writer);
2. a general correspondence (such as Anthony Minghella's highly sensitive screenwriter-director "reading" of Michael Ondaatje's poetic and lengthy novel *The English Patient*); or
3. a distant referencing (as in the Coen brothers' tacit borrowing from Homer's *The Odyssey* for *O Brother, Where Art Thou?*).

Although such descriptive categories can be used to help readers and viewers appreciate the film adaptation's intention and its right to go its own way, any preoccupation with fidelity to the literary original and its presumed superiority also tends to constrain the discussion of each film's immersion in its own particular cultural and historical moment. Part of the comedic point in the

Coen brothers' Depression-era comedy (released in 2000) is that mundane and narrow-minded facts of life surrounding antiheroes in the twentieth century can unsettle the gravity of ancient heroic epics such as *The Odyssey*. In contrast, serious costume dramas, including *Howards End* and *The English Patient*, can succeed in speaking to the present through the sheer realistic credibility of the characters and issues represented in their particular historical circumstances.[17]

All three recent adaptations—*Howards End, The English Patient*, and *O Brother*—were critically and commercially successful films despite differing degrees of closeness to and different relationships with their literary source. Interestingly, all three also show an extremely tight association between writer and director in each project's conception (especially in the case of Minghella, who assumed both roles). Each writer was closely allied with each director's intention and in addition had a thorough grounding in film tradition. The Coen brothers took their title, historical moment, and tone for their film from writer-director Preston Sturges's *Sullivan's Travels* (1942), in which the line "O brother, where art thou?" occurs. Certainly, the quality and success of many adapted films have been rooted in a strong writer-director team approach, such as that between Martin Ritt and Irving Ravetch/Harriett Frank, Jr., or Alfred Hitchcock and John Michael Hayes. The recognition of the potential power of cinema is also observable among those who have a particularly strong personal devotion to rendering a literary source. Some examples are actress Emma Thompson's script for *Sense and Sensibility* (1995, Ang Lee) and Christopher Hampton's screenplay rendition of his already adapted stage version of *Dangerous Liaisons* (1988, Stephen Frears) from the period novel by Choderlos de Laclos. Furthermore, because all of the adaptations mentioned above were well received by critics and audiences, very few negative criticisms regarding lack of fidelity to source resulted. On the contrary, a renewed appreciation of, or at least attention to, the source material was the typical consequence. The film adaptation's tendency to create or reenergize public interest in the literary source, and through this renewed interest to spark a wider discussion of the aesthetic force and cultural meanings of the page and screen texts and their temporal contexts, reinforces the intermedial as well as historiographic dimensions of adaptation study.

Classical Hollywood and the adapted screenplay

The major studios of classical Hollywood had story departments with a stable of writers who were usually assigned to adaptation projects according to their genre experience. Robert Wise observed, "In my time, all the major studios had story departments to cover all the established and upcoming books. They provided directors with all the information they needed, like synopses."[18] Studio directors didn't have to actually read their sources for adaptation, especially in the rush to produce the many films demanded by the studios' exhibitors prior to 1948. Furthermore, the formulation of and final say on a script seldom began and ended with the story department, which answered to the studio head or to the production manager in the studio system. As independent-minded director Frank Capra wrote in a letter to the *New York Times* in 1939, "about six producers today pass upon ninety percent of the scripts and cut and edit about ninety percent of the pictures."[19]

Thomas Schatz points out that David Selznick, while at MGM with Irving Thalberg, closely oversaw and proved the viability of filming classics as major productions in the 1930s, and he successfully produced several while there.[20] Even in cases where a studio sought out a specific writing talent to adapt a literary work, studios continued to rule the process. At Columbia, noted screenwriter Budd Schulberg explained why he did not write the final script used to adapt his own 1947 novel, *The Harder They Fall*.

I had a fight with Harry Coen about that, not the first or last. I had done the book on my farm in Bucks County, and I had also done the screen adaptation there. He insisted that if I did the screenplay, I must do it at the studio. ... I really had left Hollywood because I couldn't stand that routine. It just did not fit my method of work. I said I would do the screenplay at the farm and then come out for conferences. ... One thing I couldn't stand about that system was that there was a secretarial pool that typed up the pages, about four or five a day, as you wrote. They would send those pages right up to the front office. The writer could not look at the work and turn it in when it was ready. The front office was more or less looking over your shoulder every step of the way. That's counterproductive to any real creativity. I refused to work under that system, so I didn't get to do the script.[21]

Schulberg had a reputation for doing extensive and intensive hands-on research for his screenplays because he felt compelled by the sociopolitical realities of the American experience. His realist scenario for *On the Waterfront* (1954) was based partly on Malcolm Johnson's Pulitzer prize-winning articles on crime on the New York waterfront, but also on months of Schulberg's own research, which included attending longshoremen union meetings and anti-crime commission hearings. He also insisted that the film's director, Elia Kazan, and actor Marlon Brando join him in spending extended time on the docks with the longshoremen before shooting started. It was as if Schulberg were preparing a nonfiction exposé on the subject while simultaneously building a script. All of this explains why his Academy Award for *On the Waterfront* was in the category of Story and Screenplay rather than Original Screenplay. In his study of screenplay documents, Tom Stempel further discovered that the film's legendary taxicab scene, reputed to have been improvised by Marlon Brando and Rod Steiger, appeared in an early Schulberg draft, "closer to its final form in the film than almost any other scene."[22] Stempel also observes the irony related to this Schulberg and Kazan film: "the best screenplay to come out of the HUAC investigations was written by a screenwriter [and a director] who had testified."[23] Schulberg's leftist ideological bent, in any case, did not make him an easy fit with Hollywood's producer-driven and studio image-driven system of the time.

George Bluestone's landmark academic study, *Novels into Film: The Metamorphosis of Fiction into Cinema* (1957), considers two adaptations from popular sources and three from classic literature, including *The Grapes of Wrath*. He points out that whatever the cultural status of the source, cinema can find its own methods for creating quality and significance. However, in noting how linguistic metaphors can be accomplished in film only when "they arise naturally from the setting," he also shows limitations in his recognition of film's rhetorical arsenal. Nevertheless, his observations are generally wide-ranging and informative of collaborative, industrial, and political realities in Hollywood adaptation. He remarks on the way director John Ford and his cinematographer Gregg Toland created objective details for *The Grapes of Wrath* (1940) that were not in the novel (or the screenplay) in order to heighten character and story in the film. But he notes also that the strongest sociopolitical commentary in Steinbeck's novel is missing from the film, and that Darryl Zanuck at Fox was so concerned about investor resistance to the production of *The Grapes of Wrath* that he announced it under another title, *Highway 66*.[24] Bluestone also makes several references to the film's screenwriter, Nunnally Johnson, and his many contributions, including structural changes that provided a stronger story line, better pacing, and a greater unity for the film. Writer Johnson said, for example, that he moved Ma's speech and "chose it for his curtain line because he considered it the 'real' spirit of Steinbeck's book,"[25] and in fact the novelist had no public qualms with the filmmakers' results.[26] As for director Ford, he glibly claimed not to have read the novel at all,[27] which, if true, means that his visual interpretations were based almost entirely on his feel of the story from the script. Bluestone's book is not inclined to theory, but its practical realization of the industrial and creative process that is cinema, including his willingness to add the screenwriter's name alongside the director's, does recognize the screenplay's significance.[28]

Adaptations of both classic and popular literature have consistently dominated the world of Hollywood's award-winning films. Historically, the great majority of Academy Award-winning films have been adaptations. But the Motion Picture Academy did not consistently distinguish two categories of adapted versus original writing, partly owing to a tendency also to award the best story (not necessarily from a literary source). The Academy had had separate awards for Best Writing: Adaptation and Best Original Story since 1931, but those categories were ambiguous as to whether the person responsible for an original story might have also helped on the screenplay, and whether a winning screenplay in this category was necessarily also adapted. The titles for the three writing awards in 1942 were Best Original Motion Picture Story, Best Original Screenplay, and Best Screenplay (Adaptation). The category of Best Motion Picture Story was finally discarded in 1957, which marked the clear modern distinction between either an original or an adapted screenwriting award category. The distinction between the two awards concerns whether or not a screenplay is based on previously published material.[29] In copyright law, an adaptation is defined as a "derivation that recasts, transforms or adapts a previous work," which already suggests the varied forms that adaptation may take. In any case, the adapted screenplay finally gained a clear award status, whether it originated from published news reports, popular fiction, or classic literary sources. The dominance of popular material for adaptations is reflected in the number of chapters in this book that are concerned with such sources.[30]

Of greatest overall significance here is that the Academy Award for an adaptation is given to a screenplay and not to a film—there is no Oscar category for Best Adapted Motion Picture. This recognizes the distinct nature of the art of adaptive writing versus original scriptwriting, as well as the importance of the screenplay-writing stage in the adaptation process. Whether the predominance of film adaptations that win Best Film awards suggests more about the advantage of films based on already familiar stories and characters in Academy voters' minds or about the willingness of producers to back, and major directors to shoot, "presold" material is unclear. The focus on the screenplay in the competition involving adapted films, however, is a salient point, for the screenplay has always been a crucial aspect of motion picture adaptation, whether it has been recognized as such or not. In fact, one of the reasons for considering Academy Awards in this discussion is the paucity of other forms of significant evidence regarding the viewing public's historical assessment of adapted screenplays.[31]

New Wave auteurism and the new Hollywood aftermath

The French New Wave critics and filmmakers, who began work in the middle of the 1950s and continued on through the 1960s, considered film a kind of extension of creative literary authorship that used the camera instead of the pen. Canonic literature, as it was complacently adapted and filmed in France up until this time in what François Truffaut called the "tradition of quality," was to be replaced by original scripts and films, or at least by more creative, "auteurist" adaptations. André Bazin commented specifically on the adaptation of quality literature versus popular textual sources:

> The more important and decisive the literary qualities of the work, the more the adaptation disturbs its equilibrium, the more it needs a creative talent to reconstruct it on a new equilibrium not indeed identical with, but the equivalent of, the old one.[32]

This notion of equivalency in adaptation calls attention to cinema's particular need to do certain things differently in the transmediation from literature. Furthermore, the auteurists' central attack (mounted by Truffaut's 1954 essay *La politique des auteurs*) was not on adaptation in general so much as on its frequent tendency toward a complacent style and passive allegiance to literary sources. Several films by New Wave directors were in fact adaptations, including Truffaut's *Jules and Jim* (from the novel by Henri-Pierre Roché) and Jean-Luc Godard's *Masculine, Feminine* (from the story by Guy de Mauppasant). The New Wave challenge did succeed in shifting the emphasis in Western critical thinking from the literary source text and its dominant status in adaptation to the film work in the hands of a creative director—and particularly a writer-director—whose style and personal vision were of primary importance. The French auteur theory accented the director's inspiration through a personal approach that may or may not be borrowed in part from literature, and thus advanced the message of film modernism and its self-conscious experimentation with form as an ingredient of narrative and theme.

Because auteur theory touted the artistry of film as a medium that was culturally as significant as literature, New Wave critics created their own pantheon of great directors, and also called attention to hitherto underappreciated Hollywood film genres in which some of those directors worked. These genres included the film noir, the suspense thriller, the disenfranchised youth film, the thoughtful Western, and the comedy. One of the distinguishing features of so-called auteur directors, in fact, was their sole engagement with, or more frequently an active collaboration in, the composition of the screenplay, including those adapted from a previous source. Alfred Hitchcock, who virtually created the genre of the suspense thriller, not only depended on published sources for his films but also took a strong hand with his hired screenwriters in every one.[33] The French cineastes also noted that auteur directors, including Howard Hawks and Anthony Mann, among several others, asserted some degree of creative independence from mainstream Hollywood studio filmmaking even as they worked in and around it. The auteur theory was as much about originality and resistance to conservative standardization as it was about directorial inspiration and vision. This meant going further than simply creating a new artistic initiative, a romance of the great artist. There was an ideological leaning in the realist theory of Bazin and in the progressive and socially engaged writing and filmmaking of those such as Truffaut and particularly Jean-Luc Godard. Their contributions to the academic and cultural appreciation of cinema as art, as something more than casual entertainment for the whole family, encouraged a more sophisticated film audience and greatly influenced public attitudes toward film. But the focus on the director's dominance in the 1960s, which followed the producer's dominance in the Hollywood studio era, still did not raise the status of the writer per se. New Wave directors emphasized the cinematic search for truth, whatever their story's origin.

One aspect of the eventual rejection of auteurism by American film critics such as Richard Corliss had to do with the overemphasis on the director at the expense of the screenwriter, for which Corliss makes a strong case in his book, *The Hollywood Screenwriters*. In part a challenge to Andrew Sarris's cataloguing of great directors, Corliss traces the extensive contributions of many writers during the studio era that repeatedly put their stamp on major Hollywood films, including adaptations. There were many screenwriters in this category, including Samson Raphaelson (who wrote for Ernst Lubitsch), Garson Kanin (who could be said to have written for Judy Holliday and the Tracy-Hepburn combo), Jules Furthman (who wrote for Howard Hawks), and Ben Hecht (who wrote for virtually everyone who was a someone). Considering the director's role, Corliss was inclined to observe that Hollywood directors were essentially "interpretive artists" *unless they also wrote their own films*. Nor did Corliss feel that auteur critics in France or Hollywood were really adhering to the notion that auteurism was mainly about style: "visual style is not auteur criticism's major interest. The auteurist is really writing about theme criticism. And themes—as expressed through plot, characterization and dialogue—belong primarily to the writer."[34] If Corliss was on shaky ground here, he did ultimately recognize that the best Hollywood films resulted "from the productive intersection of a strong writer and a strong director—and often a strong actor—exploring mutually sympathetic themes and moods."[35] But the efforts of Corliss to boost the recognition of screenwriters had little lasting effect, especially within the narrow rubric of writer versus director as auteur.

In addition to European influences,[36] which included the French New Wave, and the demise of the hegemonic studio system and the censorship codes that survived into the 1950s, perhaps the greatest impact on writers and directors and their cultural status was felt from the historical events of the late 1960s, which also awakened America's social and political consciousness. The assassinations of key national leaders and the growing terror of the Vietnam War, along with the civil rights movement and the women's movement, which gained momentum throughout that decade, all added up to what some called a counterculture revolution, and one that the quickly dubbed "New Hollywood" took an important part in. Its launch date is usually assigned to the 1967 release of director Arthur Penn's generic hybrid *Bonnie and Clyde*, for which writers David Newman and Robert Benton received a National Society of Film Critics' Award for Best Adaptation. Novelists and screenwriters continued to lack power in the production system, though Mario Puzo's novel *The Godfather* made him an obvious choice to work with writer-director Francis Ford Coppola on the adaptations that became the main Godfather films. *The Godfather* and *The Godfather: Part II* (1972 and 1974), garnered a Best Film and Best Adapted Screenplay award (alongside Coppola's award for Best Director in 1974), which recognized both their strong stylistic and storytelling achievements. These films also showed a new angle on the treatment of the violent mafia—the underbelly of capitalism based on "family" allegiances. The new appreciation for originality in American film style, content, and genre that had begun in the late 1960s encouraged yet more flexible and innovatively cinematic adaptations of challenging literary sources. Much of what has apparently attracted modern talent to adaptation, after all, has not been so much literary sophistication in the source, which can be an obstacle to visual treatment, but something in the narrative that has immediate, significant cultural relevancy.

In 1975, the Best Adapted Screenplay award went to Laurence Hauben and Bo Goldman for transforming Ken Kesey's novel and its follow-up Broadway play, *One Flew Over the Cuckoo's Nest,* to the big screen. The film's screenwriters and director Milos Forman take full advantage of opportunities to open the novel up and to convert its internal narrator's primary metaphor of the mythical "Combine"—systemic institutional oppression—into more realistic forms. Forman's earlier Czechoslovakian film *Fireman's Ball* (1967) presented a metaphor for a system of political oppression that had been internalized by an entire nation, which partly explains the choice of Forman to direct *Cuckoo's Nest.* Beyond the latter film's political theme, Forman and writers Goldman and Hauben also created a screen text that can be read for its time as a comment on individual inspiration and passion in filmmaking over and against the forces of timidity and middle-brow conventionalism that had dominated mainstream Hollywood productions up until the advent of the New Hollywood movement. The work of Michael Douglas as producer[37] on *Cuckoo's Nest* (and on some seventeen other films that followed), moreover, is a reminder of some of the major contributions of producers, whose unwavering belief in the cultural importance of certain projects made their realization possible.

A few producers should be recognized based on their track record relative to the New Wave guidelines of an original orchestration of talent that is determined to move beyond complacent commercial cinema. Saul Zaentz, for example, produced major film adaptations such as *Amadeus*

(1984), *The Unbearable Lightness of Being* (1988), and *The English Patient* (1996). Producers, whether working inside or outside studios, are usually the ones who initiate the purchase of screen rights to published material, along with the hiring of writers and directors to create the screen adaptation. An alternative case, however, is when a screenwriter or a potential director develops a strong adaptation only to realize an unwillingness on the part of financial backers until the cultural moment seems right for such a project. For example, the script for *Brokeback Mountain* (adapted from E. Annie Proulx's short story) was shopped around by writers Larry McMurtry and Diana Ossana for four years until it was made and eventually won the Oscar for Best Film in 2005. Larry McMurtry was also credited as an executive producer.

There are always larger industrial and audience factors at work in the entertainment business, and these factors can have an impact on the kinds of adaptations that are green-lighted for production in Hollywood. The 1970s, 1980s, and 1990s saw exploding costs for films, a resulting drop in the output of big- and middle-budget films, and the financial necessity for big opening weekends across the cineplexes of America. The need for huge film openings also added to the gross inflation in film costs by requiring massive marketing campaigns that increasingly exceeded the production costs of the movie. The level of financial risk in a single major film could make or break studios and consequently put tremendous pressure on the few writers and directors who were finding their work to be commercially viable.[38] Adding to this was the fact that most of the Hollywood studios had become absorbed into huge conglomerates, which created further levels of administrative approval. Ironically, this situation may have helped the number of adaptations being considered for major backing, but it did not generally advance the quality of what was being produced. If film marketers felt a little safer with adaptations, the conservative strategy to increase the number of sequels and remakes left adaptive writers yet narrower options for creativity. More recently, conglomerates in the new millennium look particularly to adapted screenplays and films that may have strong potential for sequels (called "tent-pole" projects). Commercially, too, the exploding market in DVD sales of movies has enriched the media conglomerates while leaving directors and particularly writers, whose entire screenplay may be offered on a DVD, with small compensation. The lucrative post-theatrical market in DVDs now outgrosses most theatrical box office, and the designation of who receives these profits remains contentious, particularly for creative talent.

The contrast between adapted films that become commercial blockbusters and those that garner Best Adapted Screenplay awards is very revealing of the dimensions of the Hollywood world of adaptation projects. This has become even more pronounced in recent decades. Peter Benchley scripted his own best-seller *Jaws* (1975, Steven Spielberg) along with Carl Gottlieb, and the movie became the top box-office grosser of that year, while the Adapted Screenplay award winner was *One Flew Over the Cuckoo's Nest*. In 1986, the top box-office hit was based on an article written and then adapted by Ehud Yonay, Jim Cash, and Jack Epps for *Top Gun* (Tony Scott). The Best Adapted Script award that year went to Ruth Prawer Jhabvala for *A Room with a View* (James Ivory), based on E. M. Forster's novel. In 1993, Spielberg co-wrote with Michael Crichton an adaptation of the novelist's best-seller, *Jurassic Park*, while the Best Adapted Screenplay award went to Steven Zaillian for his script for *Schindler's List* (Spielberg). In 2002, the top-grossing film was *Spider-Man* (Sam Raima), based on the Marvel comic book series, while the Best Adapted Screenplay award went to Ronald Harwood for *The Pianist* (Roman Polanski), based on the World War II Warsaw memoir by Wladyslaw Szpilman. These contrasting examples are not overly selective for any given year, and they show the continued prominence of adapted material in the industry and its power with viewers, whether for mass appeal or for films more likely to be associated with aesthetic quality and social insight as viewed by the Academy.

For those trying to become established as screenwriters, to write a non-contract script based on someone else's published work means having money to buy at least a timed "option" on a source "property," and possibly also the money to secure the full rights. This usually requires the kind of track record and financial risk most individuals outside the Hollywood money loop cannot afford. McGilligan reflects on this: "The niches for personal expression, as Walter Hill notes … have dwindled. Young writer-directors can find a sanctuary with smaller, independent films, but Hollywood writers, as always, have to trust in bigger financing, an empathetic producer, fortitude, and luck."[39] Add to this the sheer reduction in the number of theatrical films made in Hollywood, as well as the radical current decline in feature films made for network television, and any inclination toward risk and originality in adaptation seems to have been reduced for all but a few producer-writer-director stalwarts. They too must find sufficient inspiration in literary sources to devote significant chunks of their lives and perhaps their livelihood to the effort. The screenplay thus takes its place in a world of Hollywood cinema that remains predominantly a complex entertainment business in which only extraordinary efforts by gifted collaborators have succeeded on occasion in raising it to a level of artistic as well as cultural power.

Theories of structuralisms and the disappearing author

The influence of the auteur theory began to wane with the academic rise of semiotics and structuralism. Semiotics declared the centrality of the sign and sign systems (the signifier and the signified) that could be applied to visual media as well as written language. The increased emphasis on referentiality and the problem with the notion of representation in visual communication, which Christian Metz partly formalized in the notion of the "imaginary signifier" in cinema, shifted attention from the "speaker" or writer and director to the act of language/sign usage in communication and its meaning. Interest turned also to structuralist approaches based in cultural anthropology. Structuralism accented narrative formulas and cultural constructions (often in Lévi-Straussian binary patterns of opposition) that worked both within language or signs and across audiovisual media. Structuralist theory tended to trace cultural influences and patterns in broad historical strokes. Writers and directors had not presumably invented so much as recontextualized what was already ingrained in cultural history. More relevant to adaptation, deconstructionist Jacques Derrida pushed structuralism to poststructuralist dimensions by observing not only that any sense of an original is impugned through a variety of cultural factors from the outset, but also that the original may be enhanced by a "copy" (or adaptation) through a fresh reading, which suggests a full circularity of influences. Roland Barthes attacked the status of authorship directly in his 1968 essay, "The Death of the Author." He also reified the work of critical interpretation in relation to the source under study, as if every literary source were only a reinterpretation of earlier sources, including critical ones. Michel Foucault's essay, "What is an Author?" (1969), further insisted on reduced attention to a singular "author-function" and raised additional "suspicions … concerning the … creative role of the subject." Julia Kristeva, borrowing from M. M. Bakhtin's universalist realm of direct and indirect discursive influences subsumed under the term dialogism, further developed the idea she named "intertextuality," which challenged the prestige of prior sources as opposed to the realm of discourse that circulates around them. Broad intertextual approaches increase the emphasis on the array of possible cultural and industrial influences on an author and text.[40] Taken as a whole, then, this multiple-front, evolving theory had the effect of leveling the playing field between any "high culture" presumptions of the literary source contrasted with the film adaptation that followed it. Further, however, the theoretical extreme led by Barthes and Derrida belittled the role of all authorship by reducing source novel writers, and screenwriters and directors by implication, to invisibility or mere "author-functions" in a galaxy full of textual influences and cultural signifiers.

Poststructuralism's challenge to the idea of the unified subject and the unified text remains current. Lacanian psychoanalytic theory as well as Bakhtin's reading of fiction and criticism further questioned the possibility of subject or author autonomy, and thus the discrete individuality of any author's narrative and style. Robert Stam explains further:

> The Bakhtinian "proto-structuralist" conception of the author as the orchestrator of pre existing discourses, along with Foucault's downgrading of the author in favor of a "pervasive anonymity of discourse," opened the way to a non-originary approach to all arts. Bakhtin's attitude toward the literary author as inhabiting "inter-individual territory" suggested a devalorization of artistic "originality" … adaptation becomes simply another "zone" on a larger and more variegated map.[41]

In contradistinction to approaches emphasizing unity and originality, then, poststructuralism has emphasized rather the gaps and fissures that are a part of the "subject" and the artifact, and (along with "proto-structuralism") the multivocality of influences that shape both. In all of this Stam notes Bakhtin's modification of theoretical language that allows at least for "inter-individual territory,"[42] but where subjective authorship would seem to remain of modest consequence.

Literature and film as well as language translation theorists, however, have begun to raise questions about the total erasure of the individual creative voice. Issues of personal style continue to exist alongside issues of personal worldview within specific historical eras. In his essay, "The Unauthorized Auteur Today" (1993), Dudley Andrew challenged dogmatic theorizations of adaptation that slammed the door on all claims of authorship. He had already suggested in an earlier chapter on adaptation that:

> [i]t will no longer do to let theorists settle things with a priori arguments. We need to study the films themselves as acts of discourse. We need to be sensitive to that discourse and to the forces that motivate it.[43]

The implied sense of a possible personal as well as cultural "motivation" in the process of adaptation resides here. Similarly, in Mireia Aragay's recent collection, *Books in Motion*, she observes that "a redefined notion of auteurism has become a central focus in recent writing on adaptation."[44] Intertextual study can reveal both the screenwriter's struggle for a creative take on preexisting literary materials and the collaborative process tied to the director who seeks to put his or her particular reading on the screen. An adapted film begins as a screenplay transformation of a source, and eventually becomes a film derivation from that screenplay. Recognizing this specificity of textual stages not only confirms adaptation's intertextual status but can also point more precisely to the contributions of key individuals and their most significant impact along the way. Tracing generic, institutional, ideological, and cultural influences need not entirely displace considerations of key creative decisions by individuals most directly responsible for a film. Those broader influences, if considered only in isolation, may miss the way they are finally filtered through the specific interpretations of producers, writers, and directors. Has the deterioration of the subject position in poststructuralism and postmodernity reached the point of total concession by all to a complete erasure of creative inspiration and dedicated conviction of purpose?

Having accepted the convincing theoretical case for a greater balance and more active intercourse between source and adapted texts, the tendency to highlight any variety of cultural influences while overlooking the stage of personal or interpersonal authorship remains troubling. Must we forget that in the end, it is always certain individuals who write a novel or a screenplay and who direct actors and films? And while the majority of their decisions may be recognized as resulting from larger historical and cultural contexts, and from certain guiding perspectives adapted from the source, that the primary talent in a given film adaptation can also serve as very specific individual antennae of interpretation that may be more than the sum of those larger influences? Whatever remains of the creative subject and individual inspiration and effort implies a particular voice, and not necessarily only a culturally mimetic one. Contemporary conditions of mass mediation have certainly altered the process of psychological and social development related to individual identity. Important recent adaptations such as *To Die For* (1995) and *Adaptation* (2002)[45] in fact take these very themes of the media-absorbed and degraded personal reality of the individual as their primary subject. If poststructuralism signals the death of the unified subject and text in a welter of cultural influences, and if postmodernism emphasizes reality's absorption into commercial and political mediations that leave the subject exteriorized and hollowed out, then neither theory would seem capable of doing more than reconfirming the power of larger forces already at work. What remains of the subject's "expressive voice" may be only the final resistant echoes of real cultural memory no longer able to make connections even with its own most personally and deeply felt experiences. Does this leave adaptation study with only so many cycles of textual borrowing and transference where no personal agency remains? Certainly, great cinema is not solely individual expression, but neither does it seem only a summary mirror of cultural forces.

There is a reason why so many case studies look to issues of authorship for understanding. The closer one gets to a work, the more the particulars of story treatment, visual style, performance, tone, pacing, scoring, editing, and themes become recognizable as a series of decisions attributable to individuals. And this applies equally to adaptation study. Just as an adapted film can change an entire cultural view of a source—such as Francis Ford Coppola's *Apocalypse Now* (1979) "updating" Joseph Conrad's *Heart of Darkness*—so too can special efforts by individuals such as Alfred Hitchcock or Stanley Kubrick change the way we look at the balance between literary source and adapted film. As we step back from the aesthetic particulars of a work, it is possible to see larger circumstances and trends affecting whole groups of films. Both macro- and micro-perspectives for critical interpretation are useful, and there is no reason to disparage one for the other. Hence, Foucault's ideas on author functions can be seen as his analytical distance from the daily reality and personal efforts of those caught up in the pressurized circus of adaptive screenwriting and film production, where certain decisions may breach as well as follow larger cultural norms. Significant theorists and writer-directors alike are usually reactive to culture in the sense that they can bring something unique to it and also, perchance, modify its direction. Certainly, the history of film includes its changing pantheon of theorists as well as filmmakers, however divergent their functions and methods.

In the Hollywood filmmaking contexts and constraints of rights and contracts, institutional structures of production and branding, and the assignment of screen credits, creative talent can ultimately choose either a lazy approach of audience exploitation through cultural clichés, spectacle, and commercial reification or look instead toward a careful cultural observation, uniqueness of expression, and cultural engagement. Surely it is individuals and their dedication of energy to something illuminative in film that makes the latter happen. Successful transformations such as *Million Dollar Baby* (2004, Clint Eastwood), which Paul Haggis adapted from an "F. X. Toole" short story (and just after the author's death), thematizes singular dedication to class mobility and a specific kind of fulfillment. This confirms a fundamental American myth, but one that is also placed by these authors against very specific gender, class, and racial stereotypes. The film was also made for $30 million and grossed $100.4 million within five months, figures suggesting that its particular message and aesthetic, as driven home by the personal commitment of its makers, have communicated something universal to audiences (not to mention the implication in its box-office success that art and commerce need not be mutually exclusive). Part of the significance of narrative film writing and production resides in its potential to reach millions worldwide, and thus to make a difference in ways and at levels that literature has been unable to achieve.

Nevertheless, the two narrative media share in what can be, as several theorists have already suggested, a largely beneficial synergy. And this synergy is often most in evidence through the intertextual script that links them. As I have attempted to demonstrate, the adapted screenplay asserts the main parameters and direction of authorial intention, whatever the final outcome on the big screen may be. Bazin wrote in 1948 that the public impact of films was greater than novels at myth-making, and he noted also the way film adaptations reinforce rather than eliminate the relevancy of drama and the novel.[46] There appears to be a longing for the audiovisual image in the descriptive suggestion of the word, and a longing for the word to describe the full immediacy of the film image. A critical approach to adaptation that recognizes authorial desire through the script intertext as well as the film can reveal—like the many sketches a sculptor might draw in preparation for completing a statue—the significant stages of smaller decisions that finally add up to the whole.

Beyond formalistic or poststructuralist cross-textual analyses, then, there should also be room in the equation for consideration of the adaptive writer's and director's orchestration of voice and desire in cinema short of an overly romanticized auteurism. Stam reinforces this view in his comments on authorship:

> Auteur studies now tend to see a director's work not as the expression of individual genius but rather as the site of encounter of a biography, an intertext, an institutional context, and a historical moment ... they [directors, and to this I would add screenwriters] "orchestrate" pre-existing voices, ideologies, and discourses, without losing an overall shaping role ... a director's work can be both personal and mediated by extrapersonal elements such as genre, technology, studios, and the linguistic procedures of the medium.[47]

A revised contemporary sensitivity to adaptive film authorship would therefore also include the environments of all three texts—literary, script intertext, and film. All three can be sites of personal and cultural struggle and perhaps revelation. We look to locate and recognize both definitive individual voices and extrapersonal contexts when they show themselves across the developmental writing stages of adaptation, as well as on through the multitrack dimensionality and enunciating voice of the completed film.

■ ■ ■

Questions and projects

1. Examine a literary source, the screenplay that adapts that source, and the film made from the screenplay. How would you describe the evolution of the work through these three phases? How would you account for the changes?
2. Make the claim that the screenplay is a work of literature. How would you distinguish it as an aesthetic or artistic practice different from its literary source and the final film. Support you position with reference to a particular screenplay/film.

Notes

1   The promotional factor was put to direct use, for example, in the ploy by the makers of the Hobbit book-to-film trilogy, who encouraged readers to post their suggestions for the making of the film online as these projects were being developed and written. In this case the films' fidelity not only to the fantasy novels but to their readers' imagined realizations of them was encouraged as a form of audience pretesting. This approach clearly influenced the development of the adapted screenplay.

2   Among these are Tom Stempel's *Framework: A History of Screenwriting in the American Film* (1988), Linda Seger's and Edward Jay Whitmore's *From Script to Screen: The Collaborative Art of Filmmaking,* and Pat McGilligan's *Backstory* series of screenwriter interviews, including *Backstory 4: Interviews with Screenwriters of the '70s and '80s* (2006). Long the main text on the writing of adaptations is Linda Seger's *The Art of Adaptation* (1997), followed by Kenneth Portnoy's *Screen Adaptation: A Scriptwriting Handbook,* 2nd ed. (1998).

3   These include John M. Desmond and Peter Hawkes, *Adaptation: Studying Film & Literature* (2006); Mireia Aragay, ed., *Books in Motion: Adaptation, Intertextuality, Authorship* (2005); Kamilla Elliott, *Rethinking the Novel/Film Debate* (2003); Sarah Cardwell, *Adaptation Revisited: Television and the Classic Novel* (2002); Ginette Vincendeau, ed., *Film/Literature/Heritage: A Sight and Sound Reader* (2001); James Naremore, ed., *Film Adaptation* (2000); Robert Giddings and Erica Sheen, eds., *The Classic Novel: From Page to Screen* (2000); Timothy Corrigan, *Film and Literature: An Introduction and Reader* (1990); Deborah Cartmell and Imelda Whelehan, eds., *Adaptations: From Text to Screen, Screen to Text* (1999); John C. Tibbetts and James M. Welch, eds., *Novels into Film: The Encyclopedia of Movies Adapted from Books* (1999); and Brian McFarlane, *Novel to Film: An Introduction to the Theory of Adaptation* (1996).

4   The Robert Stam titles include *Literature Through Film* (2005) and two titles co-edited with Alessandra Raengo: *Literature and Film* (2005) and *A Companion to Literature and Film* (2005). These texts tend to cover the adaptation categories of literary history, theory, and international and other influences, respectively.

5   Robert Wise writes, for example:

> I absolutely believe in getting the script in order before starting to film. On one occasion, on *Star Trek: The Motion Picture*, we had only the first half of the script ready when we had to start shooting. … In the meantime, there were delays after delays. Finally I had to start shooting. The script rewrites kept on coming until the last day of shooting. That was not a satisfactory way to work and I think the film shows it.

> —From foreword in Tibbetts and Welch, eds., *Novels into Film*, viii–ix

6   See Arthur Eckstein's "Darkening Ethan: John Ford's *The Searchers* (1956): From Novel to Screenplay to Screen," *Cinema Journal* 38, no. 1 (1998): 3–24.

7   As a complex and expensive medium and industry, film encompasses, in addition to producers, writers, directors, and often storyboard artists, the contributions of CPAs and budget analysts, performers, art directors, and set builders, agents, technicians, special effects departments, all descriptions of equipment, schedulers, composers, editors, promotion and advertising, distributors, and exhibitors, to name only some of the skills, technology, and jobs required.

8   Stempel, *Framework,* 184.

9   The shooting script is a special script alteration that more thoroughly addresses the technical requirements of production. The shooting script includes numbered scenes, expanded descriptive details for special effects, and so on. Shooting scripts may be used as the basis for storyboards, which are typically hand drawn (or created using computerized images) that lay out the approximate angle and "look" of each individual shot in the visual progression of scenes. Once production is under way, the shooting script will also carry notations by the "script girl" to indicate actual camera takes on the set that will be delivered to the film's editors as a continuity script to aid in cutting and identifying all the rough footage. See also William Horne's "See Shooting Script: Reflections on the Ontology of the

Screenplay," *Literature/Film Quarterly* 20, no. 1 (1998): 52.

10   Selznick's famous battle with Hitchcock over the control of the script for "Selznick's" production of *Rebecca* is also apropos here.

11   See Jack Boozer *Authorship in Film Adaptation* (2008) Chapter 2, on Hitchcock's working methods, and the discussion in Chapter 3 of *Eyes Wide Shut* and screenwriter Fredric Rafael's *Eyes Wide Open*.

12   Stempel, *Framework,* 121. Herman Mankiewicz and Orson Welles also shared the Academy Award for Best Original Screenplay.

13   McGilligan, *Backstory 4,* 159. Jhabvala's comments on screenplay dialogue in these interviews are also supported in reverse by writer-director Robert Benton, who tells the story of convincing an actor for his film *Bad Company* to sound more like a Jimmy Stewart than a Montgomery Clift by having writer David Newman write lines for him "so that if Daffy Duck did the part he would sound like Jimmy Stewart." When the actor read them, he gave in (p. 26).

14   See Boozer *Authorship* Chapter 10 by Cynthia Lucia on *High Fidelity,* a film that John Cusack starred in as well as co-wrote and co-produced. Another example is Emma Thompson's script adaptation of Jane Austen's *Sense and Sensibility* (1995, Ang Lee), in which she also played the lead role.

15   Interview of Carl Franklin in *Creative Screenwriting* 4, no. 1 (1997): 20.

16   Geoffrey Wagner divides what he calls "modes" of adaptation into three comparable categories of distance from the source: *transposition, commentary* and *analogy,* with analogy being the most distant. See his *The Novel and the Cinema* (Rutherford, NJ: Fairleigh Dickinson University Press, 1975), cited in Joy Gould Boyum's *Double Exposure: Fiction into Film* (New York: Plume, 1985), 69.

17   These three examples also suggest that quality in adaptation may be more closely associated with talent and conviction in story truth than in reliance on a big budget, even for historical films. The Merchant-Ivory British production was shot in 1992 for only $8 million; Minghella's sweeping project, also British, was shot in 1996 for only $31 million; and the Coen brothers' comedy was shot in the United States in 2000 for about $26 million.

18   Wise, foreword to Tibbetts and Welch, eds., *Novels into Film,* viii.

19   Richard Glatzer and John Raeburn, eds., *Frank Capra: The Man and His Films* (Ann Arbor, MI: University of Michigan Press, 1975), 15.

20   Thomas Schatz, *Genius of the System* (New York: Metropolitan Books, 1996), 75. Similarly, Albert LaValley's description of Warner Bros. producer Jerry Wald's domination of the development of the script for the film *Mildred Pierce* (1946) in Boozer *Authorship* Chapter 2 provides yet another example of how this might work in relation to writers.

21   Gary Crowdus and Dan Georgakas, *Cineaste Interviews* (Chicago: Lake View Press, 2002), 365–366. *The Harder They Fall* (1957, Mark Robson) gave the screenplay credit to Philip Yordan.

22   Stempel, *Framework,* 165.

23   Ibid., 166. Both of them nevertheless went on to create highly regarded films, such as the next one they did together, *A Face in the Crowd* (1957, Elia Kazan, based on Schulberg's short story), which details the rise and fall of a countrified media huckster.

24   Bluestone, 159. "Working titles" are often assigned to films in production for a variety of reasons, but Zanuck specifically used "Highway" in his working title to prevent possible politically motivated interruptions and controversy while shooting of this controversial novel took place out on a public highway location.

25   Ibid., 167.

26   Johnson was graciously complimented on his script by Steinbeck himself, who recognized the difficulty of transforming his more than 500-page novel into what was "more dramatic in fewer words than my book." Johnson had completed a successful populist script of *Jesse James* for Zanuck the previous year, and he seemed the obvious choice to adapt Steinbeck's progressive novel (*Framework,* 83).

27   Bluestone, *Novels into Film,* 169.

28   Ibid., 64. Bluestone writes: "An art whose limits depend on a moving image, mass audience, and industrial production is bound to differ from an art whose limits depend on language, a limited audience and individual creation." One special consequence of appealing to a mass audience in the studio

era was the conservatively imposed system of film censorship, which was effectively instituted as a mandated Production Code in 1932. The Code exerted a great influence on the writing of all types of screenplays, which had to be cleared prior to production. By 1934, screenplays had to be pre-approved by the Joseph Breen office before shooting went forward, but it was adaptations such as *The Moon Is Blue* that began to break the Code's hold in 1953.

29   See "The Best Screenplay and Writing Academy Awards" for an extended historical breakdown of the writing award categories (http://www.filmsite.org/bestscreenplays.html).

30   In the American Film Institute's current list of 100 Best American Movies of all time, for example, thirty-one of the top fifty are adaptations, and of those only five or six could be considered literary classics ("America's 100 Greatest Movies," AFI.com). Best-selling stories and novels have far outnumbered quality literary works as sources for film, and the arena of popular sources is also larger because it includes nonfiction as well as fiction, including biographies, history, and current newspaper, magazine, and TV news stories, as well as comic books, film and TV documentaries, and TV programs.

31   The Writers Guild has been recognizing screen writers since 1953 with the Laurel Award for those who "advance the literature of the motion picture through the years, and have made outstanding contributions to the profession of the screen-writer." But this award is not for individual screenplays and generally recognizes contributions in adapted and original scripts.

32   André Bazin, *What Is Cinema?,* ed. and trans. Hugh Gray (Berkeley, CA: University of California Press, 1967), 56. This statement assumes, of course, that a writer and director actually seek "equivalency" in an adaptation.

33   See Thomas Leitch in Boozer *Authorship* Chapter 2 on Hitchcock.

34   Richard Corliss, ed., *The Hollywood Screenwriters* (New York: Avon Books, 1970), 11.

35   Ibid., 20.

36   Looking back on and arguing for the numerous examples of fine films that were adaptations in the European tradition generally is Andrew S. Horton and Joan Magretta's collection, *Modern European Filmmakers and the Art of Adaptation* (New York: Frederick Ungar, 1981).

37   Kirk Douglas had bought the rights to Kesey's novel with the idea of playing the Randall P. McMurphy role, but he had difficulty getting it developed until he allowed his son Michael to take over as producer. Michael promptly chose Jack Nicholson as McMurphy, Forman to direct, and the screenwriters mentioned.

38   As David Cook observed: "This condition has been seen as inhibiting the creative freedom of people working within the industry, especially since it has become common practice for producers, directors, writers and stars to receive a percentage of the net profits of their films as well as a smaller fixed salary, or fee-for-service." David Cook, *A History of Narrative Film* (New York: W. W. Norton, 1996), 935.

Consider also the fate of scriptwriters versus producers presented in Michael Tolkin's script adaptation of his own Hollywood insider novel, *The Player* (1992, Robert Altman, who also had a major hand in the script). Hollywood screenwriter Walter Hill further reports the yet darker comment by his writing colleague David Giler, who said that "your work is only read by the people who will destroy it" (*Backstory* 4,148).

39   *Backstory* 4, 12. McGilligan's comment on young writer-directors also suggests the contradiction in the current situation, where adaptations have generally not been accessible territory for most young writers. In contrast, the expanded public interest in the screenplay, which has continued to grow over the last thirty years, has created increased numbers of new writers who have been aided by the proliferation of screenplay competitions and grants, as well as academic courses and programs in screenwriting.

40   The essays by Roland Barthes and Michel Foucault are included in John Caughie, ed., *Theories of Authorship: A Reader* (London: Routledge and Kegan Paul, in association with the BFI, 1981).

41   Stam, *Literature and Film,* 9.

42   Ibid.

43   Dudley Andrew, "The Unauthorized Auteur Today," in *Film Theory Goes to the Movies,* ed. J. Collins

et al. (New York: Routledge, 1993), 77–85. See also D. Andrew, *Concepts in Film Theory* (New York: Oxford University Press, 1984), 106.

44   See Mireia Aragay's "Introduction: Reflection to Refraction: Adaptation Studies Then and Now" in her *Books in Motion,* 28. On the same page, Aragay cites the analysis of a contributor, Margaret McCarthy, who found in German director Doris Dorrie's "auteurist identity a paradoxical blend of individual expression and adaptation to pre-existing conventions and constraints."

45   See Frank P. Tomasulo on *Adaptation,* Chapter 6 in Boozer *Authorship* . Regarding *To Die For,* see also my chapter, "Women and Murder in the Televirtuality Film," in *Killing Women: The Visual Culture of Gender and Violence,* ed. Annette Burfoot and Susan Lord (Ontario: Wilfrid Laurier University Press, 2006), 139–154.

46   André Bazin, "Adaptation or the Cinema as Digest," in Naremore, ed., *Film Adaptation,* 25–26.

47   Robert Stam and Toby Miller, *Film and Theory: An Anthology* (Malden, MA: Blackwell Publishers, 2000), 6.

References

Aragay, Mireia, ed. *Books in Motion: Adaptation, Intertextuality, Authorship.* New York: Rodopi, 2005.

Bazin, André. *What Is Cinema?,* edited and translated by Hugh Gray. Berkeley, CA: University of California Press, 1967.

Behlmer, Rudy, ed. *Inside Warner Bros. (1935–1951).* New York: Viking, 1985.

Bluestone, George. *Novels into Film.* Berkeley, CA: University of California Press, 1957.

Boozer, Jack. "Women and Murder in the Televirtuality Film." In *Killing Women: The Visual Culture of Gender and Violence,* edited by Annette Burfoot and Susan Lord, 139–154. Ontario: Wildred-Laurier University Press, 2006.

Boozer, Jack. *Authorship in Film Adaptation*, Austin, TX: University of Texas Press, 2008.

Bricknell, Timothy, ed. *Minghella on Minghella.* London: Faber & Faber, 2005.

Cardwell, Sarah. *Adaptation Revisited: Television and the Classic Novel.* New York: Manchester University Press, 2002.

Cartmell, Deborah, and Imelda Whelehan, eds. *Adaptations: From Text to Screen, Screen to Text.* New York: Routledge, 1999.

Caughie, John, ed. *Theories of Readership: A Reader.* London: Routledge and Kegan Paul, in association with BFI, 1981.

Corliss, Richard, ed. *The Hollywood Screenwriters.* New York: Aron Books, 1970.

Corrigan, Timothy. *Film and Literature: An Introduction and Reader.* Upper Saddle River, NJ: Prentice Hall, 1999.

Desmond, John M., and Peter Hawkes. *Adaptation: Studying Film & Literature.* New York: McGraw-Hill, 2006.

Elliott, Kamilla. *Rethinking the Novel/Film Debate.* Cambridge: Cambridge University Press, 2003.

Giddings, Robert, and Erica Sheen, eds. *The Classic Novel: From Page to Screen.* New York: Manchester University Press, 2000.

Glatzer, Richard, and John Raeburn, eds. *Frank Copra: The Man and His Films.* Ann Arbor, MI: University of Michigan Press, 1975.

Literature/Film Quarterly, 1979–present.

McFarlane, Brian. *Novel to Film: An Introduction to the Theory of Adaptation.* New York: Oxford University Press, 1996.

McGilligan, Patrick. *Backstory 4: Interviews with Screenwriters of the '70s and '80s.* Berkeley, CA: University of California Press, 2006.

Naremore, James, ed. *Film Adaptation.* New Brunswick, NJ: Rutgers University Press, 2000.

Portnoy, Kenneth. *Screen Adaptation: A Scriptwriting Handbook,* 2nd edn. Boston, MA: Focal Press, 1998

Schatz, Thomas. *Genius of the System.* New York: Metropolitan Books, 1996.

Seger, Linda. *The Art of Adaptation: Turning Fact and Fiction into Film.* New York: Henry Holt, 1997.

Seger, Linda, and Edward Jay Whetmore. *From Script to Screen: The Collaborative Art of Filmmaking.* New York: Henry Holt, 1994.

Stam, Robert. *Literature Through Film.* Oxford: Blackwell, 2005.

Stam, Robert, and Alessandra Raengo, eds. *A Companion to Literature and Film.* Oxford: Blackwell, 2005.

Stam, Robert, and Alessandra Raengo, eds. *Literature and Film.* Oxford: Blackwell, 2005.

Stempel, Tom. *Framework: A History of Screenwriting in the American Film.* Syracuse, NY: Syracuse University Press, 1988.

Thompson, Emma. *The Sense and Sensibility Screenplay and Diaries.* New York: Newmarket Press, 1996.

Tibbetts, John C., and James M. Welch, eds. *Novels into Film: The Encyclopedia of Movies Adapted from Books.* New York: Checkmark Books, 1999.

Vincendeau, Ginnette, ed. *Film/Literature/Heritage: A Sight and Sound Reader.* London: BFI, 2001.

2.4 NOVELS, THEATER, POETRY, AND NON-FICTION

Chapter 22

André Bazin

THEATER AND CINEMA

ORIGINALLY PUBLISHED IN FRENCH IN 1951 and translated into English in 1967, the following and other essays in Bazin's *What Is Cinema?* represent highly energized and imaginative thinking about film in general and film and literature in specific. One of the leaders of serious film study in France, Bazin introduces crucial terms and distinctions about the relationships—past, present, and future—between film and drama, about canned theater, drama versus theater, the textuality of drama, and so forth. He also identifies the distinctive powers of the cinema to create a unique and powerful identification and presence for audiences through the use of spatial realism. While Bazin remains committed to the cinema as a unique artistic form, he clearly respects the powers of traditional literature and drama. He ultimately urges a creative evolution whereby cinema builds on its literary precedents as an exchange through which the two practices continually reinvigorate each other.

■ ■ ■

THEATER AND CINEMA
ANDRÉ BAZIN

From *What Is Cinema? Vol. 1,* trans. Hugh Gray, Berkeley, CA: University of California Press, 1971, pp. 95–112

The leitmotiv of those who despise filmed theater, their final and apparently insuperable argument, continues to be the unparalleled pleasure that accompanies the presence of the actor. "What is specific to theater," writes Henri Gouhier, in *The Essence of Theater*, "is the impossibility of separating off action and actor." Elsewhere he says "the stage welcomes every illusion except that of presence; the actor is there in disguise, with the soul and voice of another, but he is nevertheless there and by the same token space calls out for him and for the solidity of his presence. On the other hand and inversely, the cinema accommodates every form of reality save one—the physical presence of the actor." If it is here that the essence of theater lies then undoubtedly the cinema can in no way pretend to any parallel with it. If the writing, the style, and the dramatic structure are, as they should be, rigorously conceived as the receptacle for the soul and being of the flesh-and-blood actor, any attempt to substitute the shadow and reflection of a man on the screen for the man himself is a completely vain enterprise. There is no answer to this argument. The successes of Laurence Olivier, of Welles, or of Cocteau can only be challenged—here you need to be in bad faith—or considered inexplicable. They are a challenge both to critics and philosophers. Alternatively one can only explain them by casting doubts on that commonplace of theatrical criticism "the irreplaceable presence of the actor."

The concept of presence

At this point certain comments seem called for concerning the concept of "presence," since it would appear that it is this concept, as understood prior to the appearance of photography, that the cinema challenges.

Can the photographic image, especially the cinematographic image, be likened to other images and in common with them be regarded as having an existence distinct from the object? Presence, naturally, is defined in terms of time and space. "To be in the presence of someone" is to recognize him as existing contemporaneously with us and to note that he comes within the actual range of our senses—in the case of cinema of our sight and in radio of our hearing. Before the arrival of photography and later of cinema, the plastic arts (especially portraiture) were the only intermediaries between actual physical presence and absence. Their justification was their resemblance which stirs the imagination and helps the memory. But photography is something else again. In no sense is it the image of an object or person, more correctly it is its tracing. Its automatic genesis distinguishes it radically from the other techniques of reproduction. The photograph proceeds by means of the lens to the taking of a veritable luminous impression in light—to a mold. As such it carries with it more than mere resemblance, namely a kind of identity—the card we call by that name being only conceivable in an age of photography. But photography is a feeble technique in the sense that its instantaneity compels it to capture time only piecemeal. The cinema does something strangely paradoxical. It makes a molding of the object as it exists in time and, furthermore, makes an imprint of the duration of the object.

The nineteenth century with its objective techniques of visual and sound reproduction gave birth to a new category of images, the relation of which to the reality from which they proceed requires very strict definition. Even apart from the fact that the resulting aesthetic problems cannot be satisfactorily raised without this introductory philosophical inquiry, it would not be sound to treat the old aesthetic questions as if the categories with which they deal had in no way been modified by the appearance of completely new phenomena. Common sense—perhaps the best philosophical guide in this case—has clearly understood this and has invented an expression for the presence of an actor, by adding to the placards announcing his appearance the phrase "in flesh and blood." This means that for the man in the street the word "presence," today, can be ambiguous, and thus an apparent redundancy is not out of place in this age of cinema. Hence it is no longer as certain as it was that there is no middle stage between presence and absence. It is likewise at the ontological level that the effectiveness of the cinema has its source. It is false to say that the screen is incapable of putting us "in the presence of" the actor. It does so in the same way as a mirror—one must agree that the mirror relays the presence of the person reflected in it—but it is a mirror with a delayed reflection, the tin foil of which retains the image. It is true that in the theater Molière can die on the stage and that we have the privilege of living in the biographical time of the actor. In the film about Manolete however we are present at the actual death of the famous matador and while our emotion may not be as deep as if we were actually present in the arena at that historic moment, its nature is the same. What we lose by way of direct witness do we not recapture thanks to the artificial proximity provided by photographic enlargement? Everything takes place as if in the time-space perimeter which is the definition of presence. The cinema offers us effectively only a measure of duration, reduced but not to zero, while the increase in the space factor reestablishes the equilibrium of the psychological equation.

Opposition and identification

An honest appraisal of the respective pleasures derived from theater and cinema, at least as to what is less intellectual and more direct about them, forces us to admit that the delight we experience at the end of a play has a more uplifting, a nobler, one might perhaps say a more moral, effect than the satisfaction which follows a good film. We seem to come away with a better conscience. In a certain sense it is as if for the man in the audience all theater is "Corneillian." From this point of view one could say that in the best films something is missing. It is as if a certain inevitable lowering of the voltage, some mysterious aesthetic short circuit, deprived us in the cinema of a certain tension which is a definite part of theater. No matter how slight this difference it undoubtedly exists, even between the worst charity production in the theater and the most brilliant of Olivier's film adaptations. There is nothing banal about this observation and the survival of the theater after fifty years of cinema, and the prophecies of Marcel Pagnol, is practical proof enough. At the source of the disenchantment which follows the film one could doubtless detect a process of depersonalization of the spectator. As Rosenkrantz wrote in 1937, in *Esprit*, in an article profoundly original for its period,

> The characters on the screen are quite naturally objects of identification, while those on the stage are, rather, objects of mental opposition because their real presence gives them an objective reality and to transpose them into beings in an imaginary world the will of the spectator has to intervene actively, that is to say, to will to transform their physical reality into an abstraction. This abstraction being the result of a process of the intelligence that we can only ask of a person who is fully conscious.

A member of a film audience tends to identify himself with the film's hero by a psychological process, the result of which is to turn the audience into a "mass" and to render emotion uniform. Just as in algebra if two numbers equal a third, then they are equal to one another, so here we can say, if two individuals identify themselves with a third, they identify themselves with one another. Let us compare chorus girls on the stage and on the screen. On the screen they satisfy an unconscious sexual desire and when the hero joins them he satisfies the desire of the spectator in the proportion to which the latter has identified himself with the hero. On the stage the girls excite the onlooker as they would in real life. The result is that there is no identification with the hero. He becomes instead an object of jealousy and envy. In other words, Tarzan is only possible on the screen. The cinema calms the spectator, the theater excites him. Even when it appeals to the lowest instincts, the theater up to a certain point stands in the way of the creation of a mass mentality. It stands in the way of any collective representation in the psychological sense, since theater calls for an active individual consciousness while the film requires only a passive adhesion.

These views shed a new light on the problem of the actor. They transfer him from the ontological to the psychological level. It is to the extent to which the cinema encourages identification with the hero that it conflicts with the theater. Put this way the problem is no longer basically insoluble, for it is a fact that the cinema has at its disposal means which favor a passive position or on the other hand, means which to a greater or lesser degree stimulate the consciousness of the spectator. Inversely the theater can find ways of lessening the psychological tension between spectator and actor. Thus theater and cinema will no longer be separated off by an unbridgeable aesthetic moat, they would simply tend to give rise to two attitudes of mind over which the director maintains a wide control.

Examined at close quarters, the pleasure derived from the theater not only differs from that of the cinema but also from that of the novel. The reader of a novel, physically alone like the man in the dark movie house, identifies himself with the character. That is why after reading for a long while he also feels the same intoxication of an illusory intimacy with the hero. Incontestably, there is in the pleasure derived from cinema and novel a self-satisfaction, a concession to solitude, a sort of betrayal of action by a refusal of social responsibility.

The analysis of this phenomenon might indeed be undertaken from a psychoanalytic point of view. Is it not significant that the psychiatrists took the term catharsis from Aristotle? Modern pedagogic research on psychodrama seems to have provided fruitful insights into the cathartic process of theater. The ambiguity existing in the child's mind between play and reality is used to get him to free himself by way of improvised theater from the repressions from which he suffers. This technique amounts to creating a kind of vague theater in which the play is of a serious nature and the actor is his own audience. The action that develops on these occasions is not one that is divided off by footlights, which are undoubtedly the architectural symbol of the censor that separates us from the stage. We delegate Oedipus to act in our guise and place him on the other side of a wall of fire—that fiery frontier between fantasy and reality which gives rein to Dionysiac monsters while protecting us from them. These sacred beasts will not cross this barrier of light beyond which they seem out of place and even sacrilegious—witness the disturbing atmosphere of awe which surrounds an actor still made up, like a phosphorescent light, when we visit him in his dressing room. There is no point to the argument that the theater did not always have footlights. These are only a symbol and there were others before them from the cothurnus and mask onwards. In the seventeenth century the fact that young nobles sat up on the stage is no denial of the role of the footlights, on the contrary, it confirms it, by way of a privileged violation so to speak, just as when today Orson Welles scatters actors around the auditorium to fire on the audience with revolvers. He does not do away with the footlights, he just crosses them. The rules of the game are also made to be broken. One expects some players to cheat. With regard to the objection based on presence and on that alone, the theater and the cinema are not basically in conflict. What is really in dispute are two psychological modalities of a performance. The theater is indeed based on the reciprocal awareness of the presence of audience and actor, but only as related to a performance. The theater acts on us by virtue of our participation in a theatrical action across the footlights and as it were under the protection of their censorship. The opposite is true in the cinema. Alone, hidden in a dark room, we watch through half-open blinds a spectacle that is unaware of our existence and which is part of the universe. There is nothing to prevent us from identifying ourselves in imagination with the moving world before us, which becomes *the* world. It is no longer on the phenomenon of the actor as a person physically present that we should concentrate our analysis, but rather on the ensemble of conditions that constitute the theatrical play and deprive the spectator of active participation. We shall see that it is much less a question of actor and presence than of man and his relation to the decor.

Behind the decor

The human being is all-important in the theater. The drama on the screen can exist without actors. A banging door, a leaf in the wind, waves beating on the shore can heighten the dramatic effect. Some film masterpieces use man only as an accessory, like an extra, or in counterpoint to nature which is the true leading character. Even when, as in *Nanook* and *Man of Aran*, the subject is man's struggle with nature, it cannot be compared to a theatrical action. The mainspring of the action is not in man but nature. As Jean-Paul Sartre, I think it was, said, in the theater the drama proceeds from the actor, in the cinema it goes from the decor to man. This reversal of the dramatic flow is of decisive importance. It is bound up with the very essence of the *mise-en-scène*. One must see here one of the consequences of photographic realism. Obviously, if the cinema makes use of nature it is because it is able to. The camera puts at the disposal of the director all the resources of the telescope and the microscope. The last strand of a rope about to snap or an entire army making an assault on a hill are within our reach. Dramatic causes and effects have no longer any material limits to the eye of the camera. Drama is freed by the camera from all contingencies of time and space. But this freeing of tangible dramatic powers is still only a secondary aesthetic cause, and does not basically explain the reversal of value between the actor and the decor. For sometimes it actually happens that the cinema deliberately deprives itself of the use of setting and of exterior nature—we have already seen a perfect instance of this in *Les Parents terribles*—while the theater in contrast uses a complex machinery to give a feeling of ubiquity to the audience. Is *La Passion de Jeanne d'Arc* by Carl Dreyer, shot entirely in close-up, in the virtually invisible and in fact theatrical settings by Jean Hugo, less cinematic than *Stagecoach*? It seems to me that quantity has nothing to do with it, nor the resemblance to certain theater techniques. The ideas of an art director for a room in *Les Dames aux camélias* would not noticeably differ whether for a film or a play. It's true that on the screen you would doubtless have some close-ups of the blood-stained handkerchief, but a skillful stage production would also know how to make some play with the cough and the handkerchief. All the close-ups in *Les Parents terribles* are taken directly from the theater where our attention would spontaneously isolate them. If film direction only differed from theater direction because it allows us a closer view of the scenery and makes a more reasonable use of it, there would really be no reason to continue with the theater and Pagnol would be a true prophet. For it is obvious that the few square yards of the decor of Vilar's *La Danse de la mort* contributed as much to the drama as the island on which Marcel Cravene shot his excellent film. The fact is that the problem lies not in the decor itself but in its nature and function. We must therefore throw some light on an essentially theatrical notion, that of the dramatic place.

There can be no theater without architecture, whether it be the cathedral square, the arena of Nîmes, the palace of the Popes, the trestle stage on a fairground, the semicircle of the theater of Vicenza that looks as if it were decorated by Bérard in a delirium, or the rococo amphitheaters of the boulevard houses. Whether as a performance or a celebration, theater of its very essence must not be confused with nature under penalty of being absorbed by her and ceasing to be. Founded on the reciprocal awareness of those taking part and present to one another, it must be in contrast to the rest of the world in the same way that play and reality are opposed, or concern and indifference, or liturgy and the common use of things. Costume, mask, or make-up, the style of the language, the footlights, all contribute to this distinction, but the clearest sign of all is the stage, the architecture of which has varied from time to time without ever ceasing to mark out a privileged spot actually or virtually distinct from nature. It is precisely in virtue of this *locus dramaticus* that decor exists. It serves in greater or less degree to set the place apart, to specify. Whatever it is, the decor constitutes the walls of this three-sided box opening onto the auditorium, which we call the stage. These false perspectives, these façades, these arbors, have another side which is cloth and nails and wood. Everyone knows that when the actor "retires to his apartment" from the yard or from the garden, he is actually going to his dressing room to take off his make-up. These few square feet of light and illusion are surrounded by machinery and flanked by wings, the hidden labyrinths of which do not interfere one bit with the pleasure of the spectator who is playing the game of theater. Because it is only part of the architecture of the stage, the decor of the theater is thus an area materially enclosed, limited, circumscribed, the only discoveries of which are those of our collusive imagination.

Its appearances are turned inward facing the public and the footlights. It exists by virtue of its reverse side and of anything beyond, as the painting exists by virtue of its frame. Just as the picture is not to be confounded with the scene it represents and is not a window in a wall. The stage and the decor where the action unfolds constitute an aesthetic microcosm inserted perforce into the universe but essentially distinct from the Nature which surrounds it.

It is not the same with cinema, the basic principle of which is a denial of any frontiers to action.

The idea of a *locus dramaticus* is not only alien to, it is essentially a contradiction of the concept of the screen. The screen is not a frame like that of a picture but a mask which allows only a part of the action to be seen. When a character moves off screen, we accept the fact that he is out of sight, but he continues to exist in his own capacity at some other place in the decor which is hidden from us. There are no wings to the screen. There could not be without destroying its specific illusion, which is to make of a revolver or of a face the very center of the universe. In contrast to the stage the space of the screen is centrifugal. It is because that infinity which the theater demands cannot be spatial that its area can be none other than the human soul. Enclosed in this space the actor is at the focus of a two-fold concave mirror. From the auditorium and from the decor there converge on him the dim lights of conscious human beings and of the footlights themselves. But the fire with which he burns is at once that of his inner passion and of that focal point at which he stands. He lights up in each member of his audience an accomplice flame. Like the ocean in a sea shell the dramatic infinities of the human heart moan and beat between the enclosing walls of the theatrical sphere. This is why this dramaturgy is in its essence human. Man is at once its cause and its subject.

On the screen man is no longer the focus of the drama, but will become eventually the center of the universe. The impact of his action may there set in motion an infinitude of waves. The decor that surrounds him is part of the solidity of the world. For this reason the actor as such can be absent from it, because man in the world enjoys no a priori privilege over animals and things. However there is no reason why he should not be the mainspring of the drama, as in Dreyer's *Jeanne d'Arc*, and in this respect the cinema may very well impose itself upon the theater. As actions *Phèdre* or *King Lear* are no less cinematographic than theatrical, and the visible death of a rabbit in *La Règle du jeu* affects us just as deeply as that of Agnès' little cat about which we are merely told.

But if Racine, Shakespeare, or Molière cannot be brought to the cinema by just placing them before the camera and the microphone, it is because the handling of the action and the style of the dialogue were conceived as echoing through the architecture of the auditorium. What is specifically theatrical about these tragedies is not their action so much as the human, that is to say the verbal, priority given to their dramatic structure. The problem of filmed theater at least where the classics are concerned does not consist so much in transposing an action from the stage to the screen as in transposing a text written for one dramaturgical system into another while at the same time retaining its effectiveness. It is not therefore essentially the action of a play which resists film adaptation, but above and beyond the phases of the intrigue (which it would be easy enough to adapt to the realism of the screen) it is the verbal form which aesthetic contingencies or cultural prejudices oblige us to respect. It is this which refuses to let itself be captured in the window of the screen. "The theater," says Baudelaire, "is a crystal chandelier." If one were called upon to offer in comparison a symbol other than this artificial crystal-like object, brilliant, intricate, and circular, which refracts the light which plays around its center and holds us prisoners of its aureole, we might say of the cinema that it is the little flashlight of the usher, moving like an uncertain comet across the night of our waking dream, the diffuse space without shape or frontiers that surrounds the screen.

The story of the failures and recent successes of theater on film will be found to be that of the ability of directors to retain the dramatic force of the play in a medium that reflects it or, at least, the ability to give this dramatic force enough resonance to permit a film audience to perceive it. In other words, it is a matter of an aesthetic that is not concerned with the actor but with decor and editing. Henceforth it is clear that filmed theater is basically destined to fail whenever it tends in any manner to become simply the photographing of scenic representation even and perhaps most of all when the camera is used to try and make us forget the footlights and the backstage area. The dramatic force of the text, instead of being gathered up in the actor, dissolves without echo into the cinematic ether. This is why a filmed play can show due respect to the text, be well acted in likely settings, and yet be completely worthless. This is what happened, to take a convenient example, to *Le Voyageur sans bagage*. The play lies there before us apparently true to itself yet drained of every ounce of energy, like a battery dead from an unknown short. But over and beyond the aesthetic of the decor we see clearly both on the screen and on the stage that in the last analysis the problem before us is that of realism. This is the problem we always end up with when we are dealing with cinema.

The screen and the realism of space

The realism of the cinema follows directly from its photographic nature. Not only does some marvel or some fantastic thing on the screen not undermine the reality of the image, on the contrary it is its most valid justification. Illusion in the cinema is not based as it is in the theater on convention tacitly accepted by the general public; rather, contrariwise, it is based on the inalienable realism of that which is shown. All trick work must be perfect in all material respects on the screen. The "invisible man" must wear pyjamas and smoke a cigarette.

Must we conclude from this that the cinema is dedicated entirely to the representation if not of natural reality at least of a plausible reality of which the spectator admits the identity with nature as he knows it? The comparative failure of German expressionism would seem to confirm this hypothesis, since it is evident that *Caligari* attempted to depart from realistic decor under the influence of the theater and painting. But this would be to offer an oversimplified explanation for a problem that calls for more subtle answers. We are prepared to admit that the screen opens upon an artificial world provided there exists a common denominator between the cinematographic image and the world we live in. Our experience of space is the structural basis for our concept of the universe. We may say in fact, adapting Henri Gouhier's formula, "the stage welcomes every illusion except the illusion of presence," that "the cinematographic image can be emptied of all reality save one—the reality of space."

It is perhaps an overstatement to say "all reality" because it is difficult to imagine a reconstruction of space devoid of all reference to nature. The world of the screen and our world cannot be juxtaposed. The screen of necessity substitutes for it since the very concept of universe is spatially exclusive. For a time, a film is the Universe, the world, or if you like, Nature. We will see how the films that have attempted to substitute a fabricated nature and an artificial world for the world of experience have not all equally succeeded. Admitting the failure of *Caligari* and *Die Nibelungen* we then ask ourselves how we explain the undoubted success of *Nosferatu* and *La Passion de Jeanne d'Arc*, the criterion of success being that these films have never aged.

Yet it would seem at first sight that the methods of direction belong to the same aesthetic family, and that viewing the varieties of temperament and period, one could group these four films together as expressionist as distinct from realist. However, if we examine them more closely we see that there are certain basic differences between them. It is clear in the case of R. Weine and Murnau. *Nosferatu* plays, for the greater part of the time, against natural settings whereas the fantastic qualities of *Caligari* are derived from deformities of lighting and decor. The case of Dreyer's *Jeanne d'Arc* is a little more subtle since at first sight nature plays a nonexistent role. To put it more directly, the decor by Jean Hugo is no whit less artificial and theatrical than the settings of *Caligari,* the systematic use of close-ups and unusual angles is well calculated to destroy any sense of space. Regular ciné-club goers know that the film is unfailingly introduced with the famous story of how the hair of Falconetti was actually cut in the interests of the film and likewise, the actors, we are told, wore no make-up. These references to history ordinarily have no more than gossip value. In this case, they seem to me to hold the aesthetic secret of the film; the very thing to which it owes its continued survival. It is precisely because of them that the work of Dreyer ceases to have anything in common with the theater, and indeed one might say, with man. The greater recourse Dreyer has exclusively to the human "expression," the more he has to reconvert it again into Nature. Let there be no mistake, that prodigious fresco of heads is the very opposite of an actor's film. It is a documentary of faces. It is not important how well the actors play, whereas the pock-marks on Bishop Cauchon's face and the red patches of Jean d'Yd are an integral part of the action. In this drama-through-the-microscope the whole of nature palpitates beneath every pore. The movement of a wrinkle, the pursing of a lip are seismic shocks and the flow of tides, the flux and reflux of this human epidermis. But for me Dreyer's brilliant sense of cinema is evidenced in the exterior scene which every other director would assuredly have shot in the studio. The decor as built evoked a Middle Ages of the theater and of miniatures. In one sense, nothing is less realistic than this tribunal in the cemetery or this draw-bridge, but the whole is lit by the light of the sun and the gravedigger throws a spadeful of real earth into the hole.

It is these "secondary" details, apparently aesthetically at odds with the rest of the work, which give it its truly cinematic quality.

If the paradox of the cinema is rooted in the dialectic of concrete and abstract, if cinema is committed to communicate only by way of what is real, it becomes all the more important to discern those elements in filming which confirm our sense of natural reality and those which destroy that feeling. On the other hand, it certainly argues a lack of perception to derive one's sense of reality from these accumulations of factual detail. It is possible to argue that *Les Dames du Bois de Boulogne* is an eminently realistic film, though everything about it is stylized. Everything, except for the rarely noticeable sound of a windshield-wiper, the murmur of a waterfall, or the rushing sound of soil escaping from a broken vase. These are the noises, chosen precisely for their "indifference" to the action, that guarantee its reality.

The cinema being of its essence a dramaturgy of Nature, there can be no cinema without the setting up of an open space in place of the universe rather than as part of it. The screen cannot give us the illusion of this feeling of space without calling on certain natural guarantees. But it is less a question of set construction or of architecture or of immensity than of isolating the aesthetic catalyst, which it is sufficient to introduce in an infinitesimal dose, to have it immediately take on the reality of nature.

The concrete forest of *Die Nibelungen* may well pretend to be an infinite expanse. We do not believe it to be so, whereas the trembling of just one branch in the wind, and the sunlight, would be enough to conjure up all the forests of the world.

If this analysis be well founded, then we see that the basic aesthetic problem of filmed theater is indeed that of the decor. The trump card that the director must hold is the reconversion into a window onto the world of a space oriented toward an interior dimension only, namely the closed and conventional area of the theatrical play.

It is not in Laurence Olivier's *Hamlet* that the text seems to be rendered superfluous or its strength diminished by directorial interpretations, still less in Welles' *Macbeth*, but paradoxically in the stage productions of Gaston Baty, to the precise extent that they go out of their way to create a cinematographic space on the stage; to deny that the settings have a reverse side, thus reducing the sonority of the text simply to the vibration of the voice of the actor who is left without his "resonance box" like a violin that is nothing else but strings. One would never deny that the essential thing in the theater is the text. The latter conceived for the anthropocentric expression proper to the stage and having as its function to bring nature to it cannot, without losing its raison d'être, be used in a space transparent as glass. The problem then that faces the filmmaker is to give his decor a dramatic opaqueness while at the same time reflecting its natural realism. Once this paradox of space has been dealt with, the director, so far from hesitating to bring theatrical conventions and faithfulness to the text to the screen will find himself now, on the contrary, completely free to rely on them. From that point on it is no longer a matter of running away from those things which "make theater" but in the long run to acknowledge their existence by rejecting the resources of the cinema, as Cocteau did in *Les Parents terribles* and Welles in *Macbeth,* or by putting them in quotation marks as Laurence Olivier did in *Henry V.* The evidence of a return to filmed theater that we have had during the last ten years belongs essentially to the history of decor and editing. It is a conquest of realism—not, certainly, the realism of subject matter or realism of expression but that realism of space without which moving pictures do not constitute cinema.

■ ■ ■

Questions and projects

1. Examine Shakespeare's *Henry V* and Laurence Olivier's adaptation in light of Bazin's argument. Where does he seem most correct and where might there be omissions or problems with his analysis of that play? Are there other useful ways of comparing the two?
2. Select two or three of Bazin's central claims and test them on more recent adaptations of theater on film such as Tom Stoppard's *Rosencrantz and Guildenstern Are Dead* (1990), Kenneth Branagh's *Henry V* (1989), or Wallace Shawn's *Vanya on 42nd Street* (1994).

Chapter 23

Leo Braudy

ACTING
Stage vs. Screen

T HE DIFFERENT STYLES AND STRATEGIES OF ACTING have always been a major
    ingredient in adaptations and distinctions between film and literature. The following excerpt
from Braudy's 1976 book introduces that often overlooked dimension in the differences
between film and literature: namely, what distinguishes the portrayal of characters in drama
and film. Braudy's analysis has a useful historical overview, which places the question in
the context of theatrical acting from Aristotle and Shakespeare through the increasingly
naturalistic acting of the nineteenth century. The heart of this piece traces the dominant
acting styles in theater and film through the twentieth century, making crucial distinctions
about how the two forms make available different meanings for characters.

■ ■ ■

ACTING: STAGE VS. SCREEN
LEO BRAUDY

From *The World in a Frame, What We See in Films*, 2nd edn, Chicago, IL:
University of Chicago Press, 1984, pp 191–201

Acting in Europe and America has been historically defined by the varying interplay of the
heightened and the normal, the theatrical and the nonchalant, in the conception of the role.
Until the Renaissance, there was little attempt to place any special value on the absorption of
the rhythm, themes, and gestures of everyday life into drama or acting style. Aristotle had taught
that the most intense feelings possible in drama were those in tragedy, when the characters and
the acting style were on a much higher plane than the normal life of the audience. Everyday life,
where the characters and the way they behave tend to be on the same or lower social levels than
the audience, was primarily a source of stylized comedy. The stage was raised above the audience
in part because the characters and their impersonators were not to be considered as individually

as the audience might assess each other. In Greek, Roman, and medieval society, actors therefore tended to portray beings purer than the audience, the somber figures of myth and the caricatures of comedy—a division of acting labor not unlike that of the silent screen.

Shakespeare helped make an enormous change in this rotation between the audience and the actors by elaborating the analogies possible between the world and the stage. He began the European theater's effort to absorb and reflect the life of the audience as much as to bring the audience out of itself into another world. Comedy could therefore become more serious because it was no longer necessary to involve emotions lower than the grand style of tragedy. More intimate theaters and better lighting permitted a more nuanced acting style. By the mid-eighteenth century David Garrick had become the first to attempt historical authenticity in costuming, once again asserting the need to ground the play and the style of acting in some possible and plausible setting rather than a special world of theater. The "fourth wall" theories of the later nineteenth century further defined theatrical space and dramatic acting as an extension of the world of the audience. Stylized acting did not disappear, of course. The broader styles remained in opera, ballet, and popular comedy, as well as revivals of classics, symbolic and proletarian drama, and the experiments with ritual theater from the end of World War Two to the present.

Acting on stage had necessarily developed a tradition of naturalness as well. In the eighteenth century Diderot had argued that the paradox of acting is that an actor must be cold and tranquil in order to project emotion. Actors who play from the soul, he said, are mediocre and uneven. We are not moved by the man of violence, but by the man who possesses himself. In the early twentieth century, Konstantin Stanislavsky turned Diderot's view of the actor self-possessed in passion into a whole style. He rejected theories of acting based on imitation and emphasized instead an actor's inner life as the source of energy and authenticity for his characterizations. More "mechanical" and expressionist styles of stage acting implicitly attacked Stanislavsky's methods by their emphasis on the intensity of emotion and the visual coherence of the stage ensemble. Minglings of the two traditions produced such hybrids as the Group Theater, in which the interplay between ensemble and individual produced a thematic tension often missing from Eisenstein's productions, whether on stage or in film. Elia Kazan's film style, for example, with its mixture of expressionistic, closed directorial style and open, naturalistic acting, is a direct descendant of this tradition.

Our ability to learn what films can tell us about human character has suffered not only from preconceptions derived from the novel of psychological realism, but also from assumptions about acting that are drawn from the stage. We know much better what our attitude should be toward characters in fiction and drama. Unlike those forms, films emphasize acting and character, often at the expense of forms and language. Films add what is impossible in the group situation of the stage or the omniscient world of the novel: a sense of the mystery inside character, the strange core of connection with the face and body the audience comes to know so well, the sense of an individuality that can never be totally expressed in words or action. The stage cannot have this effect because the audience is constantly aware of the actor's impersonation. Character in film generally is more like character as we perceive it everyday than it is in any other representational art. The heightened style of silent film acting could be considered an extension of stage acting, but the more personal style allowed by sound film paradoxically both increased the appeal of films and lowered their intellectual status. The artistic was the timeless, Garbo not Dietrich, Valentino not Gable.

But character in sound film especially was not so much deficient as it was elusive. Films can be less didactic about character because the film frame is less confining than the fictional narrative or the theatrical proscenium. Sound films especially can explore the tension between the "real person" playing the role and the image projected on the screen. The line between film actor and part is much more difficult to draw than that between stage actor and role, and the social dimension of "role" contrasts appropriately with the personal dimension of "part." Film acting is less impersonation than personation, part of personality but not identifiable with it. "Can Ingrid Bergman commit murder?" ask the advertisements for *Murder on the Orient Express* (Sidney Lumet, 1975); the casual substitution of actress for character crudely makes an assertion that better films explore more subtly. Unlike the stage actor, the film actor cannot get over the footlights. Although this technical necessity may seem to make him less "real" than the stage actor, it makes his relation to the character he plays much more real. Audiences demand to hear more about the private life of the film actor than the stage actor because film creates character by tantalizing the audience with the promise of the secret self, always just out of the grasp of final articulation and meaning. The other life of a stage character is the real life of the person who plays him. But the other life of a film character is the continuity in other films of the career of the actor who plays him. In plays the unrevealed self tends to be a reduced, meaner version of the displayed self; in films it is almost always a complex enhancement. Within the film a character may have a limited meaning. But the actor who plays him can potentially be a presence larger than that one part, at once more intimate and more distant than is ever possible on stage.

Film preserves a performance that is superior to the script, whereas stage performances and plays are separate realities, with the performance often considered second best. The stage actor is performing a role: he may be the best, one of the best, the only, or one of many to play that role. But the role and its potentials will exist long after he has ceased to play it, to be interested in it, to be alive. The film actor does not so much perform a role as he creates a kind of life, playing between his characterization in a particular film and his potential escape from that character, outside the film and perhaps into other films. The stage actor memorizes an entire role in proper order, putting it on like a costume, while the film actor learns his part in pieces, often out of chronological order, using his personality as a kind of armature, or as painters will let canvas show through to become part of the total effect. If the movie is remade and another actor plays the part, there is little sense of the competition between actors that characterizes revivals on stage. "Revival" is a stage word and "remake" is a film word. Hamlet remains beyond Booth's or Olivier's or Gielgud's performance, but Alan Ladd as Gatsby and Robert Redford as Gatsby exist in different worlds.

Filmmaking is a discontinuous process, in which the order of filming is influenced more by economics than by aesthetics. Film actors must therefore either have stronger personalities than stage actors or draw upon the resources of personality much more than stage actors do. Strong film actors can never do anything out of character. Their presence defines their character and the audience is always ready for them to reveal more. Even though studio heads like Louis Mayer forced actors and actresses to appear "in character" offscreen as well, we sense and accept potential and variety from the greatest movie actors, while we may reject less flamboyant fictional characters as "unreal" or refer to the woodenness of stage characterization. Continuity in stage acting is thematic continuity: "Watch in happiness someone whom you will soon see in sorrow" is one of the fatalistic possibilities. But the discontinuities of film acting allow the actor to concentrate on every moment as if it were the only reality that existed. No matter how conventionalized the plot, the film actor can disregard its clichés and trust instead to the force and continuity of his projected personality to satisfy beyond the more obvious forms of theme and incident. Because he must present his play in straightforward time, a stage director will work with the actor to get a "line" or a "concept" of the character that will permeate every scene. But movie acting, bound in time to the shooting schedule and the editing table, must use what is left out as well as what is expressed. The greatest difference between a film and a stage version of the same work is less in the "opening" of space that films usually emphasize than in the different sense of the inner life of the characters we get.

Going to the theater is a social occasion in a way that going to films is not. Stage characters always exist in a society, and the great plays are almost all plays about the problems of living within a social context. Any bad film brings the audience more directly in touch with human presence than the actually present human beings of the stage because on stage there is so much emphasis on the correct filling of the role, parallel to the correct filling of the social role. The Shakespearean metaphor of the world as a stage expresses the new Renaissance awareness of self-presentation as a process of social interaction in which one defined oneself by social roles, the ones rejected as much as the ones accepted. On the stage we appreciate character generally as part of an ensemble of actors or in brief individual moments, and our understanding of those characters comes from our understanding of the relations between characters—how the stage looks—much more than from the revelations of an inner life. Olivier's *Hamlet* (1948), for example, with its Oedipal interpretation, is less forceful than the play because Hamlet's secrets are not the problems of interpretation—what's really stopping him?—but problems of decision *in front of other people*. Plays, and therefore theatrical acting, emphasize acting out, being seen, being overheard, or being spied upon. A common theme of all drama from the Renaissance on is the problem of honor, fame, and reputation—in short, all the ways in which the individual is known socially. But this theme appears only rarely in films. In its place is the problem of personal identity: who is Charles Foster Kane? who is Charlie Kohler? When a film is set in the context of a mannered society (like *The Awful Truth*, Leo McCarey, 1937, or *Blume in Love*, Paul Mazursky, 1972), the question of the film involves the benevolent discovery of the "real" nature of the characters, not the satiric exposure of that real nature, which would be the theatrical way of organizing the action. The faults of hypocrisy and insincerity—two other traditional themes of drama—also appear very rarely in films. The hypocrite on stage, or the audience's awareness of a character who says one thing and does another, becomes in films the character who deceives himself as well. In films, the theatrical emphasis on the importance of the role is replaced by the authenticity of feelings, the preserved human being with whom we have come into contact. Film acting expands the ability of art to explore the varieties of the intimate self, apart from social awareness, outside of ceremonial or semi-ceremonial occasions, with a few others or even alone.

Movies therefore stand between the strongly social emphasis of theater and the strongly individual emphasis of novels, incorporating elements of both. At a play we are always outside the group, at the footlights. But at a film we move between inside and outside, individual and social perspectives. Movie acting can therefore include stage acting better than stage acting can include movie acting. George C. Scott, for example, is essentially a stage actor who also can come across very well in films. When he was making *Patton* (Franklin Schaffner, 1970), he insisted that he repeat his entire first speech eight times to allow for the different camera angles; he refused to repeat only the sections that corresponded to the rephotographing. His sense of the character was therefore what I have been describing as a stage sense of character, in which the continuity is linear and spelled out. The performance is excellent and effective, but Scott's way of doing it tells us nothing of the differences in stage and film acting. It may have a touch of the New York stage actor's almost traditional hostility to films. At best, it is only another example of the way a newer art can more comfortably embrace the methods of an older art than the other way around. In fact, virtuosity in films tends to be a characteristic of second leads or medium minor characters, not stars, and the Academy Awards perpetuate the stage-derived standards by giving so many awards to actors and actresses cast against type, that is, for stage-style "virtuosity."

The film actor emphasizes display, while the stage actor explores disguise. But stage acting is still popularly considered to be superior to film acting. An actor who does a good job disappears into his role, while the bad (read "film") actor is only playing himself. The true actor, the professional craftsman, may use his own experience to strengthen his interpretation. But the audience should always feel that he has properly distanced and understood that experience; it is another tool in his professional work-chest. The false actor, the amateur actor, the film actor, on the other hand, works on his self-image, carries it from part to part, constantly projecting the same thing—"himself." Such a belief is rooted in an accurate perception; but it is a false interpretation of that perception. The stage actor does project a sense of holding back, of discipline and understanding, the influence of head over feelings, while the film actor projects effortlessness, nonchalance, immediacy, the seemingly unpremeditated response. Thus, when stage actors attack film actors, they attack in some puritanical way the lack of perceptible hard work, obvious professional craft, in the film actor's performance. Like many nonprofessionals in their audience, such stage actors assume that naïveté, spontaneity, "being yourself," are self-images that anyone in front of a camera can achieve. A frequent Actors Studio exercise, for example, is "Private Moment," in which the student is asked to act out before the group something he or she ordinarily does alone that would be very embarrassing if someone happened to see. Private self-indulgences and private games are thereby mined for their exposable, group potential. But the concentration of film, its ability to isolate the individual, makes every moment that way, and so the problem of the film actor may be to scale down intimacy rather than discover and exaggerate it.

How do we know the "themselves" film actors play except through the residue of their playing? How much do film actors, as opposed to stage actors, model their offscreen selves to continue or contrast with their screen images? To accuse an actor of "playing himself" implies that we have seen and compared the "real" and "false" selves of the actor and reached a conclusion. Film acting deposits a residual self that snowballs from film to film, creating an image with which the actor, the scriptwriter, and the director can play as they wish. Donald Richie has recorded that the Japanese director Yasujiro Ozu said: "I could no more write, not knowing who the actor was to be, than an artist could paint, not knowing what color he was using." Ozu's remark indicates how a director takes advantage of a previously developed image in order to create a better film. But the stage actor in a sense ceases to exist from play to play; we experience only the accumulation of his talent, his versatility. In our minds the stage actor stays within the architectures he has inhabited, while the film actor exists in between as well, forever immediate to our minds and eyes, escaping the momentary enclosures that the individual films have placed around him.

"Playing yourself" involves one's interpretation of what is most successful and appealing in one's own nature and then heightening it. Film actors play their roles the way we play ourselves in the world. Audiences may now get sustenance from films and from film acting because they no longer are so interested in the social possibilities of the self that has been the metaphysic of stage acting since Shakespeare and the Renaissance, the place of role-playing in the life of the audience. The Shakespearean films of Laurence Olivier and Orson Welles clearly express the contrast. The tendency in stage acting is to subordinate oneself to the character, while the great film actor is generally more important than the character he plays. Our sense of Olivier in his Shakespearean roles is one of distance and disguise: the purified patriotism of Henry V, in which all the play's negative hints about his character have been removed; the blond wig he uses to play Hamlet, so that, as he has said, no one will associate him with the part; the bent back, twisted fingers, and long black hair of Richard III. But Welles assimilates the roles to himself.

Costume for Welles is less a disguise than a generation from within and so he presented it in various television appearances of the 1950s, gradually making up for his part while he explained the play to the audience, until he turned full face into the camera and spoke the lines. In theater we experience the gap between actor and role as expertise; in film it may be described as a kind of self-irony. The great stage actor combats the superiority of the text, its preexistence, by choosing his roles: Olivier will play Hamlet; Olivier will play a music-hall comic. The great film actor, assured that his image absorbs and makes real the script, may allow himself to be cast in unpromising roles, if only for visibility. In the audience we feel Welles's character to be part of his role, whereas we perceive not Olivier's character but his intelligence and his ability to immerse himself in a role. Olivier is putting on a great performance, but Welles feels superior enough to the Shakespearean text to cut, reorganize, and invent. Olivier is a great interpreter; Welles is an equal combatant. For both, Shakespeare is like a genre, similar to the western, that offers materials for a contemporary statement. But Olivier sticks closely to the language and form of the play itself. We judge Olivier finally by Shakespeare, but we judge Welles by other films. Both choose those Shakespearean plays that emphasize a central character. But Olivier's willingness to allow Shakespeare the last word frees him for the more assertive political roles, whereas Welles stays with the more domestic or even isolated figures of Macbeth and Othello. Olivier began his Shakespearean film career with the heroic self-confidence of Henry V, while Welles, at least for the moment, has ended his with Falstaff—the choice of the ironic imagination of film over the theatrical assertion of social power.

These distinctions between stage acting and film acting are, of course, not absolute but points on a slippery continuum. Marlon Brando's career, for example, is a constant conflict between his desire to be versatile—to do different kinds of films, use different accents, wear different costumes—and the demand of his audience that he elaborate his residual cinematic personality. Brando tries to get into his roles, and often sinks them in the process, while Cary Grant pumps them up like a balloon and watches them float off into the sky. The main trouble that Chaplin has in *A Countess from Hong Kong* (1967) is taking two actors (Brando and Sophia Loren), whose own sense of their craft emphasizes naturalistic, historically defined character, and placing them within a film world where they would best exist as masks and stereotypes. Their efforts to ground their characters destroys the film. It may be funny if Chaplin or Cary Grant vomited out a porthole, but it's not funny when Brando does it. Brando can be funny in films only as a counterpoint to our sense of "Brando," for example in *Bedtime Story* (Ralph Levy, 1964). When he is acting someone else, the ironic sense of self-image that is natural to a film actor does not exist. We share Cary Grant's sense of distance from his roles, whether they are comic, melodramatic, or whatever, because it corresponds to our sense of personal distance from our daily roles in life. The sense of "putting it on" that we get from Brando's greatest roles—*A Streetcar Named Desire, Viva Zapata!, The Wild One, On the Waterfront*—stands in paradoxical relation to Method theories of submergence in the role. Brando's willingness to cooperate with Bernardo Bertolucci in the commentary on and mockery of his screen image that forms so much of the interest of *Last Tango in Paris* may indicate that he no longer holds to the theatrical definition of great acting. His progenitor role in *The Godfather* seems to have released him to create the paradox of the self-revealed inner life of a screen image elaborated by *Last Tango*. In the films of the 1970s, character, and therefore acting as well, has taken on the central importance in film. And the stage actor in film finds that his virtuosity is more a parlor trick than a technique of emotional and artistic power. Films make us fall in love with, admire, even hate human beings who may actually in the moment we watch them be dead and dust. But that is the grandeur of films as well: the preservation of human transience, the significance not so much of social roles as of fragile, fleeting feelings.

■ ■ ■

Questions and projects

1. Analyze how Marlon Brando interprets the role of Stanley in *Streetcar Named Desire*. What, in his acting, is a product of its presentation on film and how might he portray that character differently on stage?

2. To what extent does an actor's interpretation of a character change with the time and place? Examine the history of a character, such as Jo in Louisa May Alcott's *Little Women*, and analyze the specific changes and transformations that have taken place in several film embodiments of that character from George Cukor's 1933 version with Katherine Hepburn to Gillian Armstrong's 1994 adaptation featuring Winona Ryder.

Chapter 24

George Bluestone

THE LIMITS OF THE NOVEL AND THE LIMITS OF THE FILM

G EORGE BLUESTONE'S 1957 STUDY was one of the first of the new and mounting wave of academic books to bring the study of film into the postwar era. It uses a historical perspective that builds on a growing body of research on film and a cultural sentiment that is willing to accept film as an art form with its own properties and laws. Those textual properties, separated from other social issues or theoretical concerns, are the focus of this study. More specifically, Bluestone examines the two "modes of consciousness" that describe, respectively, novels and films; within those modes he looks at how the novel and film represent time according to the formal laws of their respective materials.

■　■　■

THE LIMITS OF THE NOVEL AND THE LIMITS OF THE FILM
GEORGE BLUESTONE

From *Novels into Film*, Baltimore, MD: Johns Hopkins University Press, 1957, pp. 1–16, 46–61

The two ways of seeing

Summing up his major intentions in 1913, D. W. Griffith is reported to have said, "The task I'm trying to achieve is above all to make you see."[1] Whether by accident or design, the statement coincides almost exactly with an excerpt from Conrad's preface to *Nigger of the Narcissus* published sixteen years earlier: "My task which I am trying to achieve is, by the power of the written word, to make you hear, to make you feel—it is, before all, to make you see."[2] Aside from the strong syntactical resemblance, the coincidence is remarkable in suggesting the points at which film and novel both join and part company. On the one hand, that phrase "to make you see" assumes an affective relationship between creative artist and receptive audience. Novelist and director meet here in a common intention. One may, on the other hand, see visually through the eye or imaginatively through the mind. And between the percept of the visual image and the concept of the mental image lies the root difference between the two media.

Because novel and film are both organic—in the sense that aesthetic judgments are based on total ensembles which include both formal and thematic conventions—we may expect to find that differences in form and theme are inseparable from differences in media. Not only are Conrad and Griffith referring to different ways of seeing, but the "you's" they refer to are different. Structures, symbols, myths, values which might be comprehensible to Conrad's relatively small middle-class reading public would, conceivably, be incomprehensible to Griffith's mass public. Conversely, stimuli which move the heirs of Griffith's audience to tears, will outrage or amuse the progeny of Conrad's "you." The seeming concurrence of Griffith and Conrad splits apart under analysis, and the two arts turn in opposite directions. That, in brief, has been the history of the fitful relationship between novel and film: overtly compatible, secretly hostile.

On the face of it, a close relationship has existed from the beginning. The reciprocity is clear from almost any point of view: the number of films based on novels; the search for filmic equivalents of literature; the effect of adaptations on reading; box-office receipts for filmed novels; merit awards by and for the Hollywood community.

The moment the film went from the animation of stills to telling a story, it was inevitable that fiction would become the ore to be minted by story departments. Before Griffith's first year as a director was over, he had adapted, among others, Jack London's *Just Meat (For Love of Gold)*, Tolstoy's *Resurrection*, and Charles Reade's *The Cloister and the Hearth*. Sergei Eisenstein's essay, "Dickens, Griffith, and the Film Today,"[3] demonstrates how Griffith found in Dickens hints for almost every one of his major innovations. Particular passages are cited to illustrate the dissolve, the superimposed shot, the close-up, the pan, indicating that Griffith's interest in literary forms and his roots in Victorian idealism[4] provided at least part of the impulse for technical and moral content.

From such beginnings, the novel began a still unbroken tradition of appearing conspicuously on story conference tables. The precise record has never been adequately kept. Various counts range from 17 to almost 50 percent of total studio production. A sampling from RKO, Paramount, and Universal motion picture output for 1934–35 reveals that about one-third of all full-length features were derived from novels (excluding short stories).[5] Lester Asheim's more comprehensive survey indicates that of 5,807 releases by major studios between 1935 and 1945, 976 or 17.2 percent were derived from novels.[6] Hortense Powdermaker reports, on the basis of *Variety's* survey (June 4, 1947) that of 463 screenplays in production or awaiting release, slightly less than 40 percent were adapted from novels.[7] And Thomas M. Pryor, in a recent issue of the *New York Times*, writes that the frequency of the original screenplay, reaching a new low in Hollywood, "represented only 51.8 percent of the source material of the 305 pictures reviewed by the Production Code office in 1955." Appropriate modifications must be made in these calculations, since both Asheim and Powdermaker report that the percentage of novels adapted for high-budgeted pictures was much higher than for low-budgeted pictures.[8]

The industry's own appraisal of its work shows a strong and steady preference for films derived from novels, films which persistently rate among top quality productions. Filmed novels, for example, have made consistently strong bids for Academy Awards. In 1950, *Time* reported the results of *Daily Variety's* poll of 200 men and women who had been working in the industry for more than twenty-five years. *Birth of a Nation* was considered the best silent film; *Gone with the Wind* the best sound film and the best "all time film."[9] Originally, both were novels. The choice of

Gone with the Wind was a happy meeting of commercial and artistic interests. For when, some five years later, *Time* reported *Variety's* listing of Hollywood's "all time money makers," Miss Mitchell's title stood ahead of all others with earnings of some $33.5 million. More important, of the ten most valuable film properties, five had been adapted from novels.[10] The high percentage of filmed novels which have been financially and artistically successful may be more comprehensible when we remember how frequently Pulitzer Prize winners, from *Alice Adams* to *All the King's Men*, have appeared in cinematic form.[11]

Just as one line of influence runs from New York publishing house to Hollywood studio, another line may be observed running the other way. Margaret Farrand Thorp reports that when *David Copperfield* appeared on local screens, the demand for the book was so great that the Cleveland Public Library ordered 132 new copies; that the film premier of *The Good Earth* boosted sales of that book to 3,000 per week; and that more copies of *Wuthering Heights* have been sold since the novel was screened than in all the previous ninety-two years of its existence. Jerry Wald confirms this pattern by pointing out, more precisely, that after the film's appearance, the Pocket Book edition of *Wuthering Heights* sold 700,000 copies; various editions of *Pride and Prejudice* reached a third of a million copies; and sales for *Lost Horizon* reached 1,400,000.[12] The appearance, in 1956, of such films as *Moby-Dick* and *War and Peace*, accompanied by special tie-in sales of the novels, has continued this pattern.

But when Jean-Paul Sartre suggests that for many of these readers, the book appears "as a more or less faithful commentary" on the film,[13] he is striking off a typically cogent distinction. Quantitative analyses have very little to do with qualitative changes. They tell us nothing about the mutational process, let alone how to judge it. In the case of film versions of novels, such analyses are even less helpful. They merely establish the fact of reciprocity; they do not indicate its implications for aesthetics. They provide statistical, not critical data. Hence, from such information the precise nature of the mutation cannot be deduced.

Such statements as: "The film is true to the spirit of the book"; "It's incredible how they butchered the novel"; "It cuts out key passages, but it's still a good film"; "Thank God they changed the ending"—these and similar statements are predicated on certain assumptions which blur the mutational process. These standard expletives and judgments assume, among other things, a separable content which may be detached and reproduced, as the snapshot reproduces the kitten; that incidents and characters in fiction are interchangeable with incidents and characters in the film; that the novel is a norm and the film deviates at its peril; that deviations are permissible for vaguely defined reasons—exigencies of length or of visualization, perhaps—but that the extent of the deviation will vary directly with the "respect" one has for the original; that taking liberties does not necessarily impair the quality of the film, whatever one may think of the novel, but that such liberties are somehow a trick which must be concealed from the public.

What is common to all these assumptions is the lack of awareness that mutations are probable the moment one goes from a given set of fluid, but relatively homogeneous, conventions to another; that changes are *inevitable* the moment one abandons the linguistic for the visual medium. Finally, it is insufficiently recognized that the end products of novel and film represent different aesthetic genera, as different from each other as ballet is from architecture.

The film becomes a different *thing* in the same sense that a historical painting becomes a different thing from the historical event which it illustrates. It is as fruitless to say that film A is better or worse than novel B as it is to pronounce Wright's Johnson's Wax Building better or worse than Tchaikovsky's *Swan Lake*. In the last analysis, each is autonomous, and each is characterized by unique and specific properties. What, then, are these properties?

...

The modes of consciousness

It is a commonplace by now that the novel has tended to retreat more and more from external action to internal thought, from plot to character, from social to psychological realities. Although these conflicting tendencies were already present in the polarity of Fielding and Sterne, it was only recently that the tradition of *Tristram Shandy* superseded the tradition of *Tom Jones*. It is this reduction of the novel to experiences which can be verified in the immediate consciousness of the novelist that Mendilow has called modern "inwardness" and E. M. Forster the "hidden life." Forster suggests the difference when he says that "The hidden life is, by definition, hidden. The hidden life that appears in external signs is hidden no longer, has entered the realm of action. And it is the function of the novelist to reveal the hidden life at its source." But if the hidden life has become the domain of the novel, it has introduced unusual problems.

In a recent review of Leon Edel's *The Psychological Novel: 1900–1950*, Howard Mumford Jones sums up the central problems which have plagued the modern novelist: the verbal limitations of non-verbal experience; the dilemma of autobiographical fiction in which the novelist must at once evoke a unique consciousness and yet communicate it to others; the difficulty of catching the flux of time in static language. The summary is acutely concise in picking out the nerve centers of an increasingly subjective novel where "after images fished out of the stream of past time ... substitute a kind of smoldering dialectic for the clean impact of drama."[77]

Béla Balázs has shown us how seriously we tend to underestimate the power of the human face to convey subjective emotions and to suggest thoughts. But the film, being a presentational medium (except for its use of dialogue), cannot have direct access to the power of discursive forms. Where the novel discourses the film must picture. From this we ought not to conclude like J. P. Mayer that "our eye is weaker than our mind" because it does not "*hold* sight impressions as our imagination does."[78] For sense impressions, like word symbols, may be appropriated into the common fund of memory. Perceptual knowledge is not necessarily different in strength; it *is* necessarily different in kind.

The rendition of mental states—memory, dream, imagination—cannot be as adequately represented by film as by language. If the film has difficulty presenting streams of consciousness, it has even more difficulty presenting states of mind which are defined precisely by the absence in them of the visible world. Conceptual imaging, by definition, has no existence in space. However, once I cognize the signs of a sentence through the conceptual screen, my consciousness is indistinguishable from nonverbal thought. Assuming here a difference between *kinds* of images—between images of things, feelings, concepts, words—we may observe that conceptual images evoked by verbal stimuli can scarcely be distinguished in the end from those evoked by nonverbal stimuli. The stimuli, whether they be the signs of language or the sense data of the physical world, lose their spatial characteristics and become components of the total ensemble which is consciousness.

On the other hand, the film image, being externalized in space, cannot be similarly converted through the conceptual screen. We have already seen how alien to the screen is the compacted luxuriance of the trope. For the same reasons, dreams and memories, which exist nowhere but in the individual consciousness, cannot be adequately represented in spatial terms. Or rather, the film, having only arrangements of space to work with, cannot render thought, for the moment thought is externalized it is no longer thought. The film, by arranging external signs for our visual perception, or by presenting us with dialogue, can lead us to *infer* thought. But it cannot show us thought directly. It can show us characters thinking, feeling, and speaking, but it cannot show us their thoughts and feelings. A film is not thought, it is perceived.[79]

That is why pictorial representation of dreams or memory on the screen are almost always disappointing. The dreams and memories of *Holiday for Henrietta* and *Rashomon* are spatial referents to dreams and memories, not precise renditions. To show a memory or dream, one must balloon a separate image into the frame (Gypo remembering good times with Frankie in *The Informer*); or superimpose an image (Gypo daydreaming about an ocean voyage with Katie); or clear the frame entirely for the visual equivalent (in *Wuthering Heights*, Ellen's face dissolving to the house as it was years ago). Such spatial devices are always to some degree dissatisfying. Acting upon us perceptually, they cannot render the conceptual feel of dreams and memories. The realistic tug of the film is too strong. If, in an effort to bridge the gap between spatial representation and nonspatial experience, we accept such devices at all, we accept them as cinematic conventions, not as renditions of conceptual consciousness.

Given the contrasting abilities of film and novel to render conceptual consciousness, we may explore further the media's handling of time.

Chronological time

The novel has three tenses: the film as only one. From this follows almost everything else one can say about time in both media. By now, we are familiar with Bergson's distinction between two kinds of time: chronological time measured in more or less discrete units (as in clocks and metronomes); and psychological time, which distends or compresses in consciousness, and presents itself in continuous flux. What are the comparative abilities of novel and film to render these types of time?

To begin with, Mendilow describes language as "a medium consisting of consecutive units constituting a forward-moving linear form of expression that is subject to the three characteristics of time—transience, sequence, and irreversibility." But we must remember that Mendilow is here referring to chronological time only. And chronological time in the novel exists on three primary levels: the chronological duration of the reading; the chronological duration of the narrator's time; and the chronological span of the narrative events. That the three chronologies may harmonize in the fictive world is due entirely to the willingness of the reader to suspend disbelief and accept the authority of convention. As long as the novelist is not troubled by the bargain into which he enters with his reader, the three levels do not come into any serious conflict.

But Laurence Sterne saw a long time ago the essential paradox of the convention. If the novelist chooses to chronicle a series of events up to the present moment, he discovers that by the time he commits a single event to paper, the present moment has already slipped away. And if the novelist discovers that it takes a chronological year to record a single fictional day, as Sterne did, how is one ever to overcome the durational lag between art and life? If the present moment is being constantly renewed, how can prose, which is fixed, ever hope to catch it? Whenever a novelist chooses for his province a sequence of events which cannot be completed until the present moment, the three levels come into open conflict. In Sterne and Gide, that conflict becomes more central than conflicts between the characters.

The film is spared at least part of this conflict because one of the levels is omitted. Since the camera is always the narrator, we need concern ourselves only with the chronological duration of the viewing and the time-span of the narrative events. Even when a narrator appears in the film, the basic orientation does not change. When Francis begins to tell the story of Dr. Caligari, the camera shows his face; then the camera shifts to the scene of the story and there takes over the telling. What has happened is not so much that Francis has turned over the role of narrator to the omniscient camera as that the omniscient camera has included Francis as part of the narrative from the beginning.

The ranges of chronological time for reader and viewer are rather fluid, yet more or less fixed by convention. Where a novel can be read in anywhere from two to fifty hours, a film generally runs for one or two. *Intolerance* runs over two hours; the uncut version of *Les Enfants du Paradis* over three; and *Gone with the Wind* and *War and Peace* slightly less than four. Since the fictional events depicted in both novel and film may range anywhere from the fleeting duration of a dream (*Scarlet Street* and *Finnegans Wake*) to long but finite stretches of human history (*Intolerance* and *Orlando*), the sense of passing time is infinitely more crucial than the time required for reading or viewing.

We may note, of course, that a fifty-hour novel has the advantage of being able to achieve a certain density, that "solidarity of specification" which James admired, simply because the reader has lived with it longer. Further, because its mode of beholding allows stops and starts, thumbing back, skipping, flipping ahead, and so lets the reader set his own pace, a novel can afford diffuseness where the film must economize. Where the mode of beholding in the novel allows the reader to control his rate, the film viewer is bound by the relentless rate of a projector which he cannot control. The results, as may be expected, are felt in the contrast between the loose, more variegated conventions of the novel and the tight, compact conventions of the film.

Sometimes, to be sure, the conventions governing quantity do affect the end product. The silent version of *Anna Karenina* with Garbo (called *Love*) and the subsequent sound versions (the first with Garbo and Fredric March; the second with Vivien Leigh and Ralph Richardson) dropped the entire story of Levin and Kitty. And Philip Dunne, the veteran screen writer, tells us that the boy in the film *How Green Was My Valley* never grew up, thus leaving out half the novel; that the *Count of Monte Cristo* contained no more than 5 percent of its original; that *The Robe* and *The Egyptian* used less than a third of theirs.[80] While such quantitative deletions do alter the originals, it is, in the last analysis, the qualitative rather than the quantitative differences that militate against film adaptations of the novel.

If, as Mendilow says, "Fictional time is an ineluctable element in the novel," and fictional time treats of both kinds of time, then we discover that the moment we shift from chronological to psychological time, certain special problems arise.

Psychological time: variability in rate

We speak of psychological time here in at least two roughly defined ways. The first suggests that the human mind is capable of accelerating and collapsing the "feel" of time to the point where each individual may be said to possess his own "time-system." The second suggests, beyond this variability in *rate*, the kind of flux which, being fluid and interpenetrable, and lacking in sharp boundaries, can scarcely be measured at all.

As long as the kind of time we are talking about in any sense implies discrete units in a series, language seems roughly adequate to the task. For example, the observation that chronological time crowded with activity, the sense of time passing quickly, seems "long" in retrospect, whereas chronological time taken up with dull and undifferentiated activity (the sense of time passing slowly) seems "short" in retrospect still has built into it a concept of measurement. It assumes the clock as a standard of measurement, for this kind of psychological time seems "long" or "short" in terms of certain normative expectancies. It assumes a normative "feel" for chronological time which may be distended or compressed by the stress of the moment, or by memory.

Here language is still appropriate to its task. Mendilow points out, for example, that in *Tom Jones* each book draws on a progressively greater length of the reader's clock time to cover a progressively shorter period of fictional time. So that where Book Three covers five years, Book Nine and Ten cover twelve hours each. The implication is that both for Tom and the reader, the events of the five weeks which occupy the last two thirds of the novel will seem "longer" than the events of the twenty years which occupy the first third.

Compression and distension of time has its exact equivalent in the film's use of speed-up and slow-motion. We have already noted how Pudovkin found the creative element of film in "the discovered, deeply imbedded detail." But that the deeply imbedded detail is in constant motion has further implications for filmic structure. Like the principles of editing, the principles of movement seem to collect around centers of gravity dictated by the film's persistent, and almost willful self-assertion. "A sure folk instinct was shown," writes Panofsky, "when the photoplay immediately became known as the movies." Lawson extends this insight by making movement the pivotal element in film structure: "The conflict of individuals or groups projected on the screen has one characteristic that is not found in other story structures. *The conflict is in constant motion.*"

From this there develops a new kind of artistic reality, what Pudovkin calls filmic time and filmic space; what Panofsky calls the Dynamization of Space, and the Spatialization of Time. The theatrical producer, says Pudovkin,

> ... works with real actuality which though he may always remould, yet forces him to remain bound by the laws of real space and real time. The film director, on the other hand, has as his material the finished recorded celluloid.... The elements of reality are fixed on those pieces; by combining them in his selected sequence according to his desire, the director builds up his own "filmic" time and "filmic" space.[81]

The director, then, creates a new reality, and the most characteristic and important aspect of this process is that laws of space and time which are ordinarily invariable or inescapable become "tractable and obedient." Hollywood's silent comedians made use of this freedom in their own unique way. James Agee has noted how Mack Sennett, realizing "the tremendous drumlike power of mere motion to exhilarate,"[82] gave inanimate objects a mischievous life of their own, "*broke every law of nature* the tricked camera could serve him for and made the screen "dance like a witches' Sabbath" (italics mine). And other comedians, energized by the liberation of untrammeled movement, "zipped and caromed about the pristine world of the screen." No previous narrative art has been able to achieve such graphic effects.

Not only is space liberated, but *because* it is liberated, time is, too. In thirty seconds, we see shoot, stem, bud, and blossom grow gracefully one from the other, a process that takes weeks in ordinary time. Just as space can be molded, time can be arrested and quickened. Anyone who has seen the remarkable slow-motion sequence in *Zéro de Conduite* can attest to the dramatic power of distended time. By interfering and only by interfering with natural time was Jean Vigo able to render the dream-like essence of the pillow fight.

Similarly, it is easy to find innumerable examples of accelerated motion in Hollywood where the emphasis has always been, for example, on the murderous pace of the comic chase. Chaplin out-races the Keystone cops. W. C. Fields dodges in and out of traffic at eighty miles an hour. Time is distorted in the opposite direction, but the principle remains the same. Spatial mobility makes time more flexible. A man is trying to find a job without success. The film may suggest the dreary routine of job-hunting by intercutting shots of the man's feet walking along asphalt streets with close-ups of other men shaking their heads, saying no. Four or five such alternate shots, taking a few seconds of running time, can suggest a process taking months, or even years. Thus the film is able, in an instant, to suggest the sense of monotonous events that seem "short" in retrospect, even though the duration of those events is "long" by clock time.

As for the kind of rhythmic progression one finds in music, the film has an exact parallel in the thoroughly discussed theory of montage. Not only does each shot take its meaning both from preceding shots and future expectations, but the use of sound (music, dialogue) provides a complex system of counterpoint.

Psychological time: the time-flux

As soon as we enter the realm of time-in-flux, however, we not only broach all but insoluble problems for the novel but we also find a sharp divergence between prose and cinema. The transient, sequential, and irreversible character of language is no longer adequate for this type of time experience. For in the flux past and present lose their identity as discrete sections of time. The present becomes "specious" because on second glance it is seen as fused with the past, obliterating the line between them.

Discussing its essential modernity, Mendilow lends support to the idea that the whole of experience is implicit in every moment of the present by drawing from Sturt's *Psychology of Time*. For Sturt tries to work out the sense in which we are caught by a perpetual present permeated by the past:

> One of the reasons for the feeling of pastness is that we are familiar with the things or events that we recognize as past. But it remains true that this feeling of familiarity is a present experience, and therefore logically should not arouse a concept of the past. On the other hand, a present impression (or memory) of something which is past is different from a present impression of something which is present but familiar from the past.[83]

How this seeming contradiction operates in practice may be seen when we attempt to determine precisely which of two past events is prior, and in what manner the distinction between the memory of a past thing and the impression of a present thing is to be made. At first glance, we seem perfectly able to deduce which of two remembered events is prior. For example, on the way to the store this morning, I met a group of children going to school. I also mailed my letter just as the postman came by. I know that ordinarily the children go to school at nine o'clock and the postman comes by at eleven. Therefore, I deduce that I went to the store *before* I mailed my letter. Although I have not been able to give the act of my going to the store an exact location in the past, I have been able to establish its priority.

On second thought, however, it seems as if (apart from the deductions one makes by deliberate attention to relationships) the memory of a past event comes to me with its pastness already intended. The image I have of my friend *includes* the information that this is the way he looked the year before he died. Similarly, if I have a mental image of myself on a train to Kabul, then summon up an image of myself eating chestnuts, I know that the first is an image of a past thing and the second an image of a present thing because the image of myself on the train includes the information that the event took place last year. At the same time, I know that I am eating chestnuts right now. Here the perceptual witnessing of my present action checks and defines my mental images, confirming both the priority of the train ride and the presentness of the eating.

But suppose I bring my attention to bear on an object which is present now and which was also present yesterday at the same time, in the same place, in the same light. If, for example, I look at the lamp in my room which fulfills all these requirements, then close my eyes and behold the mental image, how am I to know if that image refers to the lamp which was there yesterday or to the lamp which is there today? In instance, which is tantamount to fusing a thing's past with its present, my present image, for all practical purposes, no longer respects the distinction between past and present. It offers me no way of knowing the exact location of its temporal existence.

This obliteration between past and present is precisely the problem which faces the novelist who wishes to catch the flux in language. If he is faced with the presentness of consciousness on the one hand, and the obliteration of the discrete character of past and present on the other, how is he to express these phenomena in a language which relies on tenses?

Whether we look at William James' "stream of consciousness," Ford Madox Ford's "chronological looping," or Bergson's "durée," we find the theorists pondering the same problem: language, consisting as it does of bounded, discrete units cannot satisfactorily represent the unbounded and continuous. We have a sign to cover the concept of a thing's "becoming"; and one to cover the concept of a thing's "having become." But "becoming" is a *present* participle, "become" a *past* participle, and our language has thus far offered no way of showing the continuity between them.

So elusive has been the *durée* that the novelist has submitted to the steady temptation of trying to escape time entirely. But here, too, the failure has served to dramatize the medium's limitations. Speaking of Gertrude Stein's attempt to emancipate fiction from the tyranny of time, E. M. Forster notes the impasse: "She fails, because as soon as fiction is completely delivered from time it cannot express anything at all."

To be sure, there seem to be intuitive moments of illumination in Proust and Wolfe during which a forgotten incident floats up from oblivion in its pristine form and seems thereby to become free of time. Proust's involuntary memory fuses the experience of his mother's madeleine cake with the former experience of Aunt Léonie's, and the intervening time seems, for the moment, obliterated. But it is the precise point of Proust's agonizing effort that—despite our ability, through involuntary memory, to experience simultaneously events "with countless intervening days between"—there is always a sense in which these events remain "widely separated from one another in Time." The recognition of this conflict helps us understand why every formulation which attempts to define a "timeless" quality in a novel seems unsatisfactory, why Mendilow's attempt to find an "ideal time" in Kafka seems to say little more than that Kafka was not plagued by the problem. In the end, the phrase "timeless moment" poses an insuperable contradiction in terms.

We can see the problem exemplified concretely in a passage from Thomas Wolfe's *The Hills Beyond*. The passage describes Eugene Gant's visit to the house in St. Louis where his family had lived thirty years before. Eugene can remember the sights, shapes, sounds, and smells of thirty years ago, but something is missing—a sense of absence, the absence of his brother Grover, of his family away at the fair:

And he felt that if he could sit there on the stairs once more, in solitude and absence in the afternoon, he would be able to get it back again. Then would he be able to remember all that he had seen and been—that brief sum of himself, the universe of his four years, with all the light of time upon it—that universe which was so short to measure, and yet so far, so endless, to remember. Then would he be able to see his own small face again, pooled in the dark mirror of the hall, and discover there in his quiet three years' self the lone integrity of "I," knowing: "Here is the House, and here House listening; here is Absence, Absence in the afternoon; and here in this House, this Absence, is my core, my kernel—here am I!"[84]

The passage shows the characteristic, almost obsessive longing of the modern novel to escape the passage of time by memory; the recognition that the jump, the obliteration, cannot be made; the appropriation of non-space as a reality in the novel—not the feeling of absence alone, but the absence of absence.

We arrive here at the novel's farthest and most logical remove from the film. For it is hard to see how any satisfactory film equivalents can be found for such a paragraph. We can show Eugene waiting in the house, then superimpose an image of the boy as he might have looked thirty years before, catch him watching a door as if waiting for Grover to return. But as in all cinematic attempts to render thought, such projection would inevitably fail. How are we to capture that combination of past absence and present longing, if both are conditions contrary to spatial fact?

The film-maker, in his own and perhaps more acute way, also faces the problem of how to render the flux of time. "Pictures have no tenses," says Balázs. Unfolding in a perpetual present, like visual perception itself, they cannot express either a past or a future. One may argue that the use of dialogue and music provides a door through which a sense of past and future may enter. Dialogue, after all, is language, and language does have referential tenses. A character whose face appears before us may *talk* about his past and thereby permeate his presence with a kind of pastness. Similarly, as we saw in our discussion of sound in editing, music may be used to counterpoint a present image (as in *High Noon* and *Alexander Nevsky*) and suggest a future event. In this way, apparently, a succession of present images may be suffused with a quality of past or future.

At best, however, sound is a secondary advantage which does not seriously threaten the primacy of the spatial image. When Ellen, the housekeeper, her withered face illumined by the fire, begins telling her story to Lockwood in *Wuthering Heights*, we do sense a certain tension between story-teller and story. But in the film we can never fully shake our attention loose from the teller. The image of her face has priority over the sound of her voice. When Terry Malone tells Edie about his childhood in *On the Waterfront*, the present image of his face so floods our consciousness that his words have the thinnest substance only. The scars around his eyes tell us more about his past than any halting explanation. This phenomenon is essentially what Panofsky calls the "principle of coexpressibility," according to which a moving picture—even when it has learned to talk—remains a picture that moves, and does not convert itself into a piece of writing that is enacted. That is why Shakespearian films which fail to adapt the fixed space of the stage to cinematic space so often seem static and talky.

In the novel, the line of dialogue stands naked and alone; in the film, the spoken word is attached to its spatial image. If we try to convert Marlon Brando's words into our own thought, we leave for a moment the visual drama of his face, much as we turn away from a book. The difference is that, whereas in the book we miss nothing, in the film Brando's face has continued to act, and the moment we miss may be crucial. In a film, according to Panofsky, "that which we hear remains, for good or worse, inextricably fused with that which we see." In that fusion, our seeing (and therefore our sense of the present) remains primary.

If, however, dialogue and music are inadequate to the task of capturing the flux, the spatial image itself reveals two characteristics which at least permit the film to make a tentative approach. The first is the quality of familiarity which attaches itself to the perceptual image of a thing after our first acquaintance. When I first see Gelsomina in *La Strada*, I see her as a stranger, as a girl with a certain physical disposition, but without a name or a known history. However, once I identify her as a character with a particular relationship to other characters, I am able to include information about her past in the familiar figure which now appears before me. I do not have to renew my acquaintance at every moment. Familiarity, then, becomes a means of referring to the past, and this past reference fuses into the ensemble which is the present Gelsomina. The spatial image of Gelsomina which I see toward the end of the film includes, in its total structure, the knowledge that she has talked to the Fool and returned to Zampano. In a referential sense, the pastness is built in.

That the film is in constant motion suggests the second qualification of film for approximating the time-flux. At first glance, the film seems bound by discrete sections, much as the novel is bound by discrete words. At the film's outer limit stands the frame; and within the frame appear the distinct outlines of projected objects, each one cut as by a razor's edge. But the effect of running off the frames is startlingly different from the effect of running off the sentence. For whether the words in a novel come to me as nonverbal images or as verbal meanings, I can still detect the discrete units of subject and predicate. If I say, "The top spins on the table," my mind assembles first the top, then the spinning, then the table. (Unless, of course, I am capable of absorbing the sentence all at once, in which case the process may be extended to a paragraph composed of discrete sentences.) But on the screen, I simply perceive a shot of a top spinning on a table, in which subject and predicate appear to me as *fused*. Not only is the top indistinguishable from its spinning, but at every moment the motion of the top seems to contain the history of its past motion. It is true that the top-image stimulated in my mind by the sentence resembles the top-image stimulated by the film in the sense that both contain the illusion of continuous motion. Yet this resemblance does not appear in the *process* of cognition. It appears only after the fact, as it were, only after the component words have been assembled. Although the mental and filmic images do meet in rendering the top's continuity of motion, it is in the mode of apprehending them that we find the qualitative difference.

In the cinema, for better or worse, we are bound by the forward looping of the celluloid through the projector. In that relentless unfolding, each frame is blurred in a total progression. Keeping in mind Sturt's analysis of the presentness of our conceptions, a presentness permeated by a past and therefore hardly ruled by tense at all, we note that the motion in the film's *present* is unique. Montage depends for its effects on instantaneous successions of different spatial entities which are constantly exploding against each other. But a succession of such variables would quickly become incomprehensible without a constant to stabilize them. In the film, that constant is motion. No matter how diverse the moving spaces which explode against each other, movement itself pours over from shot to shot, binding as it blurs them, reinforcing the relentless unrolling of the celluloid.

Lindgren advances Abercrombie's contention that completeness in art has no counterpart in real life, since natural events are never complete: "In nature nothing at any assignable point begins and nothing at any assignable point comes to an end: all is perfect continuity." But Abercrombie overlooks both our ability to perceive spatial discreteness in natural events and the film's ability to achieve "perfect continuity." So powerful is this continuity, regardless of the *direction* of the motion, that at times we tend to forget the boundaries of both frame and projected object. We attend to the motion only. In those moments when motion alone floods our attention and spatial attributes seem forgotten, we suddenly come as close as the film is able to fulfilling one essential requirement of the time-flux—the boundaries are no longer perceptible. The transience of the shot falls away before the sweeping permanence of its motion. Past and present seem fused, and we have accomplished before us a kind of spatial analogue for the flux of time.

If the film is incapable of maintaining the illusion for very long, if its spatial attributes, being primary, presently assert themselves, if the film's spatial appeal to the eye overwhelms its temporal appeal to the mind, it is still true that the film, above all other non-verbal arts, comes closest to rendering the time-flux. The combination of familiarity, the film's linear progression, and what Panofsky calls the "Dynamization of Space" permits us to intuit the *durée* insofar as it can, in spatial art, be intuited at all.

The film, then, cannot render the attributes of thought (metaphor, dream, memory); but it can find adequate equivalents for the kind of psychological time which is characterized by variations in rate (distension, compression; speed-up, *ralenti*); and it approaches, but ultimately fails, like the novel, to render what Bergson means by the time-flux. The failure of both media ultimately reverts to root differences between the structures of art and consciousness.

Our analysis, however, permits a usable distinction between the two media. Both novel and film are time arts, but whereas the formative principle in the novel is time, the formative principle in the film is space. Where the novel takes its space for granted and forms its narrative in a complex of time values, the film takes its time for granted and forms its narrative in arrangements of space. Both film and novel create the illusion of psychologically distorted time and space, but neither destroys time or space. The novel renders the illusion of space by going from point to point in time; the film renders time by going from point to point in space. The novel tends to abide by, yet explore, the possibilities of psychological law; the film tends to abide by, yet explore, the possibilities of physical law.

Where the twentieth-century novel has achieved the shock of novelty by explosions of words, the twentieth-century film has achieved a comparable shock by explosions of visual images. And it is a phenomenon which invites detailed investigation that the rise of the film, which preëmpted the picturing of bodies in nature, coincides almost exactly with the rise of the modern novel which preëmpted the rendition of human consciousness.

Finally, to discover distinct formative principles in our two media is not to forget that time and space are, for artistic purposes, ultimately inseparable. To say that an element is contingent is not to say that it is irrelevant. Clearly, spatial effects in the film would be impossible without concepts of time, just as temporal effects in the novel would be impossible without concepts of space. We are merely trying to state the case for a system of priority and emphasis. And our central claim—namely that time is prior in the novel, and space prior in the film—is supported rather than challenged by our reservations.

■   ■   ■

Questions and projects

1. Select a novel with an unusual way of organizing or representing time as a scheme (such as Emily Brontë's *Wuthering Heights*, Albert Camus's *The Stranger* or Franz Kafka's *The Trial*) and use Bluestone's argument to compare the way it structures time with a film version of that novel (such as Luis Buñuel's 1954 *Wuthering Heights*, Orson Welles's 1946 *The Stranger*, Luchino Visconti's 1967 *The Stranger* or Welles's 1963 *The Trial*).

2. In addition to the way in which the novel and film depict temporality, are there other experiences or dimensions to experience—such as the complexity of emotions, the description of nature, or the depiction of the physical features of a character—that film represents differently from the novel? Pair a recent novel and film and analyze how each accomplishes such a specific task to suggest what is at stake in the different artistic forms.

Notes

1   Lewis Jacobs, *The Rise of the American Film* (New York, 1939), p. 119.
2   Joseph Conrad, *A Conrad Argosy* (New York, 1942), p. 83.
3   Sergei Eisenstein, *Film Form*, trans. Jay Leyda (New York, 1949), pp. 195–255.
4   Jacobs, pp. 98–99.
5   In Marguerite G. Ortman, *Fiction and the Screen* (Boston, MA, 1935).
6   In Lester Asheim, "From Book to Film" (Ph.D. dissertation, University of Chicago, 1949).
7   In Hortense Powdermaker, *Hollywood: The Dream Factory* (Boston, 1950), p. 74.
8   For example, Asheim reports that of the "Ten Best" films listed in the *Film Daily Yearbook* for 1935–45, fifty-two or 47 percent were derived from established novels.
9   *Time*, LV (March 6, 1950), 92. From the point of view of thematic conventions, there may be further significance in the fact that both films deal with the Civil War and that both are sympathetic to the secessionists. To what extent has the Southern defeat haunted our national consciousness?
10 *Time*, LXV (January 17, 1955), 74. The figures are quoted from *Variety's* forty-ninth anniversary issue. The filmed novels were: *Gone with the Wind, From Here to Eternity, Duel in the Sun, The Robe*, and *Quo vadis.*
11 Among other filmed Pulitzer Prize winners: *The Good Earth, Gone with the Wind, The Late George Apley, The Yearling, The Grapes of Wrath, A Bell for Adano, The Magnificent Ambersons, So Big, Arrowsmith, The Bridge of San Luis Rey, Alice Adams.*
12 Jerry Wald, "Screen Adaptation," *Films in Review*, v (February, 1954), 66.
13 Jean-Paul Sartre, *What Is Literature?* trans. Bernard Frechman (New York, 1949), p. 245.
...
77 *Saturday Review*, XXXVIII (April 25, 1955), p. 19.
78 J. P. Mayer, *Sociology of Film* (London, 1946), p. 278.
79 See Maurice Merleau-Ponty, "Le Cinéma et la Nouvelle Psychologie," *Les Temps Modernes*, No. 26 (November, 1947), pp. 930–943.
80 Wald, p. 65.
81 Pudovkin, p. 53. See, too, A. Nicholas Vardac, *Stage to Screen* (Cambridge, MA, 1949) for the influence of nineteenth-century theater on early American cinema.
82 Agee, p. 74.
83 Quoted in Mendilow, p. 98.
84 Thomas Wolfe, *The Hills Beyond* (New York, 1941), pp. 37–38. In *Thomas Wolfe: The Weather of His Youth* (Baton Rouge, FL, 1955), pp. 28–53, Louis D. Rubin, Jr. analyzes in some detail Wolfe's handling of time.

Judith Mayne

READERSHIP AND SPECTATORSHIP

T HE FOLLOWING SECTION FROM Judith Mayne's 1985 book addresses the differences between readership and spectatorship as ways of bridging experiences of novels and films. For Mayne the most influential models for reading have been established by the nineteenth-century novel. Under the sway of a growing consumer culture late in that century, those ways of reading merge with new ways of seeing that would shape the movie experience through much of the twentieth century. While responding carefully to historical changes, her wide-ranging argument moves from nineteenth-century novels through film history of the 1940s. In the process she raises central issues in current film scholarship: about gender and women as readers and viewers; about consumerism, immigrant culture, and literacy; about the ways film and literature negotiate the boundaries between public and private life.

■ ■ ■

READERSHIP AND SPECTATORSHIP
JUDITH MAYNE

From *Private Novels, Public Films*, Athens, GA: University of Georgia Press, 1988, pp. 114–126

Central to the classical American cinema is a myth of authorship, and the importance of adaptations of nineteenth-century novels has to do largely with the sustenance of that myth. Parallel to the function of authorship in the relationship between the novel and film is that of readership. Consider, for example, the Robert Stevenson-directed adaptation of *Jane Eyre* (1944). There are many omissions and condensations in this film, some of which are examined by Asheim.[34] And following Bluestone, we might consider how successfully the Brontë novel is used as a point of departure to create an "autonomous" work of art. But there is another kind of work in this film, irreducible to either a celebration or a denial of authorship. The film begins with a close-up of a leather-bound volume of *Jane Eyre,* and closes with a symmetrical close-up of a page marked "The End." Such a "framing" of a film with reference to its literary source is common to many Hollywood adaptations of the period. *Jane Eyre* suggests some of the implications of this parallel between book cover and screen, between page and frame.

Throughout this film, pages from the book appear on the screen as structuring devices, with specific passages illuminated. The adult voice of Jane (Joan Fontaine) reads these passages aloud in voice-over. Occasionally these pages correspond to actual passages from *Jane Eyre,* but by and large they do not. "Chapter one," for example, on screen, begins: "My name is Jane Eyre. I was born in 1830, a hard time." This is a far cry from the actual opening of Charlotte Brontë's novel: "There was no possibility of taking a walk that day. We had been wandering, indeed, in the leafless shrubbery an hour in the morning."[35] These imaginary passages in the film form one of the many strategies by which the novel is condensed for the screen version. They recall producer David O. Selznick's description of "bridging scenes":

> I have discovered that the public will forgive you for any number of omissions—particularly of subordinate material which is not directly connected with the main plot—but it won't forgive you for deliberate changes. For that reason I have found it best to make the bridging scenes which span the omissions as suggestive as possible. That is, by picking up dialogue and even phrases from other parts of the book and using such to construct the bridging scenes, the audience is given the illusion of seeing and hearing that with which they are already familiar.[36]

The "illusion of seeing and hearing": such a description of those "well-beloved" works brought to the screen suggests an interesting parallel between the itineraries of reading and viewing. The pages are selectively illuminated, light separated from dark, and thus the arrangement of words on a page is not unlike the arrangement of figures in a landscape. The female voice narrates, while we read what she has ostensibly "written." The female character is thus simultaneously a reader and a narrator within the film.

The reading process represented in the film is of a special type. One might certainly criticize the substitutions that occur in the film and dismiss them in the terms used by Asheim: "The assumed level of audience comprehension is generally lower for the film than for the novel."[37] But Charlotte Brontë's novel has a rather unique status, for, like Emily Brontë's *Wuthering Heights*, it is a nineteenth-century classic frequently read by adolescent girls. The distortions of Brontë's novel in the illuminated pages on screen are as much the reflection of an adult's memory of the adolescent experience of reading this novel, as they are the result of a film industry determined to simplify for its mass audience at all costs. *Jane Eyre* is adapted to the screen in such a way, then, that film viewing becomes, through the book, through the novel, a form of memory of a certain kind of reading.

Memory is essential to the way in which the itineraries of reading and viewing are intertwined in this film. The film is structured so as to constantly refer to associations of the reading process, and to integrate those associations into the act of film viewing and comprehension. And thus the film version of *Jane Eyre* presents itself as a fantasy of how we remember the novel. I am reminded here of how Sergei Eisenstein spoke of Charles Dickens: "All of us read him in childhood, gulped him down greedily, without realizing that much of his irresistibility lay ... in that spontaneous, childlike skill for storytelling."[38] At the heart of D. W. Griffith's narrative skill was, according to Eisenstein, an understanding of the importance of that "childlike skill." Similarly, many of the cinematic adaptations of classical novels evolve from an understanding of the special function of reading in childhood and adolescent fantasies of the self in relation to the world. An essential component of classical film narrative is the memory recaptured by the experience of film viewing, and recaptured twice over: there is the memory of childhood, and the memory of reading. Cinematic adaptations evoke childhood memories of reading, and the transaction between viewer and screen is shaped by the contours of family identities, with the figure of the author as lover and father, as narrative authority.

Orson Welles' *Citizen Kane* (1941) brings together in a particularly striking way the implications, for classical film narrative, of the myths of authorship and readership inherited from the middle-class novel. *Citizen Kane* is less about one man's life than it is about the very possibility of telling that story in the first place. The film begins with the death of Charles Kane, and moves to a newsreel obituary. We then witness a series of interviews with Kane's acquaintances, conducted by the journalist Thompson whose assignment is to discover the significance of Kane's last word, "rosebud." That enigma has become one of the most classic in film history. Rosebud may represent lost innocence and mother-love, but it represents equally forcefully the impossibility of a facile understanding of one individual's life.

Yet it is not just any individual life which is impenetrable, but the life of an individual who has become a public figure. In the scene where the sled called Rosebud appears, when Mr. Thatcher comes to fetch the child Kane and take him away to the city and to wealth, it is as if Kane crosses an absolute threshold separating private and public spheres. Indeed, there is virtually no other private sphere in Kane's world after he leaves his home. First wife Emily seems to be as important as the President's niece as she is as Kane's wife, and second wife Susan Alexander is quickly transformed by Kane into a failed public figure herself.[39] The very structure of the film is informed by the potential negotiation of private and public spheres—from the newsreel, a collection of documents about the public man that is narrated by an authoritative voice-over, to the quest, a collection of different perspectives which make up a mosaic of glimpses into the private life concealed beneath the public façade. *Citizen Kane* does not correspond uniquely to what I have called the fantasy of reconciliation, nor to the nightmare of reification. Private and public selves never are totally integrated, but neither can it be said that *Citizen Kane* puts forth a private sphere invaded by the forces of the public sphere. For the private sphere in *Citizen Kane* remains, quite simply, separate and unknowable. And even if one accepts a dime-store Freudian explanation of Rosebud, the knowledge that Kane suffered all his life from separation anxiety is, to say the least, somewhat anti-climactic.[40]

More important than the figure of Kane himself is the attention given, in *Citizen Kane*, to the particular position of the film spectator vis-à-vis the complicated journey from public to private existence. As a reflection on spectatorship, *Citizen Kane* is a turning point of sorts in the history of the relation between classical film narrative and the novelistic tradition. Of central importance in *Citizen Kane* is the particular way in which the film spectator is implicated in the process of discovery of the enigma. To be sure, we are given privileged access to the meaning of Rosebud, but it would be a mistake to ignore the irony with which such privileged access is given. For the spectator within the film, that character who mirrors our own relation to the screen, is Thompson, and not his boss Rawlston, who is convinced that Rosebud will unlock a hidden meaning in Kane's life.[41] Thompson concludes his failed search with the remark that there is no single word or sign which could explain a man's life. And the "No Trespassing" sign appears at the end of the film as it did at the beginning, reminding us that Rosebud solves everything, and nothing at all.[42]

Yet Rosebud may not really be the object of Thompson's search. Robert Carringer argues persuasively that the little glass globe with its snow scene is endowed with much more narrative significance, and it is towards this object that Rosebud always leads us. Carringer writes: "The little glass globe (not Rosebud) is the film's central symbol. A mediating symbol of inner and outer, of subjective and objective, it stands at once for what we have seen and seek to recover, the psychic wholeness of Kane, and for the totality of Kane as a force, the man whose life and works are empires and private worlds. The shattering of the globe (not the appearance of Rosebud) is the film's main symbolic 'event.'"[43] That globe is, we recall, the object we see at the moment of Kane's death at the beginning of the film. It seems to occasion the utterance of 'Rosebud,' and once smashed on the floor, it is a lens through which we see Kane's room and an arriving nurse. We see another such globe on a bureau in Susan Alexander's apartment at the moment that Kane speaks of his mother and his childhood. The snow scene in the globe recalls, of course, the scene in the film of Kane's youth when Thatcher comes to take him away. And it recalls as well the estate of Xanadu, constructed by Kane as if to possess the glass globe on a large scale.

The glass globe links present and past, private and public selves. Xanadu has a similar function, but now in nearly hysterical proportions. Carringer says that the glass globe "condenses the whole experience of Xanadu, his last and most ambitious monument to himself."[44] For Xanadu is a private sphere erected as a public monument, within which there is nothing but space, never private but not quite public either. The narrative function of the glass globe in *Citizen Kane* is reminiscent, on several levels, of what writer Christa Wolf calls "miniatures," bits and pieces of the past, the results of a "furtive process hard to avoid, a hardening, petrifying, habituating, that attacks the memory in particular." Wolf writes:

> We all carry with us a collection of miniatures with captions, some quaint, some gruesome. These we occasionally bring out and show round, because we need confirmation of our own reassuringly clear feelings: beautiful or ugly, good or evil. These miniatures are for the memory what the calcified cavities are for people with tuberculosis, what prejudices are for morals: patches of once active life now shut off. At one time one was afraid to touch them, afraid of burning one's fingers on them; now they are cool and smooth.[45]

For Kane the globe is a miniature of lost innocence, and for the viewer, an equally forceful miniature of the very possibility of recapturing that past. How appropriate that Wolf should describe these miniatures as the province of cinema, and should then go on to insist that "prose should try to be unfilmable."[46] Indeed, *Citizen Kane* is informed by a resistance to that very process which, following Wolf's metaphor, is particularly characteristic of the cinema.

Citizen Kane puts forth a vision of private and public existence riddled with ambiguities. The ambiguity of the *quest* for the private man, and not the private man himself, is foregrounded in the film. Thus in *Citizen Kane* the transaction between viewer and screen in the public sphere of the movie theatre has become problematized. And perhaps the most striking ambiguity of all in *Citizen Kane* is that the film tells a story which, it insists, somewhat in the spirit of Christa Wolf, is "unfilmable."

That the evolution of spectatorship is tied to the function of readership is suggested in a different way by the presence of characters who function primarily as "spectators within the film," like the journalist Thompson in *Citizen Kane*. Whether major characters or not, the primary function of these figures is to establish narrative perspective. As is the case with many of the devices of film narrative, equivalences could be established between the use of the spectator within the film, and the forms of narration and point-of-view that occur in the novel. The intertextual links between novel and cinema are more strongly suggested, however, by the fact that frequently spectators within the film are identified as *readers*. Readership thus becomes a form of narrative participation incorporated into cinematic narrative.

In George Cukor's *Gaslight* (1944), there is a rather comic, elderly woman character who is constantly in the vicinity of the central action of the film, but never directly involved in it. She lives in the same neighborhood where the murder of opera singer Alicia took place, and is thus a bystander to the crime which determines the narrative development of the film. Throughout the film this woman functions as an observer, sometimes as a busybody who tries to glean information from servants, sometimes as a gossip who thoroughly enjoys discussing the past and present affairs of her neighbors. This character is first introduced to us in a train compartment she happens to share with Paula (Ingrid Bergman), the central female character of the film. The elderly woman is reading a suspense novel, which she describes for Paula: a man, who has murdered six wives and buried them all in his basement, has just taken a new wife. This novel parodies the film we are watching. The elderly woman has, she tells Paula, only reached page one hundred, and so she is certain that there is still more to come. Indeed there is, for the woman becomes a kind of reader of the equally suspenseful plot that thickens in her own neighborhood.

Gaslight's incorporation of a reader into its narrative reminds us of how, in the development of the middle-class novel, the conditions of readership were gradually and persistently incorporated and embedded into the narrative. We recall the significant resonances of Elizabeth's development as a reader in *Pride and Prejudice*, for instance. We have already seen this process at work in the early years of motion picture history: films would cease to bear titles like *Grandpa's Reading Class*, but those figures of vision would still be apparent, here and there and across the narrative structures of later films. So too within the classical Hollywood cinema there is the development of the novelistic in such an "embedded" way. The example of *Gaslight* is particularly striking, for the conditions of (cinematic) observation are precisely those of readership.

Spectatorship in the cinema evokes parallels between watching a film and reading a novel, and in this sense incorporates readership into the classical cinema. In a more general way, spectatorship in the cinema is structured by the relationship between private and public existence. The separation of private and public spheres to which the middle-class novel responds has, in the era of cinema, changed dimensions. Narratives of private and public life have been appropriated from one set of historical circumstances to another. The development of consumerism in the early twentieth century is an essential aspect of the changing relation between private and public spheres. With consumerism, the reification of the private sphere appears to be complete. In his study of the evolution of consumerism, for instance, Stuart Ewen describes how the home became increasingly perceived as a kind of factory in its own right:

> As the housewife assumed more of a factory-operative status, the home became a place where the values of factory production, and the conditions if not the pay of the wage worker, were replicated and reinforced on a day-to-day basis.[47]

The class dimensions of consumerism were essential to the reification of the private sphere. An imaginary ideal of homogeneity was put forth, whereby working-class and middle-class aspirations could be united around the pursuit of leisure and goods.[48]

We have seen how the early motion pictures offered glimpses of consumerist ideals; and how the audience for moving pictures developed, like the very phenomenon of consumerism, in cross-class terms. An important aspect of the classical cinema is the way in which the movie theatre seems to provide a space in which class differences temporarily dissolve. I do not mean that working-class and middle-class audiences would respond to films in identical ways; rather, film narrative would work on multiple levels, so that different class-defined responses would be condensed within a single film.

The relationship between private and public spheres, as a narrative theme and structure, would become an essential means to cut symbolically across class lines. Consider the film *My Sister Eileen* (1942), for example, in which two sisters, Ruth and Eileen, leave their Columbus, Ohio, home to look for work (Ruth as a writer, Eileen as an actress) in New York City. The Greenwich Village apartment they share—their private space—is constantly invaded by external forces, usually male figures, representing professional, sexual, or proprietal authority. The two sisters make uneasy accommodations by adopting a variety of family roles in relationship to each other: Eileen acts as housewife when her older sister goes out to look for work; Ruth comforts and gently disciplines her younger sister as a mother would a child; and when the sisters are frightened by the street activity that keeps them from sleep, they share a not-quite conjugal bed. The women's world is more gently invaded by another male figure, Ruth's professional mentor, who accepts her first story for publication and conveniently falls in love with her at the same time. The romantic resolution of the film marks a restoration of order, as the union of male and female coincides with the readjustment of private and public space to complementary rather than conflicting spheres.

Central to that resolution is the question of class. Ruth and Eileen leave a middle-class existence in a town which symbolizes a middle-class way of life, to live in an ethnic, working-class neighborhood. The middle-class life they leave represents security and boredom; the working-class environment they enter may represent danger, but it is also full of color and excitement. The editor whose entrance into Ruth's life allows a balance of personal and public selves is also a mediator of class differences. He promises *both* middle-class security and the vivacity of an urban environment. Viewers of this film encounter the potential mediation of class differences, but in order to arrive at that conclusion they can follow quite different paths. To a middle-class audience, the Greenwich village characters correspond to comic ethnic stereotypes, while to a working-class urban audience, the trials and tribulations of two middle-class provincials must have been laughable and amusing.

Given the historical parallels between cinema and the emergence of a consumerist culture, it is perhaps tempting to define American cinema as an agent of consumerist culture. Such a definition has been put forth persuasively by Charles Eckert who, in describing how cinema actively contributed to the cause of consumerist culture, says that in the first decades of the twentieth century, "the conditions were right for Hollywood to assume a role in the phase of capitalism's life-history that the emerging philosophy of consumerism was about to give birth to."[49]

Eckert's explorations into the "almost incestuous hegemony" which characterized Hollywood's connections with big business provide some of the most illuminating evidence for the very special role of cinema within consumerist culture. Inscribed within film from the very beginning, says Eckert, are:

> innumerable opportunities for product and brand-name tie-ins. But more than this, [motion pictures] functioned as living display windows for all that they contained; windows that were occupied by marvelous mannequins and swathed in a fetish-inducing ambiance of music and emotion.[50]

Throughout the decade of the 1930s, films would function as "living display windows." Extensive tie-ins with a variety of manufacturers assured the visibility of specific products and brand-names on the screen. In addition, entire industries would be built around the kinds of clothing and furnishings shown on screen. The female viewer was central throughout. If, in the novels of two centuries before, she occupied a strategic central position in the private sphere, in Hollywood narrative woman was central as consumer, as the strategic center of yet another stage in the relationship between private and public existence.[51]

Central, then, to Eckert's view of Hollywood is the decisive contribution of American cinema to the shaping of consumerist culture.

> Hollywood ... did as much or more than any other force in capitalist culture to smooth the operation of the production-consumption cycle by fetishizing products and putting the libido in libidinally invested advertising.[52]

Yet at the same time that consumerism was developing as a major phenomenon of twentieth-century capitalist societies, there persisted the nineteenth-century ideal of family life as a separate, isolated realm. Zaretsky writes that in the twentieth century, the "proletariat itself came to share the bourgeois ideal of the family as a 'utopian retreat.'"[53] If consumerism is built upon the reification of the private sphere, that ideal of a haven, of a "utopian retreat" persisted. And with a contradictory twist, that ideal was often actively foregrounded as a central image in advertising.

While it is true that moving pictures became, in Eckert's words, "living display windows" for the products of consumer society, the movies had an equally important function in the maintenance of the ideal of the private sphere as a privileged, separate realm. Cinema is a form of spectacle, governed by consumerist principles. Cinema is also a narrative form, governed by principles not so quickly nor so easily assimilable to the phenomenon of consumer society. Thus as spectacle and narrative, cinema emerges both from the new consumerist culture and from the eighteenth- and nineteenth-century novelistic tradition. The classical American cinema is spectacle and narrative; a vehicle for consumerism and a link to a narrative tradition. Put another way, the classical American cinema is an arena where the contradictions of the changing dimensions of private and public life are enacted.

Within the public space of the movie theatre, private fantasies are indulged: this has been a relative constant in the history of narrative cinema. But the contours of that public space, and of the transaction between viewer and screen, are always determined by specific historical conditions. In the 1940s those conditions led directly or indirectly to World War II. If the space of the movie theatre allowed a temporary dissolution of class differences, and if films were constructed to allow different forms of class identification, then moving pictures would serve an important function in the war effort. And if cinema of the 1940s explored in depth the relation of private and public spheres, it was in part because private and public existence had become problematized in American social life. The symbolic mediation of private and public life thus spoke to a kind of historical urgency.

The demands of war economy meant a heightened awareness of private and public life, the most striking symptom of which was the participation of women in the war industries. Indeed, the ways in which women were encouraged to take on work outside the home during the war is a fascinating case study of how consumerist culture would be grounded in a curious contradiction whereby the private sphere was at once a refuge from, *and* an extension of, the public sphere. One thinks of the various wartime images of women created by advertising, and Rosie the Riveter in particular stands out, dressed in overalls and carrying a lunchpail to the factory. However emancipated Rosie the Riveter might have appeared, the image of the working woman still focused on woman's traditional place in the private sphere. The popular image of woman which evolved during the war years suggested that American women had never worked outside the home before (even though women had in fact been entering the job market steadily for decades), and that women had never performed factory work before (even though they had been working in factories for years).[54] In particular, it was assumed that if women worked to support the war effort, they were *really* working for their men. One newspaperwoman spoke, typically, of the "deep satisfaction which a woman of today knows who has made a rubber boat which may save the life of her aviator husband, or helped to fashion a bullet which may avenge her son."[55] In short, then, the image of Rosie the Riveter and her compatriots corresponded to a pre-war ideal. Thus historian Leila Rupp writes that "the appeals used to recruit women for war work strengthened the impression that the public Rosie was, inside her overalls, the same prewar woman who cooked, cleaned, and cared for her family."[56]

One could of course criticize these images of woman as blatant distortions of the real situations of women workers, but the goal of advertising, after all, is to create myths, not to reproduce reality. Yet the myth thus created is anything but simple. Rupp points out that Rosie the Riveter is an "exotic creature" who seems somehow out of place in the public sphere of men's work, and so the potentially jarring quality of the image is softened by the appeal to women's traditional roles as wives and mothers.[57] Perhaps during any war, the relation between private and public spheres is bound to be problematic. But particular to 1940s America is that the institutions of consumerism, advertising in particular, were firmly in place. Never before had there been such fastidious orchestrations of the possible harmonious interchanges between the two spheres—the battlefront and the home-front, the world of men and the world of women. The home would be regarded, simultaneously, as a recuperative refuge *and* as a battlefront. If American films of the 1940s, whether specifically devoted to war themes or not, revealed a profound ambivalence towards private and public life, it is because the culture was straining under the tension of different ideals of private and public existence. Emblematic of that strain was the wartime woman worker. Her participation in war industries suggests an integration of the private and the public, but she was constantly addressed (through advertising in particular) as if she were a pure creature of domesticity.

We know that film attendance peaked during the war, and given the number of men overseas, women viewers were more visible than usual. Some theatre managers commented on the increasing number of unescorted females who were attending moving pictures.[58] Given the strategic importance of women's roles vis-à-vis the private and the public, we might look at how, in the 1940s, women were addressed as film viewers.[59] Newsreels were shown with virtually all feature films, and a strategy first developed in Detroit to attract women to the newsreels is an interesting example of how cinema's narrative capacities were adapted to wartime conditions. Noting that women were less inclined than men to be interested in newsreels, exhibitors put together a one-hour program, focusing when possible on footage of areas where Michigan soldiers had been sent. Advertisements were put in the newspapers offering free admission to mothers and wives of soldiers, who were asked to send in the names of their relatives in service. The program proved to be a smashing success, leading to an extended run and similar programs in other cities. The drawing card, of course, was the possibility of identifying loved ones. On opening day in Detroit, one woman saw a newsreel of a plane landing in Egypt, and recognized the plane as her son's from its number and nickname. And when she returned home that day, there was a letter from him confirming what she had just seen at the movie theatre.[60] One can hardly imagine a more striking mediation of the personal and the social: newsreel journalism becomes a narrative of family life. And it comes, perhaps, as no surprise that, as *Variety* reported, "it is believed numerous identifications are erroneous and it does not detract from the mounting interest. Houses have reported that different families have asked for film snips of the same soldier, both insisting he is their son."[61]

Not all film viewing in the 1940s would be so explicitly conditioned by the war, or by the possible connections between private and public life evidenced in this particular marketing strategy. But all commercial films of the period would connect to the war in one way or another. For the problematic relationship between private and public existence was not a simple result of the war, but rather was a fundamental aspect of that society which had undergone the transformation of consumerism.

David O. Selznick and the glass globe in *Citizen Kane*, cinematic versions of authors in *Madame Bovary* and *The Life of Émile Zola*, are suggestive of the changing dimensions of classical film narrative in the 1940s. The influence of the novel is in evidence from the earliest years of cinema. But in the 1940s, something changes. The confluence of increased production costs, a growing consciousness of the institutional quality of the medium, and an increasingly close relationship—with varying shades of mercantilism—between film and the novel, created a cinematic narrative institution of new depth and maturity. Kane, Selznick, and James Mason as Gustave Flaubert: these are the figurative sons of D. W. Griffith, and Kane's glass globe and Selznick's well-worn copy of *David Copperfield* are 1940s analogues to the sword that inspired *His Trust / His Faithful Trust*, the object which in Griffith's memory of childhood and then on the screen, represented the scope of narrative.

And casting an eye toward the film audience, the woman wartime worker is heir to another tradition. She may not be appropriately designated as Griffith's daughter, but the woman spectator in the 1940s, whether seeking imaginary narrative reconciliations of the two spheres or looking for loved ones in newsreels, is the descendant of two other traditions: that of the woman reader, and that of the immigrant spectator. Like them, American women viewers of the 1940s exemplify the changes in private and public existence which would be enacted in a variety of ways in the movie theatre.

■   ■   ■

Questions and projects

1. How is the activity of reading (or writing) foregrounded in a film—such as François Truffaut's *400 Blows* (1959), Stephen Frears's *Dangerous Liaisons* (1988), or Quentin Tarantino's *Pulp Fiction* (1996)—and what significance does reading in these movies have in the public and private lives of the characters? How are reading and writing related to the activity of seeing or viewing in the film?
2. Choose an adaptation in which the gender or sexual preferences of the characters play a prominent role (for example, one of the *Jane Eyre* adaptations [from 1934 to the 1990s] or Sally Potter's *Orlando* [1993]). Fashion an argument that discusses how gender influences the choices, changes, and omissions in moving from the literary work to the film.

Notes

34   Lester Asheim, "From Book to Film: Summary," *The Quarterly Review of Film, Radio and Television,* 6, (152): 258–273, p. 268.
35   Charlotte Brontë, *Jane Eyre* (1847; reprint, New York: Penguin, 1966), p. 39.
36   Cited in Margaret Farrand Thorp, *America at the Movies* (New Haven, CT: Yale University Press, 1939), pp. 242–43.
37   Asheim, "Summary," pp. 263.
38   Sergei Eisenstein, "Dickens, Griffith and the Film Today," *Film Form,* ed. and trans. Jay Leyda (1949; reprint, Cleveland, OH: World Publishing Co., 1957), p. 201.
39   David Bordwell, *"Citizen Kane,"* in Ronald Gottsman, ed., *Focus on Citizen Kane* (Englewood Cliffs, NJ: Prentice Hall, 1976), says that Kane sees "love solely in terms of power," p. 118.
40   Welles said of Rosebud: "It's a gimmick, really, and rather dollar-book Freud." See Joseph McBride,

Orson Welles (New York: Viking Press, 1972), p. 44.

41   Joseph McBride says of Thompson: "The reporter, who stands for the audience, also stands for the artist approaching the contradictions of his subject-matter" (Ibid., p. 38).

42   Joseph McBride says: "We see the 'solution' for which we and Thompson have been searching, and we realize that it does in fact solve nothing" (Ibid., p. 42).

43   Robert Carringer, "Rosebud, Dead or Alive: Narrative and Symbolic Structure in *Citizen Kane*," *PMLA* 91, no. 2 (1976): 187.

44   Ibid., p. 191.

45   Christa Wolf, "The Reader and the Writer," in *The Reader and the Writer*, trans. Joan Becker (New York: International Publishers, 1977), p. 190.

46   Ibid., p. 193.

47   Stuart Ewen, *Captains of Consciousness* (1976; reprint, New York: McGraw Hill, 1977), p. 164.

48   See Eli Zaretsky, *Capitalism, the Family, and Personal Life* (New York: Harper and Row, 1976), p. 67.

49   Charles Eckert, "The Carole Lombard in Macy's Window," *Quarterly Review of Film Studies* 3, no. 1 (1978): 2.

50   Ibid., p. 4.

51   Ibid., pp. 6, 19–20.

52   Ibid, p. 21.

53   Zaretsky, *Capitalism, the Family, and Personal Life*, p. 61.

54   See Leila J. Rupp, *Mobilizing Women for War: German and American Propaganda, 1939–1945* (Princeton: Princeton University Press, 1978), p. 177.

55   Ibid, p. 157.

56   Ibid, p. 153.

57   Ibid, p. 151.

58   *Variety* reported on a Pittsburgh theatre manager who said, "Gals have to get their romantic kicks vicariously since Uncle Sams been pulling so many eligibles out of circulation" (March 11, 1942, p. 1).

59   Yet it should be kept in mind that women have virtually always been regarded as key audiences for Hollywood films. *Variety* (August 4, 1942, p. 3) published the results of a new Gallup poll which claimed that as many men as women went to the movies. The following week a film critic responded: "It is not the percentage of men as against women that counts. It's *how* did *most* of them get there?" (August 12, 1942, p. 12). Whether men go to the movies or not, the critic claims, it is women who do the choosing.

60   The event is described in *Variety*, March 31, 1943, p. 23.

61   Ibid.

Chapter 26

P. Adams Sitney

THE LYRICAL FILM

T HE FOCUS OF P. ADAMS SITNEY is on the experimental or avant-garde films of the New American Cinema that developed after World War II. First published in 1974, this work aligns certain films especially with a revolutionary poetic tradition associated with William Blake and other Romantic poets. Concentrating on the films of Stan Brakhage, Sitney argues a connection with those lyrical revolutions in vision and image, as well as with the literary techniques of traditional poetry such as rhythm and metaphor. Although this selection concentrates on one filmmaker, the connection between poetic techniques and creative processes should point toward the variety of experimental film practices.

■ ■ ■

THE LYRICAL FILM
P. ADAMS SITNEY

From *Visionary Film: The American Avant-Garde, 1943–1978*, 2nd edn, Oxford: Oxford University Press, 1979, pp 148–164

... In his aesthetics Brakhage has revived and revised the Romantic dialectics of sight and imagination which had been refocused in American abstract expressionistic painting and American poetry (particularly in the work of Wallace Stevens) during the film-maker's intellectual formation. The history of that argument is worth consideration at this time. William Blake championed the imagination against the prevailing epistemology of John Locke, who maintained that both thought and imagination were additive aspects of the verbal and visual memory. Blake wrote,

> I assert for My Self that I do not behold the outward Creation & that to me it is a hindrance & not Action [—a forecast of the phraseology of Abstract Expressionism]. It is as the dirt

upon my feet, No part of me. … I question not my Corporeal or Vegetative Eye any more than I would Question a Window concerning a Sight. I look thro' it & not with it.

Wordsworth too writes of the tyranny of sight:

> I speak in recollection of a time
> When the bodily eye, in every stage of life
> The most despotic of our senses, gained
> Such strength in me as often held my mind
> In absolute dominion
> —*Prelude*, XII, 127ff

Our philosophies and psychologies have shifted from the naturalism of Locke and his confidence in the senses. For some artists in the tradition of Blake and Wordsworth the eye now had a renewed and redemptive value. As Wallace Stevens puts it,

> The eye's plain version is a Thing apart,
> The vulgate of experience.
> —"An Ordinary Evening in New Haven," 1–2

Harold Bloom has observed that:

> Modernist poetry in English has organized itself, to an excessive extent, as a supposed revolt against Romanticism, in the mistaken hope of escaping [Romanticism's] inwardness (though it was unconscious of this as its prime motive).[8]

The eye which both Stevens and Brakhage enlist in the service of the imagination confirms while striving to reconcile, as Bloom's view would have it, the Romantic divorce of consciousness and nature.

Brakhage claims to see through his eyes, with his eyes, and even the electrical patterns on the surface of his eyes. When he decided to become a film-maker he threw away his eyeglasses. At the beginning of his book he argues with the way language constricts vision and with the idea of sight built into the film-maker's tools. In "The Camera Eye," he writes:

> And here, somewhere, we have an eye (I'll speak for myself) capable of any imagining (the only reality). And there (right there) we have the camera eye (the limitation of the original liar) … its lenses ground to achieve 19th Century Western compositional perspective (as best exemplified by the "classic" ruin) … its standard camera and projector speed for recording movement geared to the feeling of the ideal slow Viennese waltz, and even its tripod head … balled with bearings to permit it that Les Sylphides motion (ideal to the contemplative romantic and virtually restricted to horizontal and vertical movements) … and its color film manufactured, to produce that picture post card effect (salon painting) exemplified by those oh so blue skies and peachy skins.[9]

He proceeds with a program for bringing the camera into the twentieth century by distorting its lens, obliterating perspective, discarding the tripod, altering camera speeds, and changing film stocks. He calls for these home-made modifications in the name of the eye, demanding of the film-maker (actually of himself) a dedication to what he actually sees, not what he has been taught to see or thinks he should see. That the resulting version of space corresponds to that of Abstract Expressionism, whose motivations are away from the physical eye, seems not to have occurred to Brakhage. His sense of vision presumes that we have been taught to be unconscious of most of what we see. For him, seeing includes what the open eyes view, including the essential movements and dilations involved in that primary mode of seeing, as well as the shifts of focus, what the mind's eye sees in visual memory and in dreams (he calls them "brain movies"), and the perpetual play of shapes and colors on the closed eyelid and occasionally on the eye surface ("closed-eye vision"). The imagination, as he seems to define it, includes the simultaneous functioning of all these modes. Thus Brakhage argues both with Blake and Locke, but his sympathies are with the former. Like the Romantics themselves, Brakhage's work attempts to refine the visionary tradition by correcting its errors.

The Romantic strain in Brakhage emerges with the creation of the lyrical film and culminates in his essay in mythopoeia, *Dog Star Man*, and its extended version, *The Art of Vision*, which will be discussed in the following chapter. Brakhage began to shoot his epic two years after finishing *Anticipation of the Night*. In the meantime, and through the shooting of that long film, he continued to make short lyrical films that mark one of the great periods in American avant-garde film. In this series of films—*Window Water Baby Moving* (1959), *Cat's Cradle* (1959), *Sirius Remembered* (1959), *The Dead* (1960), *Thigh Line Lyre Triangular* (1961), *Mothlight* (1963), *Vein* (1964), *Fire of Waters* (1965), *Pasht* (1965)—Brakhage invented a form in which the film-maker could compress his thoughts and feelings while recording his direct confrontation with intense experiences of birth, death, sexuality, and the terror of nature. These works have transformed the idea of film-making for most avant-garde artists who began to make films in the late sixties.

Window Water Baby Moving and *Thigh Line Lyre Triangular* record the births of the film-maker's first and third children respectively. Between the two, finished only two years apart, there is a great shift in style: the former treats the occasion almost dramatically, although the montage attempts to relieve the drama which Brakhage obviously felt while shooting the film and seeing his first child born; the latter film centers itself more fully in the eyes of the film-maker as a visual and visionary experience. The difference between them is not simply a measure of experience (seeing a third child born as opposed to the first), but that is part of it.

There is an interplay between the film-maker and his wife in *Window Water Baby Moving* that disappears in *Thigh Line Lyre Triangular*. The poetic fulfillment of that interplay comes at the moment late in the film when we see the excited face of Brakhage just after the child has been born. His wife, still on the delivery table, took the camera from him to get these shots. Earlier, they had photographed each other during an argument, which Brakhage intercut with negative images of them making love in the film *Wedlock House: An Intercourse* (1959).

In no other film does Brakhage make as much of the reorganization of chronological time; for the most part, his lyrical films exist outside sequential time in a realm of simultaneity or of disconnected time spans of isolated events. *Window Water Baby Moving* begins with images of late pregnancy. The first shots are of a window, framed diagonally, intercut with flashes of blackness. Throughout the film Brakhage uses black and white leader to affirm the screen and the cinematic illusion as one of several tactics for relieving the dramatic tension built up as the moment of birth approaches.

A rhythmic montage moves from the window to the light cast on the water in a bathtub where the pregnant wife is bathing. The camera is static, and the shots remain on the screen longer here than in other films of the same period. After a longish pause of blackness, we see Jane for the first time on the delivery table. At a painful moment in her labor, he cuts from her screams to her smiling face from the earlier episode and follows it with a recapitulation of the window and water shots. He flashes back to the earlier scene nine times, always showing it in a group of shots and always passing from one scene to the other on a plastic cut, as the glimpse of a window behind the held-up placenta, near the end of the film, initiates another cut to the window of the opening and a recapitulation of the sunlit images that follow it. *Window Water Baby Moving* ends with shots of the parents and the baby spaced amid flashes of white leader following the rhythmic pattern at the film's opening.

In *Thigh Line Lyre Triangular* we see a radically transformed space. The passages of black and white leader are more insistent; there are twisting, anamorphic shots of Jane in labor; the montage mixes the birth with flaring shots of animals, a flamingo, and a polar bear from the out-takes of *Anticipation of the Night*. The entire film is painted over with colored dots, smears, and lines. The film begins with a painted stripe which seems to open up on a scene of childbirth with labor already under way. Underneath the rapidly changing, painted surface, we see the doctor, the birth, the placenta, the smiling mother, but in an elliptical flow completely devoid of the suspense of the earlier film. Where Brakhage used plastic cutting to switch from present to past or future in his first birth film, he uses the painted surface to smooth out and elide the transitions from the birth to the strange upside-down appearance of the polar bear or the shot of the flamingo.

Although we do not see him in this film there is no doubt that we are looking at the birth through the eyes of the artist, whose eccentric vision is ecstatic to the point of being possessed. At the time of the birth he was sufficiently self-composed to pay close attention to the subtleties of his seeing while watching his wife give birth. In the interview at the beginning of *Metaphors on Vision*, he explains that:

> only at a crisis do I see both the scene as I've been trained to see it (that is, with Renaissance perspective, three-dimensional logic—colors as we've been trained to call a color a color, and so forth) and patterns that move straight out from the inside of the mind through the optic nerves. In other words, in intensive crisis I can see from the inside out and the outside in. ... I see patterns moving that are the same patterns I see when I close my eyes; and can also see the same kind of scene I see when my eyes are open. ... What I was seeing at the birth of Neowyn most clearly, in terms of this "brain movie" recall process, were symbolic structures of an animal nature.[10]

In the first chapter of his book Brakhage observes, "This is an age which has no symbol for death other than the skull and bones of one stage of decomposition ... and it is an age which lives in total fear of annihilation." In *Sirius Remembered* and *The Dead* he searches for a deeper image of death. When his family's dog Sirius died, his wife did not want it buried. They left the body in the woods where it froze in the winter and rotted in the spring. Brakhage made periodic visits to it and filmed the stages of its decomposition. The title of his film puns on the memory and the reconstruction of the dog's members.

Formally, *Sirius Remembered* is the densest of his films in the repetitive, Steinian style of *Anticipation of the Night*, and it introduces a new style, which finds its purest expression in *The Dead*. The opening passage resembles a fugue, as one sweep of the camera is followed by another, beginning a little earlier and going a little further, while the third carries on from the first. The speed of these alternations and the sudden changes they make by a reversal of direction, the injection of a brighter still image, or the occurrence of a long pan suggest that the fugue has been transposed to the micro-rhythms of post-Stravinskian music. The similarity of the shots and their reduction through movement to two-dimensional abstractions fixes the attention on their rhythmic structure.

The pattern of rhythms established in the opening shots continues throughout the film as its visual material becomes more complex. The film proceeds through fall to winter to spring, with some reversals and overlapping of the seasons. Brakhage arrests the movement of the winter scenes with flashes of whiteness when the dog is covered by a layer of snow, to affirm the flat screen and puncture the illusion, but here also to suggest an emanation from the dog of pure white light.

Midway the already complex rhythmic structure becomes compounded by superimposition. The second half of the film elaborates an intricate harmonics as the two layers of fugue-like rhythms play against one another.

In this film Brakhage views death as the conquest of the antagonist, nature, over consciousness. He illustrated this antagonism with a story of the visit of two friends during the making of the film:

> Suddenly I was faced in the center of my life with the death of a loved being which tended to undermine all my abstract thoughts of death.
>
> I remember one marvelous time which gave me the sense of how others could avoid it. [P. T.] and [C. B.] came to visit us and C. wanted to go out into the fields "to gather a little nature," as he put it. "Nature" was such a crisis to me at this time that I was shocked at that statement. [C] made some martinis, handed me one; and [P. and C], and I all went out into Happy Valley where they toasted the new buds of spring that were beginning to come up, etc., and marched right straight past the body of Sirius either without seeing it at all (any more than they can see my film *Sirius Remembered*) or else they saw it and refused to recognize it. [C] was envaled in the ideal of toasting the budding spring and here was this decaying, stinking corpse right beside the path where we had to walk, and he literally did not, could not, or would not see it.[11]

In the same interview he describes in detail how a mystical illumination helped him edit the film.

The skeletal head of the dog in *Sirius Remembered* was the first of several conventional images which Brakhage has attempted to redeem from the realm of the cliché by looking at them freshly and presenting them in a novel form. Others are the image of the tombstone as a significant image of death (*The Dead*), the heart as an image of love (*Dog Star Man: Part Three*), and flowers as an image of sexuality (*Song XVI*).

While passing through Paris to work on a commercial project (for a long time Brakhage supported himself and his art by taking commercial assignments), he sneaked his camera into the Père-Lachaise cemetery to film the monumental tombs in black-and-white. During the same trip he filmed people walking along the Seine in color from a slow-moving tourist boat on the river. At the end of a black-and-white roll, he took a shot of Kenneth Anger sitting in a café.

When he returned to America, Brakhage associated Europe, Anger, and the two traditional images, the river and the tomb, with his thoughts on death. He says:

> I was again faced with death as a concept; not watching death as physical decay, or dealing with the pain of the death of a loved one, but with the concept of death as something that man casts into the future by asking, "What is death like?" And the limitation of finding the images for a concept of death only in life itself is a terrible torture, i.e., Wittgenstein's Tractatus Logico-Philosophicus 6.4311: "Death is not an event of life. Death is not lived through. If by eternity is understood not endless temporal duration but timelessness, then he lives eternally who lives in the present. Our life is endless in the way that our visual field is without limit."[12]

He put the three images together—Anger, the tombs, and the Seine—to make *The Dead*.

Nearly every image in the film appears in superimposition, which serves several formal functions which I shall enumerate as they appear, and one poetic function: to make a spectral light emanate from people and things, as if the spirit showed through the flesh and burst through the cracks in marble tombs. Visually, Brakhage relates this effect to a thermal light sometimes visible to the trained eye, and to the Anglo-Saxon allusions to *aelf-scin*, a fairy light that hovers on the horizon at dusk.

The film opens with a pan up a Gothic statue, interrupted by flashes of negative. The black-and-white positive and negative have been printed on color stock, giving them a green-gray tint. From the color footage, only the blues of the water and occasional reds (sweaters, the oars of a rowboat) registered on the composite film. A quick image of Anger in the café changes to a double image of him as the negative is placed over the positive with left/right orientation reversed. The camera moves with fragments of rocking pans among gravestones and crypts upon which sporadic superimpositions briefly appear. This part of the film contains frequent sudden solarizations (the simultaneous printing of negative and positive, causing an instant flash or leap of the image on the screen).

A quick movement toward a crypt blackens the screen. Out of that darkness come deep blue images of the Seine, in a rapid montage, followed by a leisurely pan of the cemetery in tinted black-and-white. Another variation on the opening passage (Anger, Gothic ornamentation, the statue) ends in a white-out.

People, in blue and red, strolling along the banks of the river, appear over pans, sometimes upside-down, of the tombs. In this introduction of the theme of "the walking dead," as Brakhage calls these strollers, the tempo changes from slow, to staccato, to slow again, to staccato again, until the scene almost imperceptibly shifts from the superimposition of people with graves to a flow of superimposed cemetery images, a few frames out of synchronization, with its solarizing negative. The negative echoes the slow rocking of the positive images and pursues them like a ghost.

The shifting of visual themes and their gradual evolution through synthesis and elaboration constitute a meditation on death and the spirit in which thoughts, in the form of images, are tested, then refined, and finally passed over. A persistent idea of the light behind the objects of sight haunts the mind's eye of the film-maker and the structure of his film. Through the medium of the river, the stress shifts from positive to negative.

By overexposure of the film the graves appear almost washed out by the light of day. Another montage of water shots introduces a multiple-layered positive shot of the graves so white that only faint images in the corners of the screen indicate what they are. The movement on the river is contrasted with that of the cemetery through intercutting and superimposition until flashes, then long holds of pure white, break up the river shots.

The climax of the film is its breakthrough into negative following the flashes of whiteness. Brilliant, pure white trees in a black sky and dark crypts with cracks of brightness rock across the screen, paced with black leader. The long rocking motions move first in one direction, then another, shifting with the black shots. There is a long movement containing four black pauses as the camera passes so close to large tombs that the light is completely cut off. The second of these is so long that one thinks the film might have ended. But sudden flashes of solarization revive the ending structure, like final optimistic surges of sound before the end of many symphonies. A short finale brings us back to the Seine and the film ends on a slow movement across the shadow-marked marble wall of the river bank.

Like *Sirius Remembered*, some of the rhythmic texture of *The Dead* comes from the opposition, repetition, and superimposition of different movements of the camera. But here, rhythmic intricacy is less essential to the form of the film. *The Dead* uses superimposition organically, eliding the transitions from theme to theme or from one tempo to another. The abrupt element in the film is solarization. Finally the passages of pure whiteness and blackness act as poles in the spectrum from positive to negative and from black-and-white to color; they seldom interrupt the texture of the meditation. The best example of this is the long black passage in the pan of graves. The viewer can imagine the continuity of movement as he believes the camera is passing behind a large tomb. The shot a few seconds earlier prepared him for this. But gradually the overtone of movement evaporates, and the viewer is confronted with the presence of the black screen—another, most pessimistic, image of death. That too is denied the authority of a final image as the movement does eventually continue after this unnatural pause.

In *The Dead* Brakhage uses the vicissitudes of his raw materials—different kinds of film stock, the imperfect printing of black-and-white on color material, the washout effect of certain bright superimpositions—as metaphysical illuminations. Out of the specifically cinematic quality of light as it passes through these materials, he molds his vision of the light of death. In *The Dead* Brakhage mastered the strategy he had employed limitedly in *Anticipation of the Night* of presenting and rejecting tentative images of the essence he seeks to penetrate. The traditional symbols of the tombs and river and the absolute poles of blackness, whiteness, and negativity are the primary metaphors for death which he tests, varies, and rejects. In the course of the film the process of testing, contemplating, and rejecting becomes more important than the images in themselves.

His most radical exploration into the inflection of light through his raw materials initially occurred in response to his oppressive economic situation. When he had no money to buy film stock, he conceived the idea of making a film out of natural material through which light could pass. The clue to this came from his observing the quantity of glue and paint which Stephen Lovi had put on his film *A Portrait of the Lady in the Yellow Hat* (1962). Brakhage collected dead moths, flowers, leaves, and seeds. By placing them between two layers of Mylar editing tape, a transparent, thin strip of 16mm celluloid with sprocket holes and glue on one side, he made *Mothlight* (1963), "as a moth might see from birth to death if black were white."

The passing of light through, rather than reflecting off, the plants and moth wings reveals a fascinating and sometimes terrifying intricacy of veins and netlike structures, which replaces the sense of depth in the film with an elaborate lateral complexity, flashing by at the extreme speed of almost one natural object to each frame of the three minute film. The original title of this visual lyric, when the film-maker began to construct it, had been *Dead Spring*. True to that original but inferior title the film incarnates the sense of the indomitable division between consciousness and nature, which was taking a narrative form at the same time in Brakhage's epic, *Dog Star Man*.

The structure of *Mothlight*, as the film-maker observes in a remarkable letter to Robert Kelly printed in "Respond Dance," the final chapter of *Metaphors on Vision*, is built around three "Round-dances" and a coda. Three times the materials of the moths and plants are introduced on the screen, gain speed as if moving into wild flight, and move toward calm and separation; then in the coda a series of bursts of moth wings occurs in diminishing power, interspersed with passages of white (the whole film is fixed in a matrix of whiteness as the wings and flora seldom fill the whole screen). The penultimate burst regains the grandeur of the first in the series, but it is a last gasp, and a single wing, after the longest of the white passages, ends the film.

Significantly, in Brakhage's description of his interest in the moth's flight, sight, and functioning as oracular events in his life, he attributes to the appearance of a moth during the editing of an earlier film a liberation from a slump into self-consciousness that stalled his work:

> I was sty-my-eyed sinking into sty-meed in all self possession when suddenly Jane appeared holding a small dried plant which she put down on the working table, and without a word,

left me—I soon began working again … in the midst of attempts to work, what must surely have been the year's last moth began fluttering about me and along the work table, the wind of its wings shifting the plant from time to time and blowing away all speculations in my mind as to movements of dead plants and to enable me to continue working.[13]

For Brakhage, extreme self-consciousness and the seduction of natural objects are equivalents (which can, as in the present case, cancel each other) since they both inhibit the working process, which is his ultimate value.

In "Respond Dance," Brakhage, adapting Robert Duncan's view of the poet's role as a medium working for the Poet to the situation of the film-maker, writes:

Of necessity I become instrument for the passage of inner vision, thru all my sensibilities, into its external form. My most active part in this process is to increase all my sensibilities (so that all films arise out of some total area of being or full life) and, at the given moment of possible creation to act only out of necessity. In other words, I am principally concerned with revelation. My sensibilities are art-oriented to the extent that revelation takes place, naturally, within the given historical context of specifically Western aesthetics. If my sensibilities were otherwise oriented, revelation would take another external form—perhaps a purely personal one. As most of what is revealed, thru my given sensibilities clarifies itself in relationship to previous (and future, possible) works of art, I offer the given external form when completed for public viewing. As you should very well know, even when I lecture at showing of past Brakhage films I emphasize the fact that I am not artist except when involved in the creative process and that I speak as viewer of my own (no—damn that "my own" which is just what I'm trying, do try in all lectures, letters, self-senses-of, etc., to weed out)—I speak (when speaking, writing, well—that, is with respect to deep considerations) as viewer of The Work (not of … but By-Way-Of Art), and I speak specifically to the point of What has been revealed to me and, by way of describing the work-process, what I, as artist-viewer, understand of Revelation—that is: how to be revealed and how to be revealed to (or 2, step 2 and/or—the viewing process).[14]

What he reveals in the introductory interview, as the critic and explicator of his own work, is always illuminating and usually pertinent to our analysis of his films. But in the case of *Cat's Cradle*, the film does not support his expression of its theme. Brakhage recounts there how shortly after his marriage he took his wife to visit two friends, James Tenney and Carolee Schneemann, whom he had filmed in *Loving*. The film he shot of that encounter was to contain his observations on the tensions, identifications, and jealousies that it engendered. Yet the film itself effaces psychology and develops through its lightning montage of flat surfaces and gestures in virtually two-dimensional space an almost cubistic suggestion of the three-dimensional arena in which the four characters and one cat might interact, if only the furious pace of editing could be retarded and the synecdochic framing expanded.

The camera does not move. Like the montage at the opening of *Window Water Baby Moving*, the cutting at times follows an imaginary path of sunlight from the back of the cat, to a bedspread, to a bowl of flowers, to the opening of a door, etc. When there is movement within the frame, its direction and pace influence how it is cut. The various gestures of the film (a bare foot on the bedspread, Brakhage walking while buttoning his shirt, Carolee Schneemann painting and washing dishes, Tenney writing, Jane undressing) never seem complete; they are spread out evenly and often seen upside-down or simultaneously through the whole film without sequence or internal development. For the most part these activities are framed to obscure who the performer is so that together with the speed of the editing they tend to fuse the two men and two women together and even to create one androgynous being out of all four.

Floral wallpaper, an embroidered pillow, an amber bottle, and the cat's fur mix freely with the human gestures and with recurrent flashes of white leader and emphasize the flatness of the images. Off-screen looks of the human figures and changes of angle in a single subject establish axes of geometrical positioning, but with the rapidity of shot changes these axes spin wildly and eccentrically. The 700 shots in this five-minute film (remember there were some 3000 in the fifty minutes of the highly-edited *Twice a Man*) vary from two frames (1/12 of a second) to 48 (two seconds) with by far the greater number of images under half a second screen time.

Cat's Cradle suggests statis through, and despite, the speed of the colliding shots. In *Pasht*, made six years later, he again used a very rapid montage (one frame to sixty frame shots—mostly five or six frames), in a five-minute film for an even more stationary impression. In his blurb for the film in the catalogue of the Film-Makers Cooperative Brakhage tells us that the title comes from the name of a pet cat, named for the Egyptian goddess ruling cats. He shot the film while she was giving birth and edited it after her death. Without this guide the viewer would not know specifically what is happening in the film. It begins in black and soon shows a red furry image in the center of the screen—edgeless, undefined, and not filling the entire screen rectangle. Bits of black leader intercut with it make the image flicker like hot coals. The movement within the frame is slight, except for fragmentary glimpses of the discontinuous twisting of the fur by an anamorphic lens. The montage unites tiny bits of very similar images. Sometimes a moving orange spot of light appears, reminding the viewer of the cat in *Cat's Cradle*.

The whole screen seems to pulse with variations in the light intensity of the image, the degree of movement, the clarity of the fur, the time of a shot on the screen, and the number of elements in burst-of-image between passages of blackness. A typical passage has one black frame followed by six of soft focused fur, another frame of black, three of focused fur, six of blurred fur ending in a flash of light, another black, one bright orange, and three black. As the film nears its end the bursts become longer and the hairs of fur more clearly focused and at times larger images fill the borders of the screen, almost identifiable as very close views or anamorphic views of a cat scratching or giving birth.

Pasht presents a vision of an organism simultaneously seeming to die and regenerate. It is clearly animal but liberated from the specifics of species and character. The difference in rhythm between *Pasht* and the lyrical films of 1959 and 1960 indicates the general, but not absolute, shift in the film-maker's approach to the lyrical film before and after the making of *Dog Star Man*. *Pasht* and many of the films that follow it substitute an organic, retarded pulse for the earlier counterpoint and micro-rhythmic dynamics. In this later phase of the lyrical form, Brakhage seems to want to still the filmic image and catch the shimmering vibrations of the forces that inspire and terrify him.

Fire of Waters operates within a structure similar to that of *Pasht*. Here the matrix is gray instead of black, and its black-and-white images are grainy and thin, with an ascetic denial of visual contrast. The film begins with static lights at night—for again the camera does not move— and flares toward whiteness. The image seems to wait, while a house light or a streetlamp sits on the depthless surface of the screen, for single-frame occurrences of summer lightning. With these flashes the silhouettes of trees, house, and clouds appear. At times only a portion of the screen is dimly lit by the lightning, and at other times the whole screen flashes. The duration of the illuminations varies from one to five frames toward the middle of the film, and when the lightning explosion extends beyond the single frame, there is always a slight variation in each of the frames in which it occurs.

The change of streetlamps, car light, or house lights prefigures each new flash and makes the viewer expectant. A flare introduces a scene of suburban houses in the quivering daylight of a gray sky. Three slow tones are heard on the soundtrack, which had previously been silent. When the film reverts to night, the lightning flashes are edited to follow one another more quickly than in the first section. A final change to daylight accompanies the sound of fast panting.

In a previously unpublished interview with the author, Brakhage describes his thematic and formal concerns in making this film:

> *Fire of Waters*, as its title suggests, is inspired by a little postcard that Robert Kelly sent me when we were searching into the concerns of Being, Matter and Subject Matter, and Source. He sent a card which cut through all my German windiness about it. It said, "The truth of the matter is this, that man lives in a fire of waters and will live eternally in the first taste." That haunted me. First I couldn't make any sense out of it at all, other than that "fire of waters" would refer to cells, in that the body is mostly water and is firing constantly to keep itself going.
>
> That summer we were living at that abandoned theater. I had got a lot of lightning and streetlights on black-and-white film. I took a lot of daytime shots of the houses that surrounded us. There seemed to be an awful foreboding about that kind of neighborhood in which we were then living, which was a typical suburban neighborhood. I remember referring to it and saying "These houses look like inverted bomb craters." I had a sense of imminent disaster which I always seem to get more mysteriously and in a more sinister way in an American suburban area than I do even in New York City.
>
> When I finally came to edit that, which was just before Christmas '64, I was inspired by Kelly's card and I had the sense that the opening shot would come out of pure white leader and then be a streetlight blinking. The blink of the streetlight would set a rhythm which then I could repeat in flashes of both other streetlights and of lightning flashes, and that blink would be source for the whole rhythm structure of the film. I wanted to see how far I could depart from that rhythm exactly and still retain that rhythm as source.
>
> Then, as the whole concept deepened, I showed the actual source of those night house lights and house shadows by showing the daylight scenes of them. Then I could throw it back into the night with a build-up of the night structure, and then finally end with that one single house that dominated most of my concerns, directly across the street from us.
>
> Then I felt the need for sound. For years I had imposed the discipline on myself that if ever a single sound was needed anywhere on a track to go with an image I would put that sound in even if no other sound was needed in the whole film. That permitted me when I felt the need of slowed-down bird sounds (that is a bird's cry slowed down so that it became like a western musical instrument), to put it in where I felt it was needed. Then that caused me to feel the need of a sound of wind rising to a certain pitch at the very beginning. At the end then the speeded-up sound of Jane giving birth to Myrenna occurs on two levels in the last shot of the house. It definitely sounds like a dog in somebody's backyard in the drama sense of that scene, yelping in pain. It does actually carry the sense of a terror beyond that. That's how the sound come into it and balanced out.[15]

Brakhage had made one other sound film since *Anticipation of the Night. Blue Moses* (1962) uses strategies from the lyrical film without itself being a meditation firmly postulated in the eye of the film-maker. For this one time in his career he employed synchronous speech. The existence of this film within Brakhage's filmography is very curious; there is nothing else like it in his work. It explicitly postulates an epistemological principle: that there can be no cinematic image without a film-maker to take it and that the presence, or even the existence, of the film-maker transforms what he films. Formally, *Blue Moses* anticipates the participatory film that calls upon or addresses itself directly to the audience, a form that emerged in the early 1970s on the tail of the structural film. We have encountered its embryonic manifestation already in Anger's *Invocation of My Demon Brother*.

The single actor of *Blue Moses* hollers to the audience when he first appears from his cave. He is the merchant of metaphysical fear Melville knew as "The Lightning Rod Man." He tries to scare us by proposing to quiet our fears: "Don't be afraid. We're not alone. There's the cameraman ... or was ... once." Then in an elliptical way he informs us of what we should be afraid of. He points to mysterious tracks, in a desolate place, left by a man who must have been running. That narrative hint, recurring throughout the film, hovers on the edge of parody of the devices used in novels and films to draw us into illusionism and suspense. In a fugal structure of leap-frogging episodes interrupted by dissolves to the same actor in different costumes, Brakhage lets his actor assume different guises from the history of acting (a classical Greek mask is painted on his face, in robes he strikes "Shakespearean" postures), and his language, usually that of the confidence man, veers to sing-song and melodrama.

The leap-frogging counterpoint of scenes at the beginning of the film is recapitulated in superimposition, both of picture and sound, near the end. The actor pulls off a false beard and, in a Pirandelloistic cliché, reveals himself to the audience. "Look," he says, "this is ridiculous. I'm an actor. You see what I mean? ... You're my audience, my captive audience. I'm your entertainment, your player. This whole film is about us." In the course of the speech, the superimposition becomes footage from earlier in the film, projected over his chest. When he turns his back to the projector, the film images cease, and he is framed in a white rectangle of the projector operating without film.

In the middle of his speech in front of the interior film screen he repeats his consolation: "But don't be afraid. There's a film-maker behind *every scene*, in back of every word I speak, behind you, too, so to speak." When the camera suddenly swings around into the darkness, glimpsing the hand signals of the director, he adds, as if a spectator had turned his head to the projection booth: "No. Don't turn around. It's useless." It is at this point that he himself turns toward his screen and the images change to pure white light on his body.

Blue Moses ends as it began with a series of dissolves of the protagonist returning to his cave and gesturing ceremonially. In its form and substance *Blue Moses* attacks the dramatic film as an untenable convention. Brakhage temporarily accepts the principles of the realists of film theory who argue that cinema arises from the interaction of the artist with exterior reality in front of the camera. But he rebuts them with a demonstration of how fragile their sense of exterior reality is. At one point the actor of *Blue Moses* gestures to the sun and cries, "an eclipse," at which point an obvious, messy splice throws the image into blackness, and he adds, "manufactured, but not yet patented, for your pleasure." *Blue Moses* is a negative polemic, an attack on the modified Realism of the European cinema of the early sixties (Godard, Resnais, Fellini, Antonioni, etc.). In its place he proposed the investigation of the consciousness confronting (and constructing) external nature in the form of the lyrical film. ...

■ ■ ■

Questions and projects

1. Is it possible to give stricter definition of Sitney's use of the word "lyrical" as it applies to film? Might it involve questions of poetic "voice," "fragmented form," or "private communication"? Demonstrate one or more of these other defining features of lyric form in a poem, and then show how it transfers (or doesn't transfer) to a Brakhage film or to one by another experimental filmmaker (such as Kenneth Anger, Maya Deren, or others).

2. Are there other poetic traditions, besides the Romantic one (which occurred in the early nineteenth century) that relate to the cinema? The ballad tradition? Concrete poetry? Does a film like Ingmar Bergman's *The Seventh Seal* resemble certain older poetic forms? Compare a particular film with a poem or poetic form that it seems to resemble or approximate in style or perspective.

Notes

...

8   Harold Bloom, "The Internalization of the Quest-Romance," *Romanticism and Consciousness*, ed. Harold Bloom (New York: Norton, 1977) p. 6.

9   Stan Brakhage *Metaphors on Vision* in *Film Culture* 30 (Autumn 1963), p. 26.

10 *Ibid.*, p. 19.

11 *Ibid.*, pp. 9-10.

12 *Ibid.*, p. 14.

13 *Ibid.*, p. 80.

14 *Ibid.*, p. 77.

15 An unpublished interview with the author in the spring of 1965. A transcript is in the library of the Anthology Film Archives.

...

Chapter 27

Timothy Corrigan

THE ESSAY FILM
On thoughts occasioned by ... Michel de Montaigne and Chris Marker

ONE OF THE MOST OVERLOOKED RELATIONS in the exchanges between literature and film, the essay film has usually been described as a variation on documentary cinema, frequently distinguished by the use of a personal voice or perspective within that documentary practice. A professor of Cinema Studies at the University of Pennsylvania, Corrigan locates the essay film within a long literary tradition that extends back to the essays of Michel de Montaigne and forward through the twentieth-century photo essays of Chris Marker and others and the literary essays of Virginia Woolf and James Baldwin.

■ ■ ■

THE ESSAY FILM: ON THOUGHTS OCCASIONED BY ... MICHEL DE MONTAIGNE AND CHRIS MARKER
TIMOTHY CORRIGAN

From *The Essay Film: From Montaigne, After Marker*, New York: Oxford University Press, 2011, pp 13–15, 16–23, 30–49.

From its literary origins to its cinematic revisions, the essayistic describes the many layered activities of a personal point of view as a public experience. Anticipated in earlier memoirs, sermons, and chronicles, the most recognizable origin of the essay is the work of Michel de Montaigne (1533–1592), whose reflections on his daily life and thoughts appear, significantly, in the French vernacular of the streets rather than the Latinate discourse of the academy. With the term "essays" emphasizing their provisional and explorative nature as "attempts," "tries," or "tests," Montaigne's writings are views of, comments on, and judgments of his faltering memory, kidney stones, love, friendship, sex in marriage, lying, a "monstrous childe," and a plethora of other common and uncommon questions picked almost haphazardly from a mind observing the world passing before and through him. Imagined, to some extent, as an active intellectual exchange with his deceased friend Étienne de La Boétie, these essays not only describe a bond between a personal life and the surrounding events of that life in sixteenth-century France but, in the revision after revision that characterize these essays (1580, 1588, 1595), they testify not only to the constant changes and adjustments of the recording eyes and mind as they defer to experience but also to the transformation of the essayistic self as part of that process.

Since Montaigne, the essay has appeared in numerous permutations, inhabiting virtually every discourse and material expression available. Most often, the essayistic is associated with the literary essays whose historical prominence extends from Montaigne through Joseph Addison and Richard Steel in the eighteenth century and to contemporary writers like James Baldwin, Susan Sontag, Jorge Louis Borges, and Umberto Eco. From its literary foundation, the essay spreads through the nineteenth century in less obvious practices such as drawings and sketches, and even occasionally in musical forms such as Samuel Barber's "Essay for Orchestra." In the twentieth and twenty-first centuries, the essayistic has increasingly taken the shape of photo essays, essay films, and the electronic essays that permeate the Internet as blogs and other exchanges within a public electronic circuitry.

Aldous Huxley (2002: 330) has described the essay as moving between three poles:

> the essay is a literary device for saying almost everything about almost anything. ... Essays belong to a literary species whose extreme variability can be studied most effectively within a three-poled frame of reference. There is the pole of the personal and the autobiographical; there is the pole of the objective, the factual, the concrete-particular; and there is the pole of the abstract-universal. Most essayists are at home and at their best in the neighborhood of only one of the essay's three poles, or at the most only in the neighborhood of two of them. There are the predominantly personal essayists, who write fragments of reflective autobiography and who look at the world through the keyhole of anecdote and description. There are the predominantly objective essayists who do not speak directly of themselves, but turn their attention outward to some literary or scientific or political theme. ... The most richly satisfying essays are those which make the best not of one, not of two, but of all the three worlds in which it is possible for the essay to exist.

To map and distinguish the essay in its evolution from Montaigne to the essay film, I employ a variation on Huxley's three poles as not separable kinds of essays but as, in the best essays, interactive and intersecting registers. While one or the other may be more discernible in any given essay, my three variations on Huxley's versions of the essayistic describe the intersecting activity of personal expression, public experience, and the process of thinking. Other definitions and models of the essay tend to emphasize one or the other of these features as, for instance, the role of a personal voice or the search for documentary authenticity.[1] For me, however, the variable ratio and interactivity of these three dimensions creates a defining representational shape that emerges out of the literary heritage of the essay and extends and reformulates itself in the second half of the twentieth century as the essay film. If part of the power of the essayistic has been its ability to absorb and mobilize other literary and artistic practices, such as narrative or photographic practices, film has become, since the 1940s, one of its richest terrains.

While no single definition of the essayistic will probably ever be sufficiently malleable for its many variations, following this framework as it emerges from its literary foundation (and later adapted to the photographic essay) clarifies and formulates, I believe, the distinctive terms of the essay film. Across this conceptual history, the essayistic stretches and balances itself between abstracted and exaggerated representation of the self (in language and image) and a shifting experiential world encountered and acquired through the discourse of thinking out loud. If Montaigne introduces the literary beginnings of this practice, tracing this history and its emerging priorities leads almost climatically, for André Bazin and others, to Chris Marker's 1958 essay film *Letter from Siberia* and, subsequently, Richard Roud's prescient characterization of Marker as "1 to 1.33 Montaigne" (1962–63: 27).[2]

From Montaigne to Marker, the history of the essay offers a lengthy list of examples of a personal, subjective, or performative voice and vision as the definitive feature of the essayistic. Best exemplified by the "familiar essay" of nineteenth-century writers like Charles Lamb or Ralph Waldo Emerson, this connection between the essay and personal expression identifies, however, a much more complicated, dynamic, and often subversive position than is often acknowledged in the assumption that essays cohere around a singular self.[3] The history of the essay demonstrates, in fact, that the essayistic is most interesting not so much in how it privileges personal expression and subjectivity but rather in how it troubles and complicates that very notion of *expressivity* and its relation to *experience*, that second cornerstone of the essayistic. If both verbal and visual expression commonly suggest the articulation or projection of an interior self into an exterior world, essayistic expressivity describes, more exactly I think, a subjection of an instrumental or expressive self to a public domain as a form of experience that continually tests and undoes the limits and capacities of that self through that experience. At the intersection of these two planes, we find in the best of essays the difficult, often highly complex—and sometimes the seemingly impossible—figure of the self or subjectivity *thinking* in and through a public domain, in all its historical, social, and cultural particulars. Essayistic expression (in writing, in film, or in any of its other modes) thus demands both loss of self through that expression and the rethinking and remaking of the self as essayistic expression.

Montaigne's renowned combination of stoicism, skepticism, and Epicureanism consequently plays itself out across movement from a self-expression undoing itself in the process of thinking through the dynamics of the world "as perennial movement" ("Of Repentance" Montaigne (1948) 313). Aiming to be "an authority on myself" (822) and studying "myself more than any other subject" (821) Montaigne's motto 'que-sais-je?' ('what do I know?') calls into question the security of its own authority. It is one of many succinct phrases in his work that describes a principal drive in the writings as an investigation into the terms of one's self and how an individual might discover a certain knowledge of the world through its unsystematic experience of the world. Throughout this work, however, this drive continually rattles the terms of its own articulation, suggesting a self whose thinking through experience becomes a measure of the limits of its own capacities. While freely celebrating thinking about all details of his life, he acknowledges that "I speak freely of all things, even those which exceed my capacity" ("Of Books" 298).

In his monumental essay "Of Experience," Montaigne affirms "human ignorance" as "the most certain fact in the school of the world" (419/824) yet insists again and again on his goal to be "intellectually sensual, sensually intellectual" (433). Since "our life is nothing but movement," essayistic expression becomes that materialized place for a provisional self and its thoughts, free of method and authority: "for lack of a natural memory I make one of paper" (837), he quips, claiming that "all the fricassee that I am scribbling here ... record the essays of my life ... it's instruction in reverse ... not corrupted by art or theorizing" (826). Unlike systematic or formulaic approaches to knowledge, he learns "from experience, without any system, present my ideas in a general way, and tentatively" (824). While Francis Bacon's more social, more advisory, and more structured essays (published in 1597, 1612, 1625) serve as a parallel beginning of the modern essay, Montaigne's shifting and layered assertions and denials of passing thoughts on the world become the acknowledged background and touchstone for many of the first essay films, as Roud explicitly reminds us in his description of Marker as "a kind of one man total cinema ... a 1 to 1:33 Montaigne" (Roud 1962–63: 27).

On the foundation of Montaigne, essay writing accelerates and broadens considerably in the eighteenth and early nineteenth centuries when it begins to take a more distinctive shape as a public dialogue between a self and a visible world, often urban and sometimes natural. What I find most suggestive here about these historical reformulations of the essayistic—particularly as they help ground and anticipate the essay film—is precisely *not* the usual understanding of them as the coherently personalized expression of an authorized subjectivity, typically associated with some version of the romantic or modern ego. Rather these essays are most indicative of the form when they act out the subjection of that self within or before a natural or, as with the essays of Charles Lamb, Virginia Woolf, and Roland Barthes, a public urban space, dispersing or transforming that self within that space and, quite often and more exactly, its visibility.[4] In Woolf's essay "Street Haunting" (1927), for instance, London becomes a panoramic of sights, where the "eye is sportive and generous; it creates; it adorns; it enhances" (260), and, instead of the coherency of seeing oneself as "one thing only," the self becomes a reflection of the visual plenitude of a modern city, "streaked, variegated, all of a mixture" (261), a self "tethered not to a single mind," but a self that puts "on briefly for a few minutes the bodies and mind of others" (265). Just as essayists from Thomas De Quincey to Walter Pater created a certain poetic urgency in a prose aimed at describing the fleeting images of the world around them, Woolf's essayistic self in "Street Haunting" finds her quest for an instrument of self-expression, specifically a pencil, ecstatically waylaid by the a "velocity and abundance" (263) of the London streets.[5]

While many contemporary essays have continued this destabilizing encounter between the visual world and its verbal assessment, what becomes more pronounced and anticipatory of many essay films is a foregrounded linguistic drama. From explicit cases like William Gass's *On Being Blue* or any of Jorge Luis Borges's essays to the more naturalized tactics of writers like James Baldwin, this linguistic drama emphasizes the limitations of language as the vehicle for thinking a self in a public world and the necessity of reinventing that language to compensate for its public inadequacies. In Baldwin's "Stranger in the Village," the "sight" of an African American's visit by the local villagers in a small Swiss town produces Baldwin's complex inquiry into American racial history and the struggle to "establish an identity" (1998: 127). Throughout this essay and many others, including his long reflection on the Hollywood film industry, "The Devil Finds Work," Baldwin develops a rhetorical stance searching for new words that could sufficiently act as an interface between his personal experience and the images of the world that he sees and that see him. Or, as he puts it in 1999 "I will not take any one's words for my experience" ("I'll Make Me a World"). More explicitly and extremely, German writer Christa Wolf anticipates the tension and dialectic that underpins many essay films when she claims "Prose should strive to be unfilmable" (1999: 33).

If the essay film inherits many of the epistemological and structural distinctions of the literary essay especially as it plays itself out in a dialogue and tension between the verbal and the visual, a key transitional practice linking these two embodiments of the essayistic is the photo essay. The photo essay has taken many shapes, translating essayistic concerns with expression, experience, and thought into a variety of formal configurations of photographic images. Part scientific investigation, part educational sermon, part ethnographic tour, Jacob Riis's 1890 *How the Other Half Lives* figures prominently as an early transitional essay between the verbal and the visual. Here Riis investigates New York tenements in the 1880s as a public place defined as "the destroyer of individuality and character" (1996: 222). The novelty and power of this work spring directly from its use of shocking photographs of the deplorable living conditions to counterpoint the often melodramatic voice of the commentary.[6] If the 1930s are the heyday of the photo essay, during this period the dialogic tension between verbal text and photographic image becomes most pronounced, not coincidentally, as a transitional period that would lead to the first discussions and practices of the essay film in the 1940s. This verbal-visual dialectic becomes most famously seen in Agee and Evan's 1939 essayistic collaboration *Let Us Now Praise Famous Men* where the literary privileging of the verbal in tension with the pressure of the visual is reversed as a fundamental doubt about the adequacy of a language that can capture the public and concrete world of images: "If I could do it," Agee writes, "I'd do no writing at all here. It would be photographs; the rest would be fragments of cloth, bits of cotton, lumps of earth, records of speech, pieces of wood and iron, phials of odor, plates of food and of excrement" (1939: 13).

As a supplement for the subjective voice of the essayistic, the photo essay would frequently rely on a verbal or literary text to dramatize and concretize a shifting subjective perspective and its unstable relationship with the photographic images it counterpoints. In other cases, the structural formulation of the photo essay, as the linkage of separate photographs whose implied relationship appears in the implicit gaps or "unsutured" interstices between those images, becomes itself analogous to the shifting and aleatory voice or perspective of the literary essay as it attempts, provisionally, to articulate or interpolate itself within the public spaces and experiences being represented. In 1937, Henry Luce, founder of *Life* magazine, suggests, in his "The Camera as Essayist," just this ability of the image to mimic or usurp the verbal subjectivity of the literary essay when he describes the photo essay as part of a historical evolution that links practices from the seventeenth century to Riis and the heyday of the photo essay in the 1930s. Here construction of images can itself assimilate the role and language of the essayistic commentator since the camera "is not merely a reporter. It can also be a commentator. It can comment as it reports. It can interpret as it presents. It can picture the world as a seventeenth-century essayist or a twentieth-century columnist would picture it. A photographer has his style as an essayist has his" (Willumson 1992: 16). Whether with explicit or implicit voice or text, the essayistic tension between a verbal register and a visual order that resists and troubles the verbal thus creates, in W. J. T. Mitchell's words (1994: 289), "dialectic of exchange and resistance between photography and language," making it "possible (and sometimes impossible) to 'read' the pictures, or to 'see' the text illustrated in them." Contrasting Christa Wolf's unfilmable essayistic literary voice then, Alexander Kluge would later extend this logic when he remakes the tradition of the photo essay as the contemporary essay films in which, like his *Blind Director* (1985), "Language in film may be blind" (1999: 238).

Against this historical background, the essayistic has become increasingly the object of theoretical and philosophical reflections and self-reflections, starting especially in the early twentieth century. Well before this point, many essayists have themselves reflected on the practice as a particular kind of writing, yet, during the twentieth century attention to the essay as a unique representational strategy flourishes as a distinctive aesthetic and philosophical question, perhaps in anticipation of Jean-François Lyotard's provocative claim that the essay has become the quintessential form of postmodern thought in the latter half of the twentieth century (1984: 81).

Anticipating key dimensions and strategies of the essay film, several celebrated positions are especially important to theorizing its heritage, its status as a form of knowledge, and its subversion of aesthetic unity. Published in 1910, Georg Lukács's "On the Nature and Form of the Essay" is one of the earliest and most celebrated accounts of the essay in terms of a dialogic idealism that envisions essayistic experience as "an event of the soul" (7). For Lukács, successful essays are "a conceptual reordering of life" (1), "intellectual poems" (18) that either address "life problems" (3) or recreate that vitality as a critical engagement that becomes itself a work of art. Even within this framework, Lukács identifies, however, the essayistic experience as an active "questioning" that asserts the primacy of a subjective "standpoint" (15) and works to discover through that questioning the "idea" of a "life-sense" (15). In this mobile activity, the essayist becomes "conscious of his own self, must find himself and build something out of himself" (15) and so becomes extended through the conceptual revelations of this dialogue with real or aesthetic experience. Pinpointing what will become a central dialogic structure in essay films, Lukács sees Plato as "the greatest essayist who ever lived" (13) and "Socrates is the typical life for the essay" since Socrates "always lived in the ultimate questions ... to comprehend the nature of longing and to capture it in concepts" (13–14). All essays for Lukács are "thoughts occasioned by" (15), and lead to his famously pronounced motto of a self suspended in the experience of thinking through the core of life: "The essay is a judgement, but the essential, the value-determining thing about it is not the verdict (as is the case with system) but the process of judging" (18).

Contrasting Lukács's focus on the essay's Platonic heritage, mid-century discussions of the essay in Germany and Austria evolve around questions of the essay's unique epistemological resources. Significantly, the essay now begins to distinguish itself not as an aesthetic or idealistic experience but as an intellectual activity and form of knowledge that resists the lure of idealism defined primarily as an aesthetic experience. In the Robert Musil's monumental 1930 essayistic novel *The Man Without Qualities*, the essay comes to refigure thought as an experiential engagement with the world: it "explores a thing from many sides without wholly encompassing it—for a thing wholly encompassed suddenly loses its scope and melts down to a concept. ... an essay is ... the unique and unalterable form assumed by a man's inner life in a decisive thought. Nothing is more foreign to it than the irresponsible and half-baked quality of thought known as subjectivism" (1995: 270, 273). In 1947, Max Bense refines the argument in postwar terms that would be especially important to film by noting that "The essayist is a combiner, a tireless producer of configurations around a specific object. ... Configuration is an epistemological arrangement which cannot be achieved through axiomatic deduction, but only through a literary *ars combinatoria*, in which imagination replaces strict knowledge" (1947: 422). Like the configuration of fragments in a kaleidoscope or cinematic montage, the essay offers, for Bense, a creative rearrangement and play "of idea and image" (423–424), comparable to Benjamin's "constellations" of knowledge in *The Origin of German Tragic Drama* where "Ideas are to objects as constellations are to stars" (1977: 34).

Especially as it describes the conceptual and formal activities of the essayist, T. W. Adorno's "The Essay as Form" offers one of the most resonant models of the essay as it looks forward to the essay film. Here Adorno argues that the distinguishing strength of the essay is its ability to subvert systemic thought, totalities of truth, and "the jargon of authenticity" (1991: 7), through a "methodically unmethodical" (13) whereby the essay's "innermost formal law is heresy" (23). Fragmentary and "non-creative," the essay represents "reciprocal interaction of concepts in the process of intellectual experience" (13), and the essayistic subject becomes a "thinker" who "makes himself into an arena for intellectual experience" (13). Configured as "force fields" (13), essays celebrate "the consciousness of nonidentity" and the emancipation from the compulsion of identity (17), while simultaneously exploring a subjective activity that realizes "Nothing can be interpreted out of something that is not interpreted into it at the same time" (4). "The essay is concerned with what is blind in its objects," according to Adorno. It wants "to use concepts to pry open the aspects that cannot be accommodated by concepts, the aspect that reveals, through the contradictions in which concepts become entangled, that the net of their objectivity is merely subjective arrangement. It wants to polarize the opaque element and release the latent forces in it" (23). Coincidentally and appropriately, Adorno's essay appears the same year, 1958, as Chris Marker's *Letter from Siberia* and Bazin's description of that film as an essay film.

From the numerous literary and philosophical frameworks that precede it, a variety of definitions and descriptions of the essay film have circulated in recent years, including the important work of Nora Alter, Michael Renov and Laura Rascaroli. Many of these positions emphasize the role of the subjective voice or perspective in these films; some the mixing and matching of styles, genres, and aesthetic materials; and still others, a documentary heritage refashioned through a contemporary reflexivity on the epistemological assumptions of that heritage. Building on these and extending them in light of the history and theory of the literary essay, I return to my own formulation of the essay film as 1) a testing of expressive subjectivity through 2) experiential encounters in a public arena, 3) the product of which becomes the figuration of thinking or thought as a cinematic address and a spectatorial response. I will briefly unpack and describe the three parts of this definition.

An expressive subjectivity, commonly seen in the voice and or actual presence of the filmmaker or a surrogate, has become one of the most recognizable signs of the essay film, sometimes quite visible in the film, sometimes not. Just as the first-person presence of the literary essay often springs from a personal voice and perspective, so essay films characteristically highlight a real or fictional persona whose quests and questionings shape and direct the film in lieu of a traditional narrative and frequently complicate the documentary look of the film with the presence of a pronounced subjectivity or enunciating position. When lacking a clearly visible subjective voice or personal organizing presence, this act of enunciation can be signaled in various formal or technical ways, including editing and other representational distortions of the image.[7] The presence and activity of this subjectivity thus appears in many permutations: from Ross McElwee's self-dramatizations in *Sherman's March* (1986) and *Bright Leaves* to Kluge's intertitles in *The Patriot* (1979) to the restrained ironic banter of Patrick Keiller's Robinson and his interlocutor in *Robinson in Space* (1997). If Michael Moore's *Roger and Me* (1989) makes unmistakable the centrality of Moore as the subject of the film, *Waltz with Bashir* (2008) partially effaces and diffuses that subjective expression through animation, while films such as Chantal Akerman's *News from Home* (1977) obliquely repositions that enunciator through letters read by a mother and strict imagistic framings. Very often, moreover, essays and essay films anticipate these shifting enunciators with topics and subjects other than themselves who are analogously fragmented and unstable, such as Errol Morris's Fred Leuchter in *Mr. Death* (1999) or Jean-Luc Godard's housewife/prostitute/actress Juliette Janson /Marina Vlady in *2 or 3 Things I Know About Her* (1967) and typically work to destabilize the subject position of its reception through a reader or spectator, as in Derek Jarman's *Blue* (1993) or Lars Von Trier's *The Five Obstructions* (2003).

More than simply foregrounding an organizing subject on these three levels, essayistic practices have been most innovative and complex, I believe, in how they have troubled and complicated that subjectivity and their relation to public experience, that other cornerstone of the essay. If both verbal and visual expression can commonly suggest the articulation or projection of an interior self into an exterior world, essayistic expressivity describes a subjection of an instrumental or expressive self to a public domain as a form of experience that continually tests the limits and capacities of that self within the world, a questioning and rethinking that partly explains perhaps that attraction of the essay for politically, sexually, and racially marginalized persons. By essayistic subjectivity then—in contradistinction to many definitions of the essay and essay film—I refer not simply to the emplacement or positioning of an individual consciousness before and in experience but to an active and assertive consciousness that tests, undoes, or recreates itself through experience, including the experiences of memory, argument, active desire, and reflective thinking. In these cases a subject becomes the product of changing experiential expressions rather than simply the producer of expression. Following Robert Musil's claim "Nothing is more foreign to [essayism] than the irresponsible and half-baked quality of thought known as subjectivism" (1995: 273),

Walter Benjamin was hyperbolic but correct in identifying the radical potential of the essay as an expression made entirely of quotes (Lopate 246), thus implying a form of subjective expression that inhabits and reformulates itself constantly as the expressions of another or an other. In this context, improvisation, as a commonly recognized essayistic figure, refers to a primary structure in which subjectivity tries out different positions within the world. Fittingly Godard's essay *2 or 3 Things I Know About Her* begins exactly on this note with actress Marina Vlady/character Juliette telling the camera that in this film she will "speak as though quoting the truth," and in his *Notre Musique* an early commentator crystallizes the essayist subject as "Now 'I' is someone else."

The essay and essayistic subjectivity thus fundamentally distinguish themselves as a public experience, that is, as a form of expression and representation that necessarily relinquishes itself to events, actions, and objects outside the authority of those expressions and representations. Personal experience certainly encompasses a vast range of mental, social, and physical activities, but my contention is that the essayistic foregrounds the public nature of that experience even when characterized as personal (from privately public reflections on past events and relationships to imaginative encounters with historical places). Amidst the vast amount of debate and description of what defines a "public" or public sphere, two assumptions are important here: public life as multiple and changing domains of various registers and as a place of contestation through experience. Defining a public sphere often starts with Jürgen Habermas, who locates its modern formation in the eighteenth century when literary essays reached a heyday,[8] but even more suggestive for discussions of the essayistic is Hannah Arendt's description of the public as "the world" which, "like every in-between, relates and separates men at the same time" (1958: 52). Later film essayist Alexander Kluge and Oscar Negt offer an alternative public sphere precisely filtered through the concept of experience. Negt and Kluge's remaking of this public sphere as competing positions draws attention to the literary terms of Habermas's model and proposes alternative perspectives born more from a variegated "social horizon of experience" than from a cultural hegemony, more from below than from above. Experience suggests, to put it succinctly, the interface between different individuals and social groups, involving the many dimensions along that interface (the sensual, the emotional, the ideological, the local, the global, and so on). Or, in Michael Warner's characterization, in *Publics and Counterpublics*, public experience occurs as "scenes of self-activity of historical rather than timeless belonging, and of active participation rather than ascriptive belonging" (2002: 89). Built on the work of Kluge and Negt, Miriam Hansen has summed it up this way: "experience is that which mediates individual perception with social meaning, conscious with unconscious processes, loss of self with self-reflexivity; experience as the capacity to see connections and relations … ; experience as the matrix of conflicting temporalities, of memory and hope, including the historical loss of these dimensions" (1991: 12–13).

In essay films, subjective experience as a public activity accordingly takes a myriad of off-centered directions: for instance, shaped around private and public individuals (*Surname Viet: Given Name Nam*, *Mr. Death: The Rise and Fall of Fred A. Leuchter, Jr.*, *Blue*), urban, nationalistic, or natural geographies (*News from Home*, *Robinson in Space*, *Grizzly Man*), individual, local, and historical chronologies (*Lost, Lost, Lost*, *Dear Diary*, *Elephant*), political crises and institutions (*Respite*, *Waltz with Bashir*, *States of Unbelonging*), and the place and importance of art and aesthetics in social life (*Hypothesis of the Stolen Painting*, *The Five Obstructions*, *Close-Up*)—each more largely about subjectivities, public spaces, temporal vectors, social values, and aesthetic judgments. As many of these films indicate, moreover, the representation of modern experience in the essay film often becomes culturally associated with "risk" and "doubt," moving within and through a cultural "intermediary zone" of contested territories. That, as we shall see, the watershed years of the essay film are 1940–1945, also reminds us that failure, crisis, and trauma often become the experiential base of the essayistic.

That, as many of the examples in the following chapters demonstrate, the most charged essay films regularly return to the experience of the colonial and post-colonial historically broadens and builds on those crises as the often dangerous and fragile base of the essayistic.

This encounter between an open and protean self and social experience produces most significantly the activity essayistic thinking as the third distinguishing feature of the essay and essay film, what Montaigne early on identified as the testing of ideas. Both subjectivity and experience are of course the products of discourse, and, rather than stabilize and harmonize the encounter between these two discourses, the essayistic creates clashes and gaps in each and across their meeting with each other as a place that elicits, if not demands, thought. The essential form of this essayistic encounter, as Graham Good has characterized it, "aims ... to preserve something of the *process* of thinking" (1998: 20). The essay film, in Godards' words, is "a form that thinks" (1998: 54–57), or, according to Phillip Lopate, the essay film "tracks a person's thoughts . ... An essay is a search to find out what one thinks about something" (1996: 244).[9]

Large, speculative, impressionistic, and determined arguments about the way movies think or might think are as varied and old as film history itself. Most famously, Gilles Deleuze has become the icon of a thinking cinema, mainly through his extended reflections in *Cinema 2*. While the formidable complexity and reach of Deleuze's positions has been widely analyzed and debated, what interests me here is the practical and specific insistence that film can be understood as a dynamic forum and framework that produces ideas and a process of thinking that extends subjectivity through an outside world. "Thinking belongs to the outside," according to Deleuze (1989: 93), or, as he suggests in other terms about film specifically, cinematic thinking becomes a way of restoring our belief in the world (181–182): "The [modern] cinema must film, not the world, but belief in the world" (172). If modern cinema is widely and intricately implicated in the essayistic, Deleuze's motto would work especially for the essay film: "'Give me a brain' would be the other figure of modern cinema. This is an intellectual cinema, as distinct from a physical cinema" (204).

Essayistic thinking thus becomes a conceptual, figural, phenomenological, or representational remaking of a self as it encounters, tests, and experiences some version of the real as a public "elsewhere." Essayistic thought becomes the exteriorization of personal expression, determined and circumscribed by an always varying kind, quality, and number of material contexts in which to think is to multiply ourselves.

Rather than eliciting the bond of identification or activity of cognition, essay films ask viewers to *experience* the world in the full intellectual and phenomenological sense of that word. The viewing subject partially inhabits the unstable subject position foregrounded in the film itself (as if a home movie) and the discovery of new ideas and worlds (as if a documentary), and not only does that subject become made and remade through the pressure of the film's resistant reality but the lack of a single, dominant, or sometimes even coherent discourse disperses that viewing subject through its pastiche of forms, mix and subversion of generic structures, and cannibalization of narrative teleologies or lyrical voices. Essayistic thinking becomes the necessary recasting of subjective experience in the shifts and interstices that define experience itself.

For many viewers and scholars, Chris Marker's films exemplify the essay film. Not only do his films describe a central thread in the emergence of this practice in the 1940s and 1950s, but placed in the context of Marker's wide and varied efforts across different fields and disciplines, his work becomes a rich demonstration of how this cinematic practice inherits and remakes earlier essayistic traditions in the literary essay and photo essay, as well as anticipating new traditions. Marker is one of the most relentless and innovative essayists working in film and new media, with his 1982 *Sunless* considered one of the landmarks of modern cinema. It is, however, at the early crossroads of the photo essay and the essay film where one finds most visibly his complex engagement with the possibilities of creating space and time for thought between the images of a moving world, here between his 1959 photo essay entitled *Koreans* and his 1958 essay film *Letter from Siberia*. As Chris Marker demonstrates in his work just after the war, the photo essay would provide a transitional paradigm that allowed film to discover its capacity to explore the conceptual and intellectual spaces between images.

Best known for his 1962 film *La Jetée* (*The Jetty*), his futuristic "photo-roman" of still images, and the 1982 *San soleil* (*Sunless*), his extraordinary essay film about a cameraman traveling the globe between "the two extreme poles of survival," Marker has created a multi-media body of work that ranges through novels, literary criticism, museum installations, and the CD-ROM *Immemory* (1998). As different as his subjects and media practices are, however, his concerns have remained remarkably consistent: memory, loss, history, human community, and how our fragile subjectivity can acknowledge, represent, surrender, and survive these experiences. Across the continual undoing and redoing of expression in different forms and places, Marker's work becomes a concomitantly rigorous, witty, and poignant effort to document the human experience as a struggle to understand itself in an increasingly smaller, fragmented, and accelerated global space. If the literary appears as a consistent mode within his early experiments with expression (including a 1949 novel, *The Forthright Spirit*), in 1952 Marker recognizes a new cultural dominant in the public domain. Concluding a book-length literary essay on Jean Giradoux, he acknowledges that now it is the technological image and specifically the cinema that will recapture the "miracle of a world in which everything is at once absolutely familiar and completely strange" (1952: 43).

At this personal crossroads of the literary and the cinematic, for Marker the photo essay becomes a critical articulation. Just after the completion of his second short film, the 1953 *Les Statues meurent aussi* (co-directed with Alain Resnais), he edits a series of photo essays for Éditions du Seuil, produced from 1954 to 1958, an experience that lays the groundwork for his own photo essays. In her excellent book *Chris Marker: Memories of the Future* (2005), Catherine Lupton describes this first venture into the photo essay in a way that suggests the larger concerns that would permeate all of Marker's work:

> A potent sense of the prospective disorientation of world travel informs Marker's announcement of the Petite Planete series, which appeared in the Éditions du Seuil house magazine 27 Rue Jacob. He pinpoints a growing sense that the post-war world has come within reach as never before, but that as a subjective experience this prospect of increased access seems confusing and elusive: "we see the world escape us at the same time as we become aware of our links with it". To combat this disorientation, Seuil is launching a series of books that, to adapt one of Marker's metaphors, are intended to be user manuals for life on a small planet. He proposes that each volume is "not a guidebook, not a history, not a propaganda brochure, not a traveller's impressions", but is intended to be like a conversation with an intelligent and cultivated person who is well-informed about the country in question. (44)

Marker would bring his own distinctive voice to that conversation with his 1959 photo essay entitled *Coréennes* (*Koreans*), an essay fittingly published as the only volume in Éditions du Seuil's "Court métrage" ("short film") series.[10]

Koreans is a meditative travel essay about extremes and oppositions but mostly about lists and inventories—and the spaces made visible by all these organizations. Shadowing the images and text are the cold war politics dividing North and South Korea,[11] yet oppositions such as this are less central than the categorical abundance found in the experience and fabric of everyday Korean life, the multiplicity of things that, to borrow a phrase from his film *Sunless*, quicken the heart. "I will not deal with Big Issues" (Marker 1959: 135), the commentator concludes in an address to his cat. Rather it's the daily routines, legends and myths, conversations, relics of history, a "list of the spirits and stars that govern human life"(85), and fragments of a developing industrial future that are photographed and observed from numerous angles at passing moments. Even the seven-part organization of *Koreans* is a set of numerical categories, "The Six Days," "The Two Orphans," "The Seven Wonders," "The Five Senses," "The Three Sisters," "The Nine Muses," and "The Four Corners," that weave together lists and inventories of particular historical, imaginative, relational, emotional, and sensual experiences. "The Seven Wonders" mentions explicitly only the "wonder of ginseng" and, as a free association, "the seventh wonder ... the work of builders" who took "fifty years to complete a ginseng plant" (51–53). The other wonders appear in the markets and street scenes that come in and out of view as a series of ten photos:

> A great deal of Korea strolls by on Koreans' heads. ... Baskets, earthenware jars, bundles of wood, basins, all escape the earth's gravity to become satellites of these calm planets, obeying exacting orbits. For the Korean street has its cycles, its waves, its rails. In this double décor, where hastened ruins and buildings still balancing themselves in a second of incompletion, the soldier who buys a civilian's sun hat, the worker leaving the construction site, the bureaucrat with his briefcase, the woman in traditional dress and the woman in modern dress, the porter carrying a brand new allegory to the museum of the Revolution with a woman in black following step by step to decipher it all have their route and precise place, like constellations. (44)

In Adorno's words, here the "elements crystallize as a configuration through their motion" becoming a constellation or "force field, just as every intellectual structure is necessarily a force field under the essay's gaze" (1991: 13).

These lists, inventories, and oppositions are primarily fading scaffolding that constantly draws attention to the conjunctive intervals that hold them together: the "and" that momentarily connects without a teleological logic. They create continual movement, a recollection and anticipation as a serial activity whose accumulations are endlessly generative and open-ended. If the fundamental structure of all photo essays tends to approach that of a spatial categorizing of images, for Marker this inventory of images always approximates a photogrammatic series of film frames. In *Koreans*, he notes that "A market place is the Republic of things ... It all went by as quickly as a forgotten image between two shots" (1959: 39), a barely visible conjunctive place where the "and" opens potentially as the space of intelligence. As Deleuze notes about the cinema (and Godard's films specifically), through this conjunctive "and," categories are "redistributed, reshaped and reinvented" and so become "problems which introduce reflection on the image itself" (Deleuze 1989:185–186). "The whole undergoes a mutation . ... in order to become the constitutive 'and' of things, the constitutive between-two of images" (180). No episode in *Koreans* dramatizes the poignancy and power of this conjunctive place better than an encounter at the theater where the experience of a celebrated play based on the well known legend of Sim Chon suggests both a mythic categorization and the emotional and intellectual energy within anticipatory conjunctives: Marker encounters a female friend crying during an interval over the plight of the heroine, despite her having seen the play 200 times, and when he tries to assure her that all will be well in the end, she replies in bewilderment, "how could I be so sure of the future?"

Several key sections of *Koreans* are especially dramatic illustrations of that wavering line between the photo essay and essay film, places in the book where the photos become virtual photograms that draw attention to the space between the images as an interpretive "void" for the photographer/commentator. In these instances especially, the writer's voice as "expressive subject" documents the experiential expressions around him as faces "literally embodied [as] a smile that melts away, a face that comes undone" (Marker 1959: 25). At one point, a series of nine photos depicts a woman looking out of the frame telling "her life story." Or "more exactly," the text fills in, "she told us that there was nothing to be told, really nothing" (21–24). Immediately following, one of the most dramatic conjunctions in the book presents just two shots of two expressions. First there is a woman's smiling face answering questions about her personal life (her boyfriend, her prospects for marriage), but, when asked about her parents, the second photo captures the ruptured transition between the two images as she explains that her parents were killed during the Korean war: "At that moment," the commentator remarks,

> I was sunk in my [Rolleiflex] camera. It was on the Rollei's ground glass that I saw the metamorphosis, the smile vanishing into pain like water drunk by sand … and now the young woman's face was covered in tears, but she did not lower her head, and the hands that had hidden her laughter lay immobile on the table. The instant was hers. … The extraordinary hymn of hate and will power that followed would need more than a story and an image to do it justice. (25–26)

Here the camera lens itself becomes both a physical and metaphoric interface upon which the commentator engages a radical shift in the expressions of the self and its relation to a world and a history. In the "vanishing" that marks the space between his experience of her experience is precisely where he relinquishes himself, his images, and his stories—that is, his thoughts—to the unrecoverable reality that "was hers."

In a later sequence the centrality of this subjective space in its encounter with the world reappears as a typically askew or inverted exchange. In this case two photographs of construction cranes operating over an urban site show first a relatively empty lot and then the shapes of emerging buildings: "All night long, the aurora borealis of welding torches, spotlights on cranes, reflections of the moon and the headlights on the great glassy facades of new buildings," the commentator observes about the two photos. Yet comparative images such as these and the interval they document, he quickly notes, are not about that scene and the temporal passage it records, but about the experiential space from which they are seen, from which subjectivity and thought have ventured forth to test themselves: "I don't care much for propaganda photos in the style: 'Yesterday … Today.' But I still took these pictures of what I saw out my window, at fifteen days distance. In order not to mistake the room" (53–55).

Koreans follows a temporal and spatial journey through these conjunctive spaces between numerous faces, things, activities, and images, searching those "forgotten image[s] between two shots." As he notes early in the text, "There are many ways of traveling" (16), and one way to view the photographic and photogrammatic travels might be as a mimetic attempt to represent the dynamic continuity of these active and changing people and places. The journey of *Koreans*, however, is better characterized according to the ambitious model offered by Henri Michaux's surrealist travel memoir *Plume*, in which the traveler embraces the transitions in time and place as disorderly "rhythms, waves, shocks, all the buffers of memory, its meteors and dragnets" (Marker 1959: 16). The opening photo on this trip is thus appropriately a women descending from a plane, described as the "first Korean girl descended from heaven with the 'gift of transitions'" (10).

The textual commentary that documents these personal experiences of a vibrant and changing world becomes then a string of insertions or interpolations into these rhythms, waves, and shocks.

In *Koreans*, unlike the consistent voice of some traditional photo essays, this one is multi-vocal, mobile, scattered, and both historically and geographically layered. Weaving together poetry, photos, ancient maps, quotations from historical reports, literature, reproductions of paintings, Korean tales and legends, and comic book images, the commentary sometimes precedes the photos; sometimes it follows or is interspersed in the spaces between a series. It recounts parables, historical events, personal reflections, observations, and reminiscences of other places, melding myths with daily observations, anecdotes about ginseng, profoundly serious commentaries on the atrocities of war, and self-debunking and whimsical humor about the commentator's own efforts. Sometimes it describes the photos; sometimes it gives voice to the images. Each becomes a way of speaking/ seeing as a different representational encounter with a world that resists denotation. As Marker would later insist in his photo essay *Le Depays* (*Abroad*): "The text doesn't comment on the images any more than the images illustrate the text. They are two sequences that clearly cross and signal to each other, but which it would be pointlessly exhausting to collate" (Lupton 2005: 62). Like the images it responds to, the intense, inquisitive, and reflective subjectivity of this traveling voice and text dissolves into the fissures between the different representational materials they struggle to occupy, as moments of reflection and thinking, in the space between the photographic images.

These doubled fissures—between the textual commentary and the images and between that "forgotten image between two shots"—become in one sense a version of what W.J.T. Mitchell calls a "site of resistance," produced in the photo essay through its leanings towards non-fictional subjects, its subjective anchoring in a personal point of view, and its "generic incompleteness" (Mitchell 1994: 287): "The text of the photo-essay typically discloses a certain reserve or modesty in its claims to 'speak for' or interpret images; like the photograph, it admits its inability to appropriate everything that was there to be taken and tries to let the photographs speak for themselves or 'look back' at the viewer" (289). Signaled throughout *The Koreans* with faces and eyes looking directly at the camera, this spatial resistance is dramatized most poetically in one exchange featuring five sequential photos of six children playing and staring back at the camera, watching the author "watching them. A mirror game that goes on and on where the loser is the one who looks down, who lets the other's gaze pass through, like a ball" (Marker 1959: 43). As he quickly acknowledges, "My third eye was a bit like cheating" (43). In this exchange and in the photo essay in general, according to Vivian Sobchack, temporality itself becomes necessarily remade according to a spatial dynamics in which a "temporal hole" appears as a "gap" or "arena" opening up and staging the possibility of meaning:

> The lack of depth and dimension in the still photograph seems less a function of the phenomenal thickness of the subjects and objects that it displays than of the temporal hole it opens within the world in which we gaze at it. Indeed, the most "dynamic" photojournalism derives its uncanny power from this temporal hole, the transcendence of both existence and finitude within existence and finitude . ... The photograph, then, offers us only the possibility of meaning. It provides a significant gap that can be filled with every meaning, any meaning, and is itself meaningless in that it does not act within itself to choose its meaning, to diacritically mark it off. Like transcendental consciousness, the photograph as a transcendental structure posits the abstraction of a moment but has not momentum—and only provides the grounds or arena for its possibility. (Sobchak 1992: 60)

For Marker, however, the resistances and holes created in his photo essays, where language and subjectivity lose themselves in images of the world, might be best understood with the cinematic framework used by Deleuze. Here, thinking and "intelligence" occur when comprehension and understanding encounter the world on its own terms—in what Deleuze labels "a void" or an "interstice" in the time and spaces of representations: "What counts is ... the *interstice* between images, between two images: a spacing which means that each image is plucked from the void and falls back into it" (Deleuze 1989: 179). This creates neither spectatorial "identification," a position of a familiar emplacement in the world, nor a version of Brechtian "alienation," a position of unfamiliar exclusion from that world represented. Rather this is a suspended position of intellectual opportunity and potential, a position within a spatial gap where the interval offers the "insight of blindness," where thought becomes the exteriorization of expression.

If Marker's photo essays open a space, a changing geography, in which thinking may pitch its tent, the essay film must aim to retrieve the possibility of that active intelligence within the continuous landscape of film.[12] Bridging these different forms of the essayistic, the photogram describes a conceptual borderline between photography and film, a kind of "stop action," since it pinpoints the transformation of film's moving image into the suspension of "real movement and time" as a series of overlapping photographic images. No doubt, *The Jetty* represents this reflexive merging of the photographic series and film form most famously (also constructed only of still images except for a few seconds when those series of photograms become a continuous movement), but, enlisting the narrative framework of a science fiction tale rather than an essayistic framework, *The Jetty* creates a significantly different viewing position from the essay film, one based in identification, memory, and desire, rather than observation, reflection, and belief. [13]

Despite the canonical prominence of *The Jetty*, the majority of Marker's films are best understood within the framework of the essayistic.[14] Partly because of its historical proximity to *Koreans* and its place at this historically formative stage of the essay film and partly because it eschews the narrative logic of the more renowned *Jetty*, I'll concentrate here on the 1958 *Letter from Siberia*,[15] which represents an early paradigm for the essay film for Marker and for the practice in general. Writing about *Letter from Siberia* in 1958, André Bazin has the first and most prescient word: *Letter from Siberia* "resembles absolutely nothing that we have ever seen before in films with a documentary bias." It "is an essay on the reality of Siberia past and present in the form of a filmed report. Or, perhaps, to borrow Jean Vigo's formulation of *À propos de Nice* ('a documentary point of view'), I would say an essay documented by film. The important word is 'essay,' understood in the same sense that it has in literature—an essay at once historical and political, written by a poet as well" (2003: 44).[16]

Even more explicitly than *Koreans*, *Letter from Siberia* presents itself as an epistolary travelogue, whose voice-over begins with lines appropriated from that exemplary traveler in *Koreans*, Henri Michaux: "I am writing to you from a far country. ... I am writing you from the end of the world." Here too cold-war, East/West, oppositions linger in the background, and here too a traveler commentator, now a disembodied voice rather than a printed text, negotiates and reflects on serial inventories and oppositional categories: lists of Siberian plant and animal life alternate with descriptions of daily activities, and the film concludes with the polarized journeys of underground scientists burrowing to the center of the earth while their colleague-cosmonauts launch themselves into outer space. Digressions into an archeological past jump quickly forward to the industrial future: from Yakut tribal rituals and drawings of the wooly mammoths that once populated Siberia to the construction of new highways and telephone lines. The representational heterogeneity of *Letter from Siberia* also parallels that of Marker's photo essay as the film mixes black-and-white and color film, still photographs, archival footage, and animation to underline, here too, how the bond between experience and representation is the fault line between the world and our knowledge of it.

Unlike the photo essay's efforts to inhabit the spaces between these images, however, this essay film opens a second dimension to its travels, that particularly cinematic dimension of the temporality of the moving image. Together with the rhetorical and spatial gaps found in the photo essay, the film thus additionally depicts and examines the continual dynamics of movement captured on film, from the vertical ascents of flying airplanes to horizontally racing reindeer, through a visual syntax of continual tracks and pans capturing those temporal rhythms with a similar array of directional movements. Early in the film, for instance, dramatically different materials create dramatically different forms of temporality as a fabricated image of the past, a realistic transparency of the present, and a visual rhetoric of a desired future: animated drawings of mammoths precede a transition to documentary shots of the Lena river bustling with its industry and commerce, and, shortly after, the film offers a "spot commercial" spoofing the market value of reindeer as pets, transportation, clothing, and food. Bazin goes so far as to identify these constructions as a "new notion of montage" that he calls "horizontal" or "lateral" where, unlike the traditional "sense of duration through the relation of shot to shot," "a given image doesn't refer to the one that preceded it" (2003: 44). Comparable to the spatial openings mapped in *Koreans*, in these instances *Letter from Siberia* pries open the temporal "presence" of the moving images as an interstice (both spatial and temporal) containing multiple time zones ranging from past memories to future fantasies. As the commentator remarks in his conclusion, this Siberia is the image of a temporal vertigo: "between the Middle Ages and the twenty-first century, between the earth and the moon, between humiliation and happiness. After that it's straight ahead."

Two sequences stand out in this effort to open the cinematic image as planes with different temporal zones. The most famous is a single shot of a Yakutsk town bus passing an expensive car shown four times with four different types of commentary. The first is silent, the next a Soviet panegyric, the third an anti-Communistic denunciation, and the last the voice-over's description of the commentator's own impressions. Each commentary not only creates a very different interpretation of the street scene but also directs the perspective towards different details and activities in the shot: for one, the Zim luxury car dominates the scene; in another, the voice-over points out a man's injured eye. For the commentator this series of judgments without verdicts most immediately questions the impossible notion of objectivity regarding a landscape "with huge gaps and the will to fill them." Indeed a major problem with "objectivity" is that it "may not distort Siberian realities but it does isolate them long enough to be appraised." Instead, the four different commentaries here offer four interpretive planes or zones which describe the street scene and direct our attention in a way that maps the temporal fullness of a short interval where "What counts is the variety and the driving momentum."

The second, considerably longer, sequence follows these four shots to suggest that even this layering of a cinematic present is inadequate. "A walk through the streets of Yakutsk isn't going to make you understand Siberia," the commentator admits. "What you might need is an imaginary newsreel shot all over Siberia" in which "the commentary would be made up of those Siberian expressions that are already pictures in themselves." Locating and measuring its own voice in "those Siberian expressions" it aims to document, the commentator literally evokes images of those expressions by opening a second frame within the center of the image of the street scene, which then expands to fill the entire frame and become a collage of winter images. As the collage proceeds, this "imaginary newsreel" assumes a future conditional voice developing through a series of conjunctive "ands": "And then I'd show you" the snow, the Yakut, the spring festivals, and so on.

As these sequences suggest, the voice-over in *Letter from Siberia* becomes that of a time traveler and guide through a world that will always elude him and us temporally as well as spatially. Whereas the text-image relationship in *Koreans* identifies a fissure or gap, the audio commentary offers a more temporally mobile relationship with the fragmented chronologies of the film image. The changing voices, incorporated quotations, and music and sound recordings—from the lyrical to the bemused to the pedagogical—describe a series of shifting subject positions surrounding and intervening in the visuals. This address of the voice-over can even be dramatically insistent in attempting to direct the viewer according to a specific chronology: at one point, the commentator anticipates the contrast between the past and present in the image of a large truck passing a horse-drawn cart, and quickly reminds the viewer, this is "the shot you've been waiting for." The unusual mobility of this voice exploring time between images creates, in Bazin's words, a "montage ... forged from ear to eye" (2003: 44). Through it, *Letter from Siberia* insists, according to Bazin, "that the primary material is intelligence, that its immediate means of expression is language, and that the image only intervenes in the third position, in reference to this verbal intelligence" (44).

It seems to me a curious paradox that Deleuze says nothing about Marker's films in his monumental *Cinema 1* and *Cinema 2*, for few writers have theorized the cinema in terms so sympathetic to Marker's essayistic films and their aim to elicit a "cinematic thinking." Although Deleuze's perspective on "thought and cinema" casts a much wider net than the essayistic, it accommodates Marker's work and essayistic cinema in general in a manner that few theoretical models can— which is the justification for my selective appropriation of Deleuze. For Deleuze, thought is "the essence of cinema" (1989: 168), and it can be discovered in various orders throughout film history, beginning with the "movement images" of Eisenstein, Abel Gance, and Alfred Hitchcock.[17] Of a different order, however, is "the modern cinema," the cinema of the "time-image" (169) and, for me, the essayistic. In these films, of which there are no better examples than Marker's, thought in the cinema "is brought face to face with its own impossibility" (168) where "the suspension of the world" "gives the visible to thought, not as an object, but as an act that is constantly arising and being revealed in thought" (169). Just as the essayistic subjects personal expression to the public domain of experience, "Thought finds itself taken over by the exteriority of a 'belief', outside any interiority of a mode of knowledge" (175). For Deleuze and Marker, encountering the interstices and time zones between film images is thus the pathway to "belief" in a world always eliciting and refusing thought.[18]

Although the genealogical relationship between the photo essay (and literary essay) and the essay film is not a difficult argument to make, few writers, photographers, or filmmakers demonstrate their intricate and compelling connections better than Chris Marker, a writer and photo essayist who can deservedly be characterized as one of the most consistent, earliest, and most articulate practitioners of the essay film. Essay films have arguably become one of the most innovative and popular forms of filmmaking in the last fifteen years, producing a celebrated variety of examples from filmmakers around the globe. However extremely they may vary in style, structure, and subject matter, the best of these, I believe, work in the tradition of Marker, a tradition that draws on, merges, and recreates the literary essay and the photo essay within the particular spatial and temporal dynamics of film. Without assuming that one practice anticipates or prepares for the other in Marker's career, it seems certain that, in his early essayistic encounters with words and photographic images, Marker discovers an essential modern territory between images where the fading spaces and black time lines ask the film viewer to become a thinker. After all, as Marker notes in *Koreans*, the twentieth century "may have been nothing but an immense, interminable fade." (Marker 1959: 23)

■ ■ ■

Questions and projects

1. Select a film that could be described as an essay film (for example Patrick Keiller's 2010 *Robinson in Ruins* or Michael Moore's 2004 *Fahrenheit 9/11*) and argue how they employ essayistic strategies.
2. Analyze a specific literary essay and a specific essay film that may have similar topics (such as self-portrait or travel or criticism). One might choose essays with clear connections: for instance, compare a critical essay written about Werner Herzog's 1982 *Fitzcarraldo* and Les Blank and Maureen Gosling's film account of the making of that movie, *Burden of Dreams* (1982). How do their methods differ? How does the comparison reveal certain limitations or possibilities in each practice?

Notes

1   See especially Renov 2004, Arthur 2003, Alter 2006, and Rascaroli 2009 for extended, sophisticated and differentiated accounts of the essay film.

2   Whereas Marker is consistently associated with the beginnings of the essay film, other film historians and scholars identify other key films in the formation of the practice. Michael Renov, for instance, discusses, Jonas Mekas's *Lost, Lost, Lost* (1969/1976) as a key example of the essay film, and arguing that "the foundations of the essay film derive from three landmark documentaries," Paul Arthur places Alain Resnais's *Night and Fog* (1955) and Jean Rouch's *Les Maitres fous* (1955) alongside *Letter from Siberia* ("The Resurgence of History" 65-66). Alter follows Jay Leyda and aligns the essay film with an earlier history, beginning with Richter's 1928 *Inflation*.

3   Historically, this is an essentially Romantic formulation as a "personal essay."

4   An incisive examination of this relationship between subjectivity, the verbal, and the visible in the early nineteenth century is William Galperin's *The Return of the Visible in British Romanticism*.

5   This tension and dialogue between the verbal and the visual becomes particularly pronounced in the nineteenth century in ways that adumbrate the rise of the essayistic and film representation more generally. J. Hillis Miller has identified some of the precedents for this practice in his *Illustration* where he examines precursive examples such as the photographic frontispieces that accompany Henry James's *The Golden Bowl* (1904).

6   See Martha Rosler's "The Bowery: Two Inadequate Systems of Descriptions."

7   Looking at films such as *The Times of Harvey Milk*, *The Battle of San Pietro*, and *Hotel des Invalides*, about which Stella Bruzzi has argued incisively against the exclusion of subjective creativity in the more conventional documentary representations (2006: 40-67).

8   A streamlined version of Habermas's argument would forefront how his bourgeois public sphere, as it developed at the end of the eighteenth century, separated itself from the civil state, defining itself as an open dialogue between the private individual and public concerns. Not coincidentally, as an historical movement, it gives birth to the idea and place of culture within society—a bracketed sphere that, in the idealism of the late eighteenth and early nineteenth century with its foundation resting on property and family, both could influence and remain separate from the various economic and political pressures of that society.

9   Lopate's argument represents a common tack to associate the essayistic with a strong and coherent personal voice, which is very much contrary to my argument about essayistic subjectivity.

10   Besides Lupton's recent book, Nora Alter's exceptional study *Chris Marker*, which addresses many of these issues around Marker and the essayistic and which informs much of my thinking and reading about his work. Also of note is the two-part series on Marker in *Film Comment* in 2003.

11   Despite these political reminders, the book focuses largely on North Korea.

12 Telling of the critical relation between the photo essay and the essay film, two of Marker's own photo essays are in fact companion pieces to specific films: "China's Light: A film in the guise of a greeting card," a series of photos and commentaries published in *Esprit* to accompany his film *Sunday in Peking* (1956) and the 1982 companion piece to *Sunless*, the photo essay *Abroad*. Lupton notes that in these cases the "film and the photo-text publication are not designed to explain or absorb each other, but as an open-ended relay that invites fresh perspectives on their shared subject matter" (62). Marker's *If I Had Four Dromedaries* (1966) is another version of his exploration of this intermediary zone: a film made up entirely of still images whose premise is "a photographer and two of his friends look through and comment on a series of images taken just about everywhere in the world between 1956 and 1966."

13 In *Between Film and Screen: Modernism's Photo Synthesis*, Garrett Stewart describes *The Jetty* as a "text of decelerated process" where "Marker's plot is a perfect allegory of this devitalization" (103).

14 See Ross Gibson, "What Do I Know?: Chris Marker and the Essayist Mode of Cinema." *Filmviews* (Summer1988): 26-32.

15 That Marker seems to regard his work preceding *La Jolie mai* (1962) and *The Jetty* as juvenilia suits my argument in that that work clearly represents a testing and exploration of a new practice.

16 Since Bazin's observations, scholarly work on the essay film has, especially in the last ten years, grown considerably. See, for instance, Michael Renov's "*Lost, Lost, Lost*: Mekas as Essayist," Nora Alter's "Documentary as Simulacrum: *Tokyo-Ga*," and, for broader discussion about the new strategies of contemporary docuemtnary, Bill Nichol's *Blurred Boundaries*.

17 Deleuze's three relations to thought of the movement image occur in this way: 1. forces thinking and thinks under shock [critical thought]; 2. with a "second movement" or "spiral" between "intellectual cinema" and "sensory thought" or "emotional intelligence" [hypnotic thought](1989: 157-159); and 3. "identity of concept and image" or "the externalization of man" [action thought] (162-163). It is worth considering Garrett Stewart's strong counter arguments to the Deleuze bipartite, particularly as he insists on a much broader photogrammatic tension in film practice that encompasses the "movement-image" as well as the "time-image." He writes: "Everything Deleuze resists attributing to the movement-image as an already textured or textualized imprint of the scopic field seems displaced onto the time-image, where betweenness, stratigraphic layering, interstitial and lacunary process … where the whole process of opalescent faceting of indeterminancy takes place" (89).

18 There is, of course, an admirable utopianism joining the writer and the filmmaker on this never acknowledged (to my mind) common ground. It begins with an aesthetic that aims to overcome the human limits that allow a cinematic illusion of movement based on projecting twenty-four images a second and continues to a wry and relentless hope in what Marker calls in *Koreans* "a politics of understanding."

References

Abel, Richard (ed.). *French Film Theory and Criticism: A History / Anthology, 1907–1939, Volume 1: 1907–1929.* Princeton, NJ: Princeton University Press, 1988.

Adorno, T.W. "The Essay as Form." *Notes to Literature*, Vol. 1. New York: Columbia University Press, 1991. 3–23.

Agee, James and Walker Evans, *Let Us Now Praise Famous Men*. Cambridge, MA: Houghton Mifflin, 1939.

Alter, Nora. "The Political Im/perceptible in the Essay Film: Farocki's *Images of the World and the Inscription of War*." *New German Critique* 68 (1996): 165–92.

——. "Documentary as Simulacrum: *Tokyo-Ga*." *The Cinema of Wim Wenders: Image, Narrative, and the Postmodern Condition*. Ed. Roger F. Cook and Gerd Gemunden. Detroit, MI: Wayne State University Press, 1997.

——. "Mourning, Sound, and Vision: Jean-Luc Godard's *JLG/JLG*." *Camera Obscura* 15.2 (2000): 75–103.

——. *Chris Marker*. Urbana, IL: University of Illinois Press, 2006.

——. "Translating the Essay into Film and Installation." *Journal of Visual Culture* 6.1 (2007): 44–57.

Arendt, Hannah. *The Human Condition*. Chicago, IL: University of Chicago Press, 1958.

Arthur, Paul. "Jargons of Authenticity (Three American Moments)." In *Theorizing Documentary*. Ed. Michael Renov. New York: Routledge, 1993. 108–134.

———— . "Essay Questions." *Film Comment* 39.1 (2003): 53–62.

———— . "The Resurgence of History and the Avant-Garde Essay Film." In *A Line of Sight: American Avant-Garde Film Since 1965*. Minneapolis, MN: University of Minnesota Press, 2005. 61–73.

Astruc, Alexandre. *Du stylo à la camera   Et de la caméra au stylo, Écrits (1942–1984)*. Paris: L'Archipel, 1992.

————. "The Birth of a New Avant-Garde: La Caméra-Stylo." *Film and Literature: An Introduction and Reader*. Ed. Timothy Corrigan. Upper Saddle River, NJ: Prentice Hall, 1999.

Baldwin, James. *Collected Essays*. New York: Library of America, 1998.

————-. "I'll Make Me a World." PBS broadcast, 2/2/99

Bazin, André . "Bazin on Marker." Trans. Dave Kehr, *Film Comment*, 39.4 (July–Aug. 2003): 43–4.

Benjamin, Walter. *The Origin of German Tragic Drama*. London: Verso, 1977.

Baudrillard, Jean. "The Gulf War: Is It Really Taking Place?" *The Jean Baudrillard Reader*. Ed. Steve Redhead. New York: Columbia University Press, 2008.

Bensamaia, Reda. *The Barthes Effect*. Minneapolis, MN: University of Minnesota Press, 1987.

Bense, Max. "Uber den Essay und seine Prosa." *Merkur* 1.3 (1947): 414–24.

Blumlinger, Christa. "Lire entre les Images." *L'Essai et le cinema*. Ed. Suzanne Liandrat-Guigues and Murielle Gagnebin. Paris: Champs Vallon, 2004. 49–66

Bruno, Guiliana. *The Atlas of Emotion: Journeys in Art, Architecture, and Film*. New York: Verso, 2002.

Bruzzi, Stella. *New Documentary: A Critical Introduction*. 2nd edn. London: Routledge, 2006.

Burch, Noel. *Theory of Film Practice*. Princeton, NJ: Princeton University Press, 1981.

Dave, Paul. "Representations of Capitalism, History and Nation in the Work of Patrick Keiller." *British Cinema, Past and Present*. Ed. Justine Ashby and Andrew Higson. London: Routledge, 2000.

Deleuze, Gilles. *Cinema 1: The Movement-Image*. Minneapolis, MN: University of Minnesota Press, 1986.

———— *Cinema 2: The Time-Image*. Minneapolis, MN: University of Minnesota Press, 1989.

———— *Foucault*. Minneapolis, MN: University of Minnesota Press, 1988.

Deluc, Germaine. "The Expressive Techniques of the Cinema." *French Film Criticism and Theory: A History / Anthology, 1907–1939. Vol. 1: 1907–1929*. Ed. Richard Abel. Princeton, NJ: Princeton University Press, 1998. 310.

————-. "The Essence of Cinema: The Visual Idea." *The Avant-Garde Film: A Reader of Theory and Criticism*. Ed. P. Adam Sitney. New York: Anthology Film Archives, 1987.

Dumont, Francois. *Approches de l'essai*. Quebec: Éditions Nota bene, 2003.

Eisenstein, Sergei. "Notes for a Film of 'Capital'." Trans. Maciej Sliwowski, Jay Leyda, and Annette Michelson, *October* 2 (1976). 3–26

Fihman, Guy. "L'Essai cinématographique et ses transformations expérimentales." *L'Essai et le cinema*. Eds. Suzanne Liandrat-Guigues and Murielle Gagnebin. Paris: Champs Vallon, 2004.

Flitterman-Lewis, Sandy. "Documenting the Ineffable: Terror and Memory in Alain Resnais's *Night and Fog*." *Documenting the Documentary: Close Readings of Documentary Film and Video*. Eds. Barry Keith Grant and Jeannette Sloniowski. Detroit, MI: Wayne State University Press, 1998.

Foucault, Michel. *The Order of Things: An Archeology of the Human Sciences*. New York: Pantheon, 1970.

————. "What Is an Author?" *Language, Counter-Memory, Practice: Selected Essays and Interviews*. Ithaca, NY: Cornell University Press. 113–38.

Frampton, Daniel. *Filmosophy*. London: Wallflower Press, 2006.

Galperin, William. *The Return of the Visible in British Romanticism*. Baltimore, MD: Johns Hopkins University Press, 1993.

Gibson, Ross "What Do I Know?: Chris Marker and the Essayist Mode of Cinema." *Filmviews* (Summer 1988): 26–32.

Giannetti, Louis. "Godard's *Masculine-Feminine*: The Cinematic Essay." *Godard and Others: Essays on Film Form*. Rutherford, NJ: Fairleigh Dickinson Press, 1975.

Godard, Jean-Luc, *Godard on Godard*. Trans. Tom Milne. New York: Viking, 1972.

———. *Histoire(s) du cinema*. Paris: Gallimard-Gaumont,1998.

Good, Graham. *The Observing Self: Rediscovering the Essay*. London: Routledge, 1988.

Gunning, Tom. "*A Corner ofWheat*." *The Griffith Project,Volume 3*. Ed. Paolo Cherchi Usai London: British Film Institute, 1999. 130–41.

Hansen, Miriam. *Babel and Babylon: Spectatorship in American Silent Film*. Cambridge, MA: Harvard University Press, 1991.

Huxley, Aldous. "Preface to *The Collected Essays of Aldous Huxley*," *Aldous Huxley Complete Essays.Vol.VI, 1956– 1963*. Ed. Robert Baker and James Sexton. Chicago, IL: Ivan R. Dee, 2002.

Kahana, Jonathan. *IntelligenceWorks:The Politics of American Documentary*. NewYork: Columbia University Press, 2008.

Kamper, Birgit and Thomas Tode, eds. *Chris Marker: Filmessayist*. Munich: CICIM, 1997.

Kluge, Alexander, Edgar Reitz and Wilfied Reinke. "Word and Film." In *Film and Literature:An Introduction and Reader*. Ed.Timothy Corrigan. Upper Saddle River, NJ: Prentice-Hall, 1999.

Lopate, Phillip. "In Search of the Centaur:The Essay Film." In *Beyond Document: Essays on Nonfiction Film*. Ed. Charles Warren. Hanover, NH: Wesleyan University Press, 1996.

Lukács, Georg. "On the Nature and Form of the Essay." In *Soul and Form*. Cambridge, MA: MIT Press, 1974. 1–19.

Lupton, Catherine. *Chris Marker: Memories of the Future*. London: Reaktion Books, 2005.

Lyotard, Jean-François. *The Postmodern Condition:A Report on Knowledge*. Minneapolis, MN: University of Minnesota Press, 1984.

Malraux, André, *Esquisse d'une psychologie du cinema*. Paris: Gallimard, 1946.

———. *Le Musée imaginaire*. Genève: Skira, 1947.

Marker, Chris. *Giradoux par lui-meme*. Paris: Editions du Seuil, 1952.

———. *Coréennes*. Paris: Editions du Seuil, 1959.

———. *Le Depays.* Paris: Herscher, 1982.

Michaux, Henri. *Plume* Paris: Galliard, 1985.

Montaigne, Michel de. *The CompleteWorks of Montaigne*, trans. Donald M. Frame. Stanford, CA: Stanford University Press, 1948.

Miller, J. Hillis. *Illustration*. Cambridge, MA: Harvard University Press, 1992.

Milne, Tom, ed. *Godard on Godard*. NewYork:Viking, 1971.

Mitchell, W.J.T. *Picture Theory*. Chicago, IL: University of Chicago Press, 1994.

Moure, José. "Essai de definition de essai au cinéma." *L'Essai et le cinéma*. Ed. Suzanne Liandrat-Guigues and Murielle Gagnebin. Paris: Champs Vallon, 2004.

Musil, Robert. *The Man without Qualities, I*. NewYork: Knopf, 1995.

Nichols, Bill. *Blurred Boundaries: Questions of Meaning in Contemporary Culture*. Bloomington, IN: Indiana University Press, 1994.

———. "The Voice of Documentary." *New Challenges for Documentary*. 2nd edn. Ed.Alan Rosenthal and Jorn Corner. Manchester: University of Manchester Press, 2005. 17–33.

Panofsky, Erwin. "Style and Medium in the Motion Pictures." *Film Theory and Criticism*. 7th edn. Ed. Leo Braudy and Marshall Cohen. NewYork: Oxford University Press, 2009.

Pinel, Vincent. *Introduction au Ciné-club: histoire, théorie, pratique du Ciné-club en France*. Paris: Editions Ouvrières, 1964.

Porcile, François. *Defense du court metrage*. Paris: Les Editions du Cerf, 1965.

Rabinovitz, Lauren. "From Hale's Tours to Star Tours:Virtual Voyages,Travel Ride Films, and the Delirium of the Hyper-Real." *Virtual Voyages: Cinema and Travel*. Ed. Jeffrey Ruoff. Durham, NC: Duke University Press, 2006. 42–60.

Rascaroli, Laura. *The Personal Camera: Subjective Cinema and the Essay Film*. London: Wallflower, 2009.

Renov, Michael. *The Subject of Documentary*. Minneapolis, MN: University of Minnesota Press, 2004.

———. *Theorizing Documentary*. London and NewYork: Routledge, 1993.

———. "*Lost, Lost, Lost*: Mekas as Essayist." *The Subject of Documentary*. Minneapolis, MN: University of Minnesota Press, 2004. 69–92.

Richter, Hans. "Der Film Essay: Eine neue Form des Dokumentarfilms." *Nationalzeitung* (25 May 1940). Reprinted in *Schreiben Bilder Sperechen*, Ed. Christa Blumlinger and Constantin Wulff. Vienna: Sonderzahl, 1992. 195.

Riis, Jacob. *How the Other Half Lives*. Ed. David Leviatin. Boston, MA: Bedford/St. Martin's, 1996.

Rivette, Jacques. "Letter on Rossellini." *Cahiers du Cinema. The 1950s: Neo-Realism, Hollywood, New Wave*. Ed. Jim Hillier. Cambridge, MA: Harvard University Press, 1985. 192–204.

Roud, Richard. "The Left Bank." *Sight and Sound* (Winter 1962–63): 24–27.

Rosler, Martha. "The Bowery: Two Inadequate Systems of Descriptions." *3 Works*. Novia Scotia: The Press of the Nova Scotia College of Art and Design, 2006.

Sobchack, Vivian. *The Address of the Eye: A Phenomenology of Film Experience*. Princeton, NJ: Princeton University Press, 1992.

——. "Toward a Phenomenology of Nonfictional Film Experience." *Collecting Visible Evidence*. Ed. Jaine M. Gaines and Michael Renov. Minneapolis, MN: University of Minnesota Press, 1999. 241–54.

Stewart, Garrett. *Between Film and Screen: Modernism's Photo Synthesis.* Chicago, IL: University of Chicago Press, 1999.

Warner, Michael. *Publics and Counterpublics*. New York: Zone Books, 2002.

Warren, Charles, ed. *Beyond Document: Essays on Nonfiction Film*. Hanover, NH: Wesleyan University Press, 1996.

Watney, Simon. *Practices of Freedom: Selected Writings on HIV/AIDS*. Durham, NC: Duke University Press, 1994.

Williams, Linda. "Mirrors without Memories: Truth, History, and *The Thin Blue Line*." *Documenting the Documentary: Close Readings of Documentary Film and Video*. Ed. Barry Keith Grant and Jeannette Sloniowski. Detroit, MI: Wayne State University Press, 1998. 379–96.

Willumson, Glenn G. *W. Eugene Smith and the Photographic Essay*. Cambridge: Cambridge University Press, 1992.

Wolf, Christa. *The Author's Dimension: Selected Essays*. New York: Farrar, Straus, Giroux, 1993.

Woolf, Virginia. "Street Haunting: A London Adventure." In *The Art of the Personal Essay: An Anthology from the Classical Era to the Present*. Ed. Phillip Lopate. New York: Anchor Books, 1995.

2.5 MAJOR WRITERS/MAJOR FILMS
On William Shakespeare's *Macbeth* and Jane Austen's *Emma*

Chapter 28

Evelyn Tribble

"WHEN EVERY NOISE APPALLS ME"
Sound and fear in *Macbeth* and Akira
Kurosawa's *Throne of Blood*

E VELYN TRIBBLE IS A PROFESSOR OF ENGLISH at the University of Otago in
New Zealand. A leading scholar of early modern theater and film, Tribble situates her
investigation of Kurosawa's 1957 celebrated adaptation of *Macbeth* in the context of the
play's early productions. Here offstage and offscreen sounds and soundscapes become the key
points of intersection between the literature and the filmic adaptation, indicating again that
adaptation involves many different registers of exchange.

■ ■ ■

"WHEN EVERY NOISE APPALLS ME": SOUND AND FEAR IN *MACBETH* AND AKIRA KUROSAWA'S *THRONE OF BLOOD*
EVELYN TRIBBLE

Shakespeare, vol. 1 no. 1 (2005), pp. 75–90

Most discussions of Shakespearean film adaptation are structured by a persistent opposition between the verbal and the visual. In an essay that traces tensions between written word and cinematic image in the history of Shakespeare on film, Russell Jackson observes that the "anxiety about the visualised image usurping the spoken word's legitimate function has often dominated commentary on filmed Shakespeare" (2000: 24). A common strategy in Shakespeare and film criticism has been to examine the ways that verbal elements in Shakespeare's text are rendered visually in cinematic space. For instance, critics of Akira Kurosawa's *Throne of Blood* have commented on the ways that images of oppression and claustrophobia in *Macbeth* are rendered through the use of the low horizontal spaces of Japanese domestic architecture. Similarly, the moral ambiguities of Shakespeare's play appear visually through a striking emptiness and dislocation of exterior space, shown through the use of fog and the labyrinthine Cobweb Forest. As Stephen Prince writes (1991: 144):

[T]he metaphors Kurosawa develops—the labyrinthine forest in which Washizu becomes lost, the fog through which the warriors aimlessly ride, the horse that circles behind Washizu as Asaji plots the death of the lord—embody as patterns of movement these ideas of temporal circularity and the fatedness of violence and evil.

Other scholars such as Anthony Davies have stressed the "contrary dynamics of theatrical and cinematic space" (1988: 16), addressing not so much the tension between word and image as between theatrical and cinematic modes of constructing space.

Insights such as these have been very important in advancing studies of Shakespearean adaptation beyond questions of mere fidelity.[1] Nevertheless, structuring discussions of Shakespearean film around the poles of verbal/visual or theatrical/cinematic neglects a crucial element in both theatre and cinema: sound. With a few important exceptions, discussed below, sound as a category has seldom been addressed in a systematic way in Shakespearean studies.[2] Moreover, film as a discipline has been primarily interested in the visual, with discussions of sound generally subordinated to studies of the image.[3] In this essay, I will argue that examining the overlooked element of sound is profoundly important to both *Macbeth* and *Throne of Blood*, and that discussions of theatrical and cinematic space are impoverished without a careful analysis of the profound role of sound in shaping both uses of space, albeit through very different technical means. To make this case, I propose to examine the soundscape of *Macbeth* first as it might have sounded to auditors of the early modern period, and then as Kurosawa listened to it in his 1957 film *Kumonosu-jo* (*Throne of Blood*).[4] In this film, Kurosawa creates a peculiarly Japanese soundscape that responds to and revises Shakespeare's deployment of the repertory of sounds available to the early modern theatre. Both artists, I will argue, share an interest in the relationships among sound, fear, and the human body.

Bruce Smith's *The Acoustic World of Early Modern England* has recently drawn attention to sound in Shakespeare and in the early modern period generally, as has Wes Folkerth's recent study of "acoustemologies" (2002: 11), *Sound in Shakespeare*.[5] Folkerth discusses the Renaissance belief that "hearing is the sense with the greatest and most immediate access to the body's internal spirits" (2002: 55) and argues that "the characters in [Shakespeare's] plays routinely engage sound in an epistemological capacity, as a way of orienting themselves in physical space, in society at large, and with respect to other individuals" (2002: 106). Drawing on work in soundscape studies such as those of R. Murray Schafer and Barry Truax (*Acoustic Communication*), Smith and Folkerth have begun to elucidate the vital importance of sound in shaping early modern experience.

As Smith demonstrates, sound played a crucial role in the early modern theatre. Sounds heard range from the music performed on stage, to sounds of thunder made by rolling cannonballs along a wooden trench, to the cannon fire such as that responsible for burning down the Globe during a production of *Henry VIII*. Henslowe's catalogue of the properties and effects of his company include considerable expenditure for musical instruments: "As the company's costumes and props make up a palette for *visual* design, so their musical instruments and other sound-producing devices make up a 'palette' for *aural* design" (1999: 219). Viols, citterns, drums, trumpets, bells of various kinds, chimes, firearms and fireworks, all these comprised the array of acoustic devices of the Elizabethan and Jacobean stage (1999: 220–2). Most importantly, the theatres themselves were an "instrument for the production and reception of sound" (1999: 206). Smith has analysed the acoustic properties of the material environment of the Globe—"wood, plaster, thatch, mortar, air" (1999: 218)—concluding that "as a device for propagating sound, the 1599 Globe was extraordinarily efficient" (1999: 208). Shakespeare's awareness of the sonic properties of his theatrical environment is demonstrated by his probable experimentation with the acoustic properties of the indoor Blackfriars theatre. *The Tempest*, which was probably written for this new space, is the most musical and sonic of all of Shakespeare's plays.[6] We might compare Shakespeare's experimentation with this new environment with the film director experimenting with newly available technologies of sound, such as Dolby Surround-Sound.

In creating a soundscape for *Macbeth,* Shakespeare and the King's Men employ the available repertory of sounds to create a complex acoustic pattern that functions as an interpretive framework for the text. Off-stage sounds were particularly likely to be noted in promptbooks and in stage directions, showing the importance of their placement and proper timing to the production.[7] In *Macbeth,* Shakespeare employs a markedly full range of such effects, including a series of structuring or "establishing sounds" (Altman 1992: 250) as well as a number of unusually striking sound events. Its first establishing sounds are *"Thunder and Lightning"* (TLN 2).[8] Smith argues that plays tend to begin and end with "high-intensity sound" (1999: 224), in part as a way of securing audience attention and marking sonically the start of the fiction (in theatres and cinemas today the dimming of the house lights functions in a similar way). "Thunder and lightning" is a commonly used stage direction and it signifies more than just weather: this direction, like "thunder" alone, is associated with supernatural events, to figures of devils, spirits, witches, magicians and gods (Dessen and Thomson 1999: 230–1). Although the space on which the witches appear is initially geographically undefined, the acoustic stage direction—aided, no doubt, by the costumes and the verse structure of the lines, typically used by supernatural creatures in Shakespeare—instantly construct a supernatural space.[9] Each succeeding entrance of the witches is marked by this device, and thunder accompanies each apparition in Act Four Scene One. Examples include: *"Thunder. Enter the three Witches"* (TLN 97); *"Thunder. Enter the three Witches, meeting Hecat"* (TLN 1429–30); *"Thunder. Enter the three Witches"* (TLN 1527). Shakespeare, then, constructs a soundscape that exploits existing cultural associations of thunder and the supernatural, tightening the link with every appearance of the witches.

The second structuring sound-pattern in Macbeth is the alarum, which Dessen and Thomson describe as "a call to arms in the form of sound produced offstage before and during a battle helping to create an atmosphere of conflict and confusion" (1999: 3); drums were the most common instrument used, although trumpets might also be employed. This was a familiar device, and different drum rhythms would indicate attacks, parleys, marches and retreats. It is this sound that establishes the second scene: *"Alarum within. Enter King Malcome, Donalbaine, Lenox, with attendants, meeting a bleeding Captaine"* (TLN 15–17). As in the case of the first scene, setting is swiftly established through sound, coupled with visual and linguistic effects (the armour, the blood). The sound of drum and trumpet is linked with warfare and battle throughout. Indeed the sound of a "Drum within" (TLN 127) in the third scene marks the convergence of the supernatural space of the witches, marked by thunder, with the battle-space of Act Two Scene Two: "A Drumme, a Drumme: / *Macbeth* doth come" (TLN 128–29), the verse rhythms here echoing the sound of the drums. (It is worth noting here that the source of the sound is not entirely clear, since Macbeth and Banquo enter alone, without drummers.) The final scenes of the play, which register the rapid changes in fortune characteristic of Shakespearean battle scenes, are invariably marked by the martial sounds of the alarum.

The third acoustic pattern is that of the trumpet and the oboe (hautboy). The flourish marks a regal, ceremonial space; Dessen and Thomson describe it as "a fanfare usually played within on a trumpet or cornet, primarily when important figures enter and exit" (1999: 94). In *Macbeth,* flourishes are used exclusively for the entrance of royalty and thus mark shifts in power. Similarly a "Senit" (sennet, or extended flourish), announces Macbeth's first entrance "as King" (TLN 992), and the final stage direction of "Flourish" confirms Malcolm's invitation to "see vs crown'd at Scone" (TLN 2528–29) at the end of the play.

The hautboy is also a wind instrument, but with very different acoustical effects. One of a number of instruments classified under the heading of shawm, hautboys were produced in treble, alto and bass (the former two were similar to the modern oboe, the latter to the bassoon) (John H. Long 1961: 20–21). The sound of these instruments could convey a wide array of moods and meanings. The sound produced was "loud and piercing" (1961: 20), and they were used in outdoor amphitheatres rather than in indoor theatres. Dessen and Thomson suggest that hautboys might accompany: "(1) supernatural or sinister events; (2) an entrance of nobility or royalty; (3) a banquet, wedding procession or other ceremony; (4) a masque or dumb show" (1999: 115). Folkerth argues that because they were played by the watch, they were associated with the night and might be linked to the "liminal state between sleep and waking" (2002: 40). They certainly have this association in *Macbeth*, which tends to align hautboys and torches, creating an association between the sound and darkness. Hautboys and torches signal Duncan's fateful arrival at Macbeth's castle, and they also mark Duncan's last meal: "*Ho-boyes. Torches. Enter a Sewer, and diuers Seruants with Dishes and Seruice ouer the Stage*" (TLN 473–74). In an interesting play on this pattern, the show of eight kings that follows the three apparitions in Act Four Scene One is accompanied by hautboys (TLN 1651). As Folkerth has pointed out, this use of the instrument amalgamates the ceremonial and supernatural connotations of the sound (2002: 37–43, 88). The sound of the hautboy seems to have been at least potentially disturbing and sinister. As Dessen and Thomson note, it is described as "horrid noise" in *Double Marriage* (1999: 115), and the "*music of the hautboys ... under the stage*" in *Anthony and Cleopatra* strike Anthony's soldiers with fear, a scene discussed at length by Folkerth (2002: 37–43).

These, then, are the repeated, structuring acoustic patterns of *Macbeth*, its soundscape, or what Truax might call its keynote sounds: "those which are heard by a particular society continuously or frequently enough to form a background against which other sounds are perceived" (Truax 1999: Keynote.html). Against this backdrop occur several key "sound events" (Truax 1999: Sound_Event. html) that mark crucial moments in the play. These include the bell that is rung just before Duncan's murder, the knocking at the door immediately afterwards, and the "*Cry within of Women*" (TLN 2328) that heralds the death of Lady Macbeth. In listening to these sounds, it is important to recognize that they gain their extraordinary power through contrast with silence, a silence that paradoxically can be constructed only through speech and action. Moreover, as I will suggest, Shakespeare here exploits the association of sound and fear, the capacity of sound to startle, to stir a physical response and to prompt an orienting response, a search for the source of the sound.

John Cage famously wrote that there is no such thing as silence (Kahn 1999: 163). The film theorist Michel Chion, whom I discuss below in connection with Kurosawa, describes silence as relational, never absolute:

> [T]he impression of silence in a film scene does not simply come from an absence of noise. It can only be produced as a result of context and preparation. ... So silence is never a neutral emptiness. It is the negative of sound we've heard beforehand or imagined; it is the product of a contrast. (1994: 57)

If we suspend just for the moment the obvious differences between theatre and film, we can see that Chion's formulation provides a useful approach to the silences of *Macbeth*, which are similarly reliant upon sound. Sounds are used as "synonyms of silence" (1994: 58); when normally inaudible or background sounds are heard, such as the ticking of a clock or a whisper, "silence" is constructed through sound.

In the first two scenes of Act Two silence and darkness are mutually constitutive. The action of *Macbeth* is dominated by the night, presided over by the "secret, black, and midnight Hags"

(TLN 1577), the invocation of "thick Night" (TLN 401) by Lady Macbeth, and by the careful verbal construction of the night scene just prior to Duncan's murder. Act Two Scene One begins with the entrance of "*Banquo, and Fleance, with a Torch before him*" (TLN 569–70), in which explicit comment is made upon the darkness of the night; when Macbeth and "*a Seruant with a Torch*" (TLN 583) subsequently enter, the darkness is thick enough that the two cannot see one another. As the time for the murder draws near, sound and silence are used to establish the space of the night: "Now o're the one half World / Nature seemes dead, and wicked Dreames abuse / The Curtain'd sleepe" (TLN 629–31). Macbeth continues:

[MACBETH] Thou sowre and firm-set Earth
Heare not my steps, which they may walke, for feare
Thy very stones prate of my where-about,
And take the present horror from the time,
Which now sutes with it.

(TLN 636–40)

It is in this heightened atmosphere that the first of the sound events occurs: "*A Bell rings*" (TLN 642). We have learned earlier that this is a pre-arranged signal between Macbeth and Lady Macbeth (Macbeth tells the servant to bid his wife "when my drinke is ready, She strike vpon the Bell" (TLN 611–12)). This is one of three crucial sounds to which Macbeth's bodily response is noted; here he seems invisibly led by the sound: "I goe, and it is done: the Bell inuites me" (TLN 643).

As Macbeth exits in the direction of the bell, Lady Macbeth enters. In the next 50 lines is constructed the most intensive sonic environment of the play. Once the illusion of nightfall is firmly established in the broad daylight of the Globe stage, the audience, cued by the actors, is prepared to lower its auditory threshold and to attend to sound. As Truax notes (1984: 16):

The auditory system responds to the average noise level of any environment by shifting its sensitivity. ... One only has to remove all extraneous noise from the environment, dim the lights, and concentrate on one's hearing to experience the gradual dropping of the hearing threshold.

Here the lights are dimmed only in the imagination of the auditors, but the effect is none the less similar. Marvin Rosenberg's exhaustive account of performances of the scenes emphasizes the theatrical exploitation of the tension between sound and silence (1978: 316–51). Shortly after Lady Macbeth's entrance, attention is drawn to precisely this dynamic: "Heark, peace: it was the Owle that shriek'd / The fatall Bell-man, which giues the stern'st good-night" (TLN 650–1). Is this noise heard by the audience, or is it a dagger of the ear, so to speak? Dessen and Thomson mention a few examples of bird sounds, but they seem to have been relatively rare. Rosenberg cites a number of examples of productions which chose to cue a sound here, but its remains somewhat ambiguous. Indeed, Act Two Scene Two is full of sounds "heard" only internally by the Macbeths, creating the impression of a powerful and horrifying inner sonic environment unavailable to the audience.

Macbeth's first lines in Scene Two are "Who's there? what hoa?" (TLN 658). As with "Hearke, peace" the sibilants of the "h" and "s" mark the speech as a whisper. Whispering here does not necessarily denote a change in intensity or loudness of the sound;[10] rather the silibants of "Hearke" or "hoe" give the impression of difference from normal speech, a difference that is perceived as a whisper. Sound is perceived relationally, as Stephen Handel (1991: 108) points out in recounting experiments on perceiving the distance of speakers:

Listeners were asked to judge the distance for shouted, normal, and whispered voices. ... Even if the voices were the identical sound pressure, listeners judged the whispered voices closest and shouted voices farthest. Whispers denote intimacy and closeness; shouts denote distance.

Moreover, the use of short lines conveys the hyper-alertness generated by the dead night and the knowledge of the deed:

> [LADY MACBETH] Did not you speake?
> MACBETH When?
> LADY MACBETH Now.
> MACBETH As I descended?
> LADY MACBETH I.
> MACBETH Hearke, who lyes i'th'second Chamber?
> (TLN 668–73)

The actors speaking these lines must be audible to the audience, yet also convey the intense fear of being heard, an awareness of every small sound around them. The quickness with which each part of the line is picked up conveys the terrible intimacy of the moment, the heightened sensual attentiveness to the slightest sound. Ellen Terry wrote "together" in her notes for these lines suggesting that the two "exchange whispers, muttering, groans, gasps" (Rosenberg 1978: 330).

As Lady Macbeth exits to "guild the Faces of the Groomes" with blood, one of the most notorious of all sounds in Shakespeare occurs: "*Knocke within*" (TLN 715–17). Its effect—both on audience and actors—is electrifying. In part because of Thomas DeQuincey's famous essay "On the Knocking at the Gate in *Macbeth*" this sound is probably the best known of any in Shakespeare. In fact, DeQuincey's essay seems to have been prompted precisely because of DeQuincey's own inexplicable response to the sound: it "produced to my feelings an effect for which I never could account" (1896: 10.389). The physiological effect on Macbeth's body is made clear from his lines: "Whence is that knocking? / How is't with me when euery noyse appalls me?" (TLN 718–19). The film theorist Michel Chion reminds us that sound penetrates the body; we have no ear-lids to close it off: "... there is always something about sound that overwhelms and surprises us no matter what" (1994: 33). Sound has a direct effect on the body; sudden loud noises produce the acoustic startle response, a response consisting of

> the blinking of the eyes, head movement forward, a characteristic facial expression, raising and drawing forward of the shoulders, abduction of the upper arms, bending of the elbows, pronation of the lower arms, flexion of the fingers, forward movement of the trunk, contraction of the abdomen, and bending of the knees. (Landis and Hunt 1939: 21)

Studies of startle show that it is among the most invariant and immediate of human responses, though the intensity of the response varies considerably depending upon individual susceptibility, cultural attitudes towards startling, and the nature of the environment in which the stimulus occurs.[11] Not surprisingly, startles are stronger in dark and quiet spaces (Simons 1996: 129–30), just the sort of space that has been elaborately constructed through the voices and bodies of the actors.[12]

That this somatic response is cued is made clear from Macbeth's next lines, "What Hands are here?" (TLN 720). The best way of explaining the seeming *non sequitur* of Macbeth's sudden discovery of his hands before him is via the stage representation of an involuntary physiological response to so loud a noise, especially in the context of the hyper-attentiveness to sound constructed by the scene. Charles Kean, among others, drew out his hands at this point; as Rosenberg argues, "some such action as this starts Macbeth's mind in a new direction" (1978: 343–44).

In light of the extraordinary physiological effect of the knocking, Macbeth's response to an equally startling sound, the "*Cry within of Women*" (TLN 2328) in Act Five Scene Five, is particularly telling. The cry interrupts Macbeth's confident preparations for battle, which are signalled by the familiar sound of "Drum and Colours" called for at the beginning of the scene. "What is that noyse?" he asks Seyton, who answers "It is the cry of women" (TLN 2327–29). Most editors have Seyton exit to investigate its source, while Macbeth muses precisely on his lack of somatic response to the sound:

> MACBETH I haue almost forgot the taste of Feares:
> The time ha's beene, my sences would haue cool'd
> To heare a Night-shrieke, and my Fell of haire
> Would at a dismall Treatise rowze, and stirre
> As life were in't. I haue supt full with horrors,
> Direnesse familiar to my slaughterous thoughts
> Cannot once start me.
>
> (TLN 2330–36)

The horrifying nature of this "night-shriek" is here marked by Macbeth's somatic indifference to it. The bodily reactions of human beings to "direness"—the rousing and stirring of the hair (piloerection), the sudden start, the "cooling" of the senses—the very absence of these physical reactions to sound measures the effects of successive murders on Macbeth. In this musing, Macbeth seems to revisit the physiological effects of "direness" through the play. These include the famous "start" of Act One Scene Three that prompts Banquo's question—"Good sir, why doe you start, and seeme to feare / Things that doe sound so faire?" (TLN 151–52), long read as a somatic sign of the congruence between the witches' hail and Macbeth's own secret hopes, as well as the "suggestion, / Whose horrid Image doth vnfixr my heire, / And make my seated Heart knock at my Ribbes, / Against the vse of Nature" (TLN 245–48). In contrast to the appalling sound of the knocking, and the physiological effects of the inward imaginings, the night-shriek has no physiological effect on Macbeth, it cannot penetrate, it lacks the power to startle. Macbeth's lack of physiological response attests to his isolation, not only from the other characters, but also from the audience—the auditors—of the play.

Listening to Shakespeare in *Throne of Blood*

Here I wish to sketch the ways that Kurosawa listens to and revises the soundscape of *Macbeth*. Kurosawa's films are rightly praised for their stunning use of visuals, but his use of sound has been less appreciated. Kurosawa is unusually attentive to sound and music in his films. Donald Richie (1996: 240) comments:

> Ever since the silent film gave way to the talkie, sound has interfered with the image—and at the same time this flood of sound has become largely meaningless. That is why the director must be very careful—because a motion picture must be the most effective combination of both image and sound. Cinematic sound is never merely accompaniment, never merely what the sound machine caught while you took the scene. Real sound does not merely add to the image, it multiplies it.

Kurosawa's position here reminds us of Chion's observation that sound is transformative rather than additive; a film is not image plus sound (nor is a stage play, I would add), but "one perception influences the other and transforms it" (1994: xxvi). Kurosawa was known for working extraordinarily closely with his composer on his earlier films, Fumio Hayasaka. Masura Sato, Kurosawa's composer for *Throne of Blood* following Hayasaka's death in 1955, attests to Kurosawa's economy in the use of music: "There are many instances in his films where in the climatic scene no music whatever is used. He always says that music disturbs the more meaningful moments of a film" (Richie 1996: 241). Certainly the final scene of *Throne of Blood* is a telling example; the sounds of arrows, the cries and gasps of Toshiro Mifune as Washizu, the clatter of armour, and the sounds of Washizu's men retreating in fear before him—these indeed are the more powerful for the absence of music.

Stephen Prince has spoken of the visual compositional potential in Japanese architectural space, with its interior emptiness and stark geometrics, a feature also characteristic of the Noh theatre (1991: 146–8). Kurosawa's film uses this interior space to great visual effect, but equally he exploits its sonic potential, its status as a soundscape. Recurrent interior sounds include feet on wooden floors, the sound of doors sliding, the slow creaking of enormous doors and gates. Ambient or territorial sounds are also extremely important to the film, including the omnipresent sound of wind on the foggy peaks of Mount Fuji. Other diegetic sounds include the sound of galloping horses, the clatter of armour, the swish of the kimono, the distant sound of axes chopping down the trees, the sound of birds invading Forest Castle and the whistle of arrows alluded to earlier. Non-diegetic sounds and music are used very sparingly and are the more effective for that; examples include the low string tones that accompany many of the outdoor shots and, most strikingly, the sound of the Noh flute and percussion that are associated with Asaji. Kurosawa's sophisticated employment of sound and music in fact troubles the neat distinction between diegetic and non-diegetic sound, a "dichotomous schema" that reduces the complexity of the relationship between sound and space (Kassabian 2001: 42).

Michel Chion has written that film sound is primarily "vococentric", organized around and privileging the human voice ("Wasted Words" 104). If this is so, then *Throne of Blood* is an important exception to this principle, for in this film the human voice is dethroned, becoming one of many sounds, and perhaps among the least significant in the film. It is perhaps an example of what Chion has called "decentered speaking cinema" (1992: 110). Both voice and music (underscoring) are subordinated to the striking use of both on screen and offscreen sound.

The relationship between sound and image is never natural, though it may seem that way. Chion describes the process of associating sound and image as synchresis, the "spontaneous and irresistible weld produced between a particular auditory phenomenon and visual phenomenon when they occur at the same time" (1994: 63). By definition these are on-screen sounds; the filmmaker links sound with image, creating an illusion of a natural link between the two. In Kurosawa, such links are important sources of meaning; that is, the sound is not simply the sound made by the object, but the sound meant by the object. One striking instance of this effect in *Throne of Blood* is Kurosawa's attention to the sound of Asaji's kimono and the associations he constructs for this sound.

The scene in which we first hear Asaji's kimono is important for a number of reasons. Prior scenes with Asaji (the Lady Macbeth analogue) and Washizu (the Macbeth analogue) are shot with Asaji almost immobile and nearly inaudible. Her stasis infects Washizu with movement, as he paces around her, his feet audible on the wooden floor. In contrast, the wine-fetching scene reflects a striking reversal of this economy of movement and space in the film. Washizu is static and Asaji is mobile. As Asaji stands and moves for the first time, we hear the sound of her kimono swishing, as she moves in the circumscribed way that her dress demands. When she opens the sliding door to fetch the wine, she reveals one of the unexpected interior spaces that are a feature of Japanese domestic architecture. The visual deprivation—the blackness at the centre of the shot—is unsettling, and Kurosawa accentuates this element through his play with cinematic convention. The take is very long, framed by a medium-long shot from behind Asaji. As Asaji opens the door, the horizontal movement mimics the wipe cut that Kurosawa uses throughout this film.[13] Cut to a medium shot of Asaji entering the closet, framed by the door lintel. As she enters the space of the closet, she disappears, mimicking the fade. But the lintels of the door can be seen and, more importantly, the sound of the kimono can faintly be heard, revealing that this is a single take and that what we momentarily mistake for a cinematic technique is instead a dark interior space, anchored in "vectorized" sound (Chion 1994: 19), which fades, almost ceases, and then becomes gradually more audible just prior to her startling reappearance, facing the camera. Few directors would risk so long a take focused almost entirely on darkness. Within the frame the sound of rustling silk is isolated and suspending, irretrievably linking it with the murder of Lord Tsuzuki.

Throne of Blood is also rich in acousmatic sounds, those heard without seeing their source (Chion 1994: 71). "Active offscreen sound" is a form of acousmatic sound that "raises questions—What is this? What is happening?—whose answer lies offscreen and which incites the look to go there and find out" (1994: 85). Rick Altman, whose term for the same phenomenon is "sound advance" (1992: 251), has identified what he calls a "sound hermeneutic" in cinema:

> Cinema sound typically asks the question: "Where [does the sound come from]?" Visually identifying the source of the sound, the image usually responds: "Here!" The sound hermeneutic is the full question and answer process, as followed by the film spectator/auditor. (1992: 252)

Kurosawa exploits this hermeneutic, but with far more complexity than this simple question/answer model might suggest. Exploiting the conventions of suspense films, Kurosawa repeatedly protracts the process of seeking the source of the sound. Moreover, even when the source is discovered, its meaning and significance remain mysterious and frightening. Unfamiliar sounds evoke an orienting response; almost unconsciously, we turn our heads to discover the source of the sound. Kurosawa uses a repeated pattern of orienting responses that represent human responses to fear in an environment rendered unfamiliar and strange because of an originary act of violence. In these cases familiar, natural sounds are rendered terrifying because of their capacity to evoke the unknown.

The most obvious example of this pattern is the sound of the spirit in the woods. This scene begins with a long exterior shot, with the sounds of the Noh flute and percussion underscoring the diegetic sounds of rain and galloping horses. Rain, thunder and lightning mark this space; the forest is inhospitable to human beings. This long sequence plays off several recurring sounds: rain, thunder, horses galloping and whinnying, the shouts of the men as they attempt to gain control of the space. Typically the characters within the exterior space are dwarfed by it and disoriented, as they attempt to master it (the most striking example, of course, is the famous fog scene in which Washizu and Miki gallop in and out of the fog, away from and towards the camera, twelve times). The spirit seems to laugh in response to human volition; as Washizu fits a bow to his arrow, a clap of thunder is heard, followed by the sound of Washizu's arrow. Cut to the forest ceiling; the sound of laughter is heard immediately after the sound of the arrow. We cut back to a medium shot of Washizu peering upward in search of the sound, attempting to control his whinnying horse. There is no doubt about the origin of the sound; Washizu and Miki immediately identify it as supernatural. A protracted sequence of pans follows, as Miki and Washizu emit battle cries while galloping through the forest, surrounded by the sound of the spirit, until they arrive at its domain. The "what-is-it?" is answered easily; the "what-does-it-portend?" question drives the entire plot, as Washizu is driven by the words of the spirit.

The most telling series of sound hermeneutics takes place within the interior space of the castle and involve fear of penetration of the interior spaces by the world without. These scenes look ahead to the prophetic realization of the spirit's false promise to Washizu: that he will be safe until the trees of Cobweb Forest rise against the castle (an obvious reworking of the witches' prophecy about Birnham Woods coming to Dunsinane in *Macbeth*). As Davies remarks, "the major conflict in *Throne of Blood* is presented through the spatial polarity between the castle and the forest" (1988: 156). The interior spaces in this film are ordered, geometrical and regular; the exterior spaces disordered, winding and disorienting. The fear of the invasion of the former by the latter marks much of the final action of *Throne of Blood*, and these threats are revealed first sonically and only later, dramatically, revealed visually.

This series of sounds takes place through the night prior to the expected attack of Noriyasu, whose forces have gathered outside. In the first of these, a sentry is on guard on the battlements. It is the dead of night, "silent", no underscoring. The scene opens with a medium shot of the armed sentry peering out of the fortress battlements: "Can't see a thing."[14] He advances towards the camera, then turns his back and paces along the platform, where the space extends to include three sleeping soldiers below. He rouses one, speculating on what the enemy is doing in the darkness, but receives only a mumble in response. Again the sentry advances towards the camera, his face now framed in near close-up. Once the camera gets closer, a relative rarity in this film, the sentry suddenly freezes and orients towards the opening. He has heard a sound, only faintly audible, a distant repeating sound of metal on wood. Like the Macbeths, the sentry is hyper-alert to every sound; his startle and his physical orientation towards the sound mark its significance for the auditor/viewer. The sentry runs to his fellows, and we see them below, all oriented towards the sound, attempting to identify its source. The soldier below speculates that the enemy is building defences, which helps to identify the odd reverberating sound as an axe chopping wood. The scene ends as it begins, with a medium shot of the sentry peering through the opening, but now listening fearfully to the continuing sound. The sound hermeneutic is still incomplete: identifying its source—the chopping of trees—does not identify what it portends.

The scene shifts to a long shot of the council room, a geometric and symmetrical space dominated by Washizu, armed, seated on a stool, flanked by two rows of advisers and generals seated on the floor. They are drinking sake, and the room is silent except for the faint rustle of clothing and clatter of cups. Washizu breaks the silence by laughing and bragging of the fort's impregnability. As he is served sake, the sound of wood chopping is heard twice, mixed with and then dominated by another unidentifiable sound. This begins a protracted and suspenseful search for its source. Washizu and the generals orient to the sound, rising in fear. Cut to the soldiers outside on the platform, who also hear the sound and attempt to locate and identify it. As they search, we cut to a shot of the army, bearing torches, rushing into the courtyard. Now it is difficult to distinguish the unidentifiable sound from the clatter of armour and the rush of feet. Cut back to the council chamber, a longer shot revealing the low claustrophobic ceiling and the sentries on guard outside. Washizu is a tiny seated figure at the back of the room; the guards and generals are still in search of the source of the sound, looking upward. Finally the source is known; dozens of birds invade the council chamber. The camera closes in on the chamber, cutting rapidly to create a sense of consternation and chaos. In these two scenes, then, identifying the source of the sound—chopping of wood, flying birds—only increases fear and wonder. As the reactions of the generals and attendants reveal, the birds portend no good: "an ill omen", declares the eldest councillor.

Washizu laughs, scorns the generals for their cowardice, and declares the birds a good omen. But as he seats himself, and a bird briefly alights on his armour, a look of doubt crosses his face.

The next sequence begins with a brief exterior shot of the castle swathed in fog; low tones are briefly underscored. Cut to the council chamber, a long shot with four sleeping sentries in front and Washizu and his attendant visible at the rear of the room. The fog is beginning to penetrate the interior space of the castle, foretelling the coming invasion. Cut to a medium shot of Washizu, armed, dozing on his stool, his attendant sleeping cross-legged behind him. An off-screen voice, barely intelligible, crying "my lady!" awakens Washizu. First his eyebrow twitches, then he and the attendant stare in bewilderment towards the source of the sound. Washizu arises and we track him as he strides out of the room into the hall. His footsteps are counter-posed by the quick running steps of the female attendants fleeing in terror. Finally a shot from behind Washizu reveals a series of frames: the lintels of the door, the elderly maidservant, a kimono frame and a kimono. Cut to the kimono on the frame. Washizu slowly walks into the film frame, advances and starts at the sight, as yet invisible to the viewer. Washizu yanks down the kimono; for the last time we hear the swishing sound already firmly associated with Asaji and murder, and the camera closes in on Asaji, desperately cleaning her hands in an empty basin, punctuated by the sounds of gasping and rubbing.

This series of scenes reveal Kurosawa's skill in exploiting the sonic environments in the film. The chopping of wood in the dead of night and the sound of birds flying are significant, we later learn, because they are made as trees are hewn down for cover, thus fulfilling the prophecy. In the theatre, the spectacle of soldiers holding bits of tree branches can call forth an unintended laugh: here Kurosawa uses sound to set the stage for the later, horrific discovery of its source. The sound of chopping and the invasion of the birds, displaced from their trees, sets up the extraordinary visual rendering of the moving trees. The stunning effect of this image is rendered the more striking because it has already been framed by uncanny and frightening sounds.

Indeed, the most striking visual image in the film may be the shots of the moving Cobweb Forest. Seen from above, roughly from the point of view of Washizu, and punctuated by deep percussion underscore, this sequence is an extraordinary visual crescendo, as the disorienting exterior space of the forest approaches the castle. Only here is the sound hermeneutic complete, for in a film based on prophecy and the manipulation of human desires and actions by fate, we do not know what a sound is until we know what it portends.

I have argued for the importance of listening to Shakespeare, attending both to the technologies and conventions of sound available in the early modern theatre, and to the very different technologies and conventions of sound production in the cinema. Studying sound as a crucial element of adaptation forces us to see that sound is neither a natural nor a transparent phenomenon. Sounds are both physiologically determinate and culturally embedded, meaningful only when placed within a particular soundscape. Space shapes sound even as sound shapes space.

■ ■ ■

Questions and projects

1. Investigate only the use of sound (including dialogue) in a film adaptation and demonstrate how the use of sound becomes central to an understanding of that film as an adaptation.
2. Choose another Shakespeare adaptation (perhaps another cinematic version of *Macbeth*) in which there is a conscious engagement with the original language of the play or the terms of its original production. How and why does the adaptation remain faithful or unfaithful to those features of the original?

Notes

1   As Rothwell (2001) suggests, the question "Is it Shakespeare?" no longer drives most discussion of filmed Shakespeare.
2   Klimek (1992) is one of the few critics who has discussed sonic elements in Shakespearean adaptation.
3   This is perhaps something of an over-statement, as there is a large literature on sound, music, and film. However, it is dwarfed by work on the film image. The importance of considering sound in the cinema was argued in a special edition of *Yale French Studies*, edited by Rick Altman, which contained contributions from Altman, Christan Metz, Mary Ann Doane, Kristin Thompson, David Bordwell, and Claudia Gorbman, among others. In 1992, Rick Altman edited *Sound Theory Sound Practice*, a collection that re-visited the question of cinematic sound from a more material, historical and culturalist perspective. The standard anthology of writing on sound is Weiss and Belton (1985). See Kassabian (2001) for a relatively recent example of an argument based upon the under-representation of music and sound in the scholarship on film.
4   Soundscape is a term used by R. Murray Schafer and Barry Truax to describe the relationship between the acoustic environment and the perceiver of that environment. A play or a film represents a sound-scape in a particular way through the use of a series of "establishing sounds" (Altman 1992: 250). A soundscape of this type, then, is an intersection between the imagined sonic environment of the setting and the technologies of sound production and reproduction used in the theatre and the cinema.
5   The term was coined by Feld (1996).
6   See Gurr (1989); Smith (1999: 233–36) discusses the acoustic features of the Blackfriars; see also Sturgess (1987), ch. 5.
7   See William B. Long (1989) for a discussion of the importance of off-stage sounds and the efforts of the before preparer of the playbook to time them correctly.
8   All quotations to *Macbeth* are from Charlton Hinman's *The Norton Facsimile of the First Folio of Shakespeare* (1968) and cited by the through line numbering (TLN) of that edition.
9   For a discussion of the acoustic effects of the rhythm of the witches' speeches, see Kranz (2003).
10 See Truax (1999) for a definition of these terms.
11 There is a large literature on startle, in part because its study is amenable to laboratory conditions (that is, startle, especially acoustic startle, can be readily induced even among subjects who are expecting to hear a loud noise). The most comprehensive is Ronald C. Simons (1996), who includes a "museum" of startles in his book, many drawn from literature (including references to the *Macbeth* startles). See also Jenefer Robinson for a study that argues that such responses, generally seen as too low level for serious study of emotion, in fact provide a "useful model for the study of emotional response in general" (1995: 53), as well as Paul Ekman and colleagues (1985). Startle has also been widely studied in film, especially horror films, which are calculated to arouse "startle" in the audience; see Baird (2000).
12 Dessen and Thomson cite some sixty examples of the stage direction "start", a "sudden involuntary movement linked to surprise or awakening from sleep" that is sometimes "linked to a supernatural visitation or specifically to fear" (1999: 214).
13 Goodwin discusses Kurosawa's use of the wipe cut (1994: 141–6).
14 Subtitles are those of Donald Richie, *Throne of Blood* (Criterion Collection).

References

Altman, Rick. *Sound Theory Sound Practice*. New York: Routledge, 1992.
——, ed. *Cinema/Sound*. Special Issue of *Yale French Studies* 60 (1980): 3–286.
Baird, Robert. "The Startle Effect: Implications for Spectator Cognition and Media Theory." *Film Quarterly* 53.3 (2000): 12–24.
Chion, Michel. *Audio-Vision: Sound on Screen*. c. 1990. Trans. Claudia Gorbman. New York: Columbia UP, 1994.

———. "Wasted Words." In Rick Altman. (ed.). *Sound Theory Sound Practice*. New York: Routledge, 1992, 104–10.

Davies, Anthony. *Filming Shakespeare's Plays: The Adaptations of Laurence Olivier, Orson Welles, Peter Brook, and Akira Kurosawa*. Cambridge: Cambridge University Press, 1988.

DeQuincey, Thomas. "On the Knocking at the Gate in *Macbeth*." *The Collected Writings of Thomas DeQuincey*. Ed. Davis Masson. 14 vols. London: Black, 1896.

Dessen, Alan, and Leslie, Thomson. *A Dictionary of Stage Directions*. Cambridge: Cambridge University Press, 1999.

Ekman, P., Friesen, W. V., and Simon, R. C. "Is the Startle Reaction an Emotion?". *Journal of Personality and Social Psychology* 49 (1985): 1416–26.

Feld, Steven. "Waterfalls of Song: An Acoustemology of Place Resounding in Bosavi, Papua, New Guinea." *Senses of Place*. Ed. Steven Feld and Keith H. Basso. Santa Fe, NM: American Research Press. 1996.

Folkerth, Wes. *Sound in Shakespeare*. London: Routledge, 2002.

Goodwin, James. *Akira Kurosawa and Intertextual Cinema*. Baltimore, MD: Johns Hopkins University Press, 1994.

Gurr, Andrew. "*The Tempest's* Tempest at Blackfriars". *Shakespeare Survey* 41 (1989): 91–102.

Handel, Stephen. *Listening: An Introduction to the Perception of Auditory Events*. c. 1989. Cambridge, MA: MIT University Press, 1991.

Hinman, Charlton, ed. *The Norton Facsimile of the First Folio of Shakespeare*. New York: W. W. Norton, 1968.

Jackson, Russell. "From play-script to screenplay." *The Cambridge Companion to Shakespeare on Film*. Cambridge: Cambridge University Press, 2000. 15–34.

Kahn, Douglas. *Noise, Water, Meat: A History of Sound in the Arts*. Cambridge, MA: MIT University Press, 1999.

Kassabian, Anahid. *Hearing Film*. New York: Routledge, 2001.

Klimek, Mary Pat. "Imagining the Sound(s) of Shakespeare: Film Sound and Adaptation." In Altman, Rick. *Sound Theory Sound Practice*. New York: Routledge, 1992, 204–16.

Kranz, David. "The Sounds of Supernatural Soliciting in *Macbeth*." *Studies in Philology* 100 (2003): 346–83.

Kurosawa, Akira, dir. *Throne of Blood*. Perf. Toshiro Mifune, Isuzu Yamadia, and Minoru Chiaki. 1957. DVD. Criterion, 2003.

Landis, Carney, and Hunt, William A. *The Startle Pattern*. New York: Farrar & Rinehart, 1939.

Long, John H. *Shakespeare's Use of Music: A Study of the Music and Its Performance in the Original Production of Seven Comedies*. Gainesville, FL: University of Florida Press, 1961.

Long, William B. "*John a Kent and John a Cumber*: An Elizabethan Playbook and its Implications." *Shakespeare and Dramatic Tradition: Essays in Honor of S. F Johnson*. Ed. W. R. Elton and William B. Long. Newark: University of Delaware Press, 1989. 125–43.

Prince, Stephen. *The Cinema of Akira Kurosawa: The Warrior's Camera*. Rev. edn. Princeton, NJ: Princeton University Press, 1991.

Richie, Donald. *The Films of Akira Kurosawa*. Berkeley, CA: University Press of California, 1996.

Robinson, Jenefer. "Startle." *The Journal of Philosophy* 42 (1995): 53–74.

Rosenberg, Marvin. *The Masks of Macbeth*. Berkeley, CA: University Press of California, 1978.

Rothwell, Kenneth. "How the Twentieth Century Saw the Shakespeare Film". *Literature / Film Quarterly* 29 (2001): 82–95.

Schafer, R. Murray. *The Soundscape: Our Sonic Environment and the Tuning of the World*. 1977. Rochester, VT: Destiny Books, 1994.

Simons, Ronald C . *Boo! Culture, Experience, and the Startle Reflex*. New York: Oxford University Press, 1996.

Smith, Bruce. *The Acoustic World of Early Modern England*. Chicago, IL: University of Chicago Press, 1999.

Sturgess, Keith. *Jacobean Private Theatre*. London: Routledge, 1987.

Truax, Barry. *Acoustic Communication*. Norwood, NJ: Ablex, 1984.

———. *Handbook for Acoustic Ecology*. 1978. CD-ROM. Cambridge Street Publishing, 1999.

Weiss, Elisabeth, and John, Belton, ed. *Film Sound: Theory and Practice*. New York: Columbia University Press, 1985.

Chapter 29

Courtney Lehmann

OUT DAMNED SCOT
Dislocating *Macbeth* in transnational film and media culture

A N ACTIVE SCHOLAR OF SHAKESPEARE AND FILM, Courtney Lehmann examines a variety of recent films that have adapted *Macbeth*, often through the lenses of film genres such as film noir or the western. What distinguishes this study is its theoretical reading of the way the image of Scotland in Shakespeare's play becomes, despite the many textual differences in these contemporary adaptations, a transnational metaphor or ''idea'' that dramatizes the circulation and violence of global capital and the technological dislocation of modern spaces.

■ ■ ■

OUT DAMNED SCOT: DISLOCATING *MACBETH* IN TRANSNATIONAL FILM AND MEDIA CULTURE
COURTNEY LEHMANN

From Richard Burt and Lynda E. Boose (eds), *Shakespeare, The Movie, II*, New York: Routledge, 2003, pp. 231–251

Exploring the effects of verisimilitude in theater and film, Walter Benjamin observes that the concept of "place" in the theater cannot, ultimately, be severed from the spectator's location beyond the footlights, despite even the most powerful illusions of *mise en scène*. By contrast, cinema's ability to efface its own location in time and space is the very condition of its scopic seduction. It is, according to Benjamin, a kind of representational oasis, "an orchid in the land of technology" capable of removing us from the trivium of:

> [o]ur taverns and our metropolitan streets, our offices and furnished rooms, our railroad stations and our factories … burst [ing] this prison-world asunder by the dynamite of the tenth of a second, so that now, in the midst of its far-flung ruins and debris, we calmly and adventurously go traveling.

(1992: 672)

Benjamin's cautiously euphoric description of the centrifugal potential of cinematic representation uncannily invokes a far more recent arrival, digital technology, which has not only changed the landscape of film production, by making it widely affordable and accessible through digital distribution, but also revolutionized the act of reception as a mode of "production" in its own right. Indeed, the digital video disk (DVD) caters to the spectator's implied longing for supplemental spaces beyond the purview of the camera — provisional and performative places that invite us to construct our own film from the remnants of discarded footage, photo gallery stills, press kits, censored scenes, and multilanguage menus.[1] Accordingly, although this often highly privatized experience of home theater invokes a return to the solitary, orchid-like splendor that Benjamin ascribes to the hypnotic pull of celluloid, I would suggest that the experience of cinema today is more firmly rooted in the contested province of the thistle — a cross between a lone flower and a menacing mass of weeds — and, of course, the symbol of one place in particular: Scotland. Indeed, I shall argue that Scotland, and, more specifically, the dislocated "Scotland" that figures so prominently in twentieth-century media adaptations of Shakespeare's *Macbeth*, suggest a compelling metaphor for the transnational playground wherein the challenges and possibilities of globalization may be traversed. In the late 1990s and the new millennium, there have been no fewer than nine highly varied film, television, and internet adaptations of *Macbeth*, including a high-school video production available exclusively on the internet, adult straight-to-video and DVD spin-offs such as *In the Flesh* (Stuart Canterbury, 1998), and moderately successful independent films like *Scotland, PA* (Billy Morrissette, 2001).[2] What the adaptations I discuss have in common is not only a somewhat oblique relationship to Shakespeare's play but also a rather peculiar relationship to "Scotland": not one of them is set or shot in Scotland, and yet the idea of "Scotland" operates as a powerful metonymy for a place that is everywhere and nowhere in particular.[3] For example, the Glen Ridge High *Star Wars*-style *Macbeth* begins: "A long time ago in a galaxy far far away … Scotland" (Ben Conception, 2001). Similarly, *Scotland, PA* invokes "Scotland" only to displace it alongside the descriptive abbreviation "PA" rather than "UK." Ironically, though, the filmmakers started shooting in rural Pennsylvania only to find that they could not reproduce the look of middle America in the 1970s, and so the production moved to Nova Scotia — literally, "New Scotland." The portability of "Scotland" in the *Macbeth* films of the late 1990s and the new millennium is not, however, a mere capitulation to the hopelessness that Fredric Jameson ascribes to the postmodern condition, wherein the past can only be accessed through stereotypes that keep real history at arm's length but forever beyond our grasp (1992b: 19–20). Despite their obvious differences in production values and genre, these films more importantly suggest an attempt to map — "cognitively" and culturally — the co-ordinates of a new frontier that is not about taking the "high road" over the "low road" but, rather, about Scotland as a metaphor for the *road not taken*, a once and future landscape suspended between the imperatives of warfare and welfare, waiting upon our direction.

Taking the high (land) road *

Macbeth may be known as "the Scottish play," but the Scottish film is decidedly not *Macbeth* nor, paradoxically, is it "Scottish." As Brian Pendreigh (2002) observes, Scotland has historically been invoked on film as a place that is, in point of fact, anywhere *but* Scotland. A classic example is *Brigadoon* producer Arthur Freed's conclusion that, having toured picturesque locations in the highlands, "nowhere in Scotland … looked quite Scottish enough" and, therefore, he "went back to Hollywood, created Scotland in the studio and filled it with Americans in tartan."[4] Despite complaints of celluloid imperialism in classic films such as *Brigadoon* (Vincente Minnelli, 1954), however, the habit of viewing Scottish scenery and history through the lens of other national fantasies dates all the way back to the *Rob Roy* films of the silent era and culminates in their 1990s counterparts: *Rob Roy* (Michael Caton-Jones, 1995), starring Irishman Liam Neeson, and *Braveheart* (Mel Gibson, 1995), a film shot largely in Ireland starring the Australian-born "Mad Mac" himself, Mel Gibson. Although *Braveheart,* in particular, placed Scotland and Scottish history in an international spotlight, it did so, as Pendreigh points out, only by converting the character of William Wallace from lowlander to highlander, subscribing to the *Brigadoon* version of "Scotland" as a place of misty mountains, token tartans, and carefully cropped kilts. It seems only fitting that the film was most successful among Americans, who, quite unlike lukewarm audiences in Scotland, voted *Braveheart* the "second most important film of all time" (quoted in Pendreigh: 2002).[5] It is almost predictably ironic, then, that when the *real* Scottish film industry enjoyed a modest boom in the 1990s, marked by the release of *Shallow Grave* (Danny Boyle, 1994), this film — conspicuously shot in Edinburgh — opened with a disavowal of origins: "This could have been any city."

It is significant that this line is uttered as voice-over, for, as Joan Copjec argues, voice-over issues from an uncanny off-screen space, the space of the "bitemporal voice" that "cannot be situated in — nor subject to the ravages of — time or place" (1993: 185). This resolutely intemporal "place," I will ultimately argue, is the locus of the *real* Scotland, however much it may initially suggest the spectral appearances of *Brigadoon*. Voice-over narration is a staple of film noir, a genre that emerges, according to Copjec, as an attempt to cope with — and to warn of — the historical replacement of "desire" with "drive":

> the old modern order of desire, ruled over by an oedipal father, has begun to be replaced by a new order of the drive, in which we no longer have recourse to the protections against jouissance that the oedipal father once offered ... Which is to say: we have ceased being a society that attempts to preserve the individual right to jouissance, to become a society that commands jouissance as a "civic" duty. "Civic" is, strictly speaking, an inappropriate adjective in this context, since these obscene importunings of contemporary society entail the destruction of the civitas itself ....
>
> (1993: 182)

Shallow Grave, though by no means a noir detective film, opens with a voice-over that conveys a similar warning. For this initially comic story of middle-class twenty-somethings in search of a new flatmate quickly devolves into a murder rampage when the newcomer is found dead in his room with a huge stash of money. Rather than report the incident to the authorities, the roommates attempt to eliminate everyone who poses a threat to their efforts to hoard the money for themselves; and, as in *Braveheart* and *Rob Roy*, few indeed are left standing at the film's conclusion. In hindsight, then, the line issuing from the death-inflected, disembodied voice-over — "this could be any place" — functions as a powerful warning that the fetishization of drive — of private *jouissance* — has "mortal consequences for society" as "ever smaller factions of people proclaim their duty-bound devotion to their own special brand of enjoyment..." (Copjec, 1993: 183). That the "any place" featured in *Shallow Grave* is Scotland as opposed to "Scotland" is significant, not just for the obvious admonitory suggestion that such perverse self-interest has become the rule as opposed to the exception but also for the more subtle implication that understanding the difference between the two Scotlands may, in the not-too-distant future, be the difference between life and death.

Something is rotten in the state of Scotland

The fact that *Braveheart* and *Rob Roy* have been commercially more successful than films such as *Shallow Grave* and, later, *Trainspotting* (Danny Boyle, 1996) is not due to production values alone; rather, it is their contrasting ideological values, masked as differences of genre, which constitute the geopolitical gap between the Scottish film and the "Scottish" film. If *Shallow Grave* and *Trainspotting* suggest postmodern variations on the discomfiting themes of film noir, then *Braveheart* and *Rob Roy* are more at home among the maverick triumphs that are the topos of the American western. However, I would argue that whereas film noir confronts us with an alienating vision of a society that embraces drive over desire, the western — or, more accurately, the neo/"Scottish" western — only pretends to restore the reverse order. For heroes like William Wallace and Robert Roy MacGregor engage in mass military campaigns that fulfill their personal need for "revenge" and "honor," respectively, only by masking these private drives as political desires tied to land, freedom, and the sexual possession of women's bodies. The ideological upshot of *Braveheart* and *Rob Roy* is, therefore, not the isolated and, ultimately, dispensable victory of the traditional "outlaw" hero of the American western from Shane to Dirty Harry but, rather, the insidious validation of the corrupt system itself — a twist that is often missed in the glorification of individual courage that figures prominently in 1980s neo-westerns such as *Robocop, Rambo, Top Gun, Diehard,* and *Superman.*[6] In all of these films, the means — that is, drives — are never called into question so long as they achieve the desired ends. As Susan Jeffords explains, "the removal of a few bad individuals — whether incompetent police captains or hardened criminals such as Lex Luthor — will presumably return the system to its operating purpose: serving average Americans" (1994: 20). In *Rob Roy* and *Braveheart*, we need only substitute the corrupt Scottish gentry for the "police" and the arch-evil English King Edward Longshanks for "Lex Luthor" to apply Jeffords's conclusion; in the former, an already corrupt system is shored up when Rob Roy earns the respect and protection of the gentry who wish him — and each other — dead, just as in the latter film, the one-time-traitor-turned-Scottish-king, Robert the Bruce, replaces the martyred commoner William Wallace to lead the rag-tag Scots to victory over the English. The conclusion of both "Scottish" westerns boils down to the choice of a lesser evil that ultimately does little to change the system: the unpardonable English crime of genocide gives way to the provincial Scottish acceptance of indiscriminate homicide.

Where, then, does *Macbeth* enter the picture? Ever since Orson Welles failed to keep his 1948 *Macbeth* film — originally recorded in a Scots burr — from being redubbed into "accent-free" English, subsequent film versions have blatantly called the bluff of the play's setting by featuring visibly non-Scottish locations — from Ken Hughes's Chicago-based mafia film *Joe MacBeth* (1955) to Akira Kurosawa's medieval samurai setting for *Throne of Blood* (1957) to Andrzej Wajda's Yugoslavian film *Siberian Lady Macbeth* (1961) and, finally, to Roman Polanski's hallucinatory "Playboy" *Macbeth* (1971).[7] As in the traditional western genre, these films cannot be interpreted apart from the landscapes against which they emerge. But Shakespeare's *Macbeth* is neither a traditional nor a neo-western of the Reagan/Bush Sr. era; it is, rather, a "northern" western in both its topological and sentimental climate, which is to say, *Macbeth* is a noir western that is also, unarguably, Scottish. What I am calling the noir western takes as its point of departure the recognition that there never was an old "modern order of desire, ruled over by an oedipal father" in the first place. Rather, like the historical predicament of pre-modern Scotland, there are only so many chieftains posing as would-be fathers among their clans, all of whom maintain varying claims to the land and the personal ascriptions of entitlement it embodies. In other words, the Scotland of Shakespeare's play, like the unevenly globalized network of late capitalism, does not revolve around the choice between two evils but the proper choice of pleasures in a system characterized by an excess of *jouissance*.

And the range of possible articulations of drive in these films is as broad as the ideological expanse that separates the enabling heterogeneity of the Scottish clans from the oppressive singularity of the "Scottish" Ku Klux Klan. What the noir sensibility interjects into the framework of the western, then, is quite literally a change of scenery, converting the hero's mastery of the great outdoors to the menacing interior spaces — industrial and psychological — that characterize the noir anti-hero's increasingly claustrophobic sphere of action. In this spirit, the *fin-de-siècle Macbeths* I shall turn to now go one step further than their screen predecessors by dislocating Scotland from its moorings in anyplace at all, as "Scotland" becomes synonymous, for better or for worse, with a state of mind.

Macbeth meets Mad Max, or, the persistence of (Mel Gibson's) memory

In *Shakespeare, The Movie* (1997), Lynda E. Boose and Richard Burt cite *Clueless* (Amy Heckerling, 1995) as a symptom of Shakespeare's increasing displacement by marketing strategies that privilege, in the case of Heckerling's film, "knowing Mel Gibson's *Hamlet*" over knowing Shakespeare's *Hamlet* (1997: 8). The lure of Gibson's star persona, in other words, contains enough pop cultural capital to compensate for the fact that Cher (Alicia Silverstone) has lapsed momentarily from thunderdome to loserdom by watching a Shakespeare film in the first place. What's most curious about this episode, as Boose and Burt explain, is the fact that *Clueless* is based on the canonical Austen novel, *Emma,* which makes Cher's anti-intellectual equation of "success" with "pride in not knowing one's Shakespeare" a startling departure from the tradition that posits "Shakespeare and the English literary tradition ... [as] a rallying point of national superiority" (1997: 12). Thus, *Clueless* suggests the extent to which Hollywood capitalism has infiltrated even the most intractable markets. Only two years later, Michael Bogdanov's English Shakespeare Company teamed up with Channel 4 UK to create a made-for-television version of *Macbeth* that reveals an even greater, albeit selective, dependency on Mel Gibson's star power to sell Shakespeare; for this film is nothing less than *Macbeth* shot through the lens of *Mad Max* and, perhaps, a more subtle attempt to divert attention away from the recently released *Braveheart*. Though both the gun-toting Mad Max and the broadsword-bearing William Wallace serve as intriguing screen prototypes for a 1990s Macbeth, the former implies a rationale for British colonialism, whereas the latter clearly critiques it: the lawless renegades in the *Mad Max* series are the indigenous, pleasure-seeking Others who must be "civilized" or eliminated, whereas the hedonistic marauders in *Braveheart* are the English themselves. Significantly, Bogdanov's film was released in the same year as a Scottish referendum voting for the devolution and the establishment of a Scottish parliament, the first in nearly three hundred years.

Filmed on location in the Australian outback, *Mad Max* (George Miller, 1979) and its sequels, *Road Warrior* (1981), and *Beyond Thunderdome* (1985), are all set in a post-apocalyptic no-place featuring salvaged scraps of sheet-metal, motorcycles, black leather and, most memorably, Mel Gibson as the former-cop-turned-rebel-with-a-cause, seeking to avenge the murder of his wife and child. Bogdanov's setting for *Macbeth* suggests a "Scottish" variation on this theme — a dystopian *Brigadoon* that emerges from the smoke of intermittent bombs rather than whimsical highland mist, revealing, in the process, the burned-out vestiges of a once green and hilly landscape. According to the video jacket description, *Macbeth* occupies "a timeless zone," set "against a raw, urban industrial environment giving the film a surreal quality." Entering this "timeless" space as road warriors in their own right, Macbeth (Sean Pertwee) and Banquo (Michael Maloney) burst on to the scene astride motorcycles, sporting paramilitary garb replete with tartan accessories. But this is the point at which *Macbeth* and *Mad Max* appear to part company, for although Pertwee's Macbeth — with his spikey hair, tinted shades, and studied sense of road rage — bears a family resemblance to Gibson's Max, Pertwee's "Mad Mac" lacks the personal justification that is the trademark of Gibson's enraged screen personae. In reading Bogdanov's film through the lens of the noir western, however, we may discover that this Macbeth does have a battle-axe to grind after all, one that shifts our prurient gaze away from the devastated wasteland that is "Scotland" to the abject interiors that are its source, namely, "the guilty horizon of bourgeois comfort and detachment" (MacCannell 1993: 280).

The singular irony of the neo-noir revival of the early 1990s, according to Dean MacCannell, is that films such as *Public Eye* (Howard Franklin; 1992), *The Two Jakes* (Jack Nicholson, 1990), and *Barton Fink* (Joel Coen, 1991), offer a "fictional recuperation" of classic noir's interest in seamy, gritty, subproletarian city spaces "just as the actual proletarian space is historically lost" (1993: 282). The upshot for filmmakers is that they have been forced to virtualize, if not fantasize, "the imaginary boundaries of urban misery" in the form of artificial sets (1993: 282); however, the consequence for the actual occupants evicted from these spaces during the Reagan revolution is, of course, literal homelessness. It is significant, then, that in Bogdanov's film Macbeth does not come across as angry or "mad" until after his encounter with the witches — the abject threesome who are also marked as homeless. Poised over a flaming trash-heap, the witches are clad in filthy layers of tattered clothing, bandanas, and grime; they speak with thick Cockney inflections and gesture with dirty fingers poking out of hole-ridden gloves. Their open-air, makeshift dwelling is crudely assembled from discarded junk. Two of the witches are Caucasian, one is black, and their capacity to horrify resides in their uncanny familiarity — they are, in other words, not otherworldly enough but, rather, altogether too real. Accordingly, although Bogdanov's film was received both critically and commercially as a poor imitation of Baz Luhrmann's highly successful version of *Romeo + Juliet* (1996) released the year before, I would argue that the primary shortcoming of this *Macbeth* is its failure to live up to the escapist fiction it promises. Far from inviting us into a timeless zone, Bogdanov's film is a brutally timely allegory of the present.

After Macbeth's encounter with the witches, the scenery that begins in the province of the wide open spaces of the western shifts almost exclusively to interiors — large, vacant, post-industrial spaces that once served as the urban playground of film noir, which, in the noir western, have become a metaphor for the dark corners of unexamined conscience. This is the psychic landscape that Dean MacCannell identifies with "senile capitalism," a capitalism that has forgotten its once enabling relationship to three democratic ideals. MacCannell's provocative reflections on this unexplored tension at the very heart of film noir warrants quoting at length:

> After defeating its external enemies, fascism and communism, capitalism entered its "twilight years"; increasingly it began to turn its fading powers against its own partner, democracy, for harbouring and promoting a historically antiquated, inefficient ideological surplus. From the perspective of mature capitalism, the historical purpose of its partnership with democracy was (1) to break the privilege of aristocratic classes, making way for new entrepreneurial elites, and (2) to win the hearts and minds of socialists and others still tied to noncapitalist modes of production by offering them freedom of speech, choice, etcetera. Once traditional privilege is destroyed, and everyone is involved in the same system of global economic relations, there is no further need for democracy.
>
> (1993: 284)

The problem with this assertion, of course, as critics of globalization have made clear, is that not "everyone is involved" equally in this system, just as "drive" cannot enter into equilibrium with "desire" but instead only displace it. Significantly, in Bogdanov's *Macbeth,* it is Duncan (Philip Madoc) who is implicitly aligned with senile capitalism's uneven distribution of resources. Distinguished by his impeccably clean, non-combat wardrobe and his train of bodyguards who, later, sport slick, slim-lined suits and sunglasses — the dry-clean-only uniform of the corporate thug — Duncan suggests a portrait of senile capitalism in its worst incarnation, namely, "microfascism." As the seamy flip-side of postmodernism's exaltation of fragmentation, microfascism crystallizes as "smaller, more localized but equally exploitative power formations" made possible by an uneven global economy (Braidotti 1994: 5). This is the pseudo-medieval and distinctly postmodern fiefdom over which Duncan presides in Bogdanov's film.

Though Bogdanov's *Macbeth* fails to appeal to audiences expecting a sequel to *Romeo + Juliet,* his film is, in many ways, far more current than even Luhrmann's. For his updating of *Macbeth* is firmly rooted in a culture wherein the paternal metaphor has undergone a perverse mutation — a mutation that is encoded in the empty, abject interior spaces that pervade this film and signal its placement within the paranoid perceptual schemes of the noir universe. What is most striking about Bogdanov's approach to these interiors is the opaque quality of their emptiness; it is as if the emptiness itself is always already "filled" with a void. Lady Macbeth's chamber is a case in point, dwelling in an enormous horizontal space punctuated only with hurricane lamps and satin pillows clustered together on a dirty floor. Lady Macbeth (Greta Scaachi) reposes elegantly on the pillows in a conspicuous attempt to recover a sense of dignity long since eroded with the scraps of Duncan's royal favor. Far from being the benign, essentially absent, oedipal father of Shakespeare's play, then, Duncan suggests the obscenely present, noir father who serves not to protect but to prevent his subjects from threatening his control of the resources. Indeed, how could such an allegedly good king allow the thanes who bleed for him to live in such grotesque urban squalor, wherein people dwell like rats in abandoned warehouses-turned-tenements, entering and exiting their vast crawl spaces through windows, scaffolding, and fire escapes? The result of a dramatic shift in the demographics of factory work in the 1990s, this post-industrial wasteland is a clear indication that the jobs have all moved away to unnamed places where the labor is cheap and the workers are infinitely replaceable. As for the loyal drones who stayed behind — Macbeth and company — their occupations, like their surroundings, appear to be Duncan's whim.[8] At least at the beginning of the film, then, Macbeth is the figure who embodies the broken promises of senile capitalism. Prompted by the indigent witches to reflect on his own slumbering sense of self-worth and, it would seem, on Duncan's failure to provide for his kingdom, Pertwee's Macbeth can barely conceal his shock and rage when he is passed over by Duncan as the heir apparent to the throne. Even the other soldiers seem to expect Duncan to name Macbeth as his successor; but instead he singles out his son — the smug, spoiled Malcolm (Jack Davenport) — whose distinctly unsullied uniform, perfectly tilted beret, and tough-guy grimace (the product of long hours of practicing in the mirror) resembles what the young George W. Bush must have looked like when he served his cushy, dramatically abbreviated term in the Texas National Guard to avoid Vietnam. Following the forced round of applause that punctuates Duncan's unexpected announcement, Macbeth begs his leave to become "Mad Mac," violently kicking the fuselage at his feet when he is barely out of sight of the others. Like no other version of *Macbeth* before it, Bogdanov's film implies that Duncan gets exactly what he deserves. Indeed, the fact that the only high-tech moment in this putatively futuristic film occurs when the King's royal train enters Macbeth's "estate" via a stretch-water-limo — a tableau that seems to parody the lost splendor of the medieval castle moat — is a clear indication that Duncan approaches postmodernism's potentially democratic dislocations of time and space as an opportunity to revive feudal privileges. What distinguishes Bogdanov's film as a noir western, then, is the fact that such privileges are figured spatially, that is, as the masterful occupation of real and psychic space. In such a context, homelessness is not defined as the loss of "home" but as the loss of a meaningful relationship to space.

This is where Scotland enters the picture as a locus for imagining the possibilities of fortuitous dislocation, which I call "cinenomadicism," namely, the refusal to be bound exclusively to one "plot" of narrative, action, or land. For a short time, *Macbeth* seems committed to the distribution of social justice — and redistribution of resources — implied by this concept. Indeed, his murder of Duncan and, consequently, the expulsion of his privileged sons to England and Ireland, seem to leave Scotland with a clean slate, a space for renegotiating the lost contract between the free market and democratic freedoms. But under Mad Mac's leadership, "Scotland" becomes increasingly identified with nostalgia for the future, a variation on what Fredric Jameson calls "nostalgia for the present" in the form of the future that never will be?[9] For the bleak, post-industrial spaces that we see through the eyes of Pertwee's Macbeth suggest a perverse Dickensian fairy tale in which the ghost of capitalism future — microfascism — has already arrived. Thus, more than anything else, Bogdanov's setting seems to comment cynically on the Scottish tourism boom of the 1990s, which was stimulated by the creation of industrial theme parks designed "to recapture the glories of Scotland's industrial past which was now vanishing fast from the real manufacturing economy" (Devine, 1999: 596). Bogdanov's film of Shakespeare's Scottish play takes up this "theme" not from the perspective of the accidental tourist but from the specter of the intentionally evicted and occupationless.

However sympathetic Macbeth may be at the beginning of the film, Mad Mac cannot be the hero of this noir western, for this genre is marked by the refusal to anthropomorphize what is, fundamentally, a corruption of space itself. Consequently, Macbeth succeeds in vanquishing Duncan's neo-feudal, microfascist dynasty only by falling prey to the same horizon of bourgeois comfort and detachment as his predecessor. Unlike Duncan before him and Malcolm after him, though, Macbeth never looks comfortable in his borrowed robes. Rather, he wears his gaudy suits with the self-ironizing posture of an aging rock star, attuned to every coarse crackle of his leather pants and glaring shimmer of his sateen shirts, as if he were straining under their lack of breathability even as they mark him as capitalism's synthetic, that is, self-made man. Thus, when he attempts at the end of the film to restore his road warrior look with paramilitary garb and tartan trim, it is painfully obvious that the Macbeth of old, like the Scotland of the future, is a thing of the past. Indeed, in the process of wrestling with Macbeth, Macduff (Larcon Cranitch) reveals that he is now wearing the pants — in the form of long underwear bearing the royal Stuart tartan. But if, in the twilight years of capitalism, the clothes still make the man, in 1990s *Macbeths*, the tartan no longer makes the Scot; for in the very instant that Macduff finishes off Macbeth, Malcolm arrives fresh from the croquet lawn of his English mansion (or is it his Texas ranch?) to take credit for the victory. Unique to Bogdanov's version, Macduff glares resentfully at the perfectly coiffed Malcolm, but climbs into the Hummer to join him and his henchmen anyway. Malcolm proceeds to assert his mastery over the space he inherits by abandoning it, peeling away from this scene of industrial apocalypse in search of greener, undoubtedly suburban pastures. And so the Reagan/Bush revolution returns in the form of the son who is too young to be senile but old enough to repeat Daddy's mistakes by rote. In the final scene, Macbeth is dumped by a garbage truck onto a trash heap, and the witches eagerly pillage his body in search of accessories for their nomadic dwelling, assuring us with sinister certainty that the vicious formula of this noir western will, like Macbeth's body, be recycled.

Taking the low road: Shakespeare does Scotland

The next version of *Macbeth*, Stuart Canterbury's 1998 porn-feature *In the Flesh* (written by Canterbury and Antonio Passolini), ventures a step beyond Bogdanov's *Macbeth* to explore the abject "interior" spaces that define the explicit sex film. In many respects, hard-core pornography suggests the ultimate articulation of the noir western, not only for its exploration of the forbidden territories associated with sexual transgression but also for its vision of apocalyptic capitalism — that is, consumption without reproduction — based on the fetishization of the all-important "come shot". Like Bogdanov's *Macbeth, In the Flesh* takes for its point of departure the triumph of "drive" over desire in a landscape that is rife with a retro-futuristic sense of déjà vu. Macbeth (Mike Horner) and Banquo (Valentino) enter the film via a military jeep, dressed in disruptive combinations of crisply decorated military jackets and tartan kilts. And, as in Bogdanov's film, they dodge flames from detonated bombs as the jarring rattle of machine-gun fire pervades the air. Similarly, the witches are represented as homeless refugees — "probably shell-shocked," Banquo mutters — as the vaguely other-worldly women warm themselves over the flicker of a garbage can fire. Unlike Bogdanov's *Macbeth,* however, these indigents are not shunned as pariahs but, rather, marked as alluring threshold figures whose implied nomadicism is sexy, suggesting the ancient association of female mobility (*nomas*) with sexual promiscuity and prostitution. Clad in black latex body suits that leave nothing to the imagination, the witches beckon toward Macbeth and Banquo, inviting them to sample their wares. But contrary to our expectations for hard-core porn films, Macbeth blithely rejects their offer, paternalistically advising an all-too-eager Banquo that it is "best not to sleep with witches." Quite literally left to their own devices, the weird sisters proceed to get downright freaky among themselves, taking the viewer on a sexsploitation obstacle course that culminates in the head witch using a double-pronged dildo to pleasure the other two. In the broader context of the film, this image suggests the proverbial fork in the road — and, for Macbeth, the "road not taken" — to Scotland. Even before Macbeth and Banquo encounter the witches, *In the Flesh* opens with a series of allusions to the "Scottish film." With the help of an establishing shot of a medieval castle façade enveloped in highland mist and a voice-over in a heavy Scots burr, the film begins with an aura of *gravitas*, as the indignant voice exclaims:

> Kings come and kings go. That's the nature of war, that's the nature of life. How many battles have been fought for next to nothing? For a piece of land, for a piece of respect, for a piece of ass — but never for peace itself. That's the big lie. And it's what men do best. As men we build our castles of power and greed and lust — and then — like beasts we knock them down.

This is the pseudo-medieval "Scotland" of *Braveheart* and *Rob Roy,* the land frozen in time, shrouded in fog, and filled with noble barbarians. But this is the last we hear of Scottish accents as the scene shifts from the pastoral haunts of haughty highlanders to the hidden pleasures of urban bohemians, as the DVD jacket promises:

> Shot on film in the exotic locale of Budapest, IN THE FLESH is a perverse twist on the classic tale of Macbeth — complete with greed, betrayal, madness, and of course, plenty of lust. Set in a retro-future world of castles and cars, and packed with the most beautiful new actresses Europe has to offer, this lush epic depicts the rise to power of Lord Macbeth (Mike Horner) and his insatiable wife, Lady Macbeth (Kylie Ireland). Featuring the hardest action imaginable in the most breathtaking locations, IN THE FLESH is an assault on the

erotic senses, a sex spectacle of unprecedented proportions, that only Stuart Canterbury (*Dreams, Foolproof*) and Antonio Passolini (*Cafe Flesh 2, Devil in Miss Jones 6*) could create.

"Location," as it appears in this description, resonates as a naughty pun, since nothing in the film — from the castle interiors to the alfresco frolicking in the open air — signifies a place that is specifically "Budapest" other than the thick eastern European accents and swarthy, "Magyar" look of the cast members. Yet the artificial Budapest of *In the Flesh* has much more in common with Scotland — the land dislocated from the historical fictions I have been exploring here — than we might first realize.

Originally a borderland dividing settled cultures from nomadic ones, Hungary has historically been more deserving of the designation "Bohemia" than the Czech-populated land to the north-west, serving as a pivotal point of passage not only for Huns, Turks, and Mongols, but also for northern European tribes like the Finnish Magyars who eventually settled there. Like the "Scotland" of *Macbeth* and, as we shall see, the Hungary of *In the Flesh,* the concept of the "bohemian" is constituted precisely by its lack of a meaningful connection to place. Falsely ascribed to a nomadic people thought to live in Bohemia, the term "bohemian" emerged in association with "gypsy" which, in turn, is a word mistakenly tied to Egyptians. Nomadic in its own right, "bohemian" is a word that has accrued a variety of subversive associations over time to become a catch-all expression for "an extravagant sexual life, mobility in abode, and freedom from governing morality" (Peters 1999: 37). It seems only fitting, then, that these nomadic energies (spurred by the steady flow of capital into the former Soviet bloc) should return to Hungary and, in the process, transform Budapest into the new "Bohemia" as the center of the global porn industry. Porn, as Joseph W. Slade explains, has always been a matter of national self-interest, serving as a lucrative export for northern Europe and, in southern European countries like Spain, offering opportunities for increased tourism to cities where hard-core theaters are legal. The situation in Hungary is quite different, for unlike its European competitors, Budapest is known not only as a hothouse for Slavic beauties who "perform enthusiastically" but also as a place that welcomes the cinenomadic energies of the global market.[10] Budapest is, therefore, particularly appealing to American producers seeking to package their product as sufficiently "bohemian" — that is, dislocated from the sociopolitical imperatives of "place" — in order to circumvent GATT restrictions, which stipulate that half the programs broadcast in Europe be European in origin (in France they have to be 60 percent "French"). Under the deceptive aegis of "co-production," then, porn has become a truly multi- or, better put, *trans*national product, promiscuously following the flows of globalization so that an "American" film, for example, will "borrow the capital from a German bank, employ a Hungarian cast assembled by a European casting agency, shoot in English, distribute through a French company, and sell the product everywhere" (Slade 1997: 6).

Such a process is akin to what Dean MacCannell describes as "the perverse accommodation of capitalism by democracy" (1993: 289), a by-product of a distinctly noir environment wherein guilt — but not necessarily the pleasures associated with it — gets distributed "evenly," that is, "globally." Accordingly, the closer we look at the real conditions of production in Budapest, the more disturbing they become from the perspective of the ratio of guilt (expenditure) to pleasure (profit). Indeed, there is something vaguely sado-masochistic about the fact that Hungary, as Joseph W. Slade explains, uses porn as a means of reducing its foreign debt; in fact, the Hungarian government "actively encourages porn production because it injects revenue into the service sector" (1997: 8). Of course, this industry inflects the phrase "service sector" with distinctly bawdy overtones, which, ultimately, offer insufficient comic relief from the more sinister reality that Budapest has become such a popular site for porn films not only because of the comparatively low cost of production, but also because the women tend to be less educated and, consequently, less aware of AIDS (Slade 1997: 8). In this respect, a porn noir western like *In the Flesh* literalizes the trope of the femme fatale which, in classic film noir, represents "desire as something that not only renders the desiring subject helpless, but also propels him or her to destruction" (Cowie 1994: 145). Yet *In the Flesh* simultaneously poses a variation on this theme. For if, as in Shakespeare's play, this film is bound to end in an apocalyptic vision of death (and indeed, in the porn noir universe, the specter of AIDS suggests the ultimate embodiment of the obscenely present, devouring father), then "survival" is not predicated on winning the war but, rather, on enjoying all the battles along the way. In this brave new "Scottish" world of bohemian sexual coalitions, Mike Horner's Macbeth is defeated *not* because he succumbs to the femme fatale but because he *doesn't*: Macbeth is the villain of this film because of his monogamous refusal to "enjoy his symptom" of globalization.

When in Scotland, do as the Bohemians do

In the Flesh is particularly fascinating for the way in which it updates Shakespeare's Scottish play to further its own ideological enterprise. The conspicuous absence of Malcolm — along with Lady Macduff's children and Banquo's son Fleance — underscores the fact that dynasties are irrelevant in the world of non-procreative and nomadic sexual relations. But the freedom from sexual orthodoxy that is the *raison d'être* of porn is precisely what Macbeth resists in this film. After Macbeth's rejection of the witches' invitation, the scene shifts to Lady Macbeth (Kylie Ireland) satisfying herself with a dildo in preparation for Macbeth's arrival. Whether she is igniting the home fires in anticipation of more pleasure with her husband or as a pre-emptive strike against his impotence, is uncertain. It is significant, then, that Lady Macbeth casts the proposition to kill Duncan (Mike Foster) in terms of a sexual bargain; not only does she threaten to leave Macbeth for a "real man" if he doesn't rise to the occasion but, worse, upon his initial refusal, she ups the ante by resolving to dress him up in her "dirty little panties" and make him her "pet," her "puppy dog." Rather than suffer this apparent humiliation, Macbeth determines to "do whatever it takes to be a man," and proceeds to engage in the standard progression from oral to vaginal to anal sex with his demanding wife. But this is the first and last time that Macbeth has sex in a porn film in which he is purportedly the star. Moreover, his is the most uninventive, uninspired sex scene, compared with Duncan's two-women-on-one-man before and Banquo's three-men-on-, under-, and over-one-woman after. Macbeth's sudden and seemingly irreversible decline from virility to virulence is signified most dramatically by his lack of participation in the banquet, which, in this film, takes the form of an orgy. Indeed, Macbeth can only recoil in horror at the sight of Banquo's ghost participating in the tartan-trimmed flesh-fest that takes place on the long table over which he presides. In this Bacchanalian spin on Shakespeare's banquet scene, Macbeth is mortified not by Banquo's return from the dead but, rather, by the fact that he is being showed up by a ghost. The implication is that Banquo is an even more potent lover in death than he was in life, thus rendering the murder a failure and Macbeth an unlikely victim of John Ashcroft syndrome.[11]

In this "Scottish" film, then, Macbeth is what is wrong with the picture, for he is the only non-Bohemian. Consequently, Lady Macbeth's death is represented as being causally related to Macbeth's impotence.[12] Constantly assuming the sexual initiative at the beginning of the film, Lady Macbeth is, by the end, reduced to a mere spectator. Dwindling through the dungeon with candle in hand, she assumes a posture of disaffected voyeurism as the cell block denizens mock her plight with their sexual antics. The flickering and, finally, snuffing out of her "brief candle" thus signals the death of her phallic prowess. Appropriately, her masturbation and ensuing suicide in the bath tub — labeled "final fantasy" on the DVD menu — shows her dreaming of one last tryst with her once-hardy husband: the implication, according to the mercenary logic of porn, is that monogamy, not promiscuity, kills. As if to reinforce this distinctly noir suggestion, just prior to this scene Lady Macduff (Mira) is killed immediately after having sex with her well-hung Hungarian husband, which serves as foreplay to the kilt-clad Macduff's murder of Macbeth. However, the fact that Macduff (Zenza Maggie) is the implied sole survivor at the film's conclusion does not ultimately endorse the idea that monogamy kills but instead suggests that the horizon of microfascism has shifted. For in the age of AIDS, this film ultimately suggests that nomadic encounters "in the flesh" have necessarily been replaced by the prosthetic pleasures of autoeroticism. Yet these pleasures are not automatically safer than their bohemian counterparts, for they remind us — like the opening scene of self-detonating war instruments issuing intermittent flames — not only of the zero-sum game of suicidal terrorism, but also of the spectacle of remote control warfare with smart bombs and unmanned planes, which remains the isolationist prerogative of those nations with the most pleasure and the least guilt.

Macbeth, the comedy: from Luke Skywalker to Walker Shortbread

In 2001–2, three parodies of *Macbeth* emerged to mark the turn of the new millennium: the Glen Ridge High *Star Wars: Macbeth* (2001), *Scotland, PA* (2002), and *Macbeth, The Comedy* (dir. Allison LiCalsi, 2001); the first and last are digital films shot in a matter of days on next-to-nothing budgets, whereas *Scotland, PA* is an independent film featuring recognizable faces such as the inimitable Christopher Walken, *ER* star Maura Tierney, and *Ally McBeal* cast member James LeGros. The comedic aspect of these *Macbeths* in no way disqualifies them as noir westerns, for these are distinctly "dark comedies" that use place — often reflected in product placement — to spin sinister tales of corporate ambition even as they imagine the possibilities of a post-corporate cinenomadicism. What is most provocative about the Glen Ridge High *Star Wars: Macbeth* and *Scotland, PA* is that in contrast to the retro-futuristic worlds of Bogdanov's *Macbeth* and *In the Flesh*, these films stage their unintentional but relentless returns to the present with a detour through the past — and, more specifically, the recent past of the 1970s. In both films, however, the nostalgic focus on the more simple pleasures of bygone decades cannot ultimately insulate their *mise en scènes* from the ruthless pleasures of the present; for neither film can erase the specter of what Slavoj Zizek calls the "unhistorical kernel" which, by way of its inexhaustible repetition, gives the lie to every "new" epoch by dressing up the same historical crisis in different clothes (1992: 81). The central gambit of these noir westerns, then, is to mask time — and the attendant traumas of history — in spatial terms, focusing on "far far away" places in which lived temporalities are subsumed by a nostalgic fascination with space.

In peculiar respects, the Glen Ridge High School student production of *Macbeth* suggests a sequel to *In the Flesh*, for the traumatic kernel that its location can never completely repress is the notorious gang rape of a retarded girl by Glen Ridge High School jocks in 1989. Suddenly, this small, extremely affluent American town that prided itself on its above-average SAT scores, successful sports teams, and no fewer than 666 of the 3000 remaining gas lights operative in America, found itself in a seedy national spotlight. Describing the Glen Ridge community, the local Congregational Church minister explained that "[a]chievement was honored and respected almost to the point of pathology ... whether it was the achievements of high school athletes or the achievements of corporate world conquerors" (quoted in Lefkowitz 1998: 130). Teachers, parents, and citizens in this 1.5 square-mile community were accused of turning a blind eye to the increasingly disturbing behavioral patterns they witnessed among the popular boys at Glen Ridge High, which involved parsing people — mostly women — into categories of conquest, culminating in the rape of fourteen-year-old Leslie Faber. One such objectified group, however, was comprised of mostly males: the nerds that the jocks called "giggers," a derogatory combination of "gigabyte" and "niggers." Nine years later in the Spring in 1997, the giggers struck back, creating a video (digitally remastered and released in 2001) for their High School English class that represented the geeks inheriting the earth or, better put, the galaxy.

In keeping with the history of the Scottish play on screen, this version of *Macbeth* begins with the simultaneous citation and displacement of Scotland: "A long time ago in a galaxy far far away … Scotland." In this film, Scotland is identified as a revisionary landscape, a place of childhood nostalgia that is, in fact, no further away than the 1970s — the decade before the golden boys turned bad — when they were just kids hooked on the recently released *Star Wars* (George Lucas, 1977). Significantly, the filmmakers themselves weren't even born yet; but when they reached the age that the jocks had been when they first watched *Star Wars,* these giggers were bombarded with news footage of the galactic meltdown occurring in their own back yards. Their ensuing retreat in *Star Wars: Macbeth* to a space-time before they were born thus enables the filmmakers to engage in a form of nostalgia which, in Walter Benjamin's terms, is "revolutionary": by synchronizing the past with the future, *Star Wars: Macbeth* imagines thwarting the teleological march of historical inevitability that will culminate in the Glen Ridge tragedy of the late 1980s.[13] In this context, then, Scotland is identified with a once and future place in which the giggers prevail and kids with cameras are capable of digitally remastering history.

Offering a variation on the dark comedy that constitutes the American high-school experience, this film features an attractive, athletic-looking Macbeth (Ben Concepcion) being defeated by glasses-wearing, semi-preppy nerds. Following a slew of lightsaber fencing, the rather awkward "Luke Skywalker" character, Macduff (Donald Fitz-Roy), presents an African-American "Malcolm" (Robert Fuller) with Macbeth's head in a backpack. Moments later, this McForce, replete with "Hans Siward" (Raymond Perez), make their getaway from the Glen Ridge High gymnasium (a place where geeks are never at home) by departing in a replica of the Millennium Falcon spacecraft. The implication is that this multicultural entourage is now headed "back to the future" with a clean slate, having eliminated the evildoers who will give the school and its surrounding community a bad name a decade later. What remains uncertain, however, is what these whiz kids will do when they return to the future. Indeed, given the post-Columbine release of the digital version of the Glen Ridge High School *Macbeth*, it would be difficult not to infer — even amid the fairly innocuous lightsaber battle scenes — an image of the jocks and popular kids being murdered by nerdy, trenchcoat-sporting outcasts. Yet what is markedly different about the scenario posed by *Star Wars: Macbeth* is the multiracial cast; these are not the disturbed, underachieving, neofascist white boys of Columbine High but, rather, the gifted products of transnational mergers of people, places, and profit shares in the cosmopolitan north-east. It's not surprising, then, that almost all of the cast members are currently attending Ivy League universities. But the conspicuous product placement at the end of this short film makes us wonder which "forces" will prevail when these boys leave school once and for all.

Following the triumphant finale wherein the student cast is spliced into film footage of *Star Wars* itself in order to receive their rewards from a pimply-faced Princess Leia (Rebekah Heinzen), the scene suddenly cuts away to Macduff and Malcolm back at school enjoying a Coke in front of the soda machine. This moment of brotherly solidarity between young black and white men explicitly invokes another media product of the 1970s: the "I'd like to buy the world a Coke" campaign. Whether these Glen Ridge High grads teach the world "perfect harmony" or corporate conquest remains to be seen — and screened. In the meantime, they offer "Scotland" as a piece of cinenomadic real estate where, at least for now, *anyone* can be at home, as "Yoda's advice for the budding filmmaker" on their website implies:

> If you have a video camera lying around, and better yet some editing equipment (pretty cheap for computers nowadays), go experiment. Be your own director, Go Hollywood … use a skateboard for dollying shots, or a fishing rod for special effects. … You don't need The Force – just some friends with a video camera.[14]

Scotland, PA is an inherently darker film that heads west from the affluent borough of Glen Ridge, New Jersey to explore the discount dreams and working class realities of dilapidated, rural Scotland county, also known as western Pennsylvania. Unlike the escapist fiction of *Star Wars: Macbeth*, Billy Morrissette's vision of the 1970s hearkens back to the recession and disillusionment with the government that followed the Vietnam War and Watergate scandal. Here, the forces that the characters contend with are explicitly commercial, as the film tells the story of a thirty-something couple who, trapped in the abyss of lower-management, suddenly become seized with the ambition to be the wealthiest, most successful folks in town. But the "McBeths" lack the all-important punch of pedigree and, therefore, their meteoric rise to power is short-lived. In Morrissette's film, this fundamental lack has everything to do with location, which seems to inscribe the social pathology of "going nowhere" in the nondescript topography of the land itself. Like the transitory status of Budapest, western Pennsylvania is a borderland situated between the industrial-agricultural economy of the Midwest and the slick corporate ethos of the tri-state area. By default, then, western or "Scotland" Pennsylvania is the natural habitat of "American McAnybody's" — and, perhaps, McEverybody's — "duking it out over the most popular power structure around, the small business" (Rippy, 2002: B16). What makes this outrageous comedy a tragedy, as Marguerite Rippy incisively observes, is the nature of the lesson the McBeths learn from Shakespeare, namely, "that British primogeniture survives intact in American capitalism" (2002: B16). Thus, in *Scotland, PA* it is hard not to root for Joe "Mac" McBeth (James LeGros) and his wife Pat (Maura Tierney) to succeed in their quest to be *somebody's*, since we cannot avoid thinking that at one time or another, "Scotland" — the place of loss, shame, and unfulfilled dreams — is somewhere we've all been before.

The fact that Morrissette stages his version of *Macbeth* as a literal tragedy of appetite situates this film firmly within the perceptual schemes of the noir universe, wherein it is not the specter of failure — and, consequently, of desire — that propels the narrative but, rather, its relentless satisfaction. Indeed, *Scotland, PA* draws us into the void of unfulfilled desire that lends meaning to the McBeths' loser lifestyle only to render us complicit in the formation of their super-sized drive for forbidden, deep-fried *jouissance*. Most profoundly, then, *Scotland, PA* explores the insidious symbiosis between space and ambition that is the topos of the noir western. As in Bogdanov's *Macbeth*, when we initially enter this space our sympathies lie with McBeth, since we have already seen Norm Duncan (James Rebhorn) pass him over for promotion and, worse, appoint his estranged son Malcolm (who wants nothing to do with his father or fast-food) as the new head manager. Consequently, when McBeth drowns Duncan in the deep-fat fryolater, he becomes a local hero, for once the old order of Oedipal prohibition is eliminated, the illusion of the democratic right to consume takes its place and, suddenly, enjoyment becomes the ultimate expression of "civic duty" (Copjec 1993: 182). With the help of the nomadic technology of the drive-through and a traveling French fry truck, McBeth's business expands exponentially. In the process, however, Pat's psychic space suffers steady constriction, an infirmity that works its way outward to the fryolater burn on her hand, which, she believes, is only worsening with time. That's because time cannot be synchronized with drive; by its very nature, it can only be identified with lack: "We're not bad people, Mac," Pat says to her husband while urging him to kill Duncan, "we're just underachievers who have to make up for lost time." But Pat will have to settle for space, for her one moment of glory occurs when, for the first time in her life, she appears content in her surroundings; drink in hand, she is buoyed up by the sheer bliss of her location which, the camera pulls back to reveal, is an above-ground pool, marking her arrival on the scene of the modest, Midwestern American dream.[15]

Unlike the other *Macbeth* films I have examined here, *Scotland, PA* is the only one that privileges place over protagonist, underscoring the notion that this is not really Mac's tragedy but Pat's, the figure most identified with her surroundings. She is also quite clearly the brains in the operation but, like other women in the 1970s who were contemplating their autonomy for the first time, she still requires a man to execute — and, consequently, profit from — her plans. And though she attempts to safeguard the private moments *of jouissance* that come from her suddenly, solidly, middle-class existence, the "burn" on her hand which, unbeknownst to her, has healed completely, begins to drive her insane. Copjec's observations on the paranoid, increasingly claustrophobic dimensions of the noir universe are particularly apropos of Pat's predicament: "from the moment the choice of private enjoyment over community is made, one's privacy ceases to be something one savours when sheltered from prying eyes … and becomes instead something one visibly endures – like an unending, discomfiting rain" (Copjec 1993: 183). After pharmacological creams and burner mitts fail to remove Pat's sensation of pain, a meat-cleaver does the trick, and she dies with a grin on her face. Thus, if the "burn" is the symptom of Pat's forbidden enjoyment of middle-class existence (forbidden because, based on the choices she made at nineteen, she'll never be considered classy enough to deserve this lifestyle in her thirties), her smile suggests her identification with the *sinthome,* or, "the impossible junction of enjoyment with the signifier" (Zizek 1989: 123). In other words, Pat's smile of relief signifies her liberating realization, having traversed the fantasy of her impossible class ambition, that there is nothing left for her but to identify with lack itself, for "beyond fantasy," Zizek explains, "there is no yearning … only drive … pulsating around some unbearable surplus-enjoyment" (1989: 124). Thus, Pat's violent removal of her hand is not so much the mark of a guilty conscience as it is an acceptance of the absence of desire itself — the loss of the desire to desire. As Zizek contends, "the image that most appropriately exemplifies drive is not 'blind animal thriving' but the ethical compulsion which compels us to mark repeatedly the memory of a lost cause" (1991: 272). Scotland, Morrissette's film implies, is the place where dreams go to die. The remainder of the film takes shape as a battle between the pseudo-Scots McDuff and McBeth or, more appropriately, *McCloud* and *McBeal.* Indeed, Christopher Walken's unlikely crime-stopping character parodies the 1970s detective series *McCloud,* whereas James LeGros's McBeth invokes his personification of Mark Albert on the recently canceled series *Ally McBeal.* Like McBeth, Mark Albert is not a leader but a follower, hence, he is drawn to phallic women (on *Ally McBeal,* he actually dates a woman whose incomplete sex-change operation leaves her with a penis). Pat McBeth is, of course, the phallic woman par excellence and, for a time, she exercises masterful control over their new-found, fast-food kingdom. But not even she could have anticipated the Loch Ness monster that McBeth becomes, roving and ravaging the open spaces that now seem too small to contain his appetites. Appropriately, then, the vegetarian McDuff steps in to restore the old order of prohibition, turning McBeth's meat joint into a health-food restaurant where no one, the film's conclusion implies, will go to eat. Fittingly, following the melodramatic showdown on the roof of the restaurant, McBeth flees, pausing in front of his car to take one last look at the neon sign that bears his name; seizing the advantage, McDuff jumps from the roof onto McBeth, impaling him on the steer horns that adorn his car. Punished in kind for grabbing the bull of social ambition by the horns, McBeth's gruesome death implies that it is not his bad deeds that destroy him, but his bad taste. This scenario might be funny if it weren't for the fact that Morrissette's film, with its Bad Company soundtrack, bell bottoms, Cameros, and *McCloud* in-jokes, actually succeeds in making us nostalgic for 1972, and even for "low-end corporate cutthroats" like the McBeths.[16] For the problem is that *Scotland, PA* can never completely escape its real location in 2002, which makes Mac and Pat's small-time, small-town McCruelty seem like child's play compared to their sequel. Indeed, what the fetishized arches of the letter "M" in this film ominously point to is what comes after "M" — "En" — as in noir and, of course, Enron, whose solution to the forgotten pact between capitalism and democracy is to steal from *everyone*, though not necessarily in equal measure. Compared with stock land, Scotland never looked so good.

If we didn't know that *Macbeth: The Comedy* was shot on location in New Brunswick, New Jersey, and New York, its setting could be just about anywhere that Walker Shortbread ships. Indeed, even more so than in *Scotland, PA,* in Allison LiCalsi's film, "Scotland" is not so much produced as it is consumed, for Walker Shortbread, Glenlivet Scotch Whisky, "mad for plaid" fashions, and "Thank God I'm SCOTTISH" placards make all the Scottish world a stage for comedy – and commodities.[17] Yet what distinguishes *Macbeth: The Comedy* from *Scotland, PA* is the fact that rather than serving as markers of distinction and separation, the product placements form a continuum between places defined as home and the marginalized spaces of exile: "have shortbread, will travel" seems to be the only social qualification for movement in this film. *Macbeth: The Comedy* thus refuses to inscribe Shakespeare's play within the structures of loss and longing that are, according to Homi Bhabha, the province of globalization. For in the process of creating access to "a range of materials and material cultures with an ease never before imagined," globalization, Bhabha contends, erodes the prospect of "being-and-belonging by virtue of the nation, a mode of experience and existence that Derrida calls a national ontopology" (1999: ix). With the exception of LiCalsi's film, the *Macbeths* of the late 1990s and new millennium ultimately suggest a conservative reaction to this loss of national ontopology in their portraits of "Scotland." For if Bogdanov's *Macbeth* and *In the Flesh* are fueled by the diasporic energies of transnational media culture and, consequentiy, look to Shakespeare for ontological stability, then the Glen Ridge High *Star Wars: Macbeth* and *Scotland, PA* are exilic narratives that similarly appropriate Shakespeare as a source of nostalgia for better times and places that remain, nonetheless, hopelessly out of reach. Set in neither the "retro-future" nor the recent past, *Macbeth: The Comedy* privileges not a monadic conception of "Shakespeare" but, rather, a cinenomadic idea of Scotland.[18] As in the other noir westerns I have explored here, the through-line in LiCalsi's comedy is its preoccupation with the centrifugal energies of multinational capitalism. However, in this film, the act of conspicuous consumption is not visibly marked by class distinction, and capitalism itself is conceived of as a horizontal, rather than vertical, force. For example, although the three male witches appear homeless as they wander across the snowy countryside of New York bedroom communities, their clothes signify their bohemian lifestyle as fashionable, even willful. This Utopian concept is first introduced in the opening scene, where the witches huddle together for warmth over a steaming kettle until — in a moment of unimaginable horror — a Karl Lagerfeld sweater rises to the surface of the bubbling cauldron and "Sassy Sister" shrieks: "I told you it was dry clean only and now it's ruined, you bitch!" But the class markers that are absent from this seemingly non-discriminatory distribution of products are reinscribed in the frequent citations of Shakespearean verse, virtually all of which result in annoying interruptions of the dramatic action and are signaled by the sudden irruption of "serious" orchestral background music. Duncan (John little), for example, requires Donalbain (Gerald Downey) to translate for him every time a character cites lines from the play "You'll have to excuse my father," Donalbain explains, "Ever since verse came into fashion, he's been a bit confused." Unlike Karl Lagerfeld, however, "Shakespeare" is a brand name that is clearly out of fashion in this film.

For in this bizarre vision of late capitalism as all play and no work, Shakespeare himself comes to be identified with the old order of prohibition — the blocking figure who interrupts the flow of consumption as characters desperately labor to produce his lines with proper accent and inflection. According to this logic, then, Malcolm (Hugh Kelly) is represented as the heir apparent only because he is the son who practices his Shakespeare recitations at every conceivable opportunity, but, like his father, he often fails to comprehend their meaning.

Suggesting a variation on the theme of *Scotland, PA,* which sets out to answer the question "What if the McBeths were alive in '75?", Allison LiCalsi's comedy asks "What if the Macbeths could say what they were really thinking in the play?" What classifies *Macbeth: The Comedy* as a noir western is, therefore, its attempt to turn Shakespeare's play inside out: to expose, in the dark recesses of each character's conscience, the thoughts that they are cloaking in the often obscure semantics of Shakespearean verse. Consequently, the film subscribes to an entertaining form of literalism that paradoxically liberates Shakespeare's metaphor-laden language from the landscape of hidden meaning, recreating it within the topos of "plain English." The effect is the equivalent of *Macbeth* on a truth serum, for every Shakespearean line is accompanied by a Stanislavskian paraphrase that tells the real story behind the words. For example, upon determining to leave Scotland, Donalbain exclaims with conviction: "I'll go to Ireland," adding, "the beer will be cheaper there." Similarly, in the process of easing Malcolm's guilt over fleeing to England, Macduff (Ted de Chatelet) calls the bluff of his own cowardice, freely confessing: "I myself only the other day deserted my wife and kids." Plot ambiguities are likewise given logical, albeit updated explanations, according to LiCalsi's parodic approach to her Shakespearean predecessor. Consequently, the "weird sisters" are not siblings but, rather, gay male fashion mongers named Sassy Sister (Michael Colby Jones), Scary Sister (Phillip Christian), and Southern Sister (Christopher Briggs); meanwhile, Macbeth (Erika Burke), whose manhood is repeatedly indicted in the play, is literally converted to a woman in a lesbian marriage with Lady Macbeth (Juliet Furness) — a scenario that also conveniently explains why the Macbeths can't produce a legitimate heir to the throne. The most unpredictable aspect of this seemingly reductive approach, however, is the way in which it deepens and complicates the psychological layers of Shakespeare's play, as this cinematic Macbeth increasingly appears to struggle against the pull of her textual destiny. In the beginning of the film, Macbeth is fully capable of either interrupting her Shakespearean outbursts in *medias res* ("'Stars hide your fires' — no, stop that!") or decoding them in her own terms ("'So foul and fair a day I have not seen.' We really kicked some ass.") But by the end, her decisive decline into insanity is signaled when she is handed the "tomorrow" soliloquy on a scroll by her servant (Lisa Rezac), and, upon reading it, compliments the verse profusely, exclaiming: "did you write that? I gotta tell ya, it's really good." Naturally, the servant takes credit for the work, claiming enthusiastically, "there's more where that came from!"

Like Shakespeare's Macbeth before her, this female Macbeth is foiled by her pathological embrace of the witches' prophecy which, ironically, she fails to interpret *literally enough*. It never occurs to her that Macduff could be the product of a C-section, or that Birnam Wood will come to Dunsinane not of its own volition but, rather, with a little help from soldiers in search of camouflage. Often seen with book in hand and citing Shakespearean verse by rote, the witches in LiCalsi's film represent the lapse from cinematic fluidity — "an acute awareness of the nonfixity of boundaries" (Braidotti 1994: 56) — into the prescriptive assertion of textual certainty, ushering in Macbeth's tragic destiny. Ironically, in this comedy, it *is* tragic when Macbeth dies, not only because she's so likable but also because Malcolm, the new King, is devastated by her death. Indeed, he christens his reign by sobbing hysterically: "I could've changed her [from a lesbian] … I know I could've." And in some respects we can't help but believe him, for in this provisional space called Scotland, we are led to believe that anything is possible. Here, lesbians can be legally married, servants claim to authorize Shakespeare, homeless people sport Karl Lagerfeld fashions, and everyone "thanks God they're Scottish" — whatever that means. Indeed, whatever location this film gestures toward, we can be certain that it won't play in Peoria, but we can hope that it will emerge from the mists once and for all in another hundred years.

Conclusion: "If it isn't Scottish it's crap!" – Mike Myers

It seems only fitting that in *Macbeth: The Comedy,* it is the witches' weirdly worded prophecy that is associated with the menacing noir core of Shakespeare's play, much in the same way that film noir — despite its claims to esthetic autonomy — can never escape classification based on the detective fiction that precedes it. But if, as Marc Vernet provocatively claims, "Film noir is a collector's idea that, for the moment, can only be found in books" (1993: 26), then these recent *Macbeths,* remind us that Shakespeare, too, is a collector's item that, for the moment, can only be found in films. I would suggest, then, that it is not "Scotland" but *Shakespeare* who is the damned spot, Scot, or what you will, which these films relentlessly seek to traverse, inhabit and, ultimately, displace. But it is one thing to displace Scotland; it is something else entirely to replace Shakespeare as the "unhistorical kernel" that constitutes every new version of *Macbeth* as an unwitting act of repetition. Indeed, it should not surprise us that there is an outpouring of *Macbeth* films when, in the world at large, we are witnessing "an explosion of vested interests that claim their respective difference in the sense of regionalisms, localisms, ethnic wars, and relativism of all kinds" (Braidotti 1994: 146). Given the extent to which the horizon of reception has changed in the wake of the digital diaspora, the temptation has never been greater to retreat further into the private *jouissance* of our personal entertainment units. But the proper choice of pleasure, as Shakespeare repeatedly reminds us, lies not in reproducing the home theater of cruelty featured in *Macbeth* but, rather, in adopting a politics of movement that generates accountability from positionality. This, then, is the "damned spot" that marks the "X" – the point at which the high road and the low road meet in the recognition that *every* road can lead to the enabling dislocation that is Scotland, provided we are willing to leave the comforts of our homes.

■ ■ ■

Questions and Projects

1. Discuss a recent filmed adaptation of a Shakespeare play in which an image, scene, or metaphor redirects the meaning of that adaptation towards contemporary social, economic, or political issues.
2. With a Shakespeare film as an example, argue as to why this work seems especially suited (or not) to two or three central issues in contemporary life (such as debates about gender, race, technology, family, nationhood, or others).

Notes

I especially wish to thank Caroline Cox, Skip Willman, Marguerite Rippy, Allison LiCalsi, Patrick Murray, and Richard Burt.

1   My thanks to Richard Burt for letting me read his introduction and related material on digital culture and globalization from his book-in-progress, *Rechanneling Shakespeare across Media: Post-diasporic Citations and Spin-offs from Bollywood to Hollywood.*

2   In addition to the films and television adaptations I discuss, other versions include a French adult feature entitled *Macbeth* (dir. Silvio Bandinelli, 2000), *Macbeth* (dir. Jeremy Freeston, 1997), filmed in Scotland and set in the eleventh century, *Macbeth on the Estate* (dir. Penny Woolcock,1997), set in English housing projects, *Macbeth in Manhattan* (dir. Greg Lombardo, 1999), a play-within-a-film, and *Macbeth-Sangrador* (dir. Leonardo Henriquez, 1999), filmed in Venezuela. Two versions of *Lady Macbeth of Mzensk,* were also filmed, one of Dmitri Shostakovich's opera with soft-core sex scenes (dir. Petr Weigl, 1992), and the other of the short story on which the opera is based (dir. Roman Balayan, 1989). The latter is available on video but without English subtitles.

3   Richard Burt (1999: 77-125) makes the point that even Jeremy Freeston's use of Scotland in his 1997 *Macbeth* is highly mediated by *Bravehart.* On the reception of *Braveheart* in Scotland, see Maley 1998.

4   <http://www.imideouLco.uk/scots/briefhistory.shtml>.

5   *Braveheart* and *Rob Roy* also suggest conservative reactions to the multiculturalism debates of the 1990s, since these films represent places and identities that enable white men to get in on the game and "go ethnic" themselves.

6   See *Robocop* (Paul Verhoeven, 1987); *Fast Blood* (Ted Kotcheff, 1982); *Rambo: First Blood Part Two* (George Pan Cosmatos, 1985); *Rambo JJI* (Peter MacDonald, 1988); *Top Gun* (Tony Scott, 1986); *Diehard* (John McTiernan, 1988); *Superman* (Richard Donner, 1978); *Superman 2* (Richard Lester, 1980); *Superman 3* (Richard Lester, 1983); *Superman 4* (Sidney J. Furie, 1987). For a discussion of these films, see Susan Jeffords's *Hardbodies* (1994), particularly Chapter 1: "Life as a Man in the Reagan Revolution."

7   It is worth noting that Welles's *Macbeth* is now available in its "restored" form (with the Scottish accent) on both DVD and video.

8   Bogdanov's vision of Duncan as the post-industrial, obscene father may trace its imaginative origins — particularly given its production in the UK — to the Michael Gambon character in Peter Greenaway's *The Cook, the Thief His Wife and Her Lover*, 1989.

9   See Jameson's chapter in *Postmodernism* (1992b), titled "Nostalgia for the Present"

10   For a thorough analysis of the global politics of the porn industry, see Joseph W. Slade 1997.

11   John Ashcroft was defeated in the Governor's race on November 7, 2000 by Mel Carhnahan, who died before election day but nonetheless beat Ashcroft.

12   On impotence and Shakespeare porn more generally, see Burt 1999.

13   See Benjamin 1968.

14   See <http://www.glenridge.org/Macbeth.mainpage.html>.

15   Appropriately, just before the premiere of *Scotland, PA,* Pat's (Maura Tierney's) *ER* character, recovering alcoholic Abby Lockhart, fell off the wagon after six years and drank a beer. Although her fall from grace received "jeers" in the "Picks and Pans" section of *TV Guide,* what seemed gratuitous on *ER* proved the perfect backstory to Pat McBeth's single moment of glory in *Scotland, PA.*

16   <http://www.lot47 .com/scotlandpa/press,,macbeth.html>.

17   I am especially grateful to Allison LiCalsi and Patrick Murray for generously providing me with a copy of *Macbeth: The Comedy,* as well as for offering detailed information about the conception and making of the film.

18   The opening credit sequence underscores this rather contestatory relationship between Shakespeare's play and LiCalsi's film. Alluding to a line at the beginning of Sam Taylor's 1929 *Taming of the Shrew* that reads "Based on the play by William Shakespeare, with additional dialogue by Sam Taylor," LiCalsi's film ups the ante with the statement: "story and additional dialogue by William Shakespeare." It seems only fitting that this allusion to a claim that mortified purists in the first-ever Shakespearean "talkie" should be revisited as an opportunity for virtually silencing Shakespeare in this millennial parody of *Macbeth.*

Chapter 30

Hilary Schor

EMMA, INTERRUPTED
Speaking Jane Austen in fiction and film

A PROFESSOR OF ENGLISH, GENDER STUDIES, AND LAW at the University of Southern California, Hilary Schor approaches the 1995 adaptation of Emma by focusing not, as commonly happens, on casting decisions or the visuals of sets and costumes but on the use of narrative voice and disruptive voices in the film. On the one hand, this essay is a precise and illuminating example of an analysis that carefully compares the literary text and the film. On the other, it redirects readers to the fact that it is important not only to see an adaptation but also to listen to adaptations.

■ ■ ■

EMMA, INTERRUPTED: SPEAKING JANE AUSTEN IN FICTION AND FILM
HILARY SCHOR

From Gina Macdonald and Andrew Macdonald (eds), *Jane Austen on Screen,* Cambridge: Cambridge University Press, 2003, pp. 144–174

New Yorker reviewer Anthony Lane, in a characteristically intelligent review of Douglas McGrath's 1995 film production of *Emma,* offered a rather sharp condemnation of the film, one with interesting implications for most modern adaptations of Jane Austen's novels. The problem with the film, Lane argues, is not that it makes no sense, but that it makes "easy, do-it-yourself sense."[1] Reducing Emma's "artful" construction "around the ethics of plotting" to a "thinness" of romance, McGrath has made his film too easy to watch. Even such seeming accidents as its remarkable miscastings (he singles out, wonderfully, the "under the hill" Mr. Knightley of Jeremy Northam) contribute to an Austen of few narrative jolts, and of disturbingly even tone. The tensions we cannot resolve on reading her fiction (as he phrases them, "Is she affectionate or flinty? Does her tolerance float free, or does it exist to peg back her anger?") are here dissolved into a patina as even as the decorations on "the lids of cake tins," and the disturbing confusion of Emma's narration (is she in charge of her world or in the grip of it?) is here quieted into a matchmaking fantasy that never quite takes its heroine or its viewer by surprise. While remarking, as have all critics in popular and scholarly accounts, on the perfect poise and grace of Gwyneth Paltrow (her cheekbones, he asserts, "would cut a swath through communities far plusher than Highbury"), Lane finds in the very perfection of the filmic presentation a sacrifice of the true spirit of Austen's fiction: like other critics, who preferred instead the poor-theater textual faithfulness of Roger Michel's *Persuasion,* the more refined balance of Ang Lee's *Sense and Sensibility,* and even the modern high-school community of *Clueless*, he resists the charms and the ease of the McGrath/Paltrow *Emma.* The film seems, if anything, too classy to have gotten Emma right.

Lane's criticism rings true in some important ways, but it leaves unanswered (and indeed, risks leaving even vaguer than when we began) some of the principal terms by which we "read" an adaptation: What does it mean to be true to a text? What is the Austen spirit? What is celebrity and what is its relation to narrative film? And, most significantly, what is a classic? In discussing the way McGrath's adaptation works at once to center and to dislocate our automatic identification of the film of *Emma* with the novel – and indeed, troubles our identification with Emma herself – I will focus less on what we see of *Emma* and far more on what we hear of it. What has made McGrath's *Emma* seem classic to most viewers is not anything on the screen at all, but something that surrounds it: its complicated use of voice-over narration, both from the unseen female narrator who opens the film and from Emma herself in ironic commentary and epistolary confession, and its equally strategic deployment of characters' voices, both to bridge individual scenes and to interrupt our easy progress from one perspective to another. While these techniques, in particular the narratorial voice-over, have added a dated quality which has led most viewers to dismiss the film as a conservative and not terribly adventurous version of Austen's most linguistically challenging novel, the varied and disruptive nature of these different kinds of voices actually forms a most interesting attempt to "do" Austen on screen. For what is more characteristic of Austen than that voice we love to call hers, the voice of the narrator coming in to tell us what to think? What is more perplexing in *Emma* than the attempt to tell the difference between Emma herself and the wiser, but somewhat cruelly withholding, narrator who tracks her moral growth? And what is more tempting, in Jane Austen as in life, than the attempt to substitute our voice for hers; to tell others how to live and whom to love? In "voicing" Jane Austen in film, McGrath has located a troubling point in our identification with and terror at Emma herself; more than that, he has fixed on the point most vexing in moving from novel to film: who will speak for the narrator?

Opening gambits

The novel version of *Emma* opens with a calm, collected, ironic voice describing its heroine ("Emma Woodhouse, handsome, clever, and rich," I.i); the film version opens with a sphere spinning in space, pictures of people and places, and a woman with a clear, elegant English accent telling us of the world of Highbury. As the novel continues, the narrator fills in the world; as the film continues, the pictures resolve into a spinning globe held by the hand of an elegant young woman, standing at a wedding. In both cases, the voice that sends us into the narrative world sets us spinning, and then deliberately slows us down – but what is it that a narrator does, and what is the relationship of that narrative voice to the story we are beginning? Taking this question seriously leads us to ideas of knowledge, character, and adaptation at the heart of this essay – and it is worth beginning by asking, what do we know about the narrator of *Emma?*

The narrator, we might joke, is there before the novel, for the novel's famous first sentence places us squarely (indeed, almost "already") in the voice of its narrator — and one of the real achievements of the McGrath adaptation is to ask a very novelistic question: just how much are we to trust that voice, or the voice of anyone telling us a story? In a novel, we rarely begin by questioning the person speaking to us: unless a narrator is in some way marked ("Call me Ishmael") or deliberately evasive, we take the narration as so much background noise, reliable, distanced, and with no personality which might distract us from the business at hand, that of getting the plot underway. The opening sentence of Emma, with its combination of irony and humor, offers us at once a strong characterization of its heroine and the security that nothing too dreadful can happen to her in the course of our novel: "Emma Woodhouse, handsome, clever, and rich, with a comfortable home and a happy disposition, seemed to unite some of the best blessings of existence; and had lived nearly twenty-one years in the world with very little to distress or vex her" (I.i). While the "seemed" qualifies the blessings with which the sentence began, and "distress or vex her" promises a plot filled with confusion and misunderstanding, the very mildness of those verbs suggests that the plot will not bring ruination or despair, and that the heroine's happy "disposition" will see her through to a comic ending.

However, the assurance of that opening sentence might lead us to trust more than we should a series of statements that arise in following chapters, diagnosing Emma's character and orienting her world. The descriptions of Highbury and the role of Hartfield, the "comfortable" Woodhouse home, within it; the discussions of her character by other characters, in particular her governess, Miss Taylor (now Mrs. Weston), and Mr. Knightley; and the long scene we witness after the offstage wedding of the Westons which sets the plot going with its first distress of Emma and her first consciousness of loss — all this in no way seems to mitigate the narrator's somewhat curt summary of Emma, that "the real evils indeed of Emma's situation were the power of having rather too much her own way, and a disposition to think a little too well of herself" (I.i). The "indeed" keeps us from questioning the narrator's veracity — at the same time that "a little too well" keeps us from doubting Emma so much that we would refuse to follow her through the novel. From its first chapters, that is, the novel is playing a complicated game, asking us at once to identify with its heroine, and to believe a voice floating somewhere above her, which knows more than she (or we) about Emma's "real" situation.

But what is involved in believing a narrator? What kinds of epistemological leaps, games of knowledge, is Emma displaying here? In a book as involved as this one is in parading both knowledge and misinformation, in a book where everyone wants to be a narrator, how is Austen marking her own authority and making us distrust our own? One final example will suggest the difficulties of placing the Austen narrator — and the challenges a film adaptation faces. This passage seems to recreate the narrator's initial judgment of Emma's situation:

> Emma had always wanted to do everything, and had made more progress in both drawing and music than many might have done with so little labour as she would ever submit to. She played and sang; — and drew in almost every style; but steadiness had always been wanting; and in nothing had she approached the degree of excellence which she would have been glad to command, and ought not to have failed of. She was not much deceived as to her own skill either as an artist or a musician, but she was not unwilling to have others deceived, or sorry to know her reputation for accomplishment often higher than it deserved. (I.vi)

We are reasonably certain that we are listening to an authoritative voice in the first few sentences of this passage: the assurance of the diagnostic authority of the "degree" of excellence which she would have been "glad to command, and ought not to have failed of" suggest a superior intelligence, ready to measure in turn reality, degrees of excellence, and moral duty – a voice we will come, in the novel, to associate with Mr. Knightley, certain what Emma ought to "submit to." However, when we reconsider the passage, much less of it appears to be located in some external, objective perspective, and much more in Emma's own: this paragraph knows nothing Emma herself does not know. She is not "much deceived" (that smidgen allows for doubt) but by the end of the paragraph, we are firmly located in her perspective: she knows not only her own limitations, but the degree to which these limitations are unseen by others. Typically of the novel, the double negative of "not unwilling" makes her vanity seem less venal than it might – whoever is announcing her self-knowledge is willing to judge her a passive rather than an active egomaniac, willing to accept but not actively to "will" her own overvaluation – and yet the speed with which these sentences progress encourages us to more certainty in the judgment than we would have if it were announced more clearly as Emma's own. Once we trace the path of knowledge in the elegant sentences, we might be considerably less certain that authorial knowledge rests in them, and more aware that what we are hearing is not an objective narrator, but a slightly filtered account of Emma's own judgment of herself.

Thus, the novel encourages us, subtly, to distrust our distrust of Emma; it teaches us, perversely, as Mrs. Weston announces early, that there are limits to her foolishness. Some of the same lessons inhere in McGrath's filmic opening, but they push us even more directly than Austen's opening to distrust the way knowledge is understood and presented in the world of Highbury. The beautiful spinning globe of the beginning emerges against the background of what seems to be the Milky Way, and the characters and the places of the novel arise before us in hand-painted miniature form; these portraits in turn spin round with the galaxy, which turns out to be a painted ball (perhaps of silk) which the heroine, Emma, is spinning. It is her wedding present for Miss Taylor and Mr. Weston, and in the many varieties of work it will do for us (it establishes the smallness and the seriousness of this social whirl; it introduces us to groups of characters, doing the work of exposition; it introduces the motif of the heroine's artistic skills, and her want of serious practice) it stands most powerfully for the heroine's *imagined* relationship to the world around her. The narrator tells us, as the final picture of Emma appears, and as the spinning globe becomes a toy held in the heroine's hand, that in this village "there lived a young woman who knew how this world should be run."

Just as Austen's opening paragraph, with its assertion that Emma "had lived nearly twenty-one years in the world with very little to distress or vex her" cried out for a readerly insertion of "as yet," so McGrath's narrator's assertion that Emma knows how this world *should* be run conjures up our skepticism – but again, like Austen's premise of Emma's happy disposition, the smallness of this spinning globe seems to promise that (as with Emma's happy disposition) no disaster too absolute can overtake her. The combination of Gwyneth Paltrow's luminosity and her fragility strikes us as similarly vexed, offering at once certainty and vulnerability. Like the disjunction between the certainty of the narrator's confident assertion and the dizziness of the spinning world, the opening of the film seems to warn us that some gap will appear between word and image, between voice and action. This narrator, with her careful patterns of speech and cultivated accent, disappears after the film begins, leaving behind her not only the images from the revolving ball which introduce the initial changes of scene (pictures of Hartfield, Highbury, Randalls, and Donwell Abbey) but the promise of a voice that will *link* these worlds together.

Moreover, McGrath has made an interesting choice already, in choosing a female narrator for his film. Much as the beginning of the novel spins around the absence of Miss Taylor and the loss of female friendship which has centered Emma's world since the death of her mother, so the loss of that initial, comforting if slightly acerbic narratorial voice leads us to long for that absent mother – for a decidedly female intelligence who will complete Emma's moral makeover and make the world spin in the proper direction. As *Emma* moves through its various techniques of voice, suspending the narrator's own voice until the happy conclusion of the romance plot, it challenges us to listen more acutely to the vagaries of individual voice – and to listen for absent voices, as well.

Hearing voices: from free indirect discourse to voice-over

Thus, the filmmaker faces a particular problem in his adaptation: how to show the play of voices which makes up the world of *Emma,* while keeping viewers focused on the problems of knowledge that the novel highlights – and keeping them particularly focused on what Emma Woodhouse knows and how she knows it. McGrath does this quite literally by keeping us focused on voices, on what we hear and on what people say, and on the way that everyone in the story, to put it most bluntly, wants to be the narrator. If Austen's narrator makes her claim on us more directly in the striking impersonality of her opening voice, her characters wage a similar war against the text, arguing and interpreting and gossiping with a vengeance; Emma is the most imaginative but by no means the only narrator-surrogate in the novel, hardly alone in wanting her world to be more highly colored, more imaginative – in a word, more fictional, than it is. She wants, moreover, to believe that she sees the order behind the colorful events, that she can in some way both record and reorder the events of her shifting community. It is her best response to the sadness which strikes her early and hard in the novel – and it offers the relief of authority, a fiction of control which everyone in the novel longs for, and ultimately fails to achieve. Do readers long any less for such assurance? If, as Arnold Kettle has noted, "Reading *Emma* is a delightful experience, but it is not a soothing one,"[2] readers (and in particular critics) have disarmed their discomfort by trying to rid Emma of her pleasure in devising; to them (even some of the most astute), successful negotiation of the marriage plot involves an abandonment of agency, of interference, of mastery, of the desire to be a narrator.

McGrath's film attends most prominently to Emma's narratorial desire, taking it seriously, playing with her dramatic asides and ironic commentary, offering her remarkable space to comment on the action we are seeing. However, he pays careful attention as well to the games other people play with knowledge – games Austen draws out humorously, tracing from the earliest chapters the marriage plots imagined by the Westons, by both George Knightley and his brother John, and Harriet and Jane's more blighted attempts to write marriage plots for themselves. In a series of scenes, McGrath draws *our* attention to the ways the same events or documents are interpreted by different characters: in an early episode, we see person after person study a letter from Frank Churchill and pronounce upon it, these shifts of perspective conditioning us to believe that people see in their social interactions only what they are looking for – a version of themselves. Miss Bates's pronouncement that the letter is "kindly and charming" and "reminds me of Jane" expresses both her generosity and Frank's dangerous charm, as well as prefiguring Jane's engagement to Frank; Mr. Woodhouse's comment that it is "nicely expressed" but that Frank eats a dangerous amount of custard reinforces compactly his own gentleness and niceness of expression, his *status as* a valetudinarian, and Frank's as a young man of self-indulgent desires. Mrs. Goddard's announcement that Frank's penmanship is confident not only reminds us that she is a schoolteacher (and a fairly mediocre one, as Mr. Knightley points out) but that Frank's boldness transgresses norms of social behavior as surely as it does manuals of script.

This play of perspective gives *Emma* the feel of a larger social drama, integrating the view of the world as Highbury sees it, and reminding us subtly of the tedium and containment of Emma's life – as in the moment of the novel, when the "quiet prosings of three such *women* [Miss Bates, Mrs. Bates and Mrs. Goddard]" are "the long evenings she had fearfully anticipated" with the departure of Mrs. Weston. However, more than offering a comic view of the horrors of Highbury life, this dissemination of narratorial knowledge and the right to speak as a narrator suggests the problems of speaking and listening which the novel highlights throughout. It very carefully takes the problem of Austenian conversation beyond a mere dynamics of *speaking*. Consider a comparable scene in *Sense and Sensibility*, when Marianne sings for the company only to have Sir John be "loud in his admiration at the end of every song, and as loud in his conversation with others while every song lasted," and have Lady Middleton call him to order, "wonder[ing] how any one's attention could be diverted from music for a moment, [then asking] Marianne to sing a particular song which Marianne had just finished" (I.vii). Scenes of response tell us not only which characters are paying attention (as the narrator in the earlier novel says, "Colonel Brandon alone...paid her the compliment of attention") but which are worthy of our attention; when Mr. Knightley responds to Emma's anger at Jane's lack of forthcomingness about Frank Churchill, "why should you care so much about Frank Churchill," a wise viewer notes that he is paying attention *not* to Emma's treatment of Jane (to which he is accustomed) but to her attention to Frank Churchill; his critique of her conversation here, in short, is a sign of his deeper discontent with the distraction of her erotic attention.

Scenes of multiple perspective always threaten to make conversation not social but merely collective, an assortment of idiolects generated by characters so eccentric they cannot form any union; when characters speak at cross purposes, or when they seem to speak outside the frame, they are challenging more than the authority of the novel or film – they threaten to speak outside some larger social order. Or so theorists of speech in both film and novel have argued, which suggests that McGrath's play with voice, as this essay will explore, takes on larger questions of how we "speak" the self in novels and film – how the rhythm of narratorial authority and individual expression plays itself out in both media.[3] When that disembodied female voice opens his film; when characters, through cutting and sound bridges, seem to speak "for" the movie, taking over a narratorial function or interrupting other scenes; when Emma talks to herself and we seem to overhear – all these disruptions frame the issues of social discourse, individual expression, and narrative coherence herein highlighted.

The use of characters' voices to disrupt filmic coherence seems particularly appropriate for adapting Jane Austen, since the integration of voice, particularly through the technique literary critics have come to call "free indirect discourse," was one of the chief innovations Austen brought to the novel.[4] The technique suggests the kind of control Austen held over her characters' individual voices: it is conversation (discourse) which may be reported in summary rather than word for word or in third rather than first person (indirect) and is not always marked by quotation marks or other indicators (free); that is, it offers a kind of economy, breeziness, and directness we associate with the Austen style. More than that, its centrality, particularly to the later novels, suggests the importance Austen gave to the speech of individual characters – and particularly to the challenges of integrating individual voices to a larger whole – a problem we might naively think film has completely solved. However, it is worth reviewing the ways in which questions of who is speaking are central to fiction, and particularly to Austen's novels.

While direct speech, which delivers characters' voices exactly as they spoke, makes clear at every moment who is speaking and to whom, free and indirect speech, which reports speech without breaking off from a previous sentence or speech (without the helpful guides of quotation marks, and with compressions of time and space) gives a sense of rapid exchange, of greater anonymity of speech, of the characters' eccentricities of delivery – all the things we think of as characteristically Austenian. Take one example from *Emma*, for instance, where Mrs. Elton speaks in direct speech and Jane Fairfax replies in indirect, suggesting the greater loquacity of one and the greater restraint of the other: "'My dear Jane, what is this I hear? – Going to the post office in the rain! – This must not be, I assure you. You sad girl, how could you do such a thing? It is a sign I was not there to take care of you'."

Jane very patiently assured her that she had not caught any cold (II.xvi).

This quickness of presentation might seem to us almost protocinematic, and it is one associated largely with "flashy" characters in Austen. Frank Churchill speaks even more rapidly than Mrs. Elton, and his speech, although marked with quotation marks, offers a classic example of free indirect speech, what Norman Page calls an even more "telegraphic" style.[5] In this speech, he interrogates Emma about her interests: "Was she a horse-woman? – Pleasant rides? – Pleasant walks? – Had they a large neighbourhood? – Highbury, perhaps afforded society enough? – Balls – had they balls? – Was it a musical society?" (II.v). This redacted version of Frank's speech allows Austen to compress a great deal of dialogue as well as to congratulate us on our knowledge. Emma's answers are unnecessary because we have seen Highbury society and know exactly how much society it affords – it is Frank's arrival which promises more society, and the speed of his delivery, heightened by the use here of free indirect discourse, in which speeches are conflated and run jaggedly into one another, initially promises the pleasure Emma awaits. Yet, his speed also suggests the uncertainty of the behavior he in fact exhibits; it suggests a lack of interest in Emma's response which presages his lack of romantic interest in Emma. This is a man, we might observe from this passage, whose interest is firmly lodged elsewhere, in this case with his secret fiancée, Jane Fairfax, whose taciturnity above (remember, she is out in the rain trying to fetch his letters before her aunt sees the mail) conceals a similar duplicity.

Lest we think this is a fictional technique film has rendered superfluous, let us take one more example, and ask ourselves how it might become film dialogue. In a much more restrained moment later in the novel, which offers far more emotional impact, Mr. Knightley appears, and Emma believes he is about to reveal that he, like Jane, has conceived a secret engagement. This scene, which Emma believes will bring the knowledge of his attachment to Harriet, in fact brings a proposal to her. In this case, the rapidity of dialogue and its presentation in free indirect discourse suggests not haste but intimacy; the constraint will yield not to secrecy but to the revelation of affection:

> There was time only for the quickest arrangement of mind. She must be collected and calm. In half a minute they were together. The "how d'ye do's," were quiet and constrained on each side. She asked after their mutual friends; *they were all well. — When had he left them? — Only that morning. He must have had a wet ride. — Yes. — He meant to walk with her*, she found. "He had just looked into the dining-room," and as he was not wanted there, preferred being out of doors. — She thought he neither looked nor spoke cheerfully. (III.xiii, emphasis added)

Notice that the passage integrates Knightley's speech seamlessly: he refers to himself as "I", obviously, when he speaks, but the narrator does not pause to break the rhythm of the sentences, or to disturb the focus on Emma's consciousness. Free indirect speech here allows the feeling of conversation *as it is experienced* by a character, without any break. Emma's interpretation of the conversation ("she thought he neither looked nor spoke cheerfully") is withheld until the end, and we are given no idea by the narrator if Emma's perception is accurate or not – or rather, we know that it is what she believes at the moment, but whether or not Knightley's conversation is "really" cheerful, we cannot tell. We are thrown back on Emma's responses, and forced (as she is) to interpret, or more likely overinterpret, the bits of dialogue we are given in so restrained a manner. There is a complexity of thought and speech here which a film would be hard pressed to duplicate – and the literary discourse conveys the relationship of thinking and speaking in a remarkably economical way.

These scenes have appealed to recent feminist critics because they seem to offer us a view of the characters unmediated by the interfering narrator or her imagined double, the implied author,[6] but there are ways in which they show the author's hand even more clearly than scenes where she speaks directly. However, given this range of *characters'* voices, what happens at those moments, filmic as well as novelistic, when the unseen authority is heard, and begins to speak up precisely to critique the individual voices of her characters? Here, our discussion might move from novelistic depiction of individual voices (both as dialogue and as free indirect discourse) to the film's depiction of individual voices, particularly in the unusual practice of voice-overs. This essay began with the elaborate presentation of the off-stage narrator at the start of the film, suggesting that her pronouncements work in ways more complicated than a simple transcription of the implied author's voice – that voicing a narrator in film draws our attention more directly to questions of authority than does a narrator in a novel. In similar ways, when Emma Woodhouse begins to serve as a voice-over narrator herself later in the film, we are aware that she is aiming somewhat higher than the usual character's role! In acting like a narrator, Emma is seeking that position somewhere above (outside and inside, at the same time) the community of Highbury – and these moments draw our attention to her in ways that complicate the viewer's relationship to her, and to the film. It becomes impossible "merely" to listen to her voice, aware as we are that it is moving beyond the simple role of one character among many.

Similarly, just as there is no way to make a novel's narrator or a character's seemingly autonomous conversation (however cunningly presented in free indirect discourse) "purely" natural, so in film problems of who is speaking to us when a voice-over narrator speaks resist the claims of simple transcription. We know that Frank Churchill's questions were followed by some kind of answers (the "he said/she said" reporting of dialogue), and in the same way we know that characters "in" a drama do not stop to comment on it; that when Walter Neff in *Double Indemnity* and Joe Gillis in *Sunset Boulevard*[7] narrate the events of the film to us, they are involved in thinking back, looking over, talking about events we are currently "involved" in. Being a narrator works as a powerful fantasy for characters, eager to stand above the action they are immersed in, but it is no less powerful a fantasy for readers and viewers. It is no accident that when Amy Heckerling adapted *Emma*, she chose the simpler expedient of making her heroine, Cher, the voice-over narrator, addressing the viewers directly, chiding us for our impressions and confessing her mistakes to us. That impulse (to lay bare the self; to confess all; to be seen and heard directly) is at the heart of voice-over narration. When characters usurp the role of the narrator, by speaking over events, they imagine (and at times, so do we) that they have a mastery over the unfolding scene which we associate with narrators, and which we rarely feel with any certainty in our own lives. Yet, the films themselves frame that desire to achieve certainty and omniscience as troubling: when Walter Neff confesses his affair and subsequent criminal activities, he does so not directly but at one remove, speaking into a tape recorder; Joe Gillis, of course, can become a perfect narrator only (and we might add, "finally") by becoming a dead man.[8]

This is to say, then, that, as with free indirect discourse, filmic first-person narration or voice-over commentary is always and *reveals itself* always as a kind of trick; the more naturalistic it seems, the more completely it accounts for events, the less spontaneous, realistic, unmediated it in fact is.[9] Only by breaking the fiction of a "realist" film can a character talk to us – and nothing reveals the staginess of a film more than the presence of someone off stage talking to us. For this reason, the arguments against the use of voice-over narration are as heated as those circling around the use of free indirect discourse. Sarah Kozloff has laid out beautifully the contradictory ideas packed into these condemnations: voice-over narrators are considered both traces of the dramatic heritage of film and signs of something far too purely "literary"; they are imagined to "break the frame" of viewing in ways that disrupt our natural relations to film, and yet at the same time they offer a sign of a more "natural" (and hence, more personal) form of storytelling (see also her analysis of the vexed critiques of voice-over).[10] Like the use of dialogue in fiction, or moments when the narrator stops to insert himself into our readerly progress, voice-overs at once satisfy our desire to know who is talking to us, and break the fantasy that we are hearing something "true," real, absolute. Like the reminder at the end of Knightley's entrance quoted above, we are aware, suddenly, that it is "only" Emma Woodhouse we are hearing; we are no closer to knowing what Knightley "really" said or felt, only what he conveyed to one listener. The voice-over narrator, when it is not a character, can sustain the fantasy of omniscience a little longer – whoever that woman is who spoke to us at the beginning of *Emma*, when she comes back at the end, we feel some certainty that order has been restored, that a benevolent onlooker has granted us and the characters her blessing. We will consider some of the ambivalences of the narrator's return later in this essay but should first examine the ways McGrath plays with the possibility of voice-over narration in the middle of his film – those occasions when characters literally "speak over" scenes, moving from one to another; and in particular the scenes where Emma attempts to become the narrator of her own life, speaking like a first-person narrator, reporting not merely events but her "private" responses to them.

Hearing film

McGrath's *Emma* frames the act of listening primarily by making us hear before we see. One of the subtlest techniques in McGrath's repertoire of vocal styles is the separation of speaker and voice; it offers him a way of making literal a wider separation of voice and action, suggesting the way that characters' actions, speeches, and thoughts may pull them in opposing directions. Characters' internal divisions, as well as crises in the plot, are signaled as a division between visible and audible selves, much as the film uses physical comedy to suggest emotional unease. Throughout the film, scenes which are "experienced" novelistically as psychological conflict are staged as physical discomfort and jerky movement: the film's Mr. Knightley shares his novelistic namesake's habit of darting off suddenly and ending conversations abruptly; Mr. Woodhouse, in keeping with his nervous verbal dancing around conflict seems remarkably unsteady on his feet, quick to take the arms of others; in the carriage scene with Mr. Elton, Emma is forced to push him backward and forward, as well as to move quickly herself to avoid his romantic lunges. Her lack of mental preparedness for his advances is signaled economically by her physical surprise and her lightning reaction to his movements toward her: they end the scene frozen on opposite sides of the carriage, still, silent, and furious.

Yet, McGrath's use of voice as a sign of character is if anything more striking. Characters' voices routinely enter rooms before they do; a line of speech serves as a transition from one scene to another; voices proceed from space, only to have the body of the speaker emerge from a chair or from around a corner. Mr. Knightley's voice enters the room where Emma and her father sit, disconsolate, after the Weston wedding, asking "who cried the most"; Elton pops up out of nowhere to offer to take Harriet's picture to London for framing; when Emma is lamenting the failure of the Coles to invite her to their party, we see her father playing backgammon and hear Emma's voice without seeing her, only to have her follow her voice out from the depths of a chair. These voices serve a double function: a voice without a body has a curious authority, annexing, if only briefly, a narratorial position of speaking without being seen. When a voice enters the room with certainty, as Mr. Knightley's always does, it seems to assume power over those who hear it — diametrically opposite, we might imagine, to Miss Bates's meaningless prattle, which tends to continue after we see her leave, reassuring us (somewhat perversely) that we were right not to listen to her in the first place. But for both Emma and Elton, the inability to "be" where they "speak" suggests a deeper confusion: neither is behaving in a straightforward way, as indeed Elton's mistakes about Emma's affections for him and Emma's about her intention to refuse the Coles' invitation confirm. Scenes of confused mishearing (Emma's hope that Elton is proposing to Harriet when he is merely explaining his fondness for celery root; the lengthy scene in which Emma is prevented from hearing Mr. Weston's story about his son's arrival by Mr. Elton's obsequious attentions) suggest more of these psychological misunderstandings which the film must resolve, and these take the place of some of the novel's more complicated misapprehensions which the film cannot reproduce.

However, like the many scenes in which a sentence begun in one scene provides a bridge or transition to the next sequence, they suggest that hearing holds out not only "answers" but psychological truths; in films, McGrath seems to be saying, we trust what we hear more than what we see,[11] and if we are to learn *Emma's* chief lesson, that her desire to hear only what she wants to hear will persistently mislead her, then hearing becomes an essential vehicle for moral education. Scenes of verbal instruction become strangely more powerful when we hear and see them than they are when we read them, and moments like Knightley's rebuking of Emma's joke at Miss Bates's expense are if anything overstaged by McGrath.[12] Because he has compressed the strawberry-picking at Donwell Abbey and the picnic at Box Hill into one event, we lose the sense of the cumulative disappointments Emma has experienced and the sense of loneliness which leads her to flirt so outrageously with Frank Churchill. In the film, her insult to Miss Bates follows not Frank's desperate attempts to provoke her into torturing Jane Fairfax, but a snub on the part of the Eltons, who leave the picnic because of the unsuitability of games of wit. Provoked and disappointed, Emma in turn snubs Miss Bates, causing the entire party to turn silent and leading even dear Mrs. Weston to shake her head disapprovingly. Where the novel continues unbroken after Emma's comment, offering not a rebuke but Mr. Weston's ghastly pun on "m-a" "Emma," and leaving us until the end of the day and Mr. Knightley's scathing comment to realize how severe was the pain Emma inflicted, the film wastes no time and forces us to witness both Miss Bates's response and Emma's instant isolation. In part, this is the film's economy and its distrust of us, its concern that we will not notice Emma's gaffe; but it is also the film's desire that we recognize the power of speech in this tiny community. When Knightley traces the history of Emma's relation to Miss Bates, and the decline of their friendship from the days when Miss Bates's notice was "an honour to you," it encourages us to take notice of the quality of attention people pay to the speech of others. If nothing else, the film reminds us of the power any speech of Emma's will have in this world — both to wound and to honor — and makes us all the more observant of those moments of silence which fall when exactly the wrong words are spoken. As the film works to isolate Emma from her society and to make her question not only the propriety but the authority of speech acts, so the novel's chief scene of verbal damage must be even more powerfully staged by the talking pictures, and Emma's attention to her conscience (her "inner monitor") must be voiced even more loudly.

Bridging the social gap

Overall then, the film adaptation of *Emma* uses voice in three interesting ways: when the narrator speaks directly to us, at the film's beginning and end; when characters speak over scenes, forming the narrative's transitions or providing ironic commentary; and when Emma Woodhouse, in several different ways and to different ends, talks to herself. However, the latter technique in some way recapitulates the pattern of the whole, running as it does through virtually the entire film and canvassing a variety of narratorial moods. Emma's speech in itself, that is, duplicates the film's various relationships to voice: it operates as simple mockery (what can be thought but not said, as when Austen's narrator says Emma "denied none of it aloud, and agreed to none of it in private" [III.vi]); as a form between private speech and something more public, moving viewers from one, usually domestic, scene to another, usually more social; and as an attempt by Emma, usually doomed by self-blindness, to understand and enshrine her deepest feelings. Emma's private speech acts are the way the film most purely reimagines the novel's anxieties about how we are to express ourselves (reveal, conceal, and master ourselves) in public.

If they achieve this evolutionary power, Emma's first voice-over speeches begin rather more simply, in pure irony, reflecting the "clever" Miss Woodhouse of the first sentence. When she first meets Robert Martin, she says to herself, "Really, Harriet, you can do better than this"; when she sees Harriet with Mr. Elton and hopes that he is proposing (despite the suddenness of their acquaintance) she asks herself, "can this be a declaration?" These speeches become more active, both in their work of communicating Emma's distance from the social scene (that is, expressing a small form of discontent) and in doing the implied narrator's work of moving us from one scene to another, once Jane Fairfax enters the picture. Examining one such sequence of voice-over scenes, and Emma's overheard mental commentary, suggests the progression in the film's self-consciousness.

The sequence begins when Emma goes to call on Miss Bates, greeting with spoken pleasure the information that Miss Bates and her mother have news, while her voice-over self comments, "please do not let it be a letter from that ninny, Jane Fairfax." Miss Bates explains that indeed, it is a letter from Jane, in which the latter has said she is coming for a long visit. Convinced by Emma's politeness that Emma shares her joy, she announces that when Jane arrives, Emma must come to visit: she must sit just "where you are and say –." As she breaks off, the camera pans back to Emma, who is wearing a different morning dress and says, "We are so glad to have you with us." As Jane answers warmly, the voice-over Emma says, "She's more giving than I expected," but this optimism fades when Emma begins to interrogate Jane about her meeting with Frank Churchill, only to have Jane return to her customary reserve. Emma, unaware, of course, that the reserve is the sign not of Jane's coldness but of her secret engagement to Frank and her embarrassment at the concealment, interrupts Jane's response in her voice-over, saying, "I take it back. She is –." The voice-over ends the sentence with "absolutely impossible," and we fade back, discovering that Emma is now in the conservatory at Hartfield, transferring bulbs and complaining to Mr. Knightley, ever Jane's advocate, about Jane's failure to participate in what Emma considers proper social exchange.

The scene does several things for the viewers: it frames Emma's intelligence as overarching, carrying us as it does from scene to scene, and providing us with an insight we do not find in the other characters. It also conditions us, as it must for the suspense to build, to trust Emma more than any other voice we hear; its humorous changes encourage us to take the scene lightly, but like all of Emma's repartee with Mr. Knightley, it provides a different pleasure than the slower exchanges with Mr. Woodhouse, Miss Bates, even Mrs. Weston. It prepares us for a giddier form of satiric commentary, and suggests the deeper connection between Emma and Knightley, who share (even when they bicker) a position of slight superiority, intellectual as well as class-based, to the other inhabitants of Highbury. However, it also sets us up for more dangerous pleasures and more serious lessons: that voice of ironic discontent ("that ninny"; "I take it back; she is absolutely impossible") is the voice she speaks in openly when she expresses herself so bitterly to Miss Bates, and a lifetime of social self-suppression is lost in a moment: the same spirit that leads her to tell Miss Bates that she will be able to say only three boring things, leads her to mock Jane's lack of conversational interest. Curiously, of course, the later moment is a moment of attempted policing of Miss Bates's speech, which suggests the dangers of too much speech (a danger we might think Jane Fairfax has learned all too well), but Emma's earlier conversations convince her that no real danger will come to her from her own ironic perspective – or from sharing it with the likes of Knightley. Although Knightley does not approve of her comments about Jane Fairfax, his criticism is fairly light: he suggests that her dislike of Jane is related to her fear that Jane removes their collective attention from her; she remarks that he is so comical he ought to perform in the town square; and he smiles, changing the subject to announce that Mr. Elton is engaged to be married.

His comment, rather than provoking the extended self-criticism we might expect, provides instead another filmic transition, this one even more complicated. Emma announces that she does not "know what to say except that I am –," a sentence which blurs into Harriet's saying "in a state of shock." Unexpectedly, she is in a state of shock not over Elton's engagement, but over a chance encounter with Robert Martin, which she recounts in a narrative that becomes a disembodied voice-over for a flashback scene in Ford's shop; again, Emma's irony has given way to a dramatic scene that could significantly undercut her point of view, but doesn't. This unexpected switch in perspective, which is exactly the one traced in the novel, carries us visually backward in time, but it also allows Harriet her bit of narration – suggesting, more fully than does Austen's version, which depends heavily on Harriet's ineptitude of explanation, what it means to see the world differently than Miss Woodhouse; the shock when *we* hear Harriet's distress and then realize it comes from a different source, is unbuffered by Emma's response, and reminds us more powerfully of our own failures of imaginative (fanciful) narration.

This is to take sound bridges seriously as a redirection of our attention: these aural transitions (there is one final example, when Emma is explaining that she "cannot attend" a party at the Coles', only to have her break off before that key verb, finishing the sentence "tell you how delighted I am to be invited" as she walks into the Coles' lighted house) do work comically to give the film a buoyancy that we do not always expect in literary adaptations, but they also prepare us for a continual adjustment of perspective, one which reinforces the play of focalization the novel engages in, or the kind of serial commentary we saw in the communal reading of Frank Churchill's letter. The belligerent presentation of individual perspectives in that scene threatened the social unity Austen's work seems so consciously to strive for, but Emma's initial voice-overs, moments of particularized, individual interest, do not really menace the social fabric. We take them, as I believe she understands them to be, as a kind of escape valve – a necessary self-expression which allows her to continue to sacrifice her individual desires to the household god of social gossip. However, the third kind of voice-over, that which is more truly private, is harder to integrate into the ordinary exchange of social life. For the same reason, such voice-overs are harder to integrate into filmic adaptation, suggesting why they get special (and especially filmic) treatment. They are mediated for us, for the most part, by acts of writing, suggesting already a kind of literary quality to them, and their "revelation" of Emma's inner life is similarly layered and hard to read. Yet what is interesting is the way they not only, like the earlier voice-overs, carry along dramatic points of interest, but also break through and interrupt the filmic qualities we have seen so far.

The technology of privacy

When Emma Woodhouse speaks to herself of romantic love, she writes in a diary, she brushes her hair, she sits in her garden, she prays – she in all ways behaves like a literary heroine. As Lionel Trilling has observed, "Emma believes in her own distinction and vividness and she wants all around her to be distinguished and vivid"; his claim is that this is "in its essence, a poet's demand,"[13] but it is a novelist's demand as well. Emma is a creature of books, a creature in particular of romantic novels and that peculiar strain of the Gothic in which mystery, clues, and secret passions abound.[14] Notice, she does not discourage Harriet's dismay that Robert Martin has not read the Anne Radcliffe novel Harriet recommended to him, though we might imagine that she shares the narrator's slight scorn that Harriet's only literary activity is collecting riddles she cannot understand. As the narrator comments, this solitary "literary pursuit" is "the only mental provision she was making for the evening of life"; but Emma's provisions for Harriet are the stuff of fiction: secret fathers, missing inheritances, a marriage straight out of Samuel Richardson's *Pamela* (1740–1741), which assumes a servant girl's marriage to her master, Lord B, is a credible possibility. However, Emma wishes no such things for herself, and she is no confused heroine from a Gothic mind-trap. That she is finally not such a creature (such a ninny, to use her [filmic] word for Jane Fairfax) is suggested not only by her quick realization that she is not, as a heroine would be, in love with a man she has met only once, and not subject to the feline charms of Frank Churchill, but also by her inability to recognize the "real" mysterious courtship of Jane and Frank. We might observe that Emma's very realism keeps her from recognizing their affair, the one real "romance" before her eyes – a romance visible to, of all people, Mr. Knightley, who guesses long before Emma does, trapped as she is in her own ecstatic narcissism.

Ecstasy, of course, before it was associated purely with romantic love was also an out-of-body experience; to be ecstatic is to be beside the self, outside the self. Emma's voice-overs suggest repeatedly that her romantic dreams (of herself as a creature of heroic stature, the object of every erotic gaze) are far less important to her than her desire for understanding, her wish to see more of the world, to see outside of herself, to obtain some omniscient perspective. To put it vulgarly, Emma enjoys talking about (and in these scenes, particularly writing about) romance, but she is far more engaged in the pursuit of knowledge, both self-knowledge and the knowledge of the social order. She comes, and hence so do we, to associate that knowledge with Knightley's moral approval, but again we read too hastily if we subsume Emma's quest for epistemological clarity with the novel's quest to see her properly married. McGrath takes seriously Emma's desires for narratorial authority, but he also insists on our seeing through them. These scenes of self-analysis are at once lovingly filmed and more than a little mocking. They work to build our special relationship with the heroine, but also to help us learn to see beyond her vision. In important ways they advance the plot, telling us that she is first in love (though we can tell, it is only slightly) and then out of it with Churchill; but the longer scenes, following her out of her room and garden and back into the wider world, both move the story forward and reveal a knowledge of it she lacks. She may tell us that she loves Mr. Knightley; the film tells us (by virtue of allowing her voice as well as her actions to move the camera along) that she is finally correct. Yet, clever as all this is, it doesn't explain why a voice-over is necessary, or why it should be so "writerly" in its attentions.

When the film offers Emma's most private dialogues with herself, McGrath is not unleashing an old-fashioned version of literary consciousness – the kind that finds a book turning its pages or a pen moving across a screen as a novel literally turns to film before our eyes. True, Emma uses pen and ink and writes beside a lighted candle – no fluorescent lights buzz, no word-processors hum or cursors pulsate. Nonetheless, there is something technological, self-conscious, postmodern, in the moment when speaking and writing come together in this film, and reading this as a sentimental return to the novelist's moment of writing misses the point of McGrath's adaptation. These scenes "read" very differently if connected instead to some of the stranger, largely computer-based epistolary dramas of recent years. *You've Got Mail* (1998), which is self-consciously an adaptation of *Pride and Prejudice,* follows the structure of Ernst Lubitsch's *The Shop Around the Corner* (1939), introducing its lovers first as pen-pals, then as competitors, and finally as romantic soulmates.[15] In *You've Got Mail,* the romantic leads correspond exclusively by e-mail, often commenting in their letters on scenes they have just had (unknowingly) face-to-face. The amount of time the film devotes to watching them write to each other suggests its core belief: these sequences depend on the fantasy that our private selves are if anything even more adorable than our public selves – a fantasy McGrath seems in some ways to share. What is most interesting in *You've Got Mail's* scenes of writing is what happens to the voices of the writing-subjects. Obviously, the film would put us to sleep if it only watched them writing. It distrusts the simple effect of merely having them "read" in a voice-over their *received* mail, so we often see the two writing to each other, as an off-camera version of their own voices reads what they have just "written" or are "writing" to each other. Yet, often, the character seen on screen interrupts the same character's offscreen voice; that is, Meg Ryan will be "speaking" (in reality, ventriloquizing) her thoughts, only to have the Meg Ryan who is close-mouthedly typing begin to speak as well, so that we hear her in two versions – indeed, in one of them she is "reading" (ventriloquizing) a letter from Tom Hanks, only to interrupt her own reading with a question. What this suggests is not only the curiously technological nature of "inner" voices on screen today, but the curiously *doubled* nature of introspection, a necessary doubling of soliloquy, as if the self generated in writing, or in particular in correspondence, and even more particularly in e-mail correspondence, requires a "voice" as duplicitous as a multiple personality.

Emma's scenes of introspection offer a similar blend of the technologically sophisticated and the naively self-expressive; in keeping with the pattern stressed throughout this reading of the film, they accentuate the act of writing so as to give even greater emphasis to the act of speaking, but their need to negotiate so many filmic boundaries between linguistic acts lends Emma's most impassioned moments of expressiveness a significantly self-reflexive quality.[16] Emma's voice-over comments give way to the literary device of the diary almost exactly mid-way through the film, as if the deepening ironies of the plot required more self-consciousness on the part of both the heroine and the film. The initial diary entry is fairly conventional: the screen goes black after Frank Churchill says his mysterious good-bye, leaving Emma with the impression that he intends to propose to her. We see her, her voice announces, "Well, he loves me..." and then the visible heroine begins to write. The scene is filmicly conventional as well: Emma is framed by a window, robed in a negligee, her hair down, lit only by candles – all in all, she seems to be playing the part of a romantic heroine. Her voice-over suggests this as well, as she says, "I felt listless after he left and had some sort of headache, so I must be in love as well." However, her immediate concession ("I must confess I expected love to feel somewhat different from this") reminds us that she is no conventional heroine, and is incapable of fooling herself for very long; the film's next diary entry (after hearing his name at a party, she repeats, "Frank Churchill... hmmm... I must own that I am not in love with Frank") suggests again her resistance to certain kinds of romantic plotting, and her willingness to confess – to "own" her emotions.

However, in the second diary scene, what she "owns" gives way to her desire to own other people's plots: she confesses that she has not thought of him since Harriet mentioned him the other day, and immediately she begins plotting again. The staging of the scene suggests the ways her confessions give way to more enjoyable romantic episodes. As she mentions Harriet, we see Emma's face in a mirror on her writing table; that face actually speaks "Harriet... and Frank," and the mirror suggests the play of narcissism and generosity (indeed, the "romance") in her plotting. Excited by her idea, Emma leaves the writing table and moves to her dressing table, brushing her hair in front of another mirror while the voice-over continues. The appearance of one Emma, brushing her hair while some other Emma continues to voice her diary, saying, "Happy the man who changes Emma for Harriet," suggests something uncanny at work here – as if the doubling of heroines the novel persistently suggests (and which the film usually signals through the constant interweaving of the same confused lovers through the elegant rituals of ballroom dancing) called for something more than *both* writing and speech. Despite the seeming authenticity, spontaneity, and verisimilitude of voiced confession, Emma's speaking (un)consciousness seems constantly to escape the various forms of representation the film undertakes.

For all of Emma's voice-overs have a haunted (and curiously technological) nature, at the same time that the film seems to be working to present them as old-fashioned, naive, private, and romantic. Emma might wear flowing nightgowns and write before a candle-lit mirror, but the technology of the film (as it moves from voice-over to voice-over) makes this undressed quality seem mechanical trickery; the pattern of interruption and self-division again clues us in to Emma's psychic distress and the complexity of her situation. In the next long voice-over sequence, after she asserts to Mrs. Weston that she can easily "not think of Mr. Knightley," we follow her through a day in which speech constantly interrupts her attempt to prove that "I may have lost my heart but not my self-control." Emma's loss of control repeatedly punctuates the visual screen: her voice-over announcement that she tried not to think of Mr. Knightley while ordering the day's meals is interrupted by having the maid ask her if Knightley is coming to dinner, for she has ordered his favorite dish. As in the last diary scene, where she writes secretively under her "tent" of bedcovers of Mrs. Churchill's death and her attempts to renew her friendship with Miss Bates, only to interrupt herself to repeat "Mr. Knightley... hmmm... Mr. Knightley," her voice-over repetitions and slight babbling suggest a desire to speak more than she can. In that scene, the reflection on Mr. Knightley is in fact prompted by her thought that if Mr. Knightley were "privy to my thoughts" he would see her changed heart; the disruption of her speech is, obviously, our glimpse of what is only slowly becoming less private (that is, less secret) to Emma herself. However, the technological tricks, which make her thoughts as loud as any speech in the film, suggest that her secret is not private but "out" as well as out loud; she herself is not only speaking it privately (romantically, literally) to us, but publicly, to the entire world of Highbury. It is this shared knowledge, as the plot's mistakes increase and Emma risks ruining her own happiness as well as everyone else's, that persuades us to stay by her side, to remain in the private (which is, here, to say wrong) space she occupies. The revelation of her feelings, however inadvertently, to the wider "public" whom we represent, actually works, perversely, to convince us that she *has* a private self. The technology of this (writing; speaking; ordering; dictating) suggests how layered and difficult to achieve this true self-awareness is. As the gimmickry of the filmic voice-over hints, Emma's true heart must be artificially startled out of her, and her reluctant voicing of it, disruptions and all, carries the viewer through to the end.

What the film needs to bring Emma to do is to "voice" some confession, some desire, which she cannot satisfy for herself within the candle-lit hall of mirrors she has created at Hartfield. By the film's end, as the voice-overs multiply, so does our sense of Emma's loneliness, the isolation which threatened at the film's beginnings with Miss Taylor's marriage. The scenes which precede Knightley's proposal either feature Emma alone, or feature her in confused spatial relationship to others; in the most poignant of them, as she hears Harriet's confession that she is in love with Knightley, the two friends cross and recross the room, Emma unable to occupy even the same frame as her friend. After her similarly spinning encounter with Mrs. Weston, where she moves constantly from thought to thought and from garden arch to arch, unable to rest once she has realized that she loves Mr. Knightley, we follow her through the day in which she tries not to think of him, only to end with her at prayer in a private chapel, addressing God in a voice-over, asking him, if Knightley "cannot share a life with me," to ensure that he at least will share it with no one else, but remain "always the brightest part of our lives." The voice-over concludes: "If he would just stay single, lord, that would be enough for me to be perfectly satisfied," but the composure of that sentence (the "perfectly" marking Emma's perfect use of adverbs throughout the text) gives way, at the same moment her lips begin to move: the Emma on screen speaks the final two words, "Almost. Amen." Only after that concession (an admission of desire and vulnerability Emma has been slow to make) can she encounter Mr. Knightley and greet his proposal; the coming together of voice-over and heroine suggests, at this moment, a self-knowledge which Emma has hardly had before, and which alone can make possible the romantic conclusion with its pattern of mis-speech, correction, and confession.

Listening to Mr. Knightley

Highlighting the gradual emotional and cinematic evolution (voice-over into voice, we might say) that leads Emma finally to "confess" her love in the church scene is, for McGrath, part of the larger examination of a technology of self-expression I have been stressing in drawing out the curiously and self-consciously postmodern elements of this seemingly traditional film; and the strands I have been following (the inclusion of the female voice-over narrator; the interweaving of characters' voices and narratorial intelligence; Emma's divided self-narration, which makes her, as Ian Watt noted long ago, seen from both the inside and the outside, at once character and self-narrator) come together in that most important scene of resolution, the proposal of marriage.[17] This scene draws together the elements of narration, authority, speech, and attention, but it uses them to comment on the problem of adapting Austen to modern viewers and particularly to modern feminist viewers; it works to take our contemporary discomfort with happy endings and our anxiety about what to do, here almost literally, with the outspoken heroine. The problem highlighted in this essay is one of where, again almost literally, to locate the site of female speech: the film, like the novel, asks, where is that voice coming from? whom is it safe to speak for? where can Emma "go" as an independent narrator? McGrath's version responds explicitly to the problems of authority and courtship Emma raises by playing questions of female speech against, of all things, male confession, the speech act I suggested was at the heart of film voice-over in its murky antecedents in film noir, the interweaving of speech, violence, and death in *Sunset Boulevard* and *Double Indemnity*. Yet, McGrath is placing male confession not in a scene of crime, but in a scene of romantic resolution, the moment where self-revelation and social union (all the things the marriage plot stands for) come together. By doing so, he is not only responding to the challenge to marriage the novel has offered us so far, but highlighting for us a particularly modern anxiety about the nature of speech itself. Our modern intuition is to equate the successful fruition of love with self-expression, the moment when the soul (passion, deep feeling, sensibility, call it what you will) *forces* itself into speech. Jane Austen's version is considerably more complicated. The largest part of Emma's emotional development after realizing that "Mr Knightley must marry no one but herself!" comes from her fear of hearing him speak of his love for Harriet Smith; all of her self-knowledge leads her initially to suppress his desire to speak, to beg him to wait. His disappointment (for he intends to propose to her) touches her, and for the first time she begs him to speak in spite of the pain that it might cause her – real maturity revealed here in auditory rather than vocal presence. When he begins his proposal, Knightley makes a series of requests of Emma, the first of which, significantly, is that she "Say 'No,' if it is to be said." When Emma "could really say nothing," Knightley cries "with great animation, 'absolutely silent! at present I ask no more.'" He then begins his great speech, which begins, "I cannot make speeches, Emma," and continues with that most captivating of premises, that "If I loved you less, I might be able to talk about it more"; at the end of the paragraph, he says, "At present, I ask only to hear, once to hear your voice." What she says, apparently, is less important than that she says anything at all, and what she says is left largely unreported by the narrator: "She spoke then, on being so entreated. — What did she say? — Just what she ought, of course. A lady always does. — She said enough to show there need not be despair — and to invite him to say more himself." For Austen, at this climactic moment, the best speech is a promise to listen; this is some considerable boon to Emma, who has as much to conceal at this moment as to reveal, but it offers not only a rather deadly challenge to any screenwriter ("could you please write what Jane Austen knew better than to attempt") but a considerable challenge to the model of expressive subjectivity McGrath rendered increasingly problematic all along. At a moment when he dare not let the offstage Emma interrupt the visibly moved Emma, what can the heroine manage to say?

McGrath writes a perfectly acceptable speech for Emma (one which stresses her own unworthiness, allowing them to find each other in a chorus of self-dismissal) but the revision of Knightley's authority seems to me to capture something far more interesting about the film's relationship to the novel. If Emma's story is marked by the subtle correction of her thoughts, signaled in the film by the evolution of her voice-overs from self-delusion to self-awareness, Knightley's is marked both by his subtle domination of the film through voice, and his growing need to confess, to express something internal. One of the film's most striking elements is its attention to Knightley's inner life: the film cannot recapture the one chapter in the novel which is given over entirely to Knightley's point of view, the one in which he "discovers" the relationship between Frank and Jane and interrogates Emma about her cruel running joke with Frank about "Dixon," but it does give a powerful sense of how much of his life is spent following, watching, admonishing, and being amused by Emma. One of the film's signal interpolations is of banter between the two: when he witnesses Emma's request that Mr. Elton supply a riddle to Harriet's album, he asks Emma why she did not ask him. "Your entire personality is a riddle," she replies; "I thought you over-qualified." The scene where they discuss her plans for Elton and Harriet, and he (in the face of her disavowal of any such plans) informs her of what she cannot know, that when he is alone with other men, Elton talks only of marrying women with money, is staged as an archery match between them. As Emma grows increasingly upset with his new information, her aim grows worse and worse (revealing to us her own unvoiced self-doubt) and she eventually shoots an arrow far from the target; as one of his dogs gets up, whimpering, he casts Emma an affectionate glance and says, "Try not to kill my dogs."

This incident is in keeping with the general comedic emphasis which hints at characters' psychic unease; however, the archery incident suggests in addition an emphasis on Knightley's growing awareness of his affection for Emma, something the book cannot show with such clarity. In lieu of asking for Emma's silence, as he did in the book, Knightley confesses his complete misreading of the plot. In his proposal speech, he retells the plot from his point of view — a speech that reveals, as does his earlier comment that he could not tell from her actions how deep her affection for Frank Churchill was, that he has been studying her and obsessed with her romantic imaginings all along. In the novel, this speech comes after his declaration of love and is given not directly in his voice, but in a version of free indirect discourse. It is an important speech, to be sure, but it has much less dramatic weight than if it had come before Emma was certain of his love; in a sense, it comes after the suspense, in a slight let-down of reader attention, which is no doubt why it has gone unnoticed in most Austen criticism.

However, in the film the speech *is* Knightley's proposal. His proposal is nothing other than the confession that he has been as blind and jealous and confused as the supposedly much-mistaken Emma all along; that he, too, has been blind in affairs of the heart. His "did you not guess?" does reiterate our more general sense that Emma has been seeing only half the story before her eyes, but it reminds us that he, too, has been undergoing the sentimental education Austen believes necessary to move us all from our primary narcissism. He has fallen in love only to be "mortified," to realize that there are others, perhaps more attractive, in the world, and he must base his claim on something other than his self-assurance. Like Emma's realization that what she cannot stand, even more than she cannot stand to be humiliated and rejected, is to give Knightley pain (it is that realization that brings her to run after him after urging him not to speak, that brings her to confront her fear that he will tell her he loves Harriet), Knightley's return to Highbury was prompted by the desire to see Emma and comfort her. Only that moment of self-abandonment, the willingness to appear a fool, will bring him to happiness. In the film, that confession is a necessary prelude to successful courtship; even more than the heroine's full confession (which of course never comes, as she cannot tell all without revealing Harriet's secret attachment), Knightley's self-revealing speech makes possible the resolution of the din of disparate voices we have been witnessing. Also, it gives our discomfort at our own lack of understanding a curiously prominent place; if there is one thing we have been able to center our reading on, it is that Knightley will correct and tutor Emma's vision, as he attempts to restrain her wilder bursts of fanciful narration. The critics have, universally, followed Knightley's fierce running commentary on Emma's behavior (which culminates in the "badly done" that he offers so resoundingly on Box Hill), to the exclusion of all other voices in the novel – including his own when he comments, at the novel's end, that his criticism of Emma has accomplished little but to make him love her better, focusing even more of his attention on her. When McGrath centers the proposal scene on Knightley's confession that his love has made him as inaccurate a reader as he accused her of being, he similarly reorients our own reading of the novel – and our own certainty that we will always know better than Emma, that we would make the better narrator of her life. What he accomplishes is to make us listen, directly, to a confession which can only confuse our own faith that we have been listening attentively, correctly, from above, all along.

The silence of Jane Austen

If we have not been listening from above, if we have not been admonished by Mr. Knightley, if we have learned different lessons than we thought we (and our heroine) were learning, then to whom have we been listening, after all? Where is the narrator, and how are the director, the writer, the actress, the "film" as a unit, to bring us closer to that fantasized voice of Jane Austen herself, the one the novel so famously keeps just out of our reach? The problem of framing female subjectivity in speech has for recent readers been a problem of recreating Austen's own (female, if not explicitly feminist) authority. Modern adaptations of Austen's fiction are unanimous in their desire to make Jane herself speak up; even Rozema's *Mansfield Park*, an adaptation so loose as to make the plot completely nonsensical, is absolutely loyal to the spirit of Austen as it perceives it – placing the voice of Austen's juvenilia in the person of the heroine, Fanny Price, and making ridiculous the modesty which differentiated her from the more "Austenian" (wittier and more alluring) Mary Crawford. The desire to give Austen a voice resounds in the general impulse to make *everybody* in Austen film adaptations express *more;* the films dissolve in a veritable orgy of weeping, confessing, and acting-out.

Michell's *Persuasion*, which prided itself on a minimalism of dialogue and affect to mirror effectively Anne Elliot's restrained implicit narration, ratchets up its repertoire of dramatic effect and narratorial overwriting at the end: the (novel's) narrator's statement that the lovers stroll with "a most obliging compliance for public view; and smiles reined in and spirits dancing in private rapture," becomes, in the film, a parade of circus-people and fire-eaters through the streets of Bath. The scene of Wentworth's inquiry after her marriage plans which Austen excised from the original returns in the film, prompting a verbal explosion from the demure Anne Elliot, one rivaled only by her chasing after Wentworth, à la Marianne Dashwood, in the assembly rooms at Bath, and his similarly dashing entrance into the room where her family is playing at cards to demand her hand in marriage. One of the moments where Anne and the narrator nicely come together in the novel (proving that Anne has come into her own as an ironic commentator) occurs after her father's dismissal of her friend Mrs. Smith, when she thinks to herself, reminded of his friend Mrs. Clay, that Mrs. Smith was not "the only widow in Bath between thirty and forty, with little to live on, and no sirname of dignity" (II.vi); in the otherwise restrained film, this, too, becomes an outburst, as Anne astounds her family with the severity of her comment and pushes her chair away from the table, leaving them speechless.

Ang Lee's *Sense and Sensibility* similarly plays with issues of restraint and silence, needing for some reason to expand the artist's restrained palette. The film adds an astonishing (and quite moving) scene where Elinor Dashwood, lying at the foot of her sister's seeming-deathbed, cries out, "I cannot live without you... oh, please... please, dearest... Do not leave me alone." The sense that Elinor will be entirely alone in the world without her sister is poignantly vocalized here; but the comparable novelistic scene where the seducer Willoughby dangerously conveys his passion and confusion to Elinor, winning her sympathy and (against all our Austenian instincts) ours, cannot then be translated into film at all, and Marianne's equally poignant assessment of her own behavior, "I judge it by what it should have been, by yours" loses the dramatic weight it *must* have to make the point that "sense" is as powerful as "sensibility." In the film's rushing to a conclusion, sensibility has won yet once more. Throughout the film, Emma Thompson's screenplay has allied Elinor's sensibility with that of the narrator, putting Austen's narratorial comments in Elinor's mouth, and making Elinor's perspective almost entirely the camera's; in its eagerness to portray the passionate power of the sisters' love, in its sudden abandonment of its more "sensible" narrative authority, the film has tipped itself subtly onto the other side. The achievement this marks, of making us see the passion behind Elinor's restraint, cannot quite withstand the hurried romantic settlings of the endings: where the heroine of the novel leaves the room to cry behind a door (admittedly, so loudly that her lover and her family can hear her), by the film's end, Elinor is sobbing in front of all of them, and Edward (and we) can have no real suspense about her feelings.

In some ways, the return of McGrath's narrator frees *Emma* from such (to me at least) confusing additions; where other adaptations increase not only the instances of revelatory speeches but the crowds hanging around to hear them – Andrew Davies's adaptation of *Emma* (shown in the United States on A&E) adds an entire village wedding surely borrowed from Thomas Hardy, at the end of which *all* the new couples, including not only the Churchills and the Eltons but the Martins, join Mr. Knightley in toasting his bride and celebrating through a dance the life manorial – this *Emma* seems consciously to restrain itself. The narrator observes through a window the scene where Emma and Knightley inform Mr. Woodhouse of the marriage; as the narrator comments, "The elation Mr. Weston felt was soon shared by many," the other characters gradually fill the room, toasting the happy couple, and only the sobbing Harriet rushes from her encounter with Emma, devastated by her own disappointment. In the last extended scene, Harriet recounts to Emma the news of her marriage, and the narrator can conclude her script; it would seem that the opposition has been silenced.

McGrath, however, borrows one further trick from Austen – and again, its accentuation in film comes from a deliberate voicing, one that recapitulates the connection the film has been making throughout between film's vocal techniques and the problematic nature of subjectivity, particularly female subjectivity, in the text. His concluding scene follows film convention in adding the entire community to the "small band of true friends who witnessed the ceremony," perhaps on the theory that it takes a whole village to commence marital bliss, but he also retains and makes even more visible the one ironic commentator Austen's narrator cites, Mrs. Elton. Whereas the novel grants her only a small aside, in which "Mrs. Elton, from the particulars detailed by her husband, thought it all extremely shabby, and very inferior to her own, – 'Very little white satin, very few veils; a most pitiful business'" (III.xiv), in the film, she is allowed to attend the wedding, and to occupy the screen for a long moment, delivering her characteristic phrase (she does not profess to be an expert in the field of fashion, "though my friends say I have quite the eye") and concluding, "I can tell you, there was a shocking lack of satin." Moving from the novel's free, indirect discourse to direct address, a face and a voice confronting us ("you") with dissent, McGrath interrupts his own narrator, suggesting that even her certain vantage point (here reproduced cinematically by the camera's movement upward, toward omniscience and toward the church's steeple) is only one of the many available points of view, her voice only one of several to which we might equally well attend.

McGrath's Emma ends her final speech by stating sweetly, to Harriet Smith, "I only wanted your happiness," and his film does not, as my analysis might have suggested it would, end by rejecting either marital or closural bliss; but while it endorses romantic pleasure, it resists the idea most critics seem to endorse, that happiness comes from omniscience. The image of the steeple toward which the camera moved resolves into a painting like those of the spinning ball at the film's beginning; the camera moves down to a series of portraits, beginning with that of Emma and Knightley, and the film ends – but the ball does not turn itself back into the earth, spinning through the Milky Way. The return of that maternal voice, commenting and measuring and assessing, will not silence all other voices, any more than Emma's being "perfectly matched" can bring all other unions into harmony – in this version of the novel, there is no final reconciliation between Emma and Jane Fairfax; certainly, there is no harvest ball in which, as in the A&E *Emma,* the classes are reconciled into melodic and rhythmic unity.

What the play of voice and authority in the McGrath *Emma* has suggested is that what the seamlessness the novel's narrator seems to promise is a trick of narration, one that filmic narration can vex and disrupt, as it toys with our loyalty to Emma, our sense that she speaks for the film, our desire to see her vision of happiness and the film's brought back together. The very eccentricity and disassociation of character the use of voices highlights become the closest the novel comes to a moral center; only as the heroine expresses ambivalence is her narration reliable, and only as she learns to listen (or as we do) will her speech provide the true measure of her heart. Resisting as it does more conventional vehicles of speech, denying that romantic faith in self-expression the other adaptations highlight, McGrath's film comes closer to the complexity of subjectivity and realism (not mere naturalism or mimetic naïveté, but the struggle to learn and interpret) Austen's text provides to its canniest (and its least self-satisfied) readers; as in the novel, the less we are sure of what we are reading or hearing, the closer we will be to understanding the novel's hermeneutic instruction.

However, what is most moving in McGrath's *Emma* is what is most moving in Austen's: the powerful lesson that we are most estranged when we are talking to ourselves; the sense that however much society shapes what we think of as our individual selves, we are even less ourselves outside of it. *Emma* is a novel about how terribly hard it is to learn to need other voices; how dangerously self-sufficient our knowledge seems to ourselves. At the same time that it mocks our feelings of authenticity, surrounding the speaking selves with mirrors and haunting doubles, it holds up the possibility of some self which can self-correct; like the absent mother who returns only to dictate proper endings, internal monitors can give way to social harmony – and even more, to a world in which the heroine's sketch of the universe, the spinning globe in which we continue to believe Emma's portrait takes its proper place, can occupy not only our vision, but our best, listening selves.

■ ■ ■

Questions and projects

1. Listen carefully to an adaptation of a Jane Austen novel other than the 1995 *Emma*. To what extent do Schor's points about voice in *Emma* apply to this other adaptation? Does this second film mobilize voice in different ways that distinguish it?

2. Choose an adaptation by a very different writer: say, a film based on a Henry James novel or one adapted from a Virginia Woolf story. How, specifically, does voice become an integral part of the adaptation?

Notes

1   Anthony Lane, "The Dumbing of *Emma*,"*The New Yorker*, August 5, 1996.

2   Arnold Kettle, *"Emma,"* in *Jane Austen: A Collection of Critical Essays*, ed. Ian Watt (Upper Saddle River, NJ: Prentice-Hall, 1963): 113.

3   See Michael Chion, *The Voice in Cinema* (New York: Columbia University Press, 1999); Gerard Genette, *Narrative Discourse: An Essay on Method* (Ithaca, NY: Cornell University Press, 1980); Tom Levin, "The Acoustic Dimension: Notes on Cinema Sound," *Screen* 25.3 (1984): 55-68; Kaja Silverman, *The Acoustic Mirror: The Female Voice in Psychoanalysis and Cinema* (Bloomington, IN: Indiana University Press, 1988); and most particularly Mary Ann Doane's insightful essay "The Voice in Cinema: The Articulation of Body and Space," *Yale French Studies* (issue on "Cinema/Sound," ed. Rick Altman) 60 (1999): 33-50.

4   The standard account of free indirect discourse or *stile indirecte libre* is Norman Page's in *The Language of Jane Austen* (New York: Barnes and Noble, 1972): 120-138. Banfield and Cohn summarize varieties of indirect speech in fiction: Ann Banfield, *Unspeakable Sentences: Narration and Representation in the Language of Fiction* (Boston, MA: Routledge and Kegan Paul, 1982); Dorrit Cohn, *Transparent Minds: Narrative Modes for Presenting Consciousness in Fiction* (Princeton: Princeton University Press, 1978). Casey Finch and Peter Bowen's important essay "'The Tittle-Tattle of Highbury': Gossip and the Free Indirect Style in *Emma*,"*Representations* 31 (Summer 1990): 1-18 draws on similar issues.

5   Page, *Language of Jane Austen*: 124.

6   See Kathy Mezei's "Who is Speaking Here? Free Indirect Discourse, Gender, and Authority in *Emma, Howards End,* and *Mrs. Dalloway*," in *Ambiguous Discourse: Feminist Narratology and British Women Writers,* ed. Kathy Mezei (Chapel Hill, NC: University of North Carolina Press, 1996): 66-92.

7   *Double Indemnity*, Writer James Cain, Director Billy Wilder, Paramount, 1944; *Sunset Boulevard,* Director Billy Wilder, Paramount, 1950.

8   Amy Lawrence in *Echo and Narcissus: Women's Voices in Classical Hollywood Cinema* (Berkeley: University of California Press, 1991) notes the relationship between sound, technology and death almost from the beginning of recorded sound, in advertisements as simple as "His Master's Voice," in which Nipper, the faithful dog, sits on a coffin and listens to the horn of a Victrola, from which his master's voice emerges. She draws no explicit connection between this and her later stress on the "somewhat wishful insistence on the perfect fidelity of the new technology" which maintains "the recorded voice as holding a special,

essential connection to the individual" (19), but this perfection is available, in some uncanny way, only in the already-dead voice.

9   Billy Wilder recently pointed out, "The thing about voice-overs – you have to be very careful there that *you don't show what they're* already seeing. *Add* to what they're seeing. I think that you can, within seconds, really seconds, you can tell things that are much better to *hear* than to see" (Cameron Crowe, *Conversations with Billy Wilder,* New York: Knopf, 1999). Wilder's account suggests again a different order of truth-statement in sound – which he goes on to connect to the voice-over in *Sunset Boulevard,* saying, "Nobody got up and said, 'Now wait a minute, a dead man speaking, *rum-rum-rum-rah,* I don't want to see that...' They listened" (108).

10 According to Kozloff, the voice-over "Naturalizes cinematic narration," creating a special relation-ship with the viewer, couching a film "as a conscious, deliberate communication" which depends on the illusion sound creates that participants hear something more real than real (Sarah Kozloff, *Invisible Storytellers* [Berkeley: University of California Press, 1988]: 129). See 22 for her analysis of voice-over. Lawrence notes the confusion over illusion and reality in recorded sound, pointing out, "When a phonograph listener of 1898 gazed at a flat wax disc and murmured to himself, 'That's Caruso,' he was participating in a sophisticated form of make-believe" (*Echo and Narcissus: 2 1*).

11 Kozloff (*Invisible Storytellers*) comments that we put our faith in the voice of a voice-over narrator, not as created but as creator.

12 Andrew Davies's depiction of the Box Hill incident in the A&E *Emma* is if anything harsher: Miss Bates's commentary to Knightley is distinctly audible and Emma looks immediately distressed, and his Mr. Knightley is far more critical (as he is throughout) of Emma's behavior. In this version, interestingly, Davies omits Knightley's final words, which are that he must prove himself her friend "by very faithful counsel," by telling her "truths while I can"; in McGrath's version, Knightley speaks these words, imply-ing clearly that his harshness grows out of his sense that she is about to marry Frank Churchill, and he will no longer be able to speak to her in so intimate a way. Davies's version also omits the most poign-ant words of Knightley's speech, that Miss Bates "has sunk from the comforts she was born to; and, if she live to old age, must probably sink more." For Austen, as for McGrath, Emma's cruelty is a failure of forward-looking imagination, the inability to see that Miss Bates's life (and Emma's own), will grow more constrained, rather than richer, with time, and that comforts like companionship and faithful friendship are the only things that will endure.

13 Lionel Trilling, "Emma and the Legend," in *The Last Decade: Essays and Reviews, 1965-75,* ed. Diana Trilling (New York: Harcourt Brace Jovanovich, 1979): 40.

14 Austen employs Gothic conventions in a complicated way in her own fiction, invoking stereotypical Gothic anxieties in *Pride and Prejudice* and *Sense and Sensibility,* and even hinting at them in the besieged woman and men with mysterious secrets in *Emma.* Critics have attacked Catherine Morland, the heroine of *Northanger Abbey,* for her too-faithful belief in Gothic trappings, but Gilbert and Gubar offer a feminist reading in which the real Abbey horrors (including evil men, unhappy women, and dark secrets) are connected with women's lack of power in a not-so-Gothic world (Sandra Gilbert and Susan Gubar, "Shut up in Prose," in their *The Madwoman in the Attic: The Woman Writer and the Nineteenth-Century Liberary Imagination* [New Haven, CT: Yale University Press, 2000]).

15 *You've Got Mail,* Director, writer and producer Nora Ephron, Warner Brothers, 1998; *The Shop around the Corner,* Director Ernst Lubitsch, MGM, 1939.

16 In *Understanding Media: The Extensions of Man* (New York: McGraw-Hill, 1964), Marshall McLuhan sug-gests that Narcissus falls in love not with himself but with his image as reflected through a medium out-side himself, so that the myth describes our attachment to new technologies which promise to extend the self (51-56). Thus, in the writing scene, Emma quite explicitly loves not herself but her mirror, and its promise of new forms of self-expression.

17 Ian Watt, "Jane Austen and the Traditions of Comic Aggression: *Sense and Sensibility,*" *Persuasions: Journal of the Jane Austen Society of North America* 3 (December 1981): 14-15, 25-28.

Chapter 31

William Galperin

ADAPTING JANE AUSTEN
The surprising fidelity of *Clueless*

U NLIKE THE MORE CONVENTIONAL cinematic adaptations of Jane Austen's novels, which maintain a fidelity to both plot and historical setting, according to William Galperin, Amy Heckerling's comparatively freewheeling adaptation of *Emma* in the film *Clueless* registers a more profound fidelity to Austen's achievement in honoring the protocols of reading that the novel puts in place by insisting that it be read not once for story but multiple times for detail. A Professor of English at Rutgers University and the author of essays on film and television and several books, including *The Return of The Visible in British Romanticism* (1993) and *The Historical Austen* (2003), Galperin sees *Clueless* as not just a recapitulation of Austen's romantic comedy about growth and development but also about the many "differentials" involving language, fashion, and culture that add up to a meditation on change.

■ ■ ■

ADAPTING JANE AUSTEN: THE SURPRISING FIDELITY OF *CLUELESS*
WILLIAM GALPERIN

"Fidelity," as some have argued, remains a quaint or outdated concept in discussing film adaptation, given the strain that any signifying practice, much less an intermedial one, necessarily exerts on the integrity or truth of a given representation. And the problem is compounded further, Robert Stam has recently argued, by the fact that neither the novel nor the cinema is generically predisposed to a single "truth" or "essence" which could readily be transferred from one medium to the other as "an originary core" or a "kernel of meaning" or even a "nucleus of events." [1] Thus not only must any discussion of adaptation take a back seat to the respective syntheses that the novel and the cinema perform as composite genres, where questions of fidelity are best directed to the "essence of [each] medium" individually (2000: 58); such a discussion is so encumbered by the multiple dimensions in any given transfer that we are better served, Stam urges, by referring all questions of adaptation to a "dialogic" framework "rooted in a "contextual" or "intertextual history" that disposes of "hierarchies," especially those bearing on "inchoate notions of `fidelity'" (2000: 75–76). There is much obviously to admire in Stam's wariness, not the least being his sensitivity to the range and complexity of the media at issue. Still and all, the concept of fidelity is not without explanatory power here, particularly as a beginning premise. And so I begin, accordingly, with some "remarks on cinematic adaptation" delivered almost a half century ago by Jean Mitry, for whom fidelity is at the very least a pivot point in addressing the phenomenon of cinematic transfer.[2] According to Mitry, the cinematic "adaptor" of a novel has two basic options. She or he can either be "faithful to the letter," following "the procedure of the novelist step-by-step so that the chains of circumstance are exactly the same." Or, the adaptor can be faithful to the "spirit" of the novel, expressing "similar ideas and analogous sentiments, but arriv[ing] at them by slant routes" (1971: 4). As Mitry elaborates these options, however, a number of problems arise. In the first, the cinematic imperative to express novelistic "facts," including interior worlds, "visually," not only leads the adaptor "to distort the sense determined by the original literary expression," but leads also to a situation where, in "thinking only to serve the novelist," the adaptor actually "betrays" the novelist (and by implication the novel) simply "with the ... elements of [the adaptor's] own fabulation." The second option is more problematic still, "for the film, interesting as it might be, no longer has anything to do with the original work it is supposed to reflect" (1971: 4).

The "solutions" that Mitry proposes by way of mitigating these problems are not solutions really so much as concessions. But they bear usefully on the question of adapting or translating Jane Austen's novels to film, where fidelity of a certain kind remains paramount. As Mitry sees it, the adaptor has two additional options, however strained or limited: either to follow "the story" as closely as possible, "putting it into images" so as to reproduce visually the "*things* signified by words" in a novel (absent of course what is expressed or referred to in speech or dialogue) at which point the film is "no longer [a] creation but only [a] representation" (1971: 4). Or, "not troubling to remain faithful to the author," the adaptor can make what Mitry terms a "personal work," using "the original as a point of departure" or an "inspiration" but doing nothing or virtually nothing "on behalf of the novel" from which the inspiration derives (1971: 4).

Now to readers and viewers familiar with the adaptations of Austen's novels that have appeared in the last two decades, these options look less like options than extremities between which virtually every adaptation of Austen effectively oscillates. In addition to being "personal" or "inspired," both as Mitry describes it and as any viewer familiar with the novels would immediately recognize, the Austen adaptations are generally quite "faithful," both to specific aspects of the novels, chiefly plot and dialogue, and, even more importantly, to an idea or *ideal* of Austen, in which fidelity and infidelity are at times difficult to parse. The many liberties taken by the respective adaptors of *Sense and Sensibility*, *Mansfield Park* and *Persuasion*—unquestionably the most serious of the feature-length adaptations of Austen's novels to have appeared recently—cannot be dismissed as indulgences or inaccuracies. Rather they are attempts to rectify problems and to smooth out inconsistencies in the novels by way of saving Austen from her less felicitous or, as the adaptors seem to feel, less-than-Austenian tendencies.

The treatment of *Sense and Sensibility* (1995) written by Emma Thompson and directed by Ang Lee does something altogether counterintuitive, or so it seems, in foregoing the most "cinematic" moment in the entire novel: John Willoughby's tenth-hour visit in the midst of Marianne Dashwood's near-fatal illness. But this move was more likely the result of an either/or proposition posed by the novel's incoherence. After all, not only does Willoughby's visit, in which he explains his otherwise bad behavior, go a long way in retrieving him from the villainy with which he is otherwise saddled by the novel's plot to which the film in turn is pegged; his surprise visit, along with expectations it resuscitates, creates additional complications in endorsing sensibility as a mode or affect of resistance to things as they are. While the novel, like the film, is obviously aligned with something opposed to sensibility, specifically the good "sense" and propriety that Marianne's older sister Elinor continually displays in the face of disappointment or adversity, it remains, as its title suggests, just as faithful to the sisters as a unit (as opposed to a binarism) or to a sisterhood writ large, where the *desire* for something else or better finds a register in Marianne and an enabler in Willoughby. All of this might not matter much if the sisters' condition—specifically the precariousness of their lives in a culture where women typically have no control over wealth or property—were secondary or ancillary to the novel. However, with a material sanction that literally begins on page one, the resistance of the sisters' situation to the novel's story, where Marianne (to quote Eve Sedgwick) is ultimately "taught a lesson," never really flags.[3] And so the liberties that the film takes with the novel are not liberties. They are efforts to keep faith with the book as a vehicle of instruction and containment that other, equally crucial, aspects of *Sense and Sensibility* forever oppose. In striving for coherence in a text where confusion and discontent are linked, the Lee/Thompson adaptation "saves" the novel in lieu of the novel's ability, apparently, to save itself.

Driving this (in)fidelity, in which "inspiration" is mobilized on Austen's behalf regardless of what her novels may actually say, is a myth or conception of Austen as somehow flawless that has been a commonplace for over a century and a half. While some of Austen's flawlessness falls under the heading of nostalgia, particularly for Victorian readers who were much taken with the lost world of a largely gentrified community that she brings so vividly to life, most of it resides in the special place that literary history has accorded Austen as the writer who essentially invented or helped to codify the novel as a realistic instrument. As the first writer to successfully negotiate what James Thompson (echoing Ian Watt) has described as "that most fundamental contradiction of novelistic discourse ... between subjectivity and objectivity," Austen "found the means of displaying the inside and outside of human life, how her characters think and feel, along with how they interact with others." And for this she:

> occupies a crucial spot in the development of the novel; not just showing more of life, but a leap to showing all of life. As F. R. Leavis puts it, Jane Austen makes possible George Eliot: 'Jane Austen, in fact, is the inaugurator of the great tradition of the English novel.'[4]

Observations along these lines are manifold, including those by Raymond Williams, who is anything but convinced of the totality of Austen's vision:

> The paradox of Jane Austen is the ... achievement of a unity of tone, of a settled and remarkably confident way of seeing and judging, in the chronicle of confusion and change. She is precise and candid, but in very particular ways. ... Her eye for a house, for timber, for the details of improvement is quick, accurate, monetary. Yet money of other kinds, from the trading houses, from the colonial plantations, has no visual equivalent; it has to be converted to these signs of order to be recognized at all. ... Jane Austen could achieve her remarkable unity of tone—that cool and controlled observation which is the basis of her narrative method; that lightly distanced management of event and description and character which need not become either open manipulation or direct participation—because of an effective and yet unseen formula: improvement is or ought to be improvement. The working improvement, which is not seen at all, is the means to social improvement, which is then so isolated that it is seen very clearly indeed.[5]

Striking in this Marxist analysis is not just Williams' admiration, however qualified, but the horizon of perfectability it projects—the something almost perfect that needs perfecting or should be perfected—which proves an additional sanction, I would argue, for the kinds of liberties that cinematic adaptation takes with Austen.

Not always comprehensive, or as visually expansive as Williams prescribes, such "perfection" is served just as frequently by reduction or simplification. But it can also entail a more liberal collaboration along the lines of Patricia Rozema's 1999 adaptation of *Mansfield Park*, which sets out, in many ways, to complete the project that Williams' critique leaves unfinished, asserting in effect that Austen was too perfect a writer to have produced a novel as vexed as this one. In its handling of the very materials that Williams maintains are perforce hidden or evaded in Austen, *Mansfield Park* is undoubtedly enigmatic and a problem novel. What it is not is the simplistic screed that Rozema makes of it in taking the novel's many shades of gray, particularly regarding the slave trade, and converting them into primary colors. Much of the alteration centers on the heroine, Fanny Price, who goes from the self-serving moralist of the novel into a full-throated abolitionist in the film, with affinities not only with the novel's narrator but also, and more crucially, to the novelist herself of whom she is intermittently an autobiographical projection. The notion, held primarily by Austen enthusiasts, that Jane Austen *is* her narrator rather than a *writer* who might just be concerned with the mechanics of novelistic technique and form (including narrative voice) is only partly the amateur mistake here that it is for, say, Rudyard Kipling's Janeites.[6] For despite her apparent lack of interest in Austen as a technician, which a filmmaker, above all, might very well have, Rozema's way with the novel comes mostly, or so it seems, from a dogmatic adherence to its storyline, which more than in any other Austen novel is a "cover story" or vehicle of ideology that other materials, including characters who are otherwise derogated by the plot, tend mostly to undermine.[7] In seeking to justify this story, then, rather than in coming to terms with the novel as a totality, Rozema delivers a heroine who scarcely resembles the character on whom she is based.

The novel is primarily a narrative of upward mobility, centering on the rise of the initially impoverished Fanny, who goes to live with the family of her wealthy uncle Sir Thomas Bertram, who happens also to own a plantation in the West Indies. Consequently in making Fanny's rise and projected control over the Bertram family the result of her forbearance or ability to say "no" to initiatives that are openly transgressive in opposing certain of her uncle's directives, *Mansfield Park* does more than reward her on the basis of her supposed virtue.[8] It situates that virtue on a larger continuum linking domestic ideology, on the one hand, with its premium on female forbearance, and the slave trade, on the other, where virtue is obviously in short supply. For as the novel makes equally clear, the empire currently in formation is being served less by the seemingly decadent aristocracy (figured in Sir Thomas's progeny and their friends), whose members continually resist interpellation as gendered and imperial subjects, than by the more codified likes of Fanny and her sailor brother William who are the portents, along with their uncle, of the new hegemony into which British society is evolving. As a result, the novel's plot or storyline, where Fanny vanquishes her decadent and transgressive peers through demurral rather than direct action, is more than a vehicle of propaganda in which Fanny and her ideology are projected to be on the winning side of history. It is an ideological apparatus that simultaneously falls flat, both in its criticism of certain characters, who are demonstrably the most interesting and proactive in the novel, and in clearing the way for what amounts to an (un)holy alliance of domestic virtue and imperial and colonial ambition.[9]

Rozema's response to this conundrum, in which we are forced to *think* in the act of reading, is to render "perfect" or uncomplicated what is necessarily imperfect and in fact a real mess: both at the level of cultural analysis or demonstration, where Fanny's individual ambition fits hand in glove with British expansionism *tout court*, and also, and just as importantly, at the level of aesthetic or narrative performance, where Austen's signature practice of free indirect discourse—a relatively recent development in novelistic technology—comes off as a powerful but potentially sinister instrument. And so Rozema's rather liberal conflation of heroine, narrator and author is not an interpretive or collaborative indulgence so much as the result, it would appear, of reading Raymond Williams and Edward Said more closely, and with far greater sympathy, than Jane Austen.[10] The film's conversion, for example, of Fanny's woefully neutral curiosity about Antigua ("I love to hear my uncle talk of the West Indies")[11] into an angry and informed counterposition does more than whitewash what the novel subtly marks as ignorance or opportunism on her part; it converts the novel's melancholic projection of an England-about-to-be into a utopian fantasy, in which the institution of the novel as a genre, far from being part of the problem, is suddenly—in its reconstitution as film narrative—part of the solution. Unlike the adaptations of *Sense and Sensibility* or *Persuasion*, where perfection or improvement comes chiefly via simplification, Rozema's elaborate translation all but condemns the *author* of *Mansfield Park* as having failed or betrayed the values of posterity.

Rozema and other adaptors seem generally to believe, then, that Jane Austen necessarily feared change or was unequipped to deal with it in any way apart from one that was class-based and conservative. And this is why, in their quest for both perfection and fidelity, the films invariably waffle between a nearly-fetishistic delectation in the upscale and traditional environments where the narratives take place (virtually all the houses are grander in the films than in the novels) and a more progressive, if anachronistic, recasting of the novels as feminist in a more modern and recognizable way. This détente delivers more than just an Austen whose heroines can apparently jettison their impending roles as desperate housewives, as Anne Elliot does in Roger Michell's 1994 adaptation of *Persuasion*. It creates a more "perfect" Austen whose period-bound despair—or such reflexive resistance on display in *Persuasion* despite its "happy" ending—is supplanted by a full-blown feminism that, in the films of both *Mansfield Park* and *Persuasion* especially, adds melioration and change to a comedic resolution in which marriage is simply one component. The problem for the adaptors centers primarily, therefore, on how things end in Austen or, rather, in how they don't. For continually shadowing the change or improvement relegated to marriage in the novels, whose heroines marry either happily or up or both, is another horizon of change, registered primarily through accompanying details that I call "differentials," that the novels tend mostly to project or to embed in a story that can't be told or resolved by the usual means. And it is a story best summed up by the following statement from the work most often regarded—certainly by Patricia Rozema—as Austen's most sinister. Responding to an account of the changes wrought upon the chapel of an ancient estate, where further changes are being entertained, *Mansfield Park*'s Mary Crawford has this to say about what the novel's story—as distinct from the novel—patently endorses. "Every generation," she asserts smilingly, "has its improvements" (68).

There are a number of ways to interpret this statement, the most immediate being an endorsement of the kinds of improvements that the opportunistic, and therefore tradition-minded, Fanny disapproves of. Yet beyond this problematic configuration, which finds the aristocracy (Mary) in the critical vanguard and the rising middle class (Fanny) wedded to convention, there is the larger (and recurrent) sense in Mary's statement that for women, in particular, improvement has a history too long and too repetitive for there to be any hope that improvements will be "improvements." In making this statement or in being allowed to make it, Mary is indicating two distinct things: that change, especially social change, has been *at best* a repetition of the same; and second, and more important, that change *has occurred*, albeit in forms unassimilable to the usual narratives of progress or development, including progress for women, to which improvements "ought" to refer.

In the case of *Mansfield Park*, whose world is hemmed in more by the impending future than by the receding past, this latter change is invariably local in, say, the private theatrical that the Bertram children and their friends undertake during Sir Thomas's absence: an initiative that proves a reminder, first and foremost, of the performance to which all social identity or selfhood is tantamount. But it is in *Emma*, more than in any other Austen novel, that the tension between change at the local or micro level and change at the macro, and narratable, level is most evident. And it is an aspect of the novel that Austen's earliest—and most discerning readers—were able to pick up on. They did so not by necessarily discovering change in every cranny of *Emma* but simply in noting a tension between what Walter Scott (in his review of *Emma*) described as the "narrative" of Austen's novels, whose heroines are "turned wise by precept, example and experience," and what both he and the novelist Maria Edgeworth disparaged as the novels' "prosing."[12] Most of Austen's contemporaries were quite taken by this prosaic detour, and by the defamiliarizing experience of seeing everyday life and social interaction in the dynamic and unprecedented relief that Austen set it. Yet the antipathy of Scott and especially Edgeworth, who put *Emma* down after just one volume claiming (as did other contemporaries) that it had "no story in it," is equally revealing. For the anxiety for which Edgeworth's boredom is more properly a screen is an anxiety that the screen adaptations (pun intended) share equally: namely, a worry over the differentiation unleashed when there is "no story" or vehicle of ideology to anchor and direct things.

Unlike *Mansfield Park*'s heroine, whose development is entirely material rather than existential or pedagogical, Emma Woodhouse undergoes a transformation exactly as Scott outlines. In learning the error of her ways, she is not simply turned wise, or so we are given to believe; she is also turned marriageable in either learning or discovering that she has always loved Mr. Knightley, who has been her chief disciplinarian throughout. The 1996 adaptations of *Emma* by Douglas McGrath and Andrew Davies (both titled *Emma*) follow this trajectory closely, differing only in the weight they assign to pedagogy and to romance respectively. In doing so, however, both adaptations miss a great deal of what the novel is about, which, as Edgeworth unhappily surmised, has surprisingly little to do with its story. For *Emma* was written not to be read just once for story (as it were); it was written, as I've argued elsewhere, to be *reread*, particularly for what was missed or overlooked the first time around.[13] Austen's novels are obviously unique in the capacity to reward rereading. However in *Emma*, as opposed to, say, *Pride and Prejudice*, rereading is a protocol imposed by the novel directly—through the suppression, in this instance, of the courtship narrative involving Jane Fairfax and Frank Churchill, which not even the narrator, who knows or should know everything, is apparently aware of until it is disclosed by one of the characters. As an invitation to research the novel for details regarding the courtship that were overlooked and of which every other character, with the possible exception of Knightley, remains ignorant, Austen's "choice of mystery at the expense of irony" (as one critic terms it)[14] effectively endows *Emma* with an afterlife that it might not have had otherwise. But there is more to this aspect of the novel than the insider status that rereading it confers. In addition to the discovery of information on Frank and Jane that has been hiding all along in plain sight, reading *Emma* as it asks to be read now is an uncontainable process, where there is always something new and different to be discovered and to reflect upon.

Among the many things brought to light by this process is the extraordinary dimensionality of routinized existence in a small village, where change or difference, far from absent or impossible, are in fact a daily occurrence. Thus, as Reginald Ferrar noted admiringly in 1917, *Emma* "is not an easy book to read," or indeed to reread. For the "manifold complexity of the book's web" by which twelve readings of the novel provide "twelve periods of pleasure ... squared and squared again with each perusal, till at every fresh reading you feel anew that you never understood anything like the widening sum of its delights" is even on this description a sublime of sorts that "pleasure" doesn't fully describe.[15] If anything, the ongoing tension in the novel between plot and the ever "widening sum" of information, especially evident whenever Miss Bates opens her mouth, has the concomitant effect of distinguishing the heroine's improvement, on the one hand, which mimics cultural hegemony through a narrative that is tutelary and hierarchical, and change, on the other hand, which is seemingly and potentially everywhere and figured, in among other places, the heroine's attempts to unite disadvantaged women to more advantaged or entitled men. As actions pitched toward social transformation or even leveling, Emma's initiatives are relatively modest and, as she discovers to her embarrassment, not always successful. But that is in many ways the point, or the point to which we are consistently referred by the novel: not just that politics may be local in this way but that the more motivated and less contingent these politics the more vulnerable they will be to discovery and control. This is another reason why the Frank–Jane union is kept under the radar as a "shadow" narrative or parallel reality in the novel,[16] and why Emma's comparatively overt attempts at orchestrating similar change are destined to fail. For the success Frank enjoys in achieving with Jane what Emma, for her part, fails to achieve in the case of Harriet Smith, is a reminder that change or improvement may very well be abroad, but only when it doesn't ultimately matter.

The more conventional cinematic adaptations of *Emma* treat the novel very differently of course, sticking to a sense of it based on a single reading. Adhering strenuously to the main plot, in which Emma's matchmaking comes off as meddling that only threatens the happiness of the young woman she's trying to help, the adaptations by McGrath (featuring Gwyneth Paltrow) and Davies (with Kate Beckinsale) not only follow a storyline that repeats itself over and over. They use the episode of Emma's failed matchmaking as a fulcrum for a narrative that, far from one of real change, is simply a developmental account annexed to a love story. Even as it is eventually tried by many other details and characters in the novel, beginning with the arrival of Frank, Jane and Mrs. Elton and the delayed appearance of Miss Bates, all of this in the aftermath of Emma's initial failure to match Harriet and Mr. Elton, the developmental narrative remains the sum and substance of the movies, which are interested less in the novel's many details and what they might yield or signify than in getting Emma to the altar in an eminently presentable way. The adaptations seem scarcely to recall, in other words, what the novel, for its part, can hardly forget and what we are forced to remember in (re)reading it: that Emma is far more interesting and attractive as the troublemaker we first encounter than she is as Mrs. Knightley at the novel's close; that Knightley is a more suitable and age-appropriate mate for the unmarried (and now pathetic) Miss Bates than for the wife whom he will have essentially grown from seed; that Frank's flirtations with Emma are distinctly de-eroticized and pitched, if anything, toward a dialogue with the heroine regarding the uses and abuses of her agency that Knightley's top-down pedagogy ultimately nullifies; that Emma's interest in marrying Harriet is an initiative driven partly by same-sex desire; and finally, and regrettably, that in light of her exceptional independence and financial capability, same-sex solidarity—be it with Jane or Miss Bates or even Harriet—is an increasingly abject experience for Emma that she is compelled finally to suspend. And these are just a few of the differentials that the novel—or rereading it—delivers.[17]

The cinematic adaptations can also be reviewed and reconsidered. Yet all that is discoverable the second or third or fourth time around are further details and hints about Frank and Jane. Any other information of the kind I've just enumerated is nonexistent in the films, and not because it is unavailable for inclusion. It is nonexistent because to include this information by, say, casting Miss Bates as the thirty-something character she is, complicates the basic storyline in making Knightley's continual kindness to her a chivalry with a back story. Another term for these complications, then, or for what they provoke as differentials when more than the novel's story is being put into images, is thinking or reflection—something difficult to do when the impulse is either to read or to adapt for plot but eminently achievable when the adaptation rises to the interpretive model of rereading or reading for detail.

This brings me, then, to *Clueless*, which keeps faith with Austen's novel not necessarily as Mitry suggests but by effectively exchanging its nominal "story" (which the film incorporates to a surprising degree) for one lodged in the "widening sum" of its details, most of which involve change in some form. Thus while Amy Heckerling's 1995 adaptation is also a romantic comedy ending in the union—or at least the temporary union—of the Emma-character (Cher) and the Knightley counterpart (Josh), it follows the novel, or what I've been arguing *is* the novel, in being irreducible to this one narrative. In the novel, as I've suggested, the "widening" separation of story and information necessarily leaves the story of Emma's development intact, but as an object of interpretation from which the novel overall is increasingly disarticulated. And so it goes in *Clueless*, where the developmental narrative is, for all intents and purposes, nonexistent or, when existent, doggedly plot-driven and even a little pathetic, particularly at the end when Cher, like Emma, becomes a patronizing do-gooder. This is not to say that Cher does not make mistakes or even the same mistakes that Emma makes. It is simply that Cher's mistakes—including her insult to the El Salvadoran housemaid (whom she misidentifies as Mexican)—carry almost no force regarding her need for improvement or discipline. More like *Mansfield Park*'s Fanny, in fact, who arrives on the scene having learned everything she apparently needs to, Cher has learned everything that she needs or, better still, *should have learned* by the time we first encounter her in late twentieth-century Los Angeles. This is immediately derivable from her intelligence, charm, and self-irony even when they are seemingly belied by her use of language, neologism or analogy. And it receives confirmation from none other than Josh himself. Summoned to retrieve Cher after a series of mishaps in which Cher is hit on by Elton and subsequently mugged after refusing Elton's offer of a ride home, Josh finds himself in the rather awkward position of escorting not one but two girls: Cher whom he is obliged (as a step-brother) to assist and his rather opinionated date. During the car ride to the girls' respective homes the conversation migrates to the famous quote from Shakespeare's *Hamlet* ("To thine own self be true") that Josh's date attributes to the play's main character, which Cher (already offended by the former's pompous and traditional attitude) promptly and happily observes is a misattribution. Josh's date replies sardonically that she thinks (i.e., knows) that she remembers *Hamlet* accurately. But it is Cher's seemingly philistine rejoinder that she remembers Mel Gibson accurately and that it was the "Polonius-guy" who uttered the famous lines (in the movie adaptation of course) that brings a broad and approving smile to Josh's face. The novel hints at a similar attraction on Knightley's part, mostly through his constant presence at Emma's house and continued efforts to engage her. But Knightley's attraction, however palpable, is alloyed with a disposition to admonish and correct, especially when Emma is associated with the forces of change or disruption (in for example her sponsorship of Harriet) that the film—beginning by making Josh an age-appropriate companion—consistently rejects.

So at stake in *Clueless* (as in *Emma*) is a very different story than the one driving the other adaptations. More than in the novel, where the courtship narrative is at least freestanding throughout, the story in *Clueless*'s details, centering on both language and fashion, particularly in the early scenes where they literally overwhelm, aggregates to a series of ruminations—on women, on sexuality and finally on women's agency—into which the courtship plot is simply folded. Language and style are key here, both because they are at the heart of *Clueless*'s principal conceit—the "modernization" of a literary masterpiece—and, more importantly, because they proceed in the perplexed recognition that "every generation has its improvements." No one, least of all Heckerling, is claiming that Cher's cartoonish fashion sense or use of slang is truly an improvement. But it is impossible to deny that these *are improvements*—especially in certain quarters—and more crucially that they register, as language and fashion do, the change and difference occurring daily. A particularly striking example takes place in slow motion as the film lingers over a group of walkman-wearing, skateboard-toting, suburban "gangsta" wannabes, whose vanguardist fashion sense, shaped mostly by the imperative to sport underwear as outerwear, elicits a dissenting opinion from Cher, who notes apologetically that she is otherwise "no traitor to [her] generation." Whether this generational change is shocking, disruptive or just simply unappealing is beside the point; the point, in *Clueless* as in *Emma*, is the disenchanting disconnect between change, which is ongoing (and a register of possibility or, dare we say it, hope), and any narrative of real progress to which change or difference or Cher's "generation" for that matter can be assimilated.

To be sure, Cher's exasperated deployment of "as if" to refer to an order or identity to which she has been erroneously assigned—or is assumed by others to belong—hints at just such a narrative, "as if" what is happening in fashion, music, language, and manners are already the coordinates of some utopian space. And beginning indeed with the opening credits, a world elsewhere is seemingly close at hand in *Clueless* mostly in the frothy entertainment, with intertextual nods to both "chick-flicks" and screwball comedy, to which the film is at one level tantamount.[18] But this is also of course movie magic, and like all movie magic, and for that matter Cher's magical thinking here, magic with an expiration date.[19] For the real intertext that is *Clueless* includes not just *Emma* obviously, where change or difference is similarly everywhere and nowhere, but the Austen novel that follows *Emma* whose very title echoes *Clueless*'s in also describing a pathology or disposition that comes to define the heroine despite her efforts to be otherwise. In *Persuasion* this disposition refers initially to the coercion or family pressure to which the heroine Anne Elliot submits in first rejecting her suitor, Captain Wentworth. But it comes to apply equally, the novel shows, to the romantic imperative that Anne "learn[s]," or introjects subsequently, making any distinction between capitulation and desire, or between submission and will, or between "over-persuasion" and "internal persuasion" quite negligible.[20] *Clueless* proceeds in a different direction, with cluelessness as an imprecation reserved initially for other people—and a measure of the state of exception to which Cher imagines herself as belonging—and only later becoming an apparatus of self-criticism following a number of discoveries where Cher's magical thinking, or what she has imagined to be true, turns out to be otherwise. Chief among these discoveries is the realization that Cher has loved Josh all along, which echoes the famous moment in *Emma* when the heroine's conviction that "Mr. Knightley must marry no one but herself" darts through her "with the speed of an arrow."[21] The difference is that where the *éclaircissement* of the novel is primarily class-based and prompted by Harriet's presumptuous fixation on Knightley as a potential mate, Cher's recognition—though nominally provoked by a similar disclosure by the Harriet-character Tai regarding Josh—is more immediately the result of a losing battle with sexuality or impending sexualization that Cher has been waging from the very beginning. Thus even as Cher has presumably learned something by the film's close, she is at least as clueless in this putatively "enlightened state" driven by biology as she was previously, where any efforts to contain her or to coordinate her to a scenario akin to what prevails at the film's close were met with "as if."

It is here that the comparison with *Persuasion*, or with a composite Austen that includes *Persuasion*, proves instructive. For unlike Anne Elliot's struggle, which is waged primarily in the understanding that the imperatives of the body will direct her to a place—the domestic sphere—from which there is no escape and where her ability to make a difference on any scale, however subtly or quietly, will be diminished, Cher's struggle is alternately backdated and postdated. It is backdated in that, like one of Carol Gilligan's young female subjects,[22] Cher must control her sexuality lest she be controlled by it (hence, the use of fashion to attract so as to repel boys and the hilarious micromanagement of her "seduction" by Christian). And it is postdated insofar as the world of *Clueless* is no longer Jane Austen's world but a "modern" or even "postmodern" world where women can do other things apart from marrying—as the film cleverly implies in ending with a marriage that is *not* Cher's at which she is merely in attendance. That these "other things" devolve on premarital sex in the film or being able to drive rather than on something more serious or substantial, is not a joke so much as a melancholy insight. In contrast to the claustrophobic and frightened state to which the heroine is eventually consigned in *Persuasion* (but typically liberated from by the film), or to the subdued propriety that the chastened Emma eventually displays as the future Mrs. Knightley in the novel, the sixteen-year-old Cher's normative—if not quite realized—fate at the end of *Clueless* is a holding pattern that, in the spirit of *Emma* reread (or *Clueless* re-viewed) effectively honors where Cher *has been*, along with the change all around of which she is a placeholder as a member, again, of her "generation." Very near the film's end, then, amid discoveries that she has been clueless and is "majorly, totally but crazy-in-love with Josh" (that the two discoveries are linked is again no accident), Cher ambles by a shoe display and is momentarily distracted and diverted in her thinking to wonder "if they have that in my size." This is obviously a joke. But there is more to Cher's recidivism than a fetishism that the film can take easy aim at. For the calculus linking shoes to change or music to change or language to change in the movie, is, like change itself, part of the endless and dialectical work that viewing *Clueless*, like reading *Emma*, entails. Consumption of the sort Cher practices may not be the most honorable or progressive form of agency or production. However, in light of where she is literally headed at the moment she is temporarily distracted, thinking about it with her, particularly as a kind of detour or "if," is serious business indeed.

■ ■ ■

Questions and projects

1. On its surface, *Clueless* appears to be a wild and loose adaptation of Austen's novel. Summarize Galperin's argument for the "surprising fidelity" of the film. Are there other adaptations, perhaps the 2010 *Easy A* (based on Nathaniel Hawthorne's *The Scarlet Letter*), for which you can make the claim that a kind of fidelity connects the work of literature and the film? Explain with as much detail as possible.

2. Galperin identifies a crucial dimension of adaptation studies when he focuses on the similar dynamics of reading and re-reading both literature and film. Choose another film adaptation and discuss how it consciously elicits a "reading" process: Perhaps reading the film through or against the novel? Perhaps re-reading the film in the way one re-reads the novel to discover new links and meanings?

Notes

1 "Beyond Fidelity: The Dialogics of Adaptation," in *Film Adaptation*, ed. James Naremore (New Brunswick, NJ: Rutgers University Press, 2000), p. 57. See pp. 74–88.

2 "Remarks on the Problem of Cinematic Adaptation," *Bulletin of the Midwest Modern Language Association*, 4 (1971): 1–9

3   Eve Kosofsky Sedgwick, "Jane Austen and the Masturbating Girl," *Critical Inquiry* 17 (1991): 833.

4   "How to Do Things with Austen," in *Jane Austen and Co.: Remaking the Past in Contemporary Culture*, ed. Suzanne Pucci and James Thompson (Albany, NY: State University of New York Press, 2003), p. 18.

5   *The Country and the City* (New York: Oxford University Press, 1973), pp. 115–16.

6   "The Janeites," in *Debits and Credits* (London: Macmillan, 1926), pp. 147–76.

7   Sandra Gilbert and Susan Gubar, "Jane Austen's Cover Story (and Its Secret Agents)," in *Madwoman in the Attic: The Woman Writer and the Nineteenth-Century Literary Imagination* (New Haven, CT: Yale University Press, 1979), pp. 146–83.

8   Eventually Fanny also says "no" to her uncle when he insists that she marry Henry Crawford. But his directive in this instance is a mistake that he later acknowledges.

9   I discuss *Mansfield Park* along these lines in both *The Historical Austen* (Philadelphia, PA, University of Pennsylvania Press, 2003), pp. 154–79, and in "The Missed Opportunities of *Mansfield Park*, in *A Companion to Jane Austen*, ed. Claudia L. Johnson and Clara Tuite (Oxford: Wiley-Blackwell, 2009), pp. 123–33.

10 For Said's postcolonial critique of *Mansfield Park*, see *Culture and Imperialism* (New York: Knopf, 1993), pp. 80–97.

11 *Mansfield Park*, ed. James Kinsley (Oxford: Oxford UP, 2003), p. 154.

12 For a full discussion of the responses of Austen's contemporaries to her writing, see *The Historical Austen*, pp. 44–81.

13 *The Historical Austen*, pp. 180–213.

14 Wayne C. Booth, *The Rhetoric of Fiction* (Chicago, IL: University of Chicago Press, 1983), p. 255.

15 *Jane Austen: A Critical Heritage, 1870–1940*, vol. 2, ed. B. C. Southam (London: Routledge and Kegan Paul, 1987), p. 266.

16 W. J. Harvey, "The Plot of Emma," in *Emma*, ed. Stephen M. Parrish (New York: W. W. Norton, 1972), p. 456.

17 Again, for a fuller discussion of *Emma* along these lines, see *The Historical Austen*, pp. 180–213.

18 For further discussion of these cinematic intertexts, see Maureen Turim, "Popular Culture and the Comedy of Manners: *Clueless* and Fashion Cues," in *Jane Austen and Co.*, pp. 33–51, and Lesley Stern, "*Emma* in Los Angeles: Remaking the Book and the City," in *Film Adaptation*, pp. 221–38. Other relevant discussions of *Clueless* include: Deidre Lynch, "Clueless: About History," in *Jane Austen and Co.*, pp. 71–92, which sees continuities between the novel and the film in their respective engagements with historical situatedness; and Suzanne Ferriss, "Emma Becomes Clueless," in *Jane Austen in Hollywood*, ed. Linda Troost and Sayre Greenfield (Lexington, KY: University of Kentucky Press, 2001), pp. 122–9, which argues for the surprising or relative conservatism of Heckerling's remake.

19 For a more a general discussion of movie magic as a "polymorphous web" of fantasy and interpellation, see Timothy Murray, *Like a Film: Ideological Fantasy on Screen, Camera, Canvas* (New York: Routledge, 1993).

20 *Persuasion*, ed. William Galperin (New York: Longman), pp. 25, 48, 173.

21 *Emma*, ed. James Kinsley (Oxford: Oxford University Press, 2003), p. 320.

22 *Meeting at the Crossroads: Women's Psychology and Girl's Development* (Cambridge: Harvard University Press, 1992).

2.6 BEYOND FILM AND LITERARY TEXTS

Chapter 32

Simone Murray

MATERIALIZING ADAPTATION THEORY
The adaptation industry

WHILE SIMONE MURRAY'S CONTRIBUTION provides a useful historical overview of the major schools of adaptation studies since the 1950s, its main argument is for an alternative model that materializes adaptation theory within the larger framework of the "adaptation industry." While acknowledging key contributions to the field, Murray criticizes the tendency towards uncritical adherence to textual analysis as the field's primary methodology at the expense of production contexts. Murray calls for a rethinking of the adaptation as a "material phenomenon" by moving beyond aesthetic evaluation to begin to understand adaptation within its social and cultural contexts. Murray's own model for studying the "adaptation industry" innovatively seeks to create alternative methodologies by looking to contemporary research in the fields of "political economy of media," cultural theory, and history of the book.

■ ■ ■

MATERIALIZING ADAPTATION THEORY: THE ADAPTATION INDUSTRY
SIMONE MURRAY

Literature/Film Quarterly vol. 36 no. 1 (2008), pp. 4–20

> [T]he great innovators of the twentieth century, in film and novel both, have had so little to do with each other, have gone their ways alone, always keeping a firm but respectful distance.
>
> (Bluestone 2003: 63)

> I would suggest that what we need instead is a broader definition of adaptation and a sociology that takes into account the commercial apparatus, the audience, and the academic culture industry.
>
> (Naremore 2000b: 10)

Even a casual observer of the field of adaptation studies would perceive that the discipline is clearly suffering from intellectual dolours. Long regarded as the bastard offspring of literary studies and film theory, adaptation studies has struggled to achieve academic respectability since its inception in the 1950s. The field's insistence on studying screen culture was perceived as threatening by English departments predicated on the superiority of literary studies. Simultaneously, adaptation studies' residual attachment to print culture alienated it from the burgeoning discipline of film theory, whose adherents proposed jettisoning an indelibly hostile literary studies paradigm in favor of valorizing film as an art form in its own right. But more worryingly, adaptation studies is currently experiencing a welter of criticism not only from outside its own ranks, but also from within. Adaptation scholar James Naremore (2000b: 1, 11) laments the "jejune" and "moribund" nature of contemporary adaptation studies. According to Robert B. Ray (2000: 39, 46), the bulk of adaptations criticism constitutes a "dead end," "useless" in its stale models and trite suppositions. Similarly, Robert Stam—prolific scholar behind a recent three-volume series on adaptation for publisher Blackwell—asserts that adaptation studies as it currently stands is "inchoate," hamstrung by the "inadequate trope" of fidelity criticism, whereby screen adaptations are judged accordingly to their relative "faithfulness" to print originals (Stam 2000: 76, 62). For Thomas Leitch (2003: 149, 168), "adaptation theory has remained tangential to the thrust of film study," resulting in a discipline that "has been marginalized because it wishes to be."[1] Kamilla Elliott, another recent addition to this chorus of disciplinary lament, regrets "the pervasive sense that adaptation scholars lag behind the critical times" (Elliott 2003: 4).[2] Viewed in an optimistic light, such comments together suggest that adaptation studies as a field is currently bubbling with intellectual ferment, and is ripe for a sea-change in theoretical and methodological paradigms. Surveyed more pessimistically, remarks such as these suggest a field flailing to find some cohesion and to revivify its academic prospects. Regardless of which perspective is adopted, there is a substantial irony evident: as adaptation increasingly comes to comprise the structural logic of contemporary media and cultural industries, leading adaptation scholars publicly question the adequacy of the field's established paradigms to comprehend what is taking place. Adaptation studies appears deeply internally conflicted: the right discipline, at the right time, lumbered with an obsolete methodology.

Insider critics of adaptation studies base their disparaging verdicts on the discipline's production of a seemingly endless stream of comparative case-studies of print and screen versions of individual texts (Ray 2000: 39). This methodology of comparative textual analysis underpinned adaptation studies' founding critical text—George Bluestone's *Novels into Film*—and has since ossified into an almost unquestioned methodological orthodoxy within the field. Adaptation critics seek similarities and contrasts in book-film pairings in order to understand the specific characteristics of the respective book and film mediums, in what Naremore (2000b: 9) has termed an obsessive "literary formalism." Frustratingly, such studies routinely produce conclusions that provide in fact no conclusion at all: comparative case-studies overwhelmingly give rise to the frankly unilluminating finding that there are similarities between the two mediums, but also differences, before moving on to the next book-film pairing to repeat the exercise.[3] In its intellectual tail-chasing and repetitive compulsion, adaptation studies reveals all the hallmarks of a discipline in which adherence to an established methodology has become an endpoint in itself, with analytical insight and methodological innovation relegated to secondary considerations.

Particularly concerning is the fact that such advocates of methodological innovation as do exist within the field frequently hark back to models already explored. Stam, under the subheading "Proposals for Adaptation Studies," has recently called for "a thoroughgoing comparative *stylistics* of the two media" [i.e. literature and film; emphasis in original]. This statement insistently recalls Bluestone's lengthy exploration of literature and film's comparative aesthetic and formal characteristics in the first chapter of his foundational 1957 work (Stam 2005b: 41). Although Stam elsewhere argues compellingly for the cross-pollination of adaptation studies with developments in post-structuralist and post-colonial literary theory, his emphasis on investigating formal characteristics of literature and film appears merely to close the circle on nearly 50 years of adaptation studies research. That this is a widely shared critical tic is evident from surveying the titles of key books in the field over a five-decade period: the words "literature" and "film" (or their cognates "fiction," "novel," "cinema," and "movies") are rearranged in endless conjoined variations.[4]

Close attention to the published outputs of adaptation studies further evidences the becalmed nature of the discipline in highlighting the piecemeal nature of current research. Scanning one's eye down the contents pages of edited collections or journals in the field reveals a veritable forest of italics, as the titles of individual books and their companion screen versions dominate entries. The discipline suffers from a paucity of monograph-length investigations of adaptation theory, instead confining its intellectual horizons overwhelmingly to the individual case-study or to the compilation of many such case-studies.[5] A slight variation on this model is to group together a number of adaptations of a single author (or single director's) work. But this is almost never framed as an investigation of the role of the celebrity "Author" as a construct facilitating the making and marketing of adaptations, so much as an organizing device for harnessing together otherwise disparate case-studies. Most striking in such surveys of extant research is the exclusive scholarly interest in *what* adaptations have been made, and almost never *how* these adaptations came to be available for painstaking scholarly comparison. Dematerialized, immune to commercialism, floating free of any cultural institutions, intellectual property regimes, or industry agents that might have facilitated its creation or indelibly marked its form, the adaptation exists in perfect quarantine from the troubling worlds of commerce, Hollywood, and global corporate media—a formalist textual fetish oblivious to the disciplinary incursions of political economy, book history, or the creative industries.[6]

Previous waves of innovation in adaptation studies

In taking adaptation studies to task for its uncritical adherence to textual analysis as a governing methodology, I am not suggesting that adaptation studies has been devoid of innovation, only that such prior waves of innovation as have occurred have experimented within severely confined limits. To provide background and context to this article's argument for an overdue materializing of adaptation theory, it is useful briefly to survey the major schools of adaptation studies that have developed since the 1950s and to note—with a nod to adaptations studies own *modus operandi*—both their differences and their marked similarities. Characterizing virtually all academic studies of book-to-screen adaptation is an attack on the model of fidelity criticism as an inadequate schema for appreciating the richness of and motivations driving adaptations (Marcus 1971: xv; McDougal 1985: 6; Giddings, Selby, and Wensley 1990: xix, 9–10; Cartmell and Whelehan, 1999: 3, 2007: 2; Ray 2000: 45; Leitch 2003: 161–62, 2007: 16–17, 21; Hutcheon, 2006: xiii, 6–7, 2007). Such ritual rejections of fidelity criticism are frequently accompanied by revelation of fidelity critique's moralistic and sexually loaded vocabulary, with its accusations of "unfaithfulness," "betrayal," "straying," "debasement," and the like (Beja 1997: 81; Naremore 2000b: 8; Stam 2000: 54, 2005b: 3; Hutcheon 2004: 109, 2006: 7, 85, 2007). Unquestionably, rejecting the idea of film adaptation as a necessarily inferior imitation of literary fiction's artistic achievement was an essential critical maneuver if adaptation studies was to gain entry to the academy. But most striking in reading back over 50 years of academic criticism about adaptation is not the dead hand of fidelity criticism, but—quite the opposite—how few academic critics make any claim for fidelity criticism at all. Bluestone's own seminal study posited at its outset that "the film-maker merely treats the novel as raw material and ultimately creates his [sic] own unique structure," with the novel firmly put in its place as "less a norm than a point of departure" (Bluestone 2003: vii, viii).[7]

A variation on the outright rejection of fidelity as directorial goal or critical norm involves taxonomically classifying adaptations into graded "levels" or "modes" of fidelity, according to "whether the film is a literal, critical, or relatively free adaptation of the literary source" (Klein and Parker 1981: 9; also Wagner 1975: 219–31; Larsson 1982: 74; Andrew 2000: 29–34; Cahir 2006: 16–17). Certainly this goes some way toward equalizing the respective status of author and director, according film adaptors relatively greater creative and artistic agency. But fidelity is an absolute value; once a source text has been "strayed" from, the critical measuring-stick of "fidelity" loses its evaluative rigor. Given this, comparative gradings of fidelity are closer to Bluestone's outright rejection of the concept than may be apparent at first glance. In reading over several decades of adaptation criticism, the suspicion grows that, while fidelity models may remain prevalent in film and television reviewing, in broader journalistic discourse, and in everyday evaluations by the film-going public, in academic circles the ritual slaying of fidelity criticism at the outset of a work has ossified into a habitual gesture, devoid of any real intellectual challenge.[8] After all, if no one in academe is actually advocating the antiquated notion of fidelity, what is there to overturn? It appears more likely that the standardized routing of fidelity criticism has come to function as a smokescreen, lending the guise of methodological and theoretical innovation to studies that routinely reproduce the set model of comparative textual analysis. In its hermetism, it is as though parallel intellectual streams of film studies, media studies, the history of the book, and cultural theory had not all vigorously explored the interpretative significance of production, distribution, reception, and consumption contexts.

The second significant wave of adaptation studies appeared from the late 1970s with the importation of principles of narratology from the traditions of Russian formalist literary theory, structuralism, and Continental semiotics (Cohen 1979; Beja 1979; Ruppert 1980; Klein and Parker 1981; Andrew 2000). Theorists such as Roland Barthes. Gérard Genette, and Christian Metz were heavily cited in this stream of adaptation work that lingered, in some cases, well into the 1990s (Giddings, Selby, and Wensley 1990; McFarlane 1996).[9] The surprise is the tenacity of narratology's hold over adaptation studies, given that by the late 1980s post-structuralist distrust of the rule-seeking, pseudo-scientific predilections of structuralism had well and truly achieved dominance in the Anglophone academy. The structuralist-inspired quest to isolate the signifying "codes" underpinning both literature and film had the worthwhile aim of dismantling received academic hierarchies of mediums in which literature occupied the apex, and the interloper of screen studies was relegated to the lowest critical echelons (Cohen 1979: 3). It moreover recast adaptation as a two-way dynamic, where novelistic narrative techniques not only influenced film, but certain filmic devices were avidly imitated by Modernist writers well-versed in an increasingly visual culture (Cohen 1979: 2–10; Beja 1979: 51–76; Andrew 2000: 36). But the structuralist school of adaptation confines this inter-relationship of the two mediums strictly to the level of textual effects. Structuralism's characteristic isolation of texts from circuits of production and consumption, or from sociologies of media cultures generally, left its methodological impress upon adaptation studies. The effect was that, for all the narratological school's self-declared and partially justifiable revolutionary rhetoric, the movement managed to entrench further the practice of textual analysis as adaptation studies' default methodological setting and unquestioned academic norm.[10]

In what this article posits as the third major wave of innovation in adaptation studies, importing of concepts from post-structuralism, post-colonialism, feminism, and cultural studies broke down one part of the self-isolating critical wall built up around the text, and opened adaptation studies up to concepts of audience agency. This 1980s and 1990s development, handily dubbed "The Impact of the Posts" by one of its key proponents, Robert Stam, placed audience pleasure in intertextual citation front and center of its critical concerns (Stam 2005b: 8). Accordingly, fidelity criticism was deemed not only a woefully blunt instrument with which to examine adaptations, but willful *infidelity* was in fact the very *point:* adaptations interrogated the political and ideological underpinnings of their source texts, translating works across cultural, gender, racial, and sexual boundaries to secure cultural space for marginalized discourses. This post-structuralist reconceptualization of adaptation as critique—which Stam terms "intertextual dialogism" and Hutcheon dubs *"transculturation"*—borrows from Bakhtin and Kristeva to posit culture as a vast web of references and tropes ripe for appropriating, disassembling, and rearranging [italics in original] (Stam 2000: 64; Hutcheon 2006: xvi, 2004: 108–11, 2007; Leitch 2003: 165–67, 2007: 18; Aragay 2005). More specifically cultural studies-inflected concepts that also reinvigorated the study of adaptation included the permeability of high/pop cultural boundaries, overdue acknowledgement of extra-literary sources for adaptations such as pulp fiction, comic books/graphic novels, and computer games, and recognition of resistant or oppositional audience decodings of texts in ways possibly unforeseen by textual producers (Cartmell and Whelehan 1997, 2007; Hutcheon 2006; Leitch 2007). The recognition that audiences appreciate adaptations precisely because of the mass of existing pop-cultural knowledge they bring to them was decisive in weaning adaptation studies from its long preoccupation with the nineteenth-century Anglo-American literary canon, and for introducing an ethnographic dimension into the analysis of adaptation.

Yet, for all its productive theoretical innovation, this now-dominant third wave of adaptation studies has come at a price. Post-structuralism's and cultural studies' characteristic disinterest in conditions of cultural production has created a lopsidedness within adaptation studies between, on one hand, intense interest in audience consumption practices but, on the other, little countervailing attention to the production contexts, financial structures, and legal regimes facilitating the adaptations boom. The blame for this imbalance cannot, however, be entirely sheeted home to post-structuralism, cultural studies, and their affiliate "posts."

Political economy, the school of media studies dominant in UK, Canadian, and Australian (if never US) academe during the 1960s and 1970s was by the 1980s, engaged in a bitter academic turf-war with cultural studies over the relative merits of material and semiotic frameworks for analyzing media (Curran 1990). As a result, political economy was too impatient with the new wave's rejection of economically determinist Marxist cultural models to be inclined to investigate what reception theory had to offer for political economy's understanding of adaptation. Furthermore, political economy's traditional home in the social sciences (especially in politics and sociology departments) made industrial-scale cultural producers such as newspaper chains and television networks favored media for examination, in preference to the traditionally humanities-affiliated (and specifically literary studies-affiliated) format of the book. The content recycling function at the heart of adaptation was noted in passing by individual political economists of the 1970s in analyses of "synergy" within the operations of globalized media conglomerates (Murdock and Golding 1977). But as the waves of consolidation that brought book publishing into the fold of corporate media were at that time mostly still to be felt, novels and short stories were paid only glancing attention by political economy as the most common source of adapted content. More vigorous attention has been paid to such content's franchising in film, newspaper serialization, theme-park, and spin-off merchandising forms (Wasko 1994, 2001, 2003; Elsaesser 1998; Balides 2000). Neither macro-oriented political economy nor textual- and audience-focused cultural studies were therefore predisposed to examine the *how* and *why* of adaptation from the perspective of the authors, agents, publishers, editors, book prize committees, screenwriters, directors, and producers who actually made adaptations happen.

A final point to make in tracing how the study of the contemporary book-to-screen adaptation industry slipped through the intellectual net of adaptation studies, cultural studies and political economy relates to the kind of texts chosen for analysis by these respective disciplines. As outlined, adaptation studies has traditionally focused greatest attention on the nineteenth-century and Modernist Anglophone literary canon (Lupack 1999; Cartmell *et al.*: 2000). Cultural studies, for its part, originated in another disciplinary rebellion—this time against English literary studies' adamantine hostility to investigating popular culture as a legitimate topic for academic inquiry. As a consequence, cultural studies has always preferred to examine demonstrably "popular" genres such as romance novels, pulps, crime fiction, westerns, or comic books whose very non-literariness badges them as suitable new intellectual ground for cultural studies' relativist analytical project. The combined effect of these disciplines' textual orientation is that the processes by which contemporary *literary* fiction is created, published, marketed, evaluated for literary prizes and adapted for screen are still to receive sustained and detailed academic attention. That these powerful institutions comprising the contemporary literary adaptation ecosystem—with all the dynamism, symbiosis, and competition characteristic of ecosystems—have been overlooked by cognate disciplines has bequeathed to scholars a severely flawed understanding of how the contemporary adaptation industry actually functions. Attention to texts and audiences cannot of itself explain how these adaptations come to be available for popular and critical consumption, nor the production circuits through which they move on their way to audiences, nor the mechanisms of cultural elevation in which the adaptation industry is fundamentally complicit.

The costs of textual analysis as methodological orthodoxy

Having sketched the background of extant adaptation studies and noted its methodological lacunae, I want to proceed to examine in further detail how lack of attention to production contexts has compromised current understandings of adaptation. From there, I propose an alternative model that *is* capable of encapsulating the complexity of the adaptation industry and—as the current article's title states—of contributing to a long-overdue *materializing* of adaptation theory.

Adaptation critics' comparative ignorance of book industry dynamics has perpetuated a distorted understanding of adaptation, distilled here to three oft-encountered "myths" or "truisms" of adaptation studies.[11] The first of these—and by far the most frequently encountered—is the claim that books are the product of individualized, isolated authorial creation, whereas film and television function as collaborative, industrialized processes (Beja 1979: 60–62; McDougal 1985: 5; Giddings, Selby, and Wensley 1990: 2; Reynolds 1993: 8; Ray 2000: 42; Stam 2000: 56, 2005b: 17; Cahir 2006: 72). As so often when seeking the origins of adaptation studies' methodological rubric, the roots of this fallacy can be traced directly back to Bluestone (Leitch 2003: 150):

> The reputable novel, generally speaking, has been supported by a small, literate audience, has been produced by an individual writer, and has remained relatively free of rigid censorship. The film, on the other hand, has been supported by a mass audience, produced co-operatively under industrial conditions, and restricted by a self-imposed Production Code. These developments have reinforced rather than vitiated the autonomy of each medium.[12]
>
> (Bluestone 2003: vi)

In seeking to debunk this myth of isolated authorial creation, I am not denying that a clear difference in organizational and financial scale exists between the writing of, for example, a battle scene in a novel and the filmic realization of its equivalent. The problem arises from the fact that adaptation critics when they use the terms "book" or "novel" are in truth almost always speaking of "text"—that is, they are invoking an abstract *idea* of an individual author's creative work rather than the material *object* of the specific book in which that work is transmitted.[13] As the discipline known as book history has amply demonstrated since first emerging in 1950s France (curiously contemporaneous with the appearance of adaptation studies in the Anglophone academy), books have for centuries depended upon complex circuits of printers, binders, hawkers, publishers, booksellers, librarians, collectors, and readers for the dissemination of ideas in literate societies (Darnton 1990; Adams and Barker 1993). Thus the book is demonstrably as much the product of institutions, agents, and material forces as is the Hollywood blockbuster. Yet adaptation theorists regularly emphasize the power of Hollywood's political economy as though books were quasi-virginal texts untouched by commercial concerns prior to their screen adaptation (Beja 1979; Bluestone 2003; Leitch 2003). This leads to curious and easily disproved assertions that authors "have (for better or worse) been largely able to write whatever pleased them, without regard for audience or expense" (Ray 2000: 42), as "questions of material infrastructure enter only at the point of distribution" (Stam 2000: 56).

Book history has demonstrated that the commercial substructures of book culture have existed since at least the Gutenberg revolution. But these industrial characteristics have become massively more pronounced since book publishers were subsumed by global media conglomerates from the early 1980s onwards (Miller 1997; Schiffrin 2000; Epstein 2002; Murray 2006). Critics of the contemporary book publishing industry frequently observe that the potential marketability of authors, and the probability of their work being optioned for adaptation in other media, are key considerations in the signing of, especially, first-time authors (Engelhardt 1997; McPhee 2001). Moreover, these considerations all come into play *prior* to contracting; thereafter the book will also be extensively costed, edited, designed, proof-read, marketed, publicized, and distributed to retail and online outlets, (hopefully) discussed in the literary public sphere, and readers' perceptions of the work will have been extensively mediated through networks of reviews, book prizes, writers festivals, book signings, face-to-face book clubs, or their electronic and online equivalents (Hartley 2001; Long 2003; Sedo 2003; Mackenzie 2005; Hutcheon 2007). A complex literary economy therefore governs the production and dissemination of books from their earliest phases. Moreover, adaptation for the screen is not merely an add-on or after-thought to this complex economy, but is factored in and avidly pursued from the earliest phases of book production. This gives the lie to the oft-repeated mantra of authorial "autonomy" prevalent in adaptation studies and such critics' familiar juxtaposition of the Romanticized, "starving-in-a-garret" individual writer on one hand, with Hollywood's "mode of industrial production" on the other (Bluestone 2003: 34).

Further, understanding of the book industry economy fundamentally challenges adaptation theory's always implicit—and often even explicit—classification of books as "niche" whereas film is denominated as a "mass" medium (Beja 1979: 60–61; Giddings, Selby, and Wensley 1990: 2; Leitch 2003: 155; Hutcheon 2006: 5). When analyzing the weight of financial interests and industry strategizing brought to bear on the release of new books by bestselling writers such as Stephen King or Dan Brown—or even high-profile literary authors such as Salman Rushdie, Ian McEwan, or Annie Proulx—it is impossible to deny that the book industry is as thoroughly complicit in marketing and publicity processes as are its screen-media equivalents (Gelder 2004; Brown 2006; Phillips 2007; Squires 2007). The fact that book publishers and film studios increasingly find themselves affiliate divisions within overarching media conglomerates makes the incorporation of the book into the production, marketing, and distribution schedules of electronic and digital media all the more feasible and attractive (Izod 1992; Murray 2006, 2007b).

A second myth of adaptation studies deriving from critics' current dematerialized conception of the process is the belief that adaptation's trajectory is necessarily from the "old" media of the book to the "new(er)" media of film, television, and digital media. This assumed linearity is manifested explicitly in the titles of adaptation studies such as Brian McFarlane's *Novel to Film* and Linda Costanzo Cahir's *Literature into Film*.[14] Clearly, this fallacy stems from a historicist conception of media development in which mediums are seen to supersede earlier communication technologies in a process of serial eclipse. Instead, the reality of twentieth-century media environments has been that newer media do cannibalize the content of older media, but mediums continue to exist contemporaneously, rearranging themselves into new patterns of usage and mutual dependence. This complementarity of communications formats was noted in media studies as early as the work of Marshall McLuhan, and has since been regularly elaborated upon by medium theorists, notably Jay David Bolter and Richard Grusin in their exploration of cross-platform "remediation" (McLuhan 2001; Bolter and Grusin 1999; Holmes 2005). Given these intellectual trends in the broader field of communications, adaptation studies' long-held adherence to a one-way model of adaptation appears intellectually parochial.

Granted, even Bluestone (2003: 4) devoted a paragraph to the observation that "[j]ust as one line of influence runs from New York publishing house to Hollywood studio, another line may be observed running the other way." But his discussion notes only the positive impact of film versions on sales of the original novel; he does not extend his observation to examine how film content can form the basis of new print-form products.[15] Writing over 20 years after Bluestone, critic Morris Beja similarly dedicated two pages of a monograph-length work to discussing the coexistence of novelizations and original novels, but he begins this potentially innovative line of inquiry with the tellingly digressive throw-away "incidentally" (Beja 1979: 87). As far as the first two waves of adaptations studies were concerned, the book industry served as handmaiden supplying film-ready content to the screen industries; it was a relationship between mediums reciprocated only intermittently.

By the time the third wave of adaptation studies emerged in the 1980s, the increasing evidence of adaptation's print-based "afterlife" in the form of "tie-in" editions, novelizations, published screenplays, "making-off" books, and companion titles had become incontestable. Equipped with greater sensitivity to popular culture as a result of cultural studies and post-structuralist theoretical models, adaptation scholars began to note the proliferation of such book-form texts, and even their circulation simultaneous with screen versions. Again, this belated recognition of adaptation's two-way (or multi-way) traffic is flagged in the title of an influential anthology: Cartmell and Whelehan's *Adaptations: From Text to Screen, Screen to Text*. But such critics' use of these "companion texts" is—true to the discipline's generally unacknowledged textual analysis bias—to treat them as convenient additional sites for semiotic analysis, not to examine how they came to be produced or their role in cross-promoting content franchises to a variety of audience demographics (Whelehan 1999: 5–6; cf. Izod 1992: 101–02). What is currently lacking in adaptation studies is a thorough understanding of whose financial interests these "spin-off" properties serve, the intellectual property and licensing arrangements by which they are governed, and how audiences experience this multi-platform encounter with broadly similar content   specifically whether audiences invest content consumed on different platforms with varying degrees of cultural prestige or authority.

The third and final corollary of adaptation studies' prevailing indifference to the economy of book adaptation is perhaps not as strongly marked as the first two, given it concerns the more abstruse concept of the rise and fall of literary reputations. Literary prestige has remained a mostly marginalized topic in adaptation studies, being either already abundantly established in the case of "classic" authors whose canonical works are adapted for the screen or, in the case of popular culture texts such as comic books, amounting to an irrelevant concern according the relativist rubric of cultural studies (Stam 2005a: 45). Rarely examined is the phenomenon of *contemporary* writers who self-identify as "literary" authors whose work is being adapted for the screen, and how circulation of these broadly contemporaneous screen texts triggers inflation or devaluation of their literary stocks.[16] The stock-exchange metaphor invoked here is deliberate; as James F. English has observed in his analysis of cultural prizes, *The Economy of Prestige*, the fascination of questions of literary value derives from their position at the juncture of two philosophically hostile conceptual systems: the aesthetic and the commercial. The concept of literary esteem is never entirely reducible to either system operating alone, but is instead powered by its situation at the clashing tectonic plates of *both* systems. How adaptations factor into this innately volatile system for accrediting or withholding of literary reputation is a compelling topic mostly unexplored in relation to contemporary authors (as opposed to long-canonical, and more recently mass-market, authors such as Jane Austen).[17] The topic's interest stems also from its intermeshing with the broader literary and cultural economy of agents, editors, publishers, prize judging committees, book retailers, and the literary press already mentioned. Focusing critical attention on literary reputations in the process of being "brokered" within the adaptation economy provides a fascinating insight into the workings of the adaptation industry, and the shifting alliances and conflicts that inevitably arise between its nodal agents.

Proposing a new methodology for adaptation studies

From the foregoing, it will be readily apparent that this article's key aim is to rethink adaptation, not as an exercise in comparative textual analysis of individual books and their screen versions, but as a *material* phenomenon produced by a system of institutional interests and actors. In short, I am contending that adaptation studies urgently needs to divert its intellectual resources from a questionable project of aesthetic evaluation, and instead begin to understand adaptation sociologically.[18] To do so, it is necessary to move out from under the aegis of long-dominant formalist and textual analysis traditions to investigate what cognate fields of cultural research might have to offer adaptation studies in terms of alternative methodologies. These then need to be critically assessed for their own analytical blind-spots, as well as for how they might profitably be combined into a hybrid methodology supple enough to comprehend the workings of the contemporary adaptation industry.

Political economy of media

The political economy strand of media analysis originates in the critiques of the early-twentieth-century Frankfurt School, reviving with an interest in issues of ownership and control of media in the 1960s and 1970s, and informing a more recent wave of research around the commercialization of digital media. These most recent additions to the discipline have demonstrated the vital relevance of materially engaged critique for elucidating developments in the contemporary cultural sphere (Mosco 1996; Schiller 1999; Wasko 2001, 2003; Doyle 2002). Political economy's realist, materialist, and interdisciplinary methodology critically illuminates content's key role in contemporary media industries. Technological convergence around digital platforms has coincided with increasing convergence of ownership among globalized media corporations to create a commercial environment favoring the multipurposing or "streaming" of media content to orchestrate cross-platform franchises (Elsaesser 1998; Balides 2000; Murray 2003, 2005; Jenkins 2006). The key characteristic and commercial utility of contemporary media content appears to lie in its potential dissociation from any one media platform and its simultaneous replication across a range of mediums via digitization. Clearly this is adaptation operating under a different name. However, for reasons that are more institutional than theoretical, political economy of media has, as outlined earlier, tended to relegate the book to the periphery of its analytical concern because of an inherited preference for broadcast and networked media.

Cultural theory

Compelling as is political economy's materialist conceptualization of contemporary media industries, on its own it provides an inadequate schema for understanding the adaptation industry's role in brokering cultural value. In contemporary globalized media conglomerates, book publishing is of relatively minor commercial significance in terms of its contribution to overall corporate revenues. Yet publishing divisions continue to enjoy a high profile within such conglomerates as a source of prestige and as ballast for corporate claims to cultural distinction. How is it that book content is increasingly dematerialized from the book format through digital technology and adaptation, while at the same time screen producers attempt to leverage books' associations of cultural prestige and literary distinction across media platforms? Examples of such cinematic bibliophily might include the fetishizing of libraries, illuminated books, parchment maps, quills, and ink in Time Warner's film adaptations of book favorites *Harry Potter* and *The Lord of the Rings* (Murray 2003; Jenkins 2006: 169–205). On one hand, media industries would appear to be pursuing a culturally democratizing agenda of making acclaimed literary works available to demographically broader screen audiences. But, at the same time, such industrial concerns allay audience suspicions of commercial exploitation by constantly reiterating film-makers' respect for a content property's prize-winning literary pedigree. Thus cultural hierarchies are, paradoxically, kept alive by the same industry that pushes audiences to consume near-identical content across multiple media platforms.

Existing cultural theory models are inadequate to comprehend this nexus of commercial and cultural values at play in the modern adaptation industry. Most likely, this is attributable to the fact that critical theory and cultural studies have tended to develop theories of cultural value in relative isolation from the material industry contexts that preoccupy political economy. Such disparate critical foci have given rise to a disjunction between, on one hand, cultural studies' orthodoxies of textual relativism and, on the other, the media industries' avid support of cultural hierarchy as evidenced in their marketing and publicity strategies emphasizing consumer discrimination and cultural self-improvement (Collins 2002). Adaptations studies thus requires a methodological and theoretical apparatus for understanding how audiences both desire cultural relativism while also looking to the media industries for markers of cultural prestige (book prizes, film and television awards) to guide consumption and identity-formation.

History of the book

The third cognate methodology proposed here, history of the book (also termed "book history"), traces its own complex disciplinary history from French historical studies, sociology, literary studies, bibliography, and the history of ideas to coalesce as an academic discipline from the late-1970s. Like political economy, book history insists upon the material underpinnings of conceptions of culture, focusing specifically on the mechanics of print production, dissemination, and reception. The field's most productive innovation from the perspective of revitalizing adaptation studies is its devising of circuit-based models for conceptualizing the flow of print culture in host societies (Darnton 1990; Adams and Barker 1993). Specifically, these models of interlinked authors, printers, publishers, retailers, and the like maintain attention to the industrial and commercial substructures of the book trade, but they integrate these concerns with attention also to less tangible intellectual, social, and cultural currents, demonstrating the interdependence of the two spheres. Less compelling for the current project's purpose is that book history—as its self-designation suggests—overwhelmingly confines its attention to pre-twentieth-century print cultures, and has to date generally failed to embrace the contemporary book industries as part of its natural purview (Murray 2007a).

Thus the three methodologies outlined here could all already—hypothetically speaking—have converged on the issue of the contemporary adaptation industry, but have to date mostly failed to do so for reasons of their own. This anomalous state of affairs cries out to be rectified, especially at a time when leading scholars of adaptation are lamenting the methodological stagnation of the field. By combining these three fields' methodological insights, adaptation studies stands to gain a new, intellectually invigorating methodology: alert to the commercial and industrial structures of global media; wise to these systems' simultaneous invocation and disavowal of hierarchies of cultural value; and capable of holding these two domains—the material and the cultural—in dynamic relationship.

Modeling the adaptation industry

The present article's conceptual framework for a new model of what has been termed "the adaptation industry" derives from the aforementioned circuit models prominent in book history that chart the circulation and flow of print communications among various book industry stakeholders.[19] Substantially modifying such historically focused models to reflect the dynamics of contemporary English-language book cultures, the new model maps relationships among six key stakeholder groups: author societies and the construct of the celebrity author; literary agents; editors and publishers; literary prize judging committees; screenwriters; and film/television producers. Granted, this is a resiliently "bookish" model of adaptation given this article's acknowledgment elsewhere that adaptation traffics content across all media formats: film, television, computer gaming, comics, theatre, recorded music, animation, toys, and myriad other licensed commodities. But this focus upon adaptation studies' traditional book and screen mediums is defensible given the near-absence of a production-oriented stream of adaptation research to date. It is hoped that the project proposed here clears sufficient methodological ground for others to examine in detail the specific economies of adaptation between other mediums—or even, more ambitiously, to attempt to chart the workings of the entire cross-media adaptation industry in macro perspective.

Each of the nodal points in the book screen adaptation economy is connected by the two-way flow of capital (both commercial and cultural): the author sacrifices a commission payment in exchange for the increased access to publishers provided by a literary agent. Literary agents trade upon their gate-keeping function to ensure clients' submissions gain priority attention by commissioning editors. Publishing houses enhance the status of specific literary prizes in their cover-copy in exchange for the promotional fillip and exposure of a literary prize win or shortlisting. Literary prizes and their associated sales deliver proven audiences for film and television adaptations of prize-winning books, in exchange for wider promotion of the prize itself through screen-media formats. This in turn commonly stokes audience demand for (re)consumption of content in book form—the only part of the current model already touched upon by adaptation critics.

In addition to these exchanges among *adjacent* stakeholders in the adaptations circuit, there are complex capital exchanges between *non-adjacent* interests: for example, literary agents derive commission on rights sales to film and television production companies in exchange for the brand identity of an established author or book property. Publishers engineer bookshop display for film adaptation posters and ancillary marketing paraphernalia, in exchange for production stills to incorporate into the cover designs of film or television "tie-in" editions (Bluestone 2003: 4; Giddings *et al.* 1990: 22; Reynolds 1993: 10; Naremore 2000b: 13.). Similarly, successful authors can aid in establishing the house identity of their publishers, and thereby attract other desirable "name" authors to the press. Equally, authors benefit symbiotically from the imprimatur of appearing under the colophon of an esteemed publishing house. A detailed mapping of the adaptation industry would need to focus in turn upon each of these nodal agents, but with a constant emphasis upon the interdependence and tensions inherent in these deeply intertwined sectoral relationships.

One corollary of adapting circuit models from book history is an awareness of the historical specificity of book industry structures. Any mapping of the *contemporary* adaptation industry thus needs to take account of aspects of the book trade—such as the rise of the literary agent and the growth of online retailing—which have become ubiquitous only in recent decades. A suggested timeframe for such research might therefore be *circa* 1980 to the present. This timeframe is broad enough to incorporate significant structural changes to the book industry occurring as a result of corporatization and conglomeration from the early 1980s: the revolutionary impact of digital technologies on all phases of book production, distribution, and retailing; the eclipse of the editor by the agent as the author's literary mentor and champion; the elevation of book prizes in promotional campaigns by English-language publishers (notably the [Man] Booker Prize)[20]; and the marked growth of "subsidiary" rights in non-book media as a feature of standard author-publisher contracts during the period.

Focusing industry-centered adaptation research on such a recent period moreover acts as a corrective to adaptation studies' long privileging of "classic" Renaissance, eighteenth-century, nineteenth-century, and Modernist texts in its analyses (Giddings *et* al.; Lupack 1999; Cartmell *et al*. 2000; Mayer 2002; Elliott 2003; Stam 2005b).The much longer cultural histories of such texts cause them to enter the contemporary adaptation economy already freighted with critical approbation and/or notoriety. The exclusion of already-established "classics" from the proposed model ensures that the pre-existing cultural baggage of "classic" texts does not distort the findings or introduce variables that cannot be accounted for by the dynamics of the contemporary adaptation industry itself. This being said, there is no reason that the proposed materialist methodology should not also be applicable to others' studies of "classic" text adaptations occurring in earlier eras of the book, radio, film, and television industries.

A mapping of the contemporary adaptations industry must also acknowledge linguistic and geographic specificities. Overwhelmingly, adaptation studies has, to date, focused on English-language texts, or upon film adaptations in languages other than English of Anglophone "classics."[21] This is one element of extant adaptation studies that I would argue in favor of perpetuating, not for the sake of tradition itself, but because it is important to recognize the variability of the adaptations process across countries and regional language groupings (for example, the widespread audience acceptance of dubbing in Continental European screen media, the specific conventions of the *telenovela* in Hispanic media cultures, and the importance of print-format manga to the Japanese anime industry). Hence, the project advocated here would focus upon content created distributed, and consumed within the Anglophone world. The US and UK still account for the overwhelming majority of the world's English-language cultural production. Yet there are clearly points of access into these global distribution systems for content from historically "periphery" English-language cultures such as Australia, Canada, New Zealand, South Africa, Ireland, and India. That being said, there is no question that if such second-tier media-producing countries wish to gain exposure for their content to global English-language audiences, it will be in collaboration with or through acquiescence to US and UK cultural gatekeepers. Undertaking detailed mapping of the contemporary adaptations industry thus not only informs debates around cultural value but also enhances formation and implementation of cultural policy at national and supranational levels to facilitate cultural "contra-flow."

Where might adequate research resources be located to empirically bear out such an industry focused model? Perhaps textual analysis has for so long remained the default methodological setting for adaptation studies because the requisite book and screen case-studies are so readily to hand in the age of the VCR and DVD library.[22] An important practical question therefore is whether alternative resources are available to implement the proposed methodological mode and to support the theoretical suppositions raised here. As outlined above, one of adaptations studies' chief aims should be to bring academic discourses into dialogue with adaptation industry practices, an exchange that has to date barely taken place. One result of these domains' current lack of cross-pollination is that academic research analyzing contemporary industry dynamics is scanty, necessitating a multi-perspectival approach to collating research materials. Key resources would include:

- extant scholarly research in adaptation studies, media studies, film studies, history of the book, and cultural theory, as outlined above;
- memoirs/autobiographies/biographies of authors, literary agents, publishers, film agents screenwriters, screen producers, and directors;
- "cultural sphere" publications (i,e. non-academic cultural publications such as broadsheet newspaper arts and culture supplements, book review magazines, little magazines, film reviews, television guides);
- trade publications (i.e. book and screen industry-specific periodicals and commissioned reports);
- archives (e.g. the Booker Prize Archive at Oxford Brookes University (UK),[23] and British publishers' archives at the University of Reading (UK))[24];
- popular media, trade press and academic interviewing of authors, agents, publishers, literary prize judges, screenwriters, directors, and producers;
- para- and extra-textual evidence (e.g. book covers; film and television promotional materials, book prize publicity materials distributed at retail point of sale);
- popular culture meditations on the "anxiety of adaptation" (e.g. films such as Spike Jonze's *Adaptation* [2002][25]; Richard Kwieniowski's *Love and Death on Long Island* [1998]; the Coen brothers' *Barton Fink* [1991]; and book and film industry satirical novels).

Hence, myriad resources exist to verify empirically the workings of the contemporary adaptation industry; that adaptation scholars have, to date, made comparatively little use of such widely dispersed resources probably speaks of a reluctance to traverse established humanities and social sciences research protocols. But given that adaptation is itself the original interdisciplinary academic undertaking, such pusillanimous respect for boundaries for their own sake would seem to have no place in the charting of a new approach for the discipline.

Conclusion: benefits of an industry-centric adaptation model

Belated reformulation of adaptation theory to account for the industrial dimensions of adaptation in contemporary media cultures stands to benefit multiple constituencies. For academic adaptation studies, such an innovation would shake off the enervating sense of a discipline sunk in the doldrums, and would productively reconnect the field to cognate areas in cultural analysis, hybridizing its methodology and adding theoretical nuance to its governing models. Importantly for scholars already invested in the discipline, such cross-pollination would challenge other streams' pejorative verdict upon adaptation studies as a jejune theoretical backwater. A new adaptation model would take account of adaptation's role as the driving force in contemporary multiplatform media, and would seek to replicate this commercial centrality by according adaptation an equivalently central role in theorizations of twenty-first-century culture.

That adaptation is culturally ubiquitous has long been remarked upon by commentators (Orr 1992: 4; Naremore 2000b: 15; Elliott 2003: 4, 6; Hutcheon 2004, 2006: xi, 2, 2007). Without question it is steadily becoming more so. Some commentators observe this phenomenon from the specific perspective of audience and reception research, others from the more generalist vantage point of participation in "mass culture" (Larsson 1982: 81). More recently, cross-platform traffic of content has also been analyzed textually in narratological, semiotic, and post-structuralist terms (Stam 2000, 2005b: 11–12, 28). Missing from this academic equation is a third stream of research that would provide the necessary production-oriented perspective on adaptation to complement existing approaches. But rather than seeing production-focused analysis as merely a corrective to existing critical imbalances and thus as an end in itself, the current project flags how conceptualizing the industrial substructures of adaptation provides new understandings of why texts take the shape they do and how they influence or respond to audience evaluation. Hence a focus on production in the digital age provides a new dimension to adaptation research, but it also calls into question media studies' traditional tripartite division into production/text/audience categories. Production matters; but who is the producer and who is the audience in an era of infinite digital reproducibility, collective creation, and "producerly" media practice remains an open question (Bruns 2005).

More specific than these benefits accruing to the scholarly community as a whole are the payoffs such a study promises for the commonly marginalized discipline of print culture or publishing studies. Rather than perceiving the book as the rapidly obsolescing poor cousin to ever-burgeoning screen media, studying the adaptation industry reveals the continuing prominence of book-derived content in the multimedia age. This is true whether or not print formats serve as audiences' initial point of entry into a content franchise. For even a cursory glance at contemporary mainstream media culture reveals that audiences introduced to book content in screen-media versions often subsequently consume the same narratives in their original novel format, or—where the content is original to screen—audiences may seek out novelizations, making-of books, or companion volumes to prolong, enrich, and potentially complicate their content experience. Robert Stam's briefly elucidated concept of "post-celluloid" adaptation is apposite here (Stam 2005b: 11). Although Stam's use of the term appears to denote the impact upon film culture of technological developments in digital and online media, clearly digital content is also remediated into resolutely *analogue* formats such as the printed book. Audiences demand, evaluate, and sometimes "rewrite" such cross-platform content in unpredictable ways, disproving media historicists' assumptions that younger audiences are necessarily most loyal to more recently developed mediums.

Finally, the third constituency that stands to benefit from mapping of the contemporary Anglophone adaptation economy is the book, film, television, and licensing sector practitioners who are engaged in the actual mechanics of adaptation at the cultural coalface. To date, such industry participants have been inadequately served by "how to" guides that confine themselves to pragmatic issues of realizing individual adaptation projects, without providing an overview of the adaptation process from a critical, macro-oriented perspective (Seger 1992). For cultural producers in second-tier or traditionally "periphery" Anglophone nations, it is especially crucial in cultural policy and cultural nationalist terms to understand how content passes through (or bypasses) dominant US and UK cultural networks to gain exposure to global English-language audiences. What are the mechanisms by which content is brokered on the global adaptation exchange, and what complex interplays of agents, institutions, and commerce inflect cultural evaluation across different territories? What specific industry phenomena cause a rise or fall in cultural prestige for authors, publishers, directors, or studios, for what reasons and in the eyes of which audiences? Do adaptation industry agents always benefit symbiotically from the multi-platform circulation of content, or can a property's rise to mass-market exposure in one media sector trigger devaluation of a property's cultural currency in another? After all, for every reader who selects a tie-in edition on the basis of the familiar film-still reproduced on the cover, there are others who will actively seek out the "purer," more "literary" pre-adaptation cover design (Marshall 2003: A1). To what extent are relationships within the adaptation ecosystem mutually sustaining and to what extent do they evidence sectoral rivalries, commercial conflicts, and long-standing prejudices about the cultural status of specific mediums? Such issues are endlessly intellectually piquant, and unquestionably contemporary in their relevance. Together they represent an exciting opportunity to transform adaptation studies from an intellectual niche topic into perhaps the unifying discipline at the epicenter of contemporary communication studies.

■   ■   ■

Questions and projects

1. What exactly does it mean to "materialize" adaptation studies? And how does it conflict with traditional textual studies of adaptation? Are there ways that this materializing of adaptation studies might support and harmonize with more textual approaches?
2. Choose a study of the filmic adaptation of a work of literature that focuses mainly on the textual exchanges between the two works. Then explore how the often over-looked industrial and cultural contexts of that adaptation open new questions and issues.

Notes

1   Leitch makes a similar point about the cul-de-sac status of adaptation in relation to film studies in the opening chapter of his *Film Adaptation and Its Discontents*, stating that "until quite recently, adaptation study has stood apart from the main currents in film theory" (Leitch 2007: 3), relegated to the gap "between the study of literature as literature and the study of cinema as literature" (Leitch 2007: 7).

2   Such remarks echo Dudley Andrew's earlier judgment that "discourse about adaptation" is "frequently the most narrow and provincial area of film theory." However, Andrew completes his sentence with the more optimistic observation that adaptation "is potentially as far-reaching as you like"—a view of the field's potential that this article shares (Andrew 2000: 28).

3   Refer Fred H. Marcus, ed., *Film and Literature: Contrasts in Media* (Scranton, PA: Chandler, 1971); Geoffrey Wagner. *The Novel and the Cinema* (Rutherford, NJ: Fairleigh Dickinson University Press, 1975); Morris Beja. *Film and Literature: An Introduction* (New York: Longman, 1979); Michael Klein and Gillian Parker, eds., *The English Novel and the Movies* (New York: Ungar, 1981); Stuart Y. McDougal, *Made into Movies: From Literature to Film* (New York: Holt, 1985); John Orr and Colin Nicholson, eds., *Cinema and Fiction: New Modes of Adapting, 1950–1990* (Edinburgh: Edinburgh University Press, 1992); Brian McFarlane, *Novel to Film: An Introduction to the Theory of Adaptation* (Oxford: Clarendon, 1996); John M. Desmond and Peter Hawkes, *Adaptation: Studying Film and Literature* (New York: McGraw Hill, 2006).

4   Refer Fred H. Marcus, ed., *Film and Literature: Contrasts in Media* (Scranton, PA: Chandler, 1971); Geoffrey Wagner, *The Novel and the Cinema* (Rutherford, NJ: Fairleigh Dickinson University, 1975); Morris Beja. *Film and Literature: An Introduction* (New York: Longman, 1979); Keith Cohen, *Film and Fiction: The*

Dynamics of Exchange (New Haven, CT and London: Yale UP, 1979); Michael Klein and Gillian Parker, eds., *The English Novel and the Movies* (New York: Frederick Ungar, 1981); John Orr and Colin Nicholson, eds., *Cinema and Fiction: New Modes of Adapting, 1950–1990* (Edinburgh: Edinburgh University Press, 1992); Brian McFarlane, *Novel to Film: An Introduction to the Theory of Adaptation* (Oxford: Clarendon, 1996); Robert Stam, *Literature through Film: Realism, Magic, and the Art of Adaptation* (Maiden and Oxford: Blackwell. 2005); Robert Stam and Alessandra Raengo. eds., *Literature and Film: A Guide to the Theory and Practice of Adaptation* (Maiden, MA: Blackwell, 2005); Robert Stam and Alessandra Raengo, eds., *A Companion to Literature and Film* (Maiden, MA: Blackwell, 2005).

5   Hutcheon's *A Theory of Adaptation* and Leitch's *Film Adaptation and Its Discontents: From* Gone with the Wind *to* The Passion of the Christ are welcome recent exceptions to this general rule; both explicitly lament the currently fragmented nature of most adaptations research. Hutcheon diplomatically praises selected case-study-based volumes, while regretting that "such individual readings [...] rarely offer [...] generalizable insights into theoretical issues" (xiii). Despite the title of Leitch's work, which appears to herald a collection of adaptation case-studies, his volume is in fact "a study not so much of specific adaptations as of specific problems adaptations raise" (Hutcheon 2006: 20). Neither of these monographs are primarily materialist, however, in their proposed interventions in the discipline, making both books complementary rather than identical to the new research directions proposed in the current article.

6   Cartmell and Whelehan (2007: 4, 9) have recently called for adaptation studies to pay attention to the "commercial considerations [...] [of] the film and television industries" in order to better understand the production contexts out of which adaptations emerge. But, curiously, they exempt the book publishing industry from similar scrutiny. For an extended case-study example of how such an industrially focused research methodology might analyze adaptation, taking into account both the book and screen industries, refer Murray (2008: 8).

7   Bluestone (2003: 62) reiterates this analogy of the novel as raw material later in chapter 1: "What happens [...] when the film undertakes the adaptation of a novel given the inevitable mutation, is that he does not convert the novel at all. What he adapts is a kind of paraphrase of the novel—the novel viewed as raw material."

8   The tenacity of fidelity critique within film reviewing is exemplified by even internationally respected film critic David Stratton having recourse to the trope in his recent review of Ryan Murphy's film adaptation (2006) of Augusten Burroughs' memoir *Running with Scissors* (2002): "the faithful filming of a book is virtually an impossibility, and the film version has, of necessity, to be something different. The question to ask seems to be this: Is [sic] the film faithful to the spirit, to the essence, of the book" (Stratton 2007: 22).

9   Kamilla Elliott also incorporates much semiotic and formalist analysis into her recent study of adaptation, although her work historicizes "interart" debates and cross-pollinates this earlier semiotic tradition with analytical techniques derived from postmodernism and cultural studies (Elliott 2003: 5).

10   That cross-media transfer of content need not necessarily presuppose a textual analysis methodology is demonstrated by a recent wave of research into the material and institutional conditions of rights-trading and cross-promotion between book publishing and the mediums of theatre, radio, and film in the first decades of the twentieth century (refer Weedon 1999, 2007; Hammond 2004; Adam 2007).

11   There appears to be something about the glacial pace of theoretical innovation in adaptation studies that causes critics to vent their frustration in enumerated lists of "clichés," "truisms," or "fallacies" currently plaguing the field (refer Larsson 1982: 70; Leitch 2003: 149; Hutcheon 2006: 52–71).

12   Cited approvingly by Whelehan (1993: 6).

13   Refer, for example, Reynolds (1993: 16).

14   There are a handful of notable exceptions to this general view emerging from the niche adaptation studies sub-field of novelizations: e.g. Baetens 2007. The subtitle of Baetens's chapter, "Novelization, the Hidden Continent," aptly captures the currently hyper-marginalized nature of research into novelizations.

15   Many critics have similarly noted film adaptations' role in driving increased demand for the original novel: Orr (1992: 1); Izod (1992: 97, 103); Reynolds (1993: 4 10); Whelehan (1993: 18) and Hutch-

eon (2006: 90).

16   A notable exception to this general rule is John Orr, whose "Introduction: Proust, the movie" observes that (then) contemporary literary novelists such as Margaret Atwood, Ian McEwan, John Fowles, Milan Kundera, Doris Lessing, and Angela Carter were having their work adapted for highly accomplished films (Orr 1992: 4–5). Orr suggests that, in a feedback effect, these critically praised film adaptations in turn enhanced the literary reputation of the novelist.

17   Many critics have noted the role of screen adaptations of Austen's works in popularizing and expanding readerships for her novels (for example, Lupack 1999; Stern, 2000; Aragay and López 2005; Troost 2007).

18   This would seem to echo Dudley Andrew's statement that "it is time for adaptation studies to take a sociological turn" (Andrew 2000: 35). However, in the section of Andrew's much-reproduced chapter that follows his bold opening statement, it becomes clear that Andrew understands "the sociology of adaptation" as concerned with waves of artistic influence between fiction and cinema: "we need to study the films themselves as acts of discourse" (Andrew 2000:37). Hence Andrew's conception of "sociology" is still exclusively textual, bypassing the issues of production, commerce, and institutional interdependence that this discussion associates with the term.

19   "The huge growth over the last few years in what could be called the adaptation industry makes this a cultural phenomenon that cannot be ignored" (Reynolds 1993: 11).

20   The Booker Prize was established in 1969, and became the Man Booker Prize in 2002 with a change of sponsor. Refer <http://www.themanbookerprize.com>.

21   Stam and Hutcheon, both of whom trained in North American comparative literature programs, are notable exceptions to this rule; both critics' work on adaptation references a wide variety of texts from (mostly) other European language groups, in particular French-, Spanish-, Italian- and Portuguese-speaking cultures (refer Stam, 2005a: 17).

22   This plethora of research resources is in stark contrast to the laborious 1950s methodology Bluestone describes, involving sourcing the shooting-script for a given film, traveling around the US to locate a cinema currently showing the film, and then marking up the shooting-script while viewing the film to indicate scenes deleted from the film's cinema-release cut. Bluestone then compared this "accurate and reasonably objective record" of the film version to the original novel as "a way of imposing the shooting-script on the book" (Bluestone 2003: ix).

23   <http://www.brookes.ac.uk/library/speccoll/booker.html>.

24   <http://www.reading.ac.uk/library/special-collections/archives/lib-special-publishers.asp>.

25   Jonze's dizzyingly inventive film might almost serve as an unexpected (and presumably unintentional) manifesto for a new, industry-focused wave of adaptation studies. This is due to its satirical attention to the intermeshing motivations and anxieties of screenwriters, authors, agents, directors, actors, producers, and scriptwriting gurus. Not surprisingly, the film has already been extensively commented upon in recent academic adaptations work (Hutcheon 2004: 108, 2006: 2. 2007; Stam, 2005b: 1–3).

References

Adam, Jasmin. "Quo Vadis Book Culture?: The German Publishing Industry and the Emergence of Film." Paper presented at The Fourth International Conference on the Book. Emerson College, Boston. 20–22 Oct. 2006 <http://b06.cgpublisher.com/ proposals/ 226/index_html> (11 May 2007).

Adams, Thomas R., and Nicolas Barker. "A New Model for the Study of the Book." *A Potencie of Life: Books in Society*. Ed. Nicolas Barker. London; British Library, 1993, 5–43.

Andrew, Dudley. "Adaptation." [1984] *Film Adaptation*. Ed James Naremore. London: Athlone, 2000. 28–37.

Aragay, Mireia, ed. *Books in Motion: Adaptation, Intertextuality, Authorship*. Amsterdam and New York: Rodopi, 2005.

Aragay, Mireia, and Gemma López. "Inf(l)ecting *Pride and Prejudice:* Dialogism. Intertextuality, and Adaptation." *Books in Motion: Adaptation, Intertextuality, Authorship*. Ed. Mireia Aragay. Amsterdam and New York: Rodopi, 2005. 201–19.

Baetens, Jan. "From Screen to Text: Novelization, the Hidden Continent." *The Cambridge Companion to Literature on Screen.* Ed. Deborah Cartmell and Imelda Whelehan. Cambridge: Cambridge University Press, 2007. 226–38.

Balides, Constance. "Jurassic Post-Fordism: Tall Tales of Economics in the Theme Park." *Screen* 41.2 (2000): 139–60.

Beja, Morris. *Film and Literature: An Introduction.* New York: Longman, 1979.

Bluestone, George. *Novels into Film.* [1957] Baltimore: Johns Hopkins University Press, 2003.

Bolter, Jay David, and Richard Grusin. *Remediation: Understanding New Media.* Cambridge, MA: MIT Press, 1999.

Brown, Stephen. *Consuming Books: The Marketing and Consumption of Literature.* London: Routledge, 2006.

Bruns, Axel. *Gatewatching: Collaborative Online News Production.* Digital Formations series. New York: Peter Lang, 2005.

Cahir, Linda Costanzo. *Literature into Film: Theory and Practical Approaches.* Jefferson, OH: McFarland, 2006.

Cartmell, Deborah, and Imelda Whelehan, eds. *Adaptations: From Text to Screen, Screen to Text.* London and New York: Routledge, 1999.

———. eds. *The Cambridge Companion to Literature on Screen.* Cambridge: Cambridge University Press, 2007.

Cartmell. Deborah, I.Q. Hunter, Heidi Kaye, and Imelda Whelehan, eds. *Classics in Film and Fiction.* Film/Fiction series. London: Pluto, 2000.

Cohen, Keith. *Film and Fiction: The Dynamics of Exchange.* New Haven, CT and London: Yale University Press, 1979.

Collins, Jim, ed. *High-Pop: Making Culture into Popular Entertainment.* Malden, MA and Oxford: Blackwell, 2002.

Curran, James. "The New Revisionism in Mass Communication Research: A Reappraisal." *European Journal of Communication* 5.2 (1990): 135–64.

Darnton, Robert. "What Is the History of Books?" [1982] *The Kiss of Lamourette.* London: Faber, 1990. 107–35.

Desmond, John M., and Peter Hawkes. *Adaptation: Studying Film and Literature.* New York: McGraw Hill, 2006.

Doyle, Gillian. *Media Ownership: The Economics and Politics of Convergence and Concentration in the UK and European Media.* London: Sage, 2002.

Elliott, Kamilla. *Rethinking the Novel/Film Debate.* Cambridge: Cambridge University Press, 2003.

Elsaesser, Thomas. "Cinema Futures: Convergence, Divergence, Difference." *Cinema Futures: Cain, Abel or Cable?: The Screen Arts in the Digital Age.* Ed. Thomas Elsaesser and Kay Hoffmann. Amsterdam: Amsterdam University Press, 1998. 9–26.

Engelhardt, Tom. "Gutenberg Unbound." *Nation* 17 Mar. 1997: 18–21, 29.

English, James F. *The Economy of Prestige: Prizes, Awards, and the Circulation of Cultural Value.* Cambridge, MA: Harvard University Press, 2005.

Epstein, Jason. *Book Business. Publishing Past Present and Future.* New York: Norton, 2002.

Gelder, Ken. *Popular Fiction: The Logics and Practices of a Literary Field.* London: Routledge, 2004.

Giddings, Robert, Keith Selby, and Chris Wensley. *Screening the Novel: The Theory and Practice of Literary Dramatization.* London: Macmillan, 1990.

Hammond, Mary. "Hall Caine and the Melodrama on Page, Stage and Screen." *Nineteenth Century Theatre and Film* 31.1 (2004): 39–57.

Hartley, Jenny. *Reading Groups.* Oxford: Oxford University Press, 2001.

Holmes, David. *Communication Theory: Media, Technology and Society.* London: Sage, 2005.

Hutcheon, Linda. "On the Art of Adaptation." *Dœdalus* 133.2 (2004): 108–11.

———. *A Theory of Adaptation.* New York and London: Routledge, 2006.

———. "In Defence of Literary Adaptation as Cultural Production." *M/C Journal* 10.2 (2007) <http://journal.media-culture. org.au/0705/01-hutcheon.php> (16 May 2007).

Izod, John. "Words Selling Pictures." *Cinema and Fiction: New Modes of Adapting, 1950–1990.* Ed. John Orr and Colin Nicholson. Edinburgh: Edinburgh University Press, 1992. 95–103.

Jenkins, Henry. *Convergence Culture: Where Old and New Media Collide.* New York and London: New York University Press, 2006.

Klein, Michael, and Gillian Parker, eds. *The English Novel and the Movies.* New York: Frederick Ungar, 1981.

Larsson, Donald F. "Novel into Film: Some Preliminary Reconsiderations." *Transformations in Literature and Film.* Ed. Leon Golden. Tallahassee, FL: Florida State University Press, 1982. 69–83.

Leitch, Thomas. "Twelve Fallacies in Contemporary Adaptation Theory." *Criticism* 45.2 (2003): 149–71.

———. *Film Adaptation and Its Discontents: From* Gone with the Wind *to* The Passion of the Christ. Baltimore, MD: Johns Hopkins University Press, 2007.

Long, Elizabeth. *Book Clubs: Women and the Uses of Reading in Everyday Life*. Chicago, IL and London: University of Chicago Press, 2003.

Lupack, Barbara Tepa, ed. *Nineteenth-Century Women at the Movies: Adapting Classic Women's Fiction to Film*. Bowling Green, KY: Bowling Green State University Popular Press, 1999.

Mackenzie, Janet, ed. *At the Typeface: Selections from the* Newsletter *of the Victorian Society of Editors*. Melbourne: Society of Editors (Victoria), 2005.

Marcus, Fred H., ed. *Film and Literature: Contrasts in Media*. Scranton, PA: Chandler, 1971.

Marshall, Jeannie. "Judging Books by their Covers: Film Fans Split on Movie Tie-ins." *National Post* [Canada] 4 Jan. 2003: Al.

Mayer, Robert, ed. *Eighteenth-Century Fiction on Screen*. Cambridge: Cambridge University Press, 2002.

McDougal, Stuart Y. *Made into Movies: From Literature to Film*. New York: Holt, Rinehart & Winston, 1985.

McFarlane, Brian. *Novel to Film: An Introduction to the Theory of Adaptation*. Oxford: Clarendon, 1996.

McLuhan, Marshall. *Understanding Media: The Extensions of Man*. [1964] Routledge Classics. London: Routledge, 2001.

McPhee, Hilary. *Other People's Words*. Sydney. Picador, 2001.

Miller, Mark Crispin. "The Crushing Power of Big Publishing." *The Nation* 17 Mar. 1997: 11–18.

Mosco, Vincent. *The Political Economy of Communication: Rethinking and Renewal*. London: Sage, 1996.

Murdock, Graham, and Peter Golding. "Capitalism, Communication and Class Relations." *Mass Communication and Society*. Ed. James Curran, Michael Gurevitch, and Janet Woollacott. London: Arnold, 1977. 12–43.

Murray, Simone. "Media Convergence's Third Wave: Content Streaming." *Convergence: The Journal of Research into New Media Technologies* 9.1 (Spring 2003): 8–18.

——. "A Book that Will be Read as Long as Films are Seen: Book-to-Screen Literary Adaptations and the Content Economy." Proceedings of The Book Conference 2003 / *International Journal of the Book*, vol. 1. Melbourne: Common Ground, 2003: 329–35.

——. "Brand Loyalties: Rethinking Content within Global Corporate Media." *Media, Culture & Society* 27.3 (2005): 415–35.

——. "Content Streaming." *Paper Empires: A History of the Book in Australia, Volume 3 – 1946–2005*. Ed. Craig Munro, Robyn Sheahan-Bright, and John Curtain. Brisbane: University of Queensland Press, 2006. 126–31.

——. "Publishing Studies: Critically Mapping Research in Search of a Discipline." *Publishing Research Quarterly* 22.4 Winter 2007a: 3–25.

——. "Generating Content: Book Publishing as a Component Media Industry." *Making Books: Studies in Contemporary Australian Publishing*. Ed. David Carter and Anne Galligan. Brisbane: University of Queensland Press, 2007b. 51–67.

——. "Phantom Adaptations: *Eucalyptus*, the Adaptation Industry and the Film that Never Was." *Adaptation: The Journal of Literature on Screen Studies* 1.1 (2008): 5–23.

Naremore, James, ed. *Film Adaptation*. London: Athlone, 2000a.

——. "Introduction: Film and the Reign of Adaptation." *Film Adaptation*. Ed. James Naremore. London: Athlone, 2000b. 1–16.

Orr, John. "Introduction: Proust, the movie." *Cinema and Fiction: New Modes of Adapting, 1950–1990*. Ed. John Orr and Colin Nicholson. Edinburgh: Edinburgh University Press, 1992. 1–9.

Orr, John, and Colin Nicholson, eds. *Cinema and Fiction: New Modes of Adapting, 1950–1990*. Edinburgh: Edinburgh University Press, 1992.

Phillips, Angus. "Cover Story: Cover Design in the Marketing of Fiction." *Logos* 18.1 (2007): 15–20.

Ray, Robert O. "The Field of 'Literature and Film.'" *Film Adaptation*. Ed. James Naremore. London: Athlone, 2000. 38–53.

Reynolds, Peter, ed. *Novel Images: Literature in Performance*. London and New York; Routledge, 1993.

Ruppert, Peter, ed. *Ideas of Order in Literature and Film*. Tallahassee, FL: Florida State University Press, 1980.

Schiffrin, André. *The Business of Books: How International Conglomerates Took Over Publishing and Changed the Way We Read*. London and New York: Verso, 2000.

Schiller, Dan. *Digital Capitalism: Networking the Global Marketing System*. London: Pluto, 1999.

Sedo, DeNel Rehberg. "Readers in Reading Groups: An Online Survey of Face-to-Face and Virtual Book Clubs." *Convergence: The Journal of Research into New Media Technologies* 9.1 (2003): 66–90.

Seger, Linda. *The Art of Adaptation: Turning Fact and Fiction into Film*. New York: Holt, 1992.

Squires, Claire. *Marketing Literature: The Making of Contemporary Writing in Britain*. Basingstoke: Palgrave Macmillan, 2007.

Stam, Robert. "Beyond Fidelity: The Dialogics of Adaptation." *Film Adaptation*. Ed. James Naremore. London: Athlone, 2000. 54–76.

——. *Literature through Film: Realism, Magic, and the Art of Adaptation*. Malden, MA and Oxford: Blackwell, 2005a.

——. "Introduction: The Theory and Practice of Adaptation." *Literature and Film: A Guide to the Theory and Practice of Adaptation*. Ed. Robert Stam and Alessandra Raengo. Malden, MA and Oxford: Blackwell, 2005b. 1–52.

Stam, Robert, and Alessandra Raengo, eds. *A Companion to Literature and Film*. Malden, MA and Oxford: Blackwell, 2005.

Stern, Lesley. "*Emma* in Los Angeles: Remaking the Book and the City." *Film Adaptation*. Ed James Naremore. London: Athlone, 2000. 221–38.

Stratton, David. "Lacking a Cutting Edge." Review of Ryan Murphy's *Running with Scissors. Weekend Australian* 31 Mar. 2007: Review 22–23.

Troost Linda V; "The Nineteenth-century Novel on Film: Janc Austen." *The Cambridge Companion to Literature on Screen*. Ed. Deborah Cartmell and Imelda Whelehan. Cambridge: Cambridge University Press, 2007. 75–89.

Wagner, Geoffrey. *The Novel and the Cinema*. Rutherford, NJ: Fairleigh Dickinson University Press, 1975.

Wasko, Janet. *Hollywood in the Information Age: Beyond the Silver Screen*. Cambridge: Polity, 1994.

——. *Understanding Disney: The Manufacture of Fantasy*. Malden, MA: Blackwell, 2001.

——. *How Hollywood Works*. Thousand Oaks, CA: Sage, 2003.

Weedon, Alexis. "From Three-Deckers to Film Rights: A Turn in British Publishing Strategies, 1870–1930." *Book History* 2.1 (1999): 188–206.

——. "'Behind the Screen' and 'The Scoop'": A Cross-media Experiment in Publishing and Broadcasting Crime Fiction in the Early 1930s." *Media History* 13.1 (2007): 43–60.

——. "Elinor Glyn's System of Writing." *Publishing History* 60 (2007): 31–50.

Whelehan, Imelda. "Adaptations: The Contemporary Dilemmas." *Adaptations: From Text to Screen, Screen to Text*. Ed. Deborah Cartmell and Imelda Whelehan. London and New York Routledge, 1999. 3–19.

Chapter 33

Linda Hutcheon

"HOW? (AUDIENCES)"

THE AUTHOR OF NUMEROUS BOOKS on parody, postmodernism, and literary history, Linda Hutcheon examines the expanding borders of adaptation in her *Theory of Literary Adaptation*, as those borders grow historically and change their shape through contemporary media. In this essay from that work, Hutcheon discusses the often over-looked dynamics of the different ways audiences engage with adaptive works. For her, this involves the pleasure that audiences find in adaptations, the importance of "fan cultures" who follow a text's different incarnations, the differences between "knowing and unknowing" audiences, and the various "degrees of immersion" according to which audiences respond to adaptations.

■ ■ ■

"HOW? (AUDIENCES)"
LINDA HUTCHEON

From *A Theory of Adaptation*, New York: Routledge, 2006, pp. 113–139

Adapting is a bit like redecorating.

—Alfred Uhry

The content of a movie is a novel or a play or opera.

—Marshall McLuhan

After all, the work of other writers is one of a writer's main sources of input, so don't hesitate to use it; just because somebody else has an idea doesn't mean you can't take that idea and develop a new twist for it. Adaptations may become quite legitimate adoptions.

—William S. Burroughs

[T]he theatre itself is much less high-minded than those who keep a watchful eye on its purity; the stage has always cheerfully swiped whatever good stories were going.

—Philip Pullman

Unlike Don Quixote's books, digital media take us to a place where we can act out our fantasies. With a telnet connection or a CD-Rom drive, we can kill our own dragons.

—Janet M. Murray, *Hamlet on the Holodeck*

Movies not only used different materials, they had different cooking times for their great soups, and had to be consumed in public alongside eight hundred other people as opposed to by one solitary diner. A film was closer to the simulated excitement of a soccer stadium while books were a meditative and private act—you sat down to read one or write one and the first thing you did was ignore the rest of the world. Whereas film had various sous-chefs and a studio and a market to deal with. A book could be secret as a canoe trip, the making of a film more like the voyage of *Lord Jim's* Patna—uncertain of ever reaching its destination with a thousand pilgrims onboard and led by a morally dubious crew. But somehow, magically, it now and then got to a safe harbour.

—Michael Ondaatje on *The English Patient*, novel and film

The pleasures of adaptation

Obviously, the creation and reception of adaptations are inevitably going to be intertwined—and not only in commercial terms. Because audiences react in different ways to different media—thanks to social and material differences, as Ondaatje imaginatively suggests—the possible response of the target audience to a story is always going to be a concern of the adapter(s). Radio, television, and film have radically increased our exposure to stories and therefore, some claim, our ability to comprehend them (Thompson 2003:79). Arguably, these media have also increased our appetite for and delight in stories. But what is the real source of the pleasure derived from experiencing adaptations *as adaptations*?

In Chapter 1, I suggested that the appeal of adaptations for audiences lies in their mixture of repetition and difference, of familiarity and novelty. Novelist Julian Barnes satirizes part of this appeal in *England, England* when his French theorist character describes the joys of a theme park as its "*rivalisation* of reality": "We must demand the replica, since the reality, the truth, the authenticity of the replica is the one we can possess, colonize, reorder, find *jouissance* in" (Barnes 1998: 35). While parodying various French theorists, Barnes also puts his finger on one of the sources of the pleasure of replication—and adaptation—for audiences. Freudians too might say we repeat as a way of making up for loss, as a means of control, or of coping with privation. But adaptation as repetition is arguably not a postponement of pleasure; it is in itself a pleasure. Think of a child's delight in hearing the same nursery rhymes or reading the same books over and over. Like ritual, this kind of repetition brings comfort, a fuller understanding, and the confidence that comes with the sense of knowing what is about to happen next.

But something else happens with adaptations in particular: there is inevitably difference as well as repetition. Consider the words of librettist, playwright, and adapter for musicals and films, Terrence McNally: "The triumph of successful operas and musicals is how they reinvent the familiar and make it fresh" (McNally 2002: 19). The same could be said of any successful adaptation. To focus on repetition alone, in other words, is to suggest only the potentially conservative element in the audience response to adaptation. Noting that many modern operas (e.g., *The Great Gatsby* [1999]) have been based on novels that had earlier been made into films, Joel Honig has blamed the need for the adapting mediation of film on the opera audience's desire for "warmed-over comfort-food, prepackaged in Hollywood" (Honig 2001: 22). But perhaps the real comfort lies in the simple act of almost but not quite repeating, in the revisiting of a theme with variations.

Others argue, instead, that it is a particular kind of story that provides the comfort that explains the popularity of adaptations: the familiar linear and realist story-line "founded upon the principles of narration doubtlessly begun with Aesop, if not Moses, and polished by Walter Scott and Balzac" (Axelrod 1996: 201). Such a story-line has been seen as the appeal of formulaic genres of film adaptation, especially those that use what one critic refers to as Aristotle's notion of plot combined with Joseph Campbell's myth of the hero's quest (Axelrod 1996: 202). Adventure videogames clearly play with this same kind of story structure as well, but we have seen that the story itself is less important than the special effects universe to be entered and experienced or simply the gaming process itself—or at least this seems to be the case for male players.

Girls in the 7- to 12-year-old age range, it would appear, "tend to prefer narrative play and are attracted to narrative complexity" (Laurel 2005). Drawing upon interviews with 1,100 children and questionnaires completed by 10,000 children, Brenda Laurel notes that the vast majority of creators of fan fiction and video are female, suggesting that the fascination with story continues into adulthood. The stories that young women prefer to see adapted into game format, she shows, are those, like *Buffy the Vampire Slayer*, that overlap somewhat with their own lives and their personal issues with parents and siblings and with being accepted at school. Boys of the same age are more likely to be embarrassed by things too close to their own lives and escape instead into superhero exotic action scenarios. It seems that 81 percent of the more violent games are played by males, whereas females prefer role-playing games, like *Sims,* with more social interaction or else games that allow instant immersion in a story-line (e.g., an adaptation like *Nancy Drew*).

Another name for adaptation audiences here is obviously "fans," and the community they constitute is consciously nurtured by adapters, who realize that young women in particular need to be able to "appropriate cultural material to construct personal meaning" (Laurel 2005); this is why the interactive mode can be so attractive to them and why stories, in particular, are central to their pleasure in adaptations. From early childhood onward, as I can testify from experience, girls create imaginative worlds, complete with their own history, geography, people, and rules of behavior, and they inhabit these imaginatively. How different is sending e-mails to game characters, on bulletin boards set up by the adapting companies of course, from making up stories with and for their Barbie dolls? In 2004, Mattel, the Barbie doll's creators, decided to exploit this latter pastime and offered DVDs that are a kind of adaptation, for they bring the "Barbie world" to life "through storytelling," as explained on their Web site (http://www.yenra.com/barbie-dvds/): "Barbie will set the stage and then cue the girls' imaginations to take the story to the next level"—which turns out to be developing "a deeper connection with the Barbie brand." Given this, it is perhaps not surprising that experimental Irish composer Jennifer Walshe was driven to create her musical puppet opera for Barbie and her play friends: as its title (*XXX_LiveNude Girls*) suggests, this work explores the darker side of girls' narrative relationship to their dolls.

Although many of these theories and examples suggest pleasures tainted with a too conservative familiarity, not to mention commodification and commercialization, there are still other reasons for the positive reaction to the repetition with variation that is adaptation: what Leo Braudy, in discussing film remakes, calls "unfinished cultural business" or the "continuing historical relevance (economic, cultural, psychological) of a particular narrative" (Braudy 1998: 331). Part of this ongoing dialogue with the past, for that is what adaptation means for audiences, creates the doubled pleasure of the palimpsest: more than one text is experienced—and knowingly so. In Tony Richardson's 1963 cinematic adaptation of Henry Fielding's *Tom Jones* (1749), we recognize the novel's manipulating and controlling narrator in the film's disembodied voice-over that ends scenes just in time to prevent indecency or ironically explicates character motivation.

This is the intertextual pleasure in adaptation that some call elitist and that others call enriching. Like classical imitation, adaptation appeals to the "intellectual and aesthetic pleasure" (DuQuesnay 1979: 68) of understanding the interplay between works, of opening up a text's possible meanings to intertextual echoing. The adaptation and the adapted work merge in the audience's understanding of their complex interrelations, as they might in the 1997 BBC television adaptation of *Tom Jones* when we see a character called "Henry Fielding" self-reflexively enacting the narrator's role, but being ironically cut off mid-sentence by the real controlling figure, the director, when he digresses from the story-line selected for that particular filmed version.

In direct contrast to this elitist or enriching appeal of adaptation is the pleasure of accessibility that drives not only adaptation's commercialization but also its role in education. As noted earlier, teachers, and their students provide one of the largest audiences for adaptations. Many of us grew up with the *Classics Illustrated* comics or the animated cartoon versions of canonical literature. Today's young people are just as likely to interact with CD-ROM adaptations of either children's or adult literature. In 1992 *Shakespeare: The Animated Tales* offered half-hour versions of the major plays aimed at a 10- to 15-year-old audience and was accompanied by print texts published by Random House that differed, however, from the films. The films obviously made major cuts in the play texts, but retained their language. The style of animation was deliberately not Disney-like. Interestingly the stories seem to have been considered central, and so voice-overs were used to keep the action moving, thereby in a sense translating drama into narrative or showing into telling. There were, however, strong intertextual echoes of other Shakespearean films in the editing and in the appearances of characters and sets, prompting one critic to suggest that the animations prepared students for films of Shakespeare, not for the plays themselves (Osborne 1997:106).

Adults, of course, often "censor" adaptations, deciding that some are appropriate for children and others not. Or else they change the stories in the process of adapting them to make them appropriate for a different audience. For instance, *Lemony Snicket's A Series of Unfortunate Events* (2004) is a film adaptation of part of three books by Daniel Handler about the Baudelaire orphans. Although the books are aimed at preteens and adolescents, the film wanted and knew it would attract a broader audience and so made the very dark tales considerably brighter, in part by using a narrating Lemony Snicket who can assure younger children that everything will be okay in the end.

Adaptations of books, however, are often considered educationally important for children, for an entertaining film or stage version might give them a taste for reading the book on which it is based. This is what novelist Philip Pullman (2004) calls the "worthiness argument." Although most of the fans of the Harry Potter films will already have read the books, Pullman is not wrong, and this get-them-to-read motivation is what fuels an entire new education industry. The new film adaptation of C.S. Lewis' *The Chronicles of Narnia: The Lion, the Witch and the Wardrobe* is accompanied by elaborate teaching aids, from lesson plans to Web-based packages to material for after-school clubs. Today, hardly a book or a movie aimed at school-aged children does not have its own Web site, complete with advice and materials for teachers.

Novelizations of films, including what are called "junior" novelizations for younger viewers, are also often seen as having a kind of educational—or perhaps simply curiosity—value. If Internet postings are to be believed, fans of films enjoy their novelizations because they provide insights into the characters' thought processes and more details about their background. And, after all, that is what novels have always done well. Web site narratives (e.g., Max Payne) or even films (e.g., *Final Fantasy*) about videogames can offer the same kind of information in a different format. They all increase audience knowledge about and therefore engagement in the "back story" of the adaptation. These various supplements are sometimes released before the films or games and therefore generate anticipation. Not only do these kinds of adaptations provide more details, especially about adapted characters' inner lives, but in the process they also help foster audience/reader identification with those characters. They might also add scenes that do not appear in the screenplay or film versions, perhaps offering a minor character's perspective on the action. The novel often explains plot and motivation elements that remain ambiguous in the film: in Arthur C. Clarke's novelization of *2001:A Space Odyssey* ("based on a screenplay by Stanley Kubrick and Arthur C. Clarke"), the author actually allows us into the consciousness of the computer Hal.

Not everyone approves of novelizations, of course: for many they are simply commercial grabs, unmitigated commodifications, or inflationary recyclings. As we have seen, gamers are equally suspicious of games with direct successful movie links, seeing them as "transparent attempts to cash in on successful movie franchises with products that lack much in the way of compelling gameplay of their own" (King and Krzywinska 2002b: 7). But economic diversification is the name of the game: to use White Wolf Publishing as one example, its pen-and-paper role-playing games have been licensed to videogames, television series, action figures, comic books, interactive media events, arcade games, and even professional wrestlers. Although all of these different incarnations feed audience curiosity and fan instincts, not all are fully adaptations as defined here and as explored further in the concluding chapter. All, however, make money; audiences exist or can be created for them all.

Adaptations have come under the scrutiny not only of money makers but also of the censors, for they too have audiences in mind. This was certainly true in earlier centuries for dramatic and operatic adaptations for the stage. We have also seen that the Hollywood Production Code (1930–66), drafted by Father Daniel Lord SJ, and sponsored by Will Hays of the Motion Picture Producers and Distributors of America, decreed that movies must not lower the audience's moral standards by showing any sympathetic representations of evil, crime, or sin. Sinclair Lewis, Ernest Hemingway, William Faulkner, John Dos Passos—all were deemed capable of corrupting the movie-going mass audience. Instead, it was decided, people should see edifying religious dramas and patriotic stories. When Hemingway's *A Farewell to Arms* was adapted to the screen in 1932, it was already a hit on Broadway and a publishing success. But this was a story about an illegitimate birth, illicit love, and an army desertion, and it was a critique of war. It portrayed the Italian army anything but favorably. Needless to say, many compromises needed to be made before *A Farewell to Arms* could come to the screen, including so many changes to the plot and the character motivation that Hemingway refused to endorse it.

Closely related to these moral and educational concerns for audiences is the idea that television adaptations of literature, in particular, can act as substitute vehicles for bringing literature to a larger public, cutting away the class differences inherent in access to literacy and literature. But this does not always work in practice: the BBC's *A TV Dante* (1990), co-directed by Peter Greenaway and artist Tom Philips, is a case in point. Although television implies an address to a mass audience, this show remained "recondite," incomprehensible without explanatory notes (Taylor 2004: 147). The other major danger involved in the motivation to adapt for a wider audience is that a certain responsibility is placed on the adapters to make the "substitute" experience "as good as, or better than (even if different from) that of reading original works" (Wober 1980: 10). Would this experience be the same, however, for the audience that knows the adapted text as it is for the one that does not? How, in short, are adaptations appreciated *as adaptations*?

Knowing and unknowing audiences

When either the voice-over narrator or the protagonist of Sally Potter's film, *Orlando* (1994), addresses the audience, a kind of negotiation is set up between Virginia Woolf's text and our knowledge of it and its garrulous narrating biographer (Shaughnessy 1996: 50). If we know the adapted text, I prefer to call us "knowing," rather than the more common descriptors of learned or competent (Conte 1986: 25). The term "knowing" suggests being savvy and street-smart, as well as knowledgeable, and undercuts some of the elitist associations of the other terms in favor of a more democratizing kind of straightforward awareness of the adaptation's enriching, palimpsestic doubleness. If we do not know that what we are experiencing actually *is* an adaptation or if we are not familiar with the particular work that it adapts, we simply experience the adaptation as we would any other work. To experience it *as an adaptation*, however, as we have seen, we need to recognize it as such and to know its adapted text, thus allowing the latter to oscillate in our memories with what we are experiencing. In the process we inevitably fill in any gaps in the adaptation with information from the adapted text. Indeed, adapters rely on this ability to fill in the gaps when moving from the discursive expansion of telling to the performative time and space limitations of showing. Sometimes they rely too much, and the resulting adaptation makes no sense without reference to and foreknowledge of the adapted text. For an adaptation to be successful in its own right, it must be so for both knowing and unknowing audiences.

If we know the basic story outline of Shakespeare's play *A Midsummer Night's Dream*, for instance, we are likely to fill in the gaps necessitated by the distillation of the plot in the opera or ballet versions. When the complication of music is added, it certainly seems to help if the story is a familiar one. As Terrence McNally (2002: 24) puts it, "Music adds such an enormously new dimension to a piece, it's enough for any audience (or critic) to absorb at one hearing. If the characters and situation are familiar, listeners can relax and let the music take them somewhere new and wonderful". Nevertheless, it is probably easier for an adapter to forge a relationship with an audience that is not overly burdened with affection or nostalgia for the adapted text. Without foreknowledge, we are more likely to greet a film version simply as a new film, not as an adaptation at all. The director, therefore, will have greater freedom—and control.

Known adaptations obviously function similarly to genres: they set up audience expectations (Culler 1975: 136) through a set of norms that guide our encounter with the adapting work we are experiencing. Unlike plagiarism or even parody, adaptation usually signals its identity overtly: often for legal reasons, a work is openly announced to be "based on" or "adapted from" a specific prior work or works. If we know the work(s) in question, we become a knowing audience, and part of what hermeneutic theory calls our "horizon of expectation" involves that adapted text. What is intriguing is that, afterward, we often come to see the prior adapted work very differently as we compare it to the result of the adapter's creative and interpretive act. In the move from print to performance, in particular, characters (hobbits) and places (Middle Earth) become incarnate in a way that conditions how we imagine them in a literary work like Tolkien's *Lord of the Rings* when we return to reread it. Our imaginations are permanently colonized by the visual and aural world of the films. But what if we have never read the novels upon which they are based? Do the novels then effectively become the derivative and belated works, the ones we then experience second and secondarily? For unknowing audiences, adaptations have a way of upending sacrosanct elements like priority and originality.

If the adapted work is a canonical one, we may not actually have direct experience of it, but may rely on "a generally circulated cultural memory" (Ellis 1982: 3). Either way, we tend to experience the adaptation through the lenses of the adapted work, as a kind of palimpsest. It is said that producer David Selznick did not worry about adhering to the details of the novel *Jane Eyre* (1847) when adapting it in the 1940s because an audience survey determined that few had read it; however, he did worry about the details of *Gone with the Wind* (1939) and *Rebecca* (1940), because the novels had been recent best-sellers (in Naremore 2000b: 11–12). The disappointment of the fans of the DC comic book *Catwoman* was clear in the responses to Pitof's 2004 film, which kept only the name and added a new cast of characters in a new setting. Critics tended to blame the screenwriters (John Brancato, Michael Ferris, John Rogers, and Theresa Rebeck), calling them the "committee, the gang of four" who "declawed the poor creature" (Groen 2004: R1).

Knowing audiences have expectations—and demands. It may be less, as Béla Balázs tried to insist, that "a masterpiece is a work whose subject ideally suits its medium" and therefore cannot be adapted (quoted in Andrew 1976: 87) than a case of a "masterpiece" being a work a particular audience cherishes and resists seeing changed. Different adaptations solicit different audiences or fan communities: Harry Potter fans may not be Tolkien fans. When a film or musical announces itself as an adaptation of a particular work, those who like that work turn out for the adaptation, often to discover that only the name remains and that there is little resemblance to anything treasured and thus expected. Here is an early (1928) description of the problems with this process from the other end:

> A favorite money-saving habit is to make a picture that is very like a well-known popular novel or play, and then grow timorous at this similarity when the picture is almost completed, and buy the story which was used as a model. The title of the bought and popular tale is then used, but it usually happens that the similarity is not really so great as the nervous producer, haunted by dreams of plagiarism suits, first thought.
>
> (Bauer 1928: 294)

The more rabid the fans, the more disappointed they can potentially be, however. As Christopher Columbus, director of *Harry Potter and the Philosopher's Stone* (2001) put it: "People would have crucified me if I hadn't been faithful to the books" (quoted in Whipp 2002: H4).

There are also other dimensions to this "knowingness" of the audience of adaptation, in addition to the awareness of the specific adapted text(s). One such dimension is treated in detail in the next chapter, and that is context—in cultural, social, intellectual, and aesthetic terms. But this dimension overlaps with another kind of knowing; that is, about what Chapter 2 called the form of the adaptation and therefore the expectations created by it. In terms of genre switching in adaptation, we need only think of the different implied "pacts" made with the reader of autobiography and the reader of comics or graphic novels. Philippe Lejeune's idea of the "autobiographical pact" between reader and author is that we accept that an autobiography is a retrospective narrative by a real person about his or her own life (Lejeune 1975: 14). This pact undergoes an odd twist when Harvey Pekar's own blue-collar life stories become the *American Splendor* comic books drawn by R. Crumb and others and from there get adapted to the stage and screen. In terms of medium, musicals and operas both offer "drama unfolding through song" (Lachiusa 2002: 14), but they have different artistic traditions and, often, different audiences. As musical composer Michael John Lachiusa put it, the musical genre is "the child of European opera tradition transplanted to America" (Lachiusa 2002: 14), mixing high-brow and low-brow because of its cross-fertilization with ethnic immigrant theater, music, and dance (see Most 2004).

Medium change therefore involves the same kinds of expectation shifts. For example, the 2002 film version of Oscar Wilde's play, *The Importance of Being Earnest*, directed and adapted by Oliver Parker, exchanges the restricted drawing-room sets of the staged version for the streets of London and a grand country estate. Why? Because movie audiences expect the film to have local color and to be shot on location, with characters moving through real space. After several decades, British televised versions of classic novels now generate in their viewers expectations about style, "sumptuous, beautiful, pictorial images, strung together smoothly, slowly and carefully" (Cardwell 2002: 80). These expectations are not really dictated by the adapted literary texts, but rather by the television medium's desire to signal "artistry" through specifically cinematic markers of "quality": "the use of long-take, extreme long shots of grand buildings … [,] the preference for slow, smooth tracking shots … [,] their use of a certain type of elegant, decorous or wistful orchestral music on their soundtracks" (Cardwell 2002: 80). The institutionalization of a medium, in other words, can in itself create expectations: a movie of an opera may be allowed to differ from the staged version simply because of the audience's knowledge of its popular or mass dissemination (Leicester 1994: 247).

Readers obviously have different expectations than do spectators at a play or film or interactive participants in the new media. Showing is as different from telling as it is from interacting with a story. But even within one of these modes—especially showing—there are, as we have already seen, important distinctions to be made. Knowing stage audiences have different expectations and demands than knowing film or television audiences, as the hybrid case of Ingmar Bergman's *Magic Flute* reveals. The Swedish Radio commissioned this "production" of Mozart's opera, which became an "adaptation," for its golden jubilee. It was shown on television on New Year's Day 1975 in Sweden and later released as a film. It is a self-reflexive presentation of a staged production in a studio reconstruction of the famous eighteenth-century Drottningholm Theatre. The camera records not only the stage action but also the audience responses and the actors' activities backstage. Arguably, fans of the opera, watching either on TV or on film, might respond differently from others, as they watch their own rapt attention and enjoyment being represented by the filmed audience. Swedes who watched it on television as a family show may have been pleased with the charm and humor of the opera itself and of the film of it. Fans of Bergman's other films might have been disappointed at this existentialist director's rather sunny version of Mozart's most metaphysical opera, despite its clear citation of earlier Bergman motifs (Tambling 1987: 132–34). All "screen operas," however, have different viewing conditions and expectations than either staged operas or normal films, thanks to the guiding and controlling role of the camera and the differences in scale and level of distance/proximity (Citron 2000: 12–13).

Interactive art forms too involve distinct sets of expectations—at least for knowing audiences. To an audience mostly trained on private or public computers in the form of ATMs or information kiosks, being faced with an interactive electronic installation work in a public space like a museum may cause confusion and even alarm. Artist Ken Feingold admitted he was unhappy about how people engaged with one of his computerized works in a gallery because he had to accept that they expected "unambiguous" interaction: "It actually disappointed me tremendously, as I expected the audience, and the audience turned participants, to bring to interactive works the same capacity for abstraction, metaphor and ambiguity that is well-deployed and comfortable when viewing painting, or other artworks" (Feingold 2002: 124). Audiences need to learn—that is, to be taught—how to be knowing audiences in terms of medium. The expectations of videogame players, on the contrary, certainly include being made participants, being allowed to enter the narrative and visual world of, usually, a film, and being able to enact its logic both physically and cognitively.

Differently knowing audiences bring different information to their interpretations of adaptations. For example, film buffs likely see new movies through the lenses of other ones. Watching Kenneth Branagh's 1989 film adaptation of *Henry V*, they are probably going to see it as much as an adaptation of Laurence Olivier's famous 1944 film as of one of Shakespeare's play, translating the early version's shining clean world, with its self-conscious and stylized theatricalism, into the dank and dirty one of filmic realism. From the dark days of the end of World War II to the time of post-Falklands postimperialism, the message to British audiences changed, or so the differing vision of the two adapting actor-directors would suggest. Similarly, audiences that are well versed in British cinema might argue that Sally Potter's *Orlando* (1994) was adapting *that* tradition—the films of Derek Jarman, Peter Greenaway, and David Lean—as much as Virginia Woolf's literary work. Potter self-reflexively—and yet still realistically—suggests as much by having Orlando's daughter (not a son, as in the book) take a film camera in hand at the end and become both subject and object. There is yet another way of reading this scene: this female child may not possess any property (the purpose of having a son in the novel), but she, like Potter and her generation of female filmmakers, does possess the power of the male gaze that women were said to have lost with the medium of film (see Mulvey 1975). And, as Sophie Mayer (2005: 173–86) has explored at length, the filming girl and her film together solicit a female gaze from the audience: changing the adapted text here leads to a change in the adapting medium, defying audience expectations.

Similarly, although it is an American film, Philip Kaufman's adaptation of Milan Kundera's Czech novel, translated as *The Unbearable Lightness of Being* (1988) (screenplay by Jean-Claude Carrière), is arguably a response to Czech New Wave cinema as much as to the novel itself. But only a film expert might understand that level of intertextual reference. Or, to use a more straightforward example, how would we respond to an adaptation in the form of a contemporary musical, if we had only ever seen on the musical stage nineteenth-century European operas? What would we make of the amplified voices, the hyperactive choreography, the scaled-down musical resources? Genre and media "literacy," as it is often called, can be crucial to the understanding of adaptations *as adaptations*.

There are still other aspects to this knowingness to be considered in theorizing about the product and process of adaptation. If the audience knows that a certain director or actor has made other films of a particular kind, that intertextual knowledge too might well impinge on their interpretation of the adaptation they are watching. It can also make for amusing in-jokes and ironies. In the novelization of *Spider-Man* by Peter David (2002), Mary Jane finds Harry reading *Interview with a Vampire*. She tells him she has not read it, but she saw the movie and the little girl in it "creeped" her out. The joke here is that Mary Jane is played in the film by Kirsten Dunst, who played that creepy little girl, Claudia, in the movie adaptation of Anne Rice's novel. Sometimes, of course, an audience member may know too much: as an instance, Neil Sinyard found himself irritated, while watching the film *Morte a Venezia*, by Visconti's use of Mahler's *adagietto* from the Fifth Symphony, instead of the more obvious and appropriate choice of the Ninth Symphony, which is about death. His argument was that in moving from tragedy to triumph, the Fifth offers musical associations that run "contrary to the drift of the film": "Its inappropriateness is crippling to a film that prides itself on its cultural refinement" (Sinyard 1986: 129), he asserted.

But what if we do not know Mahler's music this well? What if we see a film or play a game without even knowing the work from which it is adapted or even that such a work exists? What if we are utterly new to the artistic conventions of the adaptation, say, of opera? What if we are unknowing audiences, in other words? I have been arguing that, in these instances, we simply experience the work without the palimpsestic doubleness that comes with knowing. From one perspective, this is a loss. From another, it is simply experiencing the work for itself, and all agree that even adaptations must stand on their own. After all, it was only in France that *films noirs* were actually seen *as adaptations* (of *romans noirs*; Cattrysse 1992: 58). If we do not know Pushkin's *Eugene Onegin* (1878), we cannot be bothered by the fact that it satirizes what Tchaikovsky's 1881 opera adaptation of it offers seriously as deep emotions. But if we do … .

Failure in conveying vision or tone in adaptations of classic works of science fiction seems particularly problematic for fans. The 2004 film of Isaac Asimov's *I, Robot* (1950) by director Alex Proyas and screenwriter Michael Cassutt came under just such attack, but it is only one example of many. The more popular and beloved the novel, the more likely the discontent: witness the negative fan reaction to Paul Verhoeven's 1997 adaptation (screenplay by Edward Neumeier) of Robert A. Heinlein's *Starship Troopers* (1959). Science fiction, however, may be particularly difficult to adapt. As Cassutt has suggested, things of the future in the earlier written narrative are now often things of the past, so setting, characters, and action inevitably have to shift and change (Cassutt 2004). As an adapter himself, he says that he would prefer the opening credits to warn the audience of the inevitable changes. Instead of "based on," they could read "suggested by" or "freely adapted from" to forestall the objections of knowing audiences.

Of course, all these complications of possible reception mean that adapters must satisfy the expectations and demands of both the knowing and the unknowing audience. But there are still other differences in audience experience that adaptations bring to our attention, and these involve such factors as the differences caused by the various media's diverse modes of audience involvement and of their degrees and kinds of immersion.

Modes of engagement revisited

As shown in Chapter 2, telling, showing, and interacting with stories differ in the kind and manner of engagement of the reader (spectator, player). Adapters know this; so too do those who market adaptations. The relatively small "graduate" audience who bought most of the 10,000 hardback copies of Malcolm Bradbury's 1975 ironic campus novel, *The History Man,* was not the same in size or makeup as the 10 million viewers of the BBC television adaptation a few years later (Bradbury 1994: 99). When television buys the rights for this kind of fiction, it knows it can build upon a "preconstructed and preselected audience" (Elsaesser 1994: 93), but that it must also expand that audience considerably and must use all the available persuasive means at its disposal to do so.

Even within a single mode of engagement, however, there are once again major distinctions to be made, especially with performance media. When director Peter Brook filmed Peter Weiss' baroquely entitled play *Die Verfolgung und Ermordung Jean Paul Marats, dargestellt durch die Schauspielgruppe des Hospizes zu Charenton unter Anleitung des Herrn de Sade* (1964) as the more simply named *Marat/ Sade* (1966), he sought a totally cinematic translation of what he had previously done on stage, knowing that spectators of live drama are free to choose at any moment, in any scene, what to look at, whereas with the film he would only be able to show one thing at a time with the camera—what *he* wanted to show. He attempted to break down this limitation by deploying three or four cameras, using twists, advances, and retreats and "trying to behave like what goes on in a spectator's head and simulate his experience" (Brook 1987: 189–90). But even this camera work, he realized, would not do what a stage production does: engage the viewer's *imagination* in a way that film, because of its realism, cannot. Noting the "excessive importance of an image, which is intrusive and whose details stay in the frame long after their need is over," Brook (1987: 192) finally accepted that the reality of the image is what gives to film "its power and its limitation." Or, as another critic has put the difference: "In theatre, the conflict of the hard, undeniable presence of actors together with the conventional artifice of scenery and stage required a suspension of disbelief. On the other hand, narrative cinema, with its flow of action, naturalistic acting, and photographic realism, increasingly involved not so much a suspension as a suppression of disbelief" (LeGrice 2002: 230). A young friend recently admitted to me that, although he loves adaptations, he cannot bear going to stage play versions: they seem so "stagey" and unrealistic to him because he is part of a generation raised on film and television, with their conventions of naturalism and immediacy. Curiously, the three-dimensional world of the stage is far less engaging for him than the two-dimensional screen world.

The human-computer interface offers yet another kind of engagement in a feedback loop between our body and its extensions—the monitor, the keyboard, the joystick, and the mouse, and the processing computer. Katherine Hayles (2001: 37) describes this relationship in this way: "We are the medium and the medium is us". Shelley Jackson's 1995 interactive art work called *Patchwork Girl* is an adaptation of both L. Frank Baum's *Patchwork Girl of Oz* (1913) and Mary Shelley's *Frankenstein* (1818/1831), and it involves us, through our clicking of the mouse, in the kind of activity that is like sewing a patchwork quilt from different fragments of cloth. Our physical acts also allow us to simulate the acts of two female figures: "the heroine Mary Shelley (a fictional counterpart of the author of *Frankenstein),* who assembles a female monster by sewing together body parts collected from different women; and the author, Shelley Jackson, who constructs a narrative identity for the monster from the stories of these women" (Ryan 2005: 524). The creating of mixed media hypertexts like *Patchwork Girl* is the direct result of cutting and suturing, just as is monster-making in the novel:

> The first page to come up on screen is the image of a woman pieced together and crossed by a dotted line. The next link is a title page with collaborative authors: Mary Shelley, Shelley Jackson, and presumably the monster herself. Links from its table of contents take you to rearrangements of the first image … [from which] various sequences of narrative and metafictional texts follow.
>
> (LeClair 2000/2003: 8)

Each mode of engagement therefore also involves what we might call a different "mental act" for its audience, and this too is something that the adapter must take into account in transcoding. Different modes, like different media, act dissimilarly on our consciousness (Marcus 1993: 17). Telling requires of its audience conceptual work; showing calls on its perceptual decoding abilities. In the first, we imagine and visualize a world from black marks on white pages as we read; in the second, our imaginations are preempted as we perceive and then give meaning to a world of images, sounds, and words seen and heard on the stage or screen. Kamilla Elliott calls this a reciprocal relationship between mental imaging and mental verbalizing (2003: 210–12), but more than words are at stake here. Psychoanalytic film theorists argue that audiences are more deeply involved consciously and unconsciously when watching a movie because of the processes of identification, projection, and integration (Marcus 1993: 18). In playing a videogame, of course, we are involved even more directly, physically and mentally, as we concentrate intensely and respond physiologically. Each of these different modes demands of its audiences, in turn, its own decoding processes. In reading, we gather details of narrative, character, context, and the like gradually and sequentially; in seeing a film or play or musical, we perceive multiple objects, relations, and significant signs simultaneously, even if the script or music or soundtrack is resolutely linear. In interactive media, both the simultaneity of film and the sequentiality of texted narrative come together in the game world and its rules/conventions.

Bruce Morrissette noted another important aspect of the mode of engagement involved in audience response when he posed what he thought of as a rhetorical question: "Has the novel ever evoked, even in its most intense action sequence, the physical empathy affecting the muscles, the glands, the pulse, and breathing rate that chase, suspense, and other extremely dynamic sequences in film bring about in most, if not all, viewers?" (Morrissette 1985: 26). But what about the *frisson* of which opera lovers speak, when the hair on the back of the neck stands up in ecstatic response to a soprano's high note? Has any film or novel ever managed *that*? And none of the telling or performing media can likely beat the degree of the active physical involvement of interactive art and especially videogames. The *Die Hard* films (1988, 1989, 1995), no matter how intense their "extremely dynamic sequences," would find it hard to beat the game versions' participatory excitement, intense concentration, engagement of kinesthetic skills, competitive energy, and provoking of often involuntary physical reactions (see Bryce and Rutter 2002: 78).

Part of this difference in physical response is a result of a difference in the audience's experience of space and time in each of these modes. When playing a computer game, we may be part of a multiplayer group, but we play, often at home, as solitary individuals, much as we read. We often have a dedicated space where we can concentrate and will not be bothered. We are alone with our computer, sitting close to the screen so that the game's world takes up our visual field, and the sound (thanks to earphones, often) dominates all, immersing us completely. This kind of gaming is a private mode; although gaming with a group of friends or in arcades is more public, it is still individualized.

With performance media, on the contrary, we frequently sit in the dark in a collectivity and respond to what we are all seeing and hearing (being shown) at the same time. Walter Benjamin (1968: 231) saw this as a mass response, the opposite of the contemplative individual response to viewing a painting. Peter Brook agreed, arguing that film in particular engulfs its audience with the image in all its immediacy: "When the image is there in all its power, at the precise moment when it is being received, one can neither think, nor feel, nor imagine anything else" (Brook 1987: 190). The theater audience, in contrast, is more distanced from the action; indeed it is at a fixed distance physically, even if actors can create intimacy through their "presence." Brook noted that "the degree of involvement is always varying . ... This is why theatre permits one to experience something in an incredibly powerful way, and at the same time to retain a certain freedom. This double illusion is the very foundation both of the theatre experience and of dramatic form. The cinema follows this principle with their close-up and the long shot, but the effect is very different" (Brook 1987: 190)—in part because of the difference between live and mediated action. For this reason, Christian Metz sees the film viewer as an isolated and distanced voyeur with no relation to the actors whom he or she regards with "unauthorized scopophilia" (Metz 1974: 185). In film, of course, our distance from the characters whose story we watch changes, depending on camera angle and type of shot. But in first-person new media art, we actually become the character and travel through an animated version of their world. Space is now something to navigate interactively: "being there" is as important to the pleasure of gaming as is "doing things" (Ryan 2001: 309).

Television too presents spatial challenges for the adapter: like the film spectator, the TV viewer does not share a space with the dramatic events the way a theater audience does, but is "reduced to a pair of eyes" (J. Miller 1986: 207) that look at a *picture* of actual objects that represent a world, rather than at the objects themselves (as on stage). And, like film, television is a representational and realist medium: "A television or film screen provides a window onto a world that is supposed to extend beyond the visible screen, and has the optics of reality. The audience sitting in the theatre knows perfectly well that however realistic the world on the stage appears to be it does not extend beyond the proscenium arch" (J. Miller 1986: 206). When films were watched in the once customary dark, silent, large movie theaters, with "intense light beams ... projected from behind toward luminous surfaces in front" (Flitterman-Lewis 1992: 217), there was a cocoon-like feeling of both anonymous collectivity and immersive enclosure that we cannot experience watching film DVDs at home on the television set.

It is not only space, however, but also time that is experienced differently by audiences in the various media; this difference creates new problems for adaptations across media. The much-discussed "presentness" of television (Cardwell 2002: 83–92), for instance, is both real and yet belied by the fact that, as we watch it at home, we are interrupted by advertisements, by family members and friends, and by telephone calls in a way that we rarely are when watching a film in a cinema or a musical in a theater (at least if all the cell phones are actually turned off). But the privacy and domesticity of TV when we are watching film videos or DVDs are related to those of reading and game playing. In all these modes, we control how much we experience and when. Most obviously, readers are always in control of the process of solitary reading. But novels take time and often lots of it to consume; films must be shorter, in part because of the audience's inability to halt the process, except by leaving the theater.

Artist Stan Douglas rather sadistically plays with precisely this idea of time and the movie audience's entrapment in his 16-mm film installation called *Journey into Fear* (2001). As its title suggests, it is an adaptation, not only of the 1940 Eric Ambler novel but also of the 1942 and 1975 film adaptations and of Melville's *The Confidence Man* (1857) too, in fact. The viewer is caught watching an unending loop of film that works through all possible permutations of dialogue dubbed and synched to talking heads. There is no escape, no exit for 157 hours from this particular "journey into fear." What these distinctions among media and modes point to is an obvious difference in how we become immersed in an adapted story—physically, intellectually, and psychologically.

Kinds and degrees of immersion

In Chapter 1, I suggested that all three modes of engagement can be considered immersive: the act of reading a print text immerses us through imagination in another world, seeing a play or film immerses us visually and aurally, and interacting with a story in a videogame or in a theme park adds a physical, enacted dimension. In each there is a sense of being "transported" (Gerrig 1993: 12), in psychological and emotional terms. The recent advent of interactive electronic media has engendered more talk about the desirability of this immersive experience. Yet surely the experimentation undertaken decades ago with works like the early 3-D films and "Aromarama," when perfumes and other odors were dispersed in cinemas to match the content of the screen images, betrays an even earlier desire for at least physical immersion. With that desire, however, comes a certain suspicion that intense engagement of any kind will limit the critical sense: "Movies don't help you to develop independence of mind," according to Pauline Kael (quoted in Peary and Shatzkin 1977: 3). Nor do videogames, say others (Grau 2003: 10). But each medium and each mode of engagement brings with it not only different possible kinds (imaginative, visual, physical) and degrees of immersion, identification, and distance but also different critical traditions that have valued one extreme or the other.

Reader-response theory, which flourished in Europe and North America in the 1980s, may be partly responsible for the change in the way we think about reception in the mode of telling. Thanks to the work of theorists like Wolfgang Iser, Stanley Fish, and Michael Riffaterre, readers are no longer considered passive recipients of textual meaning but active contributors to the aesthetic process, working with the text to decode signs and then to create meaning. To these theorists, it was not simply the "ambiguities and semantic resistances" of a difficult modernist writer like Joyce that demanded "a restless, active reader" (Dinkla 2002: 30); for them, *all* readers are engaged in the active making of textual meaning. Stage audiences, argued theater semioticians in the same years, are an active dimension of the meaning-making of any play, not only in their interpretive work but also in their physical and emotional responses at the time of viewing. Stage conventions distance audiences, even as the live presence of actors on stage makes for more intense identification. In operas and musicals, the unrealistic conventions of singing act to distance us, but the music counters that by provoking identification and a strong affective response. Clearly the adapter working from one mode to another has to take into account these different ways of involving the audience.

This may be no easy task, however, thanks to other critical traditions. When adapting to film, should an adapter believe the theory that the spectator is going to be self-consciously "*all-perceiving*" and all-powerful (Metz 1974: 173–74) or the rather different view that the spectator will always be in collusion, desiring "magic transport" and so resisting "recognition of the artifice in favor of immersion in the illusion" (LeGrice 2002: 230)? Can this involvement be controlled by camera movement, for instance? Take any one of the "heritage" British adaptations for film or television of a classic novel like Jane Austen's *Pride and Prejudice*. Their common long takes, combined with beautiful images, might well "elicit a contemplative appreciative gaze, giving us time both to look and to experience emotion" along with the character whose eyes the camera follows (Cardwell 2002: 141).

Given that the influential early media guru, Marshall McLuhan, felt that "hot media" like television were "low in participation" and "cool media" like literature were "high in participation or completion by the audience" (1996: 162), we can only imagine what he would have made of this description of the audience experience in the scenario for first-person shooters in a certain kind of videogame: "You find yourself, usually unintentionally, in a strange, hostile place, unarmed and vulnerable ... . You must explore the place to find weapons and other useful items, moving through the many game arenas or levels on some form of quest. In the process you must fight and/or avoid many enemies or monsters" (Morris 2002: 82–83). We move—and control our own movement—through a 3-D fictional world, with a sense of embodiment in the game space, a heterocosm we may already know in a non-animated version through the film from which the game is adapted. Our primary identification is directly through "the constant first-person point of view, the player's own sense of agency and experience of interactivity" (Morris 2002: 89). The player becomes at once protagonist and director in a way no performance spectator or reader ever can (Grau 2003: 8–9; Tong and Tan 2002: 101). Instead of just interpreting, the player intervenes in a kind of "frenetic virtual world" (Mactavish 2002: 34). Interactivity brings a greater degree of immersion, both mentally and physically, in the here and now. Response must be rapid: successful hand-eye coordination and puzzle solving involve learned skills and moves (King and Krzywinska 2002a: 22–23). And players play to win. The aim of any game is to keep the player on the verge of mastery but also on the verge of losing control, just like the avatars or characters *in* the game (Weinbren 2002: 183).

In videogames, therefore, there are aural (music, sound effects), visual, and kinesthetic provocations to response in the active gaming portion that make the mode of engagement one of real participation and thus the degree of immersion intense: we feel physically present in the mediated environment, rather than in our real world (Ryan 2001: 66). Anything that reminds us that we are only gaming destroys this illusion, for immersion in this mode relies on the transparency of the medium; effective games, like theme parks and rituals, must eschew the metafictional or the self-reflexive (Ryan 2001: 284). In the cinematic cut-scenes that frame the gaming, the narrative is both set up and brought to closure, but in them the player is transformed into a spectator, with all the formal and interpretive expectations of any film viewer (Howells 2002: 118). This bringing together of showing and interacting challenges any neat compartmentalization of modes of engagement, but the videogame player has more of an active role in shaping the story than does the audience for a film, play, or even novel (Mactavish 2002: 33). Multiplayer role-playing games involve participants in still other ways through player interaction. Tolkien's novels spawned *Dungeons and Dragons* board and computer games, which in turn became MUDs, narrative worlds in which participants can insert themselves. The programming system allows users in different places to communicate within the same virtual space, becoming characters and creating a collective narrative.

Similar things can happen in interactive fiction. Here too the viewer is not a voyeur and is connected to the story more than by means of emotional identification with a character, as in the telling and showing modes. Instead, "[t]he former audience is lifted out of their seat of distanced contemplation and placed in the limelight of subjective physical involvement: addressed as a storyboard controller, co-author, actor or self-performer" (Zapp 2002: 77). We can now become active participants in a heterocosm—either a fantastic or a realistic one (Ryan 2005: 527). Back in 1926 Virginia Woolf had seen that were it possible to capture the "exactitude of reality and its surprising power of suggestion,"

> we should see violent changes of emotion produced by their collision. The most fantastic contrasts could be flashed before us with a speed which the writer can only toil after in vain; the dream architecture of arches and battlements, of cascades falling and fountains rising, which sometimes visits us in sleep or shapes itself in half-darkened rooms, could be realized before our waking eyes. No fantasy could be too far-fetched or insubstantial. The past could be unrolled, distances annihilated.
>
> (Woolf: 1926: 309–10)

She was, of course, writing about cinema, however, and not interactive fiction.

Although again less immersive than videogames, what has been called "expanded cinema" using "multimedia data, visualization and manipulation" (Blunck 2002: 54) does allow members of the audience to become an integral part of the experience by controlling the way in which the story unfolds. If we think back to how important the soliciting of audience participation was for those classical theoreticians of rhetoric or for oral storytellers, we might get a clearer sense of how the audience can figure in the thinking of the adapter working in these emergent forms called "interactive storytelling" that are made possible by broadband and virtual technologies: "Interactive stories are certainly ideal for people who like things like thinking about how to resolve a conflict (in thrillers or courtroom films, for instance), or for people who are not just good listeners, but also like posing investigative questions" (Wand 2002: 177). Audiences have to learn new navigational strategies and accept a new and altered relationship with the creator of the work; in return they are given new kinds of encounters with virtual and fictional worlds that might inspire technological awe as much as increased physical and cognitive immersion. But someone creates those encounter possibilities beforehand. Hypertext fiction, for example, like *afternoon, a story* (1987) by Michael Joyce, one of the founding writers of this mode, offers the reader a variety of narrative threads to choose from, but all have been written by the author in advance. The form may be reader controlled, but the content is not. This is "selective interactivity" (Ryan 2001: 206), and the text is as much a database to be searched as a world in which to be immersed (Ryan 2004c: 342)—which may explain why there have been so few adaptations to or from this medium.

For this and other reasons, the new media are not without their detractors, who often suggest that it may not only be the difficulty of access or mastery that prevents adapters from rushing to use these new forms to attract new audiences. Paul Willeman has articulated many of the ideological arguments against these interactive forms. He points out that their mode of address—imperative or vocative (file, cut, paste, move)—is conducive to "authoritarian and advertising discourses," belying that rhetoric of immersion and freedom: in actual fact, he says we can only obey or ignore orders (Willeman 2002: 15). He sees this as a reduction in the scope of action "which now has to be conducted according to rigorously policed protocols, by a trivialization of the fields where interaction is encouraged, such as games and bulletin boards, and by increasing isolation of the allegedly interacting individuals" (Willeman 2002: 14–15). The so-called interactivity allowed—that is, with specific, preformatted templates—is less truly interactive, he argues, than other representational media "from religious rituals to painting, novels and cinema" (Willeman 2002: 14). According to this argument, pen and paper and the call and response of gospel and jazz music are more interactive than the electronic media today that only "allow" audiences to interact with the story.

Nevertheless, there are manifest differences in the kind and degree of immersion in the three modes of engagement. The sorts of changes and interventions by users/audiences differ. We may be as much controlled as controllers, but we are still immersed differently in a world with which we interact than with one we are either told about or shown. Think of the difference between simply sitting in a theater and seeing the film of *Pirates of the Caribbean* and going on either the original theme park ride from which the movie is adapted or DisneyQuest's interactive version of it at Disney World. As we plunge into the dark, in both versions, we are told that "Dead men tell no tales!" Neither do rides like this, at least not in the conventional narrative sense: enacting or participating replaces telling. Because people go to theme parks in groups and want to share experiences, the designers of the indoor interactive version have created what they call a virtual reality "overwhelming immersive experience on the high seas" (Schell and Shochet 2001) through a simple physical interface. One person steers at a real helm and controls the direction of the "trip"; three others man six cannons. Together they try to defeat virtual enemy pirate ships and sea monsters while collecting and defending as much gold as they can in five minutes. The designers admit to controlling the pace to make sure that, in the space of five minutes, excitement will grow to a climax. The wrap-around 3-D screens and surround sound, plus the motion platform of the boat, guarantee a sensory experience of considerable intensity that no videogame, much less novel or film can match.

Knowing or unknowing, we experience adaptations across media differently than we do adaptations within the same medium. But even in the latter case, adaptation *as adaptation* involves, for its knowing audience, an interpretive doubling, a conceptual flipping back and forth between the work we know and the work we are experiencing. As if this were not complex enough, the context in which we experience the adaptation—cultural, social, historical—is another important factor in the meaning and significance we grant to this ubiquitous palimpsestic form. When Peter Brook and Jean-Claude Carrière adapted the *Mahabharata* in 1975, they not only moved from storytelling to film but also from an Indian into a French context. In the process, they realized that they needed some way to bridge cultures and chose to add a French narrator to connect the two worlds. They were not alone in facing this kind of challenge.

■ ■ ■

Questions and projects

1. How would you describe the different pleasures of watching an adaptation? Examine one of those pleasures closely in a particular adaptation. How do those pleasures lead to a particular understanding of the film as adaptation?

2. Imagine a spectrum of viewers who possess varying degrees of "knowing" and "not knowing" the source text of a specific adaptation. Discuss how those different levels of knowledge could lead to different understandings or readings of that film.

References

Allen, Robert C., ed. 1992. *Channels of discourse, reassembled: Television and contemporary criticism.* Chapel Hill, NC: University of North Carolina Press.

Axelrod, Mark. 1996. Once upon a time in Hollywood; or, the commodification of form in the adaptation of fictional texts to the Hollywood cinema. *Literature/Film Quarterly* 24 (2): 201–8.

Barnes, Julian. 1998. *England, England.* London: Picador.

Bauer, Leda V. 1928. The movies tackle literature. *American Mercury* 14: 288–94.

Blunck, Annika. 2002. Towards meaningful spaces. In Rieser and Zapp 2002a, 54–63.

Bradbury, Malcolm. 1994. The novelist and television drama. In Elsaesser, Simons, and Bronk 1994, 98–106.

Brook, Peter. 1987. Filming a play. In *The shifting point: Theatre, film, opera, 1946–1987.* New York: Harper and Row, 189–92.

Bryce, Jo, and Rutter, Jason. 2002. Spectacle of the deathmatch: Character and narrative in first-person shooters. In King and Krzywinska 2002a, 66–80.

Cardwell, Sarah. 2002. *Adaptation revisited: Television and the classic novel.* Manchester: Manchester University Press.

Cassutt, Michael. 2004. It happens. http://www.scifi.com/sfw/current/cassutt.html. 5 August.

Cattrysse, Patrick. 1992. Film (adaptation) as translation: Some methodological proposals. *Target* 4 (1): 53–70.

Citron, Marcia J. 2000. *Opera on screen.* New Haven, CT: Yale University Press.

Conte, Gian Biagio. 1986. *The rhetoric of imitation: Genre and poetic memory in Virgil and other Latin poets.* Ed. Charles Segal. Ithaca, NY: Cornell University Press.

Culler, Jonathan. 1975. *Structural poetics: Structuralism, linguistics, and the study of literature.* Ithaca, NY: Cornell University Press.

Dinkla, Söke. 2002. The art of narrative—towards the *Floating Work of Art*. In Rieser and Zapp 2002a, 27–41.

DuQuesnay, Ian M. le M. 1979. From Polyphemus to Corydon: Virgil, *Eclogue* 2 and the *Idylls* of Theocritus. In West and Woodman 1979, 35–69.

Elliott, Kamilla. 2003. *Rethinking the novel/film debate.* Cambridge: Cambridge University Press.

Ellis, John. 1982. The literary adaptation. *Screen* 23 (May–June): 3–5.

Flitterman-Lewis, Sandy. 1992. Psychoanalysis, film, and television. In R.C. Allen 1992, 203–46.

Gerrig, Richard J. 1993. *Experiencing narrative worlds: On the psychological activities of reading.* New Haven, CT: Yale University Press.

Grau, Oliver. 2003. *Virtual art: From illusion to immersion.* Trans. Gloria Custance. Cambridge, MA: MIT Press.

Groen, Rick. 2004. Bad kitty! Very bad kitty! *Globe and Mail*, 23 July: R1.

Hayles, Katherine N. 2001. The transformation of narrative and the materiality of hypertext. *Narrative* 9 (1): 21–39.

Honig, Joel. 2001. A novel idea. *Opera News* 66 (2): 20–23.

Howells, Sach A. 2002. Watching a game, playing a movie: When media collide. In King and Krzywinska 2002a, 110–21.

King, Geoff, and Krzywinska, Tanya, eds. 2002a. *ScreenPlay: Cinema/videogames/interfaces.* London: Wallflower Press.

———. 2002b. Cinema/videogames/interfaces. In King and Krzywinska 2002a, 1–32.

———. 2002c. Die hard/try harder: Narrative spectacle and beyond, from Hollywood to videogame. In King and Krzywinska 2002a, 50–65.

Lachiusa, Michael John. 2002. Genre confusion. *Opera News* 67 (2): 12–15, 73.

Laurel, Brenda. 2005. New players, new games, http://www.tauzero.com/Brenda_Laurel/Recent_Talks/New Players. 3 June 2005.

LeClair, Tom. 2000/2003. False pretenses, parasites and monsters. http://www.altx.com/ebr. 22 May 2005.

LeGrice, Malcolm. 2002. Virtual reality—tautological oxymoron. In Rieser and Zapp 2002a, 227–36.

Leicester, H. Marshall, Jr. 1994. Discourse and the film text: Four readings of *Carmen. Cambridge Opera Journal* 6 (3):

245–82.

Lentricchia, Frank, and McLaughlin, Thomas, eds. 1995. *Critical terms for literary study*, 2nd ed. Chicago: University of Chicago Press.

Mactavish, Andrew. 2002. Technological pleasure: The performance and narrative of technology in *Half-Life* and other high-tech computer games. In King and Krzywinska 2002a, 33–49.

Marcus, Millicent. 1993. *Filmmaking by the book: Italian cinema and literary adaptation*. Baltimore, MD: Johns Hopkins University Press.

Mayer, Sophie. 2005. Script girls and automatic women: A feminist film poetics. Ph.D. diss., University of Toronto.

McLuhan, Marshall. 1996. *Essential McLuhan*. Ed. Eric McLuhan and Frank Zingrone. New York: Basic Books.

McNally, Terrence. 2002. An operatic mission: Freshen the familiar. *New York Times*. 1 Sept., Arts and Leisure: 19, 24.

Metz, Christian. 1974. *Film language: A semiotics of the cinema*. Trans. Michael Taylor. New York: Oxford University Press.

Miller, J. Hillis. 1995. Narrative. In Lentricchia and McLaughlin 1995, 66–79.

Morris, Sue. 2002. First-person shooters—a game apparatus. In King and Krzywinska 2002a, 81–97.

Morrissette, Bruce. 1985. *Novel and film: Essays in two genres*. Chicago, IL: University of Chicago Press.

Most, Andrea. 2004. *Making Americans: Jews and the Broadway musical*. Cambridge, MA: Harvard University Press.

Mulvey, Laura. 1975. Visual pleasure and narrative cinema. *Screen* 16 (3): 6–18.

Murray, Janet H. 1997. *Hamlet on the holodeck: The future of narrative in cyberspace*. New York: Free Press.

Ondaatje, Michael. 1997. Foreword to Minghella 1997: vii-x.

Osborne, Laurie O. 1997. Poetry in motion: Animating Shakespeare. In Boose and Burt 1997a, 103–20.

Peary, Gerald, and Shatzkin, Roger, eds. 1977. *The classic American novel and the movies*. New York: Frederick Ungar.

Rieser, Martin, and Zapp, Andrea, eds. 2002a. *New screen media: Cinema / art / narrative*. London: British Film Institute.

Ryan, Marie-Laure. 2001. *Narrative as virtual reality: Immersion and interactivity in literature and electronic media*. Baltimore: Johns Hopkins University Press.

——, ed. 2004a. *Narrative across media: The languages of storytelling*. Lincoln, NE: University of Nebraska Press.

——. 2004b. Introduction. In Ryan 2004a, 1–40.

——. 2004c. Will new media produce new narratives? In Ryan 2004a, 337–59.

——. 2005. Narrative and digitality: Learning to think with the medium. In Phelan and Rabinowitz 2005, 515–28.

Schell, Jesse, and Shochet, Joe. 2001. Designing interactive theme park rides: Lessons learned creating Disney's *Pirates of the Caribbean—Battle for the buccaneer gold*. http://www.gdconf.com/archives/2001/schell.doc. 31 August 2004.

Shaughnessy, Nicola. 1996. Is s/he or isn't s/he?: Screening *Orlando*. In Cartmell, Hunter, Kaye, and Whelehan 1996, 43–55.

Sinyard, Neil. 1986. *Filming literature: The art of screen adaptation*. London: Croom Helm.

Taylor, Andrew. 2004. Reflections on Phillips' and Greenaway's *A TV Dante*. In Iannucci 2004a, 145–52.

Thompson, Kristin. 2003. *Storytelling in film and television*. Cambridge, MA: Harvard University Press.

Tong, Wee Liang, and Tan, Marcus Cheng Chye. 2002. Vision and virtuality: The construction of narrative space in film and computer games. In King and Krzywinska 2002a, 98–109.

Wand, Eku. 2002. Interactive storytelling: The renaissance of narration. In Rieser and Zapp 2002a, 163–78.

Weinbren, Grahame. 2002. Mastery (sonic c'est moi). In Rieser and Zapp 2002a, 179–91.

Whipp, Glenn. 2002. Director remains faithful to Harry. *Toronto Star 21 Sept*: H4.

Willeman, Paul. 2002. Reflections on digital imagery: Of mice and men. In Rieser and Zapp 2002a, 14–26.

Wober, J.M. 1980. Fiction and depiction: Attitudes to fifteen television series and the novels from which they were made. *Special Report*. Audience Research Department, Independent Broadcast Authority.

Woolf, Virginia. 1926. The movies and reality. *New Republic* 47 (4 Aug.): 308–10.

Zapp, Andrea. 2002. net.drama://myth/mimesis/mind_mapping/. In Rieser and Zapp 2002a, 77–89.

Chapter 34

Henry Jenkins

SEARCHING FOR THE ORIGAMI
The Matrix and transmedia storytelling

FILM AND MEDIA STUDIES PROFESSOR, HENRY JENKINS, has been a pioneer in the cutting-edge study of "transmedia storytelling" – the process of telling stories across various media platforms all of which serve as self-contained stories that also contribute to an overall whole. This process of storytelling serves, on the one hand, to create potentially lucrative media franchises and, on the other, to generate immersive story worlds for the pleasure (and sometimes confusion) of a contemporary audience. Using the multiple layers of intertextual media—from movies to video games to comic books—surrounding *The Matrix* as a case study, Jenkins traces the contours and complexities of storytelling in the age of media convergence where narrative worlds become too large to be contained within a single medium. More than just a clever business model to increase profits, transmedia storytelling, Jenkins argues, is central to an active participatory popular culture and serves to define entertainment in an era of collective intelligence.

■ ■ ■

SEARCHING FOR THE ORIGAMI: *THE MATRIX* AND TRANSMEDIA STORYTELLING
HENRY JENKINS

From *Convergence Culture: Where Old and New Media Collide*. New York: New York University Press, 2006, pp. 93–130

In Peter Bagge's irreverent "Get It?," one of some twenty-five comic stories commissioned for *The Matrix* homepage, three buddies are exiting a theater where they have just seen the Wachowski brothers' opus for the first time. For two of them, *The Matrix* (1999) has been a transforming experience:

"Wow! That was Awesome!"

"*The Matrix* was the best movie I've seen in ages!"

The third is perplexed. From the looks on the faces of the prune-faced older couple walking in front of them, his confusion is not unique. "I didn't understand a word of it!"

"You mean you were sitting there scratching your head through the whole thing?"

When they retire to a local bar, one buddy persists in trying to explain *The Matrix*, patiently clarifying its concepts of manufactured reality, machine-controlled worlds, and "jacking in," while the other, being more pessimistic, grumbles, "I don't think you'll ever understand it." As their hapless pal walks away, the other two turn out to be cybernetic "agents," who concede that it's a good thing most humans don't get this movie, since "the fewer humanoids who comprehend what's really going on, the fewer we will have to destroy."[1]

Noted for his sharp social satire in *Hate* comics (1990–1998) and, more recently, *Reason* magazine, Bagge contrasts between those who "get" *The Matrix* and those who do not. Something about the film leaves some filmgoers feeling inadequate and others empowered. Bagge wrote this strip immediately after the release of the first *Matrix* movie. As we will see, things get only more complicated from there.

No film franchise has ever made such demands on its consumers. The original movie, *The Matrix*, took us into a world where the line between reality and illusion constantly blurred, and where the bodies of humans are stored as an energy source to fuel machines while their minds inhabit a world of digital hallucinations. Neo, the hacker protagonist-turned-messiah, gets pulled into the Zion resistance movement, working to overturn the "agents" who are shaping reality to serve their own ambiguous ends. The prerelease advertising for the first film tantalized consumers with the question, "What is the Matrix?" sending them to the Web in search of answers. Its sequel, *The Matrix Reloaded* (2003), opens without a recap and assumes we have almost complete mastery over its complex mythology and ever-expanding cast of secondary characters. It ends abruptly with a promise that all will make sense when we see the third installment, *The Matrix Revolutions* (2003). To truly appreciate what we are watching, we have to do our homework.

The filmmakers plant clues that won't make sense until we play the computer game. They draw on the back story revealed through a series of animated shorts, which need to be downloaded off the Web or watched off a separate DVD. Fans raced, dazed and confused, from the theaters to plug into Internet discussion lists, where every detail would be dissected and every possible interpretation debated.

When previous generations wondered whether they "got" a movie, it was usually a European art movie, an independent film, or perhaps an obscure late-night cult flick. But *The Matrix Reloaded* broke all box office records for R-rated films, earning a mind-boggling $134 million in revenues in its first four days of release. The video game sold more than a million copies in its first week on the market. Before the movie was even released, 80 percent of the American film-going public identified *The Matrix Reloaded* as a "must see" title.[2]

The Matrix is entertainment for the age of media convergence, integrating multiple texts to create a narrative so large that it cannot be contained within a single medium. The Wachowski brothers played the transmedia game very well, putting out the original film first to stimulate interest offering up a few Web comics to sustain the hard-core fan's hunger for more information, launching the anime in anticipation of the second film, releasing the computer game alongside it to surf the publicity, bringing the whole cycle to a conclusion with *The Matrix Revolutions*, and then turning the whole mythology over to the players of the massively multiplayer online game. Each step along the way built on what has come before, while offering new points of entry.

The Matrix is also entertainment for the era of collective intelligence. Pierre Lévy speculates about what kind of aesthetic works would respond to the demands of his knowledge cultures. First, he suggests that the "distinction between authors and readers, producers and spectators, creators and interpreters will blend" to form a "circuit" (not quite a matrix) of expression, with each participant working to "sustain the activity" of the others. The artwork will be what Lévy calls a "cultural attractor," drawing together and creating common ground between diverse communities; we might also describe it as a cultural activator, setting into motion their decipherment, speculation, and elaboration. The challenge, he says, is to create works with enough depth that they can justify such large-scale efforts: "Our primary goal should be to prevent closure from occurring too quickly."[3] *The Matrix* clearly functions both as a cultural attractor and a cultural activator. The most committed consumers track down data spread across multiple media, scanning each and every text for insights into the world. Keanu Reeves explained to *TV Guide* readers: "What audiences make of *Revolutions* will depend on the amount of energy they put into it. The script is full of cul-de-sacs and secret passageways."[4] Viewers get even more out of the experience if they compare notes and share resources than if they try to go it alone.

In this chapter, I am going to describe *The Matrix* phenomenon as transmedia storytelling. A transmedia story unfolds across multiple media platforms, with each new text making a distinctive and valuable contribution to the whole. In the ideal form of transmedia storytelling, each medium does what it does best—so that a story might be introduced in a film, expanded through television, novels, and comics; its world might be explored through game play or experienced as an amusement park attraction. Each franchise entry needs to be self-contained so you don't need to have seen the film to enjoy the game, and vice versa. Any given product is a point of entry into the franchise as a whole. Reading across the media sustains a depth of experience that motivates more consumption. Redundancy burns up fan interest and causes franchises to fail. Offering new levels of insight and experience refreshes the franchise and sustains consumer loyalty. The economic logic of a horizontally integrated entertainment industry—that is, one where a single company may have roots across all of the different media sectors—dictates the flow of content across media. Different media attract different market niches. Films and television probably have the most diverse audiences; comics and games the narrowest. A good transmedia franchise works to attract multiple constituencies by pitching the content somewhat differently in the different media. If there is, however, enough to sustain those different constituencies—and if each work offers fresh experiences—then you can count on a crossover market that will expand the potential gross.

Popular artists—working in the cracks of the media industry—have realized that they can surf this new economic imperative to produce more ambitious and challenging works. At the same time, these artists are building a more collaborative relationship with their consumers: working together, audience members can process more story information than previously imagined. To achieve their goals, these storytellers are developing a more collaborative model of authorship, co-creating content with artists with different visions and experiences at a time when few artists are equally at home in all media.

Okay, so the franchise is innovative, but is *The Matrix* any good? Many film critics trashed the later sequels because they were not sufficiently self-contained and thus bordered on incoherent. Many games critics trashed the games because they were too dependent on the film content and did not offer sufficiently new experiences to players. Many fans expressed disappointment because their own theories about the world of *The Matrix* were more rich and nuanced than anything they ever saw on the screen. I would argue, however, that we do not yet have very good aesthetic criteria for evaluating works that play themselves out across multiple media. There have been far too few fully transmedia stories for media makers to act with any certainty about what would constitute the best uses of this new mode of storytelling, or for critics and consumers to know how to talk meaningfully about what works or doesn't work within such franchises. So let's agree for a moment that *The Matrix* was a flawed experiment, an interesting failure, but that its flaws did not detract from the significance of what it tried to accomplish.

Relatively few, if any, franchises achieve the full aesthetic potential of transmedia storytelling—yet. Media makers are still finding their way and are more than willing to let someone else take the risks. Yet, at the heart of the entertainment industry, there are young and emerging leaders (such as Danny Bilson and Neil Young at Electronic Arts or Chris Pike at Sony Interactive) who are trying to push their companies to explore this new model for entertainment franchises. Some of them are still regrouping from their first bleeding-edge experiments in this space (Dawson's Desktop, 1998)—some of which had modest success (*The Blair Witch Project*, 1999), some of which they now saw as spectacular failures (*Majestic*, 2001). Some of them are already having closed-door meetings to try to figure out the best way to ensure more productive collaborations across media sectors. Some are working on hot new ideas masked by nondisclosure agreements. All of them were watching closely in 2003, which *Newsweek* had called "The Year of *The Matrix*," to see how audiences were going to respond to the Wachowski brothers' ambitious plans.[5] And, like Peter Bagge, they were looking at the faces of people as they exit the theaters, demanding to know if they "got" it.

What is The Matrix?

Umberto Eco asks what, beyond being loved, transforms a film such as *Casablanca* (1942) into a cult artifact, First, he argues, the work must come to us as a "completely furnished world so that its fans can quote characters and episodes as if they were aspects of the private sectarian world."[6] Second, the work must be encyclopedic, containing a rich array of information that can be drilled, practiced, and mastered by devoted consumers.

The film need not be well made, but it must provide resources consumers can use in constructing their own fantasies: "In order to transform a work into a cult object one must be able to break, dislocate, unhinge it so that one can remember only parts of it, irrespective of their original relationship to the whole."[7] And the cult film need not be coherent: the more different directions it pushes, the more different communities it can sustain and the more different experiences it can provide, the better. We experience the cult movie, he suggests, not as having "one central idea but many," as "a disconnected series of images, of peaks, of visual icebergs."[8]

The cult film is made to be quoted, Eco contends, because it is made from quotes, archetypes, allusions, and references drawn from a range of previous works. Such material creates "a sort of intense emotion accompanied by the vague feeling of a déjà vu."[9] For Eco, *Casablanca* is the perfect cult movie because it is so unselfconscious in its borrowings: "Nobody would have been able to achieve such a cosmic result intentionally."[10] And for that reason, Eco is suspicious of cult movies by design. In the age of postmodernism, Eco suggests, no film can be experienced with fresh eyes; all are read against other movies. In such a world, "cult has become the normal way of enjoying movies."[11]

If *Casablanca* exemplifies the classical cult movie, one might see *The Matrix* as emblematic of the cult movie in convergence culture. Here's science fiction writer Bruce Sterling trying to explain its fascination:

> First and foremost, the film's got pop appeal elements. All kinds of elements: suicidal attacks by elite special forces, crashing helicopters, oodles of martial arts, a chaste yet passionate story of predestined love, bug-eyed monsters of the absolute first water, fetish clothes, captivity and torture and daring rescue, plus really weird, cool submarines. ... .

There's Christian exegesis, a Redeemer myth, a death and rebirth, a hero in self-discovery, *The Odyssey*, Jean Baudrillard (lots of Baudrillard, the best part of the film), science fiction ontological riffs of the Philip K. Dick school, Nebuchadnezzar, the Buddha, Taoism, martial-arts mysticism, oracular prophecy, spoon-bending telekinesis, Houdini stage-show magic, Joseph Campbell, and Godelian mathematical metaphysics.[12]

And that's just in the first film!

The film's endless borrowings also spark audience response. Layers upon layers of references catalyze and sustain our epistemophilia; these gaps and excesses provide openings for the many different knowledge communities that spring up around these cult movies to display their expertise, dig deep into their libraries, and bring their minds to bear on a text that promises a bottomless pit of secrets. Some of the allusions—say, the recurring references to "through the looking glass," the White Rabbit, and the Red Queen, or the use of mythological names for the characters (Morpheus, Persephone, Trinity)—pop off the screen upon first viewing. Others—say, the fact that at one point, Neo pulls a copy of Baudrillard's *Simulacra and Simulation* (1981/1995) from his shelf—become clear only after you talk about the film with friends. Some—like the fact that Cypher, the traitor, is referred to at one point as "Mr. Reagan" and asks for an alternative life where he is an actor who gains political powers—are clear only when you put together information from multiple sources. Still others—such as the license plates on the cars (such as DA203 or IS5416), which reference specific and context-appropriate Bible verses (Daniel 2:3 or Isaiah 54:16)—may require you to move through the film frame by frame on your DVD player.

The deeper you drill down, the more secrets emerge, all of which can seem at any moment to be *the key* to the film. For example, Neo's apartment number is 101, which is the room number of the torture chamber in George Orwell's *1984* (1949). Once you've picked up this number, then you discover that 101 is also the floor number for the Merovingians' nightclub and the number of the highway where the characters clash in *The Matrix Reloaded*, and from there, one can't help but believe that all of the other various numbers in the film may also carry hidden meanings or connect significant characters and locations together. The billboards in the backgrounds of shots contain cheat codes that can be used to unlock levels in the *Enter the Matrix* (2003) game.

The sheer abundance of allusions makes it nearly impossible for any given consumer to master the franchise totally. In this context, the Wachowski brothers have positioned themselves as oracles—hidden from view most of the time, surfacing only to offer cryptic comments, refusing direct answers, and speaking with a single voice. Here, for example, are some characteristic passages from one of their few online chat sessions:

QUESTION: "There are quite a few hidden messages in the movie that I notice the more I watch it. Can you tell me about how many there are?"

WACHOWSKI BROTHERS: "There are more than you'll ever know."[13]

QUESTION: "Have you ever been told that The Matrix has Gnostic overtones?"

WACHOWSKI BROTHERS: "Do you consider that to be a good thing?"

QUESTION: "Do you appreciate people dissecting your movie? Do you find it a bit of an honor or does it annoy you a little, especially when the person may have it all wrong?

WACHOWSKI BROTHERS: "There's not necessarily ever an 'all wrong.' Because it's about what a person gets out of the movie, what an individual gets out of the movie."

The Wachowskis were more than happy to take credit for whatever meanings the fans located, all the while implying there was more, much more, to be found if the community put its collective mind to work. They answered questions with questions, clues with clues. Each clue was mobilized, as quickly as it materializes, to support a range of different interpretations.

So what is *The Matrix*? As one fan demonstrates, the question can be answered in so many different ways:

- Is it a "love story"? (Keanu Reeves said that in an interview.)
- Is it a "titanic struggle between intuition and controlling intellect"? (Hugo Weaving – Agent Smith said that in an interview about *The Matrix Reloaded*.)
- Is it a story about religious salvation? (*The Matrix Reloaded* was banned in Egypt, because it is "too religious.")
- Is it a story about "Believing in something" or about "Not believing in something"?
- Is it a story about "artificial humanity" or "artificial spirituality"?
- Is it a story with elements from Christianity? Buddhism? Greek mythology? Gnosticism? Hinduism? Freemasonry? The secret society Priory of Zion (Prieure du Notre Dame du Sion) (and its connection to the use of chessboard imagery at the castle Rennes-le-Chateau)?
- Is Neo a reincarnated Buddha? Or a new Jesus Christ (Neo Anderson = new son of man)?
- Is it a science-fiction movie? A fantasy movie?
- Is it a story about secret societies keeping society under control?
- Is it a story about men's history or men's future?
- Is it just a visually enhanced futuristic Kung-Fu movie? A modern Japanime?[14]

Even with all of the film releases out on DVD, and thus subject to being scrutinized indefinitely, the most dedicated fans were still trying to figure out *The Matrix* and the more casual viewers not accustomed to putting this kind of work into an action film had concluded that the parts just didn't add up.

"Synergistic storytelling"

The Matrix is a bit like *Casablanca* to the nth degree, with one important difference: *Casablanca* is a single movie; *The Matrix* is three movies and more. There is, for example *The Animatrix* (2003), a ninety-minute program of short animated films, set in the world of *The Matrix* and created by some of the leading animators from Japan, South Korea, and the United States, including Peter Chung (*Aeon Flux*, 1995), Yoshiaki Kawajiri (*Wicked City*, 1987), Koji Morimoto (*Robot Carnival*, 1987) and Shinichiro Watanabe (*Cowboy Bebop*, 1998). *The Matrix* is also a series of comics from cult writers and artists, such as Bill Sienkiewicz (*Elektra: Assassin*, 1986–87), Neil Gaiman (*The Sandman*, 1989–96), Dave Gibbons (*Watchmen*, 1986–87), Paul Chadwick (*Concrete*, 1987–98), Peter Bagge (*Hate*, 1990–98) David Lapham (*Stray Bullets*, 1995–), and Geof Darrow (*Hard Boiled*, 1990–92). *The Matrix* is also two games—*Enter the Matrix*, produced by David Perry's Shiny Entertainment, and a massively multiplayer game set in the world of *The Matrix*, scripted in part by Paul Chadwick.

The Wachowskis wanted to wind the story of *The Matrix* across all of these media and have it all add up to one compelling whole. Producer Joel Silver describes a trip the filmmakers took to Japan to talk about creating an animated television series: "I remember on the plane ride back, Larry sat down with a yellow pad and kinda mapped out this scheme we would do where we would have this movie, and these video games and these animated stories and they would all interact together."[15] David Perry described the game as, in effect, another *Matrix* movie. The actors reportedly were uncertain which scenes were being filmed for the game and which for the movie.[16] The consumer who has played the game or watched the shorts will get a different experience of the movies than one who has simply had the theatrical film experience. The whole is worth more than the sum of the parts.

We may better understand how this new mode of transmedia storytelling operates by looking more closely at some of the interconnections between the various *Matrix* texts. For example, in the animated short, *Final Flight of the Osiris* (2003), the protagonist, Jue, gives her life trying to get a message into the hands of the Nebuchadnezzar crew. The letter contains information about the machines boring their way down to Zion. In the final moments of the anime, Jue drops the letter into a mailbox. At the opening of *Enter the Matrix*, the player's first mission is to retrieve the letter from the post office and get it into the hands of our heroes. And the opening scenes of *The Matrix Reloaded* show the characters discussing the "last transmissions of the Osiris." For people who see only the movie, the sources of the information remain unclear, but someone who has a transmedia experience will have played an active role in delivering the letter and may have traced its trajectory across three different media.

Similarly, the character of The Kid is introduced in another of the animated shorts, *The Kid's Story* (2003), about a high school student who discovers on his own the truth about the Matrix as Neo and his friends try to rescue him from the agents. In *The Matrix Reloaded*, they reencounter The Kid on the outskirts of Zion, where he begs to join their crew: "It's fate. I mean you're the reason I'm here, Neo," but Neo defers, saying, "I told you, kid, you found me, I didn't find you. … You saved yourself." The exchange is staged as if everybody in the audience would know what the two are talking about and feels more like a scene involving an already established character than their first on-screen introduction. The Kid's efforts to defend Zion became one of the core emotional hooks in the climactic battle in *Revolutions*.

In *The Matrix: Reloaded*, Niobe appears unexpectedly in the freeway chase just in time to rescue Morpheus and Trinity, but for people who play the game, getting Niobe to the rendezvous point is a key mission. Again, near the end of *The Matrix Reloaded*, Niobe and her crew are dispatched to blow up the power plant, but apart from the sense that the plan must have worked to enable what we see on screen to unfold, the actual details of her operation is not represented, so that it can be played out in more depth in the game. We reencounter Niobe at the start of *The Matrix Revolutions* where she was left off at the climax of *Enter the Matrix*.

By the standards of classical Hollywood storytelling, these gaps (such as the failure to introduce The Kid or to explain where Niobe came from) or excesses (such as the reference to "the last transmission of the Osiris") confuse the spectator.[17] The old Hollywood system depended on redundancy to ensure that viewers could follow the plot at all times, even if they were distracted or went out to the lobby for a popcorn refill during a crucial scene. The new Hollywood demands that we keep our eyes on the road at all times, and that we do research before we arrive at the theater.

This is probably where *The Matrix* fell out of favour with the film critics, who were used to reviewing the film and not the surrounding apparatus. Few of them consumed the games or comics or animated shorts, and, as a consequence, few absorbed the essential information they contained. As Fiona Morrow from the *London Independent* explained, "You can call me old-fashioned—what matters to me is the film and only the film. I don't want to have to 'enhance' the cinematic experience by overloading on souped-up flimflam."[18] Those who realized there was relevant information in those other sources were suspicious of the economic motives behind what *Salon's* Ivan Askwith called "synergistic storytelling": "Even if the new movies, game, and animated shorts live up to the high standards set by the first film, there's still an uneasy feeling that Warner Bros. is taking advantage of *The Matrix's* cult following to cash in while it can." *The San Jose Mercury's* Mike Antonucci saw it all as "smart marketing" more than "smart storytelling."[19]

So let's be clear: there are strong economic motives behind transmedia storytelling. Media convergence makes the flow of content across multiple media platforms inevitable. In the era of digital effects and high-resolution game graphics, the game world can now look almost exactly like the film world—because they are reusing many of the same digital assets. Everything about the structure of the modern entertainment industry was designed with this single idea in mind—the construction and enhancement of entertainment franchises. As we saw in the previous chapter, there is a strong interest in integrating entertainment and marketing, to create strong emotional attachments and use them to make additional sales. Mike Saksa, the senior vice president for marketing at Warner Bros., couldn't be more explicit on this point: "This [*The Matrix*] truly is Warner Bros's synergy. All divisions will benefit from the property. ... We don't know what the upside is, we just know it's going to be very high."[20]

The enormous "upside" is not just economic, however. *The Matrix* franchise was shaped by a whole new vision of synergy. Franchising a popular film, comic book, or television series is nothing new. Witness the endless stream of plastic figurines available in McDonald's Happy Meals. Cross-promotion is everywhere. But much of it, like the Happy Meals toys are pretty lame and easily forgotten. Current licensing arrangements ensure that most of these products are peripheral to what drew us to the original story in the first place. Under licensing, the central media company—most often the film producers—sells the rights to manufacture products using its assets to an often unaffiliated third party; the license limits what can be done with the characters or concepts to protect the original property. Soon, licensing will give way to what industry insiders are calling "co-creation." In co-creation, the companies collaborate from the beginning to create content they know plays well in each of their sectors, allowing each medium to generate new experiences for the consumer and expand points of entry into the franchise.

The current licensing system typically generates works that are redundant (allowing no new character background or plot development), watered down (asking the new media to slavishly duplicate experiences better achieved through the old), or riddled with sloppy contradictions (failing to respect the core consistency audiences expect within a franchise). These failures account for why sequels and franchises have a bad reputation. Franchise products are governed too much by economic logic and not enough by artistic vision. Hollywood acts as if it only has to provide more of the same, printing a *Star Trek* (1966) logo on so many widgets. In reality, audiences want the new work to offer new insights and new experiences. If media companies reward that demand, viewers will feel greater mastery and investment; deny it, and they stomp off in disgust.

In 2003, I attended a gathering of top creatives from Hollywood and the games industry, hosted by Electronic Arts; they were discussing how co-creation might work. Danny Bilson, the vice president of intellectual property development at Electronic Arts, organized the summit on what he calls "multiplatform entertainment."[21] As someone who has worked in film (*The Rocketeer*, 1991), television (*The Sentinel*, 1996; *Viper*, 1994), and comics (*The Flash*, 1990), as well as in games, Bilson understands the challenges of creating content in each medium and of coordinating between them. He wants to develop games that do not just move Hollywood brands into a new media space, but also contribute to a larger storytelling system. For this to work, he argues, the story needs to be conceived in transmedia terms from the start:

> We create movies and games together, organically, from the ground up, with the same creative force driving them. Ideally that creative force involves movie writers and directors who are also gamers. In any art form, you have to like it to do well with it; in fact, you have to be a fan of it to do well at it. Take that talent and build multiplatform entertainment. The movie and game are designed together, the game deepens and expands the fiction but

does not simply repeat material from the film. It should be organic to what made the film experience compelling.

Going forward, people are going to want to go deeper into stuff they care about rather than sampling a lot of stuff. If there's something I love, I want it to be bigger than just those two hours in the movie theater or a one hour a week experience on TV. I want a deepening of the universe. ... I want to participate in it. I've just been introduced to the world in the film and I want to get there, explore it. You need that connection to the world to make participation exciting.

Bilson wants to use his position as the man who supervises all creative properties for the world's leading game publisher to create multiplatform entertainment. His first step is the development of *GoldenEye: Rogue Agent* (2004), a James Bond game where one gets to play the part of classic Bond villains like Dr. No or Goldfinger, restaging confronting 007 within digital re-creations of the original movie sets. Everything in the game is consistent with what viewers know from the Bond movies, but the events are seen from an alternative moral perspective.

This level of integration and coordination is difficult to achieve even though the economic logic of the large media conglomerates encourages them to think in terms of synergies and franchises. So far, the most successful transmedia franchises have emerged when a single creator or creative unit maintains control. Hollywood might well study the ways that Lucasfilm has managed and cultivated its *Indiana Jones* (1981) and *Star Wars* (1977) franchises. When *Indiana Jones* went to television, for example, it exploited the medium's potential for extended storytelling and character development: *The Young Indiana Jones Chronicles* (1992) showed the character take shape against the backdrop of various historical events and exotic environments. When *Star Wars* moved into print, its novels expanded the timeline to show events not contained in the film trilogies, or recast the stories around secondary characters, as did the *Tales from the Mos Eisley Cantina* (1995) series, which fleshes out those curious-looking aliens in the background of the original movies.[22] When *Star Wars* went to games, those games didn't just enact film events; they showed what life would be like for a Jedi trainee or a bounty hunter. Increasingly, elements are dropped into the films to create openings that will only be fully exploited through other media.

While the technological infrastructure is ready, the economic prospects sweet and the audience primed, the media industries haven't done a very good job of collaborating to produce compelling transmedia experiences. Even within the media conglomerates, units compete aggressively rather than collaborate. Many believe that much greater coordination across the media sectors is needed to produce transmedia content. Electronic Arts (EA) explored this model in developing its *Lord of the Rings* titles. EA designers worked on location with Peter Jackson's production unit in New Zealand. As Neil Young, the man in charge of the *Lord of the Rings* franchise for EA, explained,

I wanted to adapt Peter's work for our medium in the same way that he has adapted Tolkien's work for his. Rather than being some derivative piece of merchandise along the same continuum with the poster, the pen, the mug, or the key chain, maybe we could turn that pyramid up the side of its head, leverage those pieces which have come before, and become the pinnacle of the property instead of the basement. Whether you are making the mug, whether you are making the key chain, or whether you are making the game, pretty much everyone has access to the same assets. For me, when I took over *Lord of the Rings,* that seemed untenable if you want to build something that captured Peter's unique vision, and Howard Shore's music, and the actors, and the look of this world, and ... you needed much more direct access. Instead of working exclusively through the consumer products group, we built a partnership directly with the New Line Production company, 3 Foot 6 Productions that functioned as a clearing house for the things we needed.[23]

This system allowed them to import thousands of "assets" from the film production into the game, ensuring an unprecedented degree of fidelity to the details of Tolkien's world. At the same time, working closely with Jackson and the other filmmakers gave Young greater latitude to explore other dimensions of that world that would not appear on screen.

David Perry has described his relationship with the Wachowski brothers in very similar terms:

The Wachowskis get games. They were standing on the set making sure we got what we needed to make this a quality game. They know what gamers are looking for. With the power they have in Hollywood, they were able to make sure we got everything we needed to make this game what it is.[24]

Perry's team logged four months of motion capture work with Jada Pinkett Smith, the actress who played Niobe, and other members of the *Matrix* cast. All the movements and gestures were created by actual performers working on the set and were seen as extensions of their characterizations. The team used alpha-mapping to create a digital version of the actress's face and still preserve her own facial expressions. The game incorporated many of the special effects that had made *The Matrix* so distinctive when the film was first released, allowing players to duplicate some of the stunts that Woo-ping Yuen (the noted Hong Kong fight choreographer) had created through his wire work or to move through "bullet time," the film's eye-popping slow-motion technique.

Collaborative authorship

Media conglomeration provided a context for the Wachowski brothers' aesthetic experiment—they wanted to play with a new kind of storytelling and use Warner Bros.'s blockbuster promotion to open it to the largest possible public. If all they wanted was synergy, they could have hired hack collaborators who could crank out the games, comics, and cartoons. This has certainly occurred in other cases that have sought to imitate the *Matrix* model. More recent films, ranging from *Charlie's Angels* to *The Riddick Chronicles*, from *Star Wars* to *Spider-Man*, have developed cartoons, for example, which were intended to bridge between sequels or foreshadow plot developments. Of these, only the *Star Wars* shorts worked with a distinguished animator—in that case, Genndy Tartakovsky (*Samurai Jack*).[25] By contrast, the Wachowskis sought animators and comic-book writers who already had cult followings and were known for their distinctive visual styles and authorial voices. They worked with people they admired, not people they felt would follow orders. As Yoshiaki Kawajiri, the animator of *Program*, explained, "It was very attractive to me because the only limitation was that I had to play within the world of the *Matrix*; other than that I've been able to work with complete freedom."[26]

The Wachowski brothers, for example, saw co-creation as a vehicle for expanding their potential global market, bringing in collaborators whose very presence evoked distinct forms of popular culture from other parts of the world. Geof Darrow, who did the conceptual drawings for the ships and technology, trained under Moebius, the Eurocomics master noted for images that blur the line between the organic and the mechanical. The filmmakers hired the distinguished Hong Kong fight choreographer, Woo-ping Yuen, who was noted for having helped to reinvent Jackie Chan's screen persona, developing a distinctive female style for Michelle Yeoh, and bringing Asian-style fighting to global cinema via *Crouching Tiger, Hidden Dragon* (2000).[27] The films were shot in Australia and the directors drew on local talent, such as Baz Luhrmann's longtime costume designer Kym Barrett. The cast was emphatically multiracial, making use of African American, Hispanic, South Asian, southern European, and aboriginal performers to create a Zion that is predominantly nonwhite.

Perhaps most importantly, the Wachowski brothers sought out Japanese and other Asian animators as collaborators on *The Animatrix*. They cite strong influences from manga (Japanese comics) and anime, with Morpheus's red leather chair a homage to *Akira* (1988) and Trinity's jumpsuit coming straight from *Ghost in the Shell* (1995). Arguably, their entire interest in transmedia storytelling can be traced back to this fascination with what anthropologist Mimi Ito has described as Japan's "media mix" culture. On the one hand, the media mix strategy disperses content across broadcast media, portable technologies such as game boys or cell phones, collectibles, and location-based entertainment centers from amusement parks to game arcades. On the other, these franchises depend on hypersociability, that is, they encourage various forms of participation and social interactions between consumers.[28] This media mix strategy has made its way to American shores through series like *Pokémon* (1998) and *Yu-Gi-Oh!* (1998), but operates in even more sophisticated forms in more obscure Japanese franchises. In bringing in Japanese animators closely associated with this media mix strategy, the Wachowski brothers found collaborators who understood what they were trying to accomplish.

The Wachowski brothers didn't simply license or subcontract and hope for the best. The brothers personally wrote and directed content for the game, drafted scenarios for some of the animated shorts, and co-wrote a few of the comics. For fans, their personal engagement made these other *Matrix* texts a central part of the "canon." There was nothing fringe about these other media. The filmmakers risked alienating filmgoers by making these elements so central to the unfolding narrative. At the same time, few filmmakers have been so overtly fascinated with the process of collaborative authorship. *The Matrix* Web site provides detailed interviews with every major technical worker, educating fans about their specific contributions. The DVDs, shipped with hours of "the making of" documentaries, again focused on the full range of creative and technical work.

We can see collaborative authorship at work by looking more closely at the three comics stories created by Paul Chadwick, "Déjà Vu," "Let It All Fall Down," and "The Miller's Tale."[29] Chadwick's comics were ultimately so embraced by the Wachowski brothers that Chadwick was asked to help develop plots and dialogue for the online *Matrix* game. Chadwick might at first glance seem an odd choice to work on a major movie franchise. He is a cult comics creator best known for *Concrete* and for his strong commitment to environmentalist politics. Working on the very edges of the superhero genre, Chadwick uses Concrete, a massive stone husk that houses the mind of a former political speech writer, to ask questions about the current social and economic order. In *Think Like a Mountain* (1996), Concrete joins forces with the Earth First! movement that is spiking trees and waging war on the lumber industry to protect an old-growth forest.[30] Chadwick's political commitments are expressed not only through the stories but also through his visual style: he creates full-page spreads that integrate his protagonists into their environments, showing the small creatures that exist all around us, hidden from view but impacted by the choices we make.

Chadwick uses his contributions to *The Matrix* to extend the film's critique of the urban landscape and to foreground the ecological devastation that resulted from the war between the machines and the humans. In "The Miller's Tale," his protagonist, a member of the Zion underground, tries to reclaim the land so that he can harvest wheat and make bread. Risking his life, he travels across the blackened landscape in search of seeds with which he can plant new crops; he grinds the grain to make loaves to feed the resistance movement. Chadwick's miller is ultimately killed, but the comic ends with a beautiful full-page image of the plant life growing over the ruins we recognize from their appearance in several of *The Matrix* movies. Of all of the comics' artists, Chadwick shows the greatest interest in Zion and its cultural rituals, helping us to understand the kinds of spirituality that emerges from an underground people.[31]

While he builds on elements found in the films, Chadwick finds his own emphasis within the material and explores points of intersection with his own work. The other animators and comic artists more or less do the same, further expanding the range of potential meanings and intertextual connections within the franchise.

The art of world-making

The Wachowski brothers built a playground where other artists could experiment and fans could explore. For this to work, the brothers had to envision the world of *The Matrix* with sufficient consistency that each installment is recognizably part of the whole and with enough flexibility that it can be rendered in all of these different styles of representation—from the photorealistic computer animation of *Final Flight of the Osiris* to the blocky graphics of the first *Matrix* Web game. Across those various manifestations of the franchise, there are dozens of recurring motifs, such as the falling green *kanji*, Morpheus's bald head and mirror-shade glasses, the insectlike ships, Neo's hand gestures, or Trinity's acrobatics.[32] No given work will reproduce every element, but each must use enough that we recognize at a glance that these works belong to the same fictional realm. Consider one of the posters created for *The Matrix* Web page: an agent dressed in black is approaching a bullet-shattered phone booth, his gun in hand, while in the foreground the telephone dangles off its hook. Which of these elements is exclusive to *The Matrix*? Yet, anyone familiar with the franchise can construct the narrative sequence from which this image must have been taken.

More and more, storytelling has become the art of world building, as artists create compelling environments that cannot be fully explored or exhausted within a single work or even a single medium. The world is bigger than the film, bigger even than the franchise—since fan speculations and elaborations also expand the world in a variety of directions. As an experienced screenwriter told me, "When I first started, you would pitch a story because without a good story, you didn't really have a film. Later, once sequels started to take off, you pitched a character because a good character could support multiple stories. And now, you pitch a world because a world can support multiple characters and multiple stories across multiple media." Different franchises follow their own logic: some, such as the *X-Men* (2000) movies, develop the world in their first installment and then allow the sequels to unfold different stories set within that world; others, such as the *Alien* (1979) films or George Romero's *Living Dead* (1968) cycle, introduce new aspects of the world with each new installment, so that more energy gets put into mapping the world than inhabiting it.

World-making follows its own market logic, at a time when filmmakers are as much in the business of creating licensed goods as they are in telling stories. Each truly interesting element can potentially yield its own product lines, as George Lucas discovered when he created more and more toys based on the secondary characters in his movies. One of them, Boba Fett, took on a life of its own, in part through children's play.[33] Boba Fett eventually became the protagonist of his own novels and games and played a much larger role in the later films. Adding too much information, however, carries its own risks: fans had long debated whether Boba Fett could actually be a woman underneath the helmet, since we never actually got to see the character's face or hear its voice. But as Lucas fleshed out the character, he also closed down those possibilities, preempting important lines of fan speculation even as he added information that might sustain new fantasies.

As the art of world-making becomes more advanced, art direction takes on a more central role in the conception of franchises. A director such as Tim Burton developed a reputation less as a storyteller (his films often are ramshackle constructions) than as a cultural geographer, cramming every shot with evocative details. The plot and the performances in *Planet of the Apes* (2001), for example, disappointed more or less everyone, yet every shot rewards close attention as details add to our understanding of the society the apes have created; a hard-core fan studies how they dress, how they designed their buildings, what artifacts they use, how they move, what their music sounds like, and so forth. Such a work becomes more rewarding when we watch it on DVD, stopping and starting to absorb the background. Some fans trace these tendencies back to *Blade Runner* (1982), where urbanologist Syd Mead was asked to construct the future metropolis on the recognizable foundations of existing Los Angeles. These visions could only be fully appreciated by reading through the coffee-table books that accompany the release of such films and provide commentary on costume design and art direction decisions.

New-media theorist Janet Murray has written of the "encyclopedic capacity" of digital media, which she thinks will lead to new narrative forms as audiences seek information beyond the limits of the individual story.[34] She compares this process of world-making in games or cinema to Faulkner, whose novels and short stories added together to flesh out the life and times of a fictional county in Mississippi. To make these worlds seem even more real, she argues, storytellers and readers begin to create "contextualizing devices—color-coded paths, time lines, family trees, maps, clocks, calendars, and so on."[35] Such devices "enable the viewer to grasp the dense psychological and cultural spaces [represented by modern stories] without becoming disoriented."[36] The animated films, the game, and the comics function in a similar way for *The Matrix*, adding information and fleshing out parts of the world so that the whole becomes more convincing and more comprehensible.

Mahiro Maeda's "The Second Renaissance" (2003), for example, is a richly detailed, rapid-paced chronicle that takes us from the present moment to the era of machine rule that opens the first *Matrix* movie. The animated short is framed as a documentary produced by a machine intelligence to explain the events leading to their triumph over the humans. "The Second Renaissance" provides the timeline for *The Matrix* universe, giving a context for events such as the trial of B116ER, the first machine to kill a human, the Million Machine March, and the "darkening of the skies" that are mentioned in other *Matrix* texts. As Maeda explains,

In Part One, we see humans treat robots as objects, while in Part Two the relationship between human being and robot switches, as humans are studied by the machines. I enjoyed examining how the two sides changed . .... I wanted to show the broadness of the society, and how the robots were such a part of the background of life that they were treated as mere objects by human beings. ... In exploring the history of *The Matrix*, I wanted to show the audience how badly the robots were being treated. The images we see of the robots being abused are buried in the Archives. There are many examples of mankind's cruelty in the past.[37]

To shape our response to the images of human authorities crushing the machines, Maeda tapped the image bank of twentieth-century civil unrest, showing the machines throwing themselves under the treads of tanks in a reference to Tiananmen Square or depicting bulldozers rolling over mass graves of crashed robots in a nod toward Auschwitz.

"The Second Renaissance" provides much of the historical background viewers need as they watch Neo return to 01, the machine city, to plead with its inhabitants for assistance in overthrowing the agents. Without learning about the many times the machines had pursued diplomatic relations with the humans and been rejected, it is hard to understand why his approach yielded such transforming results. Similarly, the images showing the humans' efforts to block off the Earth from solar rays resurfaces when we see Neo's craft go above the cloud level and into the blue skies that humans have not seen for generations. "Second Renaissance" introduces many of the weapons deployed during the final assault on Zion, including the massive "mecha" suits the humans wear as they fight off the invaders.

At the same time, "The Second Renaissance" builds upon "Bits and Pieces of information," one of *The Matrix* comics drawn by Geof Darrow from a script by the Wachowski brothers.[38] The comic introduced the pivotal figure of B116ER, the robot who kills his masters when he is about to be junked and whose trial first asserted the concept of machine rights within human culture. Much like "The Second Renaissance," "Bits and Pieces of Information" draws on the existing iconography of human-rights struggles, quoting directly from the Dred Scott decision and naming the robot after Bigger Thomas, the protagonist of Richard Wright's *Native Son* (1940). If the first feature film started with a simple opposition between man and machines, the Wachowski brothers used these inter-texts to create a much more emotionally nuanced and morally complicated story. In the end, man and machines can still find common interests despite centuries of conflict and oppression.

Most film critics are taught to think in terms of very traditional story structures. More and more, they are talking about a collapse of storytelling. We should be suspicious of such claims, since it is hard to imagine that the public has actually lost interest in stories. Stories are basic to all human cultures, the primary means by which we structure, share, and make sense of our common experiences. Rather, we are seeing the emergence of new story structures, which create complexity by expanding the range of narrative possibility rather than pursuing a single path with a beginning, middle, and end. *Entertainment Weekly* proclaimed 1999, the year that *The Matrix, Fight Club, The Blair Witch Project, Being John Malkovich, Run Lola Run, Go, American Beauty*, and *The Sixth Sense* hit the market, as "the year that changed the movies." Film-goers educated, on nonlinear media like video games were expecting a different kind of entertainment experience.[39] If you look at such works by old criteria, these movies may seem more fragmented, but the fragments exist so that consumers can make the connections on their own time and in their own ways. Murray notes, for example, that such works are apt to attract three very different kinds of consumers: "the actively engaged real-time viewers who must find suspense and satisfaction in each single episode and the more reflective long-term audience who look for coherent patterns in the story as a whole … [and] the navigational viewer who takes pleasure in following the connections between different parts of the story and in discovering multiple arrangements of the same material."[40]

For all of its innovative and experimental qualities, transmedia storytelling is not entirely new. Take, for example, the story of Jesus as told in the Middle Ages. Unless you were literate, Jesus was not rooted in a book but was something you encountered at multiple levels in your culture. Each representation (a stained-glass window, a tapestry, a psalm, a sermon, a live performance) assumed that you already knew the character and his story from someplace else. More recently, writers such as J. R. R. Tolkien sought to create new fictions that self-consciously imitated the organization of folklore or mythology, creating an interlocking set of stories that together flesh out the world of Middle Earth. Following a similar logic, Maeda explicitly compares "The Second Renaissance" to Homeric epics: "I wanted to make this film as beautiful as a story from ancient Greek myth, and explore what it means to be human, as well as not human, and how the ideas are related to one another. In Greek myths there are moments where the best side of human nature is explored, and others where the protagonists are shown as very cruel. I wanted to bring the same atmosphere to these episodes."[41]

When the Greeks heard stories about Odysseus, they didn't need to be told who he was, where he came from, or what his mission was. Homer was able to create an oral epic by building on "bits and pieces of information" from preexisting myths, counting on a knowledgeable audience to ride over any potential points of confusion. This is why high school students today struggle with *The Odyssey*, because they don't have the same frame of reference as the original audience. Where a native listener might hear a description of a character's helmet and recognize him as the hero of a particular city-state and, from there, know something of his character and importance, the contemporary high school student runs into a brick wall, with some of the information that once made these characters seem so real buried in some arcane tome. Their parents may confront a similar barrier to fully engaging with the film franchises so valued by their children—walking into an *X-Men* movie with no background in comics might leave you confused about some of the minor characters who have much deeper significance to long-term comics readers. Often, characters in transmedia stories do not need to be introduced so much as reintroduced, because they are known from other sources. Just as Homer's audience identified with different characters depending on their city-state, today's children enter the movie with preexisting identifications because they have played with the action figures or game avatars.

The idea that contemporary Hollywood draws on ancient myth structures has become common wisdom among the current generation of filmmakers. Joseph Campbell, the author of *The Hero with a Thousand Faces* (1949), praised *Star Wars* for embodying what he has described as the "monomyth," a conceptual structure abstracted from a cross-cultural analysis of the world's great religions.[42] Today, many screenwriting guides speak about the "hero's journey," popularizing ideas from Campbell, and game designers have similarly been advised to sequence the tasks their protagonists must perform into a similar physical and spiritual ordeal.[43] Audience familiarity with this basic plot structure allows script writers to skip over transitional or expository sequences, throwing us directly into the heart of the action.

Similarly, if protagonists and antagonists are broad archetypes rather than individualistic, novelistic, and rounded characters, they are immediately recognizable. We can see *The Matrix* as borrowing these archetypes both from popular entertainment genres (the hacker protagonist, the underground resistance movement, the mysterious men in black) as well as from mythological sources (Morpheus, Persephone, The Oracle). This reliance on stock characters is especially important in the case of games where players frequently skip through the instruction books and past early cut scenes, allowing little time for exposition before grabbing the controller and trying to navigate the world. Film critics often compared the characters in *The Matrix* films to video game characters. Roger Ebert, for example, suggests that he measured his concern for Neo in *Revolutions* less in terms of affection for the character and "more like the score in a video game."[44] *Slate*'s David Edelstein suggests that a spectacular opening stunt by Trinity in *The Matrix Reloaded* "has the disposable feel of a video game. You can imagine the program resetting itself, and then all of those little zeros and ones reassembling to play again."[45] In both cases, the writers use the video game analogy to imply a disinterest in the characters, yet, for gamers, the experience is one of immediacy: the character becomes a vehicle for their direct experience of the game world. By tapping video game iconography, *The Matrix* movies create a more intense, more immediate engagement for viewers who come into the theater knowing who these characters are and what they can do. As the film continues, we flesh out the stick figures, adding more back story and motivation, and we continue to search for additional insights across other media as we exit the theater.

When I suggest parallels between *The Odyssey* and *The Matrix*, I anticipate a certain degree of skepticism. I do not claim that these modern works have the same depth of incrusted meanings. These new "mythologies," if we can call them that, are emerging in the context of an increasingly fragmented and multicultural society. While *The Matrix* films have been the subject of several books linking them to core philosophical debates, and while many fans see these films as enacting religious myths, articulating spirituality is not their primary function, the perspective they take is not likely to be read literally by their audience, and their expressed beliefs are not necessarily central to our everyday lives. Homer wrote within a culture of relative consensus and stability, whereas *The Matrix* emerges from a time of rapid change and cultural diversity. Its goals are not so much to preserve cultural traditions as to put together the pieces of the culture in innovative ways. *The Matrix* is a work very much of the moment, speaking to contemporary anxieties about technology and bureaucracy, feeding on current notions of multiculturalism and tapping recent models of resistance. The story may reference a range of different belief systems, such as the Judeo-Christian Messiah myth, to speak about these present-day concerns with some visionary force. At the same time, by evoking these earlier narratives, *The Matrix* invites us to read more deeply in the Western tradition and bring what we find there to bear on contemporary media.[46]

Consider, for example, this reading of the tribal celebration in *The Matrix Reloaded* through the lens of biblical interpretation:

> The feet [stamping] on the ground means that Zion is on Earth. Plain and simple. This parallels the Architect scene, and gets to the main thesis. We are cast out of the "perfection" of Heaven and living in the Real World. Symbolically, the Matrix is Heaven. Cypher makes this point in the first movie. The Real World is hard, dirty, and uncomfortable. The Matrix is, well, paradise. This point is made again in the first movie by Agent Smith, who calls the Matrix "the perfect human world" [paraphrased]. Recall that the Architect scene happens in utterly clean, utterly white perfection. The Biblical reference is clear enough. Neo, Trinity, Morpheus, and the rest of Zion have rejected God's Garden of Eden where all their needs are taken care of in favor of a hard, scrabbling existence where at least they have free will.[47]

So, even if you see classical myths as more valuable than their contemporary counterpart, works such as *The Matrix* draw consumers back to those older works, giving them new currency.

Film critic Roger Ebert ridicules this attempt to insert traditional myth into a pop science fiction/kung fu epic:

> These speeches provide not meaning, but the effect of meaning: it sure sounds like those guys are saying some profound things. This will not prevent fanboys from analyzing the philosophy of *The Matrix Reloaded* in endless web postings. Part of the fun is becoming an expert in the deep meaning of shallow pop mythology; there is something refreshingly ironic about becoming an authority on the transient extrusions of mass culture, and Morpheus (Laurence Fishburne) now joins Obi-Wan Kenobi as the Plato of our age.[48]

This criticism looks different if you accept that value arises here from the process of looking for meaning (and the elaboration of the story by the audience) and not purely from the intentionality of the Wachowski brothers. What the Wachowski brothers did was trigger a search for meaning; they did not determine where the audience would go to find their answers.

Additive comprehension

If creators do not ultimately control what we take from their transmedia stories, this does not prevent them from trying to shape our interpretations. Neil Young talks about "additive comprehension." He cites the example of the director's cut of *Blade Runner*, where adding a small segment showing

Deckard discovering an origami unicorn invited viewers to question whether Deckard might be a replicant. "That changes your whole perception of the film, your perception of the ending. ... The challenge for us, especially with *The Lord of the Rings*, is how do we deliver the origami unicorn, how do we deliver that one piece of information that makes you look at the films differently."Young explained how that moment inspired his team: "In the case of *The Lord of the Rings: Return of the King* the added comprehension is the fact that Gandalf is the architect of this plan and has been the architect of this plan for some time. ... Our hope is that you would play the game and that would motivate you to watch the films with this new piece of knowledge which would shift your perception of what has happened in the previous films." Here, Young points toward a possibility suggested by the books but not directly referenced in the films themselves.

Like his colleague Danny Bilson, Young sees transmedia storytelling as the terrain he wants to explore with his future work. His first experiment, *Majestic*, created a transmedia experience from scratch with bits of information coming at the player via faxes, cell-phone calls, e-mail, and Web sites. With *The Lord of the Rings* games, he worked within the constraints of a well-established world and a major movie franchise. Next, he is turning his attention toward creating new properties that can be built from the ground up as cross-media collaborations. His thinking races far ahead: "I want to understand the kinds of story comprehension which are unique to transmedia storytelling. I've got my world, I've got my arcs, some of those arcs can be expressed in the video game space, some of them can be expressed in the film space, the television space, the literary space, and you are getting to the true transmedia storytelling."

With *Enter the Matrix*, the "origami unicorn" takes several forms, most notably refocusing of the narrative around Niobe and Ghost. As the game's designer, David Perry, explains, every element of the game went toward helping us understand who these people are: "If you play as Ghost, who's a Zen Buddhist Apache assassin, you'll automatically ride shotgun in the driving levels, which allow you to fire out the window at agents hunting you down. Niobe is known in Zion as being one of the fastest, craziest drivers in the *Matrix* universe, so when you play the game as her, you'll get to drive through a complex *Matrix* world filled with real traffic and pedestrians, while a computer-controlled Ghost takes out the enemies."[49] Cut scenes (those moments in the game which are prerecorded and not subject to player intervention) give us more insight into the romantic triangle among Niobe, Morpheus, and Locke, which helps to explain, in part, Locke's hostility to Morpheus throughout the film. Having played through the game, you can read the longing and tension within their on-screen relationship. As for Ghost, he remains a background figure in the movie, having only a handful of spoken lines, but his screen appearances reward those who have made the effort to play the game. Some film critics complained about the degree to which Niobe's character displaces Morpheus from the center of *The Matrix Revolutions,* as if a minor character were upstaging a well-established protagonist. Yet, how we felt about Niobe would depend on whether we had played *Enter the Matrix*. Someone who had played the games would have spent, perhaps, a hundred hours controlling Niobe's character, compared to less than four hours watching Morpheus; struggling to keep the character alive and to complete the missions would have resulted in an intense bond that would not be experienced by viewers who saw her on screen only for a handful of scenes.

Perhaps the most spectacular example of "additive comprehension" occurred after the film trilogy had been completed. With little fanfare or warning, on May 26, 2005, Morpheus, Neo's mentor, was killed off in *The Matrix Online,* while trying to reclaim Neo's body that had been carried away by the machines at the end of *Revolutions*. As Chadwick explained, "They wanted to start with something significant and meaningful and shocking and this was it."[50] A major turning point in the franchise occurred not on screen for a mass audience but in game for a niche public.

Even many of those playing the game would not have witnessed the death directly but would have learned about it through rumors from other players or from some other secondary source. Morpheus's death was then used to motivate a variety of player missions within the game world.

EA's Young worried that the Wachowski brothers may have narrowed their audience by making too many demands on them:

> The more layers you put on something, the smaller the market. You are requiring people to intentionally invest more time in what it is you are trying to tell them and that's one of the challenges of transmedia storytelling. ... If we are going to take a world and express it through multiple media at the same time, you might need to express it sequentially. You may need to lead people into a deep love of the story. Maybe it starts with a game and then a film and then television. You are building a relationship with the world rather than trying to put it all out there at once.

Young may well be right. The Wachowski brothers were so uncompromising in their expectations that consumers would follow the franchise that much of the emotional payoff of *Revolutions* is accessible only to people who have played the game. The film's attempts to close down its plot holes disappointed many hard-core fans. Their interest in *The Matrix* peaked in the middle that tantalized them with possibilities. For the casual consumer, *The Matrix* asked too much. For the hard-core fan, it provided too little. Could any film have matched the fan community's escalating expectations and expanding interpretations and still have remained accessible to a mass audience? There has to be a breaking point beyond which franchises cannot be stretched, subplots can't be added, secondary characters can't be identified, and references can't be fully realized. We just don't know where it is yet.

Film critic Richard Corliss raised these concerns when he asked his readers, "Is Joe Popcorn supposed to carry a *Matrix* concordance in his head?"[51] The answer is no, but "Joe Popcorn" can pool his knowledge with other fans and build a collective concordance on the Internet.[52] Across a range of fan sites and discussion lists, the fans were gathering information, tracing allusions, charting chains of commands, constructing timelines, assembling reference guides, transcribing dialogue, extending the story through their own fan fiction, and speculating like crazy about what it all meant. The depth and breadth of *The Matrix* universe made it impossible for any one consumer to "get it" but the emergence of knowledge cultures made it possible for the community as a whole to dig deeper into this bottomless text.

Such works also pose new expectations on critics—and this may be part of what Corliss was reacting against. In writing this chapter, I have had to tap into the collective intelligence of the fan community. Many of the insights I've offered here emerged from my reading of fan critics and the conversations on discussion lists. While I possess some expertise of my own as a longtime science fiction and comics fan (knowing for example the ways that Paul Chadwick's previous work in comics connects to his participation in *The Matrix* franchise), this merely makes me one more member of this knowledge community—someone who knows some things but has to rely on others to access additional information. I may have analytic tools for examining a range of different media but much of what I suggest here about the links between the game and the films, for example, emerged not from my own game playing but from the conversations about the game online. In the process of writing this chapter, then, I became a participant rather than an expert, and there is much about this franchise which I still do not know. In the future, my ideas may feed back into the conversation, but I also will need to tap the public discussion in search of fresh information and insights. Criticism may have once been a meeting of two minds—the critic and the author—but now there are multiple authors and multiple critics.

Inhabiting such a world turns out to be child's play—literally. Transmedia storytelling is perhaps at its most elaborate, so far, in children's media franchises like *Pokémon* or *Yu-Gi-Oh!* As education professors David Buckingham and Julian Sefton-Green explain, "*Pokémon* is something you do, not just something you read or watch or consume."[53] There are several hundred different *Pokémon*, each with multiple evolutionary forms and a complex set of rivalries and attachments. There is no one text where one can go to get the information about these various species; rather, the child assembles what they know about the *Pokémon* from various media with the result that each child knows something his or her friends do not and thus has a chance to share this expertise with others. Buckingham and Sefton-Green explain: "Children may watch the television cartoon, for example, as a way of gathering knowledge that they can later utilize in playing the computer game or in trading cards, and vice versa. ... The texts of *Pokémon* are not designed merely to be consumed in the passive sense of the word. ... In order to be part of the *Pokémon* culture, and to learn what you need to know, you must actively seek out new information and new products and, crucially, engage with others in doing so."[54]

We might see such play with the possibilities of *Pokémon* or *Yu-Gi-Oh!* as part of the process by which young children learn to inhabit the new kinds of social and cultural structures Lévy describes.[55] Children are being prepared to contribute to a more sophisticated knowledge culture. So far, our schools are still focused on generating autonomous learners; to seek information from others is still classified as cheating. Yet, in our adult lives, we are depending more and more on others to provide information we cannot process ourselves. Our workplaces have become more collaborative; our political process has become more decentered; we are living more and more within knowledge cultures based on collective intelligence. Our schools are not teaching what it means to live and work in such knowledge communities, but popular culture may be doing so. In *The Internet Galaxy* (2001), cybertheorist Manuel Castells claims that while the public has shown limited interest in hypertexts, they have developed a hypertextual relationship to existing media content: "Our minds—not our machines—process—culture. ... If our minds have the material capability to access the whole realm of cultural expressions—select them, recombine them—we do have a hypertext: the hypertext is inside us."[56] Younger consumers have become informational hunters and gatherers, taking pleasure in tracking down character backgrounds and plot points and making connections between different texts within the same franchise. And so it is predictable that they are going to be expecting these same kinds of experiences from works that appeal to teens and young adults, resulting in something like *The Matrix*.

Soon, we may be seeing these same hypertextual or transmedia principles applied to the quality dramas that appeal to more mature consumers—shows such as *The West Wing* (1999) or *The Sopranos* (1999), for example, would seem to lend themselves readily to such expectations, and soap operas have long depended on elaborate character relationships and serialized plotlines that could easily expand beyond television and into other media. One can certainly imagine mysteries that ask readers to search for clues across a range of different media or historical fictions that depend on the additive comprehension enabled by multiple texts to make the past come alive for their readers. This transmedia impulse is at the heart of what I am calling convergence culture. More experimental artists, such as Peter Greenaway or Matthew Barney, are already experimenting with how they might incorporate transmedia principles into their work. One can also imagine that kids who grew up in this media-mix culture would produce new kinds of media as transmedia storytelling becomes more intuitive. *The Matrix* may be the next step in that process of cultural evolution—a bridge to a new kind of culture and a new kind of society. In a hunting culture, kids play with bows and arrows. In an information society, they play with information.

Now some readers may be shaking their heads in total skepticism. Such approaches work best with younger consumers, they argue, because they have more time on their hands. They demand way too much effort for "Joe Popcorn," for the harried mom or the working stiff who has just snuggled onto the couch after a hard day at the office. As we have seen, media conglomeration creates an economic incentive to move in this direction, but Hollywood can only go so far down that direction if audiences are not ready to shift their mode of consumption. Right now, many older consumers are left confused or uninvolved with such entertainments, though some are also learning to adapt. Not every story will go in this direction—though more and more stories are traveling across media and offering a depth of experience that would have been unanticipated in previous decades. The key point is that going in deep has to remain an option—something readers choose to do—and not the only way to derive pleasure from media franchises. A growing number of consumers may be choosing their popular culture because of the opportunities it offers them to explore complex worlds and compare notes with others. More and more consumers are enjoying participating in online knowledge cultures and discovering what it is like to expand one's comprehension by tapping the combined expertise of these grassroots communities. Yet, sometimes, we simply want to watch. And as long as that remains the case, many franchises may remain big and dumb and noisy. But don't be too surprised if around the edges there are clues that something else is also going on or that the media companies will offer us the chance to buy into new kinds of experiences with those characters and those worlds.

■ ■ ■

Questions and projects

1. Choose a film or a work of literature that has generated imitations, parodies, and other responses across the Internet (through blogs, YouTube videos, and so forth). Contrast what each brings to the transformation of the original text and how they interact with each other.
2. According to Jenkins, "transmedia storytelling" and "collaborative authorship" complicates—or perhaps makes impossible—the designation of a single or final meaning of a story. Find an example in a transmedia film or literary text that supports this point.

Notes

1   Peter Bagge, "Get It?" http://whatisthematrix.warnerbros.com, reproduced in Andy and Larry Wachowski (eds.), *The Matrix Comics* (New York: Burlyman Entertainment, 2003).
2   On the commercial success of the films, see "The Matrix Reloaded," *Entertainment Weekly*, May 10, 2001.
3   Pierre Lévy, *Collective Intelligence: Mankind's Emerging World in Cyberspace* (Cambridge, MA: Perseus Books, 1997).
4   Franz Lidz, "Rage against the Machines," *TV Guide*, October 25, 2003, http://www.reevesdrive.com/newsarchive/2003/tvg102503.htm.
5   Devin Gordon, "The Matrix Makers," *Newsweek*, January 6, 2003, accessed at http://msnbc.msn.com/id/3067730.
6   Umberto Eco, "*Casablanca*: Cult Movies and Intertextual Collage," in *Travels in Hyperreality* (New York: Harcourt Brace, 1986), p. 198.
7   Ibid.
8   Ibid.

9   Ibid., p. 200.

10 Ibid.

11 Ibid., p. 210.

12 Bruce Sterling, "Every Other Movie Is the Blue Pill," in Karen Haber (ed.), *Exploring the Matrix: Visions of the Cyber Present* (New York: St Martin's Press, 2003), pp. 23–24.

13 This and subsequent quotations are taken from Matrix Virtual Theater, Wachowski Brothers Transcript, November 6, 1999, as seen at http://www.warnervideo.com/matrixevents/wachowski.html.

14 "Matrix Explained: What Is the Matrix?" http://www.matrix-explained com/about_matrix.htm.

15 Joel Silver, as quoted in "Scrolls to Screen: A Brief History of Anime," *The Animatrix* DVD.

16 Ivan Askwith, "A *Matrix* in Every Medium," *Salon*, May 12, 2003, accessed at http://archive.salon.com/tech/feature/2003/05/12/matrix_universe/index_np.html.

17 For a useful discussion, see Kristin Thompson, *Storytelling in the New Hollywood: Understanding Classical Narrative Technique* (Cambridge, MA: Harvard University Press, 1999).

18 Fiona Morrow, "Matrix: The 'trix of the Trade," *London Independent*, March 28, 2003.

19 Mike Antonucci, "Matrix Story Spans Sequel Films, Video Game, Anime DVD," *San Jose Mercury*, May 5, 2003.

20 Jennifer Netherby, "The Neo-Classical Period at Warner; *Matrix* Marketing Mania for Films, DVDs, Anime, Videogame," *Looksmart*, January 31, 2003.

21 Danny Bilson, interview with author, May 2003. All subsequent quotations from Bilson come from that interview.

22 See Will Brooker, *Using the Force: Creativity, Community, and Star Wars Fans* (New York: Continuum, 2002).

23 Neil Young, interview with the author, May 2003. All subsequent quotations from Young come from this interview.

24 John Gaudiosi, "*The Matrix* Video Game Serves as a Parallel Story to Two Sequels on Screen," *Daily Yomiuri*, April 29, 2003.

25 "Three Minute Epics: A Look at *Star Wars: Clone Wars*," February 20, 2003, www.starwars.com/feature/20040220.

26 Interview, Yoshiaki Kawajiri, http://www.intothematrix.com/rl_cmp/rl_interview_kawajiri.html.

27 For a useful overview, see Walter Jon Williams, "Yuen Woo-Ping and the Art of Flying," in Karen Haber (ed.), *Exploring the Matrix: Visions of the Cyber Present* (New York: St. Martin's Press, 2003), pp. 122–125.

28 Mizuko Ito, "Technologies of the Childhood Imagination: *Yugioh*, Media Mixes and Everyday Cultural Production," in Joe Karaganis and Natalie Jeremijenko (eds.), *Network/Netplay: Structures of Participation in Digital Culture* (Durham, N.C.: Duke University Press, 2005).

29 Paul Chadwick, "The Miller's Tale," "Déjà vu," and "Let It All Fall Down," http://whatisthematrix.warnerbros.com/rl_cmp/rl_middles3_paultframe.html. "The Miller's Tale" is reproduced in Andy and Larry Wachowski (eds.), *The Matrix Comics* (New York: Burlyman Entertainment, 2003).

30 Paul Chadwick, *Concrete: Think like a Mountain* (Milwaukie, OR: Dark Horse Comics, 1997).

31 This shared vision may be why Chadwick was asked to develop the plotlines for the Matrix multiplayer online game. For more on Chadwick's involvement, see "The Matrix Online: Interview with Paul Chadwick," Gamespot, http://www.gamespot.com/pc/rpg/matrixonlinetentatvetitle/preview_6108016.html.

32 For a useful discussion of the continuities and discontinuities in a media franchise, see William Uricchio and Roberta E. Pearson, "I'm Not Fooled by That Cheap Disguise," in Roberta E. Pearson and William Uricchio (eds.), *The Many Lives of the Batman: Critical Approaches to a Superhero and His Media* (New York: Routledge, 1991).

33 The audience's role in fleshing out Boba Fett is a recurring reference in Will Brooker, *Using the Force: Creativity, Community and Star Wars Fans* (New York: Continuum, 2002).

34 Janet Murray, *Hamlet on the Holodeck The Future of Narrative in Cyberspace* (Cambridge, MA: mIT Press, 1999), pp. 253–258.

35 Ibid.

36 Ibid.

37   "Mahiro Maeda," interview, at http://www.intothematrix.com/rl_cmp/rl_interview_maeda2.html.

38   Geof Darrow, "Bits and Pieces of Information," accessed at http:// whatisthematrix.warnerbros.com, reproduced in Andy and Larry Wachowski (eds.), *The Matrix Comics* (New York: Burlyman Entertainment, 2003).

39   Jeff Gordinier, "1999: The Year That Changed the Movies," *Entertainment Weekly*, October 10 2004, http://www.ew.com/ew/report/0.6115.271806_7_0_.00.html.

40   Murray, *Hamlet*, p. 257.

41   Maeda, interview.

42   Betty Sue Flowers (ed.), *Joseph Campbell's The Power of Myth with Bill Moyers* (New York Doubleday, 1988).

43   See, for example, M. M. Goldstein, "The Hero's Journey in Seven Sequences: A Screenplay Structure," NE Films, September 1998, http://www .newenglandfilm.com/news/archives/98september/sevensteps.htm; Troy Dunniway, "Using the Hero's Journey in Games," Gamasutra.com, http://www .gamasutra.com/features/2000127/dunniway_pfv.htm.

44   Robert Ebert, "The Matrix Revolutions," *Chicago Sun Times*, November 5, 2003.

45   David Edelstein, "Neo Con," *Slate*, May 14, 2003, http://slate.msn.com/id/2082928.

46   Fans are not the only people seeking for meaning through *The Matrix*. See, for example, William Irwin (ed.). *The Matrix and Philosophy: Welcome to the Desert of the Real* (Chicago: Open Court, 2002).

47   Brian Takle, "The Matrix Explained," May 20, 2003, http://webpages .charter.net/btakle/matrix_reloaded.html.

48   Ebert, "Matrix Revolutions."

49   John Gaudiosi, "'Matrix' Vid Game Captures Film Feel," *Hollywood Reporter*, February 6, 2003, accessed at http://www.thelastfreecity.com/docs/7965.html.

50   Stephen Totilo, "Matrix Saga Continues On line—Without Morpheus," MTV.Com, May 26, 2005, http://www.mtv.com/games/video_games/news/story.jhtml?id=1502973.

51   Richard Corliss, "Popular Metaphysics," *Time*, April 19, 1999.

52   See, for example, Suz, "The Matrix Concordance," at http://members .lycos.co.uk/needanexit/concor.html.

53   David Buckingham and Julian. Sefton-Green, "Structure, Agency, and Pedagogy in Children's Media Culture," in. Joseph Tobin (ed.), *Pikachu's Global Adventure: The Rise and Fall of Pokémon* (Durham, NC: Duke University Press, 2004), p. 12.

54   Ibid., p. 22.

55   Marsha Kinder identified similar trends as early as 1991, arguing that children's media could be read as a site of experimentation for these corporate strategies and as the place where new consumers are educated into the demands of what I am calling convergence culture. Cartoon, series such as *Teenage Mutant Ninja Turtles* and games such as *Super Mario Bros*, were teaching kids to follow characters across media platforms, to adjust fluidly to a changing media environment, and to combine passive and interactive modes of engagement. Marsha Kinder, *Playing with Power in Movies, Television and Video Games: From Muppet Babies to Teenage Mutant Ninja Turtles* (Berkeley: University of California Press, 1991).

56   Manuel Castells, *The Internet Galaxy: Reflections on the Internet, Business, and Society* (Oxford: Oxford University Press, 2001), pp. 202–203.

PART 3

Writing about film and literature
Critical terms, borders, and strategies

EACH OF THE THREE FOLLOWING CHAPTERS represents a basic introduction to some of the techniques, organizations, and issues used when thinking about, analyzing, or writing about the interaction of film and literature. The first section calls attention to ideas and forms that film and literature share, that they modify, and that they do not share; the second sketches some common and important analytical fields and topics that adaptation studies have pursued; and the third section rehearses the fundamental strategies for writing and researching essays on film and literature. The aim here is to develop a critical vocabulary and analytical perspectives that allow students to think more carefully about how they understand and write about individual works and about the interaction between film and literary texts. Any work of film or literature will use formal or organizational techniques in a particular way and respond to important debates in their own way, and a critical vocabulary will grow more refined and insightful in response to those individual works.

Chapter 35

ANALYTICAL TERMS AND CATEGORIES

Theme or motif

The *theme* or *motif* identifies the main idea or ideas developed in a work of literature or film.

Examples

In Shakespeare's *Hamlet*, one prominent theme is the tragic isolation and indecision of the hero in a corrupt society. In *The Scarlet Letter*, the devastating effect of guilt, hypocrisy, revenge becomes a key theme in a morally dark world.

When adapted

A movie may elaborate or change the central theme of an original literary work, such as when Laurence Olivier emphasizes Hamlet's Oedipal sexual crisis in his 1948 adaptation. With its direct references to the novel *The Scarlet Letter* and to earlier film adaptations, the 2010 film *Easy A* transforms the grim themes of the Nathaniel Hawthorne's novel into a teen pic about sex, injustice, and redemption in a contemporary high school.

Characters

Characters are those individuals that populate and propel stories, plays, movies, and even poems. Traditionally, characters have been designated as major or minor, as a *protagonist* (one with heroic or positive features) or an *antagonist* (one with villainous or negative features). They may be realistic or animated; they may be described only in terms of external appearance or by means of internal thoughts and psychological depth; a character may motivate actions and events or be passively subject to them.

Examples

In *The Lord of the Rings,* Frodo is clearly one of the main protagonists, while the villainous Sauron is the unmistakable antagonist. Important secondary or minor characters include Frodo's companions Bilbo and Sam.

When adapted

Some literary works may present such a vast number of major and minor characters that it would be difficult or impossible for a film to reproduce all of them. In addition, a literary character's appearance, which is originally grounded in words and a reader's imaginative visualization of those words, is made concrete and visible in a movie. This physical realization of a character is a frequent source of confusion or dissatisfaction in measuring a film against its literary source. Thus, Vladimir Nabokov was perfectly satisfied with his Lolita incarnated through actress Sue Lyon, while Stephen King was publicly upset by Kubrick's choice of Jack Nicholson to play his character Jack Torrance. Ask: which characters are added, omitted, or changed in an adaptation? Why? In Luchino Visconti's 1971 adaptation of Thomas Mann's *Death in Venice*, the filmmaker changes the profession of the central character (from a writer to a composer). How does that alter an understanding of that character? How are movie characters a product of certain techniques and film materials? What advantages do the use of words and moving images have over a purely linguistic description of characters or even over the physical presence of a character on stage?

Point of view

Central both to visual arts and literary arts, point of view describes the position from which an individual sees—physically, psychologically, and socially—another person, object, or event. Many sorts of literature, particularly novels, allow multiple points of view to interact, and this ability to mobilize multiple points of view has been a salient connection between novels and films that likewise create dramas from confrontations and exchanges across many points of view. With a *first-person point of view,* events are seen through the eyes and mind of a single individual; with a *third-person omniscient point of view,* there are seemingly no limitations to what can be seen, known, and presented; *a limited or restricted third-person point of view* is objectively outside that of the characters but remains focused primarily on one or two characters.

Examples

In Robert Browning's poem "His Last Duchess" the reader follows the speech of the Duke as he both distorts the life of his former wife and unwittingly reveals his own egomaniacal point of view. In Japanese director Akira Kurosawa's *Rashomon* (1950), a rape and murder are recounted in four different and conflicting versions from the different points of view of a bandit, a priest, the wife, and a woodcutter.

When adapted

Movies have always had difficulty recreating the first-person point of view employed by some novels; they have also had more freedom and flexibility with point of view than available to the closed physical space of theatrical drama. What is gained and lost by these different ways of creating points of view? How does the imagistic point of view used in a movie expand or limit the power of a literary point of view? What happens to the satirical linguistic perspectives of authors such as Henry Fielding or Evelyn Waugh when those literary works are recreated as images in *Tom Jones* (1963) or *The Loved One* (1965)?

Story/plot/narration

Stories are commonly what literature and movies might share, as they provide basic materials, from fact or fiction, about events, lives, characters, and their interaction and development. Where film and literature often part ways is in the narrative construction of those stories through a *plot,* which presents those events in a certain order (either chronological or not), and a *narration* that incorporates, shapes, and colors that plot with a certain point of view. *Narrative causality* describes how a character's needs and desires motivate events and actions (often as a linear progression).

Examples

In *The Wizard of Oz,* the plot maps Dorothy's determined desire to get home, while the narration creates two different worlds by using black-and-white images for life in Kansas and Technicolor when the story moves to Oz. David Lean's adaptation of *Great Expectations* (1946) remains quite close to the story found in Charles Dickens's novel and even recreates the narrative point of view of the main character Pip, yet many of the narrative subplots needed to be abandoned and the ending of the film narrative differs from both Dickens's original and revised endings.

When adapted

The omissions, additions, and changes to a story or plot are a popular focus in discussion of adaptation. Ask: how has the narrative structure and logic changed or not changed in the conversion to a movie? Do the same causal motives drive the narrative in both versions, or have those motives been reduced or altered? To what extent does the ending settle (or not) the meaning of the story, and, if an adaptation changes that ending, how does that change the meaning of the story?

Settings/sets/*mise-en-scène*

A *setting* is a location in which to place the action and characters. *Sets* are specifically those props, backdrops, and other constructions used in theatrical productions, and can range from the minimal to the extravagant. With film criticism, settings and sets are referred to as the *mise-en-scène,* which also includes all the other theatrical and stage materials put in place before the camera begins filming. Props, lighting, costumes, and so forth are considered part of a film's *mise-en-scène.*

Examples

The Mississippi River functions as the primary setting in Mark Twain's *Adventures of Huckleberry Finn.* In Tennessee Williams's *A Streetcar Named Desire,* the sets that describe a dilapidated section of New Orleans are the significant background and stage for the collapse of the lives of some of the characters, while in Hitchcock's *Vertigo* (1958), the city of San Francisco functions as a *mise-en-scène* defined by its hilly streets, apartment rooms, automobiles, and other elements.

When adapted

Settings in novels and sets on a theatrical stage always imply a principle of selection that indicates some designated significance or meaning. Changes to both the larger setting and to the smaller objects in a cinematic *mise-en-scène* can signal a significant redirection of the meanings of the adaptation.

Language, composition, and style in literature and film

Language can be spoken, printed, and recorded. From the intertitles of silent movies to the dialogue found in all forms of written and performed literature, linguistic styles can run the gamut from the sparsely prosaic to the elaborately poetic. Along this spectrum, *prose* can be described as the everyday or ordinary use of language, reflecting the way of speaking or writing in a specific historical time and place; *poetry* usually employs the *rhythms* and sometimes the *rhymes* associated with intensified verse.

In addition to sharing these literary forms, film has developed its own formal, rhetorical, and stylistic units. These cinematic units can be classified as (1) those created by *the compositions of the film image* and (2) those created by *the editing of sound and image on film.* The *shot* describes a single, uncut segment of film. Some of the common stylistic techniques that add to the significance of the shot are: (1) the *shape of the frame* (which can have a standard Academy ratio of 1.37:1 [width to height], a widescreen shape of, typically 1.85:1 or 2.35:1, or be resized to fit a television screen); (2) the *perspective of the image* (which can range from a deep focus that clearly shows backgrounds, middle grounds, and foregrounds to a very flat shallow focus in which only one plane is clearly seen); (3) the *film speed* (which creates slow, fast, or normal motion); (4) the *distance between the camera and the figure* being filmed (resulting in close-ups, long shots, and other relations); (5) the *angle* at which the shot captures the object or event (which results in low angle, high angle, or straight-on shots); (6) *camera movements* (such as sweeping *pans* of a horizon or *tracks* that follow the action on a cart); and (7) the use of *color* or *black and white* film (both of which can discriminate among a wide range of tones).

When one or more shots like this are rhythmically linked or edited together to describe a single space or place, this is called a *scene*; a *sequence* describes a number of edited shots and scenes that are connected by a specific action or idea. Scenes and sequences are usually constructed through *editing*, which is the linking together of two or more shots. Most mainstream or classical films attempt to edit shots and sequences in a way that makes the editing unnoticeable, which is referred to as *continuity editing* or *invisible editing*. Like literature (especially poetry), editing can create rhythms and even rhymes in the style of a film. This can be done, to take two popular strategies, by pacing the editing with *takes* (long takes hold a shot for an extended period of time, while short takes cut quickly) or generating a rhythm of *shot/reverse shot* exchanges (whereby the image might cut between a person looking and the person or thing being looked at). For example, an *establishing shot*, which introduces the place where the action will take place, may introduce the setting of a film, and then be rapidly followed by a series of reverse shots of individuals looking at that same scene.

The use of sound in a film usually begins with the distinction between *diegetic sound*, when the source of the sound can be located in the world of the film such as the screeching of a car tire on screen or off, and *nondiegetic sound*, when the source of the sound is not in that world, such as orchestral background music in an intimate romantic scene. *Sound editing* is also a major part of film style and form, and can involve not only the editing of dialogue and other sounds that are part of the scene, but also *offscreen sounds*, whose source is outside the frame of the image, or *postdubbed sounds*, which are sounds extraneous to the action but which may work to support or counterpoint what is seen in the image.

Examples

In Orson Welles's *Chimes at Midnight* the rapid editing of the battle sequence portrays the energy and brutality of war more graphically but less poetically than Shakespeare was able to accomplish when his *Henry IV* plays were staged. In the remake of Henry James's novella *The Turn of the Screw* as *The Innocents* (1961), the editing of sound becomes one of the most unsettling dimensions of this ghost story as it troubles stability of a place permeated by ghostly noises.

When adapted

When a work of narrative or dramatic literature is adapted, the language and dialogue will usually be edited down to fit the shortened time restrictions of feature films. What has been retained and what has been removed can reveal much about the new version. Compositional features of an adaptation can likewise provoke insightful questions: How has the use of framing or camera angles changed or developed an understanding of the themes or characters? How has the editing changed the pace of the story—and to what effect?

Genres

As forms of classification, literary and film genres spring from a social and aesthetic contract: they assume an important economic and commercial dimension since they prepare readers and audiences for similar or new works that writers and filmmakers want them to see, enjoy, and understand. Genres also contain a tension. On the one hand, they participate in recognizable conventions and formulas that seem to transcend individual literary or cinematic examples of that genre; on the other hand, genres continually evolve in terms of specific historical periods and practices.

Generic classifications have traditionally disagreed about what are the primary genres, since genre is, to say the least, a malleable and changing way to classify films, literature, and our expectations about individual works. *Comedy* is a dramatic genre that is less about laughs than about the triumph of society and social consensus over the differences of individuals. In movie culture, there are three clear descendants of that literary paradigm: *Comedies* associated with laughs are still about the foibles and tribulations of outsiders, but the humor of the outsider's position (whether he is Jacques Tati or Bill Murray) is viewed sympathetically, allowing any eccentricities to be understood or eventually reintegrated into the community. *Screwball comedies*—particularly evident in the 1930s (like the 1939 *Bringing Up Baby*) but still popular today (as in the 2009 *The Proposal*)—replicate the plot structure of comedies but exaggerate the physical problems rather than the emotional or social problems of the characters. Perhaps the most common generic comedy in film today, *romantic comedies* develop many of the themes and forms of those earlier variations, but usually adapt a more realistic balance between the physical, intellectual, and emotional problems of the individuals at the center. Some kind of harmonious conclusion, reasserting a communal balance, remains a defining characteristic, although the standard heterosexual pairings are only one kind of happy couple now found at the movies.

Tragedy is often perceived as the generic opposite of comedy. In classical tragedy, the central character or social leader (an Oedipus, a Hamlet) acts out a tragic flaw, which is normally related to pride and which directly affects the health of the community. Inevitably this flaw leads to the leader's suffering and downfall. Unlike the main comedic characters, the tragic figure is not reintegrated into the society but must be sacrificed and expelled, leaving greater knowledge in his or her wake. In the last two centuries, *melodrama* emerges as one of the modern derivatives of tragedy. Here too, the protagonist suffers a torment, but the powers that persecute him or her are less a consequence of spiritual fates than of the material forces found in patriarchal families, restrictive societies, or oppressive governments.

Originating as medieval French tales, *romances* tell stories of chivalric, imaginary, or personal love and the search for fulfillment or completion. *Arthurian legends, quest narratives*, and *picaresque novels* (the kind parodied in works from Cervantes's *Don Quixote* to *Monty Python and the Holy Grail*) are part of this tradition, and it appears in the nineteenth century as variations on the *Bildüngsroman*, which includes novels like Goethe's *Wilhelm Meister's Apprenticeship* or Dickens's *Oliver Twist* that tell tales about growing up and the various quests associated with that maturation process. In the twentieth century, both the film and literary genres of the *hard-boiled detective stories*, as in the movie *The Big Sleep* (1946), are dark descendants of this wide-ranging genre as they entwine the complex search for truth and meaning with the search for love. Of postwar movie genres, the *road movie* represents another detour on the generic path of romances: Here, the male questors of *Easy Rider* (1969), *The Living End* (1992), and the adaptation of Cormac McCarthy's novel *The Road* (2009) have little hope of permanent love and little sense of the goal of their travels, yet each makes the search for an undefined grail a way to learn about love and relationships.

Related to romances, *epic poetry* such as Homer's *Odyssey* or William Wordsworth's *The Prelude* depict the heroic adventures of an individual as he confronts and conquers physical and mental obstacles on journeys across the world or the land. Through these encounters, epics recount the originating history of a people and the beginnings of a culture or nation. In more modern literatures, epic journeys reflect actual historical events and backgrounds, and the hero becomes a more recognizably human character who survives as an emblem of a cultural or national memory. From *Stagecoach* to *Heaven's Gate* (1980) and *Dances with Wolves* (1990), *westerns* follow the epic genre in their emphasis on the hero who conquers the western wilderness and helps establish the history of the American identity. In contemporary *action films* (the *Rambo* sequels [1982,1988], *Die Hard* [1988], and so forth), this epic fight for a national identity takes place in a global environment where the narrative length and detail of classical epics has been replaced by visual spectacles.

Since the Greek plays of Aristophanes (*Lysistrata*), *satire* has been a genre of literature that ridicules or exposes human and social follies and vices. Usually less concerned with private life than with public life, satires flourished in the late seventeenth century and eighteenth century in the plays of Molière (*Tartuffe*), the poetry of Alexander Pope ("The Rape of the Lock"), and the narrative prose of Jonathan Swift (*Gulliver's Travels*), and in the twentieth century, literary satire ranges from the dour political attacks on technological society found in George Orwell's novel *1984* to Samuel Beckett's combination of cosmic despair and slapstick mockery in *Waiting for Godot*. Indeed, the slapstick films of Charlie Chaplin, Keaton, and others represent an early and important connection between literary satire and films that continue to explore, wryly but sometimes severely, the predicament of the human individual caught in the machinery of the twentieth century.

Finally, it is worth considering the *literary film* as a film genre in its own right (just as the movie novel could be considered a literary genre). The literary film can be defined most generally as a film in which a literary work or other literary connections function, like all genres, as part of the expectations it elicits from its audience. In that sense a literary film would include two kinds of movies: (1) adaptations in which the movie draws attention to the literary work from which it is derived, presuming either familiarity with that work or at least cultural recognition of its literary status; (2) films in which a prominent literary presence—such as a writer turned filmmaker or a script by a recognized novelist or playwright—shapes expectations about the literary qualities of those films.

Examples

That the movies are such a public forum has encouraged satiric films in numerous subgenres directly descended from the literary genre. Of the many examples of the cross-overs between literature and film, there are *comedic satires*, from the Marx Brothers movies to *Austin Powers: International Man of Mystery* (1997) and Frank Oz's *Death at a Funeral* (2007). Similarly, historical epics have been a constant in both literary and film history, each incarnation reflecting its generic heritage and its cultural, formal, and historical variations: from Homer's *Odyssey* to James Joyce's *Ulysses* to Joseph Strick's experimental *Ulysses* (1967) to Joel and Ethan Coen's comic version of the Odyssey, *O Brother, Where Art Thou?* (2000).

When adapted

When considering the generic assumptions that inform a particular literary or film practice, ask how cultural history determines its specific changes and styles. If classical epics assumed an omniscient narrative perspective (tantamount to that of a god) in order to acclaim heroes who were like gods, do modern westerns rely on long shots to emphasize how grand perspectives on nature are a significant part of the tales of more democratic nations? If eighteenth-century literary satires direct verbal ironies at the hypocrisy of different classes, where do movies often direct their satire? More generally, are there movie genres without a literary past? Are there literary genres which films have not successfully adapted?

Chapter 36

MAJOR TOPICS IN ADAPTATION STUDIES

WRITING ABOUT ADAPTATION or the many other different kinds of interactions between literature and film involves a large field of critical questions and topics. These projects usually involve some (or a great deal of) textual analysis, employing the forms and structures outlined in the previous section. Yet analytical writing also engages larger topics that have traditionally defined adaptation studies. The following is a sampling and introduction to some of the more important, innovative, or debated topics that become part of writing about adaptation. A precisely focused essay may involve one or more of these topics.

Material differences in film and literature

Despite their similarities and connections, film and literature use materially different ways to describe the world or to express a point of view. Literature usually employs printed words, and often requires a longer reading time than the way we access stories through images on a screen, which are usually presented in a 90- or 120-minute format. Dramatic literature likewise distinguishes itself from film performance, most clearly through the difference of an actual physical performance versus a performance recorded on celluloid or videotape. Like novels and short stories, much poetry is written for a printed page, but many poets prefer their works to be read or performed before a live audience, thus associating their poetry with performative arts like theater.

The tools of each trade can also be quite different and, as basic as they are, they are often a good starting point for considering the different forms. Literature organizes words through sentences, stanzas, chapters, and so forth. Plays use acts and scenes whose breaks are, in most cases, clearly evident. Film may borrow some of these structures but usually works to make any scenic shifts invisible and often seamless.

Many questions and issues surround the distinction between the way individuals watch a performance of a movie and the way they read literature or view a performance of a play at the theater. These include delineating the intellectual activities that distinguish watching images and listening to recorded words from reading words on a page, as well as other psychological, social, and economic dimensions to these experiences. In this regard, television is a related but very different way of adapting literature since the size of a television image and the conditions in which we watch it (at home usually) differ considerably from those of a movie screening.

Although these basic material differences might seem obvious and are rarely considered in subtle comparisons of different forms of film and literature, keeping them in mind may be the best starting point in an examination of what film and literature finally have or do not have in common. A person may read Charles Dickens's long novel *Nicholas Nickleby* in private over the course of several months, controlling her pace and reflections along the way; she may view the 100-minute version of the 1947 film in the semidarkness of a small movie theater, following rather than controlling the pace of the story; or she may attend, on two different days at a Broadway theater, an 8-hour production by the Royal Shakespeare Company, her attention divided among the crowd around her, the sets, and the characters. In each of these cases, different meanings of the works may originate in the extremely different conditions and shapes of the specific literary or filmic form, and the value we assign each version should take into account the material possibilities available in each medium.

Recommended readings

A. Nicholas Vardac's *Stage to Screen* is a pioneering account of some of the important issues that define the transition from stage to screen in the nineteenth century; Sarah Cardwell's "Literature on the Small Screen: Television Adaptations" (p. 168) explores how television significantly changes the material terms and thus potential meaning of literary adaptation; Linda Hutcheon's *A Theory of Adaptation* is a wide-ranging discussion of the many material differences that define adaptations from movies to computer games.

Theater and film

Once the cinema progressed (early in the twentieth century) beyond the peepshow amusement of kinetoscopes and other optical toys for private viewing, theater and dramatic literature become the primary models that movie makers turned to in the early years of the cinema, for several reasons: (1) both theater and movies are public and commercial spectacles addressing audiences rather than individuals; (2) early audiences for movies have been socially and culturally prepared by the theatrical traditions of music halls and other popular shows; (3) because of the lack of camera mobility, the best way to film a story is to place the stationary camera before the characters and action and so duplicate the position of a viewer before a stage; and (4) the production materials for theater, specifically sets and actors, become readily available materials for developing the entertainment potential of movies.

Theater and film have, of course, many other structures, materials, and formulas in common. Drama's fundamental roots in conflict continue in classical cinema, as both drama and film foreground confrontations between individuals and other individuals and between individuals and societies. Nineteenth-century theater and its five-act paradigm of a "well-made play" provide film with one of the most durable formulas for structuring film action as it organized theatrical action according to exposition, complication, crisis, climax, and resolution. These remain standard developmental structures in much theater and film today.

Theatrical sets, actors, and costumes are basic elements of both theater and film, yet the physical presence and concreteness of these features in the theater become transformed in a film image. Acting style, for example, can take advantage of camera close-ups and other positions; sets and settings in the cinema naturally gravitate more toward realistic locations; and the possibilities for constructing space and time are significantly different in the two media.

Although theater remains a regular source throughout film's relationship with literature in the twentieth century, movies often change the nature of their relationship with dramatic literature. Since Vachel Lindsay's "Thirty Differences Between the Photoplays and the Stage" and other early writings, observers and practitioners of cinema quickly begin to urge film to distinguish itself from its theatrical parentage, and the history of filmmaking and film criticism has vacillated between a rejection of theatrical models and creative encounters with them. In the first quarter of the twentieth century, the ascension of film's powerful realism is one factor in moving the province and powers of cinema away from the theater, while, by the 1930s, cinema's ability to entertain large middle-class audiences brings theater spectacles and musicals back into the movies in full force. In recent years, theatrical literature has been used in a myriad of ways, sometimes to take advantage of traditional dramatic values of character and dialogue (drawing actors and filmmakers like Sir John Gielgud and Kenneth Branagh), sometimes, as in theatrical films such as the Broadway musical *Chicago* (2002), to foreground a theatrical artificiality (of space, sets, or costumes) that subverts film's realism.

More and more, the exchange between theater and film has moved in both directions. In recent years, Tom Stoppard, Caryl Churchill, Richard Foreman, Martin McDonagh and other playwrights have ingeniously incorporated film metaphors and techniques as part of their stage plays, and television drama, which creates original dramatic material for television, has become a subgenre in its own right.

Recommended readings

André Bazin's "Theater and Cinema" (p. 223) remains one of the most intelligent and complex essays on the relation of theater and cinema; Leo Braudy's "Acting: Stage vs. Screen" (p. 232) is a careful reflection on what distinguishes acting for two different media and the potentials and limits of each; Robert Knopf's *Theater and Film: A Comparative Anthology* gathers a broad collection of essays by theater and film scholars, directors, and actors to provide a multitude of perspectives on this important relationship.

Adaptation

Adaptation is the most common practice in the exchange between literature and film, describing the transposition of a novel, play, or other literary source to film. Although this term can sometimes suggest a derivative or less creative practice, it is useful to keep in mind that even the most original works of movies and literature might be considered "adaptations" of materials drawn from one source or another. Not only are famous literary works, like the plays of Shakespeare or James Joyce's *Ulysses,* drawn from historical documents or earlier literary sources but, in the broadest sense, even the most seemingly original work develops or "adapts" information or material from conversations, newspapers, dreams, or historical events.

In most discussions of adaptation, a key term is fidelity, a notion that asks to what extent an adaptation is true to or faithful to the original text. Traditional discussions about fidelity and adaptation presume five questions in determining how faithful the film adaptation is.

1. To what extent are the details of the settings and plot accurately retained or recreated?
2. To what extent do the nuance and complexity of the characters survive the adaptation?
3. To what extent are the themes and ideas of the source communicated in the adaptation?
4. To what extent has a different historical or cultural context altered the original?
5. To what extent has the change in the material or mode of communication (a printed page, a stage, 35mm film) changed the meaning of the work for a reader or viewer?

Pragmatically, these questions are answered in the way an adaptation might emphasize, for instance, action over dialogue or in how much of the plot is kept intact and where it is altered.

Although fidelity studies continue to provide insightful pathways into an adaptation, other critical approaches have reconsidered and replaced fidelity as a measure with perspectives and terms that allow for more creative exchanges between the original text and its adaptation. In Dudley Andrew's essay in this volume (p. 65), he proposes three kinds of adaptive tactics: borrowing, intersecting, and transforming. Others have suggested adaptation involving other processes: as a matter of generation and regeneration, from one work to another, or as an exchange in which the adaptation's relation to the original text can be described as translation, transposition, commentary, or analogy. More broadly, Robert Stam's arguments (p.74) address and jettison traditional ideas about textual fidelity, and offer a complex theory of adaptation as "intertextuality," a position that has informed many contemporary studies of adaptation as they turn away from fidelity as a measure of a successful adaptation.

As Linda Hutcheon argues so convincingly, it is also important to consider how the literature adapted and the audience's implied awareness of the original work shapes an understanding of a film adaptation. Well-known works of classical literature (*Hamlet* or *Moby-Dick*) may assume a viewer's familiarity with the original, and the adaptation may address its audience's awareness or recognition of that prior work through changes or omissions. Conversely, many movie adaptations work with a minor or relatively unknown piece of literature, and essentially treat it as an invisible dimension of its film, which most audiences neither know nor need to know. These and other issues about an audience's expectations should be considered with any adaptation.

One of the wittiest and most intelligent commentaries on film adaptation is Jean-Luc Godard's film *Contempt* (1963). Brilliantly weaving different notions of personal and professional fidelity, the story is of a scriptwriter attempting to negotiate a movie deal with an American producer (played by Jack Palance). Mainly interested in commercial success, the producer hopes to adapt Homer's *Odyssey* with the help of German director Fritz Lang. *Contempt* addresses the numerous cultural, linguistic, and commercial conflicts and compromises involved in the process, but, more than just presenting these issues, Godard, typically, makes them part of the complex images and structures of *Contempt* itself, which is an adaptation of a novel of Alberto Moravia.

Recommended readings

Jean Mitry's "Remarks on the Problem of Cinematic Adaptation" continues to be a key theoretical reflection on adaptation; carefully demarcating types of adaptation, Dudley Andrew's "Adaptation" (p. 65) set the tone for adaptation studies for many years; Robert Stam's "Beyond Fidelity: The Dialogics of Adaptation" (p. 74) led the way in undoing and rethinking the persistence of fidelity as a touchstone in adaptation; Simone Murray's "Materializing Adaptation Theory: The Adaptation Industry" (p. 365) is a refreshing and innovative redirection of adaptation studies to the material industries that shape the practice.

Poetry and film

Poets from all cultures and contemporary historical periods have reacted to the movies. Sometimes this response has taken the shape of a denunciation of the abrasive powers of popular movies as the center of culture. Sometimes films have furnished poets with images or figures that have become symbols or metaphors for a particular idea or problem. Sometimes the cinema describes for poets an entire way of seeing or of constructing vision that works in conjunction with poetic language or that stands out in its difference.

Of the different literary genres that film has drawn on or influenced, poetry has been the most elusive and less common. From the early years of film history, however, there have been notable examples. Griffith adapts Tennyson's poem *Enoch Arden* in 1911. Joseph Moncure March's narrative poems *The Wild Party* (1928) and *The Set-Up* (1928) are other relatively early attempts to put poetry on film, and, through the 1920s and early 1930s, the movies demonstrate an especially lively connection with poetry as part of movements such as Dadaism, Futurism, and various schools of Surrealism—all of which recognize the capabilities of film to disrupt and recreate perception that rattled common views and broke through perceptual barriers. Jean Cocteau is one of the most renowned poet-filmmakers, whose films include *The Blood of a Poet* (1930), *Beauty and the Beast* (1946), and *Orpheus* (1950). Added to a screenplay of *Blood of a Poet* is his apocalyptic remark about the regenerative powers of film as part of a literary tradition: "With the cinema, death is killed, literature is killed, poetry is made to live a direct life. Imagine what the cinema of poetry might be" (1972: xii). In the post-World War II years, experimental filmmakers such as Maya Deren and Stan Brakhage find the paradigms for their films in the confrontation with linguistic sense found in twentieth-century poetry, and that tradition has continued to the present in the non-narrative films of Bruce Baillie, Bruce Conner, and many other filmmakers. Even certain narrative films, such as Ingmar Bergman's 1957 *The Seventh Seal,* strike some viewers as more like a poetic allegory than a dramatic story; and in 1965 Pier Paolo Pasolini argues for the unique powers of film to create a distinctive poetic idiom, based in the realism of the image, in his essay "A Cinema of Poetry."

Throughout this century, poets have taken movie matters as subjects or borrowed (sometimes even anticipated) film's imagistic mobility or unique formal structures. For instance, "Imagism" describes a school of poetry active especially in the years 1912–1915; it includes the work of T. E. Hulme, H. D. (Hilda Doolittle), William Carlos Williams, and Ezra Pound (most famously, his poem "In a Station in the Metro"). The main premise of imagism is that the poetry should be, above all else, a visually concrete language stripped of the emotional and intellectual decoration associated with some nineteenth-century poetry. Like some early directors and theoreticians of the cinema, Pound and others see the Chinese ideogram as a model for this kind of poetry, and poetic imagism might be usefully related to the new aesthetics of photography and film and, in turn, to the more poetic experiments with film form through the 1920s by Man Ray, Marcel Duchamp, Hans Richter, and others.

What distinguishes poetic films from narrative films, theatrical films, or documentary films is often an exploration and distillation of the language of the medium in order to incite a viewer's imagination. Like many poems, poetic films aim to intensify or make unfamiliar the formulas of conventional or mainstream movies. With this definition, poetic films would include many experimental films that examine and test the nature of film as a language and medium of expression (such as the films of Brakhage and Michael Snow); it could also include films that border on and participate in the conventions of narrative or storytelling but that emphasize the imaginative or fantastical potential of vision and images (thus making room for the poetry of animation cinema or for the mesmerizing sequences in films such as Werner Herzog's *Heart of Glass* [1976], Glauber Rocha's *Antonio das Mortes* [1969], Terrence Malick's *The Tree of Life* [2011], and animated films such as Mamoru Oshii's *Ghost in the Shell* [1995]).

There are three fundamental ways of discussing the relationship between film and poetry: (1) how poets are influenced by or how they recreated the structures and figures of the movies in their poetry; (2) how a poetic sensibility or vision is shared by creators of both literature and cinema (and other forms as well) so that one identifies an imaginative or "poetic" quality; and (3) how a film and a poem construct metaphors, symbols, and other poetic idioms in different or similar ways.

Recommended readings

Robert Richardson's "The Question of Order and Coherence in Poetry and Film" (in *Literature and Film*) examines the different formal organizations that link and differentiate the two practices; with different emphases and arguments, P. Adams Sitney's "The Lyrical Film" (p. 262) and David E. James's "The Filmmaker as Poet: Stan Brakhage" (in Virginia Wright Wexman's *Film and Authorship*) discuss the connection between this key experimental filmmaker and various Romantic poets; Susan McCabe's *Cinematic Modernism: Modernist Poetry and Film* demonstrates the influence of the cinema on modernist poets such as Gertrude Stein and Marianne Moore.

The novel and film

The relationship between the novel (or narrative fiction) and film has always been one of the most dominant and persistent. The origins of the novel extend back through Miguel de Cervantes's seventeenth-century *Don Quixote*, but for many its most notable achievements occur in the nineteenth century, when a growing middle class of readers is also witnessing the scientific and technological birth of a new realism, a detailed realism that photography and cinema would both promote. Although theatrical structures seemed originally most suited to the stationary camera of early cinema, the development of editing techniques and camera movements point the cinema more and more toward the mobile points of view found in the novel and especially in those nineteenth-century prototypes.

Since the turn of the century, most films have used some sort of narrative storyline, making novels (and short stories) attractive to filmmakers. Movies have turned toward a variety of novels—from classics to popular or "pulp" fiction, from eighteenth-century novels like *Tom Jones* (1749) to bestsellers like *The Girl with the Dragon Tattoo* (2009) that may precede the film by only a few years. (These choices about the kind of novel and the historical period it comes from are always potentially meaningful in discussing any transposition of a novel into film.) Representing several centuries of literary materials, novels provide fully developed characters and stories that can be easily adapted. If drama offers film models for conflict and spectacle, narrative fiction provides film with materials and models for two primary features of the cinema: (1) *plots* that develop through a *character psychology* that drives the action according to a temporal pattern of (frequently) cause and effect; and (2) a mobile variety of *narrative points of view* that organize those events from one or more perspectives. Thus, in *Gone with the Wind*, the film takes advantage of the novel's chronological depiction of historical and personal change, points of view alternating between spectacles of the Civil War and the individual perspectives of characters like Rhett, the driving desires of Scarlett, and a logic of triumph over the many obstacles and tragedies that confront the characters.

Unlike short stories, novels usually require significant cutting and shrinkage if they are to be recreated in the shorter temporal format of a movie. Thus choices of what to include or omit can be either artistically significant or a matter of economics. If films bring more realism to novels, those films struggle before the novel's *selective* power of descriptive detail (whereby a description is always a meaningful choice of what to describe), the wide variety of numerous points of view available, and the full elaboration of a character's consciousness found in novels. Many novelistic techniques, such as a stream of consciousness style that moves fluidly through a central character's conscious and unconscious perceptions, are extremely difficult to recreate in a film or are considered unpopular with audiences.

Recommended readings

Kristin Thompson's "Novel, Short Story, Drama: The Conditions for Influence" (p. 130) is a precise historical account of how the publishing industry and copyright laws refashioned early adaptations; Brian McFarlane's *Novel to Film* offers a series of rich case studies of adaptations such as *Daisy Miller* (1974) and *Cape Fear* (1991); Judith Mayne's "Readership and Spectatorship" (p. 252) moves from nineteenth-century novels through films of the 1940s, arguing how the evolution of spectatorship as reading involves numerous questions about gender, consumer culture, and other issues; and Robert Stam and Alessandro Raengo's collection *Literature and Film* provides a number of sophisticated case studies of particular adaptations of novels by films.

The screenplay

As a kind of writing that precedes the filming of a topic or story, screenwriting is a practice between literary writing and a finished movie. While the first films rarely worked from a script or screenplay, this changed quickly, and movies today work from screenplays that have been revised many times. Within the studio system, the first stage of a screenplay is often a one- or two-page summary of an idea that comes from a "programming" or story department that is charged with developing potential material from newspapers or "literary properties." With a successful plot, this is followed by a thirty-to-sixty-page treatment, which is an extended summary and outline of the main idea and plot of a film. After this stage, a detailed screenplay may be developed through many stages (and sometimes by different screenwriters). A final shooting script will develop specific scenes with descriptions of the settings, actions, and dialogue.

The connections between a screenplay and a finished film can vary considerably. Some filmmakers work quite creatively and loosely from a screenplay, changing dialogue and action as they shoot the film or allowing actors to improvise (as with the films of John Cassavettes or Mike Leigh). Others insist that the script be followed strictly and often use a script that details precise camera angles and positions. In any case, a screenplay should rarely be seen as the verbal, equivalent of the film images, and to study a screenplay as literature means perceiving it as a form of writing between literature and film.

Many of the most reputable literary figures of the twentieth century have worked as screenwriters, the movie industry hoping to take advantage of both their reputations and their abilities as writers: Gabriele D'Annunzio, William Faulkner, Marguerite Duras, and Peter Handke are examples. Although many writers consider screenwriting only a prelude to the real work of filmmaking, others, such as Pasolini, have argued that the screenplay is a literary work in its own right.

Indeed there may be some justification in considering the screenwriter as controlling the perspective and ideas of a film as much as the director. Thus screenwriters like Anita Loos (*Gentlemen Prefer Blondes* [1928, 1953]), Howard Koch (*Letter from an Unknown Woman* [1948]), or Garson Kanin (*Woman of the Year* [1942]) produce scripts that often have the textual consistencies and personal voice used to identify good literature and creative writers. A number of daring directors are, in fact, first scriptwriters who emerge from the turbulence of the 1940s and 1950s to direct new kinds of movies: Richard Brooks (*The Blackboard Jungle* [1955]), Joseph Mankiewicz (*All about Eve* [1950]), Robert Rossen (*The Hustler* [1961]), and Samuel Fuller (*Pickup on South Street* [1953]) dramatize the crucial creative links between writing and filming, especially during the 1950s (and in many other decades as well).

Recommended readings

Béla Balázs's "The Script" is one of the first serious arguments for scriptwriting as a distinctive art in itself; Douglas Garrett Winston's *The Screenplay as Literature* suggests that many of the best new wave films have their source in creative screenplays; and Jack Boozer's "The Screenplay and Authorship in Adaptation" (p. 199) makes a convincing case for the screenwriter as a creative auteur.

Authors and auteurs

One central connection between literature and film is the writer. With literature, the place and function of the writer is fairly clear: he or she is the author who expresses and organizes a feeling, a perspective, an idea, or a story through words. Today we generally describe this authorial activity as creative, in part because this work is considered so personal and imaginative. This conception of the author has provided an immediate obstacle in finding a corresponding figure for the creative force in filmmaking where the literary writer has been compared to the screenwriter, the director, and even producers, stars, studios, and super-agents. That few, if any, of these movie creators have the independence and isolation associated with the activity of a literary author has invariably complicated the equation.

Of the many discussions of the filmmaker as *auteur*, Peter Wollen's is one of the more complex and discriminating. In 1969 he discusses auteurism, specifically in how it might relate to adaptation:

> What the auteur theory demonstrates is that the director is not simply in command of a performance of a pre-existing text. ... Don Siegel was recently asked on television what he took from Hemingway's short story for his film, *The Killers*; Siegel replied that "the only thing taken from it was the catalyst that a man has been killed by somebody and he did not try to run away." The word Siegel chose—"catalyst"—could not be better. Incidents and episodes in the original screenplay or novel can act as catalysts; they are the agents which are introduced in the mind (conscious or unconscious) of the auteur and react there with the motifs and themes characteristic of his work. The director does not subordinate himself to another author; his source is only a pretext, which provides catalysts, scenes, which fuse with his own preoccupations to produce a radically new work. Thus the manifest process of performance, the treatment of a subject, conceals the latent production of a quite new text, the production of a director as an auteur.
>
> (Wollen 1972: 112–113)

Auteurism may become more complicated by recognizing that even literary authors rarely have the romantic independence imagined for them, and that only since the nineteenth century have writers and societies tried to hide or disguise the amount of social and commercial machinery and social activity that shapes the writing of a novel, play, or poem. Filmmaker Atom Egoyan is, for many, an example of a contemporary auteur whose relation to that label is complicated by industrial and commercial pressures. His attitude toward adaptation suggests some of the complications in seeing the film auteur as an author of personal expression and perspectives: on adapting a Russell Banks' novel for his 1997 *The Sweet Hereafter*, he says, "I'd become impatient with my own stylistic predispositions. How do you challenge yourself? By attaching yourself to an existing property."

Recommended readings

Andrew Sarris's "Notes on the Auteur Theory in 1962" is an historically important statement of the terms of auteurism that Sarris adapted from its French paradigm; Virginia Wright Wexman's collection *Film and Authorship* gathers some of the best contemporary positions on auteurism and authorship; and Jack Boozer's *Authorship in Film Adaptation* features a variety of contributions on how adaptors might be considered auteurs.

The film novel

What most obviously defines the film novel is that the action and events take place around movies or movie culture. This could mean a setting in a film center such as Hollywood or a character whose thoughts and experiences are determined by the movies. Although sometimes described more narrowly as "the Hollywood novel," novels of this kind have been written throughout this century with increasing frequency, several having both critical and commercial success: F. Scott Fitzgerald's *The Last Tycoon,* Nathaniel West's *The Day of the Locust,* Luigi Pirandello's *Shoot!,* and Vladimir Nabokov's *Laughter in the Dark* are only a sampling. In one sense, film novels are only a particular version of what other novels do when they assimilate the different social forms and discourses into their plots and backgrounds—in this case the settings and discourses of film culture.

As with many of the novels, film novels can go beyond simply using movie culture to surround and define characters. Film novels can use film and its techniques in a variety of other ways as well: (1) as measures of historical or cultural values that introduce debates about history, gender, or other social values, as does Michael Tolkin's *The Player* or, in less obvious ways, Thomas Pynchon's *Gravity's Rainbow*; (2) as part of a style and structure, in which the language and formal shapes of the novel mimic or approach the forms and structures used by the cinema; (3) as focal points for stories about seeing and the psychology of perception; and (4) as philosophical or epistemological touchstones for discussing the relationship between different registers of reality, as in both Manuel Puig's novel and Hector Babenco's film *Kiss of the Spider Woman* (1985).

Recommended readings

Gavriel Moses's *The Nickel Was for the Movie* and Kamilla Elliott's *Rethinking the Novel/ Film Debate* ranges across multiple complex topics that bind the novels and film, including the cinematic novel.

The essay film

One of the rarely acknowledged products of the collaboration between film and literature is the essay film. The essay as a literary form has its origins, for most historians, in the writings of Michel de Montaigne who wrote short personal reflections on the facts and idiosyncrasies of his everyday life. The term *essay* comes from the French word meaning "attempts" or "testings," and remains suggestive of the provisional and fragmentary perspectives of a prose writing practiced by Bacon, Samuel Johnson, William Hazlitt, Walter Pater, Virginia Woolf, and some of the best contemporary writers from James Baldwin to Joan Didion.

As a film practice it is usually identified with the documentary forms that extend back to the beginnings of cinema history and specifically to the Lumière brothers. In the 1950s, documentary practices experiment with numerous formal innovations, including the presence of the personal voice and perspective of the filmmaker as he or she reflects on the realities before the camera. In bringing these essayistic innovations to film, postwar European cinema offers the most recognizable essay films as a merger of that literary tradition and the new investigations of realism in the 1950s.

While its most renowned practitioners in the 1950s included Chris Marker, Alain Resnais, and Agnès Varda, it is Jean-Luc Godard in the 1960s who described his own work during this period—*Made in the USA* (1966) and *La Chinoise* (1967) for example—as essayistic. According to Godard, "I consider myself an essayist; I do essays in the form of novels and novels in the form of essays: Simply I film them instead of writing them" (Giannetti 1975: 19). Variations on the essay film can also be found in the experimental documentaries of Jonas Mekas and later in the work of Raoul Ruiz, Wim Wenders, Trinh T. Minh-ha, and Michael Moore.

Characteristic of the essay film are (1) a usually—but not necessarily—short documentary subject, (2) the lack of a dominant narrative organization (although narrative may provide one of several patterns in the film), and (3) the interaction of a personal voice or vision, sometimes in the form of a voice-over. In the essay film, the interaction of that subjective perspective and the reality before it becomes a testing or questioning of both, and the structure of the film, like the literary essay, follows the undetermined movement of that dialogue.

Recommended readings

Alexandre Astruc's "The Birth of a New Avant-Garde: La Caméra-Stylo" (p. 181) is a prophetic 1948 essay that suggests some of the groundwork for the essay film; Laura Rascaroli's *The Personal Camera* is a theoretically astute study of many of the most important contemporary film essayists; and Timothy Corrigan's *The Essay Film: From Montaigne, After Marker* investigates the theoretical and historical connections between the literary essay and the essay film, and features close readings of films by Godard, Varda, Errol Morris, Werner Herzog, and others.

Novelizations and tie-ins

One of the most striking products of the movie industry's assimilation by conglomerates and media corporations has been the burgeoning business of tie-ins. Ancillary tie-ins have been a part of the film/literature relationship since the beginning of the twentieth century. They refer to the practice of marketing a variety of merchandises around the release of a movie, and the tie-ins of contemporary film culture can mean anything from tee shirts and hamburgers to toys and music compact discs. Today, most studios have their own merchandising units in their marketing departments. Responding to logic and the economics of tie-ins, publishers of literature would continue to take advantage of a successful adaptation to promote or redistribute a book, but especially in recent years, the connection becomes more common since the studio and the publisher may work for the same media corporation. The Disney Corporation may be the most notorious and successful company in spreading a movie through merchandise from, for instance, the music and collectible figures of *Pocahontas* (1995) to novelizations of the story.

Novelization is one increasingly common version of ancillary marketing of a tie-in with a literary film or a film with literary potential. It is the process of turning the story of another work, such as a play, poem, or film, repackaging a successful movie as a novel or written narrative version of that movie. The 1944 film *To Have and Have Not* (scripted by William Faulkner and propelled by Humphrey Bogart and Lauren Bacall) generates three new printings of Hemingway's novel. But, in the last few decades, through the power of novelization, the process has grown more convoluted. After Arthur C. Clarke's 1948 short story "The Sentinel" becomes the critically acclaimed movie *2001: A Space Odyssey* (1968), the same year Clarke develops it as a novel with the same title. In 1983, he writes a sequel novel, *2010: Odyssey Two*, which is made into a film in 1984, and, in 1987, that is followed by yet another novel, *2061: Odyssey Three*, in a series of spin-offs and tie-ins binding the fiction and the films. In 1970, Eric Segal writes a small novel based on Robert Evans's screenplay for the forthcoming movie *Love Story* (1970). After a major promotion campaign, the book tops the *New York Times* bestseller list just as the movie is released in December. Indeed, like these precedents, many popular novels today appear aimed at film adaptation even when they are first published as novels, and their style and structure could be considered already that of a novelization. Today it is common to see either a novelization or re-issue of a novel or play as a coordinated tie-in with the release of a movie.

In this context there are many implications for literature and the activity of reading: (1) the novelization usually becomes a reduction or literalization of the movie in which the traditional descriptive techniques and textual richness of narrative fiction are transformed into only action and character; (2) reading a novelization (or a traditional novel re-released in the spotlight of a successful movie) usually means that the reading will be mediated by the film images, characters, and so on.

Recommended readings

Justin Wyatt's *High Concept* provides an industrial base for considering the interconnections in media industries that produce both novels and films; and Henry Jenkins's "Searching for the Origami: *The Matrix* and Transmedia Storytelling" (p. 403) is part of a book-length study on "convergence culture" in which novelizations are just one earlier version of the participatory exchanges between different texts.

Shakespeare and film

"Shakespeare on film" is practically a film genre in its own right. Besides the many short silent homages to Shakespeare (detailed in Robert Hamilton Ball's book *Shakespeare on Silent Film*), the major movements of film history become, from one point of view, a history of Shakespeare on film: Douglas Fairbanks's early Hollywood sound attempt at Shakespeare in *The Taming of the Shrew* (1929), Max Reinhardt's lavishly scenic 1935 *A Midsummer Night's Dream,* Laurence Olivier's renowned *Henry V* (1945), Orson Welles's 1948 expressionistic *Macbeth*, Akira Kurosawa's remarkable 1957 cross-cultural translation of *Macbeth* as a samurai *Throne of Blood*, Franco Zeffirelli's triumphant success with the youth market in his 1968 *Romeo and Juliet,* Liz White's 1980 racially charged production of *Othello,* Jean-Luc Godard's humorously self-referential *King Lear* (1988), Gus Van Sant's postmodern *My Own Private Idaho* (1991), the abridged and animated collection *Shakespeare: The Animated Tales* (1992), Baz Luhrmann's star-studded spectacle *William Shakespeare's Romeo + Juliet* (1996), Kenneth Branagh's song-and-dance version of *Love's Labour's Lost* (2000), and Julia Taymour's gender-bending *The Tempest* (2010).

Shakespearean movies have used vastly different styles and cultural perspectives. Often these adaptations have tried to be faithful to Shakespeare's texts and the theatrical conventions of his times. At other times, these films have liberally reinterpreted the materials and the aesthetic or political intentions of the original play. Shakespeare has been put on film and television in attempts to popularize language and plots that often alienated audiences; films of his plays have also aimed to record definitively complete versions of those plays for scholarly or classroom use.

Many of the questions asked of adaptations in general apply to Shakespearean movies in particular: Is the adaptation interested in a faithful or creative exchange with the play? What motivates certain omissions or changes in the film? Or, how does the time and place of the adaptation color or determine the film? Yet there are other important questions specific to Shakespearean adaptations. (1) How is Shakespearean language used or not used and at what cost? (2) What is the relation of the language, the acting, and the images? (3) How is the cultural or literary value of Shakespeare, as perhaps the greatest icon of Western literature, being used or addressed?

Recommended readings

Judith Buchanan's *Shakespeare on Silent Film: An Excellent Dumb Discourse* is a detailed study of Shakespeare adaptations during the silent period of early cinema. Samuel Crowl's *Shakespeare and Film* is a broad and useful introduction to the plays of Shakespeare as they reappear in the language of film; Anthony Davies's *Filming Shakespeare's Plays* introduces some of the most celebrated and canonical adaptations of Olivier, Welles, Brook and Kurosawa; Lynda E. Boose and Richard Burt's, two-volume *Shakespeare, The Movie: Popularizing the Plays on Film, TV, and Video* brings together a variety of contemporary essays engaging the relationship between adaptation and popular culture; Evelyn Tribble's "When Every Noise Appalls Me": Sound and Fear in *Macbeth* and Akira Kurosawa's *Throne of Blood*" (p. 297) is a rare, sophisticated, and detailed look at the use of sound in a specific Shakespearean adaptation.

Chapter 37

WRITING ABOUT FILM AND/VERSUS LITERATURE

W RITING ABOUT THE RELATIONSHIPS of film and literature requires most of the guidelines used for all good critical writing: about organization and style, about usage and grammar, and about research and revision. As a specific kind of writing, however, writing about film offers, broadly and schematically, three particular directions: 1) writing about individual works or authors, 2) writing about historical, cultural, or industrial contexts, and 3) writing about theoretical approaches. A writer may thus concentrate on the differences in a particular adaptation of a particular work of literature, such as John Ford's 1940 version of John Steinbeck's *The Grapes of Wrath*, exploring formal or thematic connections and variations in that exchange. Another writer may wish to examine the social and industrial events of 1940 that surround and inform Ford's film, examining the two works as shaped by the Great Depression, the changes in the Hollywood studio system, and other cultural and political forces of the times. A more advanced student of the field might choose to research and address the way the film adaptation identifies and addresses a presumed audience of the story and how those changes raise larger theoretical questions about movie reception as it is shaped by the contemporaneous publication of Steinbeck's 1939 novel. While an essay may focus relatively exclusively on any one of these directions, all three could overlap in a single, if lengthy, essay.

Whether adapting one of these frameworks or other approaches, a focused and clearly articulated argument is the key to a successful essay. This requires five crucial steps in the writing process:

1. Careful notes on the literary work and/or film establish the groundwork for the subsequent analysis. Whether the focus is on literature or film, it is critical to work with exact quotations and exact descriptions of images and sequences. With film analysis, this can be particularly challenging since it means precise description of not only what happens in an important scene but also a detailed recreation of how visual and audio forms shape the scene.

2. A precisely articulated thesis often does not emerge until a writer has worked through several drafts of an essay. A working thesis—a rough description of the argument of the essay—will normally guide a writer through a first draft, but a final draft should revise that guiding idea as a lucid and precise thesis that appears early in the paper and acts as a blueprint for each step of the following argument. To engage a reader, a good thesis should make crystal clear what is at stake in the essay and why the argument is important.

3. A cogent and clear development of that thesis should be ideally reflected in topic sentences that visibly and logically advance the argument of the thesis. A topic sentence outline, done before or after a draft is completed, will make it clear whether or not the argument is completely clear and logical.

4. Precise analysis becomes the necessary evidence that should support each step of the argument as it is developed in each paragraph. Those original notes can be refined and integrated into the paragraph to show how and where the film and literary texts under discussion validate the interpretations.

5. Careful revision and proofreading can make the difference between an essay that engages and holds a reader's attention and one that is easily dismissed as not serious. Even the best writers recognize the critical importance of revising the content and style of a piece of writing since that is how sometimes vague and awkward ideas and perceptions are transformed into insightful and lively prose.

Sophisticated critical writing often demands carefully researching the topic of the essay. In this, keep in mind that research is not ornamentation: rather, it is the evidence that you have a solid and informed grasp of the topic and that you have found a way to enter into the larger scholarly conversations about that topic. In a sense, research legitimizes your analysis. The amount of research needed for an essay depends on your topic, the works under discussion, and the amount of time you can devote to the research: more time will allow you to properly research even a very popular topic (such as one on Kenneth Branagh's 1996 *Hamlet*); a precise working thesis will direct that research more efficiently and manageably (allowing you, for instance, to concentrate your research primarily on the use of sets in Branagh's film). Last but not least, properly documented research is critical since, if overlooked or done haphazardly, the work of the essay (and for the entire course) will be undone by the charge of plagiarism. For this documentation, there are two common formatting methods: the Modern Language Association MLA style and the Chicago Style, both of which are readily available in print, from library databases, and online.

This student essay on *The Searchers* (1956) is a good example of how a discriminating analysis involves comparative questions about film and literature and, in the process, demonstrates how the movie uses specific technical and formal strategies to express its themes.

* * *

"The Darkened Doorways of *The Searchers*"
Richard Geschke

Based on a 1954 novel by Alan LeMay, John Ford's 1956 adaptation of *The Searchers* dramatizes some of the critical changes that can occur in moving a story from a book to the screen. Most film adaptations require some adjustments to the plot (usually deletions). But in Ford's *The*

Searchers, we witness a major alteration in the central character, Ethan Edwards, which in turn affects the significance of the entire story. As part of Ford's transformation of Edwards, the film uses a specific image pattern based on the composition of a darkened doorway, an image pattern that indicates how a film narrative can sometimes supplement or even surpass a literary narrative.

Although most of the central plot elements remain intact, the most significant change in the adaptation is the character of Ethan Edwards. In the novel he is a fairly traditional western hero who, without much psychological complexity, rescues his niece and returns home. In the film, however, his character grows much more complicated in three ways. First, from the beginning, there is the subtle but definite indication of a mysterious and possibly criminal past: since the end of the Civil War, Ethan apparently resisted returning home and possibly participated in some unmentionably dangerous, violent, or illegal acts. Second, Ford's Ethan struggles with the turbulent dangers of sexual desire. As carefully suggested by the opening sequence with Ethan and his brother's wife Martha, Ethan has had to repress his love and passion for Martha, presumably knowing that passion would violate the domestic and family codes he lives by. Third, in the film, Ethan is clearly a racist. Unlike in the novel, here he makes sarcastic remarks about his "half-breed" nephew (who is partly Native American) and, more importantly, his mission to find Debbie is, unlike in the novel, motivated by the wish to kill her because he believes she has been sexually violated by her non-white captor.

A violent, racist, and sexually troubled Ethan thus motivates and complicates the straightforward plot of the novel in new ways. On the one hand, *The Searchers* proceeds as a linear quest: Ethan and Marty Pauley search for the lost Debbie, who has been kidnapped by the Comanche tribe of Scar. That plot is ultimately resolved, in a classical manner, when they find her and she is returned home. A counter-current within this linear, forward plot, however, is an interior search that seems to move backward and inward in the film, investigating Ethan's twisted mind and dark past. At the center of these parallel plots, Marty becomes more and more aware of Ethan's violence and racism, and increasingly confronts him, eventually attempting to stop him from killing Debbie. At first, Ethan does not appear to respond to any of these demands for self-knowledge, and his climactic confrontation with Scar suggests that nothing about him has changed: He not only kills the Comanche chief but, in an act of grotesque brutality, Ford has this cinematic Ethan actually scalp Scar (which does not happen in the novel).

When in a scene that immediately follows, Ethan chases down Debbie but does not kill her, the film indicates, however, that something has indeed changed in Ethan, that his search for Debbie has revealed something horrid about himself to himself. Perhaps the scalping of Scar, who more and more seems a reflection of Ethan, has acted as a cathartic confrontation with his own dark soul. Perhaps his entire quest has, with the help of Marty, allowed him to see his own barbaric and primitive self. His decision to spare Debbie's life becomes then, at least in part, a decision to acknowledge and free himself from his own violent desires and troubled past. Driven by the need to restore a home and domestic life, Ethan's narrative has now become an inquiry into the dark passions that threaten that home life from within.

Brilliantly dramatizing the tension between Ethan's two searches is a pattern of shots focused on darkened entryways. At the opening, a three-quarters shot from behind Martha shows her looking across the plain as she stands in a doorway. The black interior of the cabin contrasts sharply with the bright light that fills the doorway from outside. A tracking shot then follows Martha out onto the porch where she watches Ethan riding toward her in the distance. At the conclusion, virtually the same shot recurs as Ethan delivers Debbie to her new home with the Jorgensens. After Debbie and the Jorgensens enter the black interior, the newly married Marty and his wife follow. Ethan, though, hesitates on the porch and then turns back into the desert.

Both these shots position Ethan as a wanderer separated from the domestic interiors that he approaches. Complicating this image, moreover, those interiors are blackened in a way that suggests a darker reality than is usually associated with the inside of a home. In an important sense, I believe, the exteriors represent that wild and primitive world that Ethan must wander through, while the interiors of home (and self) represent for Ethan the shadowy and dangerous passion now associated with his illicit love of Martha.

Between these two scenes of darkened doorways is a third scene whose black space acts as the turning point in Ethan's story and a measure of what has changed between the beginning and end of this narrative. After killing Scar, Ethan chases the fleeing Debbie to a cave. Shot from the interior as a medium long shot, the composition here clearly replicates the doorway shots that open and close the film. After approaching the cringing Debbie, Ethan does not, as we expect, kill her but instead lifts her up and says "Let's go home, Debbie." As part of a climactic turning point that begins with his brutal scalping of Scar, the scene becomes a moment of partial and temporary redemption for Ethan as he enters that darkened interior but quietly refuses to act out his repressed violence. When he releases Debbie later at a similar threshold, Ethan has recognized his own violent passion and has resisted it. As he turns at the threshold and walks back into the desert, the long take becomes an acknowledgement that Ethan cannot enter that domestic world because of who he is. In the words of the sound track, he is a man who must continue to "search his heart and soul."

There may be many social or personal reasons for these alterations in adapting the novel to the film in this way. What is clear is that Ford's version of the story is a much more troubling and disturbing version as it injects race and sexuality into a character and the narrative. In this case adapting a literary narrative as a film narrative becomes not simply the translation of characters and themes but the creation of significantly different characters and themes.

From Timothy Corrigan, *A Short Guide to Writing about Film*

Bibliography and other resources

A BIBLIOGRAPHY should, I believe, point to the major documents without overwhelming the reader with the sheer weight of the field. That has been my goal in creating a list of works that is comprehensive without being too intimidating or exhausting. I have not included many of the innumerable articles and essays on film and literature, unless they were exceptional cases. Also missing are many of the broadly based studies that may have some discussion appropriate to the study of film and literature. A separate bibliography could be assembled of remarks by novelists, poets, and playwrights on their experiences with or perspectives on film, but I trust these can be tracked down through the sources below (such as Geduld's *Authors on Film*) or by investigating the bibliography of the individual author (to locate, for instance, James Baldwin's or Gertrude Stein's essays and comments on the movies). Students of film and literature should consult *Adaptation: The Journal of Screen Studies, Literature/Film Quarterly* and other journals that may devote special issues to adaptation or other dimensions of the relationship between film and literature. There are also many texts in foreign languages addressing this topic that have not been included.

Although many film and literature journals and books include essays on adaptation and the crossovers between film and literature, there are numerous journals, websites, and books devoted exclusively to adaptation studies and the exchanges between film and literature. Three important journals devoted to adaptation and the exchanges between film and literature are:

Adaptation: The Journal of Literature on Screen Studies. Biannual. http://www.oxfordjournals.org/our_journals/adaptation/editorial_board.html
Literature/Film Quarterly. Quarterly. http://www.salisbury.edu/lfq/
Journal of Adaptation in Film and Performance. Annual. http://www.intellectbooks.co.uk/journals/view-Journal,id=153/view,page=1/

Abel, Richard. *French Cinema: The First Wave, 1915–1929.* Princeton, NJ: Princeton University Press, 1984.
Allen, Graham. *Intertextuality.* New York: Routledge, 2000.
Altick, Richard. *The Shows of London.* Cambridge, MA: Harvard University Press, 1978.
Altman, Rick, ed. *Sound Theory, Sound Practice.* New York: Routledge, 1992.

Andrew, Dudley. *Concepts in Film Theory*. New York: Oxford University Press, 1984.

Appel, Alfred, Jr. *Nabokov's Dark Cinema*. New York: Oxford University Press, 1974.

Arheim, Rudolf. *Film as Art*. Berkeley, CA: University of California Press, 1957.

Astruc, Alexandre. "The Birth of the New Avant-Garde: La Caméra-Stylo." In *The New Wave*. Ed. Peter Graham. New York: Doubleday, 1968, pp. 17–23.

Ayock, Wendell, and Michael Schoenecke, eds. *Film and Literature: A Comparative Approach to Adaptation*. Lubbock, TX: Texas Tech University Press, 1988.

Balázs, Béla. *Theory of Film: Character and Growth of a New Art*. New York: Dover, 1970.

Ball, Robert Hamilton. *Shakespeare on Silent Film*. London: George Allen and Unwin Ltd., 1968.

Barthes, Roland. *Image-Music-Text*. Trans. Stephen Heath. New York: Hill & Wang, 1977.

—— *Camera Lucida: Reflections on Photography*. Trans. Richard Howard. New York: Hill & Wang, 1981.

Baudelaire, Charles. "The Salon of 1859." Trans. Judith Mayne. In *Modern Art and Modernism: A Critical Anthology*. Ed. F. Frascina and C. Harrison New York: Harper Collins, 1983, pp. 19–21.

Bazin, André. *What Is Cinema?* 2 vols. Berkeley, CA: University of California Press, 1971.

Beja, Morris. *Film and Literature*. New York: Longman, 1979.

Benjamin, Walter. *Illuminations*. Ed. Hannah Arendt and trans. Harry Zohn. New York: Schocken, 1969.

Bloom, Harold. "The Visonary Cinema of the Romantics." In *William Blake: Essays for S. Foster Damon*. Ed. Alvin Rosenfeld. Providence, RI: Brown University Press, 1969, pp. 22–51.

Bluestone, George. *Novels into Films*. Baltimore, MD: Johns Hopkins University Press, 1957.

Boose, Lynda E., and Richard Burt, eds. *Shakespeare, The Movie: Popularizing the Plays on Film, TV, and Video. Vols. I and II*. London and New York: Routledge, 1997 and 2003.

Boozer, Jack, ed. *Authorship in Film Adaptation*. Austin, TX: University of Texas Press, 2008.

Bordwell, David. *Narration in the Fiction Film*. Madison, WI: University of Wisconsin Press, 1985.

Bordwell, David, Janet Staiger, and Kristin Thompson. *The Classical Hollywood Cinema: Film Style and Mode of Production to 1960*. New York: Columbia University Press, 1985.

Boyum, Joy Gould. *Double Exposure: Fiction into Film*. New York: Universe Books, 1985.

Brakhage, Stan. *Metaphors on Vision*. New York: Anthology Film Archives, 1976.

Braudy, Leo. *The World in a Frame*. 2nd edn. Chicago, IL: University of Chicago Press, 1984.

Brecht, Bertolt. "The Film, the Novel, and Epic Theatre." In *Brecht on Theatre*. Ed. John Willett. New York: Hill & Wang, 1964, pp. 47–51.

Brookeer-Bowers, Nancy. *The Hollywood Novel and Other Novels about Film: An Annotated Bibliography*. New York: Garland, 1985.

Brooks, Peter. *The Melodramatic Imagination: Balzac, Henry James, Melodrama, and the Mode of Excess*. New Haven, CT: Yale University Press, 1976.

Brunetta, Gian Piero, ed. *Letteratura e cinema*. Bologna: Zanichelli, 1976.

Buchanan, Judith. *Shakespeare on Silent Film: An Excellent Dumb Discourse*. Cambridge: Cambridge University Press, 2009.

Bulman, J. C., and H. R. Coursen, eds. *Shakespeare on Television: An Anthology of Essays and Reviews*. Hanover, NH: University Press of New England, 1988.

Burch, Nöel. *Theory of Film Practice*. Trans. Helen Lane. Princeton, NJ: Princeton University Press, 1981.

Cahir, Linda Costanzo. *Literature into Film: Theory and Practical Approaches*. Jefferson, NC: McFarland & Co., 2006.

Cavell, Stanley. *The World Viewed*. Cambridge, MA: Harvard University Press, 1979.

Cartmell, Deborah ,I. Q. Hunter, Heidi Kaye, and Imelda Whelehan , eds. *Pulping Fictions: Consuming Culture across the Literature/Media Divide*. London: Pluto Press, 1996.

Cartmell, Deborah and Whelehan, Imelda, eds. *Adaptations: From Text to Screen, Screen to Text*. New York: Routledge, 1999.

——. *The Cambridge Companion to Literature on Screen*. Cambridge: Cambridge University Press, 2007.

Caughie, John, ed. *Theories of Authorship: A Reader*. London: Routledge, 1981.

Carringer, Robert. *The Making of Citizen Kane*. Berkeley, CA: University of California Press, 1996.

Carrol, Rachel. *Adaptation in Contemporary Culture: Textual Infidelities*. New York: Continuum, 2009.

Cavell, Stanley. *The World Viewed: Reflections on the Ontology of Film*. 2nd edn. New York: Viking, 1979.

Ceram. C.W. *Archeology of the Cinema*. New York: Harcourt, Brace & World, 1965.

Chatman, Seymour. *Story and Discourse: Narrative Structure in Fiction and Film*. Ithaca, NY: Cornell University Press, 1978.

——. *Coming to Terms: The Rhetoric of Narrative in Fiction and Film*. Ithaca, NY: Cornell University Press, 1990.

Cocteau, Jean. *Cocteau on the Film: Conversations with Jean Cocteau Recorded by Andre Fraigneau*. Trans. Vera Traill. New York: Dover, 1972.

Cohen, Keith. *Film and Fiction: The Dynamics of Exchange*. New Haven, CT: Yale University Press, 1979.

——. *Writing in the Film Age*. Niwot, CO: University Press of Colorado, 1991.

Colie, Rosalie L. *Shakespeare's "Living Art."* Princeton, NJ: Princeton University Press, 1974.

Collins, Jim. *High-Pop: Making Culture into Popular Entertainment*. Oxford: Blackwell, 2002.

Conger, Syndy M., and Janice Welsch, eds. *Narrative Strategies: Original Essays in Film and Prose Fiction*. Macomb, IL: Western Illinois University Press, 1980.

Corkin, Stanley. *Realism and the Birth of the Modern United States: Literature, Cinema, and Culture*. Athens, GA: University of Georgia Press, 1996.

Corrigan, Timothy. *A Cinema without Walls: Movies and Culture after Vietnam*. London: Routledge 1991.

——. *The Essay Film: From Michel de Montaigne, After Chris Marker*. New York: Oxford University Press, 2011.

——. *A Short Guide to Writing about Film*. 8th edn. New York: Longman, 2012.

Crowl, Samuel. *Shakespeare and Film: A Norton Guide*. New York: W.W. Norton & Company, 2007.

Davies, Anthony. *Filming Shakespeare's Plays*. Cambridge, MA: Cambridge University Press, 1988.

De Lauretis, Teresa. *Freud's Drive: Psychoanalysis, Literature and Film*. New York: Palgrave Macmillan, 2010.

Deren, Maya. "Cinematography: The Creative Use of Reality." In *Film Theory and Criticism*. 4th edn. Ed. Gerald Mast, Marshall Cohen, and Leo Braudy. New York: Oxford University Press, 1992, pp. 59–70.

Desmond, John and Hawkes, Peter. *Adaptation: Studying Film and Literature*. New York: McGraw-Hill, 2005.

Docherty, Thomas, ed. *Postmodernism: A Reader*. New York: Columbia University Press, 1993.

Donaldson-Evans, Mary. *Madame Bovary at the Movies: Adaptation, Ideology, Context*. New York: Rodopi, 2008.

Durgnat, Raymond. *Films and Feeling*. Cambridge, MA: MIT Press, 1967.

Eckert, Charles W. *Focus on Shakespearean Films*. Englewood Cliffs, NJ: Prentice Hall, 1972.

Edel, Leon. "Novel and Camera." In *The Theory of the Novel: New Essays*. Ed. John Halperin. New York: Oxford University Press, 1974, pp. 177–88.

Egerton, Gary R., ed. *Film and the Arts in Symbiosis: A Research Guide* New York: Greenwood Press, 1988.

Eidsvik, Charles. *Cineliteracy: Film among the Arts*. New York: Random House, 1978.

Egoyan, Atom. "Interview with Atom Egoyan." *Philadelphia Inquirer,* February 21, 1996. C3.

Eisenstein, Sergei. *The Film Sense*. Ed. and trans. Jay Leyda. New York: Harcourt, 1947.

——. *The Film Form*. Ed. and trans. Jay Leyda. New York: Harcourt, 1947.

Elliott, Kamilla. *Rethinking the Novel/Film Debate*. Cambridge: Cambridge University Press, 2003.

Ellis, John. "The Literary Adaptation: An Introduction." *Screen* 23, 1 (1982): 3–4.

——. *Visible Fictions*. London: Routledge, 1982.

Fell, John L. *Film and the Narrative Tradition*. Berkeley, CA: University of California Press, 1974.

Fleishman, Avrom. *Narrated Films: Storytelling Situations in Cinema History*. Baltimore, MD: Johns Hopkins University Press, 1992.

French, Philip, and Ken Wlaschin. *The Faber Book of Movie Verse*. London: Faber and Faber, 1993.

Geduld, Harry M., ed. *Authors on Film*. Bloomington, IN: Indiana University Press, 1972.

Geraghty, Christine. *Now a Major Motion Picture: Film Adaptations of Literature and Drama*. Lanham, MD: Rowman & Littlefield Publishers, 2007.

Giannetti, Louis D. *Godard and Others: Essays on Film Form*. Rutherford, NJ: Fairleigh Dickinson University Press, 1975.

Giddings, Robert, Keith Selby, and Chis Wensley *Screening the Novel: The Theory and Practice of Literary Adaptation*. London: Macmillan, 1990.

Giddings, Robert and E. Sheen, eds. *The Classic Novel: From Page to Screen*. Manchester: Manchester University Press, 2000.

Goldstein, Laurence. *The American Poet at the Movies: A Critical History*. Ann Arbor, MI: University of Michigan Press, 1994.

Goodwin, James. "Literature and Film: A Review of Criticism." *Quarterly Review of Film Studies* 4, 2 (1979): 227–246.

Gordon, Ian. *Film and Comic Books*. Jackson, MS: University of Mississippi Press, 2007.

Gould, Evlyn. *The Fate of Carmen*. Baltimore, MD: Johns Hopkins University Press, 1996.

Hamilton, Ian. *Writers in Hollywood, 1915–1951*. New York: Carroll & Graf, 1991.

Hansen, Miriam. *Babel and Babylon: Spectatorship in American Silent Film*. Cambridge, MA: Harvard University Press, 1991.

Harrington, John, ed. *Film and/as Literature*. Englewood Cliffs, NJ: Prentice Hall, 1977.

Harrison, Stephanie. *Adaptations: From Short Story to Big Screen: 35 Great Stories That Have Inspired Great Films*. New York: Three Rivers Press, 2005.

Heath, Stephen. *Questions of Cinema.* Bloomington, IN: Indiana University Press, 1981.

Heath, Stephen, and Patricia Melencamp, eds. *Cinema and Language.* Frederick, MD: University Publication, 1984.

Hedges, Inez. *Languages of Revolt: Dada and Surrealist Literature and Film.* Durham, NC: Duke University Press, 1983.

Higgins, Lynn A. *New Novel, New Wave, New Politics: Fiction and the Representation of History in Postwar France.* Lincoln, NE: University of Nebraska Press, 1996.

Holt, Patricia. "Turning Best Sellers into Movies." *Publishers Weekly* 22 October, 1979, 36–40.

Hopkins, Lisa. *Screening the Gothic.* Austin, TX: University of Texas Press, 2005.

Horton, Andrew, and Joan Magretta. *Modern European Filmmakers and the Art of Adaptation.* New York: Ungar, 1981.

Hutcheon, Linda. *A Theory of Adaptation.* New York: Routledge, 2006.

Jacobs, Lewis, ed. *The Compound Cinema: The Film Writings of Harry Alan Potamkin.* New York: The Teacher's College Press, 1977.

James, David. *Allegories of Cinema: American Film in the Sixties.* Princeton, NJ: Princeton University Press, 1989.

Jenkins, Henry. *Textual Poachers: Television Fans and Participatory Culture.* London and New York: Routledge, 1992.

——. *Convergence Culture: Where Old and New Media Collide.* New York: New York University Press, 2006.

Jinks, William. *The Celluloid Literature.* Beverly Hills, CA: Glencoe Press, 1971.

Jorgens, Jack. *Shakespeare on Film.* Bloomington, IN: Indiana University Press, 1977.

Jost, François. *L'Oeil/Camera: entre film et roman.* Lyon: Presses Universitaires de Lyon, 1987.

Kawin, Bruce. *Mindscreen: Bergman, Godard, and First-Person Cinema.* Princeton, NJ: Princeton University Press, 1978.

——. *Faulkner and Film.* New York: Ungar, 1977.

——. *Telling It Again and Again: Repetition in Literature and Film.* Ithaca, NY: Cornell University Press, 1972.

Kidnie, Margaret Jane. *Shakespeare and the Problem of Adaptation.* New York: Routledge, 2008.

Kittredge, William, and Steven M. Krauzner, eds. *Stories into Film.* New York: Harper Colophon Books, 1979.

Klein, Michael, and Gillian Parker, eds. *The English Novel and the Movies.* New York: Ungar, 1981.

Kliman, Bernice. *Hamlet: Film, Television, and Audio Performance.* Cranbury, NJ: Fairleigh Dickinson Press, 1988.

Kline, T. Jefferson. *Screening the Text: Intertextuality in New Wave French Cinema.* Baltimore, MD: Johns Hopkins University Press, 1992.

Knopf, Robert. *Theater and Film: A Comparative Anthology.* New Haven, CT: Yale University Press, 2004.

Kozloff, Sarah. *Invisible Storytellers: Voice-Over Narration in American Fiction Film.* Berkeley, CA: University of California Press, 1988.

Krutnik, Frank. "Desire, Transgression, and James M. Cain." *Screen* 23 (1982): 31–42.

Langer, Susanne. *Feeling and Form.* New York: Scribners, 1953.

Laurence, Frank M. *Hemingway and the Movies.* Jackson, MS: University of Mississippi Press, 1981.

Lawder, Standish. *The Cubist Cinema.* New York: New York University Press, 1975.

Leitch, Thomas. *Film Adaptation and Its Discontents: From Gone with the Wind to The Passion of the Christ.* Baltimore, MD: The Johns Hopkins University Press, 2009.

Lindsay, Vachel. *The Art of the Moving Picture.* New York: Liveright, 1970.

Luhr, William. *Raymond Chandler and Film.* New York: Ungar, 1982.

Luhr, William, and Peter Lehman. *Authorship and Narrative in the Cinema.* New York: Oxford University Press, 1977.

Lupack, Barbara Tepa. *Literary Adaptations in Black American Cinema: From Micheaux to Morrison.* Rochester, NY: University of Rochester Press, 2002.

Lurie, Peter. *Vision's Immanence: Faulkner, Film, and the Popular Imagination.* Baltimore, MD: The Johns Hopkins University Press, 2004.

McCabe, Colin. *Tracking the Signifier: Theoretical Essays.* Minneapolis, MN: University of Minnesota Press, 1985.

McCabe, Susan. *Cinematic Modernism: Modernist Poetry and Film.* Cambridge: Cambridge University Press, 2009.

MacCann, Richard Dyer, ed. *Film: A Montage of Theories.* New York: Dutton, 1966.

Macdonald, Gina and Andrew Macdonald, eds. *Jane Austen on Screen.* Cambridge: Cambridge University Press, 2003.

MacFarlane, Brian. *Novel to Film: An Introduction to the Theory of Adaptation.* Oxford: Clarendon Press, 1996.

McConnell, Frank. *The Spoken Seen*. Baltimore, MD: Johns Hopkins University Press, 1976.

——. *Storytelling and Mythmaking: Images from Film and Literature*. New York: Oxford University Press, 1970.

McDougal, Stuart Y. *Made into Movies: From Literature to Film*. Niles, IL: Holt, Rinehart, & Winston, 1985.

Magny, Claude-Edmunde. *The Age of the American Novel: The Film Aesthetic of Fiction between the Two Wars*. New York: Ungar, 1972.

Manvell, Roger. *Shakespeare and the Film*. New York: Praeger, 1972.

Marcus, Fred. *Short Story/Short Film*. Englewood Cliffs, NJ: Prentice Hall, 1977.

——. *Film and Literature: Contrasts in Media*. Scranton, PA: Chandler, 1971.

Marcus, Millicent. *Filmmaking by the Book: Italian Cinema and Literary Adaptation*. Baltimore, MD: Johns Hopkins University Press, 1993.

Mast, Gerald and Marshall Cohen, eds. *Film Theory and Criticism*. 3rd edn. New York: Oxford University Press, 1992.

Mayne, Judith. *Private Novels, Public Films*. Athens, GA: University of Georgia Press, 1988.

Meisel, Martin. *Realizations: Narrative, Pictorial, and Theatrical Arts in Nineteenth-Century England*. Princeton, NJ: Princeton University Press, 1983.

Metz, Christian. *Film Language*. Trans. Michael Taylor. New York: Oxford University Press, 1974.

Miles, Peter, and Malcolm Smith. *Cinema, Literature, and Society: Elite and Mass Culture in Interwar Britain*. London: Croom Helm, 1987.

Miller, Gabriel. *Screening the Novel: Rediscovered American Fiction in Film*. New York: Ungar, 1980.

Mistral, Gabriela. "The Poet's Attitude toward the Movies." In *The Movies on Trial*. Ed. William J. Perelman. New York: Macmillan, 1936, pp. 141–51.

Miller, J. Hillis. *Illustration*. Cambridge, MA: Harvard University Press, 1992.

Mitry, Jean. "Remarks on the Problem of Cinematic Adaptation." Trans. Richard Dyer. *Bulletin of Midwest Modern Language Association* (1971): 1.

Monaco, James. *American Film Now: The People, the Power, the Money, the Movies*. New York: New American Library, 1984.

Morrissette, Bruce. *Novels and Film: Essays in Two Genres*. Chicago, IL: University of Chicago Press, 1985.

Morse, Margaret. "Paradoxes of Realism: The Rise of Film in the Train of the Novel." In *Explorations in Film Theory: Selected Essays from Cine-Tracts*. Ed. Ron Burnett. Bloomington, IN: Indiana University Press, 1991, pp. 155–67.

Moses, Gavriel. *The Nickel Was for the Movie: Film in the Novel from Pirandello to Puig*. Berkeley, CA: University of California Press, 1995.

Münsterberg, Hugo. *The Film: A Psychological Study: The Silent Photoplay in 1916*. New York: Dover, 1970.

Murray, Edward. *The Cinematic Imagination: Writers and the Motion Pictures*. New York: Ungar, 1972.

Murray, Timothy. *Like a Film: Ideological Fantasy on Screen, Camera, and Canvas*. London and New York: Routledge, 1993.

——. *Drama Trauma: Specters of Race and Sexuality in Performance, Video, and Art*. London and New York: Routledge, 1997.

Naremore, James, ed. *Film Adaptation*. New Brunswick, NJ: Rutgers University Press, 2000.

Nicoll, Allardyce. *Film and Theatre*. New York: Crowell, 1936.

Orr, Christopher. "The Discourse of Adaptation." *Wide Angle* 2 (1984): 72–84.

Orvell, Miles. *The Real Thing: Imitation and Authenticity in American Culture, 1880–1940*. Chapel Hill, NC: University of North Carolina Press, 1989.

Parill, Sue. *Jane Austen on Film and Television: A Critical Study of the Adaptations*. Jefferson, NC: McFarland, 2002.

Parker, Deborah and Mark Parker. *The DVD and the Study of Film: The Attainable Text*. New York: Palgrave, 2011.

Pearson, Roberta and William Uricchio. *Reframing Culture: The Case of the Vitagraph Quality Film*. Princeton, NJ: Princeton University Press, 1993.

Peary, Gerald, and Roger Shatzkin, eds. *The Classic American Novel and the Movies*. New York: Ungar, 1977.

——. *The Modern American Novel and the Movies*. New York: Ungar, 1980.

Pellow, Kenneth. *Films as Critiques of Novels: Transformational Criticism*. Lewiston, NY: Mellen Press, 1995.

Pendo, Stephen. *Raymond Chandler on Screen: His Novels into Film*. Metuchen, NJ: Scarecrow Press, 1976.

Peucker, Brigitte. *Incorporating Images: Film and the Rival Arts*. Princeton, NJ: Princeton University Press, 1995.

Phillips, Gene. *Conrad and Cinema*. New York: Lang, 1995.

——. *Hemingway and Film*. New York: Ungar, 1980.

——. *Stanley Kubrick: A Film Odyssey*. New York: Popular Library, 1977.

Potamkin, Harry Alan. *The Compound Cinema: The Film Writings of Harry Alan Potamkin*. Ed. Lewis Jacobs. New York: The Teachers College Press, 1977.

Rascaroli, Laura. *The Personal Camera: Subjective Cinema and the Essay Film*. London: Wallflower Press, 2009.

Ray, Robert. *How a Film Theory Got Lost and Other Mysteries in Cultural Studies*. Bloomington, IN: Indiana University Press, 2001.

Read, Herbert. "The Poet and the Film." In *A Coat of Many Colours*. London: Routledge, 1945, 123–36.

Rentschler, Eric, ed. *German Film and Literature: Adaptations and Transformations*. New York: Methuen, 1986.

Rich, Adrienne. *Adrienne Rich's Poetry*. Ed. Barbara Charlesworth Gelpi and Albert Gelpi. New York: Norton, 1975.

Richards, Jeffrey. *Films and British National Identity*. Manchester: Manchester University Press, 1997.

Richardson, Robert. *Literature and Film*. Bloomington, IN: Indiana University Press, 1969.

Robbe-Grillet, Alain. *For a New Novel: Essays on Fiction*. Trans. Richard Howard. New York: Grove Press, 1965.

Ropars-Wuilleumier, Marie-Claire. *De la littérature au cinéma: genèse d'une écriture*. Paris: Armand Colin, 1970.

Rosen, Philip, ed. *Narrative, Apparatus, Ideology*. New York: Columbia University Press, 1986.

Ross, Harris. *Film as Literature: Literature as Film*. New York: Greenwood, 1987.

Rombes, Nicholas. *Cinema in the Digital Age*. London: Wallflower, 2008.

Rothman, William. "To Have and Have Not Adapted a Film from a Novel." In *The "I" of the Camera: Essays in Film Criticism, History, and Aesthetics*. New York: Cambridge University Press, 1988, pp. 108–116.

Rothwell, Kenneth. *A History of Shakespeare on Screen*. 2nd edn. Cambridge: Cambridge University Press, 2004.

Ruchti, Unrich, and Sybil Taylor. *Story into Film*. New York: Dell, 1978.

Sanders, Julie. **Adaptation and Appropriation**. New York, NY: Routledge, 2005.

Sarris, Andrew. "Notes on the Auteur Theory in 1962." *Film Culture* 27 (1962/63): 1-8.

Schickel, Richard. *D. W. Griffith: An American Life*. New York: Simon & Schuster, 1984.

Seeger, Linda. *The Art of Adaptation*. NY: Holt, 1992.

Sillars, Stuart. *Visualization in Popular Fiction, 1860–1960*. London: Routledge, 1995.

Shattuck, Roger. "Fact in Film and Literature." *Partisan Review* 44 (1977): 539–550.

Sinyard, Neil. *Filming Literature: The Art of Screen Adaptation*. London: Croom Helm, 1986.

Sitney, P. Adams. *Visionary Film: The American Avant-Garde, 1943–1978*. New York: Oxford University Press, 1979.

Sontag, Susan. *Against Interpretation*. New York: Farrar, Straus & Giroux, 1961.

Spiegel, Alan. *Fiction and the Camera Eye: Visual Consciousness in the Film and the Modern Novel*. Charlottesville, VA: University of Virginia Press, 1976.

Stam, Robert. *Reflexivity in Film and Literature: From Don Quixote to Jean-Luc Godard*. New York: Columbia University Press, 1992.

Stam, Robert and Alessandro Raengo, eds. *A Companion to Literature and Film*. Malden, MA: Wiley Blackwell, 2005.

——. *Literature through Film: Realism, Magic and the Art of Adaptation*. Malden, MA: Wiley Blackwell, 2004.

——. *Literature and Film: A Guide to the Theory and Practice of Film Adaptation*. Malden, MA: Wiley Blackwell, 2004.

Talbot, Daniel, ed. *Film: An Anthology*. New York: Simon & Schuster, 1967.

Thomson, Brian Lindsay. *Graham Greene and the Politics of Popular Film and Fiction*. New York: Palgrave Macmillan, 2009.

Toles, George E., ed. *Film/Literature*. Winnipeg: University of Manitoba Press, 1983.

Troost, Linda and Sayre Greenfield, eds. *Jane Austen in Hollywood*. Lexington, KY: University of Kentucky Press, 2001.

Truffaut, François. "A Certain Tendency of the French Cinema." In Ed. Bill Nichols. *Movies and Methods*. Vol I. Berkeley, CA: University of California Press, 1976.

Van Wert, William. *The Theory and Practice of the Ciné-Roman*. New York: Arno, 1978.

Vardac, A. Nicholas. *Stage to Screen: Theatrical Method from Garrick to Griffith*. Cambridge, MA: Harvard University Press, 1949.

Wagner, Geoffrey. *The Novel and Cinema*. Rutherford, NJ: Fairleigh Dickinson University Press, 1975.

Waller, Gregory. *The Stage/Screen Debate: A Study in Popular Aesthetics*. New York: Garland, 1983.

Welch, Geoffrey Egan. *Literature and Film: An Annotated Bibliography, 1909–1977*. London: Garland, 1981.

Welsh, James M. *The Literature/Film Reader: Issues of Adaptation*. Lanham, MD: The Scarecrow Press, 2007.

Wexman, Virginia Wright, ed. *Film and Authorship*. New Brunswick, NJ: Rutgers University Press, 2003.

Wicks, Ulrich. "A Researcher's Guide and Selected Checklist to Film as Literature and Language." *Journal of Modern Literature* 3, 2 (April 1973): 323–350.

Wilbur, Richard. "A Poet and the Movies." In *Man and the Movies*. Ed. W. R. Robinson. Baton Rouge, LA: Louisiana State University Press, 1967, p. 224.

Williams, Linda. *Figures of Desire: A Theory and Analysis of Surrealist Film*. Urbana, IL: University of Illinois Press, 1981.

Williams, Raymond. *Culture and Society: 1780–1950*. New York: Columbia University Press, 1983.

Wilson, George. *Narration in Light: Studies in Cinematic Point of View*. Baltimore, MD: Johns Hopkins University Press, 1986.

Winston, Douglas Garrett. *The Screenplay as Literature*. Rutherford, NJ: Fairleigh Dickinson University Press, 1973.

Wollen, Peter. *Signs and Meaning in the Cinema*. Rev. edn. Bloomington, IN: Indiana University Press, 1972.

Wyatt, Justin. *High Concept: Movies and Marketing in Hollywood*. Austin, TX: University of Texas Press, 1985.

Yacowar, Maurice. *Tennessee Williams and Film*. New York: Ungar, 1977.

Index